MW01156965

Guide to
Telecommunications Technology

Tamara Dean

THOMSON
™
COURSE TECHNOLOGY

Australia • Canada • Mexico • Singapore • Spain • United Kingdom • United States

Guide to Telecommunications Technology

is published by Course Technology

Associate Publisher:
Steve Elliot

Production Editor:
Elena Montillo

Associate Product Manager:
Tim Gleeson

Senior Editor:
Will Pitkin

Technical Editor:
James I. Conrad, Accusource CC, Inc.

Editorial Assistant:
Nick Lombardi

Senior Editor:
Lisa Egan

Senior Manufacturing Coordinator:
Laura Burns

Cover Design:
Julie Malone

Product Manager:
Amy M. Lyon

MQA Technical Leaders:
Nicole Ashton, John Bosco

Text Designer:
GEX Publishing Services

Developmental Editor:
Ann Shaffer

Product Marketing Manager:
Jason Sakos

Compositor:
GEX Publishing Services

TABLE OF
Contents

Preface

Telecommunications is a broad topic, covering telephone systems and data networks, and the ways the two can be combined. Although few data or telephone networks are exactly alike, all share some fundamental technology. This book introduces you to the technology behind telecommunications, beginning with how signals are generated by manipulating electric current. It covers the history of telecommunications technology and policy and describes how this history led to the public telephone network familiar to us all. It explains many ways data signals can be encoded and transmitted. It details the end user and connectivity equipment necessary for a complete telephone or data network. It also illustrates how telecommunications networks are designed and what transmission media they may use. The book closes with a chapter on convergence, the exchange of data, voice, and video services over the same network. The text is written in an approachable style and provides thorough explanations, so that even novice students will grasp difficult concepts. Throughout the book, technology is described in its real-world context. Each chapter offers several examples of a technology's typical use, benefits and drawbacks, costs, and impact on users and providers.

The Intended Audience

This book is intended to serve the needs of students and professionals who need to understand the basic technology that supplies voice and data telecommunications services. It is ideally suited for introductory courses on telecommunications. The text and pedagogical features are designed to provide a truly interactive learning experience, preparing readers to put their knowledge to work on a real voice or data network. By reading this text and performing the end-of-chapter projects, students also position themselves for further study in advanced telecommunications or networking. Each chapter includes Hands-on Projects that lead readers through various tasks in a step-by-step fashion. Each chapter also contains case studies that place readers in the role of problem solver, requiring them to apply concepts presented in the chapter to achieve a successful solution.

Chapter Descriptions

Individual chapters discuss the following topics:

Chapter 1, "Telecommunications Overview," introduces different types of telecommunications services and describes how they are used. It also introduces the most prominent standards organizations that contribute to global telecommunications technology specifications.

Chapter 2, "Principles of Telecommunications Technology," explains how electric current is used to generate telecommunications signals, illustrates the differences between analog and digital communications, and discusses different ways in which data is encoded and measured.

Chapter 3, "The Evolution of Telecommunications Technology and Policy," guides the reader through the evolution of telecommunications signaling and transmission, from the invention of the telephone to computerized switching. It also describes the evolution of telecommunications policy in the United States, including the growth and breakup of AT&T and the origins of today's competitive business environment.

Chapter 4, "The Public Network," outlines the types of businesses that deliver telephone and other telecommunications services to nearly every American household. It describes each part of the public network, including inside and outside plant. Finally, it explains how common carriers interact for call routing and billing.

Chapter 5, "Customer Premise Equipment and Applications," discusses telecommunications equipment and services from an end-user's standpoint. This chapter includes private switching and enhanced calling features.

Chapters 6, "Signaling and Switching," explains common modulation and multiplexing techniques used in telecommunications transmission. It also describes the different types of switching used on voice and data networks. Finally, it describes how conventional telephone switches handle call setup, routing, supervision, and other functions.

Chapter 7, "Data Networking Fundamentals," introduces data networking concepts including the OSI Model, the components of a client-server network, and protocols such as TCP/IP and IPX/SPX.

Chapter 8, "Physical Transmission Media," provides detailed information about coaxial cable, non-twisted and twisted-pair copper cables, and fiber optic cables. It also includes installation and troubleshooting guidelines for transmission media.

Chapter 9, "Wireless Transmission and Services," describes the unique signaling and transmission techniques used with wireless telecommunications, including cellular telephone networks, satellite communication, and wireless LANs.

Chapter 10, "Network Access and Transmission Methods," explains data network topologies and network access methods, such as Ethernet and ATM. It also discusses network transmission methods including T-carriers, DSL, and ISDN that can be used for both data and voice communication.

Chapter 11, "Data Network Connectivity," examines the components that allow computers, printers, IP telephones, and other devices to communicate across a data network. The chapter describes the purpose, technical requirements, and interoperability for each device.

Chapter 12, "Internet Standards and Services," explains how the Internet, the largest and most varied data network in the world, came to be. It also discusses the technology behind services unique to TCP/IP-based networks, including e-mail, the Web, and e-commerce.

Chapter 13, "Information Security," addresses the security concerns inherent in all tele-communications technology. It examines the most likely threats for both telephone and computer networks and provides techniques for countering these threats.

Chapter 14, "Convergence of Voice, Video, and Data," presents examples of how one network can carry voice, video, and data signals at the same time. It describes the end user equipment, network design, connectivity devices, transmission techniques, and protocols necessary for issuing voice and video signals over data networks.

Appendix A, "Digital Encoding Methods," provides a table of binary, hexadecimal, and ASCII codes with their decimal number equivalents.

Features

To aid you in fully understanding networking concepts, this book includes many features designed to enhance your learning experience.

- **Chapter Objectives** Each chapter begins with a detailed list of the concepts to be mastered within that chapter. This list provides you with both a quick reference to the chapter's contents and a useful study aid.

- **Illustrations and Tables** Numerous illustrations of signal graphs, theoretical mod-els, network designs, and telecommunications equipment help you to visualize and better understand technical concepts. In addition, the many tables included provide concise references on essential topics such as data transmission rates, common car-riers, cabling types, and networking standards.

- **Hands-on Projects** Although it is important to understand the theory behind telecommunications technology, nothing can compare to real-world experience. To this end, along with thorough explanations, each chapter provides numerous Hands-on Projects aimed at providing you with practical implementation experience.

- **Chapter Summaries** Each chapter's text is followed by a summary of the concepts introduced in that chapter. These summaries provide a helpful way to revisit the ideas covered in each chapter.

- **Review Questions** The chapter summary is followed by a set of review questions that reinforce the ideas introduced in each chapter. Answering these questions will ensure that you have mastered the important concepts.

- **Case Projects** Located at the end of each chapter are several cases. In these exten-sive exercises, you implement the skills and knowledge gained in the chapter through analysis of realistic telecommunications environments. Case projects stimulate you to translate technical theory into workable implementations.

Text and Graphic Conventions

Wherever appropriate, additional information and exercises have been added to this book to help you better understand the topic at hand. Icons throughout the text alert you to additional materials. The icons used in this textbook are described below.

 The Note icon draws your attention to additional helpful material related to the subject being described.

 Each hands-on project in this book is preceded by the Hands-On icon and a description of the exercise that follows.

 Tips based on the authors' experience provide extra information about how to attack a problem or what to do in real-world situations.

 The cautions warn you about potential mistakes or problems and explains how to avoid them.

 Case Project icons mark case projects, which are more involved, scenario-based assignments. In these extensive case examples, you are asked to implement independently what you have learned.

Instructor's Materials

The following additional materials are available when this book is used in a classroom setting. All of the supplements available with this book are provided to the instructor on a single CD-ROM.

Electronic Instructor's Manual The Instructor's Manual that accompanies this textbook includes:

- Additional instructional material to assist in class preparation, including suggestions for classroom activities, discussion topics, and additional projects.
- Solutions to all hands-on projects and end-of-chapter materials, including the review questions and case projects.

ExamView® This textbook is accompanied by ExamView, a powerful testing software package that allows instructors to create and administer printed, computer (LAN-based), and Internet exams. ExamView includes hundreds of questions that correspond to the topics covered in this text, enabling students to generate detailed study guides that include page references for further review. The computer-based and Internet testing components allow students to take exams at their computers and also save the instructor time by grading each exam automatically.

PowerPoint presentations. This book comes with Microsoft PowerPoint slides for each chapter. These are included as a teaching aid for classroom presentation, to be made available to students on the network for chapter review, or to be printed for classroom distribution. Instructors, please feel at liberty to add your own slides for additional topics you introduce to the class.

Figure files. All of the figures and tables in the book are reproduced on the Instructor's Resource CD, in bitmap format. Similar to the PowerPoint presentations, these are included as a teaching aid for classroom presentation, to make available to students for review, or to be printed for classroom distribution.

ACKNOWLEDGMENTS

Many generous and talented people contributed to the making of this book. Thanks to Steve Elliot, Associate Publisher and Will Pitkin, Senior Editor, for their ongoing dedication to the project. Thanks to Lisa Egan, Senior Editor, for coordinating the project from the start and to Amy Lyon, Product Manager, for brilliantly orchestrating communications, schedules, reviews, quality, design, production, and many more things I never had to think about. I am deeply grateful to Ann Shaffer, Developmental Editor and friend, for knowing exactly how to clarify and improve the text, and for offering all sorts of good advice. Thanks also to Lisa Ruffolo for editing assistance. Special thanks to Abby Reip for her tenacity and patience in obtaining the right photos. Thanks to Elena Montillo, Production Editor, and to the copyeditor, Karen Annett, who minded the details and polished the final drafts for production. Credit goes to the Course Technology quality assurance staff who checked my work at every step. I'm also grateful to the reviewers who carefully read the drafts and took the time to suggest changes for the better. Thanks to James Conrad for his insightful technical reviews. A special thanks to Vicki Hunsinger, who offered her time and expert advice in person.

Paul Bauer	University of Denver, Daniels College of Business
Sanjiv Gulshan	Verizon
Vicki Hunsinger	DeVry Training, Chicago
Gary Kessler	Champlain College
Keith Morneau	Northern Virginia Community College

For additional help with research and technical material, I'm grateful to Tom Callaci, Nancy Gibson, and Kurt Grantin at TDS Telecom, Brian Rogers and Suzanne Godfrey at Norlight Telecommunications, Peyton Engel, David Klann and Jerry Steinhauer at Berbee Information Networks, and Alicia Dunnigan and others at the Federal Communications Commission. Thanks, as ever, to Paul and Janet Dean for their encouragement and enthusiasm.

Tamara Dean

PHOTO CREDITS

Cover Image	Ron Garnett, *AirScapes*: Lower Wedgeport, Nova Scotia
Figure 2-13	Courtesy of Jameco Electronics
Figure 2-18	Vishay Intertechnology, Inc.
Figure 2-20	Courtesy of Jameco Electronics
Figure 2-22	Courtesy of Agilent Technologies
Figure 2-23	Courtesy of Tektronix
Figure 2-25	Courtesy of Jameco Electronics
Figure 2-28	Courtesy of Jameco Electronics
Figure 2-30	Courtesy of Jameco Electronics
Figure 2-31	Courtesy of Jameco Electronics
Figure 3-1	Smithsonian Photo by Alfred Harrell
Figure 3-2	Ron Christianson *www.museumphones.com*
Figure 3-3	© CORBIS
Figure 3-4	© Bettmann/CORBIS
Figure 3-6	John D. Jenkins/*www.sparkmuseum.com*
Figure 3-8	Courtesy of IBM Archives
Figure 3-9	Courtesy of University of Pennsylvania
Figure 4-2	Courtesy of Corning Cable Systems
Figure 4-3	Courtesy of Telect, Inc.
Figure 4-7	Courtesy of Marconi Corporation plc
Figure 4-9	Courtesy of the author with permission from TDS Telecom
Figure 4-11	Courtesy of the author with permission from TDS Telecom
Figure 4-12	Courtesy of the author with permission from TDS Telecom
Figure 4-14	Courtesy of the author with permission from TDS Telecom
Figure 4-15	Courtesy of Homaco
Figure 4-17	Courtesy of the author with permission from TDS Telecom
Figure 5-2a	© 2003 PhotoDisc
Figure 5-2b	© corbisstockmarket.com
Figure 5-7	© Eyewire Collection
Figure 5-10	Courtesy of Bourns
Figure 5-12	© CORBIS
Figure 5-13	Courtesy of Ultratec, Inc.
Figure 5-14a	Courtesy of Comdial
Figure 5-14b	Courtesy of Nortel Networks

Read This Before You Begin

The Hands-on Projects in this book help you to apply what you have learned about telecommunications technology. Although modern voice and data networking components can be expensive, the projects aim to use widely available and moderately priced hardware and software. The following section lists the minimum hardware and software requirements that allow you to complete all the Hands-on Projects in this book. In addition to the following requirements, students must have administrator privileges on their workstations and for some exercises, on the class server, to successfully complete the project.

Lab Requirements

- **Hardware:**

  - Each student workstation and each server computer requires at least 128 MB of RAM, an Intel Pentium or compatible processor running at 233 MHz or higher, and a minimum of 50 MB of free space on the hard disk. The computer should also have a modern sound card, speakers, and at least one free PCI slot.

  - For exploring old and new customer premise equipment, two pre-1970s rotary telephones and one newer, inexpensive touchtone telephone are necessary.

  - For installing computer equipment, students need a computer repair toolkit that includes a static mat and wrist guard, and both flathead and Phillips screwdrivers, and a utility knife.

  - For working with computer connectivity, each student needs a removable Ethernet 10/100BaseT PCI network interface card.

  - For experiments with physical transmission media, students require a networking toolkit that includes the following cable-making supplies: at least 30 feet of CAT5 or higher cabling, at least six RJ-45 plugs, a wire cutter, a cable stripper, a crimping tool, and a punch-down tool.

  - For implementing a basic client-server network, a class requires at least two Ethernet hubs that are both capable of 10BaseT or 100BaseT transmission and four or more CAT5 or higher straight-through patch cables that are each at least 3 feet long.

  - For making a homemade telegraph and other simple electromagnetic devices, students need AA and D batteries, tape, 24-30 AWG copper wire, thumbtacks, nails, paperclips, sandpaper, corrugated cardboard, a wire stripper, a wire cutter, and an electric buzzer.

- **Software:**
    - Windows 2000 Professional or Windows XP for each student workstation
    - Windows 2000 Server for each server computer
    - Either the Netscape or Internet Explorer Web browser, version 5.0 or higher
    - The latest version of WinZip file compression and expansion software
    - The latest version of Adobe Acrobat Reader

1

TELECOMMUNICATIONS
OVERVIEW

> **After reading this chapter and completing the exercises, you will be able to:**
>
> ◆ Define communication and telecommunication
>
> ◆ Illustrate components of a communication system
>
> ◆ Understand the difference between voice, video, and data telecommunications
>
> ◆ Describe how telecommunication is used in a variety of industries
>
> ◆ Identify careers available to telecommunications professionals
>
> ◆ Identify the organizations responsible for establishing significant telecommunications standards and policies

Telecommunications is a broad area of study, encompassing everything from a telephone call between neighbors to a satellite transmission across the globe. Whether you realize it or not, you are probably personally familiar with telecommunications technology. If you have ever used a computer, the Internet, a pager, cellular phone, or other telephone, you have used a telecommunications service. In addition to being critical in personal communications, telecommunication is also a vital part of success in business.

This chapter highlights some of the vital telecommunications services in use today. It also describes a number of ways in which telecommunications technology is actually being used by businesses and government organizations. Finally, it provides an overview of the careers available in telecommunications. You can think of this chapter as not only an introduction to the field, but also a roadmap for the rest of this book, which focuses on the technologies that make telephone- and computer-based telecommunications possible.

WHAT IS COMMUNICATION?

In an earlier age, the Romans used the Latin word *communicare* when they meant "to make common, to share, or to impart." The modern word **communication** is used to refer to a particular kind of sharing—the sharing of information or messages between two or more entities. The following sections introduce you to the elements of modern communications.

Personal and Data Communications

As with any kind of sharing or exchange, communication requires at least two entities. One part must send the information, whereas the other receives it—though the entities sending and receiving information need not be human.

When the parties sending and receiving information *are* human, **personal communication** occurs. **Data communication**, on the other hand, involves an exchange of information between electrical or electronic devices (such as computers).

Take a moment to think about the nature of personal communication first. The most obvious example of personal communication is a conversation between two people. But personal communication can come in other forms—for example, a student reading the novel *Jane Eyre* is taking part in a kind of personal communication. In this example, Charlotte Bronte, the author of the novel, can be considered the sending party whereas the student is the receiving party. As you can see, personal communication does not necessarily mean face-to-face conversations—it occurs whenever humans interact in some way.

By contrast, data communication is what occurs when your computer issues commands over the telephone line and a computer at your Internet Service Provider (such as America Online) receives and interprets those commands to allow you to connect to the Internet. Unlike personal communication, which may use sound waves or printed letters, data communication uses electrical means to convey information. Note that some forms of personal communication, such as a telephone call, rely on data communication to convey information from the sender to the recipient.

Despite their different methods, data and personal communications share some common elements. For example, in both cases, information must be presented in a format that the receiver can understand. In personal communications, the format is known as language. In data communications, this format is generally known as a code, and the pieces of information exchanged are known as **data**.

Elements of a Communication System

Every type of communication (whether personal or data) involves a source, transmitter, communications channel, receiver, and destination. Each of these items is depicted in Figure 1-1. The **source** is the originator of the message, whether it is a person or machine. For example, if you live in Phoenix and you phone your grandmother in Raleigh, you are the source of the communication. The **transmitter** is the equipment that modifies the message (either data or voice) into the form required for transmission. In the example above, the vibrating mechanism in your telephone handset is the transmitter. The **communications channel** is the means of carrying the signal from the source to the destination. In the context of data communications, a communication channel is more commonly referred to as the **transmission media**, or sometimes simply, **media**. Transmission media may be physical, like a copper wire or fiber optic cable, or atmospheric, like radio waves. In the phone call example, the telephone wires in your house, your local telephone company's wires, the long distance phone company's network, your grandmother's local phone company's wires, and the telephone wires in your grandmother's house are all part of the communications channel.

The **receiver** is the device that captures the message from the communications channel and converts it into a form that the person or machine at the destination can understand. One example of a receiver is the electromagnetic coil and speaker in your grandmother's telephone handset. Finally, the **destination** in a communications exchange is the person or machine to whom the message is directed—in this example, your grandmother.

Figure 1-1 Elements of a Communication Process

Although all communications systems include these elements, the nature of each element varies from one communication system to the next. For example, in a network of computers, the transmitter is part of a network interface card, whereas in a paging system, the transmitter is mounted on an antenna. In another example, the communications channel for a long distance telephone call might be a fiber optic cable across the nation, whereas the communications channel for a local telephone call might be a copper wire connected to the local telephone company's facilities.

Flow of Messages

All communication can be divided into different types, based on a number of characteristics. For instance, it's sometimes helpful to divide communications systems according to the way messages flow within the system—that is, whether messages can flow in only one direction, in two directions in turn, or in two directions simultaneously. The type of communication in which messages flow in only one direction, from source to destination, is known as **simplex**. An example of simplex communication is a high school principal using a public announcement (p.a.) system to read the day's announcements to multiple classrooms. This system does not allow for students in the classrooms to reply over the communications channel, thus it is considered one-way, or simplex.

By contrast, **half-duplex** communication occurs when messages travel in both directions between the source and the destination, but in only one direction at a time. An example of half-duplex communication is a CB radio on which you must push a button on the mouthpiece to talk, then release the button before you can listen to the other party's response. Both parties using a CB radio cannot talk at the same time.

A third type of communications is **full duplex**. In full-duplex communication, messages can travel over the communications channel in both directions simultaneously. Full-duplex communication occurs when you talk to a friend on the telephone. Because it is possible for both of you to talk and listen to each other at the same time, you are using full-duplex communication. Full-duplex communication is sometimes simply called **duplex** communication. Simplex, half-duplex, and full-duplex communications are depicted in Figure 1-2. Note that these terms apply to personal communications as well as data communications.

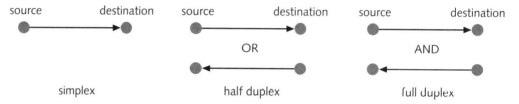

Figure 1-2   Simplex, half-duplex, and full-duplex communications

Relative Number of Sources and Destinations

Besides the flow of messages, another common method of categorizing types of communication is according to the relative number of sources and destinations. Both data and personal communications transmit information in a one-to-one, one-to-many, or many-to-many fashion, as pictured in Figure 1-3.

In **one-to-one** communication, a single source sends information to a single destination. For example, if you send an e-mail to your supervisor without copying anyone else, you are issuing one-to-one communication. A telephone call from a woman to her stockbroker is another example of one-to-one communication. In each case, the one-to-one communication allows for only one sender and one receiver. One-to-one communication is also known as **point-to-point** communication.

In **one-to-many** communication, a single source simultaneously sends information to multiple destinations. This is also known as **broadcast** communication. An example of one-to-many communication is a college professor lecturing to a room of thirty students. Another example is radio and TV broadcasting. In this example, the single source is a radio or TV station using radio frequency waves as its communications channel to reach many viewers or listeners. In yet another example, one computer on a network may issue a message to every other computer connected to the network, requesting information about the location of a printer on the network.

Many-to-many communication occurs when many sources issue messages to many destinations. For example, many-to-many communication takes place when a group of business people sit in a conference room talking and listening through a speakerphone to another group in a different conference room. In this case, the communication involves many senders and many receivers.

Figure 1-3 illustrates one-to-one, one-to-many, and many-to-many communications. You will find examples of all three types of communications throughout this book.

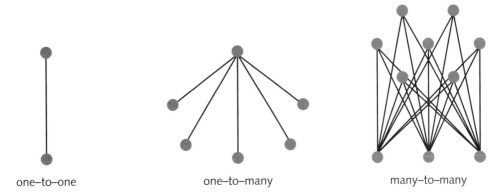

one–to–one   one–to–many   many–to–many

Figure 1-3 One–to–one, one–to–many, and many–to–many communications

WHAT IS TELECOMMUNICATION?

The word telecommunication derives from the Greek word *tele*, meaning over a distance, plus the word *communication*. Thus, putting these two parts together, you get **telecommunication**—communication that spans a distance. An ancient example of telecommunications is the use of fire signals on hilltops that are miles apart. These days, modern telecommunications is a vast field that encompasses everything from broadcasting to telephone technology to computer networks.

Within the field of telecommunications, professionals typically divide its services into three categories: voice, video, and data. **Voice telecommunication** refers to any means of using electrical signals to transmit human voice across a distance, such as telephones and radio broadcasts. **Video telecommunication** refers to the electrically-based transmission of moving pictures and sound across a distance, such as TV broadcasting or distributing live feeds of an event to the screens of networked computers. Finally, **data telecommunication** refers to the use of electrical signals to exchange encoded (in other words, specially formatted) information between computerized devices across a distance. Sending an e-mail to a colleague, retrieving a spreadsheet from your computer's hard disk, and sending a message to your spouse's pager are all examples of data telecommunications. Note that voice, video, and data telecommunications all belong to the larger "data communication" category described in the previous section, because they all rely on electrical signals. This book focuses primarily on voice and data telecommunications, including the study of telephone technology (also known as **telephony**) and computer networking. Figure 1-4 offers a view of the array of telecommunications services.

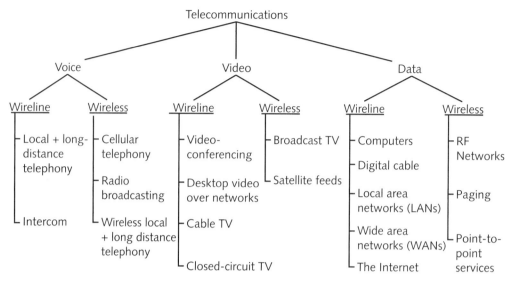

Figure 1-4   Telecommunications services

MODERN TELECOMMUNICATIONS SYSTEMS

Modern telecommunication has evolved from primitive fire signals to lightning-fast global data exchange. In this book, you learn about the steps in this evolution, including the technological and political factors that influenced the growth of the industry. This section provides you with an overview of voice and data telecommunications systems in use today and introduces you to the scope of the significant telecommunications topics discussed in this book. Don't expect to absorb all the information provided here. Instead, consider this section a guided tour of the world of telecommunications. You'll learn about the details throughout the course of this book.

Voice

We are all familiar with the most popular 20th century voice telecommunications apparatus, the telephone. The telephone is still the primary means of transmitting and receiving voice signals. From a user's perspective, the telephone changed little during the 20th century; however, its core technology underwent dramatic transformation. Each advance made telephony faster, more reliable, and capable of carrying a greater volume of signals for longer distances. In 1925, for example, each telephone call had to be physically connected by an operator at a switchboard. This not only increased the time necessary to complete a phone call, but it also limited the privacy of the information exchanged. Now, however, telephone calls are automatically and electronically routed to their destination in a matter of microseconds, and they are much more difficult to intercept. That's only one example of what modern telephone technology has achieved. Consider the advanced features, such as call waiting, caller ID, conference calling, and call forwarding, that residents can order along with their basic phone service. None of these features were possible until the late 20th century, thanks to advances in the telephone companies' equipment.

Telephony advances have also helped businesses. Imagine a world in which legal documents must be hand-delivered to be signed, colleagues have to relay messages through receptionists if they cannot connect to their called party, and a business person has to fly cross country to share figures, documents, and conversations with a group of associates. These were typical business scenarios only twenty years ago. Now, however, legal documents can be faxed and signed immediately, colleagues can bypass receptionists and leave messages on voice mail or e-mail, and associates can meet through voice or video conference calls to share figures, documents, and conversation. These are only small examples of how telecommunication has transformed business. Later in this chapter, you will read true stories illustrating how advanced telephony and computer networking are critical to the bottom line of modern businesses.

Today's telephony **infrastructure** is a collection of cables, wires, connectivity devices, users, and user equipment all working together, in ever more complex ways. The telephony infrastructure includes cross-continental fiber optic cable to facilitate international voice telecommunications and national and regional cabling to connect long distance calls. It includes numerous local, regional, and national switching centers where phone calls are routed to their destinations by computerized telephone switches. It also includes local connections (up to three miles in length) to residences and businesses capable of greater connection speed and volume than ever before. Finally, it includes the sophisticated telephone equipment and applications that users rely on. In fact, much of this progress occurred only in the last quarter century, thanks to two powerful events: the invention of the semiconductor and the breakup of AT&T. You'll learn about both of these events later in Chapter 3, along with other significant turning points in telecommunications technology and history. You will also learn how telephones integrate with computers and networks at multiple levels to provide faster, more reliable, and more feature-rich services.

Data

One of the first data telecommunications inventions was the **telegraph**, a device invented in the 1860s that uses a wire to convey electrical pulses that represent letters or numbers over a distance. From this starting point, data telecommunications evolved throughout the 20th century, thanks to innovations in materials, electricity, and encoding techniques. (In Chapter 3, you learn more about each step in the evolution of telecommunications technology.) These technological advances mean we can now send a much greater volume of data much faster and over much longer distances than in the early days of the telegraph. For example, although it might have taken ten minutes for a telegraph operator to send a one-paragraph message in 1880, a modern network can send the same amount of information to its destination in nanoseconds. Newer data telecommunications technology is not only faster, but it also ensures better accuracy due to more reliable transmission media and techniques that enable the receiver to monitor the integrity of the data it has received.

Following are some examples of present-day data telecommunications technologies:

- Encoded information transmitted over traditional telephone lines (for example, a modem connecting to an Internet Service Provider's server)

- Encoded information saved to fixed media, such as a hard disk, floppy disk, or CD ROM

- Encoded information exchanged between two computers that are directly connected by a single cable

- Encoded information exchanged by a group of connected computers on a network

- Encoded information exchanged by two devices over radio waves (for example, paging systems)

As noted in the previous list, data telecommunications are often defined by the method in which they transmit and receive data, the transmission media they use, and the types of sources and receivers involved in data exchange. This book dedicates a great deal of space to **networks**, which are groups of computers and other devices (such as printers) that are interconnected to more easily exchange data and share resources. In this book, you learn about many kinds of networks, including those that use physical transmission media (such as wire) and those that use atmospheric transmission media (such as radio waves). Networks form the foundation for most major data telecommunications systems because connecting multiple, computerized devices enables sources to send more data to more recipients in a shorter period of time than, for example, using floppy disks or two connected computers to exchange information.

Note that the distinction between voice and data communication is sometimes blurred. As you'll learn, data telecommunications are often used to transmit voice signals. For example, a computer network can be used to encode voice into bits of data and send it over a wire. This combination of voice, video, and data communication along the same communications channel is called **convergence**. Convergence is the future of telecommunications services, and this book helps you understand the technologies and driving forces behind it.

Types of Telecommunications Companies

Besides the history and technology of voice and data telecommunications, this book also delves into the types of companies that provide telecommunications services. You also learn about the agencies that make sure these companies work within established laws and conventions. You may be aware that for a majority of the 20th century, one telephone company, the Bell System (or AT&T), dominated voice telecommunications in the United States. Because the growth, maintenance, and dissolution of the monolithic Bell System are significant aspects of telecommunications development, this book examines them in depth in Chapter 3. After you understand how the Bell System evolved, you will begin to understand how today's telecommunications companies in business emerged.

The way in which the Bell System was dissolved (by first separating its Equipment Manufacturing Division from its Telephone Service Division) resulted in a similar partitioning of telecommunications companies in the United States. Companies can be roughly divided into **service providers**, those that supply the communications channels for voice and data transmission, and **equipment providers**, those that supply the user and connectivity equipment, such as telephones. For example, U.S. Cellular is an example of a service provider; it provides the infrastructure necessary for customers to make cellular telephone calls. However, U.S. Cellular does not manufacture cellular phones. An equipment provider, such as Nokia or Motorola, supplies U.S. Cellular's customers with telephones. Nor does U.S. Cellular manufacture its own radio antennas and transmitters, but rather purchases these components from equipment providers.

The distinctions between service providers and equipment providers may not always seem clear. For example, suppose you request caller ID service from your local telephone company (which is a service provider). The telephone company might supply you with a piece of equipment that displays the name and number of the party who's calling you. This piece of equipment may have the local telephone company's name on the outside, leading you to believe that perhaps they manufactured it. However, if you disassembled the box, you would probably find a different company's name inside, one that focused on manufacturing equipment. In that case, the telephone company merely distributed the device.

Another natural distinction between types of telecommunications companies separates voice, video, and data telecommunications companies. For example, your local telephone company has traditionally focused on carrying voice signals over its infrastructure, whereas a company such as NBC focused on carrying video signals. At the same time, a company such as Qwest focused on carrying data signals. Meanwhile, an equipment manufacturer such as Lucent (the latest version of the old Bell System's equipment division) focused on supplying equipment to connect voice systems, RCA focused on making equipment to connect video systems, and Cisco focused on making equipment to connect data systems. However, as you might guess, the distinctions between what each of these equipment providers manufactures and what each of the service providers carry are also blurring as voice and video signals are increasingly carried over data connections. In fact, Cisco now manufactures voice connectivity equipment, local telephone companies carry data signals over their infrastructure, and traditional broadcasting companies, such as NBC, provide services over the Internet.

Growth of the Telecommunications Industry

To say that the telecommunications industry is growing rapidly is an understatement. At the time of this writing, the United States government recently released a report citing the number of high-speed (faster than a normal telephone line) lines connecting individuals and businesses to the Internet increased 36% during the first half of the year 2001, for a total of 9.6 million high-speed connections. This is a 250% increase over the number of high-speed lines that existed by the end of 1999. The number of minutes Americans spend on interstate long-distance telephone calls has quadrupled in the last 25 years to a total of

600 billion minutes. At the same time, surveys indicate that 61% of American households have personal computers. As of July 2001, the number of computers that provide files and Web pages to users on the Internet had grown to over 125 million, maintaining a 63% annual growth rate. Many more statistics are available, and all indicate upward trends.

The explosive growth in telecommunications made a significant contribution to the world's economy during the 1990s. It also resulted in a shortage of skilled workers capable of programming software, installing and maintaining high-speed lines, configuring and troubleshooting networks, and consulting with companies on how best to implement telecommunications. Though the growth rate of some voice and data telecommunications businesses has slowed in the past few years, these companies will undoubtedly continue to succeed, and the field will continue to generate plenty of job opportunities. Later in this chapter you will learn about possibilities in the telecommunications field.

TELECOMMUNICATIONS AT WORK

Now that you know what kinds of applications and companies fall under the label "telecommunications," you are ready to learn how telecommunications are transforming modern business. Each of the following sections describe true, real-life situations that illustrate the ways voice, video, or data telecommunications in different industry segments are shaping business. As you read, make mental notes about the variety of infrastructure and expertise required to make each project a success. Later, after you learn more about specific telecommunications technologies, you can refer back to these stories with deeper understanding.

Financial Services

Financial institutions are essentially information processors, and as such, all rely on telecommunications systems to maintain customer records, inform customers about services and accounts, and conduct financial transactions. One of the most impressive instances of telecommunications in the financial services industry takes place at a multinational bank's **call center**, a facility dedicated to fielding customer calls. A call center typically consists of multiple, trained personnel (also called "agents") and multiple telephone lines. A large institution's call center handles over four million calls each year and employs 290 personnel to answer phones. Given the volume of calls the bank must handle, every opportunity to streamline responses to customers means a significant savings in operation costs.

One way a bank saves money and customers' time is by using an **interactive voice response (IVR)** system, a method of sending information over the telephone by pressing buttons in response to recorded voice prompts, to answer routine questions. An IVR is entirely automated. After greeting a caller, the system prompts him to answer a question by pressing a number on his phone. It may contain several levels of questions in its menu. Figure 1-5 shows an example of an IVR menu that can provide bank customers with information about their accounts.

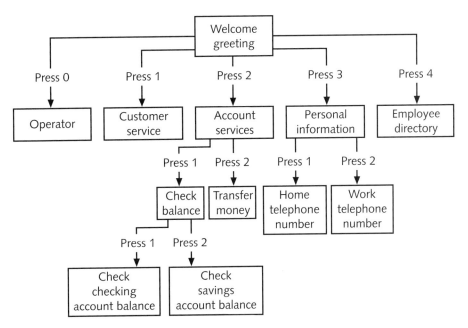

Figure 1-5 An IVR menu

IVR systems can save the information indicated by the caller during the phone call on a computer. If your bank allows you to perform accounting and administrative services by phone, it probably uses an IVR system. After you call the IVR number, you may hear a recording that says, "Press 1 now to reach our Customer Service Department, Press 2 for account services, Press 3 to change your personal information," and so on. If you press 3, you might be prompted to enter your account number and a password. These are checked against information on the bank's computer to verify your identity. Next, you might be prompted to choose the type of personal information you want to change. For instance: "Press 1 to change your home telephone number, Press 2 to change your work telephone number," and so on. If you press 1, you are prompted to enter a new home telephone number. The new number you entered is saved in the bank's computer files that contain your personal information.

In the case of a multinational bank, 25% of its customers' calls might be handled by the IVR system. That means some customers never need to speak to a live attendant. This frees call center personnel to spend time on more complex customer questions.

Another advanced telecommunications feature used in a bank's call center is an **automatic call distributor (ACD)**. An ACD system uses computerized devices attached to the phone lines to automatically route calls to specific phone extensions. Originally, ACD systems were designed to evenly distribute the volume of incoming calls to multiple agents. For example, if a call center employs five agents, and three are busy, one just hung up his phone, and one has not taken a call in twenty minutes, the ACD routes a new call to the agent who has not answered a call in twenty minutes. Newer ACD systems have even more intelligence. For example, a multinational bank might use an ACD system that relies on a customer's IVR system input to route his call to the agent who can best answer his question.

Any large organization that must field a number of customer questions is likely to have a call center with an ACD system. To function well, call centers require not only a sound telecommunications infrastructure, but also ongoing training for personnel on the company's services, products, and policies. Later in the book, you learn more about advanced telecommunications services. Next, you learn about how utility companies are using call center technology to improve customer service and hopefully, prevent their customers from choosing a different utility provider.

Utilities

Recent deregulation (the introduction of competition for services) in the utilities industry has made telecommunications even more critical to this industry. Whereas power companies used to enjoy government-sanctioned monopolies on providing gas and electricity in their territory, they are now subject to competition from any other qualified utility company that wants to offer those services. To persuade their customers not to choose another utility provider, utility companies must strive harder to please their customers, in part by answering questions as promptly as possible.

An advanced call center at a utilities company typically uses both an ACD and an IVR. Upon calling, a customer initially accesses the IVR system. If the utility company is experiencing a temporary power outage, due to an ice storm, hurricane, or flood, for example, the IVR system might begin with a message explaining approximately how long it will take the company to restore electricity or gas service. These pre-recorded messages can be entered, changed, or deleted at any time by a call center supervisor. During a power outage, such a message will likely answer most customer questions, thereby avoiding the necessity for agents to personally answer many of the incoming calls. If customers prefer to speak with an agent, however, they can always press a button to do so. Utility IVR systems also enable customers to inquire about their bills, request an extension on their payment deadline, report outages, and request disconnection or connection of services. Some IVR systems can even be programmed to automatically call customers when a power outage will affect them.

In addition to offering advanced voice telecommunications services, utility companies are also making use of advanced data telecommunications. A large power company in the southern United States, for example, provides customers the option of viewing and paying their utility bills via the Internet. Customers may also submit forms to request connection and disconnection of their services over the Internet. Finally, just as customers can call the utility for more information, this company also allows them to send questions to customer support staff through e-mail. Not long after advertising this service, the utility company began to receive hundreds of e-mail inquiries each month, and this number continues to grow.

Manufacturing

The use of advanced voice, video, and data telecommunications in manufacturing has resulted in faster and more efficient production of goods and at the same time it has also increased global competition. In the early part of the 20th century, obtaining parts from overseas suppliers was slow and expensive, thus giving an advantage to domestic suppliers. In the early 21st century, however, those barriers have been nearly erased. Manufacturers must adopt new technology, including advanced communications, to remain competitive.

Supply chain management, an electronic means for connecting a manufacturer with its suppliers and distributors is a notable example of the use of telecommunications in the manufacturing industry. Telecommunications can also be used for quality control. (For example, an auto company in Detroit currently inspects parts made in Prague using high-quality digital photos transmitted over a global network.) It can also be used in asset management—the process of identifying and tracking every asset a company owns, scheduling, entering orders, and controlling inventory.

One company that makes use of nearly all of these technologies is a large U.S. orthopedics manufacturer that supplies artificial replacements for hips, knees, and shoulders. First, salespeople from 28 locations across the United States enter customer orders into a database. This database resides on a computer to which personnel across the company have access through high-speed data connections. At the company headquarters in Texas, employees check the orders for accuracy. Then, in the manufacturing facility, production supervisors use the verified information to predict how long orders will take to fulfill, to schedule staff for necessary tasks, and to indicate the amount of material they need to requisition to replenish the stock that these orders will require. This same database drives an automated bin carousel that contains multiple component bins rotating on a conveyor system. The bin carousel translates order information into parts, rotating and depositing multiple parts before a production operator, the person responsible for completing the order. A production operator then merely needs to pick up the parts and assemble them to actually create an orthopedic device. After orders are shipped from the manufacturing facility, the order database is updated to reflect the shipment. Using such an advanced telecommunications system for manufacturing has resulted in the orthopedics company shipping all orders on the same day they are received—a very impressive accomplishment.

Transportation

Telecommunications and transportation share many similarities. Both convey things (voice, video, and data; or goods and people), both use defined routes for their conveyance, and both rely on access to public infrastructure. For example, telecommunications requires underground conduits, telephone poles, transoceanic pathways, and satellite orbits. Transportation requires highways, railroads, shipping canals, flight paths, and so on. In fact, some telecommunications links use routes, such as highway and railroad systems, that were once meant strictly for transportation. Thus, it is not surprising that the transportation industry is closely linked to and largely dependent on telecommunications.

Some examples of the transportation industry's use of telecommunications include: computerized flight control for airport traffic, software that issues maps and directions based on a given starting point and destination, government-sponsored transportation hotlines that inform callers about road construction and hazardous road conditions, and systems for suggesting the most efficient route between multiple locations (for use by taxicabs or couriers, for example).

One of the most exciting new technologies to influence transportation is designed for automobiles. For a few years, some cars have been equipped with navigational systems that use satellite transmission of geographical data to assist drivers in finding their destinations. Now those navigational systems are becoming even more sophisticated. A new telecommunications system allows drivers to create personal profiles of addresses, transportation preferences, and frequently followed routes before they get in their cars. These preferences are saved by a telecommunications service provider and made available to the driver through radio wave transmission to the car's antenna.

For example, a pharmaceutical salesman in northern Illinois might keep a list of doctors and clinicians, his customers, on his computer. After he signs up for the personalized navigation telecommunications system, he can copy this list of customers and their addresses to the navigational system, which is located on a computer at the service provider's facility. He may also decide that he does not want to travel on Chicago's Kennedy Expressway during the months of June through August, because it will be under construction. He can add this information to his personal navigational profile; during that period of time, the system will never recommend a route that uses the Kennedy Expressway.

Now suppose that after he signs up for the navigational system, he plans a day of sales calls. From home, he connects to the navigational system and identifies the doctors he wants to visit that day. He further specifies that all of his sales calls should occur within a 20 mile radius. Then, he requests that the system print a route for him to follow that leads him from one customer to the next in the most efficient manner. While in his car, if he desires, the navigational system also prompts the salesman with directions—when to take an exit, where to turn right or left, and so on. To keep the salesman's hands on the steering wheel, this system might offer **voice recognition**, a feature that enables the navigational system to recognize the user's voice and respond to spoken commands. Thus, if he is ready to visit Dr. Susan Anderson at Mercy Memorial Hospital, he can simply say to the receiver in his car, "Retrieve address for Susan Anderson" and the system responds with her address.

Retail

The big news about telecommunications and the retail industry is centered on **e-business**, or the use of data telecommunications to conduct business transactions. One well known form of e-business takes place when a company sells its goods to consumers via the Internet. Some researchers estimate that over half of the population in the United States that had Internet access in 1999 purchased something over the Web. These consumers spent an average of $460 in online goods that year. The statistics for Internet retailing are numerous and varied, but one thing is clear: Without an Internet sales presence, businesses are unable to compete in today's economy.

The apparel and sportswear segment of the retail industry uses particularly sophisticated and unique telecommunications technology for their online business. Some large apparel companies not only allow consumers to view each item in each possible color, but also allow the consumer to enter his or her body measurements and virtually try on the item. For example, suppose you are looking for a new pinstripe oxford shirt, but have never before purchased clothing from this retailer and aren't certain how their shirts fit you. You can create a "virtual model" of your body by entering dimensions for your waist, chest, neck, arm, and so on. After your model has been created, you can choose a style of shirt and with the click of a button, view that shirt on your virtual model. Based on what you see, you can decide whether you want to purchase the item. If you do want to purchase it, this can be accomplished through just one additional mouse click.

Other Web technology has made shopping online simpler and more economical for the consumer. For example, a consumer can sign up for a retailer's e-mail service that automatically notifies the consumer if one of their favorite items has been marked down. Or, to get the best possible price on an item, consumers might use sites that search a number of online retailers at once to return a list of stores that carry the item and its price. Underlying all these online sales features is a large and complex network of high-speed data links that connect computers containing databases of product information with the Internet.

Before the products even reach a retailer's point of sale (such as a Web site), telecommunications technology helps with manufacturing, quality control, inventory, distribution, and product shipping. Retailers rely heavily on advanced telecommunications in their warehouses. For example, one large apparel company with stores in malls across the country recently upgraded its entire warehouse system, including its communications infrastructure. Prior to the upgrade, the workers spent up to three days unloading shipments from clothing manufacturers and placing them in the appropriate place in the 500,000 square foot warehouse, then picking them and shipping them to their stores. As a result of the upgrade, the new clothing stays in the warehouse for as few as 12 hours before being shipped to stores.

The new process works like this: When the boxes of clothing are removed from delivery trucks, bar code scanners (handheld devices that use radio waves to read a series of light and dark lines that represents product information) automatically identify the boxes' contents and store that information on a computer. The computer then determines not only where in the warehouse that box must be stored, but also the most efficient path for a forklift driver to take to deliver the box to its proper place. Later, when a store requests that item, warehouse personnel use handheld computers containing inventory data to locate the item in the warehouse. The same computer removes the product from the warehouse's inventory when it is picked off the shelf, then automatically prints a mailing label. The package is then delivered to the warehouse docks where it is loaded onto a truck for shipping.

Healthcare

You are probably aware that clinics and hospitals use computers to maintain patient records, accounting and inventory information, and personnel schedules. They also use paging and wireless telephone systems to make sure doctors and nurses who are "on call" can be contacted 24 hours a day in case of emergency. But you may not be aware of the latest use of telecommunications in healthcare called **telemedicine**, a field that brings patients and healthcare professionals together by exchanging voice, video, and data over distances when they can't meet face-to-face.

Telemedicine improves the quality of healthcare because ailments can often be diagnosed and treated faster. It also streamlines the record-keeping process for clinicians who spend a great deal of time entering data about their cases. Telemedicine is particularly beneficial for rural patients, but it is used in urban and suburban environments as well. It is such a popular field that entire journals, conferences, classes, and Web sites (for example, *telehealth.net*) are now devoted to discussing it.

An outstanding example of telemedicine takes place in Nova Scotia, Canada. In 1997, the province made a commitment to bringing quality, timely healthcare to all citizens by investing $8 million in a telecommunications infrastructure that connects 43 major hospitals and numerous outlying clinics. Now, patients in remote areas can make electronic visits to specialists rather than traveling to a larger city to meet with a specialist face-to-face. During the visits, their health records and current vital signs can be electronically transmitted to the specialist for review.

For example, suppose an elderly woman in a small coastal town 110 miles east of Halifax, Nova Scotia, fell down a flight of stairs. When her local emergency team arrives to assist, they take her vital signs and determine that she is conscious, mobile, and responding normally. However, they are not certain whether she has sustained any bone fractures. Rather than drive the woman two hours to a large hospital in Halifax, they transport her to the local community clinic, where a general practitioner gives her an exam and takes x-rays of her right arm, right leg, and pelvic region. Meanwhile, a radiologist is summoned in Halifax. After her examination, the woman is positioned before a computer and a video conferencing device, which includes a camera, microphone, and transmitter. The general practitioner connects the videoconferencing system to the Halifax radiologist's video conferencing system. The computers at both the clinic and the Halifax hospital are already connected by the data network, and the clinic uses this network to transmit photos of the woman's x-rays to the Halifax doctor. Through the videoconferencing system, the radiologist asks the woman a number of questions and asks the general practitioner to assist her in performing a few more tests. The data from these tests are electronically transmitted to the Halifax radiologist. After viewing the x-rays and analyzing the test results, the radiologist determines that the woman has not suffered a fracture and requires only moderate painkillers and weeks of bed rest. The data from this visit, including the x-ray photos, are automatically saved in the patient's computerized health records.

Government and Education

Many government agencies use advanced telecommunications to provide faster and easier access to public services. For example, in the United States, each federal agency (for example, the General Services Administration, the Federal Trade Commission, the Securities and Exchange Commission, the Internal Revenue Service) hosts a Web site with information about its services, copies of its reports, lists of contacts for more information, a list of links to other government and business associations, the ability to search for specific information, and sometimes even an avenue for filing a complaint. For example, if you were to connect to the Internet and point your browser to the Federal Trade Commission's (FTC's) Web site, *www.ftc.gov*, you could search for "tobacco advertising" and immediately retrieve a catalog of all the speeches, reports, and press releases that the FTC has issued on this topic. In the "Hands-on Projects" section at the end of this chapter, you will have the opportunity to search the Federal Communications Commission's (FCC's) Web site for current reports about the telecommunications industry.

Local and state governments also make extensive use of telecommunications. Consider local 911 emergency dispatch services. The success of these services relies on not just a telephone line between the caller and the 911 operator, but also a system for recording each call and a computerized method of keeping call data, such as the time the call was received, the name and address of the caller, and the nature of the emergency. In most locations, the automated 911 telecommunications system can detect the caller's address based on the originating telephone number, then save that information on a computer. New technology enables dispatch computers to instantly map the caller's address and indicate the fastest route for an emergency vehicle to take to the caller. A computer may also automatically page the appropriate emergency contact after a call is entered into the system. After the emergency vehicle is en route, the 911 operator can transmit more information about the call to the emergency vehicle's driver through a wireless telephone connection.

Telecommunications also plays a significant role in education. In South Carolina, a large public school district is improving education through distance learning. **Distance learning** is the use of telecommunications technology to inform, educate, or train students across distances. It may use any type of communications channels, sources, and destinations. In South Carolina, the Aiken County Public School District, one of the state's largest, is using distance learning to provide equal quality education to all its students.

Aiken serves over 25,000 students whose homes are spread out over 1178 square miles. Some of the district's schools are in rural areas and serve smaller populations of students than their more suburban counterparts. The Aiken County Public School district, using federal and state grants, and with the help of BellSouth, installed connections to carry audio and video signals between teachers at central schools and students at remote locations. In each classroom, Aiken installed three television sets for students to watch the teacher, plus a camera and microphone for students to ask questions. Aiken's program has enabled all students to take advantage of the district's variety of classes. It has also enabled adult residents of the county to attend high school or continuing education courses. The Aiken County School District has received awards for its technological innovation that connects classrooms. Yet it is not alone. Aiken is one of thousands of districts across the nation using telecommunications to enhance educational opportunities.

New Frontiers for Telecommunications Technology

One of the most impressive wide-scale uses of telecommunications technology was at the 2000 Summer Olympics in Sydney, Australia. During the games, Australia's largest telecommunications service provider, Telstra, had to ensure that over one million cellular telephone users could make phone calls, thousands of international locations could connect to video links and receive broadcasts, and hundreds of thousands of Olympics personnel could communicate within the Olympics complex.

Telstra founded its Olympics infrastructure on a vast grid of fiber optic cable installed beneath Olympic Park, the grounds where most of the events took place. **Fiber optic cable** is a transmission media that contains thin strands of fiber in its core and uses pulses of light to convey signals. It is capable of carrying higher amounts of data, voice, or video within a given time span than any other type of media. Because the grounds for the Olympic Games had yet to be constructed, Telstra was fortunate to be able to install cable before the cement had been poured for the streets and sidewalks. Most telecommunications installers must work around obstacles, such as roads, buildings, utility poles, and cables. Because the company was not sure how much voice, video, and data would have to be carried, Telstra decided to triple the amount of cabling it thought it might need. The fiber optic cable totaled 4800 kilometers (or nearly 3000 miles) and was used as the basis for all types of telecommunications services: voice, video, and data.

For the video links, Telstra established a single broadcast center to collect video feeds, then connected multiple fiber optic links from that center to each venue in the park, as shown in Figure 1-6. Telstra also used its Olympic Park fiber network to manage automated security devices and record pictures from security cameras throughout the site. In addition to the fiber optic cable foundation, Telstra established a number of transmitters to send video signals to satellites, thus allowing TV stations in other countries to receive them. The company also built an entire cable TV network within Olympic Park so that participants and staff could watch any event at any time, not just those carried by the local cable TV company. To enable Olympic Park residents and visitors to make phone calls, Telstra installed 30,000 individual copper telephone lines.

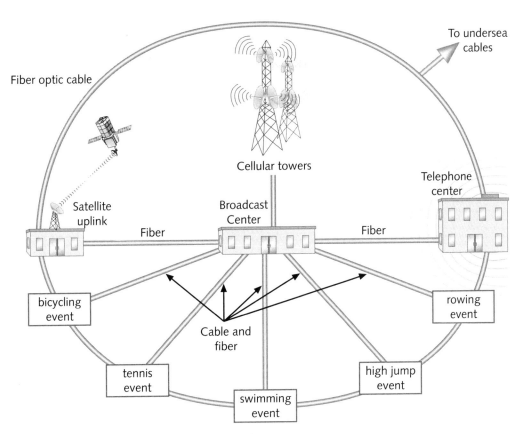

Figure 1-6   Telstra's Olympic Park network

On a much smaller scale, cutting-edge telecommunications technology is helping Girl Scouts in San Diego, California, make ordering cookies easier and more accurate. Traditionally, after a Girl Scout obtained her cookie orders, she or a parent had to tally the orders and return the completed worksheet to a troop volunteer, who would then tally the orders for the troop and submit a worksheet to the regional Girl Scout Council. The Council would then send a large order to the cookie producers, including information not only about what types of cookies to bake, but also where each different troop's stash needed to be shipped. Finally, council and troop leaders analyzed sales data and determined which girls had sold the most. Different sales levels were awarded different types of merit badges, which the troop leaders had to special order. Now, however, telecommunications has simplified this entire process.

Girl Scout cookie sales in San Diego have been streamlined by an IVR system. In the case of the San Diego Girl Scouts, troop coordinators can now call an IVR number that prompts them for a security code to access the system and identify their troop. Once in the system, the coordinators respond to prompts to enter the type and number of cookies the troop has sold. The IVR system can be accessed any time, day or night. After the cookie sales are entered, this data is saved on a computer and later supplied to bakers and shippers. In addition, the computer can tally sales information and supply troop leaders with specific sales performance data. The IVR system has not only decreased the amount of time troop volunteers spend inputting orders, but it has also increased the accuracy and efficiency of making and shipping cookies.

CAREERS IN TELECOMMUNICATIONS

Given the explosive growth of the telecommunications industry, demand for workers with skills in data and voice communications technology remains strong. And because telecommunications is such a broad field, the opportunities are varied. With solid knowledge of the industry and sufficient technology skills, you could qualify for positions as disparate as a wireless networking engineer, Web site designer, or telecommunications policy analyst.

Many careers specific to the telecommunications industry fall into the categories of engineer or technician. Typically, the difference between an engineer and a technician is that the engineer is responsible for conceiving, designing, and implementing a system, whereas a technician is responsible for installing, maintaining, and troubleshooting a system. Of course, many of the responsibilities assigned to engineers and technicians overlap. Examples of telecommunications engineering jobs include network engineer, software engineer, wireless engineer, electronics engineer, and data security engineer. Examples of telecommunications technician jobs include telephone technicians, wireless installation and repair technicians, software technicians, computer (PC) technicians, and network technicians.

No matter what type of telecommunications position you seek, the following will serve you well:

- The ability to install, maintain, and troubleshoot the system of cables and wires that carry telecommunications services
- A thorough knowledge of the public telephone network, and the carriers and regulations that are part of it
- Familiarity with enhanced telephone services (such as IVR and ACD)
- A mastery of the basic principles of electricity
- A clear understanding of how computers accept and interpret data from other computers over a network
- The ability to design, install, and troubleshoot basic networks
- An understanding of how the Internet works
- Familiarity with wireless transmission methods

Trends in the telecommunications industry make some specialized skills more desirable to employers. Following are some areas within the field of telecommunications that you might consider specializing in:

- Networked convergence of voice, video, and data
- Fiber optic media and transmission techniques
- Electronics and circuit design and engineering
- Development of telephony and computer applications
- Wireless telephony and networking
- Information security

Many Internet job listing sites allow you to search for telecommunications positions. Table 1-1 lists some examples of Web sites with searchable job databases that may help you find a job in the telecommunications industry.

Table 1-1   Web sites with searchable job databases

Web site	Description
www.telecomcareers.net	TelecomCareers.Net: a searchable recruitment center for telecommunications job seekers and employers
www.broadbandcareers.com	Broadband Careers Network: a searchable recruitment center for telecommunications job seekers and employer
www.hotjobs.com	HotJobs: a searchable site for job seekers and employers from across the world and from multiple industries
www.monster.com	The Monster Board: a searchable site for job seekers and employers from around the world and from many different industries
www.headhunter.net	Headhunter: a searchable site for job seekers and employers from around the United States and from many different industries
www.careerweb.com	CareerWeb: a searchable site for job seekers and employers from across the United States and from many different industries

TELECOMMUNICATIONS STANDARDS ORGANIZATIONS

In addition to formal regulation and legislation, the telecommunications industry is guided by standards prescribed by many national and international organizations. **Standards** are documented agreements containing technical specifications or other precise criteria that stipulate how a particular product or service should be designed or performed. Many different industries use standards to ensure that products, processes, and services suit their purpose. For example, when plastics manufacturers test their products for flexibility, the tests they perform must adhere to strict specifications set down by the

American National Standards Institute (ANSI). This ensures that the test results from one manufacturer can be accurately compared to other manufacturers' results. If each manufacturer didn't use the same ANSI test, one company might test flexibility by pulling on the plastic, whereas one might test flexibility by poking it. The flexibility numbers that each manufacturer obtained, even for the same type of plastic, would be completely different, and consumers could not compare the two products' flexibility.

Standards are especially important in the world of telecommunications. Imagine the chaos that would reign if there were no single organization responsible for assigning frequencies or determining where satellites may orbit the earth. Imagine how frustrating it would be as a consumer to buy a telephone with a plug that didn't fit into the telephone jack in your wall. These are just a few examples of the types of standards set by the telecommunications agencies.

Because the telecommunications industry includes so many different services, many different organizations oversee its standards. In some cases, a few organizations oversee a single aspect of telecommunications. For example, both ANSI and ITU are involved in setting standards for Integrated Services Digital Network (ISDN) communications. Whereas ANSI prescribes what kind of hardware the consumer needs to accept an ISDN connection, ITU prescribes how the ISDN link ensures that data arrives in the correct sequence, among other things. In addition, different standards organizations have different types of members. The ITU, for example, is an organization made of representatives appointed from each country, whereas the IEEE is an organization made of technical professionals.

A complete list of the standards that regulate the telecommunications industry would fill an encyclopedia; however, you should be familiar with the handful of significant groups that set the standards referenced by manuals, articles, and books. The groups described in the following sections are responsible for establishing the future of telecommunications.

ANSI

The **ANSI (American National Standards Institute)** is an organization composed of over a thousand representatives from industry and government who together determine standards for the electronics industry. (It also determines standards for other technical fields, such as chemical and nuclear engineering, health and safety, and construction.) In addition, ANSI represents the United States in setting international standards.

ANSI does not dictate that manufacturers comply with their standards, but requests them to voluntarily comply. Of course, manufacturers and developers benefit from compliance, because compliance ensures potential customers that the systems are proven reliable and will integrate with an existing infrastructure. New electronic equipment and measurement methods undergo rigorous testing to prove they are worthy of ANSI's approval.

An example of an ANSI standard is ANSI T1.240-1998, "Telecommunications - Operations, Administration, Maintenance, and Provisioning (OAM&P) - Generic Network Information

Model for Interfaces between Operations Systems and Network Elements."You can purchase ANSI standards documents online from ANSI's Web site (*www.ansi.org*) or find them at a university or public library.

TIA and EIA

Two closely associated standards organizations are TIA and EIA. The **EIA (Electronic Industries Alliance)** is a trade organization composed of representatives from electronics manufacturing firms across the United States. EIA began as the Radio Manufacturers Association (RMA) in 1924 and evolved to include manufacturers of televisions, semiconductors, computers, and networking devices. EIA not only sets standards for its members, but also helps write ANSI standards and lobbies for legislation favorable to the growth of the computer and electronics industry. One of the EIA's subgroups merged in 1988 with the former United States Telecommunications Suppliers Association (USTSA) to form the **TIA (Telecommunications Industry Association)**. TIA focuses on standards for information technology, wireless, satellite, fiber optics, and telephone equipment. It also has a special subcommittee devoted to multimedia standards development. In addition to lobbying and setting standards, both groups sponsor conferences, exhibitions, and forums in their areas of interest.

You can find out more about TIA from its Web site (*www.tiaonline.org*) and about EIA from its Web site (*www.eia.org*). Probably the best known standard to come from the TIA/EIA alliance is its guidelines for structured cable management (in other words, how cable should be installed in a building). You will learn more about these guidelines in Chapter 9.

IEEE

The **IEEE (Institute of Electrical and Electronic Engineers)**, or "I-triple-E," is an international society composed of engineering professionals. Its goals are to promote development and education in the electrical engineering and computer science fields. To this end, IEEE hosts numerous symposia, conferences, and local chapter meetings and publishes papers designed to educate members on technological advances. It also maintains a standards board that establishes its own standards for the electronics and computer industry and contributes to other standards setting bodies such as ANSI. IEEE technical papers and standards are highly respected in the networking profession. Among other places, you will find references to IEEE standards in manuals that accompany network interface cards.

Following are just a few examples of IEEE standards: "Information Technology Year 2000 Test Methods," "Virtual Bridged Local Area Networks," and "Software Project Management Plans." Hundreds more are currently in use. You can order these documents online from IEEE's Web site (*www.ieee.org*) or find them in a university or public library.

ATIS

ATIS, The **Association for Telecommunications Industry Solutions**, is a North American trade association made of thousands of companies that provide communications equipment and services. Its membership reviews emerging technology and agrees on standards and operating procedures to ensure that services and equipment supplied by multiple companies can be easily integrated. For example, through one of its technical forums, ATIS developed standard billing formats for wireless companies (for example, companies that provide paging services). ATIS works closely with TIA/EIA in developing standards. The adherence to ATIS standards is voluntary for their member companies. But to remain competitive, these companies usually see adherence as essential. ATIS also acts as a lobbying group for these companies, recommending policy to the government. You can find out more about ATIS by viewing its Web site at *www.atis.org*.

ISO

ISO (International Organization for Standardization) is a collection of standards organizations representing 148 countries with its headquarters located in Geneva, Switzerland. Its goal is to establish international technological standards to facilitate global exchange of information and barrier-free trade. Given the organization's full name, you might assume it should be called "IOS," but "ISO" is not meant to be an acronym. "Iso" is the Greek word for "equal," and using this term conveys the organization's dedication to standards.

ISO's authority is not limited to the telecommunications industry, but also applies to the fields of textiles, packaging, distribution of goods, energy production and utilization, shipbuilding, banking, and financial services. The fact that screw threads, bank cards, and even the names for currencies are the same worldwide are all evidence of ISO's work.

In fact, only about 500 of ISO's nearly 12,000 standards apply to communications-related products and functions. International electronics and electrical engineering standards are separately established by the International Electrotechnical Commission (IEC), a branch of ISO. And all of ISO's information technology standards are designed in tandem with the IEC. You can find out more about ISO at its Web page: *www.iso.ch*.

ITU

The **ITU (International Telecommunications Union)** is a specialized United Nations agency that regulates international telecommunication usage, including radio and TV frequencies, satellite and telephony specifications, networking infrastructure, and tariffs applied to global communication. It also provides developing countries with technical expertise and equipment to advance their technological base. The ITU was founded in Paris in 1865 but became part of the United Nations in 1947 and relocated to Geneva, Switzerland.

The ITU's standards arm contains members from 188 countries and publishes detailed policy and standards documents that can be found on its Web site (*www.itu.ch*). Typically, ITU's documents pertain more to global telecommunication issues rather than industry technical specifications. Some examples of ITU documents are: "Communications for Rural and Remote Areas," "Telecommunication Support for the Protection of the Environment," and "The International Frequency List."

> The ITU used to be called the CCITT, or Consultative Committee on International Telegraph and Telephony. You may still see references to CCITT standards in manuals and texts.

U.S. GOVERNMENT REGULATORY AND LEGISLATIVE BODIES

In addition to (voluntarily) adhering to standards, telecommunications companies must adhere to federal and state rules about how to conduct business. For example, a cellular telephone company may only transmit signals at a certain frequency, a television station must dedicate a certain amount of their programming to "child-friendly" shows, and a local telephone company is restricted in the amounts it can charge individuals for phone service. In Chapter 3, you will learn about the significant rules and decisions that shaped the growth of the telecommunications industry. But first, in this section, you will be introduced to the government entities that issue and enforce those rules. Because much of the landmark telecommunications technology and policy was developed or established in the United States, this section focuses on telecommunications in the United States.

As you will see, there are three ways to establish rules, or public policy, for the telecommunications industry: regulation, legislation, and court rulings. The term regulation refers to a policy established by a federal or state entity. The primary national regulatory agency involved in telecommunications is the **Federal Communications Commission (FCC)**, which was founded in 1934 in response to the growth and need for control over the telecommunications industry.

Legislation, on the other hand, is law passed down from federal and state elected officials, such as the U.S. Senate and House of Representatives, through majority votes. Both the Senate and House of Representatives have special committees that research telecommunications issues and make recommendations, but the elected officials make the final decision. The third method of policy setting, court rulings, takes place in the judicial branch of the government. All three spheres of government have influenced the telecommunications industry, as you will discover later in this book. Chapter 3, which focuses on the evolution of the telecommunications industry, describes the impact of government policy in great detail.

Many telecommunications policies are also generated and enforced at the state level. The states' equivalent to the FCC is the **Public Service Commission (PSC)**, in some places known as the **Public Utilities Commission (PUC)** or the state Commerce Commission. These agencies, in addition to the state legislative branches, have jurisdiction over intrastate telecommunications. They would, for example, get involved in approving a phone company's rates for local and long distance phone service within the state. Because the FCC sets policy almost exclusively for interstate telecommunications, the state public service commissions hold significant power and responsibility for establishing telecommunications policy, such as monthly rates, that directly affects consumers.

CHAPTER SUMMARY

- ❑ Communication is the conveyance and understanding of meaningful information from one entity to another. Communications can be divided into personal and data communications. Every communication system involves a source, transmitter, communications channel, receiver, and destination.

- ❑ Different types of communication are defined by whether their messages can flow in only one direction (simplex), in two directions in turn (half duplex), or in two directions simultaneously (full duplex).

- ❑ Both data and personal communications transmit information in a one-to-one, one-to-many, or many-to-many fashion.

- ❑ The word telecommunication derives from the Greek word *tele*, meaning over a distance, plus the word *communication*. Thus, putting these two parts together, you get telecommunication, or, communication that spans a distance.

- ❑ Within the field of telecommunications, professionals typically divide its services into three categories: voice, video, and data.

- ❑ Voice telecommunication refers to any means of using electrical signals to transmit human voice across a distance, such as telephones and radio broadcasts.

- ❑ Video telecommunication refers to the electrically-based transmission of moving pictures and sound across a distance.

- ❑ Data telecommunication refers to use of electrical signals to exchange encoded information between computerized devices across a distance.

- ❑ The study of telephone technology is known as telephony.

- ❑ The telephone is the primary means of transmitting and receiving voice signals. Although the telephone changed little during the 20th century from a user's perspective, its core technology underwent dramatic transformation. Each advance made telephony faster, more reliable, and capable of carrying a greater volume of signals for longer distances.

- ❑ An infrastructure is a system's collection of cables, wires, connectivity devices, users, and user equipment all working together. Today's telecommunications infrastructures are more complex than ever.

❐ One of the first data telecommunications inventions was the telegraph, a device that uses a wire to convey electrical pulses that represent letters or numbers over a distance. Throughout the 20th century, data telecommunications was transformed due to innovations in materials, electricity, and encoding techniques.

❐ Different types of data telecommunications are often defined by the method in which they transmit and receive data, the transmission media they use, and the types of sources and receivers involved in data exchange.

❐ The combination of voice, video, and data traveling over the same telecommunications infrastructure is called convergence. Convergence is the direction for the future of telecommunications services.

❐ For a majority of the 20th century, one telephone company, the Bell System (or AT&T), dominated voice telecommunications in the United States. The growth, maintenance, and dissolution of the monolithic Bell System shaped the entire telecommunications industry.

❐ Telecommunications companies can be roughly divided into service providers, those that supply the communications channels for voice and data transmission, and equipment providers, those that supply the user and connectivity equipment, such as telephones.

❐ Advanced telecommunications systems are critical to every business sector, from manufacturing to healthcare, as well as every government organization.

❐ The telecommunications industry is guided by standards prescribed by many national and international organizations. Standards are documented agreements containing technical specifications or other precise criteria that stipulate how a particular product or service should be designed or performed.

❐ Some significant telecommunications standards organizations include ANSI, ATIS, IEEE, ISO, ITU, and TIA/EIA.

❐ In addition to (voluntarily) adhering to standards, telecommunications companies must adhere to federal and state rules about how to conduct business. The organization responsible for setting federal telecommunications policy in the United States is the Federal Communications Commission (FCC). Laws pertaining to telecommunications are established by the United States Congress.

❐ At the state level, Public Service Commissions (also known as Public Utility Commissions or Commerce Commissions) are responsible for setting telecommunications policy specific to the state.

Key Terms

ANSI (American National Standards Institute) — An organization composed of over a thousand representatives from industry and government who together determine standards for the electronics industry in addition to other fields. ANSI also represents the United States in setting international standards.

ATIS (Association for Telecommunications Industry Solutions) — A North American trade association made of thousands of companies that provide communications equipment and services. Their membership reviews emerging technology and agrees on standards and operating procedures to ensure that services and equipment supplied by multiple companies can be easily integrated.

automatic call distributor (ACD) — A system that uses computerized devices attached to the phone lines to automatically route calls to specific phone extensions.

broadcast — A type of communication in which one source simultaneously sends a message to multiple destinations. Also called *one-to-many*.

call center — A facility dedicated to fielding customer calls. A call center usually consists of multiple, trained personnel (also called "agents") and multiple telephone lines.

communication — The sharing of information or messages between two or more entities.

communications channel — The means of carrying a signal that contains data from the source to the destination (for example, copper wire).

convergence — The combination of voice or video plus data signals traveling over the same networks and using the same connectivity equipment.

data — Discreet pieces of information. In the context of telecommunications, the term data usually refers to information formatted for and exchanged between computers.

data communication — The sharing of information or messages between electrical or electronic devices.

data telecommunication — The use of electrical signals to exchange encoded information between computerized devices across a distance.

destination — The person or machine to whom a message is directed.

distance learning — The use of telecommunications technology to inform, educate, or train students across distances.

duplex — *See* full duplex.

e-business — The use of data telecommunications to conduct business transactions.

EIA (Electronic Industries Alliance) — A trade organization composed of representatives from electronics manufacturing firms across the United States that helps establish standards for electronic equipment and services.

equipment provider — A company that provides telecommunications devices, such as telephones, computers, and network connectors.

Federal Communications Commission (FCC) — The primary national regulatory agency involved in telecommunications in the United States.

fiber optic cable — A transmission media that contains thin strands of fiber in its core and uses pulses of light to convey signals. It is capable of carrying higher amounts of data, voice, or video within a given time span than any other type of media.

1

full duplex — A form of communications in which messages can travel over a communications channel in two directions simultaneously. May also be simply called "duplex."

half duplex — A form of communications in which messages can travel over a communications channel in two directions, but only one direction at a time.

IEEE (Institute of Electrical and Electronic Engineer) — An international society composed of engineering professionals. Its goals are to promote development and education in the electrical engineering and computer science fields.

infrastructure — The foundation for a network or system. In the case of the public telephone network, a collection of cables, wires, connectivity devices, and user equipment make up its infrastructure.

interactive voice response (IVR) — An automated method of sending and accepting information over a telephone line by pressing buttons in response to recorded voice prompts.

ISO (International Organization for Standardization) — A collection of standards organizations representing 130 countries with its headquarters located in Geneva, Switzerland. Its goal is to establish international technological standards to facilitate global exchange of information and barrier-free trade.

ITU (International Telecommunications Union) — A specialized United Nations agency that regulates international telecommunication usage, including radio and TV frequencies, satellite and telephony specifications, networking infrastructure, and tariffs applied to global communication. It also provides developing countries with technical expertise and equipment to advance their technological base.

many-to-many — A type of communication in which multiple sources simultaneously send messages to multiple destinations.

media — *See* transmission media.

network — A group of computers and other devices (such as printers) that are connected by communications channel. Networks enable multiple users to easily share resources and exchange data.

one-to-many — A type of communication in which one source simultaneously sends a message to multiple destinations.

one-to-one — A type of communication in which one source sends a message to only one destination.

personal communication — The sharing of information between humans.

point-to-point — Communication on a network that involves one source and one destination.

Public Service Commission (PSC) — A state regulatory agency responsible for setting intrastate telecommunications policy. PSCs are known as Public Utilities Commission (PUC) or the state Commerce Commission in some states.

Public Utilities Commission (PUC) — *See* Public Service Commission.

receiver — A device that captures a message from the communications channel and converts it into a form that the destination can understand. May also be called a decoder.

service provider — A company that provides the communication channel for voice, video, or data transmission.

simplex — A form of communications in which messages can only travel in one direction.

source — The originator of a communication process.

standards — Documented agreements containing technical specifications or other precise criteria that stipulate how a particular product or service should be designed or performed.

telecommunication — Communication that spans a distance.

telegraph — An electromechanical device that uses a wire to convey electrical pulses that represent letters or numbers over a distance.

telemedicine — The use of voice, video, and data telecommunications to enable patients and healthcare professionals to exchange information over distances.

telephony — The study of telephone, or voice telecommunication, technology.

TIA (Telecommunications Industry Association) — A standards organization established in 1988 from a subgroup of the EIA and the former United States Telecommunications Suppliers Association (USTSA). TIA helps establish standards for information technology, wireless, satellite, fiber optics, and telephone equipment. It also has a special subcommittee devoted to multimedia standards development.

transmission media — The communication channel used to exchange information between electrical or electronic devices.

transmitter — The equipment that modifies a message (either data or voice) into the form required for transmission. May also be called an encoder.

video telecommunication — Any means of electrically transmitting moving pictures and sound across a distance, such as TV broadcasting or distributing live feeds of an event to the screens of networked computers.

voice recognition — A feature of some computers that enables them to recognize a user's voice and respond to spoken commands. To recognize these commands, a voice recognition system needs to be "trained" to understand the user's voice patterns.

voice telecommunication — Any means of using electrical signals to transmit human voice across a distance, such as telephones and radio broadcasts.

REVIEW QUESTIONS

1. Which part of the communications process modifies a message into a form that can be interpreted by the destination?

   a. source

   b. transmitter

   c. receiver

   d. destination

2. In data communications, what is a more common term for "communications channel?"

   a. transmission media

   b. signal

   c. throughput

   d. bandwidth

3. Describe the function of a decoder.

4. If a football coach is yelling orders to his team on the field, what type of communication is he practicing?

   a. one-to-one

   b. one-to-many

   c. many-to-many

   d. many-to-one

5. Which of the following best describes the communication method in use when you telephone a friend?

   a. quarter-duplex

   b. half-duplex

   c. full-duplex

   d. simplex

6. Which of the following is involved when you save a word processing file to a floppy disk?

   a. data telecommunications

   b. voice telecommunications

   c. video telecommunications

   d. cable telecommunications

7. Which of the following is another term for one-to-many communications?

   a. full-duplex

   b. broadcast

   c. serial

   d. simplex

8. Which of the following is an example of voice telecommunications?

   a. an alphanumeric paging system

   b. an e-mail system

   c. a satellite navigation system

   d. a cellular telephone system

9. What does the word, "tele," from which "telecommunications" is derived, mean in Greek?

    a. at a distance

    b. with electricity

    c. to make common

    d. from one point to another

10. What single company had the most impact on the way in which the United States' telecommunications industry developed during the 20th century?

    a. IBM

    b. Cisco

    c. Dell

    d. Bell System

11. More and more, modern networks are carrying not only data, but also video and voice telecommunications. What is the term used to describe this trend?

    a. mulitplexing

    b. telesharing

    c. segmentation

    d. convergence

12. Describe a way in which telecommunications may be used in banks.

13. What type of telecommunications is required for a class of students to watch and listen to an instructor who is two hundred miles away?

    a. data telecommunications

    b. voice telecommunications

    c. video telecommunications

    d. satellite telecommunications

14. Describe how telecommunications can improve healthcare for rural citizens.

15. If you call your local library for information about its hours and you hear a message that says, "press 1 to listen to the library hours…," what type of system have you accessed?

    a. automated call distribution

    b. computerized voice recorder

    c. integrated voice response

    d. computerized switchboard

16. Which of the following transmission media is capable of carrying the most data in any given time period?

    a. fiber optic cable

    b. copper wire

    c. radio waves

    d. steel wire

17. Which of the following organizations has issued standards on how cable should be installed in buildings?

    a. IEEE

    b. TIA/EIA

    c. ANSI

    d. ITU

18. Which of the following international organizations would be involved in researching ways of distributing data services to third-world countries across the globe?

    a. ANSI

    b. IEEE

    c. ITU

    d. ATIS

19. What agency is primarily responsible for issuing and enforcing telecommunications policy in the United States?

    a. FTC

    b. SEC

    c. USTA

    d. FCC

20. Which of the following organizations would guide state telecommunications policy in the U.S.?

    a. public interest groups

    b. interstate commerce commissions

    c. public service commissions

    d. intrastate common council

HANDS-ON PROJECTS

Project 1-1

To analyze, design, and troubleshoot telecommunications systems, you need to be able to identify the system's source, transmitter, communications channel, receiver, and destination. In this project, you practice identifying each element in a number of scenarios. The scenarios include both personal and data communications.

    1. On a piece of paper, draw a table with eight columns, and label the first five columns as follows: Source, Transmitter, Communications Channel, Receiver, and

Destination. Leave the last three columns blank for now. Draw eight rows beneath the column headings.

2. For each of the following scenarios, write the source, transmitter, communications channel, receiver, and destination in the appropriate columns on your table (leave the last three columns blank). If you aren't sure of the proper term for an element, describe the element as best you can. You'll learn the correct terminology throughout the course of this book.

   ❑ Marvin listens to a talk radio program while driving to work.

   ❑ Mrs. Edelman lectures her high school history class.

   ❑ Susan reads a confidential memo written to her by a colleague.

   ❑ Arnie's computer issues a request to a dozen other computers on the network.

   ❑ Heidi and Margo watch a movie on HBO.

   ❑ A computer issues a print job to a printer that is directly connected to one of the computer's ports.

   ❑ Dan and Ellen have a conversation at a restaurant.

   ❑ Dr. Wong interviews a patient 100 miles away through a telemedicine system.

3. If you are in a class, compare your answers to your peers' answers. How do they differ? Is there more than one correct answer in some cases?

Project 1-2

In this project, you expand on the table you began in Project 1-1. Recall that communications can be personal or data in nature. They may also be defined by the relationship between their sources and destinations: whether information is exchanged in a one-to-one, one-to-many, or many-to-many fashion. Finally, they may be defined by which direction information can flow at any one time: simplex, half-duplex, or full-duplex.

1. Label the last three columns of the table you created in Project 1-1 as follows: "Type," "Relationship of Source to Destination," and "Flow."

2. Re-read the scenarios listed in Project 1-1. For each scenario, indicate in the Type column whether the communication type is personal or data by placing a "P" or "D" in the row corresponding to that scenario.

3. In the Relationship of Source to Destination column, indicate whether the relationship between the source(s) and destination(s) is one-to-one, one-to-many, or many-to-many.

4. Finally, in the last column, indicate whether the communication flow is simplex, half duplex, or full duplex by the letters "S," "HD," or "FD." There may be some cases in which half or full duplex are both possibilities.

5. Discuss your answers with the class and your instructor. For which of the scenarios were the communication methods most difficult to pinpoint? Which answers varied the most?

Project 1-3

This chapter provided an overview of some possible telecommunications careers. In this project, you use some of the searchable job databases on the Web to discover specifically what jobs are available. You also note the skills those jobs require. For this project, you need a computer that can browse the Web.

1. Connect to the Internet and launch your Web browser program.

2. Go to **www.telecomcareers.net**, which is the home page of the Telecom Careers employment Web site.

3. Click the **Search Jobs** link in the menu that appears near the top of the Web page.

4. Under the "Specify Keywords and Options" heading, type **technician** in the Keywords: text box.

5. Press **Enter** to search for all the job listings that contain the term "technician."

6. A list of job listings appears. Each listing contains the date it was posted, a company name, job title, the location of the job, and a link that you can click to view more information about the posting. Scroll through the page of listings and take note of the different types included in this list.

7. Choose one job that looks interesting to you and click the job title to view more information about it. The full job posting appears.

8. On a separate piece of paper, create four columns labeled as follows: title, responsibilities, skills required, and product knowledge (for example, if a job requires familiarity with Nortel's Meridian telephone system, you would note that in the fourth column). For the job posting you are currently viewing, write the corresponding job information in the appropriate columns.

9. Click the **Back** button on your browser to return to the list of job postings.

10. Repeat Steps 7–9 for at least five other telecommunications technician job postings (you may choose to view additional pages of listings to find those that interest you most). If possible, choose postings for which the company listed is not a temporary agency or employee search firm, but rather the organization for which the job would actually be performed.

11. As you view the job postings, jot down any unfamiliar industry terms at the bottom of your paper so that you can look them up in the glossary at the back of this book.

12. After you have noted the different types of responsibilities and skills required for each job, analyze the information you gathered to answer the following questions: Which skills or responsibilities are common to most of the postings? What skills are rarely required? How many of the postings require a two-year college degree?

How many require a four-year college degree? Which telecommunications products are most frequently cited in the group of job postings you chose?

Project 1-4

As you have learned, many organizations help create policy and set standards for the telecommunications industry. In this project, you explore some of the information provided by the Federal Communications Commission (FCC) online. For this project, you need a computer that can browse the Web. To read some of the reports from the Web, you also need Adobe Acrobat Reader, which is available for download at no cost from *www.adobe.com*.

1. Connect to the Internet and launch your Web browser program.

2. Go to **www.fcc.gov**, which is the homepage of the Federal Communications Commission (FCC).

3. In the Bureaus and Offices section of the FCC home page, click **Wireline Competition**. (You may need to scroll down the page to see the Bureaus and Offices heading.)

4. The Wireline Competition Bureau (WCB) home page appears. Among other things, the WCB regulates competitive telephone services. Scroll down the page and read the headlines under the "What's New" section. Based on the news releases listed, what can you determine about the bureau's current priorities?

5. Now select one of the news releases to view, such as "FEDERAL COMMUNI-CATIONS COMMISSION (FCC) UPDATES MERGER REVIEW PROCESS," by clicking on the PDF link at the end of the news release's summary. To view this file, your computer must have Adobe Acrobat Reader installed.

6. Glance through the document you have opened. What kind of information does it contain? How did the FCC obtain the information cited in this document? What public interests is the FCC taking into account by issuing this document?

7. Click the **Back** button on your browser to return to the list of news releases on the WCB home page. Browse through additional news releases that interest you.

8. When you have finished reading the FCC news releases, exit the browser program.

CASE PROJECTS

1. You are a member of your local school board. Your state and a local corporation have just announced that they are willing to contribute $2 million to the school district for telecommunications technology. However, before the district is eligible

for the money, it must devise a plan for how best to implement this new technology. Your district serves 18,000 students and contains 32 schools, including 3 high schools. Each of the schools currently has at least one computer lab, but none of the computer labs in different schools are connected to each other. In addition, your telephones have not been upgraded since 1978. Admittedly, your school district is behind the curve in implementing advanced telecommunications. But now is the time to build a solid infrastructure. The school board has asked you to perform some online research about using telecommunications in education. They suggest you find out what other school districts of similar size are doing and present your findings at the next school board meeting. Based on these findings, they also want you to make some general recommendations on how they can best spend the $2,000,000. You may want to begin your search with Internet sites such as *www.ed.gov/Technology/* (the U.S. Department of Education's Office of Educational Technology), *www-ed.fnal.gov/net_train/resource_lists/education_telecom.html* (the FermiLab education resource list), *www.iste.org* (the International Society for Technology in Education), and *www.nea.org/cet/* (the National Education Association). Make sure your recommendations take into account the number of schools, the current status of the schools' telecommunications systems, and the most important basic elements the district requires.

2. As part of your telecommunications proposal, you have recommended that the school district hire at least one telecommunications professional to maintain the new system after it has been installed. The school board is concerned about the cost of such an employee. They also wonder what type of qualifications a person needs to maintain all the technology you have suggested. One member even suggests that one of the high school's librarians could take this on in her spare time. For the next board meeting, they want you to answer these questions, plus present a complete job description for the employee you have proposed hiring. Perform searches for a "telecommunications technician" (or similar title) on Internet job sites such as *www.monster.com* and *www.hotjobs.com* to obtain this information. You may encounter technical terms with which you are not familiar. If so, use the Web site *www.webopedia.com* to lookup the definitions of those terms. Then, based on the specifics of your telecommunications strategy and your Web research, write a job description and suggest an annual salary for this employee. Also, prepare your answer to the question of whether the high school librarian could do this job in her spare time and explain why you do or don't think it's a good decision.

3. Another school board member is concerned about new PSC regulations. She asks you to investigate any telecommunications regulation currently pending at your state's PSC (or PUC) and explain how it might affect your proposal. You follow up on her request by checking with your state's public service commission. To perform this research, you could either call the PSC to request a list of current telecommunications agenda items or you could connect to the Internet and begin by retrieving your state's homepage (whose URL would follow the convention www.state.XX.us, where XX is your state's two-letter abbreviation) and searching for the PSC (or PUC) home page. For example, if you lived in Minnesota, you

would connect to the Internet and go to the following page: *www.state.mn.us*. Once there, you could select the Public Utilities Commission's (PUC's) Web site at *www.puc.state.mn.us*. (Notice that the PUC also regulates other utilities, such as electricity and water service.) Make a note of at least three issues. Then, in preparation for your next school board meeting, jot down ways in which these issues might affect your district's telecomunications strategy, if at all. If the "hot topics" for your state's PSC do not pertain to telecommunications, find out what the agency's three latest telecommunications rulings have been. For example, in many states PSCs are attempting to deal with the decreasing amount of available telephone numbers by adding new area codes. In other states, new technology is prompting the agency to require public institutions to supply more advanced access to telecommunications for hearing- and speech-impaired citizens. Still other state PSCs are turning their attention to ensuring security for electronic transactions.

2

PRINCIPLES OF TELECOMMUNICATIONS TECHNOLOGY

After reading this chapter and completing the exercises, you will be able to:

- ◆ Describe the principles of electricity that underlie all telecommunications signaling
- ◆ Explain the concepts of current and voltage as they apply to telecommunications technology
- ◆ Describe the components on an integrated circuit
- ◆ Explain the difference between analog and digital transmission
- ◆ Use binary encoding to represent decimal numbers
- ◆ Describe various electricity and data transmission measurements

---

To understand telecommunications technology, you must have a clear knowledge of the force that drives it—electricity. Electricity is used in all types of voice and data telecommunications systems. Without electricity, communication over a distance is limited to fire signals, shouting, or hand-held signs. Although this chapter does not provide a comprehensive study of electricity, it does help you brush up on your knowledge of this critical science before delving into more complex topics concerning telecommunication. Because electricity makes signaling possible, this chapter also introduces you to the signaling methods used by all telecommunications services.

PRINCIPLES OF ELECTRICITY

You have learned that every form of telecommunication requires a source, transmitter, communications channel, receiver, and destination. Every technology discussed in this book makes use of each of these elements. These elements, in turn, rely on electricity to do their work. In the following sections, you learn the basics of electricity and how electricity is used to transmit and receive telecommunications signals.

Atomic Charges

To understand the nature of electricity, you need to first consider the nature of matter. Everything in the universe, whether living or dead, is made of atoms. As you may recall from chemistry class, atoms are the smallest particles to which an element (such as hydrogen, carbon, or copper) can be reduced and still maintain the properties of that element. Atoms themselves are made up of still smaller particles called neutrons, protons, and electrons, and these particles are held together by very small charges. A **charge** is the characteristic of a material that enables it to exert force on another material. **Neutrons**, which are found at the center of an atom, possess no charge and are said to be neutral. But protons and electrons *do* have charges. **Protons**, which are also found at the center of an atom along with neutrons, carry a positive charge. This is indicated by the symbol +. **Electrons**, which orbit the center of an atom, carry a negative charge, as indicated by the symbol −. A single atom may contain several protons and electrons. Figure 2-1 illustrates a typical diagram of a carbon atom. Notice that it contains six protons (represented by +) and six electrons (represented by −). The atoms belonging to other elements (such as nickel, silver, copper, and so on) differ in the number of protons, neutrons, and electrons they contain.

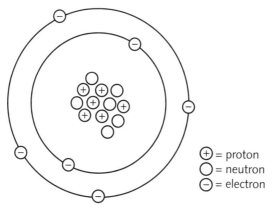

⊕ = proton
◯ = neutron
⊖ = electron

Figure 2-1   A carbon atom

Charged particles either repel or attract each other without ever making physical contact. Like charges repel each other and unlike charges attract each other. Thus, two protons tend to move away from each other. Likewise, two electrons tend to repel each other. However, a proton (which has a positive charge) and an electron (which has a negative charge) tend to come together, or attract each other.

The balance between positive and negative charges determines whether matter is stable. Stable matter is matter that is not in a state of change (for instance, matter that is not burning or boiling). In stable matter—for example, a sugar cube that is sitting on a spoon—the positive and negative charges in its atoms balance each other out. That is, an equal number of positive and negative charges (protons and electrons) are present in the atoms of the sugar cube. When an atom contains an equal number of protons and electrons, the atom as a whole does not carry a charge. In other words, the atom is considered stable in this state.

However, the atoms of some materials can be made to gain or lose electrons, causing the material to become charged. The result is a kind of electricity, called static electricity.

Static Electricity

When you move a plastic comb through your hair, some of the electrons on the surface of your hair are rubbed off onto the comb. Your hair then becomes short of negatively charged electrons and thus "positively charged." Meanwhile, the comb accumulates an excess of electrons and is "negatively charged." Nature is always trying to neutralize this charge. To restore the balance between the comb and your hair, groups of electrons jump from the comb back to your hair to reestablish a balance. (On a dry day, you may hear a crackling sound as the electrons jump.) This is an example of static electricity. **Static electricity** is the release of an accumulated charge in some material or object. Because the charges inherent in electrons and protons are bound to balance each other through static electricity, these charges are also called **electrostatic charges**.

Another common example of static electricity is lightning. During a thunderstorm, large numbers of excess electrons can accumulate in a cloud, causing it to build up a powerful negative charge. The cloud's negative charge can become so great that a spark (in the form of a lightning bolt) consisting of an enormous number of electrons jumps from the cloud to the object below (for example, a radio tower or a tall tree), in an effort to balance the difference in the relative charges of the two bodies. Because of the volume of electrons that are jumping is so huge, lightning is an extremely powerful form of static electricity. Its effects may include electrocution, a fire, or damage or destruction of electronic components.

Electric Current

You can think of static electricity as the spontaneous release of a charge imbalance. By contrast, another type of electricity, **current electricity**, or **electric current**, is the controlled movement of an electrical charge (or electrons) along the atoms of a conductor (such as wire). You can think of electric current as the flow of a charge. Figure 2-2 illustrates the difference between static and current electricity.

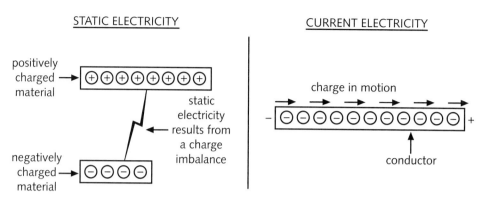

Figure 2-2   Static electricity compared to current electricity

Electric current is controlled for productive uses on a circuit. A **circuit** is a closed connection between an electric source (such as a battery) and a load (such as a lamp) over which current may flow. Following circuits, electric current powers lights, appliances, computers, power tools, and anything else that requires batteries or an electrical outlet to operate. In the field of telecommunications, electric current is commonly used to create, transmit, and receive voice and data signals. For example, the sound emitted by a telephone receiver is a result of electric current flowing over the telephone line. Likewise, the noises tapped out on a telegraph are the result of electric current. When current is manipulated to transmit information, it becomes a **signal**. You will learn more about signals in Chapters 6 and 7. But first, in the following pages, you will learn how electric current flows over different types of materials and specifically how electric current can be used in telecommunications.

Conductors and Insulator

The term "conduct" means to direct the flow of something else. Thus, a material over which electric current readily flows is known as a **conductor** (because it conducts electricity). Some of the best conductors—and the kind used to complete most electrical connections—are metals. Each type of metal has a different ability to conduct electric current. For example, silver is a better conductor than copper. But even though silver is a better conductor, copper is the most common metal used in wiring, because silver is too expensive. Water is also an excellent conductor, and for this reason, it is very important to avoid working with electric current where there is a possibility of making contact with water. Also, because human beings are largely composed of water, you make an excellent conductor if you happen to touch a wire that is carrying electric current—in other words, you can easily be electrocuted. Thus, you should always exercise extreme caution while working with electricity. One technique for protecting people and devices from being harmed by electricity is grounding. **Grounding** is the use of a conductor (such as a wire) to divert unused or potentially harmful charges to an insulator, where they will be stopped or absorbed. For example, telephone lines that come into your home are grounded to the earth.

2

Materials that do not allow electric current to flow easily are called **insulators**. Insulators are typically used to prevent electric current or signals from flowing to places they shouldn't go. For example, insulating material surrounds electrical cords to ensure that the current moves only along enclosed wires and not beyond those wires where it might cause harm. Air, ceramics, plastics, rubber, certain types of minerals, and paper are all insulators. Plastic is commonly used as an insulator in telephony wiring. The telephone line that runs through your home probably consists of four copper wires (conductors) individually surrounded by a thin coating of plastic (an insulator) and together, surrounded by a thicker plastic casing (another insulator), as shown in Figure 2-3.

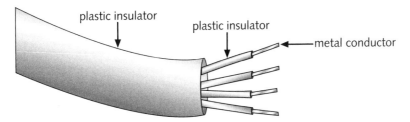

Figure 2-3   Insulators and conductors in telephone wiring

Another type of material is called a **semiconductor**, because it has some ability to conduct electricity. A semiconductor conducts electricity better than an insulator, but not as well as a conductor. The conductive ability of a semiconductor often depends on its operating temperature. Semiconductors are typically made of a solid crystalline substance such as silicon, but may be formed from a number of other materials. Semiconductors are the mainstay of modern electronics and can be found inside most modern telecommunications devices.

Now that you understand how conductors work, you are ready to learn two means of measuring the flow of electricity over a conductor. The following two sections explain how to measure the strength of a current and the amount of current.

Voltage

Electric current is frequently compared to flowing water, because they act in similar ways. The flow of both water and electricity can both be contained and directed, both exert pressure on their "containers" as they flow, and both may be stopped or slowed by obstacles in their path. For example, just as water can be sent through a hose, so can electricity be transmitted over a wire. And just as water in a hose exerts pressure on the internal walls of the hose through which it travels, electric current exerts pressure on its conductor. The pressure that the electric current exerts on its conductor is known as **voltage**. Voltage is commonly equated to the strength of the electric current. It is measured in **volts**, which is abbreviated by the letter "v."

One volt is very low pressure for an electric current. An ordinary flashlight battery may generate an electric current of approximately three volts. A car battery generates 12 volts, and a typical household lighting circuit in the United States operates at 120 volts. In the field of telecommunications, a voltage of 48 volts is used to carry signals over telephone lines in the United States. Early telephone companies settled on the 48-volt standard because any current under 50 volts does not injure people (should they accidentally make contact with the circuit) and because it is strong enough to travel over several miles of telephone wire. At the other end of the spectrum, the power lines that bring electricity to a neighborhood or business district may exert up to 13,800 volts. Electric current operating at such high voltage can be deadly.

Amperes

As you learned in the preceding section, the strength of a current is measured in volts. Next, you need to learn how to measure the amount of current flowing over a conductor. Continuing with the analogy of electric current with flowing water, consider that only a certain amount of water can move through a certain sized pipe in any given time frame. For example, you can send much more water through a four-inch pipe in one minute than you can send through a two-inch pipe in one minute. Similarly, electric current flows at different rates over different types of conductors.

The amount of current—or charge flowing through a wire each second—is measured in **amperes**, abbreviated as **amps**. The term "ampere" is taken from the name of a 19th century French physicist, André-Marie Ampère. Household appliances use approximately 15 amps of electric current. To put quantities of current and voltage in context, Figure 2-4 provides a rough "map" of how much current and voltage well-known electric devices and systems use. Notice that even your body uses electric current, at very low voltages, to regulate your cardiovascular and nervous systems!

Resistance

So far, you have learned how to measure the strength of a current flowing over a conductor (in volts) and the amount of a current over a conductor (in amps). Another important property of electrical current relates to the ease with which a conductor allows a current to flow. Just as the amount of water that can move through the pipe is affected by the pipe's size, the amount of current that can flow through a conductor is affected by the conductor's resistance. **Resistance**, then, is a material's opposition to electric current.

Resistance is a fundamental property of conductors, and depends on the conductor's structure and size. The most significant predictor of resistance is a material's atomic makeup. As you learned earlier, copper is a conductor, which means it allows a charge (in the form of electrons) to easily move through it. In other words, copper inherently has little resistance to current. On the other hand, plastic, which is an insulator, does not allow current to flow through it. Plastic has a much greater resistance than copper.

In addition to a material's atomic structure, a material's size greatly affects its resistance. Thinner wires have greater resistance than thicker wires; longer wires have greater resistance

2

than shorter wires. For example, a copper wire with a diameter of .5 mm can carry half as much electric current in the same time that a copper wire with a diameter of 1 mm can.

Resistance is measured in **ohms**. The most common type of copper wire used in telephone lines has a resistance of 16.46 ohms per 1000 feet. Thus, over a distance of 2000 feet, this wire accumulates twice as much resistance, or 32.892 ohms.

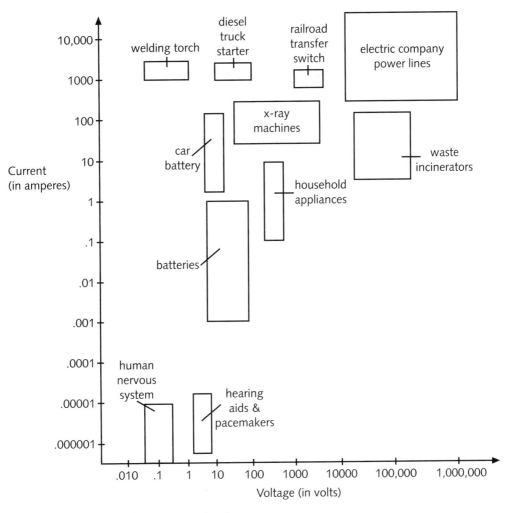

Figure 2-4   A map of currents and voltages

You now know that the strength of a current is measured in volts, the amount of a current is measured in amps, and the resistance of a conductor is measured in ohms. At this point, you may be wondering how we determine the correct measurements for a particular current flowing over a conductor. To do this, we use a mathematical formula known as Ohm's Law. This formula is explained in the next section.

Calculating Voltage, Amps, and Resistance with Ohm's Law

Ways to describe scientific phenomena are often named after the people who first recognized or quantified those phenomena. For example, in the field of Biology, Charles Darwin devised a theory of evolution in which he proposed that existing living organisms are not identical to, but rather adapted from, earlier versions of their species. This proposal is known as Darwin's Theory. A fundamental principle in the field of Electricity is Ohm's Law, named after Georg Simon Ohm, a German physicist who wrote about electricity in 1827. Simply put, **Ohm's Law** describes how electric current flows differently over different types of material.

The basic principle at the heart of Ohm's Law is this: the greater a material's resistance, the smaller the potential amount of electric current traveling over that material in a given time period. Essentially, Ohm's Law states that the amount of current flowing in an electric circuit is directly proportional to the voltage and inversely proportional to the resistance. ("Directly proportional" means that as one factor increases, the other increases. "Inversely proportional" means that as one factor increases, the other decreases.)

The relationships stated in Ohm's Law make it possible to calculate the current, voltage, or resistance of a circuit. In mathematical terms, Ohm's Law is expressed as:

$$I = \frac{E}{R}$$

Where:

- I (which stands for "intensity") represents current, the quantity of electricity flowing over a conductor, as measured in amps.

- E (which stands for "electromotive force") represents voltage, the pressure of an electric current, as measured in volts.

- R (which stands for "resistance") represents the opposition to the flow of electric current, as measured in ohms.

Suppose the ends of a 1000-foot length of No. 10 copper wire, which has a resistance of 1 ohm per 1000 feet, are connected to a 1-volt battery. When expressed in terms of Ohm's Law, E=1 and R=1. Because you know the value of these two variables, you can use Ohm's Law to determine the amount of current. First, you replace the variables with the known quantities:

$$I = \frac{1v}{1} \text{ ohm}$$

The two values of 1 on the right side of the equal sign cancel each other out, resulting in this solution:

I=1 amp

Thus, according to Ohm's Law, a 1000-foot length of No. 10 copper wire with a resistance of 1 ohm per 1000 feet, conducts a 1 amp current when connected to a 1-volt battery.

If the voltage is increased to 2 volts, the current increases to 2 amps. If the voltage is increased to 5 volts, the current is 5 amps. These equations are solved in the following list:

$$I = \frac{2v}{1 \text{ ohm}} \qquad\qquad \text{thus, I= 2 amps}$$

$$I = \frac{5v}{1 \text{ ohm}} \qquad\qquad \text{thus, I= 5 amps}$$

The preceding examples illustrate how an increase in voltage increases the amount of current traveling over a wire.

Resistance is caused not only by the material used as a conductor, but also (and usually to a greater extent) by objects in the path of electric current, such as a light bulb or a buzzer. Consider the simple electrical circuit contained in a flashlight. If three volts of battery power are connected to a lamp with 100 ohms of resistance, the amount of current flowing through the circuit is 3 volts/100 ohms, or .03 amps. This simple circuit is shown in Figure 2-5. Notice the symbols used to represent a battery and a lamp on this circuit diagram. If you continue your studies in electricity or electronics, you must be familiar with circuit diagrams and the symbols used in them.

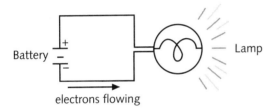

Figure 2-5   A simple circuit

You can use variations of the Ohm's Law formula to make calculations for a circuit as long as you know the value of two of the variables in the equation. If you want to find out the current flowing in a circuit, divide the voltage by the resistance (E = ⅟ᵣ). If you know the voltage and the current, you can determine the resistance by changing the formula to R = ᴱ⁄ᵢ (resistance equals voltage divided by current). If you know the resistance and the current, you can determine the voltage by changing the formula to E = I × R (voltage equals current times resistance).

Resistance is a complex property that depends on additional variables besides the type of element a conductor is made of and the size of a conductor. For example, temperature and pressure also influence a conductor's natural resistance. More complex equations quantify how these multiple factors affect resistance. However, a deeper discussion of resistance is beyond the scope of this book.

Direct and Alternating Current

There are two distinct types of electric current: direct current and alternating current. In **direct current (DC)**, an electrical charge flows steadily in one direction (either from a positively charged point to a negatively charged point or vice versa) over the conductor.

To cause this steadily flowing charge, a source must apply a constant amount of voltage to the conductor at all times. If you graph the strength of a DC charge over time, it looks like a straight line, as in Figure 2-6. A battery provides a constant amount of voltage to a conductor, thus circuits that rely on batteries use direct current.

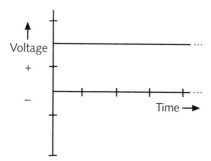

Figure 2-6 Voltage over time in a DC circuit

In **alternating current (AC)**, the electrical charge flows in one direction first, then in the opposite direction, then back in the first direction, and so on, in an alternating fashion over the conductor. In other words, electrons flow from the positively charged end of the circuit to the negatively charged end, then switch direction from negative to positive. This causes the voltage to alternate between positive and negative values. However, the amperage, or amount of charge flowing through the circuit each second, remains consistent. To cause this alternating current, the source, also known as a **generator**, sends voltage that varies consistently over regular intervals of time. If you graph the strength of an AC charge as time passes, it resembles a sine wave (so named because of its relationship to the sine function in trigonometry), as shown in Figure 2-7.

If you don't recall learning about sine waves in math class, it's important now to memorize the terms for each part of a sine wave. You'll need this terminology to discuss electrical current and telecommunication signals. In the AC sine wave, the strength of the voltage is indicated by the height of the wave—the wave's **amplitude**. The term **cycle** refers to a specific section of the wave, beginning at its starting point, up to its highest amplitude, down to its lowest amplitude, and then back to its starting point. This type of motion, in which the amplitude of the wave varies regularly as time passes, is known as **oscillation**. Oscillation is characteristic of many natural phenomena besides alternating current (for example, earthquakes shake the ground in an oscillating fashion).

The term **frequency** refers to the number of cycles in a sine wave that are completed within a specified time frame. Frequency is measured in **Hertz** (abbreviated as **Hz**). 1 Hz equals 1 cycle per second. (This unit of measurement is named after Heinrich Hertz, a German physicist who studied electromagnetic theory and radio waves in the late 19th century.) Electricity supplied to homes in the United States has a frequency of 60 Hz, which means that the current reverses its direction 120 times every second (because one cycle includes two current reversals: an ascent to the highest amplitude, then a descent to the lowest amplitude). In Europe, homes use AC with a frequency of 50 Hz, in which the current reverses its direction 100 times each second.

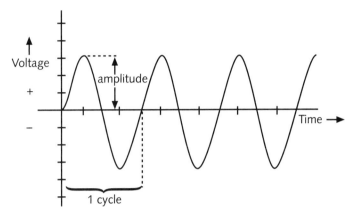

Figure 2-7 Voltage over time in an AC circuit

 Some frequencies are audible to humans. Although you don't hear the 60 Hz AC that enters your home, you may hear a "hum" when standing under a high voltage power line. This hum is generated by the 60 Hz frequency vibrating through the air around the power line.

The distance between corresponding points on a cycle is called its **wavelength**, and is expressed in meters. Wavelength is inversely proportional to frequency. The higher the frequency, the shorter the wavelength. For example, a sine wave with a frequency of 1000 cycles per second (1000 Hz) has a wavelength of 300 meters, whereas a sine wave with a frequency of 2000 Hz has a wavelength of 150 meters, as shown in Figure 2-8. Understanding frequencies and wavelengths are important to many telecommunication technologies, including telephony and radio and television broadcasting.

AC is used for home electrical service and to power some devices, such as motors. In telecommunications, the voice and data signals that travel along telephone lines are, in fact, a form of AC. DC is used to power portable electrical devices, such as radios and calculators. It's also used to power most electronic devices, such as stereo equipment, even though they don't use batteries. Although the wall outlet into which you plug your stereo, for example, supplies AC current, your stereo contains a **converter**, a device that changes AC into DC. Most telecommunications devices, such as answering machines, fax machines, computers, and telephone company equipment, run off of DC, as shown in Figure 2-9.

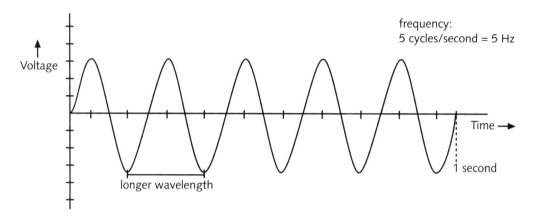

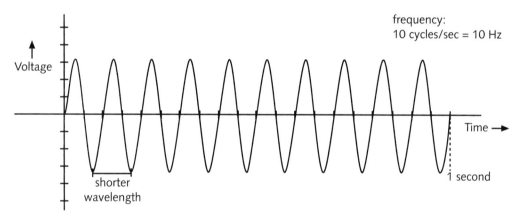

Figure 2-8   Frequencies and wavelengths

Capacitance

In addition to resistance, current, and voltage, electrical circuits are defined by two more variables: capacitance and inductance. **Capacitance** is the ability for an electric circuit or component to accumulate or store a charge. To use an analogy, capacitance is similar to the maximum amount of water a storage tank in between two pipes can hold. Capacitance is measured in **Farads** (abbreviated as F), a unit named after English chemist and physicist Michael Faraday, who experimented with electricity in the early 1800s.

Capacitance may also be imposed on a circuit by using capacitors. A **capacitor** is a device that stores electrical charge (as the tank stores water). Capacitors are usually made of two or more thin conducting plates arranged parallel to each other and separated by

2

an insulator, as shown in Figure 2-10. The plates are typically made of metal, whereas the insulator may be air, ceramic, plastic, or some other material. The maximum capacitance of a capacitor depends on the size and number of conducting plates it contains, how closely the plates are situated, and what type of insulator separates the plates. In a circuit diagram, a capacitor is represented as two plates separated by a space, as shown in Figure 2-11.

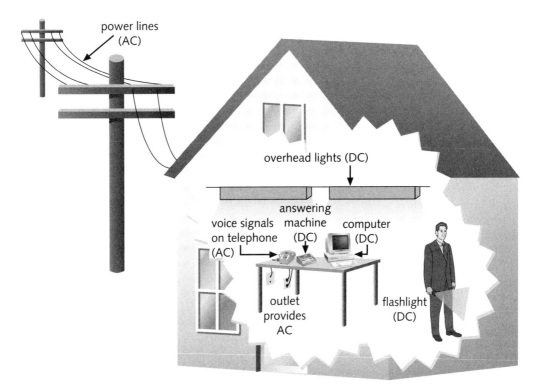

Figure 2-9   Use of DC and AC

When a capacitor is inserted into a circuit, its insulator middle stops the continuous flow of current. Although no current can flow past the capacitor, the source of electricity can continue to supply voltage to the circuit. As voltage continues to be generated, the first plate on a capacitor accumulates a negative charge. Meanwhile, the second plate loses its electrons to the other end of the circuit as the current (which is, remember, the flow of charge) continues to move. Consequently, the second plate begins building up a positive charge. As you know, opposite charges in nature want to balance out. This difference in charges between the two plates creates an imbalanced charge within the capacitor. If you remove a capacitor in this state from the circuit, the capacitor holds its stored charge. If you touch the conductive wires on the capacitors, your fingers discharge the energy it held, resulting in a shock. Some capacitors automatically release their charges when current stops flowing in the circuit (for example, when you turn off a computer); however, some do not.

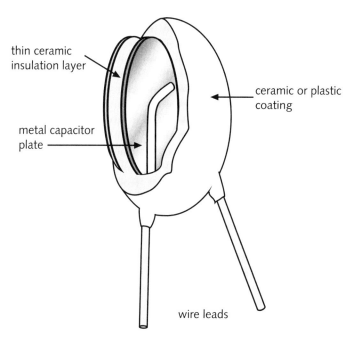

thin ceramic
insulation layer

ceramic or plastic
coating

metal capacitor
plate

wire leads

Figure 2-10   A ceramic capacitor

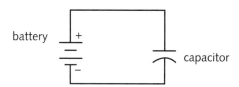

battery

+

capacitor

−

Figure 2-11   A capacitor in a circuit diagram

You might think that a capacitor could accept a charge indefinitely. But in fact, the first plate of the capacitor can only accumulate negative charge for so long. When its voltage equals the voltage of the circuit's source, it can no longer accept more electrons. At this point, it has reached its maximum capacitance. In the earlier analogy that compared a capacitor to a water storage tank, this is similar to the tank being full. Figure 2-12 depicts the buildup of charge on a capacitor.

A circuit needs to accumulate (rather than transmit) a charge because a capacitor allows the circuit to better control the current. For example, a capacitor can be used to stop potentially damaging DC current from reaching more sensitive components on the circuit. Or, a capacitor might be used to store a charge and later release it to the circuit when incoming voltage flags. This is useful for AC circuits, in which the voltage goes up and down continuously. Used on an AC current, a capacitor stores charge while the voltage is high, then releases it when the voltage dips. Capacitors are used in nearly every electronic device. They can be found in power supplies, amplifiers, monitors, and tuners for TVs, computers, and stereos as well as in automobiles, airplanes, and anything else that requires complex circuitry. A variety of capacitors are pictured in Figure 2-13.

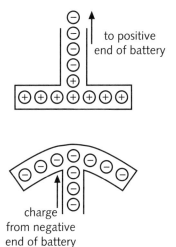

Figure 2-12   The buildup of charge on a capacitor

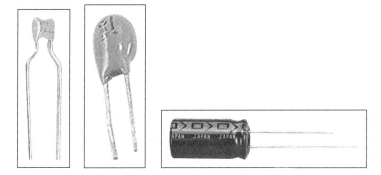

Figure 2-13   Capacitors

Inductance

When electrons move, they produce a **magnetic field**, or a region of magnetic force. Current (flowing electrons) over a wire produces a magnetic field. This field radiates outward perpendicular to the wire, as shown in Figure 2-14. The magnetic field produced by moving electrons is strongest close to the wire and weakens as you move away from the wire. Like electrostatic charge, magnetism is a force that you cannot see, but you can measure the effects. For example, if you held a compass very close to a wire carrying current in a circuit, the compass needle jumps in response to the wire's magnetic field. The magnetic effect produced by an electric current is known as **electromagnetism**. Just as fairly weak magnetism can move a compass needle, strong electromagnetism can influence larger objects.

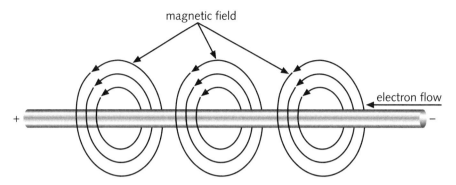

Figure 2-14   Current producing a magnetic field

A single wire doesn't produce a very strong magnetic field unless the current moving over it is extremely large. However, if the wire is coiled, the magnetic effect of a current becomes much stronger. In a coil, the weak magnetic forces around each portion of coiled wire are added to the forces around each other portion of coiled wire. Together, the forces become one large magnetic force, as shown in Figure 2-15.

When used in an electric circuit, a coil of wire is called an **inductor**, because it induces (or creates) a magnetic field. Thus, **inductance** is the capacity for an inductor to create a magnetic field. A component's inductance equals the maximum strength of the magnetic field that it can create. Inductance is measured in a unit called a **henry (H)**, named after American physicist Joseph Henry who experimented with electricity and magnetism in the early 1800s.

To further strengthen the magnetic field, wire may be coiled around a conducting core, such as iron, to produce an **electromagnet**, as shown in Figure 2-16. An electromagnet is a specific type of inductor. You may have created your own electromagnet from a battery, nail, and a few wires in early science classes. If you have never made an electromagnet, you'll have the opportunity to do so in the Hands-on Projects at the end of this chapter.

Inductors are used in electric circuits to allow direct current (DC) to pass while preventing alternating current (AC) from passing. This is precisely the opposite of what a capacitor does. An inductor accomplishes its work by building up voltage as the coil becomes magnetized, then releasing that voltage back to the circuit when the magnetic field collapses (in other words, when the current stops flowing). Inductors are used in circuits belonging in most home electronics and telecommunications devices. Another familiar use of an inductor is in car engines. When stored voltage is released, the inductor's magnetic field collapses, causing a spark that jumps across a spark plug and ignites gasoline in the engine's cylinder.

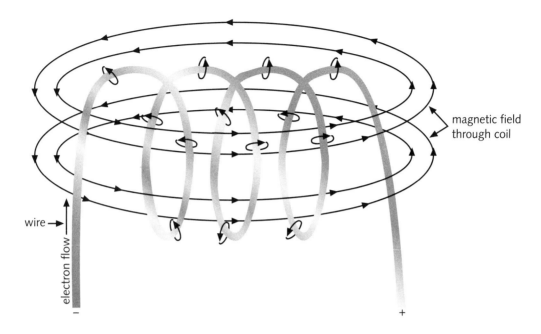

Figure 2-15 Combined magnetic forces in an inductor

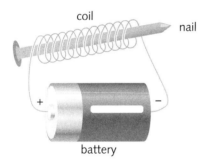

Figure 2-16 An electromagnet

Figure 2-17 shows how two different types of inductors are symbolized in circuit diagrams. In the iron-core inductor, wire is coiled around iron. In the air-core inductor, wire is coiled around air. (A number of additional types of inductors may be used in circuit designs, but an extensive discussion is beyond the scope of this book.) Figure 2-18 shows a variety of inductors.

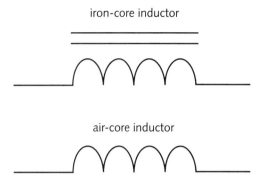

Figure 2-17   Circuit diagram symbols for inductors

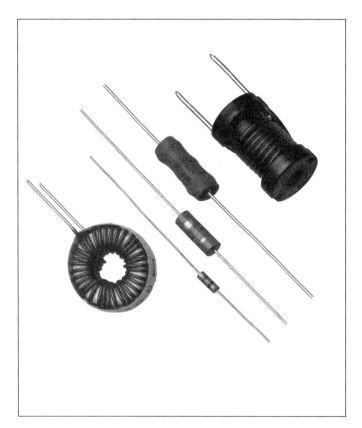

Figure 2-18   Inductors

Another use of inductors is in a transformer. A **transformer** is an electrical device that contains two electromagnetic coils and transfers electric energy from one coil to another coil through electromagnetic induction. **Electromagnetic** refers to a force (or wave) that contains a combination of electric and magnetic forces (or waves). In the case of a transformer, as one coil is subjected to current, it produces a magnetic field. If you place this coil next to another coil that has no current running through it, the first coil's magnetic field affects the second coil. In fact, it induces a voltage on the second coil. This phenomenon is known as the **mutual inductance** or the **transformer effect** and is depicted in Figure 2-19. It is through mutual inductance that a transformer transfers voltage from one part of a circuit to another part of a circuit, even though the two parts of a circuit are not physically connected.

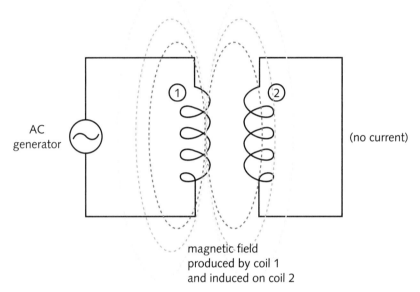

Figure 2-19   The transformer effect

Transformers only operate on AC circuits (thus, transformers are never used with batteries). Their practical application is to increase or decrease the voltage of an AC source to one more suited to a particular circuit. You may be familiar with the word transformer from discussions about high voltage power lines. As you may know, transformers help distribute electricity between lines carrying different amounts of current or voltage. Transformers are also widely used in telecommunications. For example, they are used on voice and data lines to modify available voltage into one more suited to transmitting signals. They are also used in power supplies (for radios and computers, for example) to modify the incoming voltage from an electrical outlet into one more suitable for the device. Figure 2-20 shows some transformers used in telecommunications; Figure 2-21 illustrates how transformers are represented in circuit diagrams. Notice that the symbol for a transformer looks like two parallel inductor coils.

Electrical Power

So far, you have learned about a number of ways to express the characteristics of electricity or an electric current. To review, the term "current" refers to the flow of electric charges along a conductor, volts are used to measure the pressure applied by those charges, and "resistance" refers to the amount of opposition to a current. There's just one more basic electrical concept you need to understand: power. Scientifically speaking, electrical **power** in a circuit is a multiple of the circuit's current and voltage. (In other words, voltage × current = power.) If you compare this to water through a hose, the power of the water is a combination of how fast the water is flowing and how much pressure the water is exerting on the inside of the hose. Power of a circuit at any given time is measured in **watts**, a unit named after James Watt, a Scottish engineer who experimented with engines in the mid-1700s.

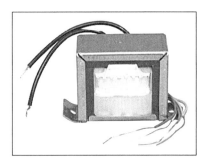

Figure 2-20   Transformers used in telecommunications

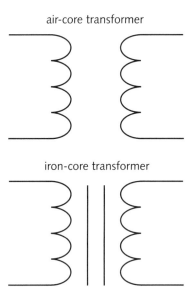

Figure 2-21   Symbols for transformers in a circuit diagram

Electrical power is calculated using this formula: volts × amps = watts. Thus, if you know the watts required by a particular load in a circuit and the voltage of the source, you can easily calculate the amount of current flowing through the circuit. For instance, a 100 watt light bulb connected to a standard 120 volt household circuit causes .83 amps of current to flow ($\frac{100}{120}$ = .83). If you hooked up twenty 100 watt bulbs to the same 120 volt circuit, the bulbs would draw 16.6 amps. (If this particular circuit were protected by a 15 amp circuit breaker, the circuit breaker would trip because it's designed to allow no more than 15 amps to flow through the circuit.) The power consumed by most telecommunications devices is so low that it is usually measured in milliwatts (1000 milliwatts = 1 watt).

Measuring Electricity

Thus far, you have learned about voltage, resistance, current, capacitance, inductance, and power. For your reference, Table 2-1 summarizes the measurements you have learned and what phenomena they measure. An understanding of these terms and how they are used is critical to understanding telecommunications technology.

Table 2-1   Measurements of electricity

Measurement	Abbreviation	Measures	Meaning
Volt	v	Voltage	Strength or pressure of electricity
Ampere	amp	Current	Rate of flow of an electrical charge
Ohm	ohm	Resistance	Opposition to current
Hertz	Hz	Frequency	Number of cycles per second in a waveform
Farad	F	Capacitance	Amount of charge that may be held by a capacitor
Henry	H	Inductance	Amount of electromagnetism that may be created by an inductor
Watt	watt	Power	Amount of power in a circuit at any given time

Often, it is simpler to express a number according to its power of 10 multiple. For instance, .004 amps is the same as 4 milliamps, 5000 volts is the same as 5 kilovolts, and 5,000,000 watts is the same as 5 Megawatts. In any scientific field, measurements may be preceded by a prefix such as "milli" or "kilo" or "Mega" to indicate what power of 10 they have been multiplied by. For your reference, the most commonly used prefixes are listed in Table 2–2, along with their power of 10 equivalents.

Bear in mind that these prefixes apply not only to amps, ohms, volts, and so on, but also to other measurements, including amounts of data. When used in the context of data storage and transfer, the prefixes equate to different powers of 2, and their values are slightly different. For example, kilo, in the context of the study of electricity, equals 10 to the 3rd power, whereas in the context of data storage equals 2 to the 10th power.

Table 2-2   Measurement prefixes

Prefix	Prefix Symbol	Power of 10	Meaning, Multiply by:
Tera	T	12	1000000000000
Giga	G	9	1000000000
Mega	M	6	1000000
kilo	k	3	1000
(no prefix – basic unit)	(none)	0	1
milli	m	-3	.001
micro	μ	-6	.000001
nano	n	-9	.000000001

Now that you have learned about basic circuits and the characteristics of electricity, you may wonder how we go about measuring them. An instrument called a **voltmeter** is connected to a circuit to measure its voltage. An **ammeter** is connected to a circuit to measure its current. An **ohmmeter** measures the resistance of a circuit. The functions of a voltmeter, ammeter, and ohmmeter may be combined into one instrument, the **multimeter**. A multimeter can measure multiple characteristics of an electrical circuit, including current, resistance, and voltage. Figure 2-22 shows an example of a modern multimeter. Another useful electrical measuring tool is the **oscilloscope**, which measures the change in voltage over time (or oscillation) on an AC circuit. Figure 2-23 shows an example of a modern oscilloscope.

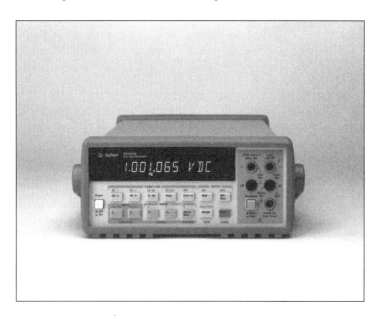

Figure 2-22   Multimeter

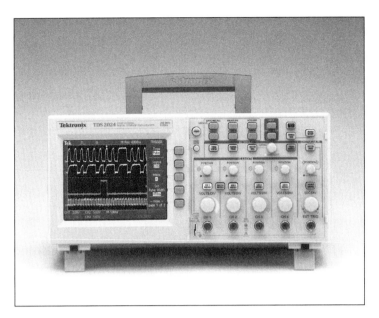

Figure 2-23   Oscilloscope

ELECTRONICS

In the scientific world, there is some debate over whether electronics is a different field from electricity, as both deal with the movement of electrons. For the purposes of this book, **electronics** is defined as a separate field of study that deals with the behavior of electric charge as it flows in a vacuum, in gases, and in semiconductors. In general, the term "electronics" applies to small control and communications devices, such as computers, whereas "electricity" applies to motors, lights, and appliances. The field of electronics has made possible such things as radios, televisions, stereo amplifiers, and computers.

In the following section, you are introduced to the two major categories of electronic components as well as the most widely used type of electronic circuit, the integrated circuit. If you can recognize these components and understand how they are used, you will be better able to comprehend the many types of telecommunication technology discussed later in this book.

Passive Electronic Devices

Electronic components are divided into two categories: passive devices or active devices. A **passive device** is a component that contributes no power gain to a circuit; in other words, it does not modify the current or voltage it receives from the power source. Thus, a passive electronic device cannot control the current that passes through it, but merely accepts the signals that it receives.

You have already learned about a few types of passive electronic devices, including capacitors and inductors. Recall that capacitors and inductors accept an incoming charge and either store the charge (in the case of a capacitor) or generate a magnetic field as a result of the charge (in the case of an inductor). Although these devices may use the incoming current or voltage to influence the rest of a circuit, neither has the ability to increase the current or voltage of the circuit.

Another important passive electronic device is a resistor. Earlier, you learned that a device, such as a light bulb or buzzer, creates resistance in a circuit. These devices reduce the amount of current that can flow through a circuit by using that current to produce light or sound. In electronics, a **resistor** is a component inserted into a circuit to provide a specific amount of resistance (measured in ohms). This resistance makes it possible to control the amount of current moving through the circuit, whether the current is AC or DC. The symbol for a resistor on a circuit diagram is shown in Figure 2-24. Notice how the resistor symbol (with its zig-zag shape) implies the resistor's function of impeding the flow of current. Resistors are the most ubiquitous passive electronic component. If you open an electronic device, you will find a number of tiny, cigar-shaped resistors, with differing amounts of resistance, as shown in Figure 2-25.

Figure 2-24   Symbol for a resistor in a circuit diagram

Figure 2-25   Resistors

Active Electronic Devices

An **active device** is an electronic component that is capable of controlling voltages or currents it receives. An active device requires a minimum level of incoming voltage to perform its job. Usually this voltage is provided by a DC source. After it receives that voltage, an active device may amplify signals, create AC signals, and perform other functions. Active devices play critical roles in many telecommunication devices, including television and radio transmitters and receivers. Some examples of active devices are filters, diodes, transistors, and integrated circuits, all of which are discussed in the following sections.

2

Diodes

A **diode** is an electronic component that allows current to flow in only one direction. You can think of them as one-way valves for electricity. For example, if you insert a diode into an AC circuit, whose current alternates its flow between positive and negative ends of a circuit, the diode accepts only the positive voltage (the current flowing from the positively charged end of the circuit to the negatively charged end of the circuit) and prevents the negative voltage from passing, as shown in Figure 2-26. The result is a series of positive voltage pulses that flow in one direction, as opposed to oscillating voltage that continuously reverses direction. (Note that until the AC is applied to the circuit, the diode does nothing.) As a result of filtering out one direction of the current's flow, the diode effectively converts AC into DC electricity. This is useful in devices, such as stereos, that require DC but must plug into an AC source.

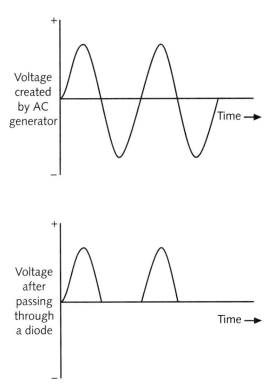

Figure 2-26   AC circuit voltage before and after passing through a diode

When connected to a DC power source, a diode can perform two different functions, depending on the direction of the current. When the current flows from the negatively charged end of the circuit to the positively charged end of the circuit, the diode stops the current from flowing completely. When the current flows from the positively charged end of the circuit to the negatively charged end of the circuit, the diode lets the current pass with little resistance. When used to perform these two tasks, a diode is considered a **switch**, a device that can start and stop current on a circuit.

You may think of a switch as something that requires human intervention—for example, the switch that turns on your overhead light only works when you flip it on with your finger. But as you can infer from the discussion on diodes, switches can also be small components that are controlled through the application of electricity. These types of switches require no human intervention, and thus are considered to be automated.

Diodes come in a variety of forms and can be made from variety of materials, but most modern diodes are made from semiconductors. Each type of diode can accept only a specific amount of current before it overheats. Figure 2-27 illustrates the symbol used to represent a diode in a circuit diagram. Figure 2-28 depicts two different diodes. Notice that diodes look very similar to resistors.

Figure 2-27   Symbol for a diode in a circuit diagram

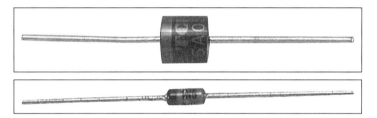

Figure 2-28   Diodes

Transistors

Another common active electronic component is the **transistor**. The word "transistor" derives from the phrase, "transferring current over a resistor." This reflects a transistor's ability to allow current to overcome the resistance of a component. This function can be very useful in controlling current. Inside, a transistor is essentially two diodes sandwiched together into a single unit that allows current approaching from either direction to overcome resistance provided by the two (internal) connected diodes. The result is either a halt to current or a great increase (amplification) in current. Notice that a transistor can accomplish the switching function of a diode, but the same transistor can also amplify current. Like diodes, transistors are made of semiconductors. And like diodes, transistors come in a variety of sizes, depending on their intended use. Note that you can't make a transistor simply by placing two diodes together in a circuit. To properly overcome the resistance (due to the molecular structure of the semiconductor inside a diode, which is beyond the scope of this book), they must be manufactured as one component.

Because transistors can act as amplifiers (that is, they can strengthen signals), or they can act as switches (that is, they can turn signals on and off), they are very useful and are found in many telecommunication devices. In fact, they were first invented in the mid-20th century to amplify and improve the quality of a telephone voice signal. You learn more about the evolution of the transistor and other telecommunication technology in Chapter 3. Now, nearly every electronic device contains transistors, from satellite broadcasting systems to computers to cellular telephones. Figure 2-29 illustrates the symbol used to represent a transistor in a circuit diagram. Figure 2-30 depicts three different transistors.

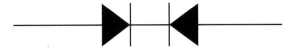

Figure 2-29   Symbol for a transistor in a circuit diagram

Figure 2-30   Transistors

Integrated Circuits

You have learned that a circuit is a closed electrical connection with an applied voltage. You have also learned that circuits may contain many different types of components, including resistors, inductors, capacitors, transistors, and so on. An **integrated circuit (IC)** is a circuit that combines the conductor and the attached components of a circuit in one small unit, as pictured in Figure 2-31. Note the IC's telltale rows of pins that enable it to be connected to a circuit board. A **circuit board** is a thin sheet of an insulating material (in other words, material such as plastic that does not readily conduct electricity) with a circuit made of a very thin conductor (usually copper) built into it that acts as the circuit. Some electronic components are soldered permanently onto a circuit board, whereas others are connected to the board through rows of tiny metallic pins.

Figure 2-31   An integrated circuit

An integrated circuit no larger than a penny may contain millions of individual components. This small size is its chief advantage. In fact, engineers developed the IC in response to a desire for smaller electronic devices during World War II (though the integrated circuit was not perfected until after the war ended). An integrated circuit's size is also its chief disadvantage. If one of an IC's internal components (for example, a transistor) fails, that component cannot be effectively repaired or replaced. This is because the internal circuitry of an IC is so tiny and complex that replacing a component is more time consuming and costly than simply replacing the entire IC. Thus, if an IC contains a faulty component, it is typically thrown away. Luckily, another advantage to integrated circuits is that they are inexpensive. In addition, they are reliable, require little power, and generate little heat. With all these advantages, you can understand why ICs are found in virtually every modern electronic device.

Integrated circuits come in many varieties, and each IC is designed to fulfill a specific purpose. For example, an IC may act as a stereo amplifier or a converter for changing AC into DC in a household appliance. A special kind of IC is the **microprocessor**, which contains all the components and intelligence necessary to accept and carry out all instructions on a computer.

TRANSMISSION CONCEPTS

Now that you have a solid foundation in electricity, you are prepared to learn how electricity is used to communicate information across distances. The remainder of this chapter describes ways in which voice and data signals are transmitted and encoded. It also covers ways in which these signals can be distorted or damaged by nearby electromagnetic fields.

Signals

Every type of communication depends on signals. Earlier in this chapter, you learned that when an electric current is manipulated to convey information, it is called a signal. However, some signals do not depend on electric current (for example, sign language). Thus, a more general definition for signal is a method for representing information to convey that information from one entity (such as a person or computer) to another. Records indicate that humans communicated via fire signals as early as 1200 BC. In modern times, we use small amounts of electricity to generate most of our signals. To produce a signal, the transmitter applies an electrical charge to the communications channel. Because signals used in telecommunication are electrical impulses, their magnitudes are expressed in voltage. For example, earlier in this chapter, you learned that voice signals carried over telephone lines use a voltage of 48 v.

Signaling is the movement of signals over a communications channel. In the context of telecommunications, signaling refers to the movement of electrical charges along a transmission media, such as wire or the air, according to a predefined format. Bear in mind that charges may also move along a wire randomly, but without a format; such charges do not convey information. In other words, random charges do not transmit signals. Later in this section, you learn about different ways in which signals may be formatted.

Signals carry not only the content of the message (for example, the words that you speak into a telephone mouthpiece), but also information about the source and destination, the message's coding techniques, the message's order and length, the duration of the communication, and the signal's route. This type of information does not contribute to or change the essential message being transmitted. In a comparison between telecommunication and the U.S. mail, such information is like the envelope and address you add to a letter before you send it. The envelope and address do not change the thoughts your letter expresses, but enable those thoughts to be conveyed. Many complex systems have evolved to generate, capture, and analyze this type of signaling information. For example, long distance companies use this information for billing purposes and to optimize the routes that data takes between source and destination. You learn about the most common signaling technology in Chapter 6.

Signals can be either analog or digital. You learn the importance of this distinction in the next two sections.

Analog Transmission

In everyday English, the word "analog" means a thing that is similar to another thing. In telecommunications, **analog** refers to electromagnetic signals that continuously vary in their strength and speed. An electromagnetic signal is a signal that relies on electromagnetic forces, or waves. Recall that an electromagnetic wave is one that contains a combination of electric and magnetic properties. Radio waves, such as those you receive on a clock radio, are examples of electromagnetic signals. Analog transmitters use variable voltage to create continuous waves—that is, voltage that increases and decreases continuously but never completely stops until the signal is complete. An analog signal results in an inexact (or approximate) replica of the original message. In other words, an analog version of your voice is not identical to your speech.

To understand why, think of two tin cans connected by a wire. When you speak into one of the tin cans, you produce analog sound waves that vibrate over the wire until they reach the tin can at the other end, as shown in Figure 2-32. These sound waves are only approximations of your voice, and they are significantly affected by the quality of the wire. For example, if you try the tin can experiment with a pure copper wire with no twists or bends in it, your voice arrives sounding clearer than if you use an unfolded coat hanger. But no matter what medium you use, the sound waves become distorted as they traverse the wire, arriving at the second tin can at least a little muddled.

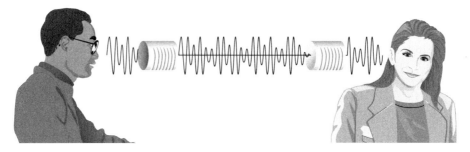

Figure 2-32   Sound transmitted over a wire

To learn more about an analog signal's properties, recall the sine wave you learned about earlier in this chapter during the discussion of AC. Just as an AC signal is based on a sine wave, so are analog signals based on sine waves. As such, they may be described by their oscillation, frequency, wavelength, and amplitude, and are depicted in graphical form as voltage (on the Y axis) over time (on the X axis), as shown in Figure 2-33. Notice how the voltage continuously varies as time passes.

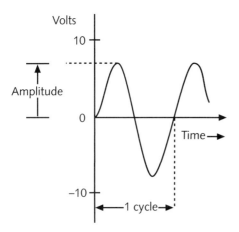

Figure 2-33   A simple analog signal

When discussing analog signals, the most important characteristics are the signal's amplitude and frequency. Recall that amplitude measures the strength of the signal and is expressed in volts. The term frequency refers to the number of cycles in an analog signal, and is measured in Hertz (abbreviated as Hz) which is equal to one cycle per second. A sine wave, such as the one pictured in Figure 2-33, consists of a single, fundamental frequency. Some frequencies are audible to humans. A dial tone (the sound that you hear when you pick up a telephone receiver) is an example of a sine wave containing one frequency. However, voices and instruments emit a complex composite of several fundamental tones whose frequencies and amplitudes rapidly vary. Human speech generally occurs in the range of 300 to 3300 Hz, though the human ear can detect frequencies in a much wider range. A human perceives a low frequency as a deep sound, whereas a high frequency sounds shrill. For instance, a few notes from a tuba might have a frequency of 45 to 300 Hz, whereas a flute can generate notes with frequencies as high as 3,300 Hz.

Figure 2-34 provides an example of an analog signal of a person speaking a full sentence. Because each person's voice patterns vary, a representation of the signal you generate when speaking the same sentence may look somewhat different.

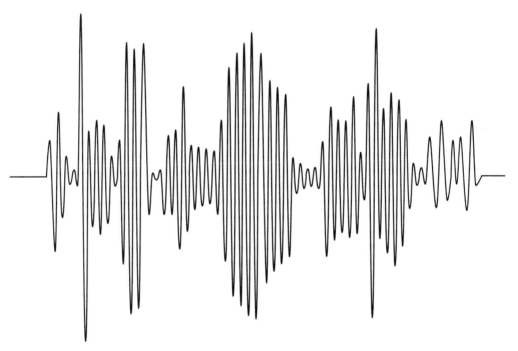

Figure 2-34   Analog signal of an actual voice

Digital Transmission

In addition to analog signals, telecommunications devices often make use of digital signals. To get an immediate appreciation of the differences between the two types of signals, compare the analog signal (shown earlier in Figure 2-33) to the digital signal shown in Figure 2-35. As you can see in Figure 2-35, **digital** signals are composed of individual pulses of voltage. In other words, in a digital signal, voltage switches on and off; it equals either 0 volts or a specific, positive voltage. The 0 voltage part of a digital signal represents the number 0. The other part of the signal (the positive voltage) represents the number 1. (The precise amount of voltage used to indicate a "1" in a digital signal varies depending on the technology used to send the signal.)

Digital signals are the only type of signals that computers can interpret, and the only type of signals that computers can issue. Thus, in computer circuits, 0s and 1s are used exclusively to convey information. So, it follows that computers rely on pulses of 0 voltage or positive voltage to represent information. The difference between the two types of pulses is established by electronic switches. Recall from the discussion about electronics that a transistor or a diode may act as a switch, a device that may alternately stop charge from passing or allow it to flow. When the transistor allows current through, a positive voltage results, indicating a 1. When the switch prevents current from flowing, there is no voltage, indicating a 0.

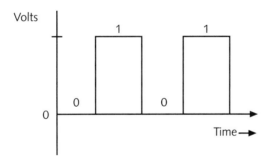

Figure 2-35   A simple digital signal

A system that uses 1s and 0s to transmit information is known as a **binary** system. Every pulse (whether equal to 0 or 1) in the digital signal is called a binary digit, or **bit**. A bit can *only* have a value of 1 (for "on") or 0 (for "off"). Eight bits together form a **byte**. One byte carries one piece of information, such as a single letter or number. You learn more about how data are transmitted in bits and bytes later in this chapter.

Comparing Analog and Digital Transmission

Because a network only has to send and receive patterns of 1s and 0s (or "on" and "off" indicators), digital transmission is more reliable than analog transmission, in which the signal's voltage continuously varies. And because of their reliability, digital signals can be transmitted at higher speeds, for longer distances and with higher quality than analog signals.

Most data networks rely exclusively on digital transmissions. One situation in which you are likely to use analog signals to transmit data is when using a modem to connect two systems. The modem may transmit analog signals over the phone lines, but the signals must be converted into digital signals by the modem at the receiving computer. The word **modem** derives from its function as a *mod*ulator/*dem*odulator, modulating analog signals into digital signals at the transmitting end, then demodulating digital signals into analog signals at the receiving end. You learn more about modem communications later in this book.

Digital transmission requires many pulses to transmit the same amount of information that an analog signal can transmit with one wave. For example, you might convey the letter "A" with a single wave in analog format, but in digital format, the same message requires 8 bits, or 8 separate pulses. Still, the high reliability of digital transmission makes this extra signaling worthwhile. In the end, digital transmission is more efficient than analog because it causes fewer errors.

In most circumstances, digital signals are preferred over analog. However, one benefit to analog signals is that, because they are more variable than digital signals, they can convey more subtleties. For example, think of the difference between your voice (which produces an analog signal) and the digital voice of an automated teller machine. This type of digital voice has a poorer quality than your own voice—that is, it sounds "like a machine." It can't convey the subtle changes in inflection that you expect in a human voice. However, more expensive and sophisticated digital devices can approximate the human voice with little discernible difference in quality.

It is important to understand that in both the analog and digital worlds, a variety of signaling techniques are used. For each different technique, standards dictate what type of transmitter, communications channel, and receiver should be used. For example, the type of transmitter used for radio broadcasts and the way in which this transmitter manipulates current to produce signals is different from the transmitter and signaling technique used on a network. Although not all signaling methods are covered in this book, you learn about the most common methods used for data and voice telecommunications.

Transmission Flaws

One of the most common transmission flaws affecting telecommunication signals is noise. **Noise** is unwanted interference from external sources, which can degrade or distort a signal. It affects both analog and digital signals, but affects analog signals much more profoundly. Many different types of noise can affect transmission. Most of these are caused by one of two electromagnetic phenomenon: **Electromagnetic Interference (EMI)** or **Radio Frequency Interference (RFI)**. Both RMI and EMI are waves that emanate from electrical devices or cables carrying electricity. Motors, power lines, televisions, copiers, fluorescent lights, and other sources of electrical activity (including a severe thunderstorm) can cause both EMI and RFI. In addition, RFI may be caused by strong broadcast signals from radio or TV towers. The extent to which noise affects a signal is influenced by the type of wire or other transmission media used to carry the signal. Wireless transmission is typically more susceptible to noise.

You may be familiar with noise if you have talked on a phone and heard a hissing sound in the background or if you've tried to tune into a distant radio station while driving under strong power lines. When noise affects analog signals, this distortion can result in the incorrect transmission of data, just as if static on the phone line prevented you from hearing the person on the other end of the line. Figure 2-36 shows an analog signal affected by noise.

Although noise affects digital signals, it affects them less severely than analog signals. As shown in Figure 2-37, a digital signal distorted by noise can still be interpreted as a pattern of 1s and 0s.

Another transmission flaw is **attenuation**, or the loss of a signal's strength as it travels away from its source. To compensate for attenuation, both analog and digital signals are boosted, or strengthened, en route to allow them to travel farther. However, the technology used to boost an analog signal is different from that used to boost a digital signal.

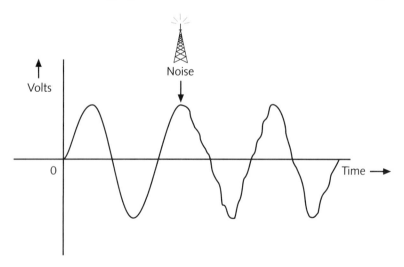

Figure 2-36   An analog signal distorted by noise

2

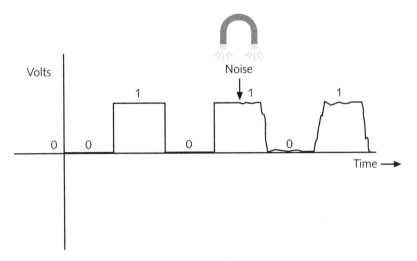

Figure 2-37 A digital signal distorted by noise

Analog signals pass through an **amplifier**, an electronic device that increases the voltage, or power, of the signals. When an analog signal is amplified, the noise that it has accumulated is also amplified. This indiscriminate amplification causes the analog signal to progressively worsen. After multiple amplifications, an analog signal becomes difficult to decipher. Figure 2-38 shows an analog signal distorted by noise and then amplified once.

Whereas a weakening analog signal must be amplified, a weakening digital signal must simply be repeated. When digital signals are repeated, they are actually retransmitted in their original, pure form, without any noise. This process is known as **regeneration**. A device that regenerates a digital signal is called a **repeater**. You learn more about repeaters in Chapter 11. Figure 2-39 shows a digital signal distorted by noise and then regenerated by a repeater.

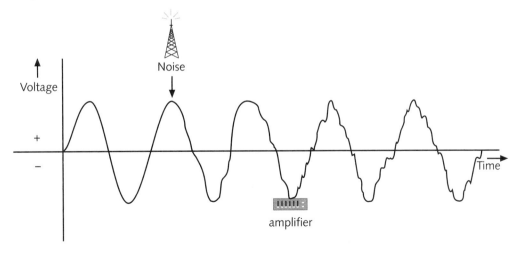

Figure 2-38 An analog signal distorted by noise and then amplified

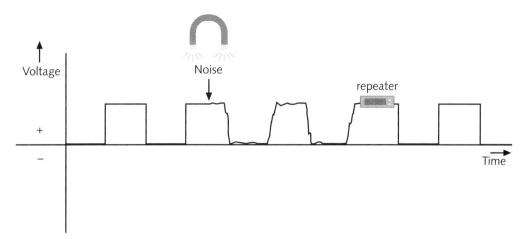

Figure 2-39   A digital signal distorted by noise and then regenerated

Encoding and Numbering Systems

Encoding is the process of modifying data so that it can be interpreted by the receiver. Data can be encoded in a variety of ways, depending on the nature of the receiver (which could be a software program, a piece of hardware, or a human). Most computer users rarely need to know how data is encoded, because the computer hardware or software performs the translation from code into language they can understand. However, as a telecommunication professional, you need to understand the most basic encoding schemes.

Encoding takes place all around you. You encode your thoughts when you present them in a language that your listener can understand. A sound wave is encoded by a radio station transmitter so that it can be received by your radio. These are both examples of analog encoding. However, digital systems make extensive use of encoding as well, and different encoding schemes are used for different technology. Software programs, for example, may be encoded in languages such as C++ or Java. The following sections discuss several methods for encoding data.

The Decimal System

The numbering system that we all learn as children is called the **decimal system**. Because you are so familiar with this numbering system, you probably don't often consider its origin or realize that you can break it down. But in fact, the decimal system uses a total of 10 digits (0 through 9), multiplied by an exponential of 10 to represent any number. The exponent equals the value's position, which may be any whole number (including a negative number to represent digits after the decimal point). For example, in the decimal system the number 25 is actually 2×10^1 (or 20) plus 5×10^0 (or 5). The number 256 is actually $2 \times 10^2 + 5 \times 10^1 + 6 \times 10^0$, or 200 + 50 + 6. The number 5489.732 is actually $5 \times 10^3 + 4 \times 10^2 + 8 \times 10^1 + 9 \times 10^0 + 7 \times 10^{-1} + 3 \times 10^{-2} + 2 \times 10^{-3}$, or 5000 + 400 + 80 + 9 + .7+ .03 + .002. There is no limit to the number of digits in a decimal number. Thus, any quantity of multiples of 10 may contribute to a decimal number's value.

The Binary System

As you have learned, bits and bytes form the basis for all digital communications. A byte consists of eight bits, each of which represents a 1 or a 0. Thus, for example, one byte might look like this: 1 0 0 1 0 0 0 1. In the decimal system, you read that number as 1×10^7 plus 1×10^4 plus 1×10^0, or ten-million, ten-thousand one. But to determine the value of a byte, you actually have to use the binary system. According to the binary system, you multiple each digit by 2 raised to a specific power (for example, 2^7 or 2^4). To refresh your memory of exponents, 2^4 is $2 \times 2 \times 2 \times 2$, which equals 16. Similarly, 2^7 is $2 \times 2 \times 2 \times 2 \times 2 \times 2 \times 2$, or 128.

In the binary system, each bit position, or placeholder, in the number represents a specific multiple of 2. In a byte, which contains 8 placeholders, the placeholder farthest to the right is known as the zero position. Thus, a digit in that position must be multiplied by 2 to the 0 power, or 2^0, to determine its value. Recall from early math classes that any number raised to the power of 0 has a value of 1. Thus, if a 1 is in the zero position, its value equals 1×2^0, or 1×1. If a 0 is in the zero position, its value equals 0×2^0, or 0×1. (As you know, however, 0 times anything equals 0.)

The placeholder positions in a binary number increase as you move from right to left, starting with zero. In a byte, which has eight placeholders, the placeholder farthest to the left is the 7th position. Any digit in the 7th position must be multiplied by 2 to the 7th power, or 2^7, to determine its value. If a 1 is in the 7th position, its value equals 1×2^7 or 1×128. Similarly, a digit in the 4th position would be multiplied by 2^4 to determine its value. Thus, a 1 in the 4th position would indicate a value of 16. Figure 2-40 shows the different values that are represented by a 1 in each different position within a byte.

Bit position:	7	6	5	4	3	2	1	0
Binary exponential:	2^7	2^6	2^5	2^4	2^3	2^2	2^1	2^0
Value if bit = 1:	128	64	32	16	8	4	2	1

Figure 2-40   *The binary coding scheme*

If a bit in the byte equals 1 (in other words, if it's "on"), its numerical equivalent in the coding scheme is added to the total. If a bit equals 0, that position has no value and nothing is added to the total. For example, the decimal number 8 equals 2^3, which means a single "on" bit is indicated in the third position as follows: 00001000. The decimal number 9 equals 8+1, or $2^3 + 2^0$, and is represented by the binary number 00001001. Following are some additional examples of bytes translated into decimal format:

- The byte 11111111 equals: $1 \times 2^7 + 1 \times 2^6 + 1 \times 2^5 + 1 \times 2^4 + 1 \times 2^3 + 1 \times 2^2 + 1 \times 2^1 + 1 \times 2^0$, or $128 + 64 + 32 + 16 + 8 + 4 + 2 + 1$. Its decimal equivalent, then, is 255.

- The byte 01010101 equals: $0 \times 2^7 + 1 \times 2^6 + 0 \times 2^5 + 1 \times 2^4 + 0v2^3 + 1 \times 2^2 + 0 \times 2^1 + 1 \times 2^0$, or $0 + 64 + 0 + 16 + 0 + 4 + 0 + 1$. Its decimal equivalent, then, is 85.

- The byte 00100100 equals: $0 \times 2^7 + 0 \times 2^6 + 1 \times 2^5 + 0 \times 2^4 + 0 \times 2^3 + 1 \times 2^2 + 0 \times 2^1 + 0 \times 2^0$, or $0 + 0 + 32 + 0 + 0 + 4 + 0 + 0$. Its decimal equivalent, then, is 36.

- The byte 10101010 equals: $1 \times 2^7 + 0 \times 2^6 + 1 \times 2^5 + 0 \times 2^4 + 1 \times 2^3 + 0 \times 2^2 + 1 \times 2^1 + 0 \times 2^0$, or $128 + 0 + 32 + 0 + 8 + 0 + 2 + 0$. Its decimal equivalent, then, is 170.

If all the bits preceding a bit with the value of "1" in a byte have a value of "0," sometimes the preceding 0s are simply left off. For example, the decimal number 8 could be represented by either of the following binary numbers – 00001000 or 1000 – because their value is the same.

Note that the binary numbering scheme may be used with more than eight positions. However, in the digital world, bytes form the building blocks for messages, and bytes always include eight positions. In a data signal, multiple bytes are combined to form a message. Thus, if you were to peek at the 1s and 0s used to transmit an entire e-mail message, for example, you might see millions of zeros and ones passing by. A computer can quickly translate these binary numbers into codes, such as ASCII, that express letters, numbers, and even punctuation marks. You learn about ASCII and other codes next.

To fully understand the binary coding scheme, you should practice manually coding decimal numbers as binary numbers and vice versa. But to make conversion quicker and easier, you may use a scientific calculator, such as the one available with the Windows operating system.

For example, to convert the number 192 to a binary number:

1. On a Windows computer, click **Start**, point to **Programs**, point to **Accessories**, and then click **Calculator**.

2. Click **View**, then click **Scientific**. You want to translate a decimal number into a binary number, so first you need to make sure that the decimal option is selected.

3. Verify that the **Dec** option button is selected.

4. Type **192**. Now that you have typed the decimal number, you can convert it to its binary equivalent.

5. Click the **Bin** option button. The number 1100000, appears in the display window. This is the binary equivalent of 192.

You can reverse this process to convert a binary number to a decimal number.

The Hexadecimal System

When working with large decimal numbers, the binary numbering scheme, which is the only one that computers can understand, becomes unwieldy. For example, the 3-digit number 188 in the binary numbering system is an 8-digit number, 10111100. Translating decimal numbers into binary form is tedious for humans. A simpler and more efficient way for both humans and computers to communicate is by using the **hexadecimal** numbering system (or hex system), which uses 16 symbols (0 through 9 and A through F) to represent decimal digits 0 through 15, respectively. (The word hexadecimal is derived from the Greek word *hex*, meaning "six" and *decem* meaning "ten.") In the hexadecimal system, a number has the decimal equivalent of the digit multiplied by 16 to the power of its position. As with the binary and decimal systems, digit positions begin at the far right of the number with the 0 position. For example, if the digit in the 0 position equals 1, its hexadecimal value would be 1×16^0, or 1. If the digits in both the 0 and 1st positions equal 1, the hexadecimal value of the number would be 1×16^1 (or 16) + 1×16^0 (or 1), for a total of 17. A more complex example is the hexadecimal number 388, which equals $3 \times 16^2 + 8 \times 16^1 + 8 \times 16^0$ in the hexadecimal system and has the decimal equivalent of 768 + 128 + 8, or 904. The translation can be performed in reverse to convert decimal numbers into the hexadecimal format. For example, the decimal number 62 equals 48 (the highest multiple of 16 contained in 62) plus 14, or $3 \times 16^1 + 14 \times 16^0$, or 3 E (recall that the decimal number 14 is represented by the letter E in hexadecimal code). You can find a table of decimal, binary, and hexadecimal equivalents in Appendix A.

As with converting between decimal and binary numbers, converting between decimal and hexadecimal notation is simplified by using a scientific calculator, such as the one available with the Windows operating system.

For example, to convert the decimal number 256 to a hexadecimal number:

1. On a Windows computer, click **Start**, point to **Programs**, point to **Accessories**, and then click **Calculator**.

2. Click **View**, then click **Scientific**. Make sure that the **Dec** option button is selected.

3. Type **256**, then click the **Hex** option button. The hexadecimal equivalent of the number 256, 100, appears in the display window.

EBCDIC

The **binary coded decimal (BCD)** system was one of the first code sets that represented a complete English alphabet as binary numbers. IBM devised this code and used this system on its earliest computers. But BCD could only use up to 64 symbols to represent letters, numbers, and other characters (such as punctuation marks). Later, in the 1960s, IBM expanded BCD. The new version was called **Extended BCD Interchange Code (EBDIC)**. EBCDIC (pronounced eb-suh-dik) is an 8-bit encoding system adopted by IBM for use with its mainframe computers. 8-bit means that EBCDIC uses eight binary placeholders to encode characters. Given that each of eight placeholders has two possibilities (1 or 0), EBCDIC can encode up to 2^8, or 256, different characters, including letters, numbers, and punctuation marks.

Even though EBCDIC has been replaced by better encoding systems, it remains in use on some large IBM computers. During the late 1990s, organizations upgraded their software to make sure the programs could interpret dates that included the year 2000. Many companies also took this opportunity to upgrade their older EBCDIC encoding system to ASCII, which you will learn about next.

ASCII (American Standard Code for Information Interchange)

Most text messages exchanged between computers are encoded in a simple scheme known as **ASCII** (pronounced *as-kee*), which stands for American Standard Code for Information Interchange. A few different types of ASCII encoding exist. The standard kind, and the one used in the United States, is a 7-bit encoding system. This means that it uses seven binary digits to represent any single character. Because a combination of 1s and 0s in seven different places (2^7) allows for 128 possible permutations, ASCII represents English letters, numbers, special characters, and punctuation marks as numbers from 0 to 127. In ASCII, for example, the letter T is represented by the number 84, which in binary format would be 1010100. Notice that the number has seven placeholders.

ASCII is frequently used for basic e-mail messages, but it does not have a mechanism for encoding formatting, such as margins, tables, bold, or underline attributes, so it cannot be used for sophisticated documents or spreadsheets. A complete table of characters and their ASCII numerical equivalents can be found in Appendix A. Because ASCII is a standard method of translating letters into numbers, any kind of computer system can use this coding to communicate with another computer system.

To convert a word into binary format using the ASCII encoding scheme, you can look up each letter on an ASCII conversion chart (such as the one found in Appendix A), then convert the ASCII number to its binary equivalent. For example, the word BAT (all capital letters) in ASCII code is 66 65 84. Converted to binary notation, BAT becomes 1000010 1000001 1010100.

Unicode

Unicode is an internationally recognized 16-bit encoding scheme developed in the early 1990s. Because Unicode can make use of 16 binary placeholders, it may represent up to 2^{16}, or up to 65,536 characters. Recall that ASCII, which is an American standard, can only represent 256 characters. This limitation presents a problem when attempting to encode languages, such as Japanese, which use many more characters to create words than English uses, or numeric systems, such as Arabic, which use different digits than the Roman numerals (0 through 9) with which we are all familiar. Unlike ASCII, Unicode has enough placeholders to represent each major language's letters, numbers, and special characters with a unique code. Unicode even contains codes to represent economic, political, religious, business, and zodiac symbols. Because Unicode offers an alternative to ASCII that can help bridge encoding differences between countries, some scientists predict that Unicode will replace ASCII in the future. Many software companies (such as Microsoft) are currently writing their software so that it complies with Unicode standards.

When reading about software, you may see references to "UTF-*n*" where "*n*" is a number. **Unicode transformation format (UTF)** refers to the way in which a software program uses Unicode. The number represents which UTF method that software program employs. It may help to think of the UTF distinctions as different dialects of the same language. Just as someone from New York uses the same language as someone from Georgia, chances are they pronounce their words and use expressions in a different way.

Because Unicode has so many character codes, the entire code set is not included in Appendix A. However, you should know that the first 128 Unicode codes are the same as the 128 ASCII codes, which are included in Appendix A.

Measuring Data

Because bytes are used to represent data, the more data, the greater the number of bytes required to represent it. As a telecommunications professional, you will hear quantities of data, whether stored on a computer's hard disk or traveling over a computer's connection to a network, expressed in magnitudes of bytes. The most common magnitudes of bytes used to express amounts of data storage are listed in Table 2-3. In some contexts (for example, if precise numbers are not necessary or if referring to storage on a floppy disk rather than a hard disk), these quantities may be rounded down to the nearest multiple of 1000. For example, sometimes when people say "1 Kilobyte," they actually mean 1000 bytes rather than 1024 bytes.

Table 2-3   Data storage terminology

Term	Abbreviation	Quantity
Byte	B	8 bits
Kilobyte	KB	2 to the 10th power (1024) bytes or 1000 bytes, depending on the context
Megabyte	MB	2 to the 20th power (1,048,576) bytes (1024 kilo bytes) or 1000 kilobytes, depending on the context
Gigabyte	GB	2 to the 30th power (1,073,741,824) bytes (1024 megabytes) or 1000 megabytes, depending on the context
Terabyte	TB	2 to the 40th power (1,099,511,627,776) bytes (1024 gigabytes) or 1000 gigabytes, depending on the context

Throughput and Bandwidth

In addition to measuring data storage, telecommunication professionals often need to know how much data can be transferred over a communications channel. For example, you may need to download a file that is 4 MB in size and have a modem that's capable of accepting 56,000 bits of data per second (bps) or 56 Kilobits per second (Kbps). Under optimal circumstances, how long will this data transfer take? If 4 MB equals 4,194,304 bytes (4 × 1,048,576) and each byte equals 8 bits, then the total number of bits to be transferred equals 33,554,432. When you divide the total by the 56,000 bps capacity of the modem, you get approximately 600 seconds, or 10 minutes. (Modems rarely reach their optimal connection speed due to noise or other characteristics of the communications channel; however, so the actual time to download this file would probably be longer.)

Another word for the amount of data that a communications channel can carry during a given period of time is **throughput**. As in the previous example, throughput is commonly measured in bits per second (bps). In the case of a modem, it may be Kilobits (1,000 bits) per second (Kbps), but in most modern data communications, throughput is measured in Megabits (1,000,000 bits) per second (Mbps). Throughput may also be called **capacity**.

All media are limited by the laws of physics that prevent signals from traveling faster than the speed of light. Beyond that, throughput is limited by the signaling techniques used on a given media. In general, the signaling techniques used on fiber-optic cables can achieve higher throughput than those used on copper or wireless connections. Noise and devices connected to the transmission media can further limit throughput. A noisy communications channel spends more time compensating for the noise and therefore has fewer resources for transmitting data.

Often, the term bandwidth is used interchangeably with throughput. However, strictly speaking, **bandwidth** is a measure of the difference between the highest and lowest frequencies that a media can transmit. This range of frequencies is expressed in Hz and is proportional to throughput. For example, if the Federal Communications Commission (FCC) told you that you could transmit a radio signal between 870 and 880 MHz, your allotted bandwidth would be 10 MHz. The higher the bandwidth, the higher the throughput. This is because higher frequencies can transmit more data in a given period of time than lower frequencies. In Chapters 8 and 9, you will learn the bandwidth characteristics of different types of communications channels.

2

You may hear the term "baud" used interchangeably with the bits per second (bps) designation, but this is incorrect. One **baud** equals one cycle of an analog wave, but it does not necessarily equal one bit of data. For example, a 2400 baud modem can transmit 2400 analog wave cycles per second. However, due to digital coding and compression techniques, this same modem may achieve 9400 bits per second in actual data transferred. Baud rates are only used to describe analog transmission. You will never hear baud rates used in the context of fiber optic networks, for example. The term baud is named after French telegrapher Jean-Maurice Baudot who invented a code for sophisticated telegraph transmissions.

CHAPTER SUMMARY

- A charge is a fundamental property of a material to exert a force on another material. Electrons carry negative charges, whereas protons carry positive charges. In stable matter, these charges are balanced. When matter has an excess of either protons or neutrons, it is said to be electrically charged.

- Electricity may exist as either static electricity, the imbalance of charges, or as current electricity, the flow of charge along a conductor.

- When electric current is manipulated, it can generate and transmit information as signals.

- The three main characteristics of a circuit are voltage, current, and resistance. If two of these characteristics are known, the third can be calculated using Ohm's Law, which states that the amount of current flowing in an electric circuit is directly proportional to the voltage and inversely proportional to the resistance.

- There are two distinct types of electric current: direct current and alternating current. In direct current (DC), an electrical charge flows steadily in one direction over the conductor. In alternating current (AC), the electrical charge flows in one direction first, then in the opposite direction, then back in the first direction, and so on, in an alternating fashion over the conductor.

- AC voltage follows a sine wave in which the strength of the voltage is indicated by the wave's amplitude and the number of times each second the wave cycles (from its starting point through a full oscillation back to its starting point) is known as its frequency. Frequency is measured in Hertz (abbreviated as Hz).

- Devices useful for controlling current include capacitors, inductors, and transformers.

- A wire may be coiled around a conducting core, such as iron, to produce an electromagnet, which is a specific type of inductor. Electromagnets are used in motors and in some telecommunications devices.

- Electrical power in a circuit is a multiple of its current and voltage (in other words, voltage $\times$ current = power).

❐ In a circuit, voltage is measured by a voltmeter, current is measured by an ammeter, and resistance is measured by an ohmmeter. A device that can measure all three of these variables is called a multimeter. An oscilloscope measures the change in voltage over time (or oscillation) on an AC circuit.

❐ Electronics is a field that deals with the behavior of electric charge as it flows in a vacuum, in gases, and in semiconductors. In general, the term "electronics" applies to power controls and communications devices, such as computers, whereas electricity applies to motors, lights, and appliances.

❐ Electronic devices may be active or passive. Examples of passive devices are capacitors and inductors. Examples of active devices are transistors and diodes.

❐ Integrated circuits contain many tiny components in one enclosed unit. They are inexpensive, reliable, small, and they require little power and generate relatively little heat.

❐ Analog refers to signals that use variable voltage to create continuous waves, resulting in an inexact replica of the original message.

❐ Digital signals are composed of pulses of zero voltage and precise positive voltage that represent values of either 0 or 1, respectively.

❐ The use of 1s and 0s to encode information is known as a binary system. Every pulse in the digital signal is called a binary digit, or bit. A bit can *only* have a value of 1 or 0, which equate to "on" and "off," respectively. Eight bits together form a byte.

❐ Digital transmission is more reliable than analog transmission. Because of their reliability, digital signals can be transmitted at higher speeds, for longer distances, and with higher quality than analog signals.

❐ Noise is unwanted interference from external sources that may degrade a signal. It affects both analog and digital signals, but affects analog signals much more profoundly.

❐ Attenuation is the loss of a signal's strength as it travels farther away from its source. To compensate for attenuation, both analog and digital signals are boosted en route to travel farther. However, analog signals pass through an amplifier, whereas digital signals are regenerated in their original, pure form.

❐ In the binary numbering system, each bit has a decimal equivalent of 2 to the power of its position if the bit is on (in other words, equals 1).

❐ The hexadecimal numbering system uses 16 symbols, 0 through 9 and A through F, to represent decimal digits 0 through 15, respectively.

❐ Most text messages are encoded in a simple scheme known as ASCII (pronounced *as-kee*). ASCII represents English letters, numbers, special characters, and punctuation marks as numbers from 0 to 127.

2

❑ Unicode is an internationally recognized 16-bit encoding scheme developed in the early 1990s. Because Unicode can make use of 16 binary placeholders, it may represent up to 2^{16}, or up to 65,536 characters and encode the letters of many different languages. In the future, Unicode may replace ASCII as the most common encoding system for data.

❑ The amount of data that a communications channel can carry during a given period of time is throughput or capacity. Throughput is commonly measured in bits per second (bps).

❑ Bandwidth is a measure of the difference between the highest and lowest frequencies that a media can transmit. This range of frequencies is expressed in Hz and is directly proportional to throughput.

KEY TERMS

active device — An electronic component that is capable of controlling voltages or currents it receives.

alternating current (AC) — An electrical charge flowing in one direction first, then in the opposite direction, then back in the first direction, and so on, in an oscillating fashion over a conductor. To cause this AC, the source sends voltage that varies consistently over regular intervals of time. Home electrical outlets provide AC.

American Standard Code for Information Interchange (ASCII) — An encoding scheme used for simple text messages that represents English letters, numbers, special characters, and punctuation marks as numbers from 0 to 127.

ammeter — An instrument used to measure the current flowing through a circuit.

ampere (amp) — A measure of the amount of current flowing through a conductor. The ampere is named after 19th century French physicist André Marie Ampère.

amplifier — An electronic device that increases the voltage, or power, of a signal.

amplitude — The height, or strength, of a current's or signal's wave. Amplitude is measured in volts.

analog — The signals that use variable voltage to create continuous waves, resulting in an inexact (or approximate) replica of the original sound.

attenuation — The loss of a signal's strength as it travels farther away from its source.

bandwidth — A measure of the difference between the highest and lowest frequencies that a media can transmit.

baud — One cycle of an analog wave. Though used to describe modem transmission speeds, a baud is not necessarily equivalent to one bit of data. The term baud is named after French telegrapher Jean-Maurice Baudot who invented an early code for telex transmission.

binary — A system that uses only 1s and 0s to encode information.

binary coded decimal (BCD) — One of the first code sets that represented a complete English alphabet as binary numbers. IBM devised this code and used this system on its earliest computers. BCD can only use up to 64 symbols to represent letters, numbers, and other characters. It was replaced by EBCDIC.

bit — A pulse in a digital signal which has a value of either 1 or 0. Abbreviation for "Binary Digit."

boost — To strengthen a signal.

byte — The equivalent of eight bits. One byte carries one piece of information, such as a single letter or number.

capacitance — The ability for an electric circuit or component to accumulate or store a charge. Capacitance is measured in Farads.

capacitor — A device that stores electrical charge. Capacitors are usually made of two or more thin, conducting plates arranged parallel to each other and separated by an insulator.

capacity — The amount of data that can traverse a communication channel within a given time period.

charge — The characteristic of a material that enables it to exert an atomic force on another material.

circuit — A closed connection between an electric source (such as a battery) and a load (such as a lamp) over which electric current may flow.

circuit board — A thin sheet of an insulating material that holds electronic components (for example, resistors and diodes) plus conductive pathways (typically made of copper) to connect those components in a circuit.

conductor — A material over which electric current readily flows.

converter — A device (found in most household appliances) that changes AC into DC.

current electricity — *See* electric current.

cycle — A section of a sine wave, beginning at a starting point, up to the wave's highest amplitude, down to its lowest amplitude, and then back to the starting point. One cycle per second equals one Hertz.

decimal system — A numbering system that uses a total of 10 digits, 0 through 9, multiplied by an exponential of 10 to represent any number.

digital — A method of expressing information in signals composed of pulses of zero voltage and positive voltage that represent values of either 0 or 1, respectively.

diode — An active electronic device made from a semiconducting material that allows current to flow in only one direction.

direct current (DC) — An electrical charge flowing steadily in one direction over a conductor. To generate DC, a source must apply a constant amount of voltage to the conductor at all times. Batteries are examples of DC power sources.

EBCDIC (Extended BCD Interchange Code) — An 8-bit encoding system developed by IBM and adopted for use with its mainframe computers. EBCDIC can encode up to 2^8, or 256, different characters, including letters, numbers, and punctuation marks.

electric current — The controlled movement of an electrical charge (or electrons) along the atoms of a conductor (such as wire).

electromagnet — A central conducting core surrounded by a coil that produces an electromagnetic field when current is applied to the coil. An electromagnet is a specific type of inductor.

electromagnetic — A type of force (or wave) that contains a combination of electric and magnetic forces (or waves).

electromagnetic interference (EMI) — A form of noise, or waves that emanate from electrical devices or cables carrying electricity. Motors, power lines, televisions, copiers, fluorescent lights, and other sources of electrical activity (including a severe thunderstorm) can cause EMI.

electromagnetism — The magnetic effect produced by an electric current.

electron — An atomic subparticle that orbits the center of an atom and carries a negative charge.

electronics — In general, the study of moving electrons. More specifically, electronics is a field that deals with the behavior of electric charge as it flows in a vacuum, in gases, and in semiconductors.

electrostatic charges — The charges inherent in electrons and protons that are bound to balance each other through static electricity.

encode — To modify a set of data into a specific representation that can be interpreted by the receiver (whether it is a software program, piece of hardware, or human).

Farads (F) — A measure of capacitance. The Farad was named after English chemist and physicist Michael Faraday, who experimented with electricity in the early 1800s.

frequency — The number of times a wave cycles from it's beginning point to its highest amplitude, to its lowest amplitude and back to where it started before it repeats. Frequency is measured in cycles per second, or Hertz.

generator — A power source that supplies AC.

giga (G) — A prefix that indicates a quantity multiplied by 2 to the 30th power (1,073,741,824) in the context of data transfer or storage or 10 to the 9th power (1,000,000,000) in the context of mathematics, physics, and electronics.

gigabyte (GB) — A quantity of data equivalent to 2 to the 30th power (1,073,741,824) bytes (1024 megabytes) or 1000 megabytes, depending on the context.

grounding — The use of a conductor (such as a wire) to divert unused or potentially harmful charges to an insulator, where they will be stopped or absorbed.

henry (H) — A unit used to measure inductance. The henry was named after American physicist Joseph Henry who experimented with electricity and magnetism in the early 1800s.

Hertz (Hz) — The unit of measure in which frequency is expressed, equal to cycles per second. The term was named after German physicist Heinrich Hertz who, in the late 19° century, studied electromagnetic theory and radio waves.

hexadecimal numbering system chex system — A numbering scheme based on 16 symbols, 0 through 9 and A through F.

inductance — The capacity for an inductor (or coiled wire) to create a magnetic field.

inductor — A coil of wire that generates (or induces) a magnetic field as electric current flows over it.

insulator — A material over which electric current doesn't readily flow.

integrated circuit (IC) — A chip made of a semiconductive material (usually silicon) that contains embedded electronic components, such as resistors, diodes, and transistors.

kilo (k) — A prefix that indicates a quantity multiplied by 2 to the 10th power (1024) in the context of data transfer or storage or 10 to the 3rd power (1000) in the context of mathematics, physics, and electronics.

kilobyte (KB) — A quantity of data equivalent to 2 to the 10th power (1024) bytes or 1000 bytes, depending on the context.

magnetic field — A region of magnetic force. Electrons moving through a wire cause a magnetic field that radiates outward from the wire.

mega (M) — A prefix that indicates a quantity multiplied by 2 to the 20th power (1,048,576) in the context of data transfer or storage or 10 to the 6th power (1,000,000) in the context of mathematics, physics, and electronics.

megabyte (MB) — A quantity of data equivalent to 2 to the 20th power (1,048,576) bytes (1024 kilobytes) in the context of data transfer or storage or 10 to the 6th power (1,000,000) bytes (or 1000 kilobytes) in the context of mathematics, physics, and electronics.

micro (µ) — A prefix that indicates a quantity multiplied by 10 to the −6th power (.000001).

microprocessor — A special kind of integrated circuit that contains all the components and intelligence necessary to accept and carry out all of the incoming instructions on a computer.

milli (m) — A prefix that indicates a quantity multiplied by 10 to the −3rd power (.001).

modem — A device that derives its name from its function as a *modulator/demodulator*, modulating analog signals into digital signals at the transmitting end, then demodulating digital signals into analog signals at the receiving end.

multimeter — An instrument that can measure multiple characteristics of an electrical circuit, including its current, resistance, and voltage.

multiplexing — The process of simultaneously transmitting multiple signals over one circuit.

mutual inductance — A phenomenon in which one inductor (that has current flowing through it) produces a magnetic field and thereby induces a voltage on a nearby coil. Also known as the *transformer effect*.

nano (n) — A prefix that indicates a quantity multiplied by 10 to the −9th power (.000000001).

neutrons — An atomic subparticle found at the center of an atom, which possesses no charge (and is said to be neutral).

noise — Unwanted interference from external sources, such as fluorescent lights, cathode ray tubes, or broadcast towers, that may degrade a signal. Noise may include electromagnetic interference or radio frequency interference.

ohm — A measure of resistance.

ohmmeter — An instrument used to measure the resistance of a circuit.

Ohm's Law — A principle of electricity that states that the amount of current flowing in an electric circuit is directly proportional to the voltage and inversely proportional to the resistance. Ohm's Law is named after German scientist Georg Simon Ohm.

oscillation — A type of wave motion in which the amplitude of the wave varies regularly as time passes. Oscillation is present in AC current, analog signals, and other natural phenomena.

oscilloscope — An instrument that measures the change in voltage over time (or oscillation) on an AC circuit or an analog signal.

passive device — An electronic component that contributes no power gain to a circuit; in other words, it does not modify the current or voltage it receives from the power source.

power — In an electrical circuit, a multiple of the circuit's current and voltage (in other words, voltage x current = power). Power is measured in watts.

proton — An atomic subparticle found at the center of an atom, which carries a positive charge.

radio frequency interference (RFI) — A form of noise, or waves that emanate from electrical devices or cables carrying electricity. RFI may also be caused by strong broadcast signals from radio or TV towers.

regeneration — The process of retransmitting digital signals in their original, pure form. Regeneration is used by repeaters to compensate for attenuation.

repeater — A device inserted at intervals in the communications channel that regenerates a digital signal or amplifies an analog signal that has been degraded by attenuation.

resistance — The opposition to electric current. Resistance is a fundamental property of conductors that depends on the conductor's structure and size. It is also caused by loads or resistors in a circuit. Resistance is measured in ohms.

resistor — A passive electronic device that is inserted into a circuit to provide a specific amount of resistance and thus help control current.

semiconductor — A material (such as silicon) that has some ability to conduct electricity. A semiconductor conducts electricity better than an insulator, but not as well as a conductor.

signal — A method for representing information in order to convey the information from one entity (such as a person or computer) to another. A signal may be formed by manipulating an electric current.

signaling — The movement of signals, or electrical charges that represent encoded information, along a communications channel.

static electricity — The sudden transfer of an accumulated charge from one material to another.

switch — An electronic or electromechanical device that can open and close a circuit.

tera (T) — A prefix that indicates a quantity multiplied by 2 to the 40th power (1,099,511,627,776) in the context of data transfer or storage or 10 to the 12th power (1,000,000,000,000) in the context of mathematics, physics, and electronics.

terabyte (TB) — A quantity of data equivalent to 2 to the 40th power (1,099,511,627,776) bytes (1024 gigabytes) or 1000 gigabytes, depending on the context.

throughput — The amount of data that a communications channel can carry during a given time period. Throughput may also be called "capacity."

transformer — An electrical device that contains two electromagnetic coils and transfers electric energy from one coil to another coil through electromagnetic induction.

transformer effect — *See* mutual inductance.

transistor — An active electronic device made from a semiconducting material that allows current to overcome the resistance of a component. A transistor can be used as an amplifier or a switch.

Unicode — An internationally recognized 16-bit encoding scheme developed in the early 1990s. Because Unicode can make use of 16 binary placeholders, it may represent up to 2^{16}, or up to 65,536 characters and encode the letters of many different languages.

Unicode transformation format (UTF) — The way in which a software program uses Unicode encoding.

volt (v) — A measure of voltage, or current strength.

voltage — The pressure that the electric current exerts on its conductor. Voltage is measured in volts.

voltmeter — An instrument that is connected to a circuit to measure its voltage.

watt — A unit for measuring electrical power. The watt was named after James Watt, a Scottish engineer who experimented with engines in the mid-1700s.

wavelength — The distance between corresponding points on a wave's cycle. Wavelength is expressed in meters and is inversely proportional to frequency.

REVIEW QUESTIONS

1. Lightning is an example of what kind of electricity?

2. What atomic subparticle carries a negative charge?

   a. proton

   b. neutron

   c. electron

   d. photon

2

3. What measurement is used to describe the strength of an electric current?

   a. ohms

   b. volts

   c. amperes

   d. Hertz

4. Which of the following ideas is reflected in Ohm's Law?

   a. The greater a material's resistance, the greater the amount of potential current that can flow through it during a given time period.

   b. The greater a material's resistance, the lower the amount of potential current that can flow through it during a given time period.

   c. The lower a current's voltage, the greater its frequency.

   d. The lower a material's resistance, the greater its frequency.

5. Which of the following is considered an insulator?

   a. copper

   b. silver

   c. aluminum

   d. rubber

6. What type of current does a battery provide?

   a. alternating

   b. direct

   c. oscillating

   d. opposing

7. What measurement is used to describe the magnitude, or strength, of an electric current?

   a. frequency

   b. bandwidth

   c. ohms

   d. voltage

8. Frequency is an expression of:

   a. frames per second

   b. meters per second

   c. cycles per second

   d. volts per second

9. What type of electronic component is made of two parallel plates of conducting material separated by an insulating material?

   a. capacitor

   b. inductor

   c. transformer

   d. resistor

10. What could cause voltage in a coil that has no current running through it?

    a. a nearby inductor emitting an electromagnetic field

    b. a resistor on the same circuit that redirects voltage

    c. a nearby capacitor that has stored and must discharge its voltage

    d. a nearby insulator that has absorbed and must release its charge

11. If a circuit has very low volts and amps, it will also have low:

    a. Hertz

    b. ohms

    c. Farads

    d. watts

12. Which of the following is equivalent to 3 milliwatts?

    a. .03 watts

    b. .003 watts

    c. .00003 watts

    d. .0000003 watts

13. A transistor is an active electronic device. True or false?

14. Which of the following electronics components is a passive device?

    a. transistor

    b. resistor

    c. capacitor

    d. microprocessor

15. Both diodes and transistors can act as:

    a. amplifiers

    b. processors

    c. transformers

    d. switches

2

16. What telecommunications device was the transistor initially invented to improve?

    a. telephone

    b. satellite

    c. computer

    d. television

17. If an engineer discovered that an IC in her computer contained a faulty transistor, what should she do with the IC?

    a. dismantle it and replace the faulty transistor

    b. dismantle it, remove the portion of the circuit that contained the faulty transistor, and replace that portion of the circuit

    c. throw it away and replace it with a new IC

    d. dismantle it and fix the faulty transistor

18. In digital signaling, what does a pulse of positive voltage represent?

    a. 0

    b. 1

    c. 00

    d. 11

19. How many bits are in a byte?

    a. 2

    b. 4

    c. 6

    d. 8

20. Which of the following represents a byte of information in the binary numbering scheme?

    a. 10330081

    b. 10000000

    c. 0hF3EC10

    d. 110101010

21. How is attenuation compensated for differently in analog and digital signals?

22. What is the binary equivalent of the decimal number 59?

    a. 111011

    b. 00110201

    c. 3B

    d. 73

23. What is the decimal equivalent of the hexadecimal number FF?
    a. 16
    b. 48
    c. 255
    d. 586

24. What is the hexadecimal equivalent of the decimal number 83?
    a. 0f
    b. 123
    c. 01010011
    d. 53

25. Which of the following may be a source of RFI?
    a. broadcast tower
    b. smokestack
    c. excessive heat
    d. leaking hose

26. Which of the following cannot be represented in ASCII code?
    a. colon
    b. margin setting
    c. alphabetic characters
    d. the number 9

27. What single encoding system is capable of representing the characters of many different alphabets, including Japanese?
    a. BCD
    b. EBCDIC
    c. ASCII
    d. Unicode

28. One gigabyte equals how many bytes?
    a. 2 to the 10th power
    b. 10 to the 3rd power
    c. 2 to the 30th power
    d. 10 to the 10th power

29. If a modem is capable of accepting 28 Kbps of data, how long would it take to download a 2 MB file (assuming optimal line conditions)?

30. Throughput and bandwidth are the same thing. True or false?

HANDS-ON PROJECTS

Project 2-1

2

This project demonstrates how electrostatic charges cause objects to repel or attract each other. Although it is a simple experiment, it should prompt you to think about electricity on the atomic level. As you perform this experiment, consider what is happening to the electrons and protons on the surfaces of each material. For this project, you need a roll of transparent tape (such as the kind you use to wrap presents). This experiment works best in a dry place and may not work as well in a humid environment.

1. Pull two strips, each approximately 9 inches in length, from the roll of tape.

2. Dangle both strips of tape, one in each hand, with their ends approximately a foot apart. Now slowly bring the strips of tape closer together (adhesive sides pointing away from each other), until they are touching. What happens? Based on this, do you think the two strips of tape possess like or unlike charges?

3. Now take each piece of tape and rub it between your fingers for a few seconds (if your fingers are too dry, this will not work as well; you might want to breathe on them to dampen them). Repeat Step 2. What happens this time? Why did rubbing the pieces of tape change the results?

4. Now fold over an inch at the top of each strip of tape to form a tab. This tab allows you to hold the strips of tape more easily in the next few steps.

5. Place the adhesive side of one strip of tape against the non-adhesive side of the second strip of tape so that you have two layers of tape stuck together in one strip.

6. Holding the two tabs, quickly pull the two strips of tape apart.

7. Now bring the two steps of tape closer together. What happens? Why is this different from what happened when you attempted to bring the strips of tape close in Step 1?

Project 2-2

In this project, you have the opportunity to create your own induction coil and an electromagnet. This is another simple experiment which you may have conducted years ago in a science class. Even so, you should bring a deeper understanding of the concepts involved when you perform the experiment now. For example, as you construct the electromagnet and vary its properties, consider how the same principles you're using to manipulate the amount of magnetism it creates may be used in motors. Also, think about how the electromagnet could affect nearby analog or digital signals. For this project, you need a AA (1.5 V) battery with a full charge, a spool of thin copper wire coated with enamel (24 to 30 gauge wire works well), a wire cutter, some sandpaper, a pencil, at least a dozen paperclips, and a large nail (at least three inches long).

1. Using the wire cutter, cut a length of wire approximately 30 inches long off the spool of copper wire.

2. Leave about 5 inches of wire straight, then wind the wire around the pencil (in one direction) approximately 15 times. Be careful not to allow one coil of the wire to touch another coil.

3. Remove the pencil. You should have two straight ends of wire with a coil in the middle.

4. Using the sandpaper, rub approximately ¾ inch of the enamel from each end of the wire. You will know when you have removed the enamel when the shiny copper is revealed.

5. To complete your induction coil, hold one end of the (bare) copper wire against the positive side of the AA battery and hold the other end of the wire against the negative side of the battery. The coil should be extended to the side, parallel to the battery. After you have completed these contacts, current will flow through the coil. As you know, current will flow through a coil causes a magnetic field.

6. Now, hold the coil over the paperclips and use it as a magnet. How many paper-clips can it pick up?

7. Release your hold on the battery and the wire ends. Next, you are going to see what happens to the coil's magnetism when you make the coil longer. To begin, insert the pencil into the coil.

8. Now, wind more of the straight wire around the pencil, making sure to wind in the same direction as you were winding before.

9. Remove the pencil and repeat Steps 5–6. How has the coil's magnetic field changed? How many paperclips can you pick up?

10. Next, you will create an electromagnet, which uses a conductor in the center of its coil, rather than air. To begin, cut another length of copper wire from your spool, this one approximately 20 inches long.

11. Remove about ¾ inch of enamel off each end of the wire with the sandpaper.

12. Leave about 5 inches of wire straight, then wind the wire around the nail approximately 20 times. Remember to wind in only one direction and don't let one part of the wire touch any other part.

13. Leave the nail inside the coil.

14. To complete your electromagnet, hold one end of the copper wire against the positive side of the AA battery and hold the other end of the wire against the negative side of the battery. The nail and its coil should be extended to the side, parallel to the battery. After you have completed these contacts, current flows through the electromagnet.

15. Use the electromagnet to pick up paperclips. How many can it pick up? How does this compare to the induction coil you made?

Project 2-3

In this project, you exercise your knowledge about numbering systems by manually translating familiar decimal numbers into hexadecimal and binary equivalents. You then devise a ternary (base 3) numbering system and perform further translation based on that system. For this project, you need a pencil and paper.

1. To refresh your memory of how the decimal system works, write out the number 43,019 in an expanded notation as its separate base-10 components (for example, x multiplied by 10^y).

2. To exercise your skill at translating binary and decimal numbers, calculate and write down the binary equivalent of the following decimal numbers: 16, 127, 202. (If necessary, use the numbering system key in Figure 2-40 for reference.)

3. Translate the following binary numbers into decimal format: 00000110, 00110011, 11111111.

4. Translate the following hexadecimal numbers into decimal, then into binary format: 7A, 4D, 31.

5. If you want to check your work, use a scientific calculator (such as the one that comes with the Windows operating system) to verify your manual calculations.

6. Binary, decimal, and hexadecimal numbering systems rely on bases of 2, 10, and 16, respectively. However, any number can be used as the basis for a numbering system. To illustrate this, write a row of 8 binary position holders as shown in Figure 2-40, beginning with 2^7. Below those, write the corresponding ternary position holders, beginning with the 7th position and progressing to the 0th position (for example, start with 3^7).

7. Under the row of ternary position holders, write the following values: 95169, starting at the 4th position.

8. Below that, expand the ternary number by multiplying the value times the ternary exponent (for example, begin with 9×3^4).

9. Now, calculate the ternary number's decimal equivalent by adding the expanded values you calculated in Step 8.

10. Use your row of ternary position holders as a reference to convert the decimal numbers 66, 121, and 300 into their ternary equivalents.

Project 2-4

In this project, you explore the frequency allocations assigned by the United States Commerce Department's National Telecommunications and Information Administration (NTIA) and the Federal Communications Commission (FCC). For this project, you need a workstation with Internet access, modern browser software, such as Netscape Navigator or Internet Explorer, and the Adobe Acrobat Reader software (available for free at Adobe's download Web site: *http://www.adobe.com/products/acrobat/readstep2.html*).

1. Connect to the Internet, open your browser and go to **www.ntia.doc.gov/osmhome/allochrt.pdf**.

2. In the left frame, click **View full chart** to see an overview of all frequency allocations.

3. Search through the chart's frequencies to find some familiar wireless services. What range of frequencies is allocated to AM broadcasting? What range of frequencies is allocated to TV broadcasting? Find three ranges of frequencies that are allocated to amateur radio broadcasters.

4. While viewing the chart, notice that many services are allocated multiple frequency ranges, often far apart on the spectrum. What might be the cause for these seemingly illogical assignments?

CASE PROJECTS

1. A friend has asked you to help him with some home electronics projects. He has decided to build his own simple amplifier for fun, but he doesn't know the first thing about circuits or electricity. Using what you have learned in this chapter in addition to electronics references either from the library or off the Web (you may want to find an electronics hobbyist site that offers simple amplifier kits), help your friend answer the following questions:

   ⊐ Will the amplifier use static or current electricity?

   ⊐ Will the amplifier require AC or DC voltage to run?

   ⊐ How much voltage will it require?

   ⊐ How much current will it use?

   ⊐ What kind of components will he need to buy to build the amplifier? (For example, will it require capacitors, inductors, resistors, etc.?)

   In your research, you will probably find that many different types of amplifiers may be created out of simple electronics. Based on your understanding of your friend's knowledge, what type of amplifier do you suggest that he make?

2. Your friend decides to buy one of the simple electronic kits you recommended. Weeks later, he thinks he has the amplifier working. He wants to prove that it's working by talking through it in his basement and having you listen in the upstairs kitchen. However, you cannot hear your friend at all. When you tell him this, he thinks the problem is a type of RFI causing problems with the signal. How do you know that this is not, in fact, the problem?

3. The next day your friend tells you that he has solved the problem with his amplifier. But now, he wants to make the amplifier more powerful. Can you suggest any ways in which he could accomplish this? What components in his simple design might he have to change?

3

THE EVOLUTION OF TELECOMMUNICATIONS TECHNOLOGY AND POLICY

After reading this chapter and completing the exercises, you will be able to:

- Describe the growth of telecommunications technology since the late 19th century
- Identify key inventions and their current equivalents in telephony technology
- Explain the impetus for and impact of AT&T's divestiture
- Discuss how government has influenced the way in which consumers obtain telecommunications services
- List current policy trends that affect the telecommunications industry

To fully understand our current telecommunications industry, you need to understand the historical forces that shaped it. In this chapter, you learn about both the technical and policy evolution that has resulted in the modern field of telecommunications. Because a healthy telecommunication system is so vital to all parts of a society, governments frequently intervene to ensure that new technology is deployed in a way that furthers the common good. Often, this involves forcing one telecommunications company to provide services for another, or to make some other type of concession. For example, the FCC may order a local phone carrier to allow a competitor to use its underground cable because doing so would allow the competitor to provide new or better services. In the United States, government involvement has transformed the telecommunications industry. One of the most significant government actions took place in 1984 when the courts and the FCC deliberately dismantled AT&T, which had been a monopoly phone system for much of the 20th century. Currently, open competition potentially offers greater innovation and favorable pricing, but also holds the threat of a return to large, conglomerate telecommunications providers.

THE EVOLUTION OF TELECOMMUNICATIONS TECHNOLOGY

Today's telecommunications technologies have evolved from the earliest smoke signals to almost instant global transmission of large amounts of data. In later chapters, you learn specifically how modern voice and data communications technology work. But first, you should understand the technical advances that made it possible. After all, even the most advanced network still relies on basic scientific principles that were discovered and exploited over a century ago. The following pages provide a condensed view of telecommunication technology's history, highlighting these critical discoveries.

Early Signaling and Telegraphy

In the late 1700s, two French brothers, Claude and Ignace Chappe, lived across Paris from each other, but within seeing distance. They developed a system of communication involving moveable arms attached to a vertical pole. Each position of the arms represented a different letter, and by manipulating the arms, the brothers could create words and have a conversation. This type of signaling, in which visual cues represent letters or words, is known as a **semaphore**, from the Greek *sema*, which means "signal" and *phóros*, which means "bearer." One of the brothers later improved on their early semaphore system to establish a nationwide signaling system and code that was later adopted by much of Europe. Other semaphore systems used flags or boxes with multiple panels that could open and close. One disadvantage to semaphores over long distances was that they required considerable manpower to manipulate and observe (through telescopes) the signaling. In addition, because semaphores depend on clear weather, in places such as England, where fog and smog were common, they were unreliable.

In the early 1800s, scientists were experimenting with electrical impulses that traveled along wire and caused a magnetized needle at the other end of the wire to move. In 1837, Samuel Morse expanded on this idea by using an electromagnet and a hand-operated switch, known as a key, to alternately open or close an electrical circuit over a wire. What he transmitted was a series of short and long pulses (dots and dashes) that represented characters, known as **Morse code**. In 1840, just as the U.S. Congress was considering funding a cross-country semaphore system, Samuel Morse applied for his telegraph patent and urged the government to invest in a telegraph system instead. In 1844, to demonstrate his telegraph, Morse sent the following famous message between Baltimore, MD and Washington, DC: "What Hath God Wraught?" The telegraph key used to send that message is pictured in Figure 3-1. Telegraph lines spread quickly over the United States. In 1856, Western Union Telegraph Company was founded. The company then quickly began acquiring a number of other telegraph companies. By 1861, over two thousand telegraph offices operated across the United States.

Figure 3-1 Telegraph key used to send Morse's famous telegraph message in 1844

Advances on Morse's simple telegraph continued throughout the 19th century. A German scientist invented a method of **duplexing**, or simultaneously transmitting a signal in both directions along the same wire. Next, Thomas Edison invented a telegraph in which four signals could travel in either direction simultaneously along a wire. And in 1871, in France, Jean Baudot invented a method of **multiplexing**, or simultaneously transmitting an indeterminate number of multiple signals over one circuit. This concept is still used today, albeit transformed through many technological advances, in complex voice and data networks. By the end of the 19th century, telegraph wires spanned the Atlantic and had become pivotal communications channels for commerce and government.

Telephone Technology

As telegraph technology matured, inventors were developing early versions of its successor, the telephone. During the 1870s, two Americans, Elisha Gray and Alexander Graham Bell, designed similar, but slightly different devices that could transmit speech over wires. Both devices depended on electromagnetic coils which prompted vibrating elements (in Gray's case, reeds and in Bell's case, membranes and later, liquid) in a transmitter to reverberate according to varying frequencies. The first sounds transmitted by these early telephones were barely recognizable as speech. Figure 3-2 shows Bell's original liquid-based telephone transmitter.

Figure 3-2   Bell's original liquid-based telephone transmitter

On February 14, 1876, Alexander Graham Bell filed for his telephone patent, beating Elisha Gray's patent filing by less than three hours. Bell's early telephone patent is considered the most valuable patent in American history, as it described not only the telephone apparatus, but also telephone technology, and spawned an entire industry that has endured for well over a century. Bell offered his patent to Western Union for $100,000, but they declined the offer, explaining that "this device is of no use to us." Because of the early telephone's poor sound quality, Western Union officials doubted it could ever carry voice over long distances. In 1880, Bell founded his own company, American Bell, which by 1882 had gained a controlling interest in Western Union.

The quality of telephone transmission improved through the continued research of Bell, Gray, and Thomas Edison. One of the most valuable advances was Edison's invention of a pocket of carbon granules to conduct electric current and cause vibration in a thin iron membrane in telephone transmitters. This invention, which enabled voices to be heard more distinctly, was used in telephone transmitters until the 1970s.

The look, feel, and mechanics of telephone devices evolved quickly between the 1880s and the mid-1900s. In the very first telephones, the funnel-like apparatus served as both transmitter and receiver, requiring both parties to switch their position from ear to mouth when listening or speaking. Because this was cumbersome, in 1878, a telephone was developed with separate pieces, either of which could be used for transmitting or receiving. Later, wall-mounted telephones had a fixed transmitter attached to the front of the box and a hanging receiver that could be held to the ear. An example of such a wall-mounted telephone is shown in Figure 3-3. Different types of both wall-mounted and desk telephones proliferated during the 1890s and at the turn of the century.

Figure 3-3   A turn of the century wall-mounted telephone

In 1880, 30,000 telephones were in use in the United States, and by the end of the 19th century, telephone technology had become universally accepted. Before this could occur, however, a method for overcoming the problem of connecting one telephone directly with another had to be devised. Although directly connecting two telephones only requires one wire, connecting 1000 telephones in this manner requires up to a half-million separate wires! The solution was the telephone exchange. Alexander Graham Bell envisioned an infrastructure of wires criss-crossing cities and states and terminating in several **exchanges**, or **central offices**, where operators would connect the circuits to complete a call. (As you will learn, modern central offices, which still terminate and connect multiple customer lines, are almost entirely automated.) Each phone line had a jack for its connection and the operators had flexible circuit cords with plugs at their ends, which the operator inserted into the appropriate jacks to complete the connection.

An exchange was also known as a switching point because, as you learned in Chapter 2, the device used to open and close a circuit is known as a switch. The terms switch and switching are still used in telecommunications, though modern switches are exclusively electronic (not electromechanical). People who owned telephones could subscribe to use the phone company's wire infrastructure and central office's services (hence the term **subscriber** to refer to a telephone company customer). As operators connected calls, they noted the duration of the calls for billing purposes. The first telephone exchange opened in New Haven, Connecticut in 1878 and connected 21 separate lines. Figure 3-4 shows an 1885 telephone switchboard.

Figure 3-4   A telephone switchboard in 1885

The next significant advance in telephone technology was the adoption of an automatic switch developed by Almon Strowger in 1889. His invention, called the **step-by-step switch**, used a cylinder with an arm that brushed against rows of electrical contacts in a ratcheting motion. The movement of the arm was controlled directly by pulses from the telephone. Thus, although callers did not have to rely on operators to manually connect their calls, they did have to press buttons in specific patterns to request a number—a feature that proved unwieldy and unsatisfactory. By 1896, Strowger replaced the button-pushing method with a rotary dialer, a technology that was used through much of the 20th century.

In 1913, N.J. Reynolds, a Western Electric engineer, developed a better automatic switch, the crossbar switch. The **crossbar switch** used a grid of horizontal and vertical bars, with electromagnets at their ends. The horizontal bars could rotate up and down to connect to specific vertical bars and thus complete circuits. Each possible permutation of the vertical and horizontal bars' positions represented a different connection. The original version of this switch could complete up to 10 simultaneous connections. As crossbar technology improved through the 20th century, the number of connections such a switch could complete also increased. In the 1970s, a single crossbar switch could handle up to 35,000 connections.

In the mid-20th century, advances in electronics led Bell Labs, and later AT&T (American Telegraph and Telephone), to begin integrating electronics into crossbar switches to make them more efficient. In 1965, AT&T placed into service its first electronic switching system (ESS), which used magnetized reeds sealed within glass tubes to complete circuits. This switch could simultaneously handle up to 65,000 two-way voice circuits. Until the 1970s, all the telephone switches depended on a continuous physical connection to complete and maintain a call. However, in 1976, a new type of electronic switch was put into service that could handle multiple calls. This new switch relied on **time division switching**, a transmission technique in which samples from multiple incoming lines are digitized, then each sample is issued to the same circuit, in a predetermined sequence, before finally being transmitted to the correct outbound line, as shown in Figure 3-5. Previous switches (such as the crossbar and step-by-step switches) connected calls by **space division switching**, or by manipulating the physical space between two lines, thereby closing a circuit to connect a call. Although space division switching required a continuous electromechanical connection to maintain a single closed circuit, time division switching enabled one switch to handle hundreds of thousands of calls. You learn more about modern telephone switching technology in Chapter 6.

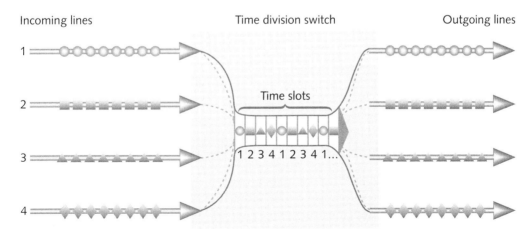

Figure 3-5   Time division switching

While switching technology evolved, a hierarchy of switching locations was established to handle different types of calls in different places and to facilitate the connection of every phone line to every other phone line. The three types of exchanges are: local, tandem, and toll. As its name implies, a **local switching center** (often called a **local office**) is a place where multiple phone lines from homes and businesses in one geographic area converge and terminate. For example, your home phone line and the phone lines of every home on your block probably end at the same local office. A **tandem switching center** is an exchange where lines from multiple local offices converge and terminate. Finally, a **toll switching center** is an exchange where lines from multiple tandem switching centers converge and terminate. This facility is called a toll office because it handles long-distance, or toll, calls.

At the same time that scientists and inventors were working on telephone technology, multiple businesses and governmental factors were affecting how the industry grew in the United States. In particular, throughout the 20th century, the government made several attempts to curb AT&T's growing monopoly and potential abuse of power in the nation's phone system. The history of the telephone industry and the roles of significant business and government entities are covered later in this chapter.

Wireless Technology

Telegraphs and telephones are examples of **wireline**, or **wire-bound** technology, because they rely on physically connected wires to transmit and receive signals. Another way of communicating is via **wireless** technology, which relies on the atmosphere to transmit and receive signals. Examples of modern day wireless technology include cellular phones, radios, television, and satellite communications. You learn more about modern wireless technology in Chapter 9.

Wireless technology, like wireline telephony, got its start in the late 1800s. In 1894, an Italian physicist named Guglielmo Marconi invented a method of transmitting electromagnetic signals through the air. His invention relied on an induction coil. Recall from the Hands-on Project in Chapter 2 that an induction coil is a made by winding wire in either one or multiple layers around a metal rod to form a coil, then applying a charge to the wire. The charged wire induces an electromagnetic field that generates more voltage. Induction coils come in many varieties and are used for many purposes. Marconi connected an induction coil to a telegraph key. Each time the key was pressed, the coil discharged voltage (in the form of a spark) through the air between two brass surfaces. The resulting disturbances in the air could be issued through an antenna and detected by a distant receiver. The receiver consisted of a glass cylinder filled with metal filings. When electromagnetic waves reached an antenna connected to the glass cylinder, the metal filings became charged and cohered, or aligned themselves to close a circuit. The length of time they cohered translated into short or long pulses. These pulses were relayed to a Morse code printer and resulted in a message encoded with dots and dashes. In other words, Marconi's invention used the same type of signals sent and received by a telegraph.

In 1896, Marconi applied for a patent for this device, which he called the radio. Figure 3-6 shows one of Marconi's early induction coil radio transmitters. Marconi continued work on this primitive radio, gradually improving the quality of its signal, and increasing the distance the signal could travel. By 1901, people were using his devices to transmit wireless signals across the Atlantic.

Figure 3-6 Marconi's induction coil radio transmitter

At the same time Marconi was refining his radio technology, other inventors were developing competing devices. American engineer Lee DeForest was working with vacuum tubes. A **vacuum tube** (which evolved from the light bulb) is a sealed container made of glass, metal, or ceramic, that contains, in a vacuum, a charged plate that transmits current to a filament. Original vacuum tubes contained two electrodes (one positive—the plate—and one negative—the filament) and maintained an electromagnetic current between them. However, these vacuum tubes were not capable of modulating (for example, amplifying) the current they maintained.

In 1907, DeForest patented the **Audion**, a type of vacuum tube that contained an additional electrode in the middle of the positive and negative electrodes. When subjected to voltage, the third electrode could control current inside the tube. The result was that the Audion could amplify (or boost) a signal. DeForest's Audion was a significant development in radio technology. It provided the first instance of signal amplification, and it formed the basis for all subsequent radio and television advances. Because the Audion was capable of producing radio waves of greater strength and stability than those produced by Marconi's transmitter, it soon replaced Marconi's older invention. In 1915, actual voice signals, rather than telegraph code, were successfully transmitted via radio using DeForest's technology. After that was proven possible, radio technology evolved quickly.

Not long after DeForest patented his Audion tube, another inventor improved on it. In 1912, Edwin Armstrong, an electrical engineering student at Columbia University, discovered how to greatly increase the power of the Audion by repeatedly feeding a radio signal back through the tube. His continued experimentation led to his best-known invention, frequency modulation. Frequency modulation is the technology used for FM radio and other forms of wireless communication. Recall from Chapter 2 that frequency is the number of times each second that a sine wave completes a full cycle.

In **frequency modulation**, one wave containing the information to be transmitted (for example, on a classical FM radio station, a violin concerto) is combined with another wave, called a carrier wave, whose frequency is constant. The addition of the information wave modulates the carrier wave, resulting in a third wave with unique characteristics that, when interpreted by a receiver, reveals the information transmitted. You learn more about FM and other forms of modulation in Chapter 6. Suffice it to say that the advent of FM technology began a new era for wireless communication. FM afforded the best clarity (with little static and a full range of audible frequencies) than any other wireless technology then available.

Through World War I, wireless technology was used almost exclusively by the military and the scientific community. For example, ships used Marconi's wireless devices to communicate with land. As a soldier in World War I, Edwin Armstrong repaired and maintained radios on the battlefields. In World War II, the Army and Navy began using secretly encoded radio transmissions to send messages about position and battle plans over land and sea. During that time, troops on the ground were also able to communicate using Motorola's new invention, the **Walkie-Talkie**—a two-way hand-held communication device that uses frequency modulation techniques.

By the end of World War II, radio technology had matured, and was widely available to the public. The next development in wireless communication was wireless telephony. In 1946, AT&T Bell Laboratories connected the first wireless car phone to the St. Louis phone network. AT&T called its system the "Improved Mobile Telephone Service" (IMTS). To use the limited number of available frequencies more efficiently, they spread many low-power transmitters across the city. As a car phone user moved from one area of the city to another, his call was handed off between transmitters, and the frequency issued from the previous transmitter became available for another user. The area serviced by one of these transmitters was called a **cell**, and this hand-off technique formed the basis for modern day cell phone communications. However, the technology took a long time to perfect. It wasn't ready for commercial use until 1970.

In the early 1980s, AT&T began a test of its wireless phone network in the Chicago metropolitan area. The pilot was a huge success and soon new wireless phone companies were opening for business across the country. By 1995, more than 25 million people had subscribed to wireless phone service.

Meanwhile, scientists were looking beyond earth for new wireless pathways. In 1945, Arthur C. Clarke (the author of *2001: A Space Odyssey*) wrote an article discussing the possibility of communicating through space. He envisioned communication between manned space stations that continually orbited the earth. But other scientists recognized the worth of using satellites to convey signals from one location on earth to another. In December 1958, the U.S. government launched its first experimental satellite, which stayed in orbit for 12 days before its batteries failed. In 1962, a satellite named Telstar successfully transmitted television signals and telephone conversations across the Atlantic for the first time.

Most satellites circle the earth approximately 22,300 miles above the equator in a geo-synchronous orbit. **Geosynchronous** means that satellites orbit the earth at the same rate as the earth turns. Consequently, at every point in their orbit, the satellites maintain a constant distance from a point on the earth's equator. Information sent to earth from a satellite first has to be transmitted to the satellite in an uplink. An **uplink** is a broadcast from an earth-based transmitter to an orbiting satellite. Often the uplink information is scrambled (in other words, its signal is encoded) before transmission to prevent unauthorized interception. At the satellite, a **transponder** receives the uplink, then transmits the signals to another earth-based location in a **downlink**. A typical satellite contains 24 to 32 transponders. Each satellite uses unique frequencies for its downlink. These frequencies, as well as the satellite's orbit location, are assigned and regulated by the Federal Communications Commission (FCC). Back on earth, the downlink is picked up by a dish-shaped antenna. The dish shape concentrates the signal, which has been weakened by traveling over 22,000 miles, so that it can be interpreted by a receiver. Figure 3-7 provides a simple view of satellite communication.

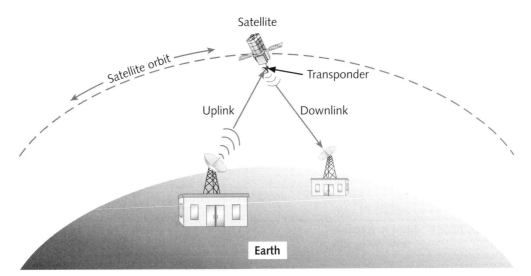

Figure 3-7 Satellite communication

Many advances in satellite technology were necessary to launch satellites, maintain a satellite's position relative to the earth, and to keep it in orbit. Although early satellites could stay in orbit for a matter of weeks, modern satellites are much lighter and powerful and can stay in orbit for over a decade. Satellites are used for TV and radio signals, as well as for transcontinental telephony.

This section has provided a very brief introduction to the evolution of wireless technology. As you can imagine, many additional inventors and technologies were responsible for bringing wireless communication to its current level of sophistication. You learn more about modern wireless technology and its uses in Chapter 9.

Early Computing

You have now learned about the evolution of the telegraph, telephone, and wireless communications. Another significant technology used in telecommunications is the computer. In fact, most modern telecommunication systems (for example, the telephone network that allows you to complete a call from New York to Los Angeles) rely on some type of computer.

Long before computers came into existence, humans were busy inventing various devices for automating mathematical calculation. One of the earliest of these devices was the abacus, a frame that contains markers along wires or grooves that can be manually moved to solve arithmetic problems. A form of the abacus has been dated to Mediterranean civilizations living in 300 B.C. But true **computing** (that is, the automatic manipulation of input based on logical instructions) wasn't really a possibility until 1822. In that year, Charles Babbage, an English mathematics professor, proposed an automated calculating machine as large as a locomotive and powered by steam. Babbage's invention was called the **difference engine**. Though a working difference engine was never actually built, Babbage's ideas were adopted by other inventors working on automated calculating machines. In 1889, an American inventor, Herman Hollerith, used the idea of punch cards to input data into a calculating machine. A single punch card could represent one number, whereas combinations of two punch cards could represent a letter. Hollerith, who worked for the U.S. Census Bureau, proposed his device as a means of speeding up time-consuming census calculations. And in fact, Hollerith's invention did just that. The Census Bureau spent seven full years tabulating the results of the 1880 census. But thanks to Hollerith's invention, tabulating the 1890 census results took just six weeks. Hollerith used his punch card invention to found the Tabulating Machine company, which later became International Business Machines (IBM). Punch cards continued to be used with computers even into the 1980s.

Computing technology improved quickly throughout the twentieth century. As with telephone and wireless technology, much of this development was spurred by military interests. For example, during World War II, German scientists developed a computer to help design aircraft. At the same time, the British invented a computer named Colossus, which could decode German messages. Also at the same time, the U.S. Army worked with the University of Pennsylvania to develop the **Electronic Numerical Integrator and Computer (ENIAC)**, a multipurpose computer so large that it required its own 30 foot by 50 foot room. ENIAC was first used to assist with ballistics calculations. Part of this giant computer is shown in Figure 3-8. These early computers were a great advance, but they did have several major drawbacks that limited their usefulness. For one thing, they were not capable of retaining any information supplied to them, nor any information that they generated.

Figure 3-8   The ENIAC computer

In the mid-1940s, a U.S. scientist named Jon Von Neumann designed a computer that was capable of retaining logical instructions for use at any time, even after the computer had been turned off, then on again. That is, the computer had a memory. **Memory**, in the context of computing, refers to a feature or physical part of a computer that enables it to store information for later retrieval. Memory allowed Von Neumann's computer to not only store logical instructions, but also to store data and as a consequence, to perform instructions on the data at any time. The addition of memory to computers led to greater flexibility (for instance, a computer could now be turned off, then turned on again without losing calculations it had already performed) and opened the way for further advances in computing, which occurred rapidly after Von Neumann's invention.

The first computer designed for business (and not merely scientific purposes), was called **UNIVAC (Universal Automatic Computer)** and became available in 1951. It weighed 16,000 pounds and performed approximately 1000 calculations per second. It was used to predict the outcome of the 1952 election based on only 1% of the total poll data. By 1957, Remington-Rand, the company that manufactured UNIVAC, had sold 46 of the computers. However, UNIVAC was about as big as a one-car garage—still too large to be practical for widespread use. Figure 3-9 shows a picture of the UNIVAC computer, with the console on the left.

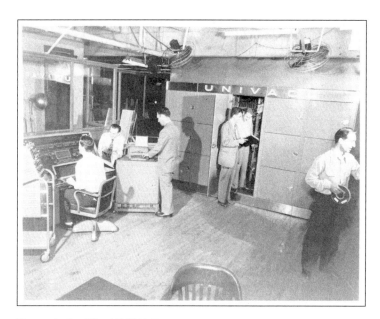

Figure 3-9   The UNIVAC computer

UNIVAC and the computers that preceded it relied on thousands of vacuum tubes (recall that vacuum tubes were used to amplify voltage). However, the need for so many vacuum tubes and pipelines of circulating water (used to reduce heat generated by the vacuum tubes) resulted in huge, unwieldy computers. This problem of size in early computers was solved by the invention of transistors. In the mid-1950s, engineers created computers that used transistors rather than vacuum tubes and thus began to build smaller and smaller computers. But computers didn't become small enough for practical business use until 1958, when the integrated circuit (IC) was introduced. Invented by Jack Kilby, an engineer with Texas Instruments, the integrated circuit combined electronic components, such as resistors, diodes, and transistors, into a small silicon disk. Scientists later condensed more components on a single silicon chip, called a semiconductor.

Throughout the 1960s, the size of circuits continued to shrink, and the number of components that could be squeezed onto a single chip grew into the thousands. The result was a dramatic increase in power with a decrease in size. By 1965, many large businesses used computers for financial calculations. In 1971, Intel condensed the functions of data storage, data input, data output, and data processing into one chip. Prior to this development, each chip was manufactured and used for one, specific purpose. Even better, Intel's chips could be mass produced to fit in multiple computers. Together with smaller size, the ability to be used interchangeably in different brands of computers and for multiple functions in all these computers paved the way for even smaller and still less expensive computers. These less expensive computers were dubbed "personal computers," because they were affordable to the ordinary citizen, not just for businesses. Apple and Commodore released some early personal computers in the 1970s, which came with user-friendly spreadsheet and word processing programs. In 1981, IBM unveiled its first affordable and user-friendly personal computer (PC).

Personal computers soon filled the workplace. In the 1980s, engineers realized that connecting multiple computers and enabling them to share resources (for example, data storage space, printers, and programs) was a more economical use of often limited or expensive computing resources. Thus, the first business networks were constructed. Today, networks form a vital component of almost any business. In telecommunications, networks assist with not only data sharing, but also sharing telephone lines and consolidating switching and messaging functions.

THE EVOLUTION OF TELECOMMUNICATIONS POLICY

As the first part of this chapter explains, telecommunications technology is continually advancing. When new technology becomes available to the public, both the technology and the companies that produce and supply the technology are subject to government regulation and legislation. In the remainder of this chapter, you learn how changing policies in the United States have affected the evolution of the telecommunications industry. By the end of the chapter, you will understand the different types of companies that the nation's policy trends have created. You will also gain insight into the direction further policy changes may lead.

As you learned in Chapter 1, several entities work together to develop and enforce telecommunications regulation and legislation. To recap, in the United States, the Federal Communications Commission (FCC) sets rules for the telecommunications industry—for example, the frequency band used by a cellular phone company or the maximum rates a telephone company can charge its customers for certain types of calls. Congress passes acts of legislation that further guide telecommunications companies' actions—for example, imposing restrictions on what type of service a telephone company can offer in a certain location. At the state level, similar regulatory and legislative controls apply to intrastate telecommunications. At all levels, the government aims to set policies that foster competition and technological innovation while ensuring that quality, affordable service is equally available to all consumers.

In the early part of the 20th century, the telecommunications industry was characterized by significant regulation and little competition. Later in the 20th century, the government attempted to reduce the restrictions on telecommunications companies. This trend in telecommunications policy resulted in lengthy legal battles over such fundamental concepts as geographical boundaries, what constitutes a monopoly, and definitions of "equipment" and "services." Changing policy has also molded the industry into what some consider a confusing mix of regulated and non-regulated telephone companies. The advent of digital transmission, which blurs the distinction between service types and renders geography less important, has generated still more confusion and legal debates.

Early Antitrust Measures

To understand the history of telecommunication in the United States, you need to understand the history of American Telegraph and Telephone company (AT&T), which begins with Alexander Graham Bell's invention of the telephone in 1876. In 1877, Bell and two other men formed the Bell Telephone Company, a business through which Bell planned to sell his telephones and provide service between telephone users. After acquiring dozens of new patents from other companies and exponentially increasing its value, the Bell Telephone Company became American Bell in 1880. In 1882, American Bell gained a controlling interest in the **Western Electric Company**, the firm that was founded in 1856 as Western Union Telegraph (discussed earlier in this chapter) and that had an existing network of telegraph wires.

Together, American Bell and Western Electric became known as the **Bell System**. In 1885, American Telegraph and Telephone (AT&T) was incorporated as a subsidiary of the Bell System, with the aim of constructing a long distance telephone network and providing long distance service (to Bell System subscribers only). But by 1899, AT&T bought out American Bell and became the parent company of the Bell System. Until 1984, AT&T consisted of the following:

- AT&T, the parent company and long-distance provider

- 22 **Bell Operating Companies (BOCs)**, the telephone companies that provided local service in different regions of the nation

- Western Electric, the manufacturing arm of the company

- **Bell Telephone Laboratories**, the research and development arm of the company, responsible for innovation and new technology

Informally, AT&T and its subsidiaries were known as "Ma Bell."

Once established, AT&T quickly began buying independent telephone companies across the nation, concentrating first on metropolitan areas. From the 1880s to the turn of the century, telephone subscribers had their choice of thousands of service providers (each of which supplied its own network of telephone wiring and a means of interconnecting subscribers) and equipment providers (which supplied the actual telephones). But AT&T was buying so many companies that by the turn of the century, sixty percent of U.S. telephone subscribers used a Bell System local line.

AT&T's majority stake in the industry caught the attention of the government during a time when anti-monopoly sentiment was gaining strength. A monopoly, such as AT&T's at the turn of the century, has the potential to abuse its favorable position by, for example, charging inflated prices or preventing other companies from entering the market. Most notably, AT&T was refusing to allow other telephone companies to connect with its expansive network of telephone lines. Fearing that the government might use its anti-trust laws against it, AT&T approached the U.S. Department of Justice in 1913 with a proposal for reducing its monopoly. This solution, called the **Kingsbury Commitment** (after the

AT&T vice president who drafted the proposal) promised that AT&T would divest itself of Western Union, stop buying independent telephone companies, and allow independent telephone companies to connect to its lines and switching centers.

As a result of the Kingsbury Commitment, AT&T functioned as a regulated monopoly from 1913 to 1984. Being a **regulated monopoly** meant that although AT&T was allowed to provide services without any competitors, it was subject to a great deal of constraints dictated by the government. Among other things, the government determined the rates AT&T could charge for service, how quickly it could depreciate its equipment, and how much it could charge other phone companies to connect to its network. In its capacity as a regulated monopoly, AT&T continued to provide phone service to most areas of the United States (some independent local phone companies, such as GTE, continued serving subscribers in limited areas). In addition, AT&T continually developed new technology for voice and data communications and provided phone equipment to the public.

The Communications Act of 1934

The first telecommunications regulations imposed in the United States were under the auspices of the Interstate Commerce Commission (ICC). From 1910 to 1934, the ICC regulated telegraph and radio service. In 1934, Congress passed the Communications Act of 1934, which established the Federal Communications Commission (FCC), state Public Utilities Commissions (PUCs), and initial guidelines for the telephone industry. The Communications Act of 1934 also put into law the provisions of the Kingsbury Commitment—namely, that AT&T was a regulated monopoly responsible for providing nationwide telephone service and that as a regulated monopoly, AT&T was subject to limits on the types of services they could provide and the prices they charged for those services.

The entire text of the Communications Act of 1934 (including amendments that have been made to it since 1934) can be found on the Internet at *www.fcc.gov/Reports/ 1934new.pdf*. If you read it, you'll note that the first paragraph of the Act describes the founding and purpose of the Federal Communications Commission.

Challenging the Monopoly

From 1913 to 1984, AT&T's dominance in the telecommunications industry was continually challenged. For example, companies that had developed phone attachments, such as early answering machines and fax machines, protested AT&T's stronghold on the customer equipment market. According to regulations at that time, a customer couldn't even attach a shoulder rest to the phone, much less an answering machine. This prohibition was reversed in 1956 with the **Hush-a-Phone decision**, a Supreme court ruling that allowed "foreign attachments," or devices that were not manufactured by AT&T to be affixed to AT&T telephones. The decision was named after a hollow metal, cup-like device, shown in Figure 3-10, that could be attached to a telephone mouthpiece to keep a conversation more private and less affected by background noise.

Figure 3-10   The Hush-a-phone telephone attachment

However, the Hush-a-Phone decision did not allow other companies' equipment to interconnect with AT&T lines. The restriction against interconnecting to AT&T's telephone network was challenged in 1965 and eventually lifted in 1968 through the **Carterfone decision**. The Carterfone decision was named after a means of connecting private, radio-controlled telephones to the local telephone lines, which was invented by Tom Carter—the same man who invented the Hush-a-Phone device.

Meanwhile, in the mid-1950s, the Department of Justice became concerned about AT&T's forays into electronic switching, in which telephone switches are controlled through electronic, rather than electromechanical, means. Because electronic switching was an early form of computing, the government worried that AT&T had an unfair advantage over other computer-related research and manufacturing companies. To prevent AT&T from taking over yet another industry, the Department of Justice challenged AT&T under anti-trust laws, suggesting that AT&T should divest itself of Western Electric. The result of this challenge was that AT&T signed a consent decree, a settlement between a court and an accused party, in 1956. In this decree, which resolved the dispute, the Department of Justice forced AT&T to restrict itself to providing telephone service. According to the decree, AT&T was prohibited from branching out into the computer services industry. In return, AT&T could keep its research and manufacturing facilities and maintain its regulated monopoly status for telephone service.

Many of the challenges to AT&T's dominance involved competing companies attempting to bypass AT&T's infrastructure. As you learned in Chapter 1, infrastructure is a term often used in voice and data telecommunications to refer to the framework of a system or network. AT&T's infrastructure included its transcontinental network of telephone lines, switches, and exchanges. Because AT&T was a regulated monopoly, law prohibited other companies from using its infrastructure or building a similar infrastructure to provide public telephone service. However, the law wasn't clear on whether a company could build an entirely different type of infrastructure to provide private telephone service and connect such private lines to AT&T's public infrastructure. This ambiguity allowed competitors to further challenge AT&T's dominance.

In 1969, a company called Microwave Communications International (MCI) began carrying business phone calls over a private microwave link between St. Louis, Missouri and Chicago. (A **microwave link** is a path used for transmitting and receiving signals via microwaves, a technology discussed in Chapter 9. The microwave link established by MCI was private because the signal's path directly connected only the two participating businesses.) Because MCI didn't use the Bell System, it did not have to pay AT&T for use of its infrastructure. AT&T protested that MCI was unfairly bypassing its system. It claimed that because MCI was not responsible for universal public service, as AT&T was, it could offer much lower prices and more attractive service than AT&T could. The FCC, however, upheld MCI's right to use its private microwave link because private microwave services were not part of AT&T's regulated monopoly. This opened the door to other companies that wanted to supply private, long-distance telephone service and was the start of many battles over long-distance competition.

AT&T Divestiture

Though AT&T was the predominant public telephone company in the mid-to-late 20th century, subscribers were dissatisfied with the company's service. At the same time, advancing technology spawned a new generation of companies unveiling innovative products. These companies had to fight AT&T every step of the way to get their new products into the market. As a result of growing public discontent and increasing alternatives to the phone giant's sub-par service, the Justice Department once again investigated AT&T for possible antitrust abuse in 1974. The investigation lasted seven years. Finally, in 1982, the Department of Justice ruled that AT&T should be split into multiple, smaller companies. Some of these new, smaller companies—for example, those that provided local telephone service—would continue to be regulated monopolies. Others would be open to competition. This ruling, called the **Modified Final Judgment (MFJ)**, was accompanied by over 500 pages of instructions detailing exactly how AT&T should be divided. The ruling was written by Judge Harold Greene, a district court judge in Washington, DC. According to the MFJ, the actual divestiture of AT&T was scheduled to take place on January 1, 1984.

The Justice Department's primary goal for breaking up AT&T was to spur innovation and competition in a field that would prove even more vital in the latter part of the century than it had in the first. AT&T, hampered by its giant size and government restrictions, couldn't possibly adapt to changing technology as quickly as hundreds of newer, more nimble companies could. But dismantling the phone company proved both politically and technically complex. And, as expected, the original MFJ was challenged and amended continually, beginning practically the day it was released. Still, the MFJ was the first major crack in the dam for an industry that was primed for a flood of growth.

As part of the MFJ, AT&T, which included Western Electric, Bell Laboratories, the local Bell Operating Companies, and the Long Lines division, was forced to divide. The courts allowed AT&T to choose which portions of its business it wanted to keep and which would become new, separate entities. AT&T kept its most profitable businesses, national long distance services, and the manufacture of new telecommunications technology. It divested itself of the least profitable business, local phone service. Figure 3-11 shows AT&T (or "The Bell System") before divestiture. Figure 3-12 shows AT&T after divestiture.

From the 22 former Bell Operating Companies that provided local phone service and phone directories, the MFJ created seven **Regional Bell Operating Companies (RBOCs)**. The RBOCs remained regulated monopolies but were independent from AT&T and from each other. These seven new companies were called: NYNEX, Bell Atlantic, Bell South, Ameritech, Southwestern Bell Corporation, US West, and Pacific Telesis. As regulated monopolies, the local RBOCs were not allowed to provide any type of long distance services. However, the RBOCs could provide customer telephone equipment. To do this, each RBOC had to create a subsidiary company that was exclusively devoted to providing telephone equipment. Each equipment subsidiary had to be self-sustaining; it could not rely on revenue generated by the RBOC's local phone service business.

The business that AT&T kept was separated into two divisions: AT&T Technologies, which handled the innovation and production of new technologies (such as transmission and switching equipment, telephones, networks, and computer systems), and AT&T Communications, which handled long distance phone service. Western Electric ceased to exist. The research and development business, formerly Bell Laboratories, became **Bell Communications Research (Bellcore)** and was jointly owned by the new RBOCs.

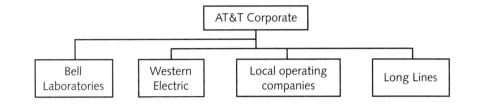

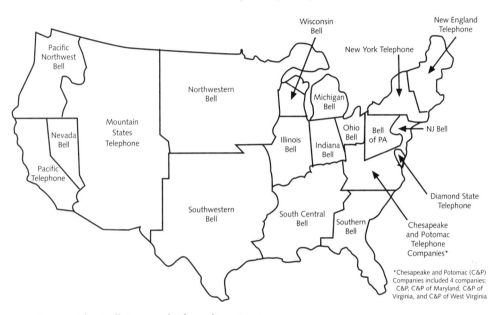

Local Bell Operating Companies:

Figure 3-11   The Bell System before divestiture

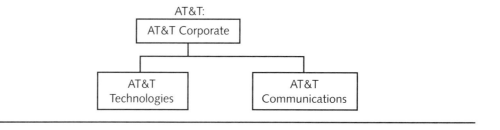

And 7 Regional Bell Operating Companies:

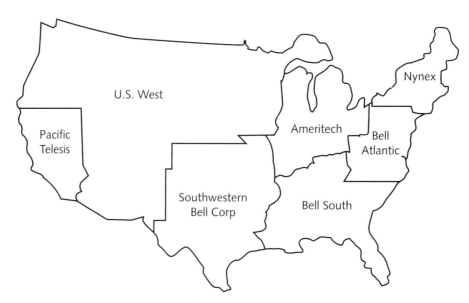

Figure 3-12 The Bell System after divestiture

Until the divestiture of AT&T, the distinction between local service and long distance service was not clear. In most cases, it didn't need to be, because a call across the nation and a call between two city suburbs (which might now be considered local) were typically carried by the same provider. However, once the RBOCs were responsible for local service, the definitions of local and long-distance service had to be clarified. In the MFJ, Judge Harold Greene attempted to set these legal boundaries. He subdivided each RBOC region into **Local Access and Transport Areas (LATAs)**, roughly equivalent to area codes at that time. A total of 160 LATAs were established across the United States. RBOCs were limited to providing service within specific LATAs. Phone service within a specific LATA was known as **intraLATA** service. (IntraLATA service is what we commonly term local phone service.) Companies that supply local, or intraLATA telephone service are known as **local exchange carriers (LECs)**.

Figure 3-13 provides an example of LATA boundaries in the northeast region of the United States. Notice that although the boundaries of LATAs roughly correspond to area code boundaries, the LATA numbers are different from the area code numbers. LATA boundaries are now regulated by the FCC, and from time to time, phone companies petition the agency to modify those boundaries (for example, to make phone calls between two suburbs of the same city considered local).

3

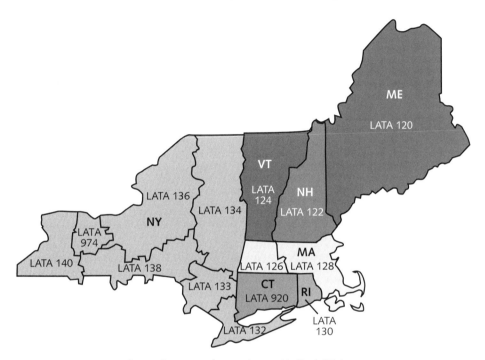

Figure 3-13   LATA boundaries in the notheast United States

As you might expect, long distance calls were defined as those that took place between LATAs. A service that allowed for calls between LATAs was known as **interLATA** service. InterLATA service providers are also called **interexchange carriers (IXCs)**. (As you learned earlier in this chapter, "exchange" is another term for a switching location where telephone lines terminate and can be interconnected. In the context of interexchange carriers and service, an exchange refers to the geographical area served by one switching location.) InterLATA service is what we consider long-distance service. An IXC is what telephone customers typically call a long-distance telephone company. Examples of IXCs include Sprint, MCI (now WorldCom), and AT&T.

After the distinction between long distance and local service had been established, it was necessary to provide some means for the long distance providers (the interLATA providers) to gain access to the local phone systems. After all, the long distance carriers couldn't provide long distance phone service unless they had a connection to each subscriber. The connection to each subscriber was owned by the local (intraLATA) service provider. According to the MFJ, RBOCs had to allow interLATA providers to access and lease their facilities, including local phone lines and switches. Most importantly, the RBOCs had to charge each interLATA provider the same price, and provide the same quality of access to its local customers. This concept is known as **equal access**. Requiring local phone companies to provide equal access to their facilities meant that AT&T no longer had an unfair advantage over new competitors in long distance services.

Another complex question the MFJ had to solve was how the new RBOCs would recover their costs for modifying their switching and billing systems to conform with the new LATA boundaries and equal access requirements. After significant wrangling with AT&T, the courts declared that the RBOCs could charge every customer a set IXC access fee for each line they leased, whether or not they ever used a long distance provider's service. The money collected through this fee would subsidize the required changes to the RBOC's infrastructure. Although subscribers and long-distance carriers disputed the necessity for the access fee, it remained in effect until the Telecommunications Act of 1996. (You learn about this important piece of legislation in the next section.)

Although AT&T's leaders spent millions of dollars fighting the lawsuits that led to divestiture, the MFJ proved beneficial for them in the end. It allowed AT&T to concentrate its efforts on the more profitable and quickly growing computer and data networking fields. In both emerging fields and in long distance service, the company was forced to become more competitive.

The Telecommunications Act of 1996

The breakup of AT&T in 1984 went a long way towards reducing monopolistic practices in the telecommunications industry. Yet, the MFJ (and the subsequent modifications to it) still allowed for regulated monopolies (such as the RBOCs) to control local telephone service. In the 1990s, the U. S. government decided that the existence of these regulated monopolies hindered competition. As a result, Congress passed the Telecommunications Act of 1996, a sweeping piece of legislation that affected competition in local phone service, wireless telecommunications, cable TV, broadcasting, and the Internet. The act also imposed restrictions on obscene content, provided technology funding for schools and healthcare, and redefined the role of the FCC. According to the Act's introduction, lawmakers sought: "To promote competition and reduce regulation in order to secure lower prices and higher quality services for American telecommunications consumers and encourage the rapid deployment of new telecommunications technologies." (The entire text of the Telecommunications Act of 1996 can be viewed on the Internet at *www.fcc.gov/Reports/tcom1996.txt*.)

Table 3-1 summarizes the provisions of the Telecommunications Act of 1996. Although the Act applied to all forms of telecommunication (its provisions being divided into seven distinct topical areas), the remainder of this section focuses on policies that affected telephony and emerging digital services.

Table 3-1   A Summary of the Telecommunications Act of 1996

Topic	Provisions
Telecommunications Services	Allowed competition for local telephone service and imposed many requirements on LECs to ensure smooth and economical interconnection between competitors
Broadcast Services	Removed previous limits on the number of broadcast outlets one entity could own, increased spectrum availability, modified the process for renewing broadcast licenses and the terms of those licenses, and allowed broadcasters more flexibility in programming
Cable Services	Repealed previous rate caps on cable service charges, repealed restrictions on telephone companies owning a stake in or providing cable services, and prohibited local or state regulation of services provided via cable systems
Regulatory Reform	Eliminated unnecessary regulations and modified roles of FCC and state public service commissions with the intent of preventing any further barriers to competition
Obscenity and Violence	Modified prohibitions against obscene or harassing phone calls set forth in the Communications Act of 1934 to include any form of telecommunications service and increased penalties for these violations, prohibited the use of telecommunications services to make available obscene communication or make indecent communication available to minors, required cable providers to scramble indecent content, allowed cable operators to refuse to carry obscene content, and required television manufacturers to allow parents to control obscene or violent programming
Effect on Other Laws	Explained how the provisions of the Telecommunications Act of 1996 pertain to previous communications laws (for example, what parts of the Act supercede or replace the 1984 MFJ, the Communications Act of 1934, and state and local communications regulation)
Miscellaneous Provisions	Instituted the national educational technology fund, the universal service fund, and the technology development fund, and required state and federal communications commissions to encourage the deployment of advanced telecommunications capability to all Americans

The Act codified requirements for the interconnection of all local exchange carriers. These policies included:

- Interconnecting with other service providers and not imposing any barriers to interconnection

- Enabling nondiscriminatory resale of their services to competitors

- Providing **number portability**, or the ability of telecommunications service users to retain their same telephone number—no matter what service provider they choose—without hampering the quality, reliability, or convenience of their phone service

- Allowing competitors to access and connect to their facilities (such as switches, poles, conduits, and rights-of-way)

Local exchange carriers that enjoyed a monopoly on telephone service until the Act went into effect are known as **incumbent local exchange carriers (ILECs)**. All RBOCs are ILECs, but not all ILECs are RBOCs. Recall that when AT&T became a regulated monopoly in the early 1900s, some other independent telephone companies (for example, GTE) still existed and were allowed to maintain a monopoly on telephone service in their jurisdictions. Local exchange carriers that have begun competing with the ILECs for local telephone service since passage of the Act are known as **competitive local exchange carriers (CLECs)**.

To increase competition in local phone service, the Act placed a number of additional requirements on all ILECs. With the additional ILEC restrictions, Congress intended to limit powers of the ILECs and, in particular, RBOCs, which at the time supplied 95% of the nation's local phone service. These requirements included:

- Negotiating interconnection agreements in good faith

- Providing competitors with the same type and quality of access to their facilities that they themselves could obtain at their cost

- Providing competitors with access to subscriber information, such as telephone numbers and billing data

- Offering nondiscriminatory, wholesale prices for telecommunications services (such as line termination, enhanced calling features, and switching) to all competitors

- Allowing competitors to locate equipment in their central offices

- Supplying timely public notices about changes in their network that might affect a competitor's ability to connect with or provide services through their facilities

Notice that through these provisions, the Act attempted to minimize inconvenience to individual subscribers. For example, as long as ILECs share their facilities and subscriber database with competitors, consumers can choose a new local phone company while keeping their old phone number, due to the number portability requirement. The ILECs could not, for example, change a subscriber's phone number or add digits to numbers they provided to competitors (which might make a customer regard the competitor's service less favorably). At the same time, the Act allowed ILECs to enter into competition for interLATA phone service (but not interstate phone service) and manufacture telephony equipment upon approval from the FCC.

These changes helped break up the RBOC's regulated monopolies, which in turn helped increase competition. But at the same time, the Telecommunications Act sought to prevent any problems for consumers that might result from these changes. For example, using a regulated monopoly for local phone service provided the guarantee of affordable phone service in every part of the country. If the RBOCs had not been forced to provide a local line to one rancher on an isolated 5000-acre plot in Montana, they probably would not have done so because the cost of getting a line to that rancher exceeded any proceeds the company collected from his use of the line. By deregulating all telecommunications services, the government risked the possibility that competition would bring lower costs and better services only to the highly profitable and densely populated areas. To prevent loss of services to rural areas, the government created the **universal service fund (USF)**, essentially a subsidy for less populated areas, to which each telecommunications provider and business user contributed on a monthly basis.

Some policy analysts have been skeptical of the Act's capability to meet its goals of increasing competition in the local phone service market. The government anticipated that it would take time for new companies to emerge and build their own infrastructures so that they could be wholly independent and truly competitive with the RBOCs. Indeed, by the end of 2000, ILECs (mostly the RBOCs) still provided 81.5% of the local phone service. That number had decreased from 84.6% the previous year. However, according to the latest FCC data, in nearly 45% of the nation's ZIP codes, the ILECs still had no competitors. Although competitors (especially wireless carriers) are numerous in densely populated areas, they have been slow to emerge in less populated areas of the country.

The Telecommunications Act of 1996 anticipated that the RBOCs, particularly those with adjacent jurisdictions, would be in healthy competition not only with new service providers, but also with each other. However, in an effort to pool their resources and maintain their dominance, many of the RBOCs merged. For example, Bell Atlantic and NYNEX merged in April 1996, and the new company retained the Bell Atlantic name. In 2000, the FCC approved a merger between Bell Atlantic and GTE to form Verizon, the largest local telephone company in the nation at the time. In the same way, Southwestern Bell merged with Pacific Telesis and later, with Ameritech. Critics of the Telecommunications Act of 1996 point to these mergers and argue that, although the spirit of the Act was good, its execution was largely flawed. They claim that restrictions on the RBOCs did not go far enough to prevent the once-monopolies from taking advantage of their entrenched positions. Figure 3-14 depicts the current four RBOC territories. Compare these territories with the original seven territories outlined in the MFJ and shown in Figure 3-12.

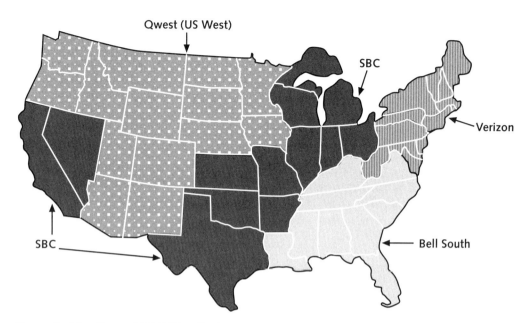

Figure 3-14   Current RBOC territories

In an effort to extend the use of cutting edge technology and Internet access equally to all citizens, the Telecommunications Act of 1996 established the **e-rate** program, which provided funds to schools, libraries, and other public entities for technology-related spending. E-rate granted up to $2.25 billion for improving network infrastructures and purchasing new computers and networking infrastructure. Schools and libraries participating in the program can purchase technology-related products for a fraction of their typical cost. The money for e-rate comes from the USF, which as you'll recall, is generated by access fees on telephone services. The e-rate program has proved immensely successful, with nearly 90% of the country's schools and libraries applying for the money by 1999. Clearly, these public entities had been eager to adopt new technology but lacked the funds to do so.

For your reference, Figure 3-15 depicts a timeline of the significant events in telecommunications policy you have just read about. Because policy is continually changing, new events could likely extend this timeline in the near future. In the following section, you learn about some emerging trends that are currently affecting the telecommunications industry.

3

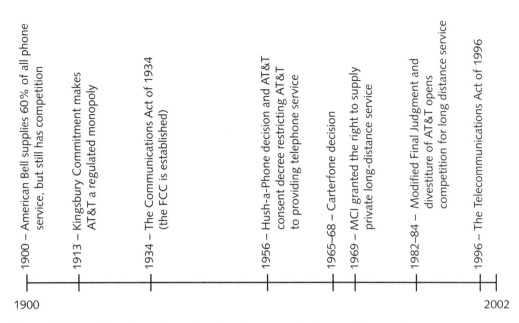

Figure 3-15   A timeline of significant telecommunications policy events

Emerging Policies

Since the Telecommunications Act of 1996, policies governing the telecommunications industry in the United States have continued to evolve. Meanwhile, new and old telecommunications providers, as well as lobbying organizations that promote citizen interests, continually challenge the latest policies. For example, in the late 1990s, some RBOCs began applying to the FCC to provide long distance communications. The FCC initially denied their requests, claiming that the RBOCs didn't yet face enough competition and might therefore benefit unfairly from their majority holdings. However, RBOCs have continued to raise this issue, and in some limited cases, have been granted permission to provide interLATA service. At this time, Congress is debating a bill that would remove all long-distance and high-speed Internet access service restrictions on RBOCs.

Another issue the RBOCs continue to battle is the access fees applied to each connection with a customer or another carrier. These fees are gradually decreasing due to the expanding facilities and competition of new telecommunications providers. Some lawmakers are eager to accelerate that trend, arguing that RBOCs and other telephone service providers are unfairly carrying the burden of funding universal telecommunications service programs, such as e-rate. Instead, these lawmakers argue, everyone should share this burden through some type of tax, whether on services or equipment. Watch for this issue to be debated in Congress throughout the next few years. A third RBOC restriction under threat is the requirement to provide competitors (such as CLECs) and IXCs with equal access to their circuits at a discounted rate. Opponents to repealing this measure argue that the RBOCs still own enough of the telephony and Internet infrastructure to gain unfair advantage unless the equal access restrictions remain in place. Proponents argue that the RBOCs' profitability and business development potential are being hampered by this remaining restriction.

At the same time, the FCC is approving more business opportunities for ILECs, such as the RBOCs; it is also examining whether more restrictions are necessary to improve service quality and ensure adherence to equal access provisions set forth in the Telecommunications Act of 1996. For example, soon the FCC may require that ILECs make their circuits available to CLECs within a certain time after the CLEC requests it, or failing that, pay the CLEC a fine.

Although many of the provisions established by the Telecommunications Act of 1996 are now in dispute, the importance of maintaining the universal service fund is not. Increasingly, the more urban and affluent citizens in the United States are enjoying greater access to the "information superhighway," whereas many rural, disabled, and poor citizens have no access to the advantages that an Internet connection can provide. This difference between the haves and have-nots is known as the **digital divide**. The digital divide issue has caught the attention of all levels of government, including the president. Congress and the FCC will likely continue to implement measures that foster affordable and universally available access for all citizens.

Besides measures that change or repeal provisions of the Act, new legislation on telecommunications services is continually being introduced in the House and the Senate. Some recent bills have included provisions for enhancing rural Internet access, methods of ensuring efficient allocation of phone numbers, methods for ensuring privacy for wireless communications, and measures to guard against excessive consolidation of telecommunications companies. In the wake of the 1998 antitrust lawsuit against Microsoft, the government is carefully eyeing the proliferation of mergers among service and equipment providers. (In fact, the FCC has had to streamline its procedures for approving mergers due to the volume of merger applications.) However, few of these mergers have yet to be prevented. Some recent large telecommunications mergers include SBC and Ameritech, US West and Qwest, and AT&T and MediaOne.

Although it has allowed the mergers to occur, the FCC has imposed requirements on the large carriers to ensure that they do not abuse their position of geographical dominance and size. In 1999, for example, Congress mandated cable service providers to allow any Internet company to distribute content over its infrastructure without any extra cost (rather than only allowing content from their own Internet networks to traverse the lines). So, for example, in an area where AT&T owned most of the underground cable, it was required to allow a competitor, such as AOL, to transmit content over that cable at the same rates it would charge a broadcast network affiliate. AT&T will likely continue to fight this, and in fact, has won reversals of the decision in some local areas.

Now that you have learned about the evolution of the Bell System and government actions related to fostering competition, you are prepared to learn specifically how the ILECs, IXCs, and competitive local telephone companies interconnect to form the public telephone network, the topic of Chapter 4.

3

CHAPTER SUMMARY

❐ In 1837, Samuel Morse invented the telegraph, which consisted of an electromagnet and a hand-operated switch, known as a key, to alternately open or close an electrical circuit over a wire. What he transmitted was a series of short and long pulses (dots and dashes) that represented characters, known as Morse code.

❐ In 1876, Alexander Bell filed his patent for the telephone. In 1880, he founded his own company, American Bell, which both produced telephones and supplied telephone service to houses and businesses.

❐ To connect multiple subscribers, Alexander Graham Bell devised the telephone exchange, where subscriber lines terminated and operators connected the circuits to complete a call. Each phone line had a jack for its connection and the operators had flexible circuit cords with plugs at their ends, which the operator inserted into the appropriate jacks to complete the connection.

❐ The next significant advance in telephone technology was the adoption of the first automatic switch, called a step-by-step switch, which was developed by Almon Strowger in 1889.

❐ In 1913, N.J. Reynolds, a Western Electric engineer, developed a better automatic switch, the crossbar switch. As crossbar technology improved through the 20th century, the number of connections such a switch could complete also increased. In the 1970s, a single crossbar switch could handle up to 35,000 connections.

❐ In the mid-20th century, advances in electronics led Bell Labs, and later AT&T, to begin integrating electronics into crossbar switches to make them more efficient. In 1965, AT&T placed into service its first electronic switching system (ESS).

❐ In 1896, Gugliemio Marconi applied for a patent for a device that issued electromagnetic waves into the air, which he called the radio. By 1901, people were using his devices to transmit wireless signals across the Atlantic.

❐ In 1907, American inventor Lee DeForest patented the Audion, which was the first vacuum tube that could amplify a signal. DeForest's Audion formed the basis for all subsequent radio and television advances, and it soon replaced Marconi's older invention.

❐ In 1946, AT&T Bell Laboratories connected the first wireless car phone to the St. Louis phone network. AT&T called its system the "Improved Mobile Telephone Service" (IMTS). IMTS used cells, or areas served by low power transmitters, which are the basis for modern cell phone technology.

❑ In 1822, computers found their start with Charles Babbage's proposed steam-powered automated calculating machine, called the difference engine.

❑ Computing technology improved quickly throughout the twentieth century. During World War II, the U.S. Army worked with the University of Pennsylvania to develop the Electronic Numerical Integrator and Computer (ENIAC), a multipurpose computer so large that it required its own 30 foot by 50 foot room.

❑ The first computer designed for business (and not merely scientific purposes), the Universal Automatic Computer (UNIVAC) became available in 1951. It weighed 16,000 pounds and performed approximately 1000 calculations per second.

❑ By 1965, many large businesses used computers for financial calculations.

❑ To understand the history of telecommunications in the United States, you must understand the history of AT&T. AT&T grew out of Alexander Graham Bell's company, American Bell, which quickly bought other, smaller telephone companies. By the turn of the 20th century, it supplied service to sixty percent of U.S. telephone subscribers.

❑ In fear of the government using anti-trust laws against it, AT&T approached the U.S. Department of Justice with the Kingsbury Commitment in 1913. The Kingsbury Commitment promised that AT&T would divest itself of Western Union, stop buying independent telephone companies, and allow independent telephone companies to connect to its lines and switching centers.

❑ In 1934, Congress passed the Communications Act of 1934, which established the Federal Communications Commission (FCC), state Public Utilities Commissions (PUCs), and initial guidelines for the telephone industry.

❑ In 1956, AT&T signed a consent decree to resolve a dispute over its foray into electronic switching and the potential abuses of its monopoly power that these developments might lead to. The Department of Justice forced AT&T to restrict itself to providing telephone service. AT&T was prohibited from branching out into the computer services industry. In return, AT&T could keep its research and manufacturing facilities and maintain its regulated monopoly status for telephone service.

❑ In 1982, the Department of Justice ruled that AT&T should be split into multiple, smaller companies. Some of these new, smaller companies—for example, the seven Regional Bell Operating Companies (RBOCs) that provided local telephone service—would continue to be regulated monopolies. Others, such as AT&T's long distance division, would be open to competition. This ruling was called the Modified Final Judgment (MFJ). AT&T's divestiture took place in 1984.

❑ According to the MFJ, RBOCs had to allow interLATA providers to access and lease their facilities, including local phone lines and switches. Most importantly, they had to charge each interLATA provider the same price, and provide the same quality of access to its local customers. This concept is known as equal access.

❑ In the 1990s, the U. S. government decided that the existence of regulated monopolies in local phone service hindered competition. As a result, Congress passed the Telecommunications Act of 1996, a sweeping piece of legislation that affected competition in local phone service, wireless telecommunications, cable TV, broadcasting, and the Internet.

❑ Among other things, the Telecommunications Act of 1996 opened competition for local telephone service and imposed many requirements on LECs to ensure smooth and economical interconnection between them and their competitors.

3

KEY TERMS

Audion — A type of vacuum tube invented by Lee DeForest that contained an additional electrode in the middle of the positive and negative electrodes. When subjected to voltage, the third electrode could control current inside the tube. The result was that the Audion could amplify (or boost) a signal.

Bell Communications Research (Bellcore) — The research and development business that was created as a result of the Modified Final Judgment. Bellcore, which was formerly known as Bell Laboratories, was jointly owned by the Regional Bell Operating Companies (RBOCs).

Bell Operating Companies (BOCs) — The 22 telephone companies that belonged to AT&T and provided local service in different regions of the nation (for example, Michigan Bell). As part of the Modified Final Judgment, the Bell Operating Companies were separated from AT&T and transformed into seven Regional Bell Operating Companies (RBOCs).

Bell System — The company initially formed when American Bell took a controlling interest in Western Electric. Later, the Bell System came to refer to AT&T and all its subsidiaries, which controlled U.S. telephone service until the 1984 divestiture.

Bell Telephone Laboratories — The research and development arm of AT&T prior to divestiture. Bell Telephone Laboratories was responsible for innovation and new telephone technology.

Carterfone decision — A 1968 court decision that lifted the restriction against interconnecting to AT&T's telephone network. The Carterfone decision was named after a means of connecting private, radio-controlled telephones to the local telephone lines invented by Tom Carter.

cell — A geographic area that is serviced by a single low-power transmitter for wireless communications.

central office — A telephone company facility where lines are terminated and can be connected with other lines to complete calls. Central offices come in different classes depending on the geographic area and type of lines they serve. Central offices are also known as exchanges.

competitive local exchange carriers (CLECs) — The local exchange carriers that have only begun offering local phone service since competition was introduced. CLECs may build their own facilities, but they usually also lease lines from ILECs to cover the local loop portion of their subscribers' connections.

computing — The automatic manipulation of input based on logical instructions.

crossbar switch — An automatic telephone switch that used a grid of horizontal and vertical bars with electromagnets at their ends. The horizontal bars could rotate up and down to connect to specific vertical bars and thus complete circuits. Each possible permutation of the vertical and horizontal bars' position's represented a different connection.

difference engine — An automated calculating machine as large as a locomotive and powered by steam that was proposed in 1822 by Charles Babbage, an English mathematics professor. Though a working difference engine was never actually built, Babbage's ideas were adopted by other inventors working on automated calculating machines, which were precursors to modern computers.

digital divide — The discrepancy between the greater Internet access enjoyed by more urban and affluent citizens in the United States compared to the lack of access experienced by many rural, disabled, and poor citizens.

downlink — The transmission of a signal from an orbiting satellite to an earth-based receiver.

duplexing — The simultaneous transmission of a signal in both directions along a single transmission pathway.

ENIAC (Electronic Numerical Integrator and Computer) — An early computer developed in cooperation between the U.S. Army and the University of Pennsylvania. ENIAC was a multipurpose computer so large that it required its own 30 foot by 50 foot room. ENIAC did not contain memory and, therefore, could not retain any information once it was turned off.

equal access — A provision set forth in the MFJ that requires local phone service providers to allow all long distance service providers to access and use their facilities at the same, reasonable cost.

e-rate — A program for funding technology in schools and libraries across the nation that was established by the Telecommunications Act of 1996. E-rate money is generated by the universal service fund (USF).

exchange — (1) *See* central office. (2) The geographical area served by one central office.

frequency modulation (FM) — A method of transmitting signals that uses one wave containing the information to be transmitted combined with another wave, called carrier wave, whose frequency is constant.

geosynchronous — A satellite that at every point in its orbit maintains a constant distance from a point on the earth's equator.

Hush-a-Phone decision — A 1956 Supreme Court ruling that allowed the attachment of devices not manufactured by AT&T to AT&T telephones as long as the device did not harm the public telephone network.

incumbent local exchange carriers (ILECs) — The phone companies, including the RBOCs, that provided local phone service as regulated monopolies before the introduction of competition for intraLATA service.

inter-exchange carriers (IXCs) — The service providers that connect calls between LATAs, also known as long distance carriers.

interLATA — The service that is initiated and terminated between LATAs, or long distance service.

intraLATA — The service that initiates and terminates within a LATA, or local service area.

Kingsbury Commitment — The 1913 agreement between AT&T and the U.S. Department of Justice (and named after the AT&T vice president who drafted the proposal) that forced AT&T to divest itself of Western Union, stop buying independent telephone companies, and allow independent telephone companies to connect to its infrastructure. AT&T initiated the settlement, fearing that if it didn't take proactive measures, the government would use anti-trust laws against it.

local access and transport area (LATA) — A geographical area that defines local phone calls. LATAs were established by Judge Harold Greene as part of the MFJ. They were roughly equivalent to area codes at that time, and a total of 160 LATAs were established across the United States.

local exchange carrier (LEC) — A carrier that supplies subscribers with intraLATA telephone connections. CLECs and ILECs are two types of LECs.

local office — *See* local switching center.

local switching center — An exchange where multiple phone lines from homes and businesses in one geographic area converge and terminate. It may also be called a local office.

memory — In the context of computing, a feature or component of a computer that enables it to store information for later retrieval.

microwave link — A path used for transmitting signals via microwaves.

Modified Final Judgment (MFJ) — A 1982 government ruling that split AT&T into multiple, smaller companies, some of which, like Regional Bell Operating Companies (RBOCs), that provided local phone service, would continue to be regulated monopolies and others of which (such as AT&T's long-distance arm) would be open to competition.

Morse code — A method of representing characters with a series of dots and dashes. Morse code is named after Samuel Morse, the inventor of the telegraph.

multiplexing — The simultaneous transmission of multiple signals over one transmission pathway.

number portability — The ability of telecommunications service users to retain their same telephone number, no matter what service provider they choose, without impairment of quality, reliability, or convenience. The Telecommunications Act of 1996 required that every local service provider allow for number portability.

Regional Bell Operating Companies (RBOCs) — The seven local phone service carriers created from the 22 former Bell Operating Companies as part of the MFJ that broke up AT&T in 1984. These seven new companies were called: NYNEX, Bell Atlantic, Bell South, Ameritech, Southwestern Bell Corporation, US West, and Pacific Telesis.

regulated monopoly — A company that is allowed to exist without competition, but is subject to a great deal of constraints dictated by the government.

semaphore — A type of signaling in which visual cues (for example, flags) represent symbols, such as letters. The word semaphore comes from the Greek *sema*, which means "signal" and *phoros*, which means "carrying."

space division switching — A technique for switching calls that manipulates the physical space between two lines, thereby closing a circuit. Space division switching was electromechanical and required that the switch be dedicated to a connection until the subscriber terminated the call.

step-by-step switch — An automatic telephone switch developed by Almon Strowger in 1889. The step-by-step switch used a cylinder with an arm that brushed against rows of electrical contacts in a ratcheting motion. The movement of the arm was controlled directly by pulses that were issued by a subscriber's telephone.

subscriber — A telephone company customer (so called because they subscribe to telephone service).

tandem office — *See* tandem switching center.

tandem switching center — An exchange where lines from multiple local switching centers converge and terminate.

time division switching — A switching technique in which samples from multiple incoming lines are digitized, then each is issued to the same circuit, in sequence, at a different time interval, and finally transmitted to the correct outbound line. This method of switching did not require a continuous electromechanical connection and meant that one switch could handle hundreds of thousands of calls.

toll office — *See* toll switching center.

toll switching center — An exchange where lines from multiple tandem switching centers converge and terminate. This facility is called a toll office because it handles long-distance, or toll, calls.

transponder — A piece of equipment on a satellite that receives an uplinked signal from earth, amplifies the signal, modifies its frequency, then retransmits it (in a downlink) to an antenna on earth.

UNIVAC (Universal Automatic Computer) — The first computer designed for business (and not merely scientific purposes). UNIVAC became available in 1951. It weighed 16,000 pounds and performed approximately 1000 calculations per second. It was used to predict the outcome of the 1952 election based on only 1% of the total poll data. However, UNIVAC was still too large and expensive to be practical for widespread use.

uplink — A connection from an earth-based transmitter to an orbiting satellite. (Also, a broadcast over such a connection.) Often uplink information is scrambled (in other words, its signal is coded) before transmission to prevent unauthorized interception.

universal service fund (USF) — A fund established by the Telecommunications Act of 1996 to subsidize telecommunications services in less populated areas and to which each telecommunications carrier and business user contributes a small fee on a monthly basis.

3

vacuum tube — A sealed container made of glass, metal, or ceramic, that contains, in a vacuum, a charged plate that transmits current to a filament.

Walkie-Talkie — A two-way communication device developed by Motorola that uses frequency modulation techniques.

Western Electric Company — The firm that was founded in 1856 as Western Union Telegraph. Within two decades, Western Electric had established a national network of telegraph wires. In 1882, Western Electric's competitor, American Bell gained a controlling interest in the company. Combined, Western Electric and American Bell became known as The Bell System.

wire-bound — *See* wireline.

wireless — A communications technology that transmits and receives signals via the atmosphere.

wireline — A communications technology that depends on physically connected wires to transmit and receive signals.

REVIEW QUESTIONS

1. What term is used to describe a signaling system that uses visual cues across distances?

    a. telephone

    b. telegraph

    c. semaphore

    d. time division switching

2. In what year did Alexander Graham Bell receive a patent for the telephone?

    a. 1855

    b. 1872

    c. 1876

    d. 1882

3. What profession was eliminated by automatic switching?

    a. telephone technician

    b. lineman

    c. radio operator

    d. telephone operator

4. The step-by-step and crossbar are examples of what type of telephone switches?

    a. electromechanical

    b. electronic

    c. digital

    d. pressurized

5. What type of signals did Marconi's first radio transmit?

   a. touch tone

   b. amplitude modulation

   c. frequency modulation

   d. Morse code

6. What was significant about Lee DeForest's Audion?

   a. It was the first vacuum tube that could amplify signals.

   b. It was the first vacuum tube that could convert DC to AC.

   c. It was the first vacuum tube that could issue electromagnetic signals.

   d. It was the first vacuum tube that did not risk overheating.

7. What company was responsible for introducing the Walkie-Talkie?

   a. AT&T

   b. Motorola

   c. IBM

   d. MCI

8. What was the power source conceived for Babbage's difference engine?

   a. gas

   b. steam

   c. coal

   d. electricity

9. What mid–20th century invention replaced the vacuum tube in computers and led to much smaller machines?

   a. diode

   b. memory

   c. transistor

   d. semiconductor

10. Which two advances led to the proliferation of personal computers?

    a. the capability to complete more than 1000 instructions per second

    b. shrinking size

    c. affordability

    d. television marketing campaigns

11. What devices were used to input data into computers from the 1890s up to the 1980s?

    a. floppy disks

    b. magnetic platters

    c. keyboards

    d. punch cards

12. What was the name of the 1913 agreement between AT&T and the U.S. government in which AT&T agreed to stop buying independent telephone companies?

    a. Kingsbury Commitment

    b. Hush-a-Phone Agreement

    c. Sherman Antitrust Act

    d. Modified Final Judgment

13. What did the Carterfone decision allow that had been previously restricted?

    a. competitive local phone service

    b. competitive long distance phone service

    c. third-party local loop infrastructure

    d. third-party devices to attach to Bell System phones

14. What company won the first battle to compete against AT&T in providing long distance service?

    a. Sprint

    b. Nortel

    c. Verizon

    d. MCI

15. What kind of competition was opened up as a result of the MFJ?

    a. local phone service

    b. local microwave service

    c. long distance phone service

    d. open access for Internet content on cable lines

16. How many RBOCs were formed as a result of AT&T's divestiture?

    a. 5

    b. 7

    c. 12

    d. 22

17. Which government agency is responsible for enforcing the provisions of the Telecommunications Act of 1996?

    a. FTC

    b. FCC

    c. ICC

    d. NTIA

18. What provision of the Telecommunications Act of 1996 prohibits ILECs from requiring customers to dial an extra digit when calling someone who subscribes to a competitor's local phone service?

    a. equal access

    b. number portability

    c. universal service

    d. wholesale pricing

19. What does the e-rate program fund?

    a. technology upgrades for schools and libraries

    b. technology training for disadvantaged youths

    c. technology access for rural U.S. residents

    d. technology training for adults re-entering the workforce

20. As part of the Telecommunications Act of 1996, what were RBOCs allowed to do that had previously been prohibited?

    a. provide local phone service

    b. provide interstate phone service

    c. provide inter-LATA phone service within a state

    d. provide international phone service

21. Describe the problem known as the "digital divide" and what measures the government is taking to address it.

22. Why do RBOCs encounter more competition in urban areas than in rural areas?

    a. because RBOCs are more entrenched in urban areas

    b. because rural areas are less profitable to serve

    c. because there are fewer government restrictions on competition in urban areas

    d. because customers in rural areas show less desire to change local service providers

23. Which of the following is the best example of an IXC?

    a. Bell Atlantic

    b. AT&T

    c. Union River Telephone Company

    d. Urban Media

24. Which two of the following ILECs merged to form Verizon?

    a. Bell Atlantic

    b. Ameritech

    c. GTE

    d. SBC

25. On what basis does the FCC determine whether it will approve a request from an RBOC to provide long-distance phone service?

    a. the number of subscribers the RBOC currently has compared to its competitors

    b. the RBOC's annual revenue

    c. the extent to which the RBOC has contributed to the USF

    d. the amount of capital the RBOC has spent on local service equipment upgrades

HANDS-ON PROJECTS

Project 3-1

In this project, you create your own simple telegraph, similar to the one that Samuel Morse created in 1837. You need the following materials: two pieces of corrugated cardboard approximately 9 inches by six inches, two pieces of corrugated cardboard approximately 1 inch by 3 inches, three pieces of insulated copper wire approximately one foot long, three pieces of insulated copper wire approximately 5 feet long, one new "D" cell battery, four thumbtacks, two 1.5 volt-compatible buzzers (available at hardware or electronics stores), wire strippers, pliers, electrician's tape, and masking tape.

1. Using the wire strippers, remove approximately ¾-inch of the insulation from both ends of each of the six copper wires.

2. To distinguish between the three long copper wires, apply a piece of masking tape to each and label the wires 1, 2, and 3.

3. Using the masking tape, affix one small piece of cardboard about one inch from the edge of the large piece of cardboard as shown in Figure 3-16. This serves as the key, or switch, that completes the circuit. Therefore, the cardboard needs to be bendable. Crease the small piece of cardboard near the tape so that it can be pressed flat against the large piece of cardboard, but will spring back to its bent position. Repeat the same process with the other small and large pieces of cardboard.

4. Press a thumbtack into the one of the large pieces of cardboard underneath the end of the small piece of cardboard.

5. Press another thumbtack into the smaller piece of cardboard so that when the two pieces of cardboard are pressed together, the thumbtacks make contact.

6. Using electrician's tape, tape the battery to the center of that same large piece of cardboard, with the positive side facing you, as shown in Figure 3-16.

7. Using electrician's tape, connect one end of a short copper wire to the negative (flat) side of the battery and insert the other end of that wire under the thumbtack, looping it around the tack if necessary.

8. Use pliers to bend the sharp point of the tack against the bottom of the large piece of cardboard.

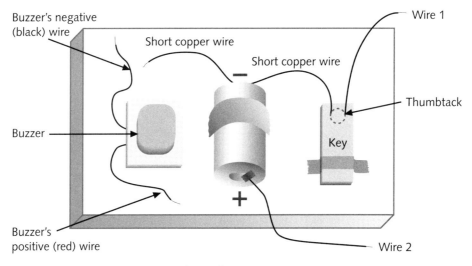

Figure 3-16 Constructing a telegraph set

9. Using electrician's tape, tape another one of the short copper wires to the negative (flat) side of the battery, making sure that the copper is touching the metal underneath the tape.

10. Tape one of the buzzers to the large piece of cardboard next to the battery, as shown in Figure 3-16. The buzzer should be equipped with a red wire (its positive side) and a black wire (its negative side).

11. Twist the end of the second short copper wire attached to the battery together with the end of the buzzer's black (negative) wire. Make sure that the two copper wires are making good contact. Wrap a small piece of electrician's tape around the twists.

12. Twist the end of the long copper wire marked "1" around the base of the thumbtack that you pressed into the small piece of cardboard in Step 5. Use pliers to bend the sharp point of the tack over on the other side of the cardboard.

13. Using electrician's tape, tape one end of the long copper wire marked "2" over the positive end of the battery.

3

14. Take the long copper wire marked "3" and twist one of its ends together with the positive (red) wire from the buzzer, making sure the two wires have plenty of contact. Use electrician's tape to secure the twists.

15. Now, repeat Steps 4–5 using the other pair of large and small pieces of cardboard to create a second key.

16. Hook both the free end of wire "2" and one end of the remaining short wire under the thumbtack affixed to the second large piece of cardboard, as shown in Figure 3-17. Use pliers to bend the sharp point of the tack against the back of the cardboard.

17. Attach the second buzzer to the same large piece of cardboard, as shown in Figure 3-17.

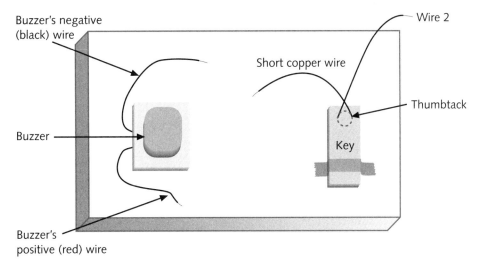

Figure 3-17   A second telegraph set

18. Twist together the ends of the short wire you just affixed to the thumbtack and the buzzer's negative (black) wire. Secure the twists with a small piece of electrician's tape.

19. Now, twist together the remaining end of copper wire number 1 with the second buzzer's positive (red) wire. Secure the twists with a small piece of electrician's tape.

20. Wrap the free end of copper wire number 3 around the thumbtack in the second telegraph set's cardboard switch. Use the pliers to bend the sharp end of the tack against the other side of the cardboard switch.

21. All wires should now be terminated. When you press the cardboard switch on either one of the telegraph keys, you should cause the buzzer on the other set to sound. If this doesn't happen, verify that you have terminated the wires in the right places and that all your contacts are good.

Project 3-2

In this project, you create a rudimentary telephone system and experiment with various grades of transmission media to determine how their physical properties affect the sound quality. You need the following materials: two (or more) empty, clean yogurt containers, a needle, two paper clips, one 5-foot length of polyester thread, two 5-foot lengths of uninsulated copper wire, one 5-foot length of uninsulated aluminum wire (available at a hardware store), and one 5-foot length of fishing line. To listen and talk through your homemade telephone, you need a partner.

1. Using the needle, make a single hole in the center of the bottom of each yogurt container.

2. Insert one end of the polyester thread through the hole of one yogurt container and on the open of the container, tie the thread to the paper clip so that it cannot be pulled out of the container.

3. Repeat Step 2 with the other end of the polyester thread, another paper clip, and another yogurt container.

4. While holding one of the yogurt containers, you and your partner should walk as far apart as the polyester thread allows, until the thread is taut.

5. Take turns talking and listening through the telephone you've created. On a separate piece of paper, rate the quality of the sound this instrument provides on a scale of 1 to 10, where 1 is barely discernable and 10 is as good as your home telephone.

6. Repeat Steps 2–5 for the fishing line, the aluminum wire, and a single length of copper wire, in this order, making sure to note how the sound of each differs.

7. Now, you should be left with a telephone made of a single copper wire. Rather than holding it taut, experiment with moving four feet closer to your partner and note the difference in sound quality, if there is one. Next, wrap the copper wire around your arm and try talking and listening again through the yogurt containers. What happens to the sound?

8. Finally, remove the single copper wire from your experimental telephone. Take the second copper wire and twist it around the first copper wire so that the wires are twisted approximately twice every inch. Now, try talking and listening again and note the sound quality.

Project 3-3

In this project, you learn about the effects of the Telecommunications Act of 1996 by studying documentation provided by the FCC. Through this project, you should get an impression of each party's point of view on the court's decision and how they attempted to sway subsequent decisions in their favor. For this project, you need a computer with Internet access. If you find that you can't fully view some of the Web pages discussed in these steps, you may need to install a more up-to-date browser.

1. Connect to the Internet and go to **www.fcc.gov**, the Federal Communications Commission home page.

2. In the Search text box, type **telecommunications act** and click **Go**.

3. A page listing documents that match your search appears. Scroll down the page until you find a document titled "FCC – Telecommunications Act of 1996." Click this listing to connect to a page dedicated to the Telecommunications Act of 1996.

4. Scroll down the page until you reach a heading titled "Common Carrier Bureau." (This is the division of the FCC that handles regulation for local and long distance carriers.)

5. Note how many modifications and reports the FCC issued on the Telecommunications Act of 1996 after the Act was implemented in early February, 1996.

6. Scroll down until you reach a report titled "Notice of Proposed Rulemaking on BOC provision of out-of-region, interstate, interexchange services, (CC Docket No. 96-21) (February 14, 1996)."

7. Click the **Text Version** link for this document to review the document.

8. What is the purpose of this document? What implications does it have for an RBOC that wants to provide service outside of its old territory? Was the policy stated in this document law when the document is issued?

9. Note the number of the FCC document: "CC Docket 96-21."

10. Use the **Back** button on your browser three times to return to the FCC home page.

11. Scroll to the very bottom of the FCC's home page. Click the **Search** link to access a page offering different types of searches.

12. Scroll down the Search page and click the **Search for Filed Comments – ECFS** link to access a search engine page.

13. The FCC Search for Filed Comments page appears, with a search form. In the text box titled "Proceeding," type the FCC docket number: **96-21**.

14. Click the **Retrieve Document List** button to begin searching for comments that carriers and other entities have filed regarding the FCC document you just read. (The search engine should retrieve approximately 50 documents.)

15. Choose to view one of the shorter documents (because this Web site may be slow) submitted by an RBOC, such as Bell Atlantic or Pacific Telesis. As you read the document, try to figure out why the RBOC would oppose the FCC's proposal, which allows them to compete for service in areas outside their regulated jurisdiction.

16. Continue selecting documents to view, noting each carrier's opinion on the FCC's Notice of Proposed Rulemaking and whether their opinion changed from the time the ruling was originally issued. Also note how the IXC's opinions (such as Sprint) differ from the RBOC's opinions on the matter.

CASE PROJECTS

1. You were hired by New York Bell in 1970 as an engineer, and since then, you have changed jobs many times. Now, you're a top manager. Though you still work in the same corporate location, many things about your job and your company have changed since you began working there. The company's Human Resources Department asks you, as one of the most senior employees, to write a column for the company employee newsletter. In this column, they want you to summarize the changes—in corporate structure, technology, and policy—that you've witnessed since you first began working there. Also, they ask you to identify which of these changes you believe to be the most advantageous for your company's customers, and why.

2. As a manager, one of your responsibilities is to participate in company orientation for new RBOC employees. During your presentation on carrier interconnection, one of the participants interrupts and asks you to explain why your company has to allow its competitors to use all its facilities at such low rates. He adds that it doesn't seem fair to him. How do you answer this? In what ways might this situation change in the next ten years?

3. As a telecommunications expert, you are also asked to consult with the FCC on how to address the digital divide. As part of your research, you read a report called "Falling Through the Net," published in October 2000 by the National Telecommunications and Information Administration (NTIA), a division of the Department of Commerce, that contains detailed statistics on what type of Americans enjoy fast access to the Internet and which citizens don't. The report can be found on the Internet at *www.ntia.doc.gov/ntiahome/fttn00/falling.htm*. Based on what you read, how would you characterize the digital divide between races in the United States? What would you suggest to address this? Also, how would you characterize the situation of Internet access for disabled persons? How would you address that problem? What methods seem most promising to you for funding rural telecommunications infrastructure? What do you conclude about the future of the USF in helping to bring equal access to all citizens?

4

THE PUBLIC NETWORK

After reading this chapter and completing the exercises, you will be able to:

♦ Explain, in general terms, the structure of the public telephone network

♦ Describe the types of carriers who currently participate in the public telephone network

♦ Recognize the elements of outside plant and describe their purposes

♦ Recognize the elements of inside plant and describe their purposes

♦ Describe the hierarchy of central offices that participate in the public telephone network

♦ Explain issues related to interconnection and billing between common carriers

♦ Describe the current telephone numbering plan and explain how it has evolved

All of the telephone calls and many of the data connections completed in the United States rely on an intricate, transcontinental collection of wires, poles, switches, fiber optic cables, microwave towers, and other components known informally as the public network. This infrastructure is considered to be public, because it can be accessed and used by any and all telephone service customers. Because the network is public, its services are regulated by the FCC and the state public utilities commissions.

The public network originated at the end of the nineteenth century in the form of copper wires strung from pole to pole. Back then, these wires were owned by several different telephone companies. As you learned in Chapter 3, the public network eventually became the domain of a single company, AT&T; however, since 1984, its ownership and use have been open to competitors. Because the public network provides a common foundation for a multitude of telecommunications services, you need to understand its different parts and be able to explain how they work together. This chapter focuses on the companies and facilities that form the public telephone network in the United States. Later in this book, you learn about specific data and voice telecommunications services that rely on the public network.

AN OVERVIEW OF THE PUBLIC NETWORK

In the context of computing, a network is a group of computers and other devices (such as printers) that are connected to each other to facilitate data exchange and resource sharing. In the context of telephone service, networks consist of multiple telephones, computers, and the cabling that connects them. It also includes telephone switches (which may or may not be computerized), telephone poles, underground tunnels, pay phones, and other components.

Most of what you have learned so far about the evolution of telecommunications has pertained to the **Public Switched Telephone Network (PSTN)**, also known as the **Plain Old Telephone System (POTS)**. The PSTN consists of all the facilities and connections maintained by all local and long distance providers. Among other things, the PSTN includes switches, copper wire, fiber optic cable, and many connection points at central offices. These facilities are used for public voice (and more recently, data) communications. You may also think of the PSTN as the old Bell System plus its post-1984 competitors. The PSTN does not include private lines (for example, a fiber optic connection between two buildings on a company's campus). However, it may include public connections that are used for private purposes—for example, telephone lines that are used by company employees to connect to the Internet and exchange company data.

A unique set of terms is used to refer to the companies and elements belonging to the PSTN. Although you are already familiar with some—such as LEC and IXC—you will learn a number of new terms throughout this chapter. Before going any further, however, you should become acquainted with a few terms, which are introduced in the following paragraphs, that will help you understand all topics discussed in this chapter.

You may use the word "line" to refer to your home telephone connection without thinking about its technical meaning. In telecommunications, **line** is used frequently to refer to one of two things. The most obvious definition of "line" is the physical connection between a subscriber and the telephone company's facilities—for example, the copper wire that connects your home to the PSTN. But "line" can also refer to a single communications channel (or circuit) between a subscriber and the central office. For greater efficiency, multiple lines are often connected to a switch and consolidated on one cable either before or at the central office. Thus, a cable can simultaneously carry multiple communications channels, or lines. This is made possible by a digital transmission technique called multiplexing, which is explained in Chapter 6. For now, bear in mind that one line does not necessarily equal one wire. Consequently, if you read that a switch can handle 20,000 lines, it does not mean that it can accept 20,000 separate wires. However, one line does equal one telephone circuit.

The place where a wire is connected to another part of the public telephone network (for example, a switch or a customer's home) is known as a **termination**. Throughout this chapter, you will recognize instances of wire terminations at residences and central offices, as well as points in between.

Another important term, **point of presence (POP)** refers to a carrier's facilities that allow it or its customers access to the public network. An ILEC's central offices are examples of POPs. An Internet Service Provider's data center, which contains equipment that allows its customers to dial in to the Internet, is another example of a POP.

COMMON CARRIERS

4

Most telecommunications service providers within the PSTN are common carriers. **Common carriers** are entities directly involved in supplying regulated telecommunications services to the public. To be considered a common carrier, a company must make its services available to any member of the public who chooses to subscribe to its services. Some examples of large common carriers include AT&T, SBC, Verizon, Sprint, WorldCom, and U.S. Cellular. However, many smaller companies also participate in the PSTN as common carriers. One kind of common carrier is a **reseller**, or a company that leases another company's facilities, and then sells services over those facilities under its own name. For example, Third Millenium Telecom is a company that offers wireless communication services. Rather than build its own wireless facilities, Third Millenium leases facilities from WorldCom Wireless. Companies that only supply private connections or services (for example, a company that offers microwave data transfer between two buildings of the same company) are not considered common carriers.

In Chapter 3, you were introduced to LECs, ILECs, CLECs, and IXCs, all of which are common carriers. The following section discusses common carriers in greater detail. Later in this chapter, you learn how a common carrier's infrastructure connects with facilities supplied by consumers and other common carriers.

Local Exchange Carriers (LECs)

Earlier, you learned that a local exchange carrier (LEC) handles intraLATA, or local, phone service. Currently, two types of common carriers provide local phone service: incumbent local exchange carriers (ILECs) and competitive local exchange carriers (CLECs). The term incumbent local exchange carriers refers to companies that have been providing local phone service since before competition was allowed for intraLATA traffic (that is, before the Telecommunications Act of 1996). All RBOCs are incumbent local exchange carriers, but they are not the only ones. Some independent phone companies existed—and were allowed to remain in business—when the Bell System became a regulated monopoly in 1913. Thus, these companies, such as GTE (now part of Verizon) and smaller, rural telephone companies—for example, Richmond Telephone Company in Richmond, Massachusetts—are also ILECs.

Companies that began offering local phone service after the Telecommunications Act of 1996 introduced competition, and are called competitive local exchange carriers (CLECs). Examples of CLECs include Covad Communications, KMC Telecom, and Fairpoint Communications. The CLEC category also includes several well-established long-distance service providers that are now attempting to compete in the local service market. Some CLECs are **facilities-based**—that is, they build their own facilities (such as microwave links and underground cables) in addition to leasing and using ILEC facilities to provide service under their name. Other CLECs are resellers. As such, they merely purchase a large amount of lines at a discounted rate from an ILEC or a facilities-based CLEC and resell the service under their own names.

Interexchange Carriers (IXCs)

AT&T and other carriers, such as WorldCom and Sprint, are considered Interexchange Carriers (IXCs) because they carry long distance traffic between exchanges. ILECs are still, in most cases, prevented from carrying interstate long distance calls, but they may carry interLATA long distance calls (for example, long distance calls within a part of one state). However, some IXCs may compete in the intraLATA market. For example, because AT&T is no longer a monopoly and has been freed from unique restrictions associated with that status, it has also begun competing in other telecommunications services, such as local phone service and Internet connectivity.

The terminology used when discussing common carriers can be quite confusing. To help you sort out all the details, Table 4-1 summarizes the acronyms for and distinctions between different types of traditional common carriers.

Table 4-1   Traditional common carriers

Acronym	Full Name	Description	Industry Examples
RBOC	Regional Bell Operating Company	One of the local phone companies created when AT&T was divested; until the Telecommunications Act of 1996, RBOCs enjoyed a monopoly in their region. Since the Act, they have been subject to competition, and some have merged with each other or with other telephone service providers.	US West (now Qwest), Southwestern Bell Corporation, BellSouth
LEC	Local exchange carrier	A company that provides public, intraLATA telephone service.	All ILECs and CLECs are LECs
ILEC	Incumbent local exchange carrier	A type of LEC that, before the Telecommunications Act of 1996, had a monopoly on intraLATA (or local) telephone service. All RBOCs are ILECs.	All RBOCs, Verizon (formerly Bell Atlantic and GTE), CenturyTel, TDS Telecom, and many others, including rural telephone companies such as Emery Telephone in Orangeville, Utah

Table 4-1   Traditional common carriers (continued)

Acronym	Full Name	Description	Industry Examples
CLEC	Competitive local exchange carrier	A type of LEC that never enjoyed a monopoly on telephone service, but since the Telecommunications Act of 1996 has competed with the ILECs.	COVAD Communications, KMC Telecommunications, Fairpoint Communications, and many others
IXC	Interexchange carrier	A carrier that provides interLATA telephone service (also known as long-distance service).	AT&T, Sprint, WorldCom, and many others

Nontraditional Common Carriers

Not all modern common carriers can be clearly identified as either LECs or IXCs. The definition of a common carrier (according to the FCC) includes companies that supply regulated "telecommunications services." Since the origin of the FCC, "telecommunications services" has come to include more than traditional, wireline voice communications. Now, it also includes wireless and data communications. Consequently, wireless communications providers (including those that provide paging, cellular telephone, and satellite communication services) are also considered common carriers. Examples of such nontraditional common carriers include Cingular, Iridium, and U.S. Cellular. In addition, some companies that offer connections to the Internet, such as high-speed cable operators or ISPs, may be considered common carriers. Examples of this type of common carrier include Aerie Networks, Level 3 Communications, and Norlight Telecommunications. However, despite the proliferation of nontraditional common carriers, regulators such as the FCC are still primarily concerned with monitoring basic telephone service providers.

OUTSIDE PLANT

Outside plant refers to the system of cabling, poles, towers, and other connectivity equipment between the customers and central offices. In the telecommunications business, outside plant is sometimes known as simply **OSP**. Although most of the elements of outside plant are indistinguishable to a layperson, each portion has a different purpose and a different name, all of which are familiar to telecommunications technicians. The following sections detail each component of a carrier's outside plant.

Demarcation Point

The **demarcation point** (or **demarc**) is the location where one entity's telephone or network facilities connect to another entity's telephone or network facilities. The term "demarcation point" does not technically refer to a physical item, but rather a logical distinction, similar to the boundary between neighborhoods in a city. The physical equivalent of the demarcation point is the **network interface device (NID)**. In the case of the public network, this is where a telephone subscriber's wires terminate and connect with the local service provider's wires. (You learn more about wires and how they are terminated in Chapter 8). The NID is typically enclosed in a box (which may or may not be locked), both to prevent unauthorized tampering and to protect it from environmental damage. In most cases, this **demarc box** is the property of the LEC.

On a residence, the demarc box is attached to the outside of the house or is located in the basement. Figure 4-1 depicts a typical residential demarcation point. Inside the box, one or two wire pairs terminate (depending on if the residence has one or two phone lines) and connect to a jack, which in turn connects with the LEC's incoming telephone lines. On the LEC's side of the box, each line is connected to a grounded **station protector**, which prevents the customer's telephone equipment from being damaged in the event of excessive current affecting the line. Figure 4-2 shows the inside of a demarc box. Notice the customer wire pairs terminating on the right hand side of the box while the LEC wire pairs terminate on the left side.

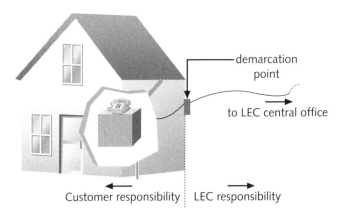

Figure 4-1   A residential demarcation point

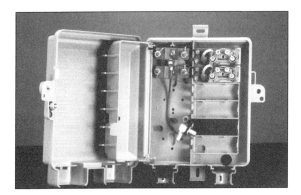

Figure 4-2   A residential demarc box

The demarcation point for a business is usually found in a much larger box, containing dozens of numbered wire pair terminations. Alternatively, the network interface device may terminate fiber connections between the business and the carrier. A business demarc is often located in a room specially designed for telecommunications equipment. Figure 4-3 shows a business demarcation box designed for use with fiber optic cable.

Figure 4-3   A business demarcation box

A demarcation point typically marks the end of the LEC's responsibility for a telephone connection. If a problem arises in the connection, the LEC is only required to assess and repair the problem up to the demarcation point, unless the subscriber has paid in advance for a maintenance plan. If the subscriber has not paid for a maintenance plan, the wire inside a residence or business must be maintained by the owner of that residence or business. If the subscriber has paid for a maintenance plan, the LEC sends a technician to assess and correct the problem beyond the demarcation point.

The Local Loop

The portion of a business or residential telephone network that connects the demarcation point to the local phone company's nearest central office is called the **local loop**. Traditionally, local loops are made of twisted copper wire pairs that carry only one or two signals and extend no more than three miles. However, the local loop is not simply one long stretch of wire. It is made of several different sections of cable that connect at different points between the subscriber's location and the phone company's facility. The components that make up the local loop belong to a telephone company's outside plant, because they are facilities located outside of the telephone company's buildings. Figure 4-4 shows a simplified view of the local loop portion of a traditional telephone connection.

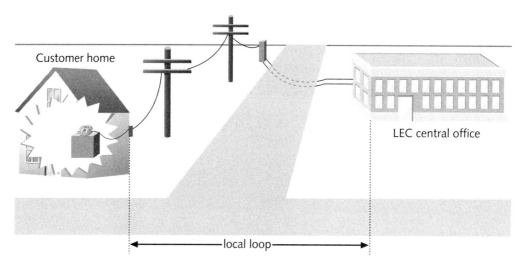

Figure 4-4   Local loop portion of a phone connection

The local loop portion of a connection, also known as the **last mile**, is the most expensive for a carrier to provide because separate lines must be installed for each individual subscriber. The first local loops were installed with the advent of local telephone service, prior to 1900. By World War I, virtually every city block was outfitted with telephone wires. Rural areas took longer to get service, because of their remote nature. In many cases, farmers banded together to install their own poles and wires, forming the first telephone cooperatives. In early local loop installations, copper wire was the chosen medium because it was inexpensive, plentiful, and of sufficient quality for most business and household needs. Copper wire continues to form the basis of most local loops today.

Although it's expensive to supply, the last mile is also the place where carriers stand to make the most money. Whichever company supplies the local loop service to your house is the one that bills you. (In the case of a CLEC, the local service provider may not own the physical local loop, but still "owns" the customer.) After providing the local loop, a carrier can sell you multiple services (such as voice mail, caller ID, and call waiting) to generate more revenue. This control over the consumer also explains why it was necessary for the Telecommunications Act of 1996 to require that the Bell System allow competitors to use its last mile infrastructure at a reasonable cost. If the government had not required the RBOCs to share their facilities, new competitors would have been forced to install their own, new local loops. This would not only be prohibitively expensive, but also disruptive, ultimately limiting competition in the last mile.

The local loop is the part of a connection most likely to have the lowest throughput and, further, be the most susceptible to damage or noise. (As you'll recall, the concepts of throughput and noise were discussed in Chapter 2.) Local loops may carry analog signals or digital signals. Traditional telephone service uses analog transmission over local loops made of copper wire. Such traditional local loops are limited to a theoretical maximum throughput of only 56 Kbps. However, in reality, the maximum throughput is limited to

53 Kbps by the FCC. Due to noise, analog local loops may experience significantly lower throughput. This is usually not a problem when the line carries voice conversations. But when it must carry data (as in the example of your computer modem dialing in to an Internet Service Provider), the low throughput of a traditional analog local loop can be problematic. Although more and more local loops can now carry digital signals, most local loops in service today still carry analog signals.

Modern digital signaling techniques can increase the local loop's potential throughput to 1.5 Mbps. This higher throughput is desirable when transmitting data over the local loop, or when using the local loop for multiple purposes (for example, to transmit voice conversations and data simultaneously). You will learn more about digital signaling over local loops later in this book.

To transform a traditional analog local loop into a faster digital line, LECs must upgrade their facilities. First, they must upgrade central office switches to switches that are capable of modern digital transmission techniques. In some cases, they must also upgrade the copper wire or replace it with fiber optic cable. Despite the hurdles involved, LECs are eager to replace their old analog facilities with digital ones. In fact, the conversion from analog-capable lines to digital-ready lines is taking place all across the nation. Even less densely populated areas are now getting a choice of fast, digital local loops at approximately twice the cost of traditional phone service. In densely populated urban areas, many carriers are completely rebuilding the local loop infrastructure. They are replacing old copper wiring with fiber optic cables or wireless links, which are capable of much greater throughput. As you might expect, this new media is more expensive to install than the old copper wiring. However, because so many customers are demanding higher bandwidth technologies in these areas, carriers reason that the revenue from greater local loop usage and additional services will overcome the cost of this new infrastructure.

Figure 4-5 shows the slow increase in copper local loops (represented by the number of copper wire terminations at a local CO) compared to the surge in fiber optic local loops (represented by the number of fiber optic terminations at a local CO), which have dramatically increased between 1991 and 2000. Still, however, copper local loops are almost 75 times more common than fiber local loops, with over 217 million copper lines installed compared to 2.9 million fiber optic local loops, according to recent FCC statistics.

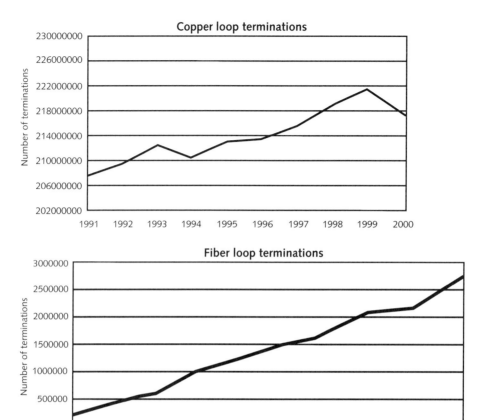

Figure 4-5 Copper vs. fiber optic local loop installation

Serving Area Concepts (SAC)

Outside plant is organized so that individual lines aggregate into pools of local lines, which aggregate into larger conduits, which together feed into a central office. The Bell System introduced this plan to simplify installation, service, billing, and troubleshooting. In suburban and urban areas, outside plant is organized according to the **Serving Area Concepts (SAC)** plan. In rural areas, outside plant is organized according to the **Rural Area Network Design (RAND)** scheme. A rural plan's service area is up to ten times larger than an urban service area, and usually handles a fraction of the number of lines handled by one urban service area.

The SAC scheme is more common than the RAND one; thus, as a telecommunications professional, you are more likely to work with it. The following discussion uses the SAC plan to describe outside plant organization, beginning just beyond the demarcation point and progressing to the central office. For simplicity's sake, this discussion assumes an entirely wire-based outside plant, though as you have learned, outside plant may include other transmission media. Figure 4-6 provides a simplified view of the components that make up outside plant. As you read the discussion that follows, be sure to refer to this diagram.

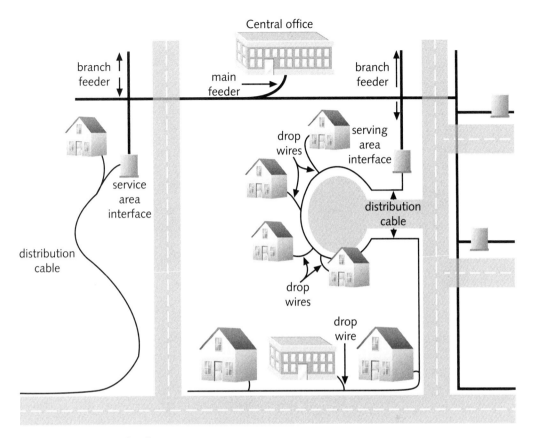

Figure 4-6   Outside plant

The cable that runs from a subscriber's demarcation point to a telephone pole or underground conduit is called the **drop wire**. The drop wire connects the subscriber's home or business line to a **distribution cable**, which gathers multiple drop wires from a neighborhood. Distribution cable is almost always installed underground and encased in a thick tube (usually made of PVC plastic) known as a **conduit**. The conduit protects the wires within the cable from environmental damage. Some drop cables and distribution cables, however, are still aerial (that is, they are strung from a demarc to a telephone pole or from one telephone pole to another).

Distribution cables lead to a **service area interface (SAI)**, a facility in which multiple wire pairs terminate, as shown in Figure 4-7, and connect to a cable called a **branch feeder**. Essentially the SAI consolidates multiple lines into one cable—the branch feeder—that contains enough wire pairs to carry the combined traffic of all the lines. You have probably seen these gray-green boxes behind large buildings or near street intersections, but may not have realized what they contain. Sometimes SAIs are called **terminal boxes**, or colloquially, "terminals," "terms," "cabinets," or "boxes." Because they allow access to hundreds, if not thousands, of phone lines, SAIs are always kept locked to prevent damage or illegal wiretapping. SAIs are owned by the LEC.

Figure 4-7   The inside of a service area interface cabinet

A group of branch feeders are then connected to the backbone of the telephone system, called main feeders. **Main feeders** are responsible for connecting a group of branch feeders to the central office. They may contain as many as 3600 wire pairs. Branch and main feeders, like distribution cable, are installed at least six feet underground in conduits made of a thick plastic sheathing; very rarely will these critical connections run between telephone poles. Main feeder conduits are usually pressurized and may contain a gel or gas that helps to insulate and protect the cables they house. In addition, this conduit may be encased in concrete. Figure 4-8 illustrates a typical installation of underground conduit.

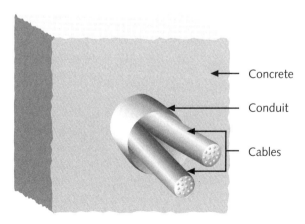

Figure 4-8   Main feeder conduit

In suburban or rural areas, cable is usually buried beneath or alongside streets. In densely populated urban areas, cabling conduits are typically located in underground tunnels that also house other utility lines and equipment. Telephone technicians can access these tunnels via **utility access holes**, more commonly known as **manholes**.

This section has provided a general description of outside plant layout. Each LEC, however, may use a slightly different plan. To keep track of their outside plant, LECs assign numbers to each SAI, branch, and main feeder cable and keep this information, along with subscriber information, in a centralized database. Each LEC maintains drawings of its outside plant that reference these numbers. Figure 4-9 shows part of one LEC's outside plant drawing.

4

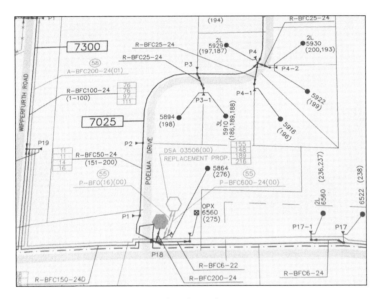

Figure 4-9   A LEC's outside plant drawing

You should now be familiar with the part of a telephone company's infrastructure that connects a subscriber to the central office. You have also been introduced to the types of transmission media, which you learn more about in later chapters. Next, you learn about customer and carrier equipment that is located indoors.

INSIDE PLANT

If outside plant is the cabling and equipment located outside a carrier's central offices, then it makes sense that **inside plant** is the cabling and equipment located inside these places. Every piece of equipment inside a central office must conform to strict government and industry standards. The standards cover not only technical specifications, so that each device integrates seamlessly with every other, but also environmental specifications (such as heat and humidity), electrical specifications (such as grounding and power draw), and safety specifications. The following sections describe the significant facilities found inside a central office and their functions.

Cable Vaults

You have learned that all the lines that connect subscribers to a service provider are encased in a large conduit known as the main feeder. The main feeder conduit, usually a fiber optic cable, enters the CO from underground at a **cable vault**, or **cable entrance facility (CEF)**, a secure, environmentally-controlled room at the central office. Because main feeders enter the cable vault from underground, the cable vault is usually located in the basement of the CO. Figure 4-10 depicts how the cable enters a cable vault; Figure 4-11 shows the view inside a small cable vault.

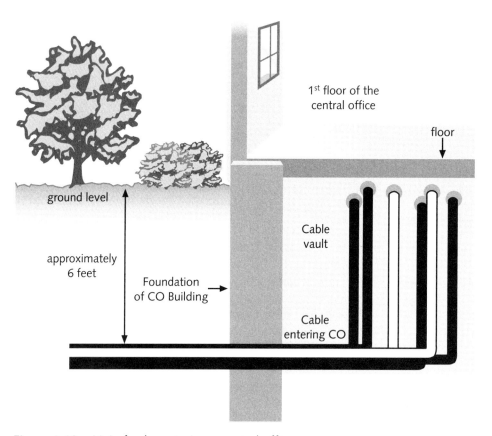

Figure 4-10   Main feeder entering a central office

From the cable vault, the large cables are separated into smaller groups of wire that lead to the main distributing frame, discussed next.

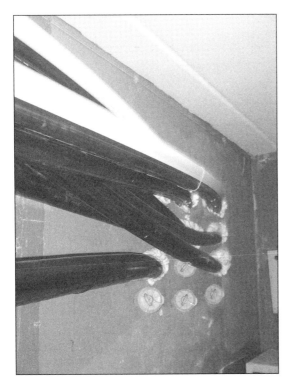

Figure 4-11   Inside a small cable vault

Distributing Frames

A **main distributing frame (MDF)** is a piece of equipment where incoming wires terminate and their circuits are connected to another set of wires that lead to central office equipment. Each distributing frame is actually made up of a large array of smaller panels called punch-down blocks. A **punch-down block** is a row of metallic clips (or receptors) that accept a wire termination. Because of their function, punch-down blocks are also known as **terminal blocks**. Each physical line entering a central office terminates at punch-down blocks on one side of the MDF. Figure 4-12 shows a picture of cables from the cable vault rising through the floor and being separated to terminate on an MDF.

On the opposite side of the MDF, lines exit a separate set of punch-down blocks to eventually connect with the central office switches. Short cables, known as **jumper wires**, are used to connect incoming lines' punch-down blocks with the outgoing lines' punch down blocks, as shown in Figure 4-13. This type of arrangement, in which wires terminating at two sets of punch-down blocks are interconnected, is known as a **cross-connect**.

Each line is identified on the MDF's punch-down blocks with a circuit number. Thanks to the MDF's centralized organization and labeling system, one line can easily be tested, disconnected, or moved from one location without disrupting other lines. In addition to separating and connecting lines, an MDF contains protectors that prevent excess electrical charge that might be carried by outside plant from reaching the equipment inside the central office.

Figure 4-12   Cables separated and terminated at an MDF

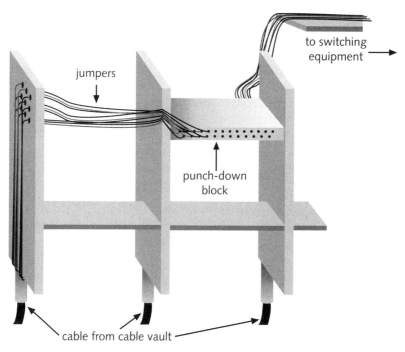

Figure 4-13   Cross-connects in an MDF

The size of a central office's MDF depends on the number of lines, or circuits, it handles. In a small central office, an MDF may be as small as a one-car garage; at a large central office, the MDF may be hundreds of feet long. One MDF may actually consist of many smaller panels. Figure 4-14 shows a main distributing frame at a large central office.

Figure 4-14   A main distributing frame

Racks

Just as you might house your audio/video equipment in specialized cabinets at home, a telecommunications service provider houses its equipment in specialized racks. **Racks** are typically heavy metal frames designed to hold equipment (such as switches) and keep equipment stable, even in the event an earthquake. Equipment is either directly bolted into the rack or outfitted with braces that are then bolted into racks. Racks also enable simple interconnection between different pieces of equipment and pathways for cabling going to and from this equipment. Finally, racks position equipment so that technicians can easily work on it. In the telecommunications professions, racks are an integral part of maintaining an organized workspace.

As you can imagine, racks come in a variety of dimensions, depending on their use. Typical racks used in central offices (for example, those that hold MDF or switching equipment) range from one to seven feet in height and from 19 to 23 inches wide. In the telephony field, racks may also be called **relay racks**, because of their role in relaying lines from the cable vault to the switching equipment. Racks equipped with doors (which may or may not be locked) are also called cabinets. Some racks may be attached to walls, though freestanding racks are, in some environments, more stable. Figure 4-15 shows two different racks that might be used in a central office.

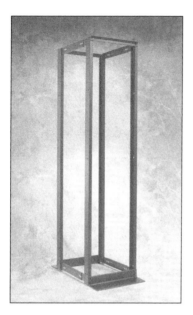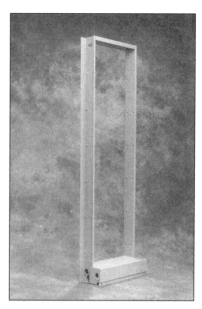

Figure 4-15   Racks used in a central office

When cabling leaves racks, it is often collected in overhead trays, or **runways**. (In exceptional cases, runways may be located above the ceiling.) Runways are not only critical in helping to organize cabling, but also to keep it flat and straight. If cabling (either copper or fiber) is kinked or looped, it may not reliably carry signals. Figure 4-16 shows how runways and racks together help organize central office cabling.

Switching Equipment

As you know, the primary function of a central office is to act as a central connection point and complete calls between customers. Whereas all the outside and inside plant discussed thus far merely helps to transport a signal, a switch interprets the signal and, based on its interpretation, makes decisions about what to do next with the call.

Recall from Chapter 3 that the first telephone switches required an operator to connect lines by plugging a cable into each line's jack on the switchboard. Later switches, such as the step-by-step switch, were electromechanical and required no human intervention. Although some electromechanical switches are still in use, most modern switches are electronic and use digital signals. They are actually types of computers that contain central processing units, software, memory, expansion slots, and network adapters, just like a desktop workstation. A sophisticated, fully-featured telephone switch can cost millions of dollars, and can process telephone calls in nanoseconds. The two major manufacturers of telephone switches used in the United States are Lucent Technologies and Nortel Networks.

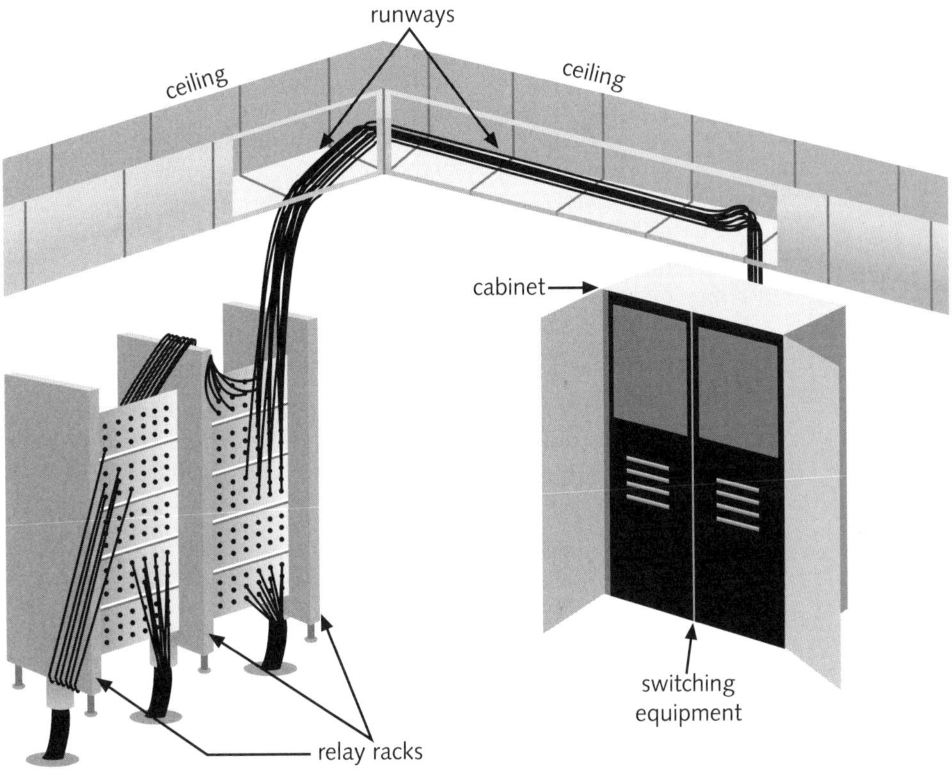

Figure 4-16   Runways and racks in a central office

The following list includes the major functions of switching equipment at a central office:

- Dial tone—**Dial tone** is a sound made up of two frequencies—350 Hz and 440 Hz—that you hear when you pick up your telephone. In the case of residential telephone service, when a customer picks up her telephone handset, her line sends a direct current signal to the switch at her local central office. This signal indicates to the switch that her telephone is **off-hook**, or that the handset has been lifted. In response to this signal, the switch issues a dial tone to her telephone. All of this occurs so quickly that it seems instantaneous to the customer. Switches are also responsible for the other tones, such as busy signals and call waiting signals, that a customer hears under different circumstances.

- Customer and phone number identification—When a line is off-hook and creates a circuit with the switch, it also sends signals to indicate what telephone number the line is associated with. The switch accepts this information and relies on a computerized database to correlate the phone number with billing information. (This is not necessarily the same signal that is used for the Caller ID feature).

- Call setup—**Call setup** is the establishment of a circuit between the caller and the party whose number she has dialed. A switch usually works with other switches at other COs to complete the circuit.

- Call routing—**Call routing** is the determination of the path (through switches and COs) a call's circuit will travel in order to be completed. The route of a call is not necessarily the most geographically direct route. Because of congestion on the public network, or even facilities that happen to be down (for example, in case a construction error has resulted in the severing of a main feeder) a call's route may be indirect. Switches determine this route.

- Call supervision—**Call supervision** is the maintenance of the circuit between a caller and the called party. This function includes knowing when both of the parties have hung up and terminating the connection. It also includes detecting whether the call needs attention (for example, if a customer has the call waiting feature and is accepting a second call on his line). Switches are responsible for call supervision as long as a call is connected.

- Line testing and maintenance—A central office tests its telephone lines regularly to ensure not only that they are operational, but also that they are capable of carrying the traffic they need to carry. With so many customers relying on telephone lines to transmit data and faxes or carry digital signals, it is more important than ever to make sure the connections are free from noise or other factors that might limit their potential bandwidth. Switches can quickly test lines, save the resulting information to a computerized database, and alert CO personnel about faulty circuits. Switches may also indicate the location of a line's fault—for example, they can distinguish between a fault in the local loop versus a fault in the MDF.

The previous list includes just some of the automated functions switching equipment may perform. In addition, switch functions can be controlled by a manual operator through a terminal attached to the switch. This is useful, for example, if a customer calls to complain that his calls keep getting cut off. A maintenance person at the CO could enter commands at the switch's terminal to check the customer's line for problems. If the switch doesn't detect any problems in the LEC's facilities, the maintenance person might suggest that the problem resides in the customer's home wiring (which the switch cannot test).

When placing a call, it is rare that a single switch is responsible for performing all the listed functions. Instead, the switch that accepts your local loop at your closest central office works with other switches, which may be located at other central offices, to complete your call. Later in this chapter, you learn more about how call switching occurs between central offices. In Chapter 6, you will learn specifically how modern telephone switches operate.

Power Equipment

For a telephone to receive and transmit signals, the local loop must carry a small amount of electrical current. This current is provided by the central office. Thus, if the CO loses power, its subscribers lose their dial tone. In addition, because switches rely on electricity, calls cannot be detected or completed without a reliable source of electricity. To ensure that a power loss does not affect telephone communications (which may be necessary in emergencies), each CO has provisions for making its own power, including large batteries and electrical generators. Figure 4-17 shows a bank of batteries at a central office. If a power failure occurs, the CO's batteries take over until the generator (which may be powered by natural gas or diesel) is started and fully functioning. Large COs maintain underground fuel storage tanks that can supply them with power for days. Carriers regularly test their COs for disaster preparedness to make sure that their phone service is reliable.

4

Figure 4-17   Batteries at a central office

Structured Cabling

Just as the layout of the cables and equipment that belong to outside plant follow standard patterns, so too does the cabling that makes up inside plant. **Structured cabling** is the design recommended by standards organizations for uniform, enterprise-wide, multivendor cabling systems. Structured cabling suggests how networking media can best be installed to maximize performance and minimize upkeep. It specifies standards without regard for the type of media or transmission technology used on the network.

Before you can understand the rules governing the organization of inside plant cabling, however, you need to learn more about wireline transmission and media characteristics. Chapter 8 is dedicated to these topics. For now, just keep in mind that the two most popular organizing principles for inside wiring are the TIA/EIA and NEC (national electric code) standards.

CENTRAL OFFICE HIERARCHY

As you know, a central office (CO) is a phone company facility where multiple lines terminate and are then interconnected. The PSTN contains over 25,000 central offices across the United States. But not all central offices are alike. In fact, depending on the type of calls they switch, central offices may belong to one of three different categories: local, tandem, or toll.

As you learned in Chapter 3, a local office is the central office that is closest to the customer. Local offices terminate customer lines and are responsible for customer services, including dial tone, call setup, and call services, such as call waiting. Local offices may also be called **end offices**, because they reside at the end of the PSTN; that is, they are the last switching location in the network before the local loop. Recall that local loops are typically no longer than three miles. Thus, the **serving area** of a local office—the geographical boundary that includes all its subscribers—extends roughly three miles in all directions from the CO. Calls between subscribers whose lines terminate at the same local office (for example, a call between you and your next-door neighbor) can be handled exclusively by that local office's switch. Most calls, however, do not fall into this category. Instead, they rely on local offices to direct their call to a tandem office.

A tandem office is a type of central office that handles calls between central offices. Tandem offices are connected to each other via trunks. A **trunk** is a transmission route between switches that typically has a great deal more capacity than a feeder. Note that a tandem office does not connect directly with subscriber lines. Instead, it serves as an intermediate switching point for all calls that do not start and end in the same local office. Such calls could still be local to one city, or they might be long distance (either intrastate or interstate). For example, if you live in Pittsburgh, PA and you dial the telephone number for your uncle in State College, PA, approximately 135 miles away, the number you dialed is initially interpreted by a switch at your local office. After that switch recognizes that the number you've dialed is not serviced by that same local office, the switch passes the call to a tandem office. The tandem office may pass your call to one or more other tandem offices before it reaches your uncle's local office in State College.

The original meaning of a toll office was a central office that handled calls that originated and terminated within the same area code or LATA, but not within the same local office. They were historically the office to which end offices would route calls that did not terminate in the end office's serving area. Toll offices, like tandem offices, are intermediate switching points between other central offices. As such, they do not connect directly with local loops. Since the breakup of AT&T, a toll office has come to mean any central office that handles the intermediate switching of a toll (or non-free) call between central offices. In fact, you may hear the term "toll office" used synonymously with "tandem office."

COs may also be organized according to class, with Class 1 being the largest (in other words, the COs that handle the most traffic). These class designations are assigned according to the central office's function in the PSTN. Class 1 COs, which are a type of toll office, are also known as **regional offices**. There are only a few of these large, Class 1 COs in the United States. At the bottom of the hierarchy sit the Class 5 COs, which are the same as local (or end) offices. When the PSTN was owned entirely by the Bell System, Class 2, 3, and 4 offices were each assigned unique functions in the hierarchy, related to the geographic range they serviced (for example, long distance within a state versus long distance within a region of the country). However, now that switching equipment and trunks can handle more traffic and competitive carriers participate in the public network, all central offices between Class 1 and Class 5—whether they accept intrastate or interstate calls—are simply known as tandem or toll offices. Thus, the hierarchy of the central office network is not as deeply stratified as it used to be.

4

Figure 4-18 depicts a simplified view of the central office hierarchy, with each type of office identified by its class and its more familiar name.

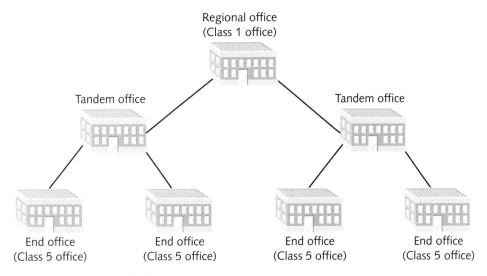

Figure 4-18   Central office hierarchy

Two phone calls from one city in the United States to another city across the country may or may not go through all the same central offices, depending on telephone traffic patterns at the time the calls are placed. Phone call routing, which is computer controlled, follows the best, fastest path available at the moment each call is placed. Sometimes, the fastest path may route a call away from the destination before going back to it, because the roundabout route is less congested. No matter what its route, however, a call must go through the end offices for both the source and destination parties.

CARRIER CONNECTIONS

Now that you are familiar with the hierarchy of central offices in the PSTN, you might wonder how many different common carriers work within this hierarchy to complete calls. This is a good question, and the answer is, "It all depends." You'll learn why this is true in the following sections.

LEC-to-LEC Connections

As you have learned, the easiest type of call to understand is one that stays within a single LEC's local office. This type of call can be handled exclusively by the LEC's local office switch. But if a call leaves the local office's serving area or is between parties who subscribe to two different LECs' services, a connection between carriers is necessary.

Because a call's circuit must always involve at least one LEC, it is useful to remember that a LEC's local office can connect either to subscribers through the local loop, or to other central offices through trunks, as shown in Figure 4-19.

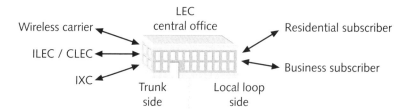

Figure 4-19   LEC connection point

When an IXC or another LEC wants to use the LEC's facilities, it connects to the LEC's central office through its trunks. For example, suppose a facilities-based CLEC in Texas called AMA Telecom establishes its own small end office and some local loops to customers in downtown Austin. Because Southwestern Bell Corporation (SBC) is the dominant ILEC in that area, most Austin residents probably get their local loop service from SBC. AMA Telecom would need to arrange a connection from its POP in Austin to a Southwestern Bell trunk that leads to the nearest SBC tandem CO, as shown in Figure 4-20. This allows AMA Telecom to complete local calls between its subscribers and SBC subscribers.

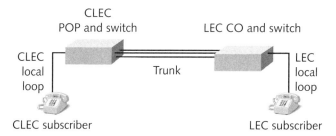

Figure 4-20   Example of a facilities-based CLEC connection to a LEC

In this example, a call initiated by an AMA Telecom subscriber signals the AMA Telecom switch to route the call to SBC. SBC's switch accepts the call and, using the signaling information from the AMA Telecom switch, completes the call to the number specified.

As you have learned, switches in different central offices communicate with each other over trunks to pass off calls. For example, if an end office switch interprets the number a person dials and determines that the call cannot be completed within its CO, the switch transfers the call over a trunk to a switch at a tandem CO. After the switches determine the best route for a call's circuit, the end office switch retransmits the dialed number to the receiving switch. In modern switching systems, it also transmits information about the call, including the source's phone number and special billing information. This information, in addition to call status and routing information, are communicated over a separate path on the network than voice signals use, a technique known as **out-of-band signaling**. Using a separate path ensures that the signals are more secure and less likely to cause network congestion. Out-of-band signaling makes it possible to connect calls very quickly.

The most common form of out-of-band signaling that occurs between switches today is signaling system 7 (SS7), a standard approved by the ITU in 1984. Prior to SS7, switches used the common channel interoffice signaling (CCIS) standard, a similar signaling system that preceded SS7. Both signaling systems are explained in detail in Chapter 6. For now, it is enough to know that switches use out-of-band signaling primarily to expedite call setup. Once a call is connected, the two switches continue to exchange data about the call status so that, for example, the original end office switch knows when the customer's line is free again.

By purchasing its own switch, the CLEC reaps the benefit of not having to pay the ILEC monthly switch and trunk leasing fees. However, some CLECs prefer to **collocate**, or lease space, for a switch in another carrier's point of presence (the location where a CLEC leases space may be an ILEC, CLEC, or IXC central office or even an ISP's data center). By leasing space, CLECs benefit from the ILEC's well-established, robust infrastructure. An example of a CLEC collocating in another carrier's facility, and then connecting to an ILEC, is shown in Figure 4-21.

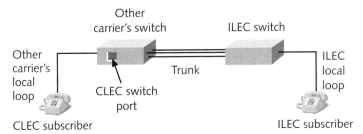

Figure 4-21   Example of a collocating CLEC connecting to an ILEC

 You may see the term "collocate" spelled "colocate" or co-locate." Any of these three spellings is acceptable. The FCC prefers "collocate," although many businesses in the telecommunications industry prefer one of the other two spellings.

As described earlier, if a telephone call originates and terminates within the same local office, the call does not need to be passed to a tandem or toll office. But if a CLEC has collocated its switches within an ILEC's end office, a telephone call may be handled in one end office and yet still need to be transferred from one switch to another if the calling party uses a different LEC than the called party uses.

As you learned earlier, CLECs may be facilities-based (as in the previous example of AMA Telecom) or resellers. Recall that CLEC resellers merely lease facilities from other LECs and then resell the local telephone service under their name. In this case, the CLEC's telephone service uses the other LEC's infrastructure and is indistinguishable in a drawing such as the preceding figures. Moreover, the reseller's services are indistinguishable in quality from the LEC's services. However, the LEC's switching software tracks the call's origin, destination, duration, and other particulars so that the LEC can accurately bill the reseller for services.

LEC-to-IXC Connections

Of course, many calls do not stay within LATAs and therefore must connect to an interLATA carrier, or IXC. Every IXC must interconnect with every LEC that it intends to transmit calls to and receive calls from. Thus, a nationwide long distance carrier, such as AT&T, creates interconnection agreements with every LEC in the nation. As with most CLECs, IXCs connect to LECs via trunks from their POPs, as shown in Figure 4-22.

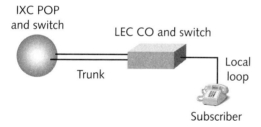

Figure 4-22   Example of an IXC connecting to a LEC

The full picture of an IXC's interconnection with LECs during a long distance call is displayed in Figure 4-23. Bear in mind that this is a great oversimplification of the process. In fact, several types of COs could be involved between the local subscriber and the IXC's POP. To complicate matters further, the two local subscribers might subscribe to different LECs.

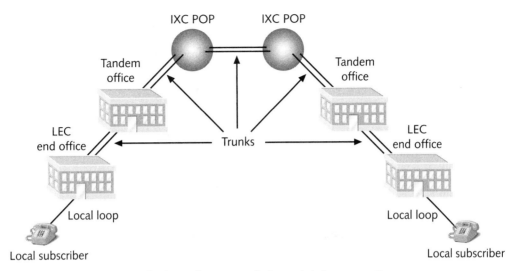

Figure 4-23   Example of a long distance call through interconnections

To demonstrate how a call travels between subscribers located in different parts of the country, let's trace one possible path of a phone call from Angela, who lives in Seattle, to her father, Jose, in Tampa. In this hypothetical situation, Angela picks up her phone. The switch at Angela's Class 5 central office (or end office) issues a dial tone to her line. Next, Angela dials her father's number, and her request to connect with this number is transmitted over the local loop to her end office, called "Seattle Main," just a few miles from her house. The switching equipment at Seattle Main interprets her request and recognizes that the destination number belongs to a different exchange. In other words, the switch acknowledges that the call cannot be handled within the Seattle Main end office. Thus, it transfers the request to its closest available tandem office—for example, a CO in Portland, Oregon. That central office's switching equipment recognizes that the call does not belong in the region and passes it off to a regional, Class 1 CO in Sacramento, California. This central office in turn passes the call off to another regional, Class 1 CO that is closer to the Jose's local office. Perhaps this Class 1 CO is in Atlanta. The Atlanta regional office passes the call to a tandem office in Tampa, Florida, which finally passes off the call to Jose's end office, a Class 5 CO called "Tampa Main," which is just a few miles from his house. Notice that, in this case, the call was routed through four central offices. If Angela called Jose again at another time, the call might be routed through different or more central offices, due to the traffic on the PSTN at that time.

Because of the long history of the telecommunications industry and the government's involvement in it, interconnection agreements between carriers are inordinately complex. Rates for using another carrier's facilities are regulated by the FCC or the state PUC, depending on whether the services are interstate or intrastate, and these rates may frequently change. Billing is even more difficult to understand, and thankfully, computers have automated that process. The following section simply attempts to provide an overview of what services are billed between carriers and how service fees are set.

BILLING BETWEEN CARRIERS

To understand the concepts involved in billing, it helps to begin with a discussion of interconnection with the LECs, which are an ever-present factor in each telephone call. As you have learned, ILECs are required by the Telecommunications Act of 1996 to allow other carriers to interconnect with or lease their facilities at reasonable rates. The federal government left it up to the state PUCs to establish what these rates should be within each state. The fees charged by ILECs are based on the leasing carrier's:

- Grade of service received
- Number of trunks used
- Amount of traffic transmitted
- Placement of equipment in ILEC's facility, also called collocation
- Facilities and circuit installation
- Maintenance and support agreement

In varying situations, some of these charges may not apply, and rates may differ from state to state. In addition, carriers have a large menu of options from which to choose, making the fees even more variable. But to begin with a simple example, suppose a CLEC leases facilities from BellSouth in Florida and pays approximately $6000 per month for full use of an entire access switch. If the CLEC doesn't expect to carry enough traffic to warrant an entire switch, it can lease merely a port on a switch for much less. In addition to the monthly switch fee, the CLEC pays BellSouth a per-minute use fee for carrying traffic over the local loop. Before the CLEC can begin providing its service, it must pay BellSouth a one-time installation and configuration fee. Optional services, such as technical support and maintenance, may be added if the CLEC chooses to pay for them.

When an IXC uses LEC facilities to originate or terminate a call, it pays a per-minute use charge for the local switch, a per-minute use charge for the local loop, and a per minute use charge for the LEC's infrastructure. In addition, the IXC also pays a one-time installation and configuration fee for each switch connection. As with the CLEC/ILEC interconnection, many optional services can add to the cost of interconnection. Most of these charges are regulated by state PUCs. In some interstate cases, however, the FCC regulates these rates.

As you may have already concluded, switches gather most of the information that makes billing possible. Switches use a **Carrier Identification Code (CIC)**, a unique four-digit number that identifies an IXC as its traffic is carried by LEC facilities. The CIC is used for both call routing and billing between carriers. In addition, the switches track originating and terminating phone numbers, route, and duration of the call to determine fees. One or more CICs may be assigned to a single carrier. Carriers then use software programs to regularly compile the data collected by their switches and issue bills to other carriers. Developing software to analyze this billing information is an industry of its own, and one of the latest features developers are touting is real-time billing between carriers. That is, each carrier would be billed for its use of another carrier's facilities while or directly after the use occurred. Similar software can verify the accuracy of bills that carriers receive from other carriers.

NORTH AMERICAN NUMBERING PLAN (NANP)

A number of standards need to be followed for carriers to facilitate billing and interconnection. One important standard governs how telephone numbers are assigned. In 1947, AT&T established the **North American Numbering Plan (NANP)**, a scheme for assigning unique phone numbers to every line in the country. This plan allowed subscribers to dial long distance directly (without having to go through an operator) for the first time. Although the numbering plan has undergone some changes, that system is essentially the same one used in North America today. However, recent projections indicate that at the rate new numbers are being assigned (due to the growth and popularity of cellular phones, second home telephone lines, fax modems, pagers, PC modems), the remaining available numbers may only last another twelve years. Industry experts are already working on developing a new numbering plan.

For numbering purposes, North America is divided into several smaller geographic regions called **Numbering Plan Areas (NPAs)**, more commonly known as area codes. The format of an NPA code is Nab, where N is any digit 2 through 9, a is any digit 0 through 9, and b is also any digit 0 through 9. For example, if you live in downtown Chicago, your NPA code is 312. If you live in Fresno, California, your NPA code is 559. Prior to 1995, the middle digit of an NPA code had to be "0" or "1," and this allowed for only 152 different area codes across the continent. However, the middle digit restriction was removed thanks to newer switching technology and the increasing demand for new numbers. Now, up to 640 NPAs are available, and many states have quickly taken advantage of the release of new numbers.

Although there are 800 possible permutations of the Nab format, only 640 are available for use as geographically-based area codes. This is because some numbers are reserved for special purposes. The following list describes these reserved NPAs:

- Easily Recognizable Codes (ERCs)—When the second and third digit of the NPA are identical (for example, the numbers 888 or 411), the NPA is known as an **Easily Recognizable Code (ERC)**. These NPAs are reserved for special purposes—for example, 888 is reserved for toll-free calls.

- N9b—These 80 NPA codes have been reserved for use when the current NANP numbering scheme undergoes further expansion.

- 37b and 96b—These 20 NPA codes have been reserved in case a previously unanticipated need for blocks of 10 contiguous NPAs arises.

The next part of any telephone number is its central office prefix, or **NXX number**. For example, if your telephone number is 246-8888, your NXX is "246." NXX numbers follow the same format as NPA codes, N*ab*, where N is any digit 2 through 9, *a* is any digit 0 through 9, and *b* is also any digit 0 through 9. If two phone numbers share the same NPA and NXX numbers, you can assume that their local loops terminate at the same CO. For example, if your telephone number is 246-8888 and the number of your friend who lives a few blocks away is 246-9999, you know that both your telephone lines terminate at the same CO. One central office can service several NXXs. For example, although you and your next door neighbor share the same local CO, your telephone number might be 246-8888 whereas hers is 235-9191.

The final four digits in the North American Numbering Plan indicate the subscriber's line. Within a single NPA-NXX, each four-digit number must be unique so that calls can be routed properly. For example, if your number is (559) 246-8888, another subscriber line ending with "8888" in the 246 NXX within the 559 area code cannot exist. However, the number 246-8888 may exist in a different area code.

If you already have a telephone line, but want to subscribe to your carrier's high-speed digital access service, your telephone company representative will ask you for your NPA-NXX number. This number helps determine what type of service you are eligible for and which central office must accommodate your service request.

A fairly new addition to the NANP is the **Automatic Numbering Identification (ANI)**. ANI numbers are two digits transmitted in a telephone signal from a customer's phone to the central office switch that identify the calling party's line number for billing purposes. The line number is often, but not always, the same as the calling party's telephone number. In a large business with many telephone lines, each line may have a different phone number, but they may share the same ANI. That is, each number indicates that its calls are billed to a single telephone number. Unlike Caller ID, ANI does not indicate the name of the subscriber. ANI is strictly for use by the central office's switching equipment, and it is only used with calls placed over digital telephone connections.

CHAPTER SUMMARY

- ❑ The Public Switched Telephone Network (PSTN), also known as the Plain Old Telephone System (POTS), is defined as the collection of local and long distance providers' facilities and connections that are available for public voice (and more recently, data) communications. You may also think of the PSTN as the old Bell System plus its post-1984 competitors.

❏ Common carriers are entities directly involved in supplying regulated telecommunications services to the public. To be considered a common carrier, a company must make its services available to any member of the public who chooses to subscribe to those services. LECs and IXCs, as well as many non-traditional service providers, such as wireless communications companies, are common carriers.

❏ Outside plant refers to the system of cabling, poles, towers, and other connectivity equipment between the demarcation point and central offices. Included in outside plant are: the demarcation point, local loop, and serving area concepts.

❏ The demarcation point indicates where the LEC's responsibility for a line ends and the subscriber's facilities begin. Also known as a network interface device, the demarcation point is usually contained within a demarcation box to protect it from tampering and environmental damage.

❏ The local loop, or "last mile," is the connection between a subscriber and the nearest central office. The original local loops were all copper wiring, and although most are still made of copper, they may also be fiber optic or wireless.

❏ Local loops are supplied by local exchange carriers. Though they are the most expensive part of the public network, they are also the place where the most money stands to be made, because they are the link to the customer.

❏ Outside plant is organized so that individual lines aggregate into pools of local lines, which aggregate into larger conduits, which together feed into a central office. In most areas, this organization follows the Serving Area Concepts (SAC) plan, which was originally developed by the Bell System.

❏ According to SAC, the cable that runs from a subscriber's demarcation point to a telephone pole or underground conduit is called the drop wire. The drop wire connects the subscriber's home or business line to a distribution cable, which gathers multiple drop wires from a neighborhood.

❏ Distribution cables lead to a service area interface (SAI), a facility in which multiple wire pairs terminate and connect to a cable called a branch feeder. Sometimes SAIs are called terminal boxes, or colloquially, "terminals," "terms," "cabinets," or "boxes."

❏ A group of branch feeders are then connected to the backbone of the telephone system, called main feeders. Main feeders are responsible for connecting a group of branch feeders to the central office. Branch and main feeders, like distribution cable, are installed at least six feet underground in conduits made of a thick plastic sheathing. This conduit may be encased in concrete.

❏ The main feeder conduit, usually a fiber optic cable, enters the CO from underground at a cable vault, or cable entrance facility (CEF), a secure, environmentally-controlled room at the central office.

❏ From the cable vault, the large cables are separated into smaller groups of wire that lead to the main distributing frame (MDF). Each line entering a central office terminates at punch-down blocks one side of the MDF. On the other side of the MDF, lines exit a separate set of punch-down blocks to eventually connect with the central office switches.

❏ Racks, or relay racks, are typically heavy metal frames designed to hold equipment (such as switches) and keep equipment stable. Racks also enable simple interconnection between different pieces of equipment and pathways for cabling going to and from this equipment. Finally, racks position equipment so that technicians can easily work on it.

❏ Part of a central office's inside plant is the switching equipment. Switches provide dial tone, along with other tones, such as busy signals and call waiting signals, to telephone customers. They interpret dialed numbers and determine how to route calls to their destination. They establish calls, supervise and maintain calls, and track information about calls for billing purposes. They also perform automated line testing and maintenance.

❏ Every central office must have reliable sources of power in case of a power failure so that the switches can operate and customers will continue to have telephone service. For immediate emergency power, the CO relies on banks of batteries. After a short period of time, electrical generators can begin supplying emergency power.

❏ A local office is the central office that is closest to the customer. Local offices terminate customer lines and are responsible for customer services, including dial tone, call setup, and call services, such as call waiting. Local offices may also be called end offices, because they are the last switching location in the network before the local loop.

❏ A tandem office is a central office that handles calls between multiple central offices. Tandem offices are connected to each other via trunks. A trunk is a transmission route between switches that typically has a great deal more capacity than a feeder. A tandem office does not connect directly with subscriber lines. Instead, it serves as an intermediate switching points for all calls that do not start and end in the same local office.

❏ Since the breakup of AT&T, a toll office has come to mean any central office that handles the intermediate switching of a toll (or non-free) call between central offices.

❏ Class 1 COs, which are a type of toll office, are also known as regional offices. There are only a few of these large, Class 1 COs in the United States. At the bottom of the hierarchy sit the Class 5 COs, which are the same as local (or end) offices.

❏ Information about a call, including the source's phone number, special billing information, call status, and routing information, is communicated over a separate path on the network than voice signals use, a technique known as out-of-band signaling. Using a separate path ensures that the signals are more secure and less likely to cause network congestion. Out-of-band signaling also enables calls to connect very quickly.

❑ A call that stays within a single LEC's local office can be handled exclusively by that CO's switching equipment. But if a call leaves the local office's serving area or is between parties who subscribe to two different LECs' services, a connection between carriers is necessary. The connection between carriers occurs along trunks between tandem or toll offices.

❑ Rates for using another carrier's facilities are regulated by the FCC or the state PUC, depending on whether the services are interstate or intrastate, and these rates may frequently change.

❑ Fees charged by ILECs to other carriers are based on the leasing carrier's: grade of service received, number of trunks used, amount of traffic transmitted, placement of equipment in ILEC's facility, facilities and circuit installation, and maintenance and support agreement. In varying situations, some of these charges may not apply, and rates may differ from state to state. In addition, carriers have a large menu of options from which to choose, making the fees even more variable.

❑ Switches use a Carrier Identification Code (CIC), a unique four-digit number that identifies an IXC as its traffic is carried by LEC facilities. The CIC is used for both call routing and billing between carriers.

❑ North America is divided into several geographic regions called Numbering Plan Areas (NPAs), more commonly known as area codes. The format of an NPA code is N*ab*, where N is any digit 2 through 9, *a* is any digit 0 through 9, and *b* is also any digit 0 through 9.

❑ The next part of any telephone number is its central office prefix, or NXX number. NXX numbers follow the same format as NPA codes, N*ab*, where N is any digit 2 through 9, *a* is any digit 0 through 9, and *b* is also any digit 0 through 9. If two phone numbers share the same NPA and NXX numbers, you can assume that their local loops terminate at the same CO.

❑ The final four digits in the North American Numbering Plan indicate the subscriber's line. Within a single NPA-NXX, each four-digit number must be unique so that calls can be routed properly.

KEY TERMS

Automatic Numbering Identification (ANI) — Two digits transmitted with a phone number to identify the number to which the call should be billed.

branch feeders — The part of the outside plant that connects service area interfaces to the main feeders in the telephone network's outside plant.

cable entrance facility (CEF) — The point where a main feeder conduit, which usually contains fiber optic cable, enters the CO from underground. Also called a *cable vault*.

cable vault — *See* cable entrance facility.

call routing — The determination of the path (through switches and COs) that a call's circuit will travel in order to be completed. The route of a call is not necessarily the most geographically direct route. Because of congestion on the public network, or even facilities that happen to be down (for example, if a construction error resulted in the severing of a main feeder), a call's route may be indirect. Switches perform call routing.

call setup — The establishment of a circuit between the caller and the party whose number she has dialed.

call supervision — The maintenance of the circuit between a caller and the called party. This function includes tracking when both of the parties have hung up and then terminating the connection. It also includes detecting whether the call needs attention. Switches are responsible for call supervision as long as a call is connected.

Carrier Identification Code (CIC) — A unique four-digit number that identifies an IXC as its traffic is handled by LEC facilities. The CIC is used for both call routing and billing between carriers.

collocate (also colocate, co-locate) — To lease space and house equipment within at another organization's facilities. Companies usually collocate to take advantage of another organization's superior infrastructure or location.

conduit — A thick tube (usually made of PVC plastic) in which cables are housed to remain protected from environmental damage.

common carrier — A direct provider of a public telecommunications service that is subject to regulation by the FCC and state public utilities commissions and that is available to any member of the public who wishes to subscribe to the services.

cross-connect — An arrangement in which wires terminating at two sets of punchdown blocks are interconnected.

demarc box — A box (at the demarcation point between a customer's facilities and a service provider's facilities) that contains a network interface device. Demarc boxes prevent both unauthorized tampering and environmental damage to the network interface device. In most cases, the demarc box is the property of the LEC.

demarcation point (demarc) — The place that marks the difference between a LEC's facilities and the subscriber's CPE. On a residence, the demarcation point is usually a small termination box attached to the side of the house.

dial tone — A sound made up of two frequencies—350 Hz and 440 Hz—that you hear when you pick up your telephone. Local office switches issue dial tone to a line when they detect that it is off-hook.

distribution cable — The cabling that connects multiple subscriber drop wires in a neighborhood to a larger conduit.

drop wire — The cable that runs from a subscriber's demarcation point to a telephone pole or underground conduit.

Easily Recognizable Code (ERC) — An NPA in which the second and third digit are identical (for example, the numbers 888 or 411). In the North American Numbering Plan, these NPAs are reserved for special purposes—for example, 888 is reserved for toll-free calls.

end office — A Class 5 COs that accept local loop connections. End offices are the only COs that terminate local subscriber lines.

facilities-based — A type of carrier that builds its own facilities (such as microwave links and underground cables) in addition to leasing ILEC facilities to provide service under their name.

inside plant — The cabling and equipment located within a carrier's central offices.

jumper wires — The short cables often used to complete circuits between punchdown blocks.

last mile — *See* local loop.

line — A circuit used for voice or data transmission. Line may also refer to the physical wire used to complete a circuit.

local loop — The portion of a subscriber's connection to a carrier's network that links a residence or business to its local phone company's central office.

main distributing frame (MDF) — The place where numerous individual incoming lines first terminate at a central office. The MDF contains several punch-down blocks that allow incoming lines to be cross-connected with another set of lines that leads to the carrier's switching equipment.

main feeder — The part of the outside plant that connects all the aggregated branch feeders to a central office.

manhole — *See* utility access hole.

network interface device (NID) — The physical point at which a subscriber's facilities connect with a service provider's facilities.

North American Numbering Plan (NANP) — The scheme for assigning unique numbers to every telephone line in North America. NANP was originally developed by AT&T in 1947. Due to the increasing need for new numbers, NANP standards are continually being assessed and revised.

Numbering Plan Areas (NPAs) — The geographically divided regions that indicate the first three digits of a North American phone number. NPAs are more commonly known as area codes.

NXX number — A prefix that represents a line's central office prefix, the NXX comes after the NPA in the North American Numbering Plan.

off-hook — The condition of a line after a subscriber has lifted the handset on his telephone.

OSP — *See* outside plant.

out-of-band signaling — A technique in which signals between switches, including all status and routing information, are communicated over a separate path on the network than voice signals use. Out-of-band signaling offers greater security and reduced call setup time than if signaling were carried over voice network paths.

outside plant — The system of cabling, poles, towers, and other connectivity equipment between the demarcation point and central offices (in other words, the physical components that make up the local loop).

Plain Old Telephone System (POTS) — *See* Public Switched Telephone Network.

point of presence — A carrier's facility, where they typically have either a switch or router to connect to a network.

punch-down blocks — An array of small metallic clips (or receptors) that accept wire terminations.

Public Switched Telephone Network (PSTN) — The collection of local and long distance providers' switching facilities and networks that are available for public voice communications, also known as the Plain Old Telephone System (POTS).

rack — A heavy metal frame designed to hold equipment (such as switches) and keep equipment stable.

regional office — A Class 3 central office. Regional offices service large regions of the country and handle toll calls from tandem COs.

relay rack — *See* rack. (The term "relay rack" is more commonly used in the telephony field, because of the rack's role in relaying cables from the cable vault to the switching equipment.)

reseller — A type of telecommunications carrier that leases links or other facilities in wholesale amounts from another carrier and resells the service to consumers under its name.

runway — An overhead tray designed to hold cables.

Rural Area Network Design (RAND) — The method of organizing outside plant in rural areas according to a distribution scheme, in which individual lines aggregate into pools of local lines, which aggregate into larger conduits, which together feed into a central office.

service area interface (SAI) — A cabinet in which multiple wires from a limited geographical area terminate. SAIs are also known as *terminal boxes*, or colloquially as "terminals," "boxes," or "cabinets."

serving area — The geographical boundary that includes all of a central office's or a carrier's subscribers.

Serving Area Concepts (SAC) — The method of organizing outside plant in suburban and urban areas according to a distribution scheme, in which individual lines aggregate into pools of local lines, which aggregate into larger conduits, which together feed into a central office.

station protector — A device attached to incoming LEC lines at the network interface that prevents a customer's telephone equipment from being damaged in case excessive current affects the line.

structured cabling — The design recommended by cabling standards organizations for uniform, enterprise-wide, multivendor cabling systems. Structured cabling suggests how networking media can best be installed to maximize performance and minimize upkeep. It specifies standards without regard for the type of media or transmission technology used on the network.

terminal block — *See* punch-down block.

terminal box — *See* service area interface.

termination — The place where a wire ends (for example, in a connector) or is connected with another part of the network (for example, at a punch-down block).

trunk — A transmission route between switches, either within one central office or between different central offices. Trunks typically have a great deal more capacity than feeders.

utility access hole — An access point to underground tunnels that house branch feeder or main feeder conduits plus other utility lines and equipment. Utility access holes are also known as manholes.

4

REVIEW QUESTIONS

1. What is the term used to describe a LEC that does not own its own facilities but leases other carriers' facilities?

   a. IXC

   b. ILEC

   c. facilities-based CLEC

   d. reseller

2. Which of the following is an example of a nontraditional common carrier?

   a. Verizon

   b. Southwestern Bell

   c. Iridium

   d. AT&T

3. On a residence, where would you find the network interface device?

   a. telecommunications closet

   b. serving area interface

   c. cable vault

   d. demarc box

4. What organization is responsible for building and maintaining the local loop?

   a. IXC

   b. FCC

   c. IEC

   d. LEC

5. What class of central office connects the local loops to a carrier's network?

   a. 5

   b. 4

   c. 2

   d. 1

6. Which of the following is also known as a "regional office?"

   a. a Class 5 central office

   b. a Class 1 central office

   c. a tandem switching office

   d. an end office

7. Where does the maintenance of a telephone line become a resident's responsibility?

   a. drop wire

   b. branch feeder

   c. distribution cable

   d. demarcation point

8. What is one reason for the last mile being the most expensive part of the telecommunications network?

   a. It is responsible for the least amount of revenue.

   b. It requires frequent upgrades.

   c. It must be supplied separately for each individual subscriber.

   d. It is difficult to troubleshoot.

9. What medium has traditionally been used for local loops?

   a. fiber optic cable

   b. copper wire

   c. aluminum wire

   d. microwave

10. Which of the following would be found in a central office's relay racks?

   a. batteries

   b. main feeder

   c. switching equipment

   d. demarc box

11. What type of outside plant connects a main feeder to a serving area interface?

    a. main feeder cable

    b. backbone

    c. distribution cable

    d. branch feeder cable

12. Which of the following is one function of a central office's MDF?

    a. terminating subscriber lines

    b. call setup

    c. call supervision

    d. issuing dial tone

13. At what part of a central office does the main feeder enter?

    a. cable vault

    b. service area interface

    c. branch feeder

    d. MDF

14. What does a central office rely on for electricity immediately after its main power source fails?

    a. hydrogen fuel cells

    b. diesel or gas electrical generator

    c. a bank of batteries

    d. its closest tandem office

15. Once a central office receives a subscriber's call, what type of device determines whether the call can be handled solely by a Class 5 CO?

    a. switch

    b. modem

    c. multiplexer

    d. CPE

16. What are the two significant advantages of using out-of-band signaling?

17. What does a CLEC gain by collocating a switch in an ILEC's CO, as opposed to reselling ILEC services?

    a. faster call routing

    b. less equipment maintenance

    c. use of a robust infrastructure

    d. discounts on traffic fees

18. Which of the following types of calls might never leave a Class 5 CO?

    a. interstate

    b. intrastate interLATA

    c. intrastate intraLATA

    d. interstate interLATA

19. Which of the following organizations helps to determine how much an ILEC charges an IXC for use of its facilities?

    a. PUC

    b. ITU

    c. IEEE

    d. TIA/EIA

20. How would a CLEC typically connect to a LEC's local office?

    a. along a trunk

    b. along a local loop

    c. along a main feeder

    d. along a branch feeder

21. What do LEC central office switches use to identify IXC traffic?

    a. ANI

    b. SAI

    c. POP

    d. CIC

22. If two phone numbers have the same NPA and NXX, what can you assume about the subscribers?

    a. They share a leased line.

    b. They live on the same block.

    c. They connect to the same Class 5 CO.

    d. They connect to the same Class 1 CO.

23. What is a synonym for NPA?

    a. NXX

    b. area code

    c. exchange number

    d. ANI

24. Why was it necessary in the 1990s to allow area codes to include a middle digit other than 0 or 1?

25. Which of the following NPAs cannot be used for a residential subscriber's telephone number?

   a. 212

   b. 569

   c. 808

   d. 411

4

HANDS-ON PROJECTS

Project 4-1

In learning about physical elements of a network, such as switches, cabling, racks, and MDFs, there is no substitute for having worked with these elements on a daily basis. Because you probably do not work in a central office, the next best thing is to tour a central office and interview the people who do work there. For this project, you need only a curious mind, cooperative LEC personnel, a pencil, and paper. If you are undertaking this project as part of a class, you might want to arrange your tour with other classmates and go as a group.

1. Contact your local telephone company to schedule a central office tour of a Class 5 (end) office. (If you aren't certain what LEC to call, take a look at your most recent phone bill.) You can obtain the number for your LEC from the phone book. (Although your LEC lists a telephone number on your monthly bill, it may not be a local number and it probably won't connect you with personnel who can help you arrange a tour.)

2. Politely explain that you are a student in telecommunications who is doing research for a class project. You will find that most professionals are happy to offer their knowledge and time to help with an educational endeavor. Ask for the number of the nearest Class 5 central office. Then call the central office and schedule a tour with the manager or supervisor at that CO.

3. During your tour, make certain to see the cable vault, batteries (and electrical generator, if possible), MDF, and switching equipment. Attempt to follow the path of an incoming line (or circuit) from cable vault to switch.

4. Ask lots of questions and take notes on the responses you receive. Following is a list of questions to get you started:

   ❐ How many circuits can the CO's switch handle at one time?

   ❐ How many subscribers does the CO connect with?

   ❐ Has the CO ever had to use its backup power? If so, what were the circumstances?

   ❐ How and when is routine line testing performed? What actions do personnel take when they find a fault on one of the lines?

- ❑ What brand and model of switches does the CO use? Why did they choose these switches?

- ❑ How has the trend toward more data connections affected their inside and outside plant?

- ❑ Where do long-distance calls go from this CO?

5. Ask to see the drawings that describe the layout of the CO's outside plant. Because they will probably be full of unfamiliar codes, ask the manager to describe what the drawing represents. Ask him or her to point out drop cables, SAIs, branch feeders, and main feeders (if shown).

6. Also take this opportunity to ask the CO manager how he or she chose telecommunications as a career and ended up in his or her current position.

7. After the tour, thank the manager for spending his or her time with you. Follow up with a thank you note to the person who arranged and escorted you on your tour.

Project 4-2

In this project, you draw a flowchart that follows a call through LEC and IXC switches, based on what you know about the type of data switches accept, how they analyze data, and the decisions they make based on its analysis. For this project, you only need a piece of paper and a pencil or pen. A knowledge of flowchart shapes and connectors is also useful.

1. Assume your flowchart will illustrate the progress of a long distance call that travels from one LEC's territory, across an IXC's network, and into another LEC's territory.

2. In response to the subscriber's signal, draw the outcome of the first switch's decision in your flow chart.

3. Once the switch has forwarded the call, what kind of data is it sending? Note this on your flow chart.

4. What kind of switch responds, and what decision does it make based on the signal it receives? (Note that there may be more than one intermediate switch, thus this decision may be repeated by multiple switches.) Draw the possible outcomes and follow the switch's decision to the next step.

5. Based on the last switch's decision, what kind of data is transmitted over what kind of connection? Draw this on your flowchart.

6. Finally, what kind of switch accepts the information passed on from Step 5? What decision does it make based on the information? Draw this on your flow chart.

7. How does the subscriber being called learn that someone is calling?

8. Without adding any more decision boxes to your flowchart, draw in the signaling process that allows the originating subscriber to recognize that her call has been answered.

Project 4-3

In this project, you use the Internet to learn more about the current state of the North American Numbering Plan. For this project, you need a computer with Internet access and a browser capable of interpreting frames in Web pages. You also need WinZip software that you can use to decompress a data file, and a text editor or word processing program to read the data file. Finally, you need Adobe Acrobat Reader, software that you can use to view other files.

1. After connecting to the Internet, launch your browser and go to the following Web page: **www.nanpa.com**. You will see the home page for the North American Numbering Plan Administration (the page is administered by a company called Neustar, Inc.).

2. On the left side, you'll notice a list of links. Click the **CENTRAL OFFICE CODES (Prefixes)** link. The CENTRAL OFFICE CODES page appears in the center frame.

3. Scroll down the page until you see the category called "Central Office Code Assignments and Summary Reports." Under this heading, click the **Download Assignment Records** link . The Central Office Code Assignments page appears, with an introduction that briefly explains how to retrieve the NANP documents. After reading the instructions, scroll down the page until you see a table that includes columns of regions and their states.

4. Find the row that includes your home state. In the far right column of the table, find the file containing utilized codes for your region. Click the filename to download the file to your computer's hard disk.

5. When asked if you want to save the file to disk, confirm by choosing the **Save this file to Disk** option, and then click **OK**.

6. The Windows Save As dialog box appears. Choose a path for the file and save it to your disk by clicking **Save**.

7. Launch WinZip and unzip the file that you just saved to your hard disk. After unzipping, the file will be in a .txt format.

8. Launch your word processor, and open the file you just unzipped.

9. Note that the columns contained in the file include the following: State, NPA-NXX, OCN (carrier number), company, and rate center.

10. From the menu bar, click **Edit**, and then click **Find**. The Find dialog box opens.

11. In the Find what text box, type your home NPA-NXX (for example, 212-432).

12. Click **Find Next** to begin searching the document.

13. Note the OCN and rate center for your NPA-NXX.

14. If you are part of a class, check with your fellow students to find out whether anyone else shares your CO.

15. If you also have a cellular phone, try Steps 10 through 12 using that NPA-NXX. Does anyone in the class share the same cellular CO?

16. Close your word processing program and return to the NANPA Web site's home page, **www.nanpa.com**.

17. In the menu in the left frame, click the **NPAs IN JEOPARDY** link. The NPAs in Jeopardy page appears in the center frame.

18. Read the introductory text on this page. Specifically, what does it mean for an NPA to be declared "in jeopardy?" What can the LECs do about it?

19. Now scroll down the page until you reach a table of states and their "in jeopardy" NPAs. What state has the most area codes in jeopardy right now? What might be a reason for this?

20. Click on any one of the files in the sixth column of that table titled "Extraordinary Measures." Because the file is in PDF format, your browser should automatically load Adobe Acrobat Reader to view the file.

21. Peruse the measures that the state has taken to conserve the remaining numbers in an area code. How do you think this will affect residential subscribers? What about business subscribers?

22. If time permits, continue exploring the NANPA site. The most recent numbering plan news will be listed under the "Press Releases" link.

CASE PROJECTS

1. You are an experienced telecommunications engineer with a major ILEC. Recently, your company has acquired a very small CLEC headquartered not far from your office. This CLEC serves 5000 subscribers from its single end office. It also collocates switching equipment at three end offices belonging to another LEC in the region. Your supervisor asks you to outline some considerations for merging the small CLEC's inside and outside plant with your company's inside and outside plant. She also asks you to indicate any circumstances that might make you recommend replacing the CLEC's facilities, rather than attempting to integrate them with your ILEC's facilities.

2. After working as an engineer in the telecommunications industry for fifteen years, you have mastered the technical aspects of every element belonging to both inside and outside plant. You are also aware that the local loop is the most expensive part of the PSTN. Your company (an ILEC) has asked you to serve on a committee that is currently investigating ways of making the local loop less costly (and therefore more profitable). What cost reduction ideas do you suggest to the other committee members? In generating your ideas, consider why it is currently the most expensive part of the PSTN, including costs involved in building the local loop, connecting it to the rest of the outside plant, terminating it at the CO, servicing it, and also billing the customer for it.

3. You have just been promoted to Director of Engineering at the ILEC, and one of your duties is to hire new talent. Based on what you know about the elements of outside plant, write a position description for an Outside Plant Engineer, a person generally responsible for the upkeep of your company's outside plant. In addition to the specific job responsibilities, be sure to include necessary schooling, types of work experience and soft skills (for example, "detail-oriented") required for this position. After you've written it, search some Internet job boards, such as Monster.com, to compare your listing with real outside plant engineer job descriptions. Were you surprised by any of the job duties listed in the actual position descriptions? Based on what you discovered, revise your original position description.

4. Your colleagues greatly admire your technical expertise in the world of telephony, and they invite you to help a standards organization develop a new numbering plan for North America. Based on what you know about the limitations of the existing NANP, what types of changes would you recommend for the new telephone numbering system? What kind of capacity do you predict might be needed in twenty years? What factors does this capacity depend on? What types of infrastructure changes or upgrades would your numbering plan require?

4

5

CUSTOMER PREMISE EQUIPMENT AND APPLICATIONS

After reading this chapter and completing the exercises, you will be able to:

♦ Discuss the purpose of customer premise equipment in a telecommunications network

♦ Identify the significant components of a modern telephone

♦ Discuss the varieties of station equipment

♦ Explain how private switching systems integrate with both CPE and the PSTN

♦ Describe how enhanced CPE services and applications work and how businesses benefit from using them

The telephone is probably the most familiar part of a telephony system. It's a simple device whose technical principles have not changed much over the last century. For example, it still requires a small amount of electrical current to transmit voice signals, and it still includes a handset (containing both a transmitter and receiver) to allow a person to conduct a conversation over great distances. However, over the past century, the simple telephone has matured into a critical apparatus for personal and business communications.

In this chapter, you learn about the technical advances that have affected telephones and other related customer premise equipment. You discover how a business with thousands of telephone users can avoid paying the local phone company for every call between its offices. You also learn about modern telephony applications, such as automatic call distribution, that make businesses more efficient. Material in this chapter provides the foundation for learning about switching and signaling, covered in Chapter 6, as well as telephony provided over data networks, covered in Chapter 14.

INTRODUCTION TO CUSTOMER PREMISE EQUIPMENT

In Chapter 4, you learned about the demarcation point, where the LEC's responsibility to maintain telephone equipment ends and the consumer's responsibility begins. Everything on the consumer's side of the demarcation point is known as **customer premise equipment (CPE)**, because it resides on the customer's premises. CPE includes the telephone wires inside a home or business (also known as **inside wiring**), telephones, modems, fax machines, answering machines, and specialized equipment, such as terminals that assist deaf callers by translating speech into text. Although CPE is in the customer's home or business, it may not always belong to the customer. For example, a modem used to send and receive digital signals over a cable connection to the Internet usually belongs to the cable company, even though it is installed inside the customer's house.

The purpose of most customer premise equipment is to receive and transmit signals. Naturally, customer premise equipment cannot function alone. Although customer premise equipment is treated separately in this chapter, bear in mind that it is only the interface, or the place where a customer interacts, with a telecommunications system. It depends on a network of cabling and switches to connect with other customer premise equipment. At a customer site, CPE connects to a carrier's local loop. Signals issued and received by CPE are interpreted and redirected by the carrier's switches. Switching methods are covered in detail in Chapter 6. Between the switches and CPE, signals are carried by cabling, which is discussed in Chapter 8.

Telephones are the most common example of customer premise equipment. In telecommunications, a telephone and any connected parts are known as **station equipment** because in the business world, they are located at a person's station, or desk. Next, you learn about the components inside a modern telephone.

INSIDE A MODERN TELEPHONE

In Chapter 3, you learned about the basic components of the first telephones, such as those invented by Alexander Graham Bell. These early devices depended on an electrical source, plus a transmitter and receiver to issue and accept voice signals. In addition, they contained a mechanism for alerting a subscriber to an incoming call and provided a means for a subscriber to indicate which number she wanted to call.

These are essentially the same components found in a modern telephone, which, like its predecessors, is a surprisingly simple instrument. In fact, many modern telephone parts are just newer versions of Alexander Bell's original components, modernized to provide better sound quality and greater reliability. In the following sections, you learn about the inner workings of a modern telephone.

Basic Components

Before learning the functions of each telephone component, it is useful to view a telephone with its components labeled. Figure 5-1 illustrates the many parts of a modern telephone. You may want to refer to this diagram as you read through this section to better understand how the components work together.

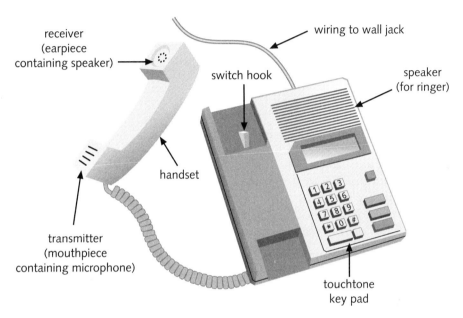

receiver
(earpiece
containing speaker)

wiring to wall jack

switch hook

speaker
(for ringer)

handset

transmitter
(mouthpiece
containing microphone)

touchtone
key pad

Figure 5-1   Components of a modern telephone

The telephones and other CPE described in this chapter are those designed for use with the PSTN and its conventional local loops. Customer premise equipment designed to take advantage of newer digital local loop technology is discussed later, in Chapters 10 and 14.

Handset

A **handset** is the part of the telephone that contains a transmitter and receiver and can be removed from the stationary equipment to allow the user to be mobile while talking. It may be connected to the stationary equipment by a cord or, in the case of cordless phones, by a wireless signal. Figure 5-2 shows handsets for both corded and cordless telephones.

A transmitter, located in the mouthpiece of a telephone handset, converts the speaker's voice into electrical pulses (specifically, fluctuating DC current) so that it can be delivered to a receiver. A receiver, located in the earpiece of a telephone handset, does the opposite. It accepts electrical pulses and converts them into speech that the listener can understand.

Figure 5-2   Handset for corded and cordless telephones

As you learned in Chapter 3, the first telephones used a vibrating reed, a thin membrane, or a liquid-filled chamber to transform electrical pulses into speech. The type of telephone transmitter most common in the twentieth century, however, was the sack of carbon granules invented by Thomas Edison. Because it is economical and rugged, this type of transmitter is still used in some telephones today.

Figure 5-3 depicts a carbon-filled transmitter. DC voltage applied to the carbon granules compacts them, changing the amount of current that can flow through them in relation to the strength of the signal. In early telephone technology, this fluctuating current was sent to the receiver through a central office, where an operator completed the circuit. It began as an analog signal and remained an analog signal all the way to its destination.

Today, the fluctuating DC current is transformed into a digital signal by the local office's switch, which first receives the current. After it has passed through the telephone company's switches, the signal is converted back to analog form and sent to the receiver. For the most part, modern telephones no longer use the compacted carbon granules in their transmitters. Instead, they use tiny electronic microphones. However, the signals issued by modern telephone transmitters are still analog signals and must be converted to digital format in order for any computerized device to interpret them.

Telephone receivers have changed even less than transmitters over the last century. Early receivers used a vibrating diaphragm, similar to a stereo speaker, but much smaller. Incoming DC current caused an electromagnetic coil next to the diaphragm to issue waves. As the diaphragm vibrated in response to those waves, it made sounds like speech. Many modern telephone receivers still use this technology. However, some have been replaced by smaller, lighter electronic components.

Figure 5-3 A carbon-filled transmitter

Local Loop Current

To transmit signals, telephone systems use direct current (DC) electricity. In the earliest telephones, individual telephone batteries supplied this current, just as you used a battery in the Hands-on Project in Chapter 3 to create a working telegraph. However, by 1900, telephone companies realized it was more reliable and efficient to supply this power over the existing telephone wires from a battery at the telephone company's central office. The standard voltage was set at 48 V (a voltage that is sufficient to carry signals, but does not cause serious physical harm). Today, local telephone companies in North America still provide 48 V current over local loops from their Class 5 central offices. The current travels over the same wires that carry voice signals to and from a subscriber's telephone.

Although current is always present on a telephone line, a circuit is not actually completed until a subscriber lifts the handset. When the handset is lifted, the circuit between the central office and the subscriber's telephone closes (that is, current is allowed to flow from one end of the circuit to another). In the case of a cordless telephone, the circuit is completed by pressing a button on the handset. In early telephones, the device that held a handset and closed a switch when the handset was lifted to complete the circuit was called a **switch hook**. Today, the mechanism that is depressed when a handset is hung up is still called a switch hook, though it depends on an electronic circuit rather than an electro-mechanical circuit. In addition to closing a circuit, lifting a switch hook alerts the switch at the end office that the party wants to make a call. As long as the handset is resting on the switch hook, the end office's switch assumes that the telephone line is not in use. (You learn more about switches in Chapter 6.) In modern telephony, depressing the switch hook may provide additional functions, for example, accepting an incoming call when using the three-way calling or call waiting features. Figure 5-4 illustrates the principle of completing a local loop circuit using a switch hook.

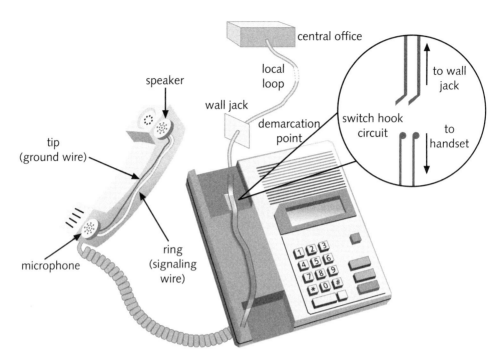

Figure 5-4   Completion of a local loop circuit using a switch hook

Wiring

The phone line that enters a residence usually contains at least four wires (or two pairs of wires). Generally speaking, in homes wired before the 1990s, the four wire strands are black, red, green, and yellow, as shown in Figure 5-5. When a subscriber has only one phone line activated, the green and red wires are used to complete the circuit. If the subscriber adds another phone line, the second line uses the black and yellow wires. Inside the subscriber's home, the wires terminate at a standard jack known as an **RJ-11** (for "registered jack number 11," an FCC standard). This type of jack contains space for two or three wire pairs (in other words, four or six separate wire strands) and accepts a standard telephone plug, as shown in Figure 5-5. In newer telephony installations, wires with more than two or three wire pairs are often installed. In fact, many new homes are outfitted with four wire-pair cables to allow for either additional phone lines or digital services. You learn more about the different types of telephone wires in Chapter 8.

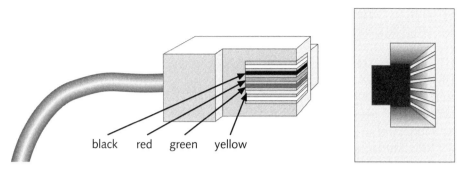

Figure 5-5   Residential telephone wire, plug, and RJ11 jack

When telephones were first introduced, the two charges necessary to complete a telephone circuit were called tip and ring, after the electrical contacts on a plug, or male connector, that an operator at a central office inserted into a jack to complete a call. The plug's tip grounded the connection, and just above it, a ring, or metal band, carried the electrical charge, as shown in Figure 5-6. Note that this plug looks similar to the one you use today to connect your headphones to a stereo. The terms tip and ring have lingered in the telephony lexicon. A **tip** is the wire that supplies the ground (or zero charge) from the central office's battery to the telephone. A **ring** is the wire that carries a negative charge (-48 V) from the central office's battery to a telephone. In other words, the ring is the wire that carries signals. The ring wire may also be referred to as the transmission wire, because it transmits signals. In a typical residential telephone wiring scheme, the tip is the green wire whereas the ring is the red wire. A tip (ground) wire and a ring (signaling) wire together make up a pair.

Figure 5-6   Tip and ring on an early telephone plug

The tip and ring wire together carry all of the signals to and from your telephone handset, including your speech (transmission), the other party's speech (reception), and the signals, such as the dial tone and the ringing sound you hear when you're receiving a call. After the two wire strands enter the telephone set, however, the transmit and receive circuits must be separated, so that the transmit circuit leads to the transmitter (where a telephone user speaks) and the receive circuit leads to the receiver (where a telephone user listens) portion of the handset.

Recall from Chapter 3 that Bell's first telephone used the same tube for a mouthpiece and earpiece, and that the transmit and receive signals both used the same wire all the way from the local loop through the handset. This arrangement was inconvenient and difficult to use, because a person making a call had to speak into the tube, and then quickly move it to her ear in order to hear the response. During technology advances of the early 1900s, a **hybrid coil** was introduced into telephone sets to separate the incoming transmit and receive signals into their own two-wire connections. This technique was used until the late twentieth century. Now, integrated circuits perform the same function.

Ringer

In the preceding section, you learned that a circuit is not complete until a person lifts the telephone's handset. But, strictly speaking, this is not entirely true. In fact, a telephone's ringer can accept voltage from an end office before the handset is removed from the switch hook. A **ringer** is the device that sounds a bell or tone to indicate an incoming call. When a subscriber's number is called, the end office's switch sends a unique signal, using the local loop's current, to the subscriber's phone. This signal activates the ringer. In the earliest telephones, the ringer was an electromechanical device that used a clapper to strike a small gong. In most modern telephones, however, the ringer is an electronic device that relies on an integrated circuit. In the United States, the FCC classifies types of ringers and regulates which ringers are acceptable.

Standard PSTN-connected telephones in North America ring with a tone of two combined frequencies of 440 Hz plus 480 Hz. These tones ring for two seconds, then are followed by a four-second silence. This pattern repeats until someone removes the handset from its switch hook. This frequency, with its repeating pattern, is commonly known as the **ringing tone**, or **ringback**. It is issued by the telephone company's local office switch. Although service providers could use different ringbacks, they usually conform to the same pattern within a country. (If you travel abroad, you will notice different ringing patterns in different countries.) Some service providers supply **distinctive ringing**, a unique ringing sound or cadence for different types of calls. For example, your employer may subscribe to a service that prompts your telephone to ring differently when you receive a call from a colleague's extension within the building than when you receive a call from an outside line, such as your home.

 People who have difficulty hearing the standard telephone ringback may purchase and install different-sounding ringers on their telephones. These devices may change the frequency or amplitude of the ringing, lowering its pitch or making it louder, for example. Alternatively, they may substitute a flashing light or a vibrating wristband for an audible ringer.

Dialer

Telephone dialers may be one of two types: rotary or touch tone. In **rotary** dialing, a user chooses a number and turns a wheel from that number to the finger stop (a small metal bar), then releases the wheel. When the user sets the wheel in motion, the circuit opens. When the user releases the wheel, the circuit alternately opens and closes, issuing a series of pulses as the dial returns to its position. The local central office's switch can translate those pulses into numbers. Rotary dials like the one shown in Figure 5-7 were used during most of the twentieth century, but have been replaced with touch tone dialers.

5

Figure 5-7   A rotary dialer

The concept of touch-tone dialing was introduced in 1964. It is faster (typically, over 10 times faster) and more convenient than rotary dialing. **Touch-tone** dialers (often called **tone** dialers) operate by transmitting a combination of two frequencies each time a button is pressed. Pressing each button issues a different combination of frequencies. For example, pressing the number 6 sends a unique combination of a 770 Hz tone and a 1477 Hz tone. This type of encoding is known as **dual-tone multifrequency (DTMF)**. The local CO's switch translates these combined frequencies into numbers with a DTMF receiver. Figure 5-8 illustrates the combination of frequencies used in DTMF in a table format. For example, pressing "9" issues the combination of a 852 Hz plus a 1477 Hz tone, whereas pressing "4" issues a combination of a 770 Hz plus a 1209 Hz tone. Notice that additional frequencies (in the fourth column of squares in Figure 5-8) can be interpreted by the switch, but are not accessible from the touch tone keypad. These frequencies, which can be generated by auxiliary telephone equipment, such as fax machines, are reserved for special signals.

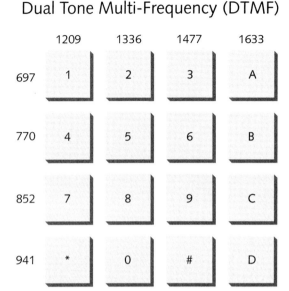

Figure 5-8   Frequencies used in DTMF

Station Protection

Several environmental factors may hamper or even sever a local loop connection, including physical damage, lightning, and water. Of these threats, the most treacherous is lightning. Consider that a telephone local loop carries an average of 48 V and may be capable of withstanding approximately seven times that amount of current. A bolt of lightning, however, carries millions of volts of electricity. Even if lightning didn't directly hit a telephone wire, but struck nearby, it could discharge thousands of volts toward the wire. Such a surge, or sudden impulse of voltage, could instantly damage telephony equipment beyond repair and potentially injure the telephone user.

To shield against this remote possibility, telephone companies have installed station protection devices at both their central offices and at the demarcation point for every subscriber line. Most of these devices use either a sealed gas discharge tube to short the circuit and divert incoming high voltage to a ground. At a demarcation point, the station protection device connects to a grounding wire that might be connected to a nearby metal pipe, such as a water pipe. For further protection, the telephone itself is insulated so that any extra voltage that does pass the ground will not be conducted through the instrument and injure the user. Figure 5-9 illustrates how a station protector and ground can safeguard a telephone at the demarcation point. Figure 5-10 shows a photo of a gas tube station protector that might be used at a home demarcation point. Notice that this protector uses two gas tubes, one that connects to the tip wire and one that connects to the ring wire. Also notice the brass connector used to attach it to a ground.

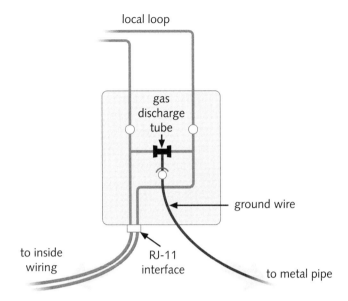

Figure 5-9   Use of a station protector at the demarcation point

Figure 5-10   A station protector for residential use

VARIETIES OF STATION EQUIPMENT

In the preceding section, you learned what all types of telephones have in common: power, wiring, transmitters, receivers, ringers, dialers, and a means of protecting them from power surges. In this section, you learn about ways in which some station equipment differs from the standard desk or wall-mounted telephone. Each specialized telephone discussed in the following sections was developed with a specific user and purpose in mind. You have probably employed some, if not all, of these devices.

Pay Telephones

A **pay telephone** (or **pay phone**) is a telephone provided for public use that requires coin, collect, or credit card payment to complete telephone calls. Pay telephones have been available in the United States since the middle of the twentieth century. Until the FCC allowed competition for this service in 1984, the Bell Operating Companies owned and maintained all pay telephones. Now, however, a multitude of private companies and even individuals can own and operate pay telephones. In the telecommunications industry, a pay phone is more commonly called a **COCOT (customer-owned coin-operated telephone)**. COCOTs can be lucrative, but they are also more difficult to manage than regular subscriber telephone sets. In particular, they are susceptible to vandalism and fraud.

Pay telephones operate according to the same principles as other telephone sets, but they require extra mechanisms to detect the types of coins deposited by a user and to collect and refund coins. When a user lifts the coin telephone handset, the telephone transmits a signal to the end office switch indicating not only that a caller wants to place a call, but also that the telephone is a coin telephone. The switch then prevents the caller from placing a call until he or she has first inserted money or entered a credit card number. If a coin is inserted, its magnetism, weight, and diameter are tested to verify that it is a coin and not a fraudulent replica (also known as a "slug"). Next, a device called a **totalizer** determines what type of coin was deposited and relays that information to the switch through pulses of brief dual-frequency tones. Each pulse represents five cents. For example, if you insert a quarter into a coin telephone, the totalizer sends five brief pulses of both 1700 Hz and 2200 Hz tones to the end office switch. The end office switch recognizes that this series of pulses represents a quarter. To prevent line fraud, the limits on the duration, amplitude, and frequency of these pulses are very strict. The switch only responds to those tones that fall precisely within those limits. Telephone companies have implemented additional restrictions to prevent fraud through the transmission of these tones directly into the telephone mouthpiece. To deter vandals, COCOTs may sound alarms and issue messages to the local CO when they have been physically damaged.

After inserting the correct amount of money, the caller can then dial a number, at which point the switch accepts the DTMF signals just as it accepts those from a conventional telephone. However, only if the called party answers are the coins retained. If no one answers, the coins are redirected to the refund chute, as shown in Figure 5-11. A coin telephone contains mechanisms to handle the timing, collection, and return of deposited coins. If the call is long distance, the switch determines when additional coins must be deposited and issues a synthesized voice signal to prompt the caller for more money. In COCOT calling, as in other types of calling, all of the call setup, routing, and charging decisions are made by the switch.

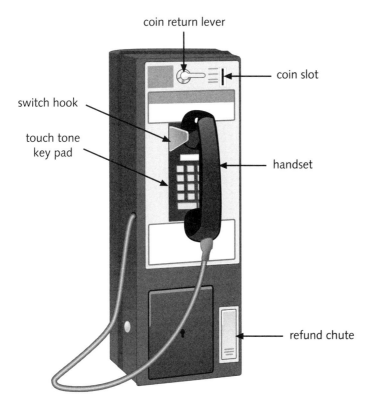

coin return lever

coin slot

switch hook

touch tone key pad

handset

refund chute

5

Figure 5-11 A standard pay telephone

Today, many COCOT calls do not involve coins but are billed to credit cards, so COCOTs are frequently equipped with credit card readers. If not, the pay phone user may be required to enter a series of numbers listed on a calling card. In both cases, the pay telephone typically forwards the credit card information to the service provider's switch, which saves the information in a computer. This information is later used to bill the credit card company or the carrier who issued the calling card for the call.

Cordless Telephones

Cordless telephones are those that can be used without a physical connection to a telephone set, but still rely on a stationary telephone, or **base station**, to connect to the PSTN. A base station receives the signal from the inside wiring and then transmits it to the cordless phone over one or more frequencies. These frequencies may belong to one of several ranges, depending on the make and model of cordless phone. The geographical range of a base station (that is, the distance it can transmit signals to the cordless handset) depends on the frequency. The higher the frequency a cordless phone uses, the longer its range. For example, cordless phones that use a 49 MHz frequency can transmit only up to 200 feet, whereas the newest models, which use a 2.4 GHz frequency, can transmit up to

2000 feet. To allow for the exchange of signals, both the cordless handset and the base station contain a radio transmitter, antenna, and receiver. Though the first cordless telephones were purely analog, they may now transmit signals in digital or analog format. As you would expect, those that use digital signaling offer better sound quality. Figure 5-12 depicts a cordless telephone and base station.

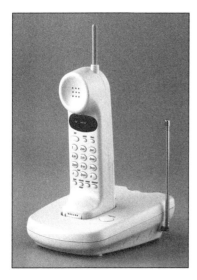

Figure 5-12   Cordless telephone and base station

 Be careful not to confuse cordless telephones with mobile telephones. Mobile telephones have a much wider transmission range (depending on the telecommunications provider, it may be virtually unlimited across the country) and do not require a stationary telephone set nearby. Wireless technology, which is discussed in detail in Chapter 9, is significantly different from cordless technology.

The main drawback to cordless phones is the ease with which these signals can be picked up by eavesdroppers. Anyone tuned into the same frequency used by a cordless phone can listen to the signals (the conversation) it is transmitting and receiving. To guard against this intrusion, some cordless phones offer **spread spectrum** transmission, in which a signal is separated and its separate pieces distributed over a wide range of frequencies. The receiver understands how to decode this signal, but less specialized receivers cannot. Spread spectrum signaling may be used with either digital or analog transmission. It is so secure that it is used by the U.S. armed forces as they transmit information between ships at sea. In addition to guarding against eavesdropping, spread spectrum technology can improve transmission in places (such as hospitals) where interference limits the range of a single-frequency signal.

Answering Equipment

Answering machines have existed in some form for almost as long as the telephone has been in use. In fact, in 1878, Thomas Edison predicted that one use of his recording technology would be to take telephone messages. By the 1930s, many European residential telephone subscribers used answering equipment. However, AT&T, which owned the United States telephone system for most of the last century, banned the use of third-party answering machines with its telephones. When the FCC declared in 1946 that auxiliary equipment manufactured by any company could be attached to telephones, the market for answering machines in the United States finally opened up. But the devices were cumbersome and tightly regulated. As a result, few average citizens used them. After 1984 and the breakup of AT&T, a proliferation of new telecommunications companies set up shop and began selling simpler and less expensive answering machines. Only then did the use of answering equipment in the United States explode.

Modern answering equipment may include small cassette recorders, voice mail systems, computerized answering machines, and centralized messaging services. Many answering machines are digital, although analog tape recorders are still available. Digital answering equipment makes it unnecessary to change tapes. It also provides more reliable call recording.

The switch at the central office does not make a distinction about who or what has "picked up the phone." Therefore, when an answering machine responds to a call, the switch completes the call circuit. The caller then waits to hear the greeting and leaves a message. When the caller hangs up, the call is terminated at the telephone company's switches. However, the switches do not send a special signal to the local loop and the answering equipment to indicate the call's termination. Thus, an answering machine has to listen for a period of silence to know when the call has ended. After it detects this period of silence, it stops recording. If the caller decides not to leave a message and hangs up before the answering machine has begun recording, the equipment simply finishes its greeting, waits for a message, then stops after the same period of silence. This process keeps the called party's line busy for a short while.

The popularity of answering machines since the late twentieth century has changed the way we communicate. We can now screen calls, deciding whether we want to pick up the phone depending on who has called. Before Caller ID, this was the only way of finding out who was calling before picking up the handset. People no longer have to worry about missing important calls if they are away from home. And although speaking into voice mail systems and answering machines was initially difficult for people to accept, most people have now adopted an abbreviated, businesslike speech especially for these machines. We may even be startled when we expect to talk with a machine and a live person answers the phone!

TTY and TDD

TTY stands for *TeleTYpewriter*, a device invented by the Teletype Corporation that uses alphanumeric characters entered through a keyboard to communicate over a voice or data network. **TDD** stands for **T**elecommunications **D**evice for the **D**eaf, which is a specially-designed device that uses a TTY and a terminal or computer screen to help speech- and hearing-impaired people communicate over the PSTN. Though they are technically slightly different, TTY and TDD are often used synonymously to refer to an interface designed to assist those who have difficulty listening and speaking using traditional telephones. For the purposes of this discussion, the more correct term, TDD, is used to refer to this interface.

A TDD uses a keyboard and a small screen so that the caller can input words, then see the typed response. TDDs can use **relay centers**, or call centers with operators who translate the typed input for the nonhearing-impaired party and type responses for reception by the hearing-impaired party's TDD. For example, if you do not own a TDD but want to call a relative with impaired hearing (say, your Aunt Margaret in Ohio), you call a relay center's toll free number first. A communications assistant answers your call, then dials the number of your Aunt Margaret's TDD. Because your Aunt Margaret cannot hear, a flashing light or vibrating wrist band alerts her of the incoming call. When your Aunt Margaret's TDD answers, the communications assistant enters a greeting. Thereafter, the communications assistant at the relay center types your conversation and sends those words to your Aunt Margaret's TDD, while reading aloud her responses to you. Modern TDDs bypass the relay centers and instead communicate directly through internal modems. But this scenario requires both parties to have TDDs. Some TDDs are also equipped with printers or large screen displays. Others are specially designed for public phone use. Figure 5-13 shows a modern TDD supplied with a printer and an internal modem. As TDD technology evolves, they are becoming more like computers. In fact, software that emulates a TDD may be installed on a typical PC.

Figure 5-13 A modern TDD

PRIVATE SWITCHING EQUIPMENT

For most residential subscribers, using the PSTN is an economical and simple way of completing telephone calls. But consider the volume of calls traveling in and out of a large organization, such as a university. Many of these calls take place between staff and students at the university. If the university had to pay the telephone company for each call that took place within the university, its telephone bills would be astronomical. **Private switching**, in which calls are connected independent of the local telephone company's CO, enables organizations to set up and route internal calls at a much lower cost. Just as a CO prevents every single telephone in the country from having to be wired directly to every other telephone, a private switching system prevents every single telephone within an organization from having to be wired directly to every other telephone within that organization. Thus, a student in a dorm room can call another student in a dorm room through the university's private switch. The call is never passed on to the telephone company's central office and the university is never charged for the call. If you have ever worked for a company in which you dialed a four-digit extension to call a colleague, you have used some type of private switching.

A private switching system not only manages internal calls, but also allows multiple individuals to share a single local loop. Private switching is more economical than public switching because by sharing lines, the organization saves money. Private switching is also more efficient. By avoiding the local loop and the carrier's central office, calls are completed much faster within an organization. However, organizations must invest money and technical expertise to establish and manage private switching systems. The following sections discuss the significant types of private switching and explain their common uses.

Key Telephone Systems

A **key telephone system (KTS)** is a system that gives all telephone users within an organization centralized access to one of many incoming PSTN lines. A KTS also provides intercom access (the ability to communicate between stations within an organization using only internal lines), plus other enhanced services. A KTS typically consists of a wall-mounted control console that connects to the organization's internal phones and to the telephone company's end office. This console, called a **key service unit (KSU)**, signals the telephone attendant about incoming calls, controls busy indicator lights on line buttons, and tracks call information, among other tasks. Through the KSU, a telephone user on one line can access any of the multiple incoming PSTN lines. Small offices of up to 50 users are most apt to use a KTS. It is called a "key" telephone system because the user must press a key before she can access one of the shared phone lines. Figure 5-14 shows a popular type of KTS telephone and KSU.

Figure 5-14   Key telephone system equipment

In a KTS telephone system, each telephone has several buttons representing multiple outgoing lines. Next to each line's button is a small light that illuminates when that line is busy, or when a call is incoming on that line. Before dialing a number outside the organization, you must push one of the buttons to select an outgoing line, a process known as **call pickup**. In contrast, other, more sophisticated types of private switching systems automatically choose an outgoing line for you once you press a digit. When using other private switching systems, for example, you press 9 to "get an outside line." Pressing a digit is not necessary in KTS; instead, the user simply presses a button representing an outside line. The user can tell if the line is free by looking to see if the light next to the button is on or off.

Another characteristic that distinguishes a KTS from other private switching systems is that it relies on the telephone company's CO to provide dial tone and to set up a call. Other types of private switching systems supply their own dial tone. Figure 5-15 depicts a simple KTS arrangement.

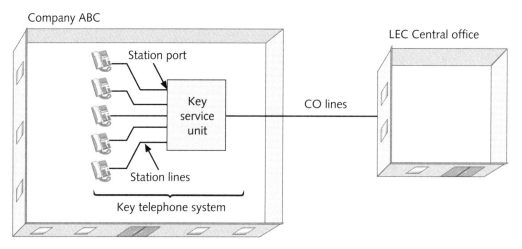

Figure 5-15   A simple KTS model

Thanks to the **intercom** feature of a KTS, you can push a one- or two-digit number to speak directly with a colleague in the same office. A call attendant in an office (often the receptionist) might use the intercom feature on a KTS to notify you of an incoming call. The intercom feature works because a KTS provides a shared path between every phone to every other phone.

In addition to call pickup, supervisory signals and intercom, all KTSs provide **call hold**, the ability to place an active connection on hold while using the telephone for something else (such as making an outgoing call).

The first KTSs were introduced in the mid-1920s. These electromechanical systems relied on complex wiring schemes and ancillary equipment that were cumbersome to maintain. In the 1970s, the Bell System began incorporating electronic components in KTSs. As a result, the equipment shrunk in size and assumed new features. Modern day KTSs are almost exclusively electronic and depend on a fully electronic KSU. Electronic KTSs provide many more features than electromechanical KTSs. The following list describes only some of these enhanced features:

- *Call forwarding*—A feature that allows a user to send a call to another telephone connected to the KTS

- *Caller identification*—A feature that displays the name and telephone number of the party who is calling; requires that the switches at the local central office are capable of transmitting this information and that the called party has a telephone set capable of displaying it

- *Direct inward dialing*—A feature that enables parties from outside the organization to dial an extension's seven digit number directly, rather than going through an attendant to complete the call

- *Do not disturb*—A feature that allows a user to disable her telephone from ringing and accepting incoming calls

- *Message waiting*—A light on the telephone that indicates if a party has a message waiting in his voice mail (defined later in this list)

- *Music on hold*—A feature that plays music or promotional recordings while a caller is placed on hold

- *Privacy*—A feature that prevents other parties from picking up a line that is in use; in newer KTS equipment, the privacy feature is standard

- *Station restriction*—A feature that can prevent specific telephones from making certain types of calls (for instance, a guest telephone in a hotel lobby might not allow long distance calls, except for 1-800 and credit card calls) or using certain features

- *Voice mail*—A system of recording messages for later retrieval, used when a party does not answer an incoming call

5

The enhanced features listed previously were not available in the early KTSs; they only became available once electronic KTSs were introduced in the 1970s. Before that time, organizations requiring these features had to use a more sophisticated type of private switching system, such as a private branch exchange (discussed in the following section).

KTS technology continues to evolve and offer more and more features. Although traditional KTSs cannot connect to a data network (which would allow the KTS to interact with computerized calling services, for example), newer, digital KTSs can. Digital KTSs are so similar to private branch exchanges that they are called **hybrid telephone systems**. In other words, they are not traditional KTSs, yet they are not considered private branch exchanges. Popular KTS and hybrid telephone system manufacturers include IBM, Lucent, and Nortel.

Private Branch Exchanges (PBX)

A **private branch exchange (PBX)** is a switch owned and operated by a business or other private organization that connects multiple telephone sets to one or more of the telephone company's central offices. You can think of a PBX as a miniature CO. It provides call setup and routing within an organization, plus a host of enhanced features. A PBX differs from a KTS in that it offers more complex features. For example, whereas a KTS waits for a telephone user to choose a line, a PBX automatically chooses an open line when a user presses a digit on her telephone keypad. Also, a PBX can operate independently of the telephone company for internal calls. Whereas a KTS depends on a CO for dial tone, a PBX actually provides its connected telephones with dial tone. And whereas KTSs typically connect an organization to the PSTN through a handful of lines, a PBX can connect an organization to the PSTN through a trunk, a connection with significantly more bandwidth than a local loop which serves to directly connect switches.

The evolution of PBXs followed the same path as the evolution of public switching exchanges. The first PBXs were controlled by operators who asked the caller for a number and manually connected the call. These operators were located at the front desk or in a basement room of an office building. Thereafter, PBXs adopted electromechanical switching. These early electromechanical PBXs were cumbersome devices that were difficult to maintain. Like public switching systems, PBXs started incorporating electronic components in the 1970s. As a result, they became more compact and more complex. These days, all new PBXs are electronic. Major PBX manufacturers include Nortel and Lucent. Figure 5-16 depicts some modern PBX equipment.

Figure 5-16   Modern PBX equipment

Components of a PBX

A PBX consists of four significant elements:

- *Station lines*—The lines that connect individual telephone sets to the switch

- *Central processor*—The computer that oversees all PBX operations, including processing incoming calls, outgoing calls, call setup, routing, supervision, and data gathering

- *Switching module*—The equipment that accomplishes call setup, routing, and supervision, just as a switch in a central office does; it connects outgoing calls from the station lines with the CO trunks and incoming calls from the CO trunks to the station lines

- *Trunks*—The lines that connect the switch to COs

As shown in Figure 5-17, the PBX accepts multiple incoming trunks from the CO at trunk interface circuits. These circuits connect with the central processing unit, which connects to the switching module. The PBX contains station line interfaces that allow the connection of an organization's internal station lines. Inside the PBX, each station line is associated with an electrical circuit on a circuit board.

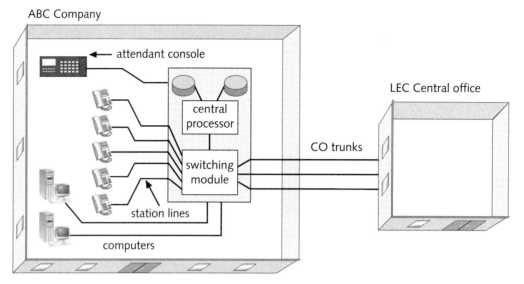

Figure 5-17 A simple PBX model

Because PBXs are designed to save money, they do not have the same number of available trunks as they have connected telephones. This arrangement assumes that not every phone in the organization will be in use simultaneously. The relationship between the number of station lines and the number of available trunks varies from one organization to another, depending on the organization's calling habits. A typical office uses about 10 percent of its lines at any given time. A telemarketing office, in which most employees are expected to be on the phone all day, might use 60 percent. On the other hand, a chemistry research facility in which most employees are expected to be experimenting in the laboratory all day might use only two percent. The fewer trunks an organization purchases, the more money it saves. However, with fewer trunks, a caller is more likely to get a busy signal during periods of high call traffic.

Although all PBXs share the four components previously listed, PBX equipment can vary widely. For example, PBXs may have separate interfaces to handle both analog and digital station lines. If a PBX supports analog station lines, any type of telephone set can be connected to that interface. However, digital PBX lines typically use a proprietary method (in other words, one that is unique and not necessarily compatible with methods used by other manufacturers) of communicating with telephones. Because each PBX's method is unique, an organization must purchase its digital phones from the same company that made its PBX.

5

In addition to individual telephone stations, a PBX system includes at least one attendant console. The attendant console is a specialized telephone used by a person (often the company receptionist) who receives incoming calls, greets callers, and forwards calls to their destination within the organization. Some PBX systems bypass a person and use an automated attendant, in the form of a voice recording, to help callers reach their inten°ded recipient. Although less personal, this method is much less expensive.

PBXs may support digital or analog transmission over its trunks and PBX trunks may connect to LECs, IXCs, or other private switching systems. Two PBXs can be connected via a permanent circuit called a **tie trunk**. A tie trunk is used, for example, to connect the PBX at a company's manufacturing facility with the PBX at its corporate headquarters 20 miles away. In this arrangement, the two PBXs communicate directly, without going through the PSTN, to complete calls between the two locations. A foreman at the manufacturing facility could call an accountant at the corporate headquarters by simply pressing a four-digit extension number. The physical trunk facilities that make up tie trunks are leased from a local telephone company, but these trunks are not part of the PSTN.

Another type of PBX trunk is the direct inward dialing (DID) trunk. A **DID trunk** is a connection to the CO that allows outside callers to dial a seven-digit number and reach a PBX telephone directly, rather than first going through an attendant. Usually a separate trunk, in addition to the standard CO trunk, is required for the DID feature to work. This is because a PBX must have a standard trunk to the PSTN to handle regular incoming and outgoing calls.

Trunks entering a PBX from the CO are pooled into groups for easier administration. To obtain access to one of these trunk groups, a user must dial an access number, in many cases, the digit "9." In response, the trunk group assigns the user's station a free line to the CO.

Features Offered by a PBX

Like modern KTSs, PBXs support a number of enhanced features, and in fact, have provided these features long before KTSs were capable of doing so. Some additional features that PBXs may provide include:

- *Automatic call distribution (ACD)*—A method of distributing incoming calls evenly over multiple stations, according to quantity of calls handled, free time, or availability. For example, if only one station line in a group is idle, the next incoming call is routed to that station. This feature is useful in call centers where multiple parties are responsible for answering incoming calls. You learn more about ACD later in this chapter.

- *Automated route selection (ARS)*—A method of determining over which trunk an outgoing call should be routed to incur the lowest cost.

- *Computer-telephony integration (CTI)*—A method of combining the features of a PBX with the features of a networked computer. Among other things, CTI allows a PBX administrator to program changes into the PBX from a networked workstation. You learn more about CTI later in this chapter.

- *Power failure provisions*—A means of providing power in the event of a power failure. Because the PBX is an electronic device, it will fail during a power failure unless it is connected to a battery. Some PBXs provide for this scenario by automatically releasing their control over connected telephone sets if the power fails, thereby allowing the telephones to dial directly to a CO and bypass the PBX.

- *Station message detail recording (SMDR)*—A method for recording call details, such as the caller's and the call recipient's identification, when the call was made, how long the call lasted, and so on.

- *System management*—A centralized method of reporting and controlling PBX parameters, such as telephone inventory, traffic patterns, extension moves and additions, and troubleshooting functions.

- *Trunk queuing*—A feature that enables a user to be notified when a trunk becomes available.

- *Unified messaging*—A feature that combines PBX voice mail with e-mail, fax, and paging services so that users only need consult one source to pick up their messages.

- *Wireless capabilities*—A feature that enables PBX users on wireless phones to have full access to PBX functionality while they roam within range of the PBX.

Note that this list of features highlights the more advanced PBX options, but it is by no means exhaustive. Virtually every call dialing, handling, notification, and reporting feature you can imagine is included with some type of PBX.

Each feature offered by a PBX system can be programmed to a series of digits on a phone. For example, at one office, a user may access her voice mail using the number 890. Rather than requiring employees to remember a number for each feature, most organizations program buttons on their PBX telephones to dial these extensions. That way, a user only has to press the button that says "voice mail." Although such phones are more expensive than standard PBX phones, they are much more convenient. A business may purchase and install any one of a great variety of PBX equipment and configurations. The ultimate choice depends on the business's size, budget, technical expertise, and geographical distribution.

PBX technology continues to improve. One area in which PBX technology is currently evolving is in its method of signaling. Whereas communication between a PBX and its connected telephones has traditionally been proprietary, newer PBXs are using standard networking communication methods to exchange information with telephones. This is good news for businesses that want to purchase equipment from different manufacturers and for those who want to integrate their PBXs with their data networks.

Centrex Systems

Centrex is a switching system that provides features similar to those offered by a PBX. However, in a Centrex system, services are supplied from the LEC's central office. (The word Centrex derives from *Central Exchange*.) A Centrex system prevents an organization from having to purchase and maintain its own switching equipment (as is necessary with a PBX).

Yet although a Centrex system uses public switching equipment, it is still a private switching system. In a Centrex system, a business's lines are separated from other PSTN lines at the LEC's CO so that only the subscribing business can use them. In addition to the basic dial tone, the LEC assigns services to those lines, such as call forwarding, voice mail, and station call reporting. A computer at the CO controls those features as well as call setup, routing, and supervision. The range of services that a customer can purchase for its Centrex depends on what the LEC offers. In some cases, a LEC does not offer all the features that a customer could get if he purchased a sophisticated PBX.

Centrex systems were very popular when PBXs were still unwieldy and required a significant amount of electricity and attention to maintain. Because PBXs have become smaller and easier to operate, the use of Centrex systems has decreased. But they still suit the purposes of some small organizations, even those with as few as two telephones. An example of a business that might prefer a Centrex system over a PBX is a brand new clothing store with only three extensions—one at the cash register, one in the inventory room, and one on the sales floor. If the owners have just moved into their space and do not have the time, expertise, or money to purchase and set up a PBX, the LEC's Centrex service could be a quick and easy solution. A company can save money using a Centrex because it does not have to purchase equipment, nor train employees on how to configure and troubleshoot switching equipment. On the other hand, routine calls cost an organization more with a Centrex than with a PBX.

Another advantage to using a Centrex system is its reliability. Because Centrex service runs from a CO, it can depend on the continuous power supply, security, and problem detection that a CO maintains. Contrast this to the vulnerability of a PBX that is stored in a basement closet in a shared office building. In addition, consider how long phone service might be disabled if a PBX fails at 4:00 a.m. on the day after the head technician left for a long vacation.

A Centrex can also make connecting multiple offices in a region easier, because the LEC would already have the trunks between offices installed. In fact, some of the multiple offices might be able to use the same CO and the same Centrex lines. Finally, leasing a Centrex system means that businesses can depend on the LEC to keep their technology current. They do not have to risk spending a large sum of money on a piece of equipment that may be obsolete in a few years.

However, for the organization that has technical expertise and the money to spend, Centrex services may not be the best private switching solution. Any changes in service or addition of lines to a Centrex must be requested of, then performed by, the LEC. A

LEC will probably take longer to do this than if a company's own employees were assigned to the task. Also, with a PBX, all the features are bundled into one purchase; they only need to be activated or programmed by a skilled technician. A Centrex package, however, includes monthly charges for each different group of services. Those charges are in addition to the basic per-line charge. If a large organization wants to use all the features available on modern private switching systems, it might be more economical to purchase a PBX in the long run.

ENHANCED TELEPHONE APPLICATIONS

In the discussion of private switching systems, you were introduced to some of the more popular enhanced telephone applications, such as computer telephony integration. Undoubtedly, you have used some of these simple applications, such as call forwarding, either at school or at work. In this section, you learn about the more complex telephone applications that may be part of a business's telecommunications strategy. Some of these applications are bundled with private switching systems, whereas others must be purchased separately (usually as a software package) and integrated with a private switch.

Call Accounting

Call accounting is the process of collecting call information in a database format and making it available through a user interface, such as a software program. Call accounting systems can analyze the collected data and prepare formatted reports. For each outgoing call, a call accounting system can record:

- Who initiated the call (from what extension)
- The number and identification of the called party
- How the call was dialed and routed (for example, did an inside employee use the four-digit extension to call his colleague down the hall or did he choose an outside line?)
- Whether the call was completed
- How long it took to complete the call
- Whether the call was local or long distance
- How long the call lasted
- How much the call cost

Much of the same information, other than the cost data, can be obtained for incoming calls. Incoming call data may also include how the call was routed within the organization.

Organizations may have several reasons for using a call accounting system, the most common being to find out who's calling whom. For example, a call accounting system can detect whether an employee is using the company's phone system to call his girlfriend across the country. A call accounting system may also be used for budget or chargeback purposes. For example, if call accounting indicates that the Sales Department in a company makes 50 percent of its long distance calls, the company's Accounting Department can charge the Sales Department for half of the long distance bill. In another example, a motel may use call accounting to determine how much to charge a guest for phone use when he checks out. Call accounting can also help determine general calling patterns within an organization. A hospital emergency room, for example, might be inundated with phone calls that are not true emergencies and must be routed elsewhere. The hospital management may obtain the call forwarding data and determine that an attendant should be dedicated to answering the emergency room phone number.

Some call accounting features are included with private switching systems. However, call accounting software can also be purchased separately from a PBX or KTS. Many different types of call accounting software exist. The software runs on a computer attached directly to the private switch. The switch must have a mechanism to collect this data and make it available for the computer's software. The software then allows users to view the data, in addition to analyzing and issuing customized reports based on the data.

Automatic Call Distribution

As you learned earlier in this chapter, automatic call distribution (ACD) is a method of distributing incoming calls evenly over multiple stations, according to quantity of calls handled, free time, or availability. The most common implementation of ACD takes place in call centers. For example, the computer help desk at a university would use an ACD to answer calls as quickly as possible. ACDs are used by almost all large service organizations, including hotel and airplane reservation lines, ticket counters, software and hardware support organizations, insurance companies, retailers, and so on.

An ACD answers an incoming call, then analyzes information about the call. For example, it may recognize the caller's number and based on that number, route the call to a help desk operator who last worked with that client. If all stations are busy, the ACD system places incoming calls in a queue until a station becomes free. You have probably called for assistance with a product or a service and waited in a queue. Some ACDs alert the callers to the expected wait time before a station will become free, and some play music or recorded messages. When a station becomes free, the ACD transfers the call to that station. Companies can program ACD systems to send a greater percentage of calls to certain stations. For example, in a help desk situation, two operators might be on primary duty between 8:00 a.m. and 10:00 a.m., taking calls as often as possible. But at the same time, two operators may be on secondary duty, taking calls only when the two primary stations are busy and meanwhile performing other tasks. The ACD system could be programmed to always send calls to the primary stations unless they were busy.

ACDs can also generate information about calls, including how many calls were sent to a queue, how long the callers waited in the queue, and whether they hung up before the ACD could forward their call to an operator. This data is valuable for an organization's planning purposes. If more than twenty percent of a company's callers hang up before reaching an operator, for example, the company might decide to hire more operators or change the way the ACD handles calls.

Computer Telephony Integration

Computer telephony integration (CTI), as you learned earlier, is a method of joining the features of a private switch with the features of a networked computer. With the combined functionality of both, CTI enables an organization to better control and assess its telecommunications use and strategy. CTI computerizes the switching process. At the same time, it provides the intelligence behind other applications, such as ACD and interactive voice response (discussed in the next section). Its features can be divided into three major categories: call control, media processing, and customer data management. Some of the significant call control functions that CTI enables include:

- Automatic dialing from a PC interface
- Call screening based on incoming phone number identification
- Call forwarding programmed through a simple PC interface (for example, if you are planning to work in the lunch room, you could program your telephone, using your networked computer, to ring the phone in the lunch room, but only if it is a call from your husband or boss)
- Automated attendant services
- Call logging and the collection of call accounting data

Some of the significant media processing features that CTI enables include:

- Voice message recording and playback
- Fax storing and sending
- Speech recognition and text-to-speech translation (for instance, your CTI-enabled computer could read an e-mail message to you)
- Online call recording

And some of the customer data management features that CTI enables include:

- Access to personal phone books saved on the network
- Caller database records that appear when a number is selected from the phone book (for example, a sales representative might use a CTI system to view the text of a previous conversation with a customer and remind the customer that he promised to meet with the salesperson that month)
- Retrieval of customer calling patterns and billing information
- Access to customer schedules

CTI software operates on a networked computer attached directly through a cable to the private switch. Through this link, the computer exchanges data with, and controls, the switch. The communication between the computer and the switch may be based on proprietary standards according to the switch manufacturer's requirements, or open standards. Within the software, standard programming interfaces enable the software code to interact with the switch's circuitry. Figure 5-18 depicts a simple CTI setup.

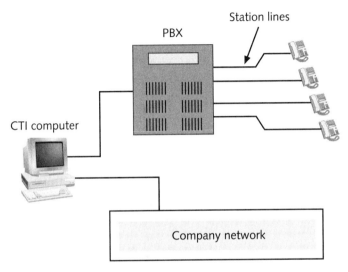

Figure 5-18   A simple CTI installation

A CTI software package ships with standard features, but once a technician installs the software, she must customize it for her organization's environment. For example, if a retailer wants to route all of the calls to its toll free service number to the east coast call center in the morning and to the west coast call center in the afternoon, the retailer's technician would have to configure the CTI software to make this happen. Numerous other parameters may need to be set for each specialized function an organization wishes to use.

CTI is most useful in the service and hospitality industries, where it provides the foundation for ACD. It can streamline the process of helping customers. For example, when a customer calls, the CTI software can identify the customer's number and correlate that with the customer's call history. Based on that call history, the CTI software can direct the switch to route the call to the same operator with whom the caller spoke the last time he called. This potentially saves the organization time and money. It may also improve customer relations.

Interactive Voice Response (IVR)

Like ACD, interactive voice response (IVR) is an application that depends on CTI. IVR systems enable individuals to provide and retrieve information to and from a computer through a touch-tone phone. IVR saves money by allowing customers to help themselves rather than speak to a person and ask questions. It may also be more convenient for customers to use an IVR than to wait for an operator to answer. Rather than a human answering a customer's call, the IVR system answers with a synthesized voice (generated by a computer attached to the private switch) and prompts the caller to select a number that corresponds to his interest. An IVR may provide information, accept information from a customer (to be saved into a database), allow the customer to help direct his call through a series of options, or allow the caller to choose to speak with an operator.

For example, you might call a large financial institution to find out how to open an account. When you call the customer service number, you are presented with a series of options that correspond to buttons on your keypad. Let's say that the IVR instructs you to press the number "2" if you want to open an account. The IVR recognizes the DTMF signal from the number "2" and proceeds to the next set of options. It may prompt you to select a checking or savings account, for example. At any point in the series of options, an IVR may allow the caller to exit the system or press a number (such as "0") to speak with a live operator. Another person might call the same customer service number to transfer money from her savings account to her checking account. In this example, the IVR accepts the caller's input and makes changes to her account based on that input. IVR responses can be either generic or personalized. If they are personalized, the IVR must rely on a customer database on the CTI computer.

More sophisticated IVR systems can interpret speech. For example, if an IVR wanted to verify the dollar amount that a caller wanted to transfer from one account to another, a synthesized voice could read back the figure, then ask the caller to "Press 1 or say 'yes' if this is correct." When the caller says "Yes," the IVR recognizes the simple command, interprets her response, and continues with its programmed sequence of actions.

As with ACD systems, IVR is most commonly used by large service organizations that field a number of calls, such as banks, universities, hotels, insurance companies, utilities, ticket counters, and so on. IVR is especially economical if many of the calls are routine—in other words, if many callers want the same type of information. For example, a theater may customize their IVR to enable callers to choose a number to find out when the next performance of a particular play takes place. The IVR may also rely on a ticketing database to inform callers whether any seats are left for a specific performance. The fact that a human does not have to answer this type of routine question saves the theater a significant amount of money and time.

Voice Mail

If you have worked in an office, you are undoubtedly familiar with voice mail. To some people, voice mail is a wonderful, time-saving application, while to others it is a frustrating obstacle to communication. As you learned earlier in this chapter, voice mail is a computerized system that allows callers to leave messages when a party does not answer the phone. Greetings and messages are saved in digital format on the computer's hard disk.

The computer also holds the voice mail system software, including standard directions spoken by a synthesized voice, such as "Press 1 to leave a message." By allowing callers to communicate even when their intended recipient doesn't answer, a voice mail system aids communication between time zones, reduces the incidence of "phone tag" (repeated, unsuccessful attempts at communication), improves communication between workers on different shifts, and can even make communication more succinct and more secure.

Many different vendors provide distinct types of voice mail systems. But each system belongs to one of two categories: standalone or integrated. A standalone voice mail system works independently of a private switching system. It may consist of a service supplied by a LEC's CO or it may be a separate device, similar to an answering machine, connected to one or more station lines. A standalone voice mail system suits a small business or one whose employees do not urgently need to keep their messages. Standalone voice mail systems are limited in their ability to reveal details about the call, such as what the originating number was. Also, standalone systems cannot automatically determine what voice mail box (the specific area on the computer used to store one person's messages) a subscriber belongs to based on the subscriber's telephone number or extension. Consequently, when someone wants to forward her incoming calls to voice mail, in a standalone voice mail system, she must specify her telephone extension. Similarly, she must call the voice mail system and identify her extension to retrieve voice mail messages. Standalone voice mail systems do not provide any signals, such as a message waiting light, to the user's telephone, because they are not connected to the private switching system (for example, a PBX).

An integrated voice mail system is one that is connected with a private switching system through a direct cable, similar to the way in which a CTI computer connects with a private switching system. Because it is integrated, the voice mail system can work with the switch to retrieve and store call data and routing information. For example, imagine that a scientist decides to work in the corporate library for the day and forwards her telephone to an extension in the library. If she is on that extension's telephone when someone tries to call her, the integrated voice mail system has the intelligence to direct the caller to her voice mail box, rather than the voice mail box for the library's extension. An integrated voice mail system can also send supervisory signals to the users' telephones to indicate that a voice mail message is waiting in the system. When users access an integrated voice mail system, they need not supply their extension number, because the system can obtain that information from the switch. Integrated voice mail systems suit organizations with many extensions and those that must save and record details about voice mail messages.

CHAPTER SUMMARY

❏ Customer premise equipment includes telephones, modems, fax machines, answering machines, and so on. It may or may not be owned by the customer.

❑ To transmit signals, telephone systems use direct current (DC) electricity. Local telephone companies in North America provide 48 V current from their Class 5 central offices. The current carries voice signals, tones (such as dialing and ringing tones), and signals about call status.

❑ The mechanism that is depressed when a handset is hung up is called a switch hook. In addition to closing a circuit, lifting a switch hook alerts the switch at the end office that the party wants to make a call. Depressing the switch hook may provide additional functions.

❑ The phone line that enters a residence usually contains at least four wires, or two pairs of wires. A wire used to transmit signals is known as a ring wire; the wire used to ground the loop is known as the tip. A ring and tip together form a pair. Inside the subscriber's home, the wires terminate at a standard jack known as an RJ-11.

❑ Touch tone, or simply tone, dialers operate by transmitting a combination of two frequencies each time a button is pressed. This type of encoding is known as dual-tone multifrequency (DTMF). The local CO's switch translates these combined frequencies into numbers with a DTMF receiver.

❑ To shield against surges, telephone companies use station protection devices at both their central offices and at the demarcation point for every subscriber line. These devices use a gas tube to short the circuit and divert incoming high voltage to a ground. At a demarcation point, a grounding wire might be connected to a nearby metal pipe, such as a water pipe.

❑ In the telecommunications industry, a pay telephone is more commonly called a COCOT (customer-owned coin-operated telephone). COCOTs are more difficult to manage than regular subscriber telephone sets. In particular, they are susceptible to vandalism and fraud.

❑ After the caller drops a coin into a pay telephone, its magnetism, weight, and diameter are tested to verify that it is a coin and not a fraudulent replica. To deter vandals, COCOTs may sound alarms and issue messages to the local CO when they have been physically damaged.

❑ Cordless telephones are those that can be used without a physical connection to a telephone set, but still rely on a base station to connect to the PSTN. A base station transmits the telephone signals it receives from the inside wiring to the cordless phone over a single frequency, which may belong to one of several ranges.

❑ To exchange signals, both the cordless handset and the base station of a cordless phone contain a radio transmitter, antenna, and receiver.

❑ Not until 1946 could third-party auxiliary equipment, such as answering machines, be attached to telephones. After 1984 and the breakup of AT&T, a proliferation of new telecommunications companies set up shop and began selling simpler and less expensive answering machines.

❑ TTY stands for TeleTYpewriter, a device that uses alphanumeric characters entered through a keyboard to communicate over a voice or data network. TDD stands for Telecommunications Device for the Deaf, a device that uses a TTY and a text display to help speech- and hearing-impaired people communicate over the PSTN.

❑ Private switching, in which calls are connected independent of the local telephone company's COs, enables organizations to set up and route internal calls at a much lower cost.

❑ A key telephone system (KTS) is a private switching system that provides centralized line and intercom access, plus other enhanced services, for multiple telephone users within an organization. It consists of a wall-mounted control console that connects to the organization's internal phones and to the end office. This key service unit (KSU) signals the telephone attendant about incoming calls, controls busy indicator lights on line buttons, and tracks call information, among other tasks.

❑ A KTS usually handles multiple lines from the telephone company and connects multiple telephones inside an organization. Small offices of up to 50 users are most apt to use a KTS.

❑ A private branch exchange (PBX) is a switch owned and operated by a business or other private organization that connects their multiple telephone sets to one or more central offices. It provides call setup and routing within an organization, plus a host of enhanced features.

❑ A PBX differs from a KTS in that it is more sophisticated and can operate independently of the telephone company for internal calls. A PBX provides its connected telephones with dial tone and can connect an organization to the PSTN through a trunk.

❑ A PBX consists of three significant elements: station lines, the lines that connect individual telephone sets to the switch; common control, the computer that processes incoming calls, outgoing calls, call setup, routing, supervision and data gathering; and trunks, the lines that connect the switch to COs. PBX equipment can vary widely.

❑ PBXs may support digital or analog transmission over its trunks and PBX trunks may connect to LECs, IXCs, or other private switching systems. A permanent circuit that connects two PBXs is called a tie trunk.

❑ The word Centrex derives from Central Exchange. Centrex is a switching system that provides similar features as a PBX, but the services are supplied from the LEC's central office.

❑ In a Centrex system, a business's lines are separated from other PSTN lines at the LEC's CO and only the subscribing business can use them. In addition to the basic dial tone, the LEC assigns services to those lines, such as call forwarding, voice mail, and station call reporting. A computer at the CO controls those features as well as the call setup, routing, and supervision.

❏ One advantage to using a Centrex system is its reliability. Because Centrex service runs from a CO, it can depend on the continuous power supply, security, and problem detection that a CO maintains.

❏ Automatic call distribution (ACD) is a method of distributing incoming calls evenly over multiple stations, according to quantity of calls handled, free time, or availability. An ACD answers an incoming call, analyzes information about the call, then forwards the call.

❏ Computer telephony integration (CTI) is a method of joining the features of a private switch with the features of a networked computer. CTI computerizes the switching process. It provides the intelligence behind other applications, such as ACD and interactive voice response.

❏ CTI software operates on a networked computer attached directly to the private switch. Through this link, the computer exchanges data with, and controls, the switch. Within the software, standard programming interfaces enable the software code to interact with the switch's circuitry.

❏ Interactive voice response (IVR) is an application that depends on CTI. IVR systems enable individuals to provide and retrieve information to and from a computer through a touch-tone phone. IVR saves money by allowing customers to help themselves rather than speak to a person and ask questions.

❏ Each voice mail system belongs to one of two categories: standalone or integrated. A standalone voice mail system works independently of a private switching system. An integrated voice mail system is connected directly to a private switch.

KEY TERMS

automated route selection (ARS) — A method of determining over which trunk an outgoing call should be routed to incur the lowest cost.

automatic call distribution (ACD) — A method of distributing incoming calls evenly over multiple stations, according to quantity of calls handled, free time, or availability.

base station — The stationary half of a cordless telephone set. A base station contains wiring to connect to the PSTN, plus a radio antenna, transmitter, and receiver to exchange signals with the cordless telephone handset. Depending on the type of phone, it may use one of several different frequencies and may have a range from 200 to 2000 feet.

call accounting — The process of collecting call information in a database format and making it available through a user interface, such as a software program. Call accounting systems can analyze the collected data and prepare formatted reports.

call forwarding — A feature that allows a user to send a call to another station connected to a private switching system.

5

call hold — The ability to place an active connection on hold while using the telephone for something else (such as making an outgoing call).

caller identification — A feature that displays the name and telephone number of the party who is calling. This feature requires that the switches at the local central office are capable of transmitting this information and that the called party has a telephone set capable of displaying it.

call pickup — A characteristic of key telephone systems that requires the user to push a button on the telephone station to select a line before placing a call.

Centrex — A switching system that provides similar features as a PBX, but the services are supplied from the LEC's central office. The word Centrex is derived from Central Exchange.

COCOT (customer-owned coin-operated telephone) — A coin operated telephone (as it is called in the telecommunications industry).

computer-telephony integration (CTI) — A method of combining the features of a PBX with the features of a networked computer.

customer premise equipment (CPE) — The part of a telecommunications system that resides at the customer's home or business. Usually, but not always, a customer owns and is responsible for CPE. Traditional telephony CPE includes inside wiring, telephones, PBX, and key systems.

DID (direct inward dialing) trunk — In a PBX, the connection to a central office that allows callers outside an organization to directly dial PBX users inside an organization using a seven-digit number.

direct inward dialing (DID) — A feature that enables parties from outside the organization to dial an extension's seven digit number directly, rather than going through an attendant to complete the call.

distinctive ringing — A unique ringing tone or cadence that identifies different types of calls.

do not disturb — A feature that allows a user to disable her telephone from ringing and accepting incoming calls.

dual-tone multifrequency (DTMF) — The coding scheme used by touch-tone dialers. DTMF transmits a combination of two frequencies each time a button is pressed.

handset — The part of the telephone that contains a transmitter and receiver and can be removed from the stationary equipment to allow the user to be mobile while he talks. When a handset is removed from the switch hook, the local loop's circuit is completed.

hybrid coil — A device introduced into telephone sets in the early 1900s to separate the incoming transmit and receive signals into their own two-wire connections.

hybrid telephone system — A private switching system that has some characteristics of a KTS and some characteristics of a PBX. Digital KTSs are considered hybrid telephone systems.

inside wiring — The telecommunications system wiring that is located inside the customer's home or business.

intercom — A feature found in private switching systems that enables users to push a one- or two-digit number to speak directly with a colleague in the same office.

key service unit (KSU) — A centralized, wall-mounted control console that provides the intelligence behind a KTS. A KSU connects to the organization's internal phones and to the telephone company's end office. It signals the telephone attendant about incoming calls, controls busy indicator lights on line buttons, and tracks call information, among other tasks.

key telephone system (KTS) — A device that provides centralized line and intercom access, plus other enhanced services, for multiple telephone users within an organization. Unlike a PBX, a KTS relies on the telephone company's CO to supply its users with dial tone.

message waiting — A light on the telephone that indicates if a party has a message waiting in his voice mail.

music on hold — A feature found in some private switching systems that plays music or promotional recordings while a caller is placed on hold.

pay telephone (pay phone) — A telephone provided for public use that requires coin, collect, or credit card payment to complete telephone calls.

privacy — A feature standard in most private switching systems that prevents other parties from picking up a line that is in use.

private branch exchange (PBX) — A private switching system owned and operated by a business or other organization that connects multiple phone lines within an organization to one or more central offices. You can think of a PBX as a miniature CO. It provides call setup and routing within an organization, plus a host of enhanced features.

private switching — A method of switching in which calls within an organization are completed independent of the local telephone company's CO. Private switching enables organizations to set up and route internal calls at a much lower cost.

relay center — A centralized call center with live operators who translate input typed into a TDD for the non hearing-impaired party, listen to the response, then type the response for reception by the hearing-impaired party's TDD.

ring — The wire in a telephone wire pair that carries a negative charge (48 V) from the central office's battery to a telephone.

ringback — A repeating pattern of combined 440 Hz plus 480 Hz tones that ring for two seconds, then are followed by a four-second silence. Ringback is issued by an end office telephone switch. Ringback is also known as ringing tone.

ringer — The device that sounds a bell or tone on a subscriber's telephone to indicate an incoming call.

ringing tone — *See* ringback.

RJ-11 (registered jack number 11) — The jack used to terminate two- or three-pair telephone connections.

rotary — A dialing scheme in which the turning and releasing of a numbered wheel alternately opens and closes the local loop circuit, issuing a series of pulses as the dial returns to its position. The local central office's switch can translate those pulses into numbers. Rotary dialing was replaced by touch-tone dialing in the late twentieth century.

spread spectrum — A method of transmission in which a signal is separated and its separate pieces distributed over a wide range of frequencies. Using spread spectrum in wireless transmission is more secure than using a single frequency.

station equipment — Any type of telephone and its ancillary parts.

station message detail recording (SMDR) — A method used by PBXs for recording and printing call details for each connected station, such as the caller's and the call recipient's identification, when the call was made, how long the call lasted, and so on.

station restriction — A feature available in most private switching systems that can prevent specific telephones from making certain types of calls or using certain features.

switch hook — The device that holds a handset and closes a switch when the handset is lifted to complete the local loop circuit. In modern telephony, depressing and releasing switch hooks may provide additional functions, such as accepting an incoming call while using the call waiting feature.

tie trunk — A dedicated circuit that connects two PBX systems.

tip — The wire in a telephone wire pair that supplies the ground (or nearly zero charge) from the central office's battery to the telephone.

tone — touch tone.

totalizer — A device inside a coin operated telephone that determines what type of coin was deposited and relays that information to the switch through pulses of brief dual-frequency tones.

touch tone — A method of dialing that uses dual-tone multifrequency encoding, in which pressing any number on the telephone keypad transmits a combination of two frequencies. These frequencies can be translated into numbers by the end office switch.

TDD (Telecommunications Device for the Deaf) — A specially designed device that uses a TTY and a visual interface to help speech- and hearing-impaired people communicate over the PSTN.

TTY (TeleTYpewriter) — A device invented by the Teletype Corporation that uses alphanumeric characters entered through a keyboard to communicate over a voice or data network.

unified messaging — The combination of telephone, voice mail, e-mail, fax, and paging services so that users only need consult one source to pick up their messages.

voice mail — A computerized system of recording messages for later retrieval, used when a party does not answer an incoming call.

REVIEW QUESTIONS

1. What type of electricity does a local loop use to transmit and receive voice signals?

   a. alternating current

   b. frequency modulated current

   c. direct current

   d. sinusoidal current

2. How many wire pairs can a typical RJ-11 jack accept?

   a. 1 or 2

   b. 2 or 3

   c. 3 or 4

   d. 4 or 6

3. What device was invented to separate telephone transmission and reception into two distinct wire paths within the telephone set?

   a. hybrid coil

   b. totalizer

   c. switch hook

   d. handset

4. Which pair of wires is typically used if a subscriber has only one telephone line connected to his house?

   a. blue and white

   b. green and red

   c. black and yellow

   d. orange and blue

5. Which wire, in a local loop connection, acts as the ground for the transmission circuit?

   a. tip

   b. sphere

   c. ring

   d. pair

6. Explain the difference between rotary and touch-tone dialing.

7. In DTMF, pressing each number on the keypad issues how many different frequencies to the local switch?

   a. 1

   b. 2

   c. 3

   d. 4

8. In DTMF, what is the fourth column of frequencies used for?

   a. dialing letters that aren't represented by numbers on the keypad

   b. dialing long distance numbers

   c. signaling between specialized equipment

   d. absorbing extra local loop current

9. Which of the following is *not* considered when a coin telephone is verifying the authenticity of an inserted coin?

   a. the diameter of the coin

   b. the weight of the coin

   c. the magnetic properties of the coin

   d. the imprint (or "face") of the coin

10. What would happen if you tried to pry a coin telephone off its base with a crowbar?

   a. The coin telephone would sound an alarm.

   b. The coin telephone would issue a small electric shock.

   c. The coin telephone would issue a signal to the local police department.

   d. The coin telephone would easily come apart.

11. What three components must a base station and a cordless handset contain to exchange signals?

12. What technique can be used to make conversations over cordless phones more secure?

   a. line-of-sight transmission

   b. frequency modulation

   c. passcode modulation

   d. spread spectrum transmission

13. How does an answering machine know when to hang up after a message has been recorded?

   a. It waits for a signal from the end office switch.

   b. It waits for a signal from the other party's handset.

   c. It waits for a specified period of silence.

   d. It waits for a drop in voltage on the local loop.

14. If you don't own a TDD, but you are calling someone who uses a TDD, where do you have to call first?

   a. the TDD user's end office switch

   b. a TDD relay center

   c. a TDD service provider

   d. a TDD substation

5

15. Which of the following is one significant advantage of private switching over public switching for a large organization?

    a. lower setup costs

    b. less technical expertise required

    c. less space required

    d. faster internal call completion

16. From what requirement did the "key telephone system" derive its name?

    a. A caller must push a key to select an outgoing line.

    b. A caller must enter an accounting key before he can select an outgoing line.

    c. The private switch must transmit a key to the CO before it can gain access to the PSTN.

    d. The private switch assigns a key to each station line for call accounting purposes.

17. What is the term for a private switching system that contains some characteristics of a KTS and some characteristics of a PBX?

    a. KTS-PBX

    b. hybrid telephone system

    c. digital private switch

    d. layer 3 switch

18. Which of the following features are standard with every KTS installation?

    a. voice mail

    b. caller identification

    c. trunk queuing

    d. supervisory signals

19. Although KTS is becoming more like a PBX system, what is one remaining difference between the two?

    a. KTS can only connect up to twelve stations.

    b. KTS cannot impose station restrictions.

    c. KTS does not provide its own dial tone.

    d. KTS is not capable of connecting to a voice mail system.

20. What type of trunk connects two PBXs over a distance?

    a. DID trunk

    b. carrier trunk

    c. POP trunk

    d. tie trunk

21. What has the invention of the semiconductor (and integrated circuit) done for PBX systems?

    a. made them less expensive

    b. made them easier to install and configure

    c. made them more compact

    d. made them disposable

22. What part of a PBX system oversees all of its operations?

    a. trunk interface

    b. station line interface

    c. central processor

    d. switching module

23. What's the primary difference between a PBX and a Centrex system?

24. Which of the following is an advantage of using a Centrex system over using a PBX?

    a. lower installation costs

    b. quicker call setup

    c. easier modifications

    d. lower ongoing costs

25. Which of the following *cannot* be determined by a call accounting system?

    a. the time at which a call was placed

    b. the extension that originated an outgoing call

    c. the cost of an incoming call

    d. the duration of a call

26. Provide three examples of organizations that would benefit from using an ACD system.

27. How does a CTI computer connect to a private switch?

    a. through the CO trunk

    b. through a cable

    c. over a network

    d. over the Internet

28. What does the "I" in IVR stand for?

    a. integrated

    b. interactive

    c. institutional

    d. incoming

29. What feature, found in IVR, enables a caller to speak his response rather than press a number?

    a. speech recognition

    b. ACD

    c. speech-to-text conversion

    d. speech-to-number conversion

30. What type of voice mail system does not require a PBX?

    a. integrated

    b. self-service

    c. networked

    d. standalone

HANDS-ON PROJECTS

Project 5-1

In this project, you explore, first hand, the insides of an older, rotary phone. Specifically, you witness the kind of technology that has since been replaced by integrated circuits. For this project, you need a desktop rotary phone that was manufactured anytime between 1930 and 1975, such as the Western Electric model 500. If your school does not have old rotary phones available for the experiment, you may obtain one through a telephone surplus store on the Web, through E-bay, or at a local flea market. Older rotary phones may cost anywhere from $2.00 to $500.00 for the more valuable antique phones. The average price is about $15.00. Because you will disassemble the phone in this project, find the least expensive equipment you can, and if possible, perform this experiment with a partner. In addition to the phone, you also need a basic tool kit that includes a small Phillips-head screwdriver, a medium-sized flathead screwdriver, and an X-acto knife. Finally, you need a piece of paper and pen to write down your answers to the questions included in the following steps.

1. Examine the outside of the phone. Look on the bottom of its base to find out who manufactured the phone and see if the year is indicated. Notice if the phone has "Property of Bell Telephone Company" or a similar warning stamped on its casing.

2. On a separate piece of paper, note the color of the phone (if it was made before the 1960s, it is probably black). Describe what the cord and the wall plug look like. Does this phone use an RJ-11 plug?

3. Lift the handset. Notice where the cord enters the handset. Can you remove the cord?

4. Notice how the transmitter (mouthpiece) and receiver (earpiece) are sealed. Remove the cover from the transmitter by unscrewing it as you would remove a jar lid.

5. What type of transmitter technology does this telephone use? Can you remove it from the handset? If so, note how the transmitter connects to the transmission wires.

6. Remove the cover from the receiver. What kind of receiver technology does this phone use?

7. If possible, remove the receiver from the handset and observe how it connects to the reception wires.

8. Check to see if it has screws holding the metal base to its cover. If so, remove those screws before prying off the plastic cover (this will probably require a small Phillips-head screwdriver). Also check to make sure the fingerwheel (the rotary dial) is not fastened through the cover. If so, take off the fingerwheel. Now, using the flathead screwdriver, pry the plastic casing off the base station.

9. After you have removed the telephone's plastic cover, observe its internal components. Describe what the ringer or buzzer looks like. Can you manually make it sound? If not, what kind of sound do you suppose it makes?

10. Notice where the wires enter the base and where they exit in order to connect to the cord. Can you tell which wires go to the transmitter and which wires go to the receiver? Identify the hybrid coil and notice how it separates the incoming wires.

11. Now take a look at the switch hook. Press the buttons in the handset cradle to move the switch hook. Notice how the circuit is closed as you do so.

12. Attempt to move the dialer. What happens on the opposite side of the dialer when you do this?

13. Make some general conclusions about this telephone. What component takes up the most room inside the casing? Which components were good candidates for replacement by integrated circuits and why? Which components might become obsolete and why? Which components have modern equivalents with much greater functionality? Can you think of any advantages that this phone has over modern electronic phones?

14. Put the phone back together by replacing its plastic cover and the cover for both the transmitter and receiver.

Project 5-2

In this project, you find out what is inside a newer, electronic phone. You compare this technology to the components you witnessed in Project 5-1 and note the similarities and differences between the two phones. For this project, you need a slim electronic, touch-tone phone that was manufactured anytime after 1980 and that has touch-tone buttons on the inside of the handset. If your school does not have any old touch-tone phones available for the experiment, you may obtain a used one through a telephone surplus store on the Web, through E-bay, or at a local flea market. Alternatively, you can purchase a new one from a discount store for less than $10. Because you will disassemble the phone in this project (though you probably won't render it unusable), find the least expensive equipment you can, and if possible, perform this experiment with a partner. In addition to the phone, you also need a basic tool kit that includes a small Phillips-head screwdriver and a larger flathead screwdriver. Finally, you need a piece of paper and pen to write down your answers to the questions included in the following steps.

1. First, examine the outside of the phone, just as you examined the rotary phone. Look on the bottom of its base to find out who manufactured the phone and see if the year is indicated.

2. On a piece of paper, note the color of the phone, describe what the cord and the wall plug look like. Does this phone use an RJ-11 plug?

3. Lift the handset. Notice where the cord enters the handset. Can you remove the cord?

4. Notice how the transmitter and receiver are sealed. In most inexpensive touch-tone phones, the handset is made of two pieces of plastic, wedged together. The plastic may also be screwed together. If you cannot pop the two pieces of plastic apart by wedging a flathead screwdriver into the seam, they probably are screwed together. Check under the keypad or under the small plastic window (which is meant to hold a piece of paper bearing the phone number of the extension) for screws. Remove the screws (this will probably require a small Phillips-head screwdriver).

5. What type of transmitter technology does this telephone use? How does it compare (in size and function) to the transmitter in the rotary phone? Can you remove it from the handset? If so, note how the transmitter connects to the transmission wires.

6. Look at the receiver. Remove it from the handset if you can (you may need the Phillips-head screwdriver for this). What kind of receiver technology does this phone use? How does it compare to the receiver in the rotary phone?

7. Follow the wires out from the receiver. To what do they connect? What can you presume about the function of this component?

8. Follow the wires away from this component to the phone's RJ-11 jack. What color are the two incoming wires? Notice how the two incoming wires are split into four wires, two for transmission and two for reception.

9. Press the switch hook on the other side of the handset and see what happens on the inside of the handset. How does this compare to the switch hook in the rotary phone?

10. Given all the components that are in the handset, what can you conclude about the components in the telephone's base station?

11. Press the touch-tone buttons on the inside of the handset and attempt to view their affect on the inside of the handset. Continue to take apart the phone and experiment with its moving parts.

12. Make some general conclusions about this telephone. What component takes up the most room inside the casing? Which components are now made of ICs that in the rotary phone were electromechanical? Which components do you think might continue to become more sophisticated with time? What advantages does this phone have over the rotary phone?

13. Put the phone back together by replacing any parts you removed and replacing the handset's plastic casing.

Project 5-3

In this project, you have the opportunity to interact with an IVR system. For this project, you only need a working touch-tone phone and telephone line that allows you to dial a 1-800 telephone number.

1. Because the U.S. government provides a great deal of information to citizens, many of its agencies use IVR systems. One program that uses an IVR system is Medicare. To hear how Medicare's IVR works, call their toll free number at 1-800-633-4227 (1-800-MEDICARE).

2. The IVR operator welcomes you to the Medicare telephone system, then asks whether you want to listen to the messages in English or Spanish. Press 1 or 2, depending on whether you want to hear messages in English or Spanish, respectively.

3. Listen to the main menu of options, and then press 5 to hear Medicare's answers to frequently asked questions.

4. Listen to the frequently asked questions options, and then press the * key to repeat the list of options.

5. Next, press 3 to hear answers to the question, "What are my Medicare health plan choices?"

6. Listen to the complete answer, and then press 2 to listen to more frequently asked questions.

7. Listen to the frequently asked questions options again, and then press 2 to hear answers to the question, "What medical supplies and equipment does Medicare cover?"

8. Listen to the answer, and then press 9 to return to the main menu and listen to the list of options.

9. Press 2 to hear about to hear about Medicaid programs available for paying healthcare costs. According to the IVR, you can retrieve information specific to your area by pressing 1.

10. Press 1, and then enter your zip code to find the number of the nearest Medicare office. The IVR will repeat the numbers you entered. Press 1 to verify that those numbers are correct.

11. Listen to the information on your local office, and then return to the main menu and try choosing different options. Based on the options you have listened to, draw a hierarchical menu of Medicare's IVR system.

12. What IVR features do you think had to be custom programmed and what IVR features do you think came with the system? List the two types of features in two separate columns.

13. At what point in the IVR system did you hear a synthesized voice, as opposed to a recording of a real, human voice?

5

CASE PROJECTS

1. You are a professional telecommunications consultant to Southern Technical College. Your mission is to research private switching solutions and recommend software, hardware, and an installation plan for this solution. The college currently has 600 students in its dorm rooms, but intends to triple its enrollment over the next five years. It also has 100 faculty and staff. Thanks to some recent private foundation grants, Southern Tech. has enough money to purchase a quality private switching system and prefers to do this rather than to buy new equipment in a few years to replace obsolete hardware and software. The administrators also want a private switching solution that includes voice mail and that can connect to the college's LAN. Before you can research solutions and make a suggestion, list six additional questions you need to ask the administrators to better understand the college's private switching needs.

2. Now that you have met with all the key administrators, you have learned that they currently use a Nortel PBX and telephone sets that were installed in 1992. Further, they agreed that they need call waiting, automated attendant, call forwarding, message waiting indicators, and at some point, they may want to add a CTI system, but one that isn't necessarily by the same manufacturer that supplies their PBX. You also learned that their PBX must be available to accept calls 24 hours a day. Spend some time on the Web researching a variety of PBX solutions. What type of private switching system do you recommend to the Southern Tech. administrators and why? Specifically what features does this system offer? How long will it last before they might have to purchase new equipment? How much do you think this system might cost? (Although cost information is often not available from the vendors' Web sites, it may be available through articles in Telecommunications journals that compare solutions. Alternatively, you can call the vendor to speak with a sales representative and get some pricing information.)

3. Now that you have presented your PBX solution to Southern Tech., you decide that they might also benefit from having an IVR system to answer routine questions about registration, admissions, classes, office hours, and so on. If you were the technician configuring the IVR menu system for Southern Tech's general assistance phone number, how would you organize this menu system? Think about where you would place the most frequently used options on the telephone keypad. Draw a diagram of your proposed menu system, using at least four levels of options.

6

SIGNALING AND SWITCHING

After reading this chapter and completing the exercises, you will be able to:

◆ Define modulation and explain its four basic versions

◆ Explain the different types of multiplexing techniques, their benefits, and hardware requirements

◆ Discuss the fundamental types of switching used in voice and data communications

◆ Identify the differences between local and tandem switching

◆ Describe modern signaling techniques used to route calls to their destination

In previous chapters, you learned the difference between analog and digital transmission, the history and nature of telephone equipment, and the way in which telecommunications carriers interconnect. This chapter explains the concepts of signaling and switching.

To understand the difference between signaling and switching, an analogy might be helpful. One way to think of a telephone network is to compare it to your body's central nervous system. In this analogy, a switch would be centered in your brain, the part of your body that accepts information from the rest of your body and makes decisions based on that information. At the other end of your central nervous system are nerve endings in your limbs and digits that can detect external stimuli, such as the difference between hot and cold. Similarly, telephone equipment receives signals from callers and transmits them to the switch. The signals that travel from your skin through your central nervous system, up your spinal cord, and to your brain are similar to telephone signals. Both depend on a small amount of electrical current to carry messages. In a telephone network, however, the nerve pathways are equivalent to local loops and interoffice trunks. To handle more information faster, telephony engineers have developed methods of combining several signals over one pathway. You learn about these techniques, as well as how a telephone network's "brain" operates, in the sections that follow.

MODULATION

Recall from Chapter 2 that electromagnetic energy is a field of both electric and magnetic waves combined. Uncontrolled electromagnetic energy radiates freely and chaotically in many directions, much like waves of water in a large pool that contains a number of splashing children. Left uncontrolled, electromagnetic waves, and thus, the signals they carry, continually interfere with each other, making clear communication impossible.

One way to control signals and ensure that they arrive at their intended destination in their intended form is modulation. **Modulation** is a technique for processing signals in which two waves are combined to produce a wave that possesses characteristics of both and can be decoded to separate these characteristics. The wave containing the signal you want to transmit is called the **information wave**. The wave that is modulated, and whose properties are constant and known to both the sender and receiver, is called the **carrier wave**. The information wave is imposed on a carrier wave to create a unique wave pattern.

For example, in the case of an FM radio station, the predetermined carrier wave may have a frequency of 88.7 MHz. If your favorite radio station is at 88.7 FM, you can always tune the radio to that carrier wave's frequency and rely on the radio to interpret the information wave's signal—for example, the morning news. Waves that are bound to a carrier wave's frequency are said to be **guided waves**. (An information wave, such as the one that transmits the morning news, is considered a guided wave.) The device that imposes the information signal on the carrier signal at the transmission end is known as a **modulator**. A **demodulator** then separates the information from the carrier signal at the receiving end.

You may recall from earlier science classes that two (or more) waves can be combined to make a single, new wave. As you can see in Figure 6-1, the resulting wave is more complex than the two original waves and contains characteristics of each.

Let's return to the pool analogy to explore the topic of modulation in more detail. As mentioned earlier, uncontrolled waves are similar to the waves produced by a group of splashing children. By contrast, a more sedate group of adults rhythmically swimming the breaststroke in lanes produces a more orderly series of waves analogous to guided waves. Now, suppose the adults were swimming laps in a wave pool—a special kind of pool, common at water parks, that generates regular waves from one side of the pool to the other. The wave generated by the pool is analogous to the carrier wave in a modulated signal. The waves generated by the swimmers are analogous to information waves. As each swimmer moves forward within his lane, the waves he creates combines with the waves generated by the pool, much as information waves combine with carrier waves. A carrier signal alone transmits no meaningful information without the changes added by the information signal.

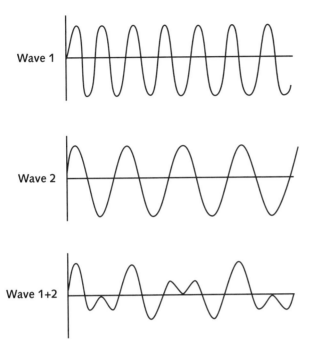

Figure 6-1   A combination of two waves

Modulation is used in both analog and digital communications. In the following sections, you learn about several types of both analog and digital modulation. Later in the chapter, you learn about multiple types of digital modulation. Modulated analog signals are used in some modern telecommunication services, notably transmission via the PSTN—but these days, digital modulation is much more common. Sometimes, it's necessary for digital equipment to send a signal over an analog system. In that case, the digital equipment must convert its digital signals to analog.

One common example of converting a digital signal to an analog signal occurs when computers must send data over analog telephone wires. To convert its signal, a computer requires **modem**, a device used to convert digital into analog signals and analog into digital signals. The word modem derives from the words **mod**ulator and **dem**odulator, which together describe its function. For example, when you use your computer to dial into your ISP's network, your computer first issues digital signals to the modem. The modem translates the digital signals into analog signals, then sends the analog signals over the telephone line. When a computer at the ISP's data center picks up your connection, its modem accepts the analog signals and translates them into digital signals that the computer can understand.

Using a modem to dial into an ISP's network is just one example of modulation and demodulation. Although every modulated signal requires a modulator to create it and a demodulator to separate the carrier from the information, the actual method of modulation can vary. You learn about several types of modulation in the following sections.

AMPLITUDE MODULATION (AM)

Amplitude modulation (AM) is a method of modulation in which the amplitude of the carrier signal is modified by the addition of the information signal. Recall from Chapter 2 that amplitude is the strength of a signal (which is indicated in a graph by the wave's height). Frequency is the number of times a wave cycles from its beginning point to its highest amplitude, to its lowest amplitude and back to where it started within a given time frame. In amplitude modulation, the carrier wave's amplitude, but not its frequency, changes with the addition of the information wave. Figure 6-2 depicts the creation of an AM wave. Notice how the carrier wave and the information wave have different amplitudes and frequencies. When the information wave is combined with the carrier wave to create an AM wave, the carrier wave's amplitude becomes variable. The carrier wave's frequency, however, does not change.

AM is the oldest type of radio broadcasting. It is still used in radio broadcasting and in shortwave, long-distance radio. But due to its limitations, AM is rarely used for modern applications, such as data transfer. You learn more about radio waves in Chapter 9, which discusses wireless transmission methods.

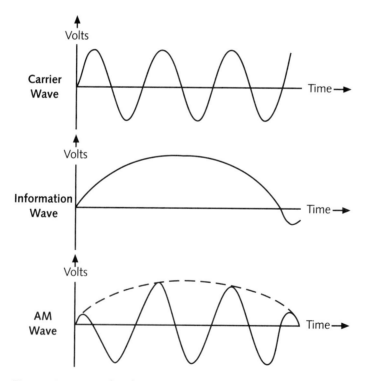

Figure 6-2   Amplitude modulation

When AM signals are converted into digital signals, parts of the wave with differing amplitudes are conveyed as either 0s or 1s, as shown in Figure 6-3. This conversion is known as amplitude shift keying, or **ASK**. (You can think of ASK as the digital version of AM.) In the simplest form of ASK, the shifts in amplitude are translated into 0s and 1s, as shown in Figure 6-3, so that the signal can be interpreted by a digital system. ASK is used on voice-grade telephone lines and older modems. However, it is not used in modern modem transmission.

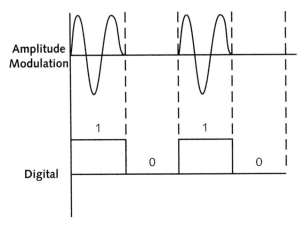

Figure 6-3   Amplitude shift keying

Frequency Modulation (FM)

Frequency modulation (FM) is a method of modulation in which the frequency of the carrier signal is modified by the addition of the information signal. Unlike with AM signals, in FM signals, the addition of the information signal does *not* change the amplitude of the carrier wave. Only the frequency of the carrier wave changes.

FM is used in microwave, cellular, mobile radio, and of course, radio broadcasting services. It is also used for the audio portion of many TV signals. FM is preferred over AM primarily because it is more resistant to noise. Figure 6-4 depicts a carrier wave using FM to transmit information. Notice how the carrier wave's amplitude is identical to the FM wave's amplitude, although their frequencies differ.

When FM signals are converted into digital signals, the differing frequencies are conveyed as either 0s or 1s, as shown in Figure 6-5. This technique is known as **frequency shift keying (FSK)**. In the simplest form of FSK, one frequency represents 1s while another frequency represents 0s. You can think of FSK as the digital version of FM. FSK is used on some modern modems.

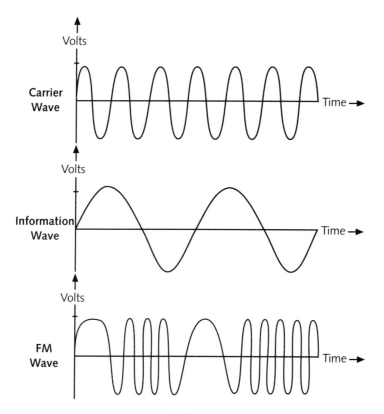

Figure 6-4 Frequency modulation

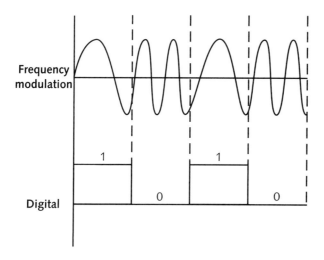

Figure 6-5 Frequency shift keying

Phase Modulation (PM)

To understand the third type of modulation, phase modulation, you need to understand the concept of a phase. In addition to its amplitude and frequency, each wave is characterized by its **phase**, or the relationship between its cycle and time. For example, imagine you had a twin with a voice identical to yours—that is, both your voice patterns possessed identical amplitude and frequency characteristics. Now, suppose you and your twin spoke the same word at precisely the same moment. If you accomplished this, the sound waves corresponding to this word would have identical phases. (In other words, the waves would be "in phase.") However, if you spoke the word a nanosecond before your twin spoke the same word, your sound waves, though identical in amplitude and frequency, would be out of phase—in other words, the waves would not have identical phases.

Phase differences between two waves are expressed in degrees. You may be familiar with the concept of degrees to describe angles or circles in geometry. For example, a triangle contains 360 degrees. In describing a wave, one full cycle equals 360 degrees. Thus, one quarter of a cycle equals 360 degrees divided by 4, or 90 degrees. Figure 6-6 shows two waves with the same amplitude and frequency whose phases vary by 90 degrees.

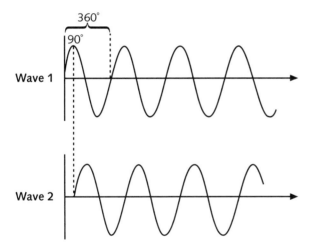

Figure 6-6   Two waves with a 90 degree phase difference

Phase modulation (PM), then, is a type of modulation in which an information wave modifies a carrier wave's phase. In phase modulation, neither the frequency nor the amplitude of the carrier wave is changed by the addition of an information wave. Figure 6-7 depicts a PM wave. Notice how the PM wave's phase is different from the carrier wave's phase. Also notice how the PM wave's phase changes each time the information wave completes a full (360-degree) cycle. Phase modulation is used to transmit color information in TV signals and for other, specialized functions.

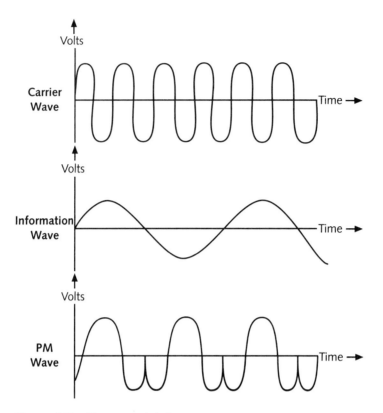

Figure 6-7   Phase modulation

The digital equivalent of PM is phase key shifting. In **phase shift keying (PSK)**, changes in phase are translated to 1s and 0s, as shown in Figure 6-8. In the simplest form of PSK, a 180-degree phase shift is used to indicate changes between 1s and 0s in the digital signal, as shown in Figure 6-8. PSK is used for sophisticated modem transmissions.

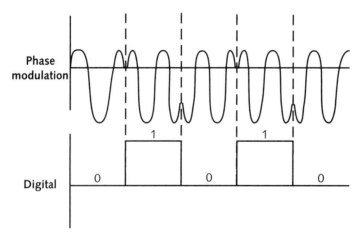

Figure 6-8   Phase shift keying

Note In addition to the types of modulation just described, more sophisticated forms of modulation are used on digital networks today. Some modulation techniques superimpose two of the techniques described previously. For example, amplitude and phase modulation may be applied to a single carrier signal for use in digital cellular systems.

Pulse Code Modulation (PCM)

In the previous sections, you learned how analog waves can be used to express analog information (for example, in AM, FM, and PM) and also how analog waves can be used to express digital information (for example, in ASK, FSK, and PSK). In these types of modulation, the way that a signal is encoded, be it analog or digital, does not change. For example, speech broadcast over AM radio is analog encoded. Modulating the carrier wave with an information wave (speech) does not change the fact that the speech is analog. In the same way, a word processing file is digitally encoded; its information is expressed in 1s and 0s. Modulating the carrier wave with an information wave (which represents the file's 1s and 0s as shifts in the wave's characteristics) does not change the fact that the file is digital.

In contrast to the types of modulation previously discussed, some types of modulation do affect the signal's encoding. In many cases, it is necessary to convert analog waves to digital signals before transmission. For example, because computers can only understand digital signals, sounds must be digitally encoded before your computer can play them. In this section, you learn how digital signals can approximate complex analog signals, such as the human voice and music.

The process of converting analog signals into digital signals is called **pulse code modulation (PCM)**. PCM is used to record instruments playing on a compact disc or to record voice messages on a digital answering machine, for example. It is also used in preparing speech to be transmitted over a data network. PCM is more complicated than the types of modulation you learned about earlier. The following sections describe each step of PCM.

Sampling

The first step in converting analog signals to digital signals is to measure the amplitude of an analog signal at multiple instants, a technique known as **sampling**. Each sample of the analog signal is converted to a small piece of digital information (using a process discussed in the following section). Together, many small digital samples resemble the larger analog signal. Numerous devices can be used to sample an analog wave, although the number of times a particular device samples the wave can vary. The higher the **sampling rate**, the more closely the digital signal resembles the original analog signal. For most voice communications, 8000 samples per second is sufficient for the signal to be received with quality that sounds like the original speech, largely because human speech does not span a very wide range of frequencies. However, for recording music on audio compact discs that you play on a stereo, a much higher sampling rate of 44,100 samples per second is used. When all the samples are assembled, a wave made of small excerpts of the original wave results. This wave, as shown in Figure 6-9, is called a **pulse amplitude modulated (PAM)** signal.

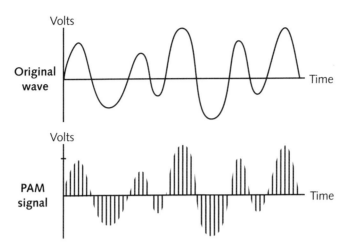

Figure 6-9 Pulse amplitude modulation

Quantizing

To create a replica of the audio wave in digital format, each sample is converted into its binary equivalent in a process called **quantizing**. For example, suppose you decide to digitize an analog wave using a sampling rate of three times per second. (Note that this is an unrealistically low sampling rate compared to the typical CD recording rate of 44,100 samples per second.) Dividing one second into three equal time periods means that you would sample a signal at .33 seconds, .67 seconds, and 1.0 seconds. Suppose the wave's amplitude equals 2 volts at .33 seconds, 10 volts at .67 seconds, and 15 volts at 1.0 second. Translating these amplitudes into digital format gives you 00000010 (or 2), 00001010 (or 10), and 00001111 (or 15). Thus, the binary transmission used to represent this analog wave, at a sampling rate of three samples per second, is 00000010 00001010 00001111.

However, such a low sampling rate would result in too little information to accurately reconstruct an analog wave. To demonstrate the importance of a sufficient sampling rate on sound quality, Figure 6-10 compares an analog wave with two quantized digital equivalents, one using twice as many samples as the other. Notice that the digital signal using a higher sampling rate more closely resembles the analog signal.

One problem with quantizing is that it introduces noise. (As you'll recall from Chapter 2, noise is an undesired signal that adversely affects the desired signal.) This occurs because a signal composed of quantized values is not as precise as the original analog signal, which is made of one continuous wave. Noise from quantizing affects the signal at lower amplitudes more dramatically than at higher amplitudes. For example, at an amplitude of 100 volts, an error (or deviation) of 1 volt means the quantized signal differs from the original signal by only 1%. But, at an amplitude of 4 volts, a deviation of 1 volt means that the quantized signal differs from the original signal by 25%.

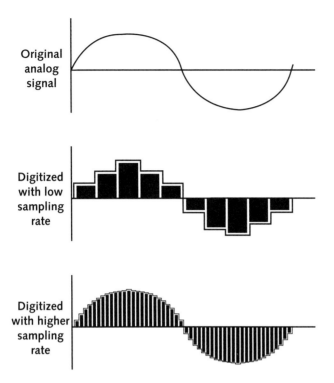

Figure 6-10 An analog signal quantized at two sampling rates

One way to mitigate the effects of quantizing noise is to take more frequent samples at the lower amplitudes and fewer samples at higher amplitudes, as shown in Figure 6-11. Notice how the combination of more samples at the lower amplitudes, where the slope of the analog wave's line is steepest, leads to a digital signal that follows the lines of the analog signal more closely. To accomplish this, the digital signal is compressed during quantizing to create more pulses in low amplitudes and expanded to create fewer pulses at high amplitudes, according to a pre-established formula. This process of compressing and expanding a signal is called **companding**. (The word itself is a combination of "compressing" and "expanding.") At the receiving end, the digital signal's compression and expansion must be reversed to restore the signal to its true waveform.

Filtering

The last step in reproducing an analog signal in digital form is filtering. **Filtering** is a process that removes inessential information from the signal, including very high and very low frequencies. Filtering is necessary to reduce the amount of bandwidth the signal requires. It is the last step in processing the signal before it is transmitted.

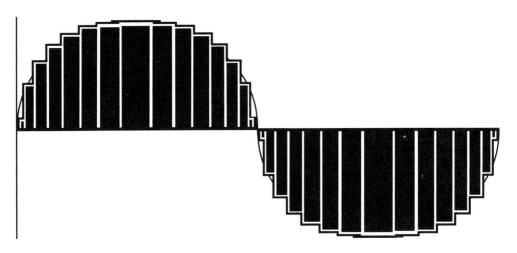

Figure 6-11   Compression and expansion in a quantized signal

Keep in mind that pulse code modulation is not the only way of converting analog signals to digital signals. In your work as a telecommunications professional, you will probably encounter other, more sophisticated methods. For the time being, however, you really only need to understand pulse code modulation, including sampling, quantizing, and filtering. These concepts provide the foundation you need to understand how digital signals are sent across networks. In the following section, you learn how multiple digital signals are transmitted at once over the same media.

MULTIPLEXING

As you learned in Chapter 1, multiplexing is the process of sending multiple signals simultaneously over one communications channel. This technique makes it possible to send more information over a single channel in a shorter period of time than relying on simplex transmission, or sending only one signal at a time over a communications channel. Many forms of multiplexing exist, and they are used to expedite both voice and data communications. The type of multiplexing used in any given situation depends on what the media, transmission, and reception equipment can handle. All types of multiplexing require two important devices. At the sending end of the channel, a **multiplexer (mux)** is required to combine multiple signals on the one channel. At the receiving end, a **demultiplexer (demux)** is required to separate the combined signals and recreate the information in its original form. In most systems, the mux and demux are combined into one unit.

In the following sections, you learn about the most common forms of multiplexing found in voice and data communications today, their required hardware, and the situations to which they are best suited.

Frequency Division Multiplexing (FDM)

Frequency division multiplexing (FDM) is a method of sending multiple analog signals simultaneously over one channel by separating the channel into subchannels, or **bands**. Each band in the channel has its own carrier signal with a unique frequency. The carrier signal for each band is then modulated by an information signal, just as in FM. A **guardband**, or a narrow range of unused frequency between each band's frequency, ensures that signals do not interfere with each other. Each band in an FDM signal is reserved for the information assigned to it. If no information is being sent, the frequency remains unused—a fact that, along with guardbands, which reserve unused frequency ranges, makes FDM somewhat inefficient.

FDM was developed in the 1930s by telephone companies to combine multiple voice signals over one wire. It can be used for voice, video, or data signals, but its most common applications are radio broadcast transmission and cable TV. It may also be used to transmit multiple voice signals over long distance analog lines. Because FDM is an older, inefficient form of multiplexing, its use on modern data networks is limited. Figure 6-12 depicts a simple FDM system.

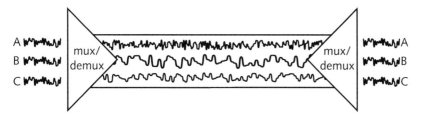

Figure 6-12   A frequency division multiplexing system

Time Division Multiplexing (TDM)

Time division multiplexing (TDM) is a method of multiplexing digital signals that has replaced FDM (an analog multiplexing technique) on modern data networks. TDM assigns a period of time—or time slot—in the sequence of communications to every device that exchanges signals over the network. Within that time slot, the channel carries data from only that node. For example, suppose five workstations are connected to a network over one wire. In this case, the multiplexer establishes five different time slots in the communications channel. Workstation A may be assigned time slot 1, workstation B time slot 2, workstation C time slot 3, and so on. In TDM, time slots are reserved for their designated nodes regardless of whether the node has data to transmit. If a node does not have data to send, its time slot remains empty. This arrangement, although logical, can be inefficient (in other words, it does not conserve limited bandwidth resources) if some nodes on the network rarely send data. Figure 6-13 shows a simple model of TDM.

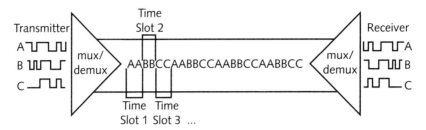

Figure 6-13   Time division multiplexing

An analogy may help you to understand TDM better. Think of each time slot as a car on a train, and the transmission of devices on a network as train stations. The train stops at every station. If a station has material to add to its car, it does so during the stop. But, if that station does not have any payload to add to its car, then the car remains empty. Furthermore, the train does not fill one station's car at another car's station.

In this analogy, the trains, or sequences of time slots, keep moving, stopping regularly at every station. As shown in Figure 6-13, at the transmitting end, a multiplexer combines the signals into one channel according to time slot. At the receiving end, a demultiplexer pulls the data from each time slot and assembles a separate, continual stream of data for each node.

For the receiver to be able to decipher mutliplexed signals in different time slots, TDM uses a technique called framing. **Framing** is the process of inserting special bits (or binary digits) in the data stream to indicate where one series of data–carrying time slots ends and another begins. Framing bits are usually assigned to their own time slot. In the train analogy, the engine resembles a framing bit, because it separates one series of cars from the next series of cars. Figure 6-14 provides a simple example of the use of framing in a TDM signal. A TDM channel can make use of many different arrangements, or schemes, of framing bits. To reassemble the separate data streams contained in a TDM signal, the demultiplexer has to understand the framing scheme for that channel.

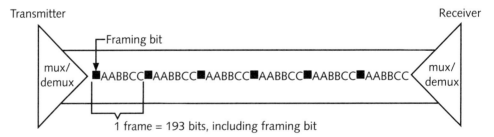

Figure 6-14   Framing in a TDM signal

Different types of digital communication use different framing and timing conventions. Some popular TDM transmission methods, discussed in Chapter 10, include T-carriers and SONET. In Chapter 9, you learn about cellular telephone networks that use technologies based on TDM.

Statistical Multiplexing

Statistical multiplexing is similar to time division multiplexing, but rather than assigning a separate time slot to each network device in succession, it assigns time slots to devices according to priority and need. This method is more efficient than TDM because it results in fewer empty time slots.

To begin with, statistical multiplexing, like TDM, assigns one time slot per device. However, if a device doesn't use its time slot, statistical multiplexing devices recognize that fact and assign the empty slot to another device that needs to send data. To do this, the multiplexer needs a way of determining (or arbitrating) which device should take over an empty time slot. The multiplexer may arbitrate on the basis of priority (for example, a server's transmission may have higher priority than a workstation's transmission) or more sophisticated factors, depending on the network. Most importantly, statistical multiplexing allows networks to maximize available bandwidth. Figure 6-15 depicts a simple statistical multiplexing system.

Figure 6-15   Statistical multiplexing

To differentiate one signal from another, statistical demultiplexers may use frames, as in TDM. Alternatively, they may transmit data in fixed-length groups (such fixed-length groups are known as **cells**). Some examples of transmission systems that use statistical multiplexing include ISDN, ATM, and frame relay. These transmission methods are discussed in detail in Chapter 10.

Note

In Chapter 1, you learned that a cell is a geographical region defined by cellular telephone networks. With this introduction of a second definition for the term "cell," you are discovering that in the world of telecommunications, one word may have two (or more) meanings. To understand which meaning applies, it's important to pay attention to the context in which the term is used. In this example, if you are discussing mobile communications with a colleague, the word "cell" probably refers to an area covered by one low power transmitter to carry cellular signals. If you are discussing high-bandwidth WANs, the word "cell" probably refers to a fixed unit of transmission used in ATM. (To further complicate matters, a "cell" may also be a data field in a spreadsheet or a part of a battery.)

Wavelength Division Multiplexing (WDM)

Wavelength division multiplexing (WDM) is a relatively new technology that enables one fiber optic connection to carry multiple light signals simultaneously. In WDM, the communications channel (in this case, a strand of glass fiber within a fiber optic cable) is divided into subchannels according to wavelength. This is similar to the way in which FDM creates separate subchannels according to frequencies. (Recall from Chapter 2 that wavelength is a property of a wave that is inversely proportional to its frequency.) Each signal in WDM is assigned a different wavelength. In this manner, multiple signals can be transmitted simultaneously in the same direction over a length of fiber optic cable. Depending on the type of equipment and fiber used, WDM may send multiplexed signals in one or two directions at the same time.

Figure 6-16 shows a simple WDM system. Note that, unlike in the other forms of multiplexing discussed so far, the device that multiplexes and demultiplexes a signal is not typically called a mux/demux, but rather a **fiber optic modem (FOM)**. At the transmitting end, a fiber optic modem creates the WDM signal, and at the receiving end, an FOM separates the multiplexed signals into individual signals according to their different wavelengths. When the sending and receiving ends are separated by long distances (for example, over 50 miles), it is sometimes necessary to regenerate (or recreate) the multiple signals in between. With fiber optic technology, it is simple for network devices to quickly regenerate signals.

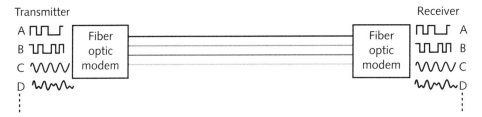

Figure 6-16   Wavelength division multiplexing

WDM is very useful on a network because it increases the amount of information that over-taxed fiber cables can carry. In addition, unlike TDM and statistical multiplexing, WDM can transmit multiple types of telecommunications services on the same length of fiber. For instance, a videoconference can share the same fiber as telephone conversations and network data. Another advantage to WDM is that bandwidth is only limited by the number of FOMs and fibers available to carry subchannels. Each subchannel on a fiber strand is assigned a signaling rate in accordance with the particular cable's WDM scheme. For example, one subchannel may be capable of 2.5 Gbps throughput, whereas another fiber may be capable of 9.953 Gbps. Consider that fiber optic cables may contain thousands of fibers, resulting in much greater capacity than another form of multiplexing (such as TDM) over traditional copper wiring.

The most common form of WDM in use today is **dense wavelength division multiplexing (DWDM)**. DWDM is a version of wavelength division multiplexing that can support a larger number of different wavelengths on the same strand of fiber, thus greatly increasing the bandwidth capacity of that fiber. The earliest WDM supported up to only four different carrier wavelengths. DWDM can currently support up to 40 different carrier wavelengths, and with continued development of the technology, this number will probably grow. Because of its high capacity, DWDM has proved to be a tremendous boon for transoceanic telecommunications networks whose fiber capacity was nearly maximized; without DWDM, network providers would have had to go through the arduous and expensive process of laying more cable across the oceans.

6

SWITCHING

Switching is a method of establishing connections and sending information between nodes on a network. It is used in both voice and data communications, and until very recently, telephony switching was quite different from data network switching. Switches were originally invented to eliminate the need to connect every telephone line directly with every other telephone line, providing a much leaner and less expensive communications infrastructure. As you learned in Chapter 1, early telephony switches, such as the step-by-step and crossbar switches, were electromechanical. Later, after the semiconductor was invented, switches became digital. In this section, you learn about switching fundamentals that apply to both voice and data networking and about modern telephony switching equipment. Data networking switches involve different technology; they are discussed, along with other networking hardware, in Chapter 11.

It may be helpful at this point to clarify the distinction between modulation, multiplexing, and switching. Modulation is a way of coding and directing signals; it does not have anything to do with sending the information to the correct destination, nor does it affect any other signal that might be traveling along the same communications channel. Multiplexing, on the other hand, is a technique for combining many signals over a single communications channel; it does not affect how a signal is modulated, where it's going, or which path it follows to its destination. Switching, meanwhile, is a technique for deciding where information needs to go and determining the best possible path to its destination. Switching makes use of both modulated and multiplexed signals, as you discover in the following sections.

Circuit Switching

In **circuit switching**, a connection is established between two devices on a network before they begin transmitting data. Bandwidth is dedicated to this connection and remains available only to the source and destination devices until the connection is terminated. While the devices are connected, all data follows the same path first selected by the switch or other connectivity device (in the case of data networks).

When you place a telephone call, your call is carried on a circuit-switched connection. Almost all telephone connections (including dial-up modem connections) use circuit switching; however, this is likely to change in the near future. Figure 6-17 provides a simple illustration of a telephone call transmitted via circuit switching.

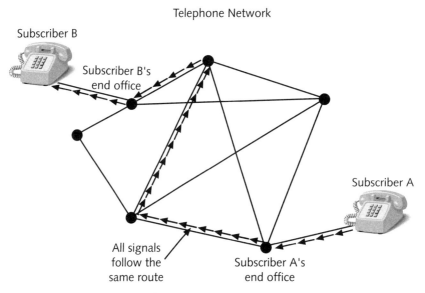

Figure 6-17   Circuit switching

Because circuit switching monopolizes a piece of bandwidth all the while the two stations are connected, it is not a bandwidth efficient technology. The advantage of circuit switching, however, is that it guarantees two devices exclusive use of a communications channel. Thus, transmission between the two circuit-switched devices does not compete with transmission issued by other devices on a network. This attribute makes it well suited to services applications, such as live audio or video conferencing, that require data to be received in the same order as it was transmitted, with little delay. Circuit switching is used for modem connections across PSTN, ISDN, and T-carriers.

Message Switching

Message switching is a method of switching in which any nodes between the data's source and its target accept and store the data before passing it on to the next node. This "store and forward" routine continues until the message reaches its destination. All information follows the same physical path, but unlike with circuit switching, the connection is not continuously maintained. Thus, unlike circuit switching, message switching has the advantage of not dominating an entire communications channel. It allows the channel to be used by other nodes. Message switching requires that each device in the signal's path has sufficient memory and processing power to accept and store the information before passing it on. Message switching is depicted in Figure 6-18.

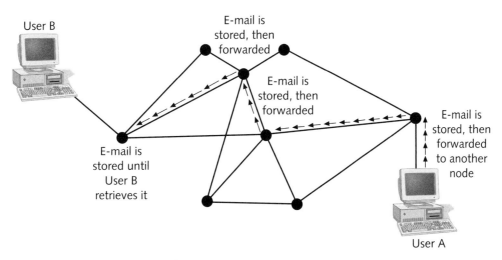

Figure 6-18   Message switching

Because message switching was succeeded by a better technology called packet switching (discussed next), few examples of message switching still exist in data networking. Telephony circuits do not use message switching at all. There is, however, one notable exception: E-mail. When you send an e-mail message, your message does not travel directly from your computer, over the Internet, and to your recipient's computer. Instead, it makes at least a few stops at servers in between. You learn more about e-mail transmission in Chapter 12.

Packet Switching

A third method for directing digital data from one node to another on a network is packet switching. **Packet switching** is a form of switching that breaks data into **packets**, or small groups of data, before they are transported. The size and content of each packet conform to some predefined standard. In addition to a piece of the data being transmitted, each packet contains a destination address and information about how to combine it with other packets to recreate the original transmission once the packets reach their destination. Packets are then free to travel any path on the network to their destination. Thus, packet switching makes it possible to find the fastest circuit available at any instant. It is a much faster and efficient technique than circuit or message switching.

An analogy may help you to understand packet switching better. Imagine that you organize a field trip for 20 colleagues to the New England Aquarium in Boston, Massachusetts. You give your colleagues the aquarium's precise address and tell them to leave precisely at 7:00 a.m. from your office building across town. However, you do not tell them which route to take. Naturally, each colleague wants to take the fastest route to the aquarium;

however, some might choose the subway whereas others might hail a taxi cab and still others might choose to drive their own cars. No matter which transportation method your colleagues choose, you all arrive at the aquarium and reassemble as a group. This is similar to how packets travel in a packet-switched network, as shown in Figure 6-19.

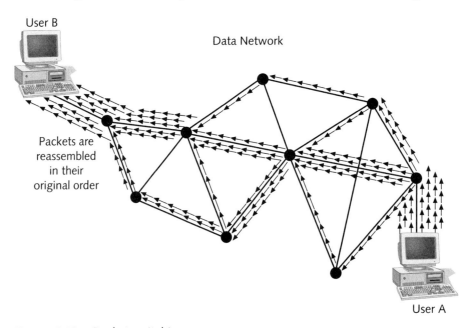

Figure 6-19 Packet switching

The destination device on a packet-switched network reassembles the packets based on the information about order included in each packet. It takes a very small amount of time to reassemble a group of packets. Because of this time delay, packet switching is not suited to live audio or video transmission. But, it is a fast and efficient mechanism for transporting typical network data, such as word processing or spreadsheet files. The greatest advantage to packet switching is that it does not waste bandwidth by holding a connection open until a message reaches its destination, as circuit switching does. And unlike message switching, it does not require devices in the data's path to hold a piece of information and determine where to send it next.

Examples of packet-switched networks include Ethernet, FDDI, and frame relay. You learn about these technologies in Chapter 10. For now, just keep in mind that many parts of the Internet rely on packet switching.

SWITCHING SYSTEMS

Every network uses one (or more) of the three switching methods described previously. Although connections between devices on a data network may be established by different types of devices, on a telephone network, a switch is the device that manages connections.

The combined collection of hardware and software that establishes connections between lines and trunks to complete calls is known as a **switching system**. Switching systems can perform many additional functions, such as monitoring lines for faults, storing information about telephone subscribers, converting analog signals to digital signals, modifying long-distance routes based on traffic patterns, and providing enhanced services, such as caller ID and voice mail.

In Chapter 3, you learned about early electromechanical switches, such as the step-by-step switch and the crossbar switch. The invention of the transistor made these early devices obsolete and revolutionized telephone switching. In 1965, after many years of research, AT&T's Western Electric Manufacturing Division (which later became the company now known as Lucent) implemented the first **Electronic Switching System (ESS)**. This system, which used transistors and electronic circuitry, greatly increased switch-processing capacity and speed. Since the introduction of ESS, all new switches have been electronic. Modern switches are actually large computers with databases, memory, and multiple processors.

In the following sections, you learn how telephone switching systems complete both local and long distance calls. All of the switching systems described use circuit switching. Subsequent sections introduce you to two of the most popular telephone switches: Lucent's latest ESS and Nortel's DMS.

Although makes and models differ between manufacturers, all modern switches share four essential elements.

- *Switching matrix*— The internal connections between incoming and outgoing lines, or circuits (may also be called switching fabric).

- *Line or trunk circuits*—The means of connecting to local lines or other trunks (may also be called switch interfaces). Line circuits may be digital or analog, depending on the line being connected.

- *Central control computer*—The part of the switch that interprets incoming data, retrieves data, and issues commands to the rest of the switch. The central control computer typically includes multiple processors, among other components.

- *Common equipment*—The components necessary to keep the switch running at all times, such as a power supply, battery, testing equipment, and distributing frames for incoming wires.

In addition to the core components previously listed, switches may contain connected peripherals, specialized software, modules to extend the switch's reach to remote locations, extra (or redundant) components (such as multiple input and output ports, multiple power supplies, multiple instances of software, and so on), or emergency power supplies.

Private Switching Systems

In some large organizations, routing each call through the nearest central office is inefficient and time-consuming. In this situation, it makes more sense to use a **private switching system**, which can direct calls independent from the telephone company's facilities. A private switching system may interact with a public switching system. Or, in the case of one employee calling another employee within the same building, they may never connect with the telephone company's facilities.

For an organization with many phone lines, a private switching system saves time and money. For example, if you have ever directly dialed a colleague's phone extension (merely the last four digits of their number), you have used a private switching system and your employer has avoided paying the local phone company to carry that call. As you would expect, private switching systems are usually not as complex or expensive as central office switching systems (though in some very large organizations, they may be).

Common examples of private switching systems are Private Branch Exchange (PBX), Centrex, and key systems. Recall that these systems were discussed in detail in Chapter 5, with other CPE. Private switching systems are often considered part of CPE, because although they operate on the same switching principles as public switches, they belong to a customer and are closely integrated with other CPE equipment.

Public Switching Systems

As described in Chapter 4, a **public switching system** is a switching system that routes calls and interconnects telephone subscribers across the PSTN. To refresh your memory, the primary functions of the public switching system include:

- Providing a dial tone when a subscriber picks up a telephone handset
- Accepting and interpreting signals issued by the subscriber's telephone (for example, a dialed number)
- Determining a call's path between a source and destination over the PSTN
- Establishing the actual connection between the source and destination over the PSTN
- Determining when the call has been terminated and releasing the connection over the PSTN
- Tracking and saving information about subscribers and calls for billing purposes

Additionally, public switching systems may perform the following functions:

- Monitor its own performance (for example, tracking the speed with which it interprets signals and establishes a route)
- Allow subscribers access to operators and emergency services
- Provide enhanced services, such as call waiting, voice mail, or caller ID
- Modify characteristics of lines or routes with input from an operator

Telephone companies divide public switching systems into two broad categories: local switching and tandem switching. As you learn in the following sections, some of the functions previously listed are performed by local switching systems only, whereas others may be performed by both local and tandem switching systems. The equipment used for local and tandem switching is similar. In fact, some sophisticated switches can be used for either local or tandem systems, depending on how they're programmed. The distinction between local and tandem switches lies in the functions they perform.

Before reading the rest of this chapter, you might want to review what you learned about central office hierarchies and carrier interconnection in Chapter 4. The following material builds on that, adding more technical details about exactly how a switch interprets signals and determines the best path for a phone call.

Local Switching Systems

You have learned that telephone subscriber lines are connected through central offices where switching actually occurs. Further, you know that the central office where a subscriber's local loop terminates is called an end office, or Class 5 central office. At a Class 5 CO, a switch receives and interprets the signal from a subscriber's telephone. An end (or local) office switch is known as a **local switch**, and it is used by ILECs, CLECs, and local wireless telephone carriers. You will find a local switch only at an end office. All other COs use tandem switches.

A local switch performs the following functions:

- Provides dial tone to a local subscriber

- Accepts and interprets signals (including off-hook notification, dial tones, and so on) from the local subscriber

- Receives signals from the destination's local switch about when to terminate the call

- Records local subscriber billing information

- Stores information about subscribers (such as what type of service they have chosen) in a subscriber database

- Tests and maintains the subscriber's local loop

- Modifies subscriber account and line configuration

- Provides enhanced services, such as caller ID, call waiting, number blocking, and voice mail

- Provides operator assistance and access to emergency services

Analog-to-Digital Conversion

Before you learn the steps involved in switching a local call, you need to learn more about some of the basic components of a local switch—particularly the parts responsible for converting an analog signal to a digital one. As you have learned, analog signals are converted to digital signals through pulse code modulation (PCM). Because voice signals are analog and modern switches transmit digital signals, voice signals must be converted to a digital format in order to be transmitted. In a telephone circuit, this conversion occurs where the subscriber line terminates at the local switch, and it involves two parts of a switch: the codec and the subscriber line interface circuit.

First, the analog line connects to a **subscriber line interface circuit (SLIC)** that provides battery power to the line (recall that a small amount of electrical current must travel over a phone line to provide signals) and detects when the telephone handset is off-hook. **Off-hook** is simply a telecommunications term that means the condition of the line when a telephone handset is lifted, or taken off its hook. (Or, in the case of cordless telephones, when the Talk button is pressed.) The SLIC can tell that the line is off-hook because taking a telephone off its hook closes the local loop circuit and allows electrical current to flow on the line.

After the incoming analog signal passes through the SLIC, it is converted into a digital signal by a part of the switch known as a **codec** (a word that derives from its function as a **cod**er/**dec**oder). The codec converts the analog signal to digital via PCM. (You learned about this form of modulation earlier in this chapter.)

To summarize then, the SLIC detects the off-hook condition and a codec converts analog signals to digital signals. Understanding where the SLIC and codec function in a switching system helps you follow the steps involved in connecting a telephone call through a local switch.

Switching an Intra-Office Call

The following steps illustrate how a local switch completes a local telephone call. Note that the components and terminology may differ slightly from one switch model and manufacturer to another, but the underlying process remains the same. To keep the example simple, the call is an **intra-office call**, in other words, one in which the local loops from the caller and her intended receiver connect to the same end office. This type of call does not need to be transferred from one local switch to another local switch. For the following example, we'll name the caller Marni and the intended recipient of the call Brian.

1. Before Marni even picks up her phone, the local switch at her end office is waiting. Inside the switch, the **line group controller (LGC)**, a component that monitors the status of hundreds of SLICs, is continually scanning the switch's incoming lines for an off-hook condition.

2. When Marni picks up her handset, she closes the line's circuit and allows electrical current to flow along her line. The SLIC detects this current and alerts the LGC that her line's telephone is off-hook. The LGC, in turn, informs the switch's central control computer that Marni wants to make a call.

3. The central control computer consults the subscriber database, which may be stored on a separate computer, to retrieve information about Marni, such as what type of customer she is (residential or business) and what services she subscribes to. Data about her phone call will also be saved in this database after the call has been terminated.

4. The central control computer then opens one end of a connection and assigns it to Marni's line.

5. The central control computer tells the LGC to stop looking for an off-hook condition for Marni's telephone. The LGC then transmits a dial tone to Marni's telephone. As you know from lifting your own telephone and hearing a dial tone, a switch can perform Steps 1-5 in microseconds.

6. After Marni hears the dial tone, she presses the buttons for Brian's telephone number. Each number on her telephone keypad transmits a unique frequency, or tone, which the switch uses to interpret the number. The LGC waits to collect all seven digits of Brian's number, then sends them to the central control computer.

7. The switch's central control computer accepts the seven digits and attempts to match them with a subscriber line in its database. When it makes a match, the central control computer searches for Brian's telephone line's SLIC.

8. The central control computer sets up a circuit from Marni's telephone's LGC to Brian's telephone's LGC.

9. Brian's LGC establishes a connection to his telephone's SLIC and instructs the SLIC to start physically ringing his telephone. At the same time, the central control computer sends Marni's name and number to Brian's telephone set. If Brian has subscribed to the service known as caller ID, this information about Marni appears in his caller ID display.

10. The central control computer commands Marni's SLIC to send a ringing sound to her telephone handset. This is the ringing she hears before Brian picks up his handset. Bear in mind that this ringing sound is separately controlled from the ringing that Brian hears at his apartment. This is why sometimes when you call someone, they seem to answer before the phone has even rung. Your LGC causes the ringing in your handset only after the ringing has begun on your intended recipient's phone. The two ringing sounds are not synchronized.

11. Because Marni originated the call, her line and her LGC are in control of the call. Marni's LGC waits for a signal from Brian's LGC that his phone is off-hook (in other words, that he has answered). When Brian answers, both his and Marni's LGCs stop their ringing tones. (If Brian's line was busy, Marni's LGC would issue a **busy signal**, a tone of two combined frequencies that repeats in bursts of .5 seconds.)

12. Marni's LGC notifies the central control computer that the call, and the circuit, can be completed. In other words, transmission of voice signals between the two lines may proceed.

13. The central control computer issues commands to complete the voice connection between Brian's LGC and Marni's LGC. Recall that telephone switches use the circuit-switching technique. That means that after this circuit has been established, Marni and Brian use it for the remainder of their telephone call.

14. When Marni and Brian finish conversing, they each hang up their phone. Let's assume that Marni hangs up first. In that case, her line's **on-hook** condition is detected by her SLIC. Her SLIC triggers her LGC to inform the central control computer about this on-hook condition. The central control computer indicates to both LGCs that the circuit may be dismantled and that the lines are once again free.

15. While the central control computer transmits information about the call to the subscriber database, the LGCs return to waiting for another off-hook condition.

In Figure 6-20, you can see the connection between a phone, its line port, and the components of a local switch.

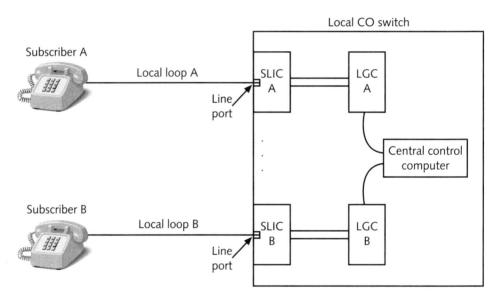

Figure 6-20   A telephone's connection to a switch

Let's return for a moment to the comparison between a network and the human body's nervous system introduced at the beginning of the chapter. It may help to think of the switch's central control computer as its brain whereas the SLICs are the nerve endings in the limbs, touching lines, and the LGCs make up its central nervous system, accepting cues and transmitting them to the central control computer. The central control computer accepts the LGC's input and based on that, makes decisions about what to do next. In the same way, if your hand makes contact with a hot burner, the nerves in your hand (the SLIC) send a message to your central nervous system (the LGC). The central nervous system sends a signal to your brain. Your brain interprets the signal and makes a decision based on that information. It then conveys its decision through the nervous system to the hand (the LGC to the SLIC) to immediately remove your hand from the burner.

Inside a real local switch, the LGCs, SLICs, and CPU are small and integrated with electronic circuit boards. In addition, modern switches contain many more components. However, the components described in the process still perform the majority of the functions.

Tandem Switching

If local switches handle signals from local loops, you can guess that **tandem switches** handle calls between central offices. In fact, tandem switches operate at any type of CO other than a Class 5. ILECs, CLECs, and IXCs own and operate tandem switches in their COs. (Even though LECs are called "local exchange carriers," recall from Chapter 3 that they may provide inter-LATA traffic, which must be passed from one CO to another.) Other carriers, such as ISPs, may also operate tandem switches as they diversify their services to include telephony. A tandem switch may perform the following functions:

- Provide termination for trunks at Class 1, 2, 3, and 4 central offices
- Gather and transmit information about telephone network traffic and congestion
- Determine the fastest path over the PSTN for long-distance calls
- Carry data and voice signals between central offices
- Test and maintain trunks
- Assist in trunk configuration

Notice that tandem switches do not perform any functions related to local loops or subscribers. For example, a tandem switch does not provide dial tone to a telephone. Nor does it interpret an incoming phone number, check lines for off-hook conditions, or issue busy signals to a handset. Tandem switches are only used in communication between central offices.

As you might expect, modern tandem switches are entirely digital. They accept only digital input and transmit only digital output. They do not typically have provisions (such as a codec) for converting analog signals to digital signals and vice versa, because this is accomplished by the local switch.

In the following steps, you learn the role that tandem switches play in a long-distance call. To keep the example fairly simple, the call is interstate—an unambiguously, a long-distance call. Once again, the terminology and components may differ between different makes and manufacturers of switches, but the underlying process remains the same. In this example, we'll name the caller Calvin and the intended recipient of the call Anna. As you read the steps, follow along with Figure 6-21, which depicts a series of tandem switches and their significant components and connections.

1. A long-distance call begins just like a local call. At Calvin's end office, an LGC is scanning the SLICs, waiting for one of them to indicate an off-hook condition. When Calvin picks up his phone to call Anna, his SLIC alerts his LGC that his line is off-hook.

2. Calvin's LGC alerts his local switch's central control computer that he wants to make a call.

3. The central control computer consults the subscriber database to retrieve information about Calvin.

4. The central control computer assigns one end of a connection to Calvin's line.

5. The central control computer establishes a connection to the LGC and tells the LGC to stop looking for an off-hook condition. The LGC then transmits a dial tone to Calvin's telephone. Notice that thus far, the steps involved in a long-distance call are identical to those involved in a local call, and further, a tandem switch has not yet been involved.

6. After Calvin hears the dial tone, he presses the buttons for Anna's telephone number. The LGC waits to collect all 10 digits of Anna's number (10 digits are necessary because the call crosses area codes), then sends them to the central control computer.

7. Calvin's local switch's central control computer recognizes that Anna's number is not one of the lines that connects to a SLIC in its central office. The central control computer requests a digital trunk connection that allows it to pass the call to another switch. This request does not go directly to Anna's central office, but rather to an intermediate switching point that processes information about the best available routes over the PSTN at that moment. (You learn more about this process of finding the best available route later in this chapter, in the section called "Switch Signaling.") For now, keep in mind that a great deal of computing goes into finding the optimal path for the call before Calvin's switch retransmits the dialed number to Anna's central office.

8. After the signal has arrived at Anna's end office switch, its central control computer checks with her LGC to determine the status of her line. Anna's switch's central control computer indicates to Calvin's switch's central control computer whether her telephone is on-hook or off-hook.

9. If Anna's line is not busy, her switch sends a confirmation to Calvin's switch that indicates the process of setting up a circuit can continue.

10. Anna's LGC establishes a path to her SLIC and instructs it to ring her telephone. At the same time, Calvin's LGC requests that his SLIC send a ringing tone through his earpiece.

11. At the same time, Calvin's switch's central control computer sends his name and number, over the A-Link to Anna's telephone.

12. When Anna answers, her switch issues a message to Calvin's switch indicating that the connection may be completed. At this point, the circuit between Calvin's and Anna's LGCs is established.

13. Calvin's LGC begins timing the call until either he or Anna hangs up. After the circuit has been terminated, a billing record is created and Calvin is billed for the call.

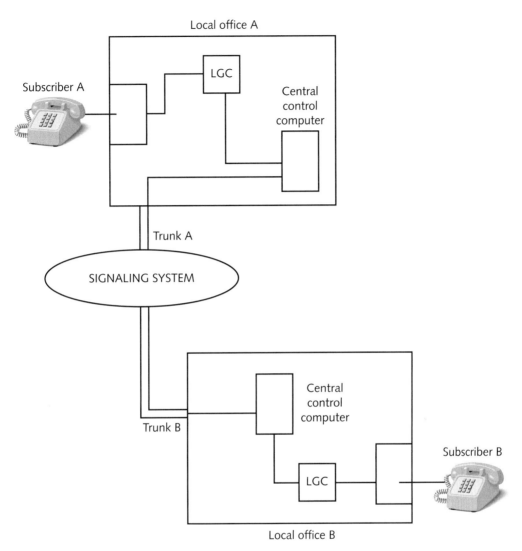

Figure 6-21   Tandem switching

Because tandem switches are primarily responsible for directing traffic over highly-utilized trunks, they must be able to sense traffic patterns and adjust phone call routing quickly. All of this is accomplished through signaling, which is controlled by sophisticated software. You learn about the two most common signaling systems, CCS and SS7, later in this chapter.

Trunks between tandem switches are entirely digital. If they rely on copper wire media, such as a T-carrier, they use a version of TDM. (You learned about this form of multiplexing earlier in this chapter.) With TDM, a digital trunk can carry up to 24 channels on one wire pair. Newer digital trunks use another type of multiplexing, DWDM, and rely on fiber optic media. These trunks have much more capacity than the copper wire trunks. As a result, carriers are quickly replacing their **backbones** (that is, major and most heavily trafficked routes) with fiber optic cable.

Lucent's ESS Switch

As you have learned, the **1ESS** switching system deployed by Western Electric (a division of AT&T) was the first electronic switch used in North America. Since its release in 1965, AT&T, and later, Lucent, have released several more versions of ESS, each with increased capacity and a variety of software and hardware enhancements. By the 1980s, ESS switches were fully digital.

The most current Lucent ESS switch is version 5, or **5ESS**. It is capable of providing both local and tandem features, depending on what type of hardware and software the telecommunications carrier requires. However, not every central office is equipped with the 5ESS, or other cutting edge equipment. Many small end offices, for example, make do with older versions of the ESS, including the original 1ESS.

A fully-featured ESS can cost several millions of dollars and handle up to 750,000 calls per hour. It may connect tens of thousands of digital trunks to other switches. In addition to digital trunks, the 5ESS can accept incoming analog, ISDN, and ATM lines. It is capable of circuit switching as well as packet switching. Furthermore, to ensure that telephone customers never lose service, this switch contains many extra (or redundant) components. For example, a 5ESS may include two power supplies, one that is used on a daily basis and one that is not routinely used but can take over should the first one fail. And finally, the software on the 5ESS can perform call routing, customer billing, line maintenance and testing, and of course, call setup and enhanced calling features, such as caller ID. Furthermore, because it is entirely digital, the 5ESS can be also used in data networking frameworks. Figure 6-22 shows an example of a Lucent 5ESS.

Figure 6-22   A Lucent 5ESS

Nortel's DMS Switch

Nortel (formerly Northern Telecom) released its first **DMS** switch in 1978. These days, Nortel's line of DMS switches are competitors to Lucent's ESS switches. (DMS stands for **digital multiplexed system**, but the full name for the product is almost never used.)

Nortel makes many version of the DMS. The DMS-10 is a small, end-office switch that relies on TDM and is used exclusively for local switching. The DMS-100, also uses TDM, but is designed for larger local offices. It can handle up to 100,000 incoming subscriber lines. The DMS-200 switches are primarily designed for tandem switching, but may also be used for local switching. Nortel's tandem-specific switches include the DMS-250, the DMS-300, and the DMS-500, the largest and most sophisticated type of tandem DMS switch.

A carrier can easily upgrade from one type of DMS switch to another to gain added features and benefits. Interestingly enough, many of the RBOCs, which were at one time part of the same company that invented the ESS, use Nortel DMS switches. A Nortel DMS-200 is pictured in Figure 6-23.

Figure 6-23   A Nortel DMS-200

Nortel switches, like Lucent switches, vary in the types of inputs and outputs they can accommodate. The latest Nortel switches can accept fiber optic connections as well as analog and digital wire connections. Thus, Nortel's high-end switches can handle data networking as well as telephony, with inputs for T-carriers, wireless, ISDN, ATM, and PSTN lines. Finally, like 5ESS, high-end Nortel DMS switches can perform call routing, customer billing, line maintenance and testing, and of course, call setup and enhanced calling features, such as caller ID.

Although switches by different manufacturers perform the same functions, software that manages one manufacturer's switch cannot be used to manage another manufacturer's switch. For this reason, and to keep maintenance and staff training costs lower, most central offices purchase all their switches from the same manufacturer.

In the preceding pages, you learned about the different categories and most popular types of switches. You have also heard references to different types of switches covered in other chapters, such as PBXs and data networking switches. To put what you have learned into context, Figure 6-24 provides an overview of switching. Notice that various kinds of switching may take place in the same industry. You may find it helpful to refer to this diagram later, when you read about data switches in Chapter 11.

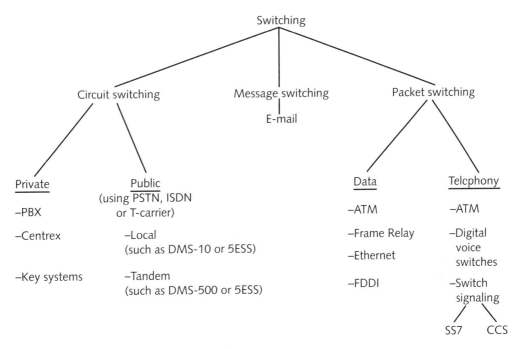

Figure 6-24   Switching categories and types

SWITCH SIGNALING

Now that you have learned about how switches function and the different types of switching equipment, you are ready to learn how switches communicate with each other.

When telephones were first invented, callers had to crank an electromechanical device on their home telephone that generated current on the line and rang a buzzer or lit a bulb at their end office. In response, an operator connected to the caller's line and asked for the number he wanted to call. The operator would then manually make the connection by plugging in a wire to complete the circuit. This series of communications is really the precursor to modern-day switching. A switch performs the same basic functions electronically as hand cranks, operators, and line plugs and jacks performed at the beginning of the twentieth century.

Earlier in this chapter (during the discussion of tandem switching), you learned that switches at different central offices communicate through signaling. **Signaling** is the exchange of information between the components of a telephone network or system for the purposes of establishing, monitoring, or releasing phone circuits as well as controlling system operations. In the call between Calvin and Anna described in the tandem switching section, you read about signaling functions, though they weren't identified as such. The following is a complete list of the three main switch-signaling functions.

- *Transmitting Address Information*—Sending the dialed phone number from one switch to another

- *Supervising*—Determining when the call has been established and when it is terminated, also knowing the status of circuits to help in call routing decisions

- *Transmitting Information*—Conveying signals, such as a busy signal, dial tone, and recorded announcements to callers

In fact, most of the information that switches gather and generate may be shared with other switches through signaling. In the following sections, you learn about the two common "languages," or signaling systems, that switches use to exchange information: CCS and SS7. Many of the signals exchanged by switches, lines, and trunks will sound familiar to you from reading the examples of how local and long distance calls are switched. In fact, you may want to return to those examples after reading the rest of this chapter to see whether you can identify which signals are part of the subscriber loop and which are interoffice signals.

Subscriber Loop Signaling

Subscriber loop signaling is the exchange of information about a telephone circuit over the local loop. Many of these signals contain information about the local loop's status. For example, one alerting function associated with subscriber loop signaling is the ringing signal that causes the recipient's phone to sound a ringing tone. This ringing signal is AC voltage that follows a 20 Hz waveform frequency that is on for two seconds, off for four seconds, then repeats until the handset is lifted.

The signal from the local loop that indicates when a ringing phone has been answered is part of the signal's supervision function. The primary types of supervisory signals include:

- *Idle circuit*—An indication that a subscriber's telephone is on-hook (in other words, the line is not in use) and the circuit is available for connection

- *Busy circuit*—An indication that a subscriber's telephone is off-hook (in other words, the line is in use) and the circuit is not available for connection

- *Seizure*—The request for service signal that is transmitted to the local switch when a subscriber takes her handset off-hook and closes the local line circuit

- *Disconnect*—The indication that a subscriber's telephone is on-hook after being off-hook (in other words, she has hung up the phone)

The subscriber loop also carries addressing signals, including tones that represent the intended recipient's phone number. Most telephones now use **touch tone dialing**, or the combination of two frequencies to identify a number on the telephone keypad. Recall from Chapter 4 that telephone numbers follow a pattern of area code, followed by central office code, followed by local extension. This pattern uniquely identifies every individual subscriber line. Switches accept these signals from the subscriber loop to determine where they will connect the call.

The subscriber loop also plays a role in the last category of signaling functions, transmitting information. Information signals carried by a subscriber loop may consist of tones or recorded announcements. For example, when you attempt to dial a number that is out of service, your subscriber loop signaling system issues a message telling you that the number you dialed is no longer in service.

Interoffice Signaling

Interoffice signaling is the exchange of alert, supervisory, and other information between switches at different central offices. Because switches interconnect through trunks, interoffice signaling takes place over trunks. One of the primary functions of interoffice signaling is routing a call to its destination over the quickest path available. Thus, the switch must be able to access all information about available trunks and lines immediately. This requires a sophisticated integration of software, hardware, and intelligence stored in databases. However, interoffice signaling was once very simple.

The earliest versions of interoffice signaling used tones carried in direct current (DC) pulses along the same circuits that carried voice conversations. This type of signaling is known as **in-band signaling**. The signals did not interfere with conversations because they were issued before talking began (in the case of setting up a call) and after the talking stopped (in the case of terminating a call). A popular way to convey these signals from switch to switch was by issuing a 2600 Hz tone. Recall that telephones carry frequencies in the range of approximately 300 to 3300 Hz. Therefore, the 2600 Hz tone fell into the range of normal transmission and reception on a telephone. This signal was easy to reproduce from a subscriber line, and with enough know-how, people could make free long-distance telephone calls by fraudulently transmitting the 2600 Hz tone over the wire. In other cases, speech signals could inadvertently disconnect a call.

Because of the major disadvantages to in-band signaling, it was replaced with out-of-band signaling, a more secure means of transmitting call information. In out-of-band signaling, switch signals are carried by a separate communications subchannel than the subchannel that carries conversations. Besides being more secure, out-of-band signaling is more efficient than in-band signaling. For example, it establishes connections more quickly. In the next two sections, you learn about the best known and most frequently used methods of interoffice signaling, CCS and SS7. Both use the out-of-band signaling method.

Common Channel Signaling (CCS)

The **common channel signaling (CCS)** system was developed by AT&T in the 1970s after they had lost significant revenues to fraudulent use of the in-band signaling technique. CCS was first installed in the Bell System in 1976. It is distinguished by the fact that it carries signal information on a dedicated data link between central offices. In CCS, no signal information is carried over the voice connections. Therefore, CCS is an out-of-band signaling technique.

6

As you have learned, out-of-band signaling is more secure and efficient than in-band signaling. But CCS provided other benefits. For one thing, it paved the way for optional calling features, such as call waiting, call blocking, automatic callback, and caller ID. These features were not only convenient for subscribers, but also supplied additional revenue for the RBOCs. CCS also enabled number portability, the ability for a subscriber to change carriers in a local area without having to change his or her phone number.

CCS relies on a digital network of switches, trunks, control software, and informational databases. CCS uses a packet-switched network (remember, no voice signals travel over CCS, only signal data) to connect these elements. This packet-switched network is entirely separate from the network that voice circuits use, as illustrated in Figure 6-25.

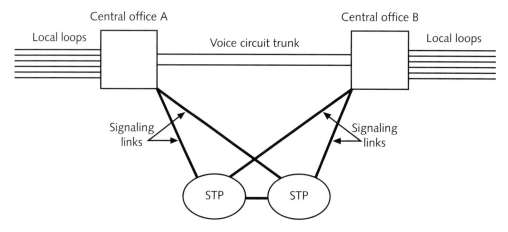

Figure 6-25   Common-channel signaling

To communicate through CCS, a switch connects to a **signal transfer point (STP)**, a packet switch designated to carry out-of-band signaling data. The STP switches the signal to either another STP or to the end office belonging to the destination subscriber. Multiple STPs across North America ensure that even if one STP is down, a switch can still connect to another switch to exchange signaling information.

Signaling System No. Seven (SS7)

Signaling System No. 7 (SS7) is a particular type of CCS employed on modern telephony networks. It is a standard developed and published by the ITU. (As you learned in Chapter 1, the ITU is a specialized United Nations agency that regulates international telecommunication usage.) The standards published by the ITU specify how switches should exchange alert, addressing, supervisory, and transmission information over a digital network. SS7 provides switch signaling guidelines for both wire-based and wireless telephony. Further, it is used around the world, though with slightly different variations in North America and Europe.

According to the ITU standard, SS7 involves multiple nodes on the packet-switched signaling network, as depicted in Figure 6-26. In addition to the STPs used in a basic CCS system, SS7 relies on multiple **service control points (SCPs)**, or databases that store information about customer preferences. For example, the SCP knows that Arlene at number 523-1234 does not have call waiting whereas the subscriber she is calling, Gary, at 555-9876, does have call waiting. Every time Arlene calls Gary, the SCP supplies the signaling network with the instruction that should Gary's line be busy, his central office's switch should send a beeping noise over his active voice circuit to indicate that he has another incoming call. In SS7 terminology, central switches are known as **service switching points (SSPs)**. In fact, the ITU termed any central office or other telecommunications switching facility a service switching point (SSP), but for the sake of simplicity, you can think of SSPs as central offices.

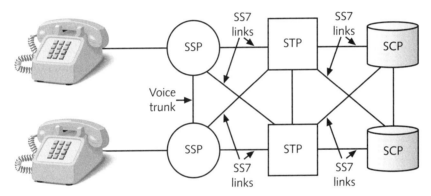

Figure 6-26   Signaling System No. 7

SCPs do not transmit customer information directly to a central office switch, however. They supply it to one of several STPs on the telephony network. In SS7, STPs simply act as intermediaries for signals moving between SCPs (customer information databases) and SSPs (central office switches). Their function is to move messages quickly and reliably from one point to another. Although SS7 seems like a mess of acronyms, its underlying architecture is fairly simple, as shown in Figure 6-26. Its complexity springs from the volumes of information it must analyze and the instantaneous decisions about service and routes it must make.

You may hear the term **Advanced Intelligent Network (AIN)** used in conjunction with many of the capabilities of SS7. This was a term coined in the early 1990s by telephony manufacturers around the world to describe the new type of telephony architecture made possible by SS7. The concept behind AIN is that switches rely on vast, centralized databases to make instant decisions on the best available voice circuit path and to provide custom services based on individual subscriber preferences. Before SS7, services this sophisticated would have been impossible.

CHAPTER SUMMARY

❏ Modulation is a signal-processing technique in which an information wave is imposed on (combined with) a carrier wave to create a unique wave pattern. It is one way to control those signals and ensure that they arrive at their intended destination in their intended form.

❏ Three major ways of modulating analog signals are amplitude modulation (AM), frequency modulation (FM), and phase modulation (PM).

❏ Three major ways of representing digital signals through modulation are amplitude shift keying (ASK), frequency shift keying (FSK), and phase shift keying (PSK).

❏ The process of converting analog signals into digital signals is called pulse code modulation (PCM). It begins by measuring the amplitude of an analog signal at multiple instants, a technique known as sampling. These samples are then digitized through a process known as quantizing. The last step in reproducing an analog signal in digital form is filtering. Filtering removes inessential information from the signal, including very high and very low frequencies, thereby reducing the amount of bandwidth the signal requires.

❏ The higher the sampling rate, the more similar the audio signal is to the digital signal. For most voice communications, 8000 samples per second is sufficient. However, audio CDs use a much higher sampling rate of 44,100 samples per second.

❏ Multiplexing is sending multiple signals simultaneously over one communications channel. It enables more information to be sent over a single channel in a shorter period of time than simplexing, the process of sending only one signal over a communications channel. Many forms of multiplexing exist and may expedite either voice or data communications.

❏ Common methods of multiplexing include frequency division multiplexing (FDM), time division multiplexing (TDM), statistical multiplexing, and wave division multiplexing (WDM). A unique form of WDM is dense wave division multiplexing (DWDM), which allows fiber optic cables to carry many more signals than the original version of WDM.

❏ Switching is a method of establishing connections and sending information between nodes on a network. It is used in both voice and data communications, and until very recently, telephony switching was quite different from data network switching.

❏ In circuit switching, a connection is established between two nodes before they begin transmitting data. Bandwidth is dedicated to this connection and remains available only to the original source and destination nodes until those users terminate communication.

❏ Message switching is a method of switching in which each intermediate node between the source and its target accepts and stores the data before passing it on. All information follows the same physical path, but unlike with circuit switching, the connection is not continuously maintained. E-mail uses message switching.

❑ Packet switching breaks data into packets before they are transported. Packets are free to travel any path on the network to their destination, because each packet contains a destination address and information about where its data belongs in the data stream.

❑ Although switch makes and models differ between manufacturers, all switches share these four essential elements: switching matrix, line or trunk circuits, central control computer, and common equipment.

❑ A local switch performs the following functions: provides dial tone; accepts and interprets signals from the local subscriber; receives signals from the destination's local switch about when to terminate the call; records local subscriber billing information; stores information about subscribers in a subscriber database; tests and maintains a subscriber's local loop; modifies subscriber account and line configuration; provides enhanced services, such as caller ID, call waiting, number blocking, and voice mail; and provides operator assistance and access to emergency services.

❑ A tandem switch may perform the following functions: provides termination for trunks at Class 1, 2, 3, and 4 central offices; gathers and transmits information about telephone network traffic and congestion; determines the fastest path over the PSTN for long distance calls; carries data and voice signals between central offices; tests and maintain trunks; and assists in trunk configuration.

❑ AT&T's Western Electric division's 1ESS was the first electronic switch used in North America. Since its release in 1965, AT&T, and later, Lucent, have released several more versions of ESS, each with increased capacity and a variety of software and hardware enhancements. By the 1980s, ESS switches were fully digital.

❑ Nortel's DMS line of switches are competitors to Lucent's ESS switches. Nortel released its first DMS switch in 1978. DMS stands for digital multiplexed system, but the full name for the product is almost never used.

❑ Signaling is the exchange of information between the components of a telephony system for the purposes of establishing, monitoring, or releasing phone circuits, as well as controlling system operations. The four basic functions of switch signaling are: alerting, transmitting address information, supervising, and transmitting information.

❑ The common channel signaling (CCS) system was developed by AT&T in the 1970s after they had lost significant revenues to fraudulent use of the in-band signaling technique. It is distinguished by the fact that it is an out-of-band signaling technique.

❑ Signaling System No. 7 (SS7) is a particular type of CCS employed on modern telephone networks. It is a standard developed and published by the ITU. This standard specifies how switches should exchange alert, addressing, supervisory, and transmission information over a digital network.

❑ In SS7, any central office or other telecommunications switching facility is called a service switching point (SSP). SCPs supply customer information to one of several STPs on the telephony network. STPs simply act as intermediaries for signals moving between SCPs (customer information databases) and SSPs (central office switches).

KEY TERMS

1ESS — The first electronic telephone switch. AT&T's Western Electric division released the 1ESS in 1965.

5ESS — Lucent's most current all-digital switch. A 5ESS may serve as a local or tandem switch, depending on what features are ordered and programmed into its software.

Advanced Intelligent Network (AIN) — A term coined by telephony manufacturers in the early 1990s to describe the new type of telephony architecture made possible by SS7. The concept behind AIN is that switches rely on vast, centralized database to make instant decisions on the best available voice circuit path and provide custom services based on individual subscriber preferences.

amplitude modulation (AM) — A method of modulation in which the amplitude of the carrier signal is modified by the imposition of the information signal. In AM, adding the information wave does not change the frequency of the carrier wave.

amplitude shift keying (ASK) — A method for converting analog amplitude modulated signals into digital signals. In ASK, areas with differing amplitude are conveyed as either 0s or 1s.

band — A subchannel within a communications channel.

backbone — A major, heavily trafficked connection between a carrier's POPs.

busy circuit — A signal that indicates that a subscriber's telephone is off-hook (in other words, the line is in use) and the circuit is not available for connection.

busy signal — A tone of two combined frequencies that lasts for .5 seconds and repeats after .5 seconds of silence. A busy signal is issued to the caller's local switch by the recipient's local switch after it detects that the recipient's line is busy.

carrier wave — In modulation, the wave whose characteristics (for example, amplitude, frequency, or phase) are modified by the addition of an information wave.

cell — A fixed-length group of data used in statistical multiplexing transmission, such as ATM.

central control computer — The means by which a switch interprets incoming data, retrieves data, and issues commands to the rest of its components. The central control computer typically includes multiple processors, among other components.

circuit switching — A method of switching in which a connection is established between two nodes before they begin transmitting data. In circuit switching, bandwidth is dedicated to the connection and remains available only to the original source and destination nodes until those users terminate communication. While the nodes are connected, all data follows the same path first selected by the switch.

codec (coder/decoder) — A device that can encode and decode a signal. Codecs are found inside switches, for example, to convert an analog signal into a digital signal.

common channel signaling (CCS) — A method of out-of-band signaling developed by AT&T in the 1970s. It is distinguished by the fact that it carries signal information on a dedicated data link between central offices. In CCS, no signal information is carried over the voice connections.

companding — The process of compressing and expanding areas of low and high amplitudes, respectively, to better quantize an analog signal that's being converted to a digital signal.

demodulator — A device that separates the information from the carrier signal at the receiving end of a modulated wave.

demultiplexer (demux) — A device that separates signals combined by multiplexing and regenerates them in their original form at the receiving end.

dense wavelength division multiplexing (DWDM) — A version of wavelength division multiplexing that can support a larger number of different wavelengths on the same strand of fiber, thus greatly increasing the bandwidth capacity of that fiber.

DMS (Digital Multiplexed System) — A series of local and tandem switches supplied by Nortel. DMS competes with and provides similar features to Lucent's ESS line of switches.

disconnect — The indication that a subscriber's telephone is on-hook after being off-hook (in other words, he has hung up the phone).

electronic switching system (ESS) — The brand name of Lucent's local and tandem switch that relies entirely on electronics. The first ESS was released in 1965 and since then, the switch has gone through many improvements. Today's ESSs are entirely digital.

fiber optic modem (FOM) — A device located at the both the transmitting and receiving ends of a wavelength division multiplexed channel. The FOM separates the multiplexed signals into individual signals according to their different wavelengths.

filtering — The part of the analog-to-digital conversion process that removes inessential information from the signal, including very high and very low frequencies, to reduce the amount of bandwidth the signal requires.

framing — In TDM or statistical multiplexing, a technique of inserting special bits in the data stream to indicate where one series of data-carrying time slots ends and another begins.

frequency division multiplexing (FDM) — A method of sending multiple analog signals simultaneously over one channel by separating the channel into subchannels, or bands. Each band in the channel has its own carrier signal with a unique frequency.

frequency modulation (FM) — A method of modulation in which the frequency of the carrier signal is modified by the application of the information signal. In FM, adding the information signal does not change the amplitude of the carrier wave.

frequency shift keying (FSK) — The method by which FM signals are converted into digital signals. In FSK, areas with differing frequency are conveyed as either 0s or 1s.

guardband — A narrow band of unused frequency that separates two information-carrying bands and ensures that signals do not interfere with each other.

guided wave — An information wave that is added to (and thus, guided by) a carrier wave in the process of modulation.

idle circuit — An indication that a subscriber's telephone is on-hook (in other words, the line is not in use) and the circuit is available for connection.

in-band signaling — A type of switch signaling that uses the same communications channel as the information being exchanged over the channel.

6

information wave — In modulation, the wave that represents the signal to be transmitted. An information wave is added to the carrier wave to result in a unique wave that possesses characteristics of both waves.

interoffice signaling — The exchange of alert, supervisory, and other information between switches at different central offices.

intra-office call — A call in which the local loops from the caller and her intended receiver connect to the same end office. An intra-office call doesn't get passed on to another CO.

line group controller (LGC) — A part of a local switch's central control computer that monitors the status of hundreds of SLICs (which are attached to subscribers' lines).

local switch — A switch that receives and interprets the signal from a subscriber's telephone at the central office where a subscriber's local loop terminates (a Class 5 CO, or end office). ILECs, CLECs, and local wireless carriers own and operate local switches.

message switching — A method of switching in which each intermediate node between the source and its target accepts and stores the data before passing it on. This "store and forward" routine continues until the message reaches its destination.

modem (modulator/demodulator) — A device used to convert digital into analog signals at the transmission end and analog into digital signals at the receiving end so that computers can communicate over analog channels, such as a phone line.

modulation — A signal-processing technique in which an information wave is imposed on a carrier wave to create a unique wave pattern.

modulator — The device that imposes an information wave on a carrier wave at the transmission end.

multiplexer (mux) — A device that can combine and transmit many signals on a single channel.

off-hook — A telecommunications term that means the condition of the line when a telephone handset is lifted, or taken off its hook. An off-hook condition closes the local line circuit, causing a small amount of current to flow over the line.

on-hook — A telecommunications term that means the condition of the line when a telephone handset is resting on its hook. While a telephone is on-hook, its local line circuit cannot be closed.

packet — A small group of data organized according to standards. Packets are used in packet switching.

packet switching — A method of switching in which data are separated into packets before they are transported. Packets are free to travel any path on the network to their destination, because each packet contains a destination address and information about where its data belongs in the data stream. Packets are reassembled in their proper order at the receiving end.

phase — The relationship between a wave's cycle (specifically, the point in the cycle when the wave crosses the zero voltage line) and time.

phase modulation — A method of modulation in which an information wave is applied to a carrier wave to modify the carrier wave's phase. Phase modulation is used to transmit color information in TV signals and for other specialized functions.

phase shift keying (PSK) — A method by which analog, phase modulated waves are transformed into digital signals. In PSK, changes in phase indicate a change in the value of bits to either 1 or 0.

private switching system — A means of routing calls from source to destination independent from the telephone company's facilities. A private-switching system may interact with a public-switching system. Or, in the case of one employee calling another employee within the same building, they may never connect with the telephone company's facilities.

public switching system — A means of routing calls and interconnecting telephone subscribers across the PSTN.

pulse amplitude modulation (PAM) — The assembly of multiple analog wave samples to create a wave that approximates the original wave.

pulse code modulation (PCM) — The process of converting analog signals into digital signals.

quantizing — The process of converting the sampled amplitude of an analog wave into its binary equivalent.

sampling — The process of measuring the amplitude of an analog wave at regular, multiple instants to generate an approximation of that wave in digital form.

sampling rate — The number of samples of an analog wave's amplitude taken each second in order to create a digital representation of the wave. For example, the sampling rate of an audio CD is 44,100 samples per second.

seizure — The request for service signal that is transmitted to the local switch when a subscriber takes her handset off-hook and closes the local line circuit.

service control points (SCP) — Databases that store information about customer preferences, which are used in SS7 signaling.

service switching points (SSP) — Central switches, as defined in the SS7 signaling protocol, or any telecommunications switching facility, according to ITU standards.

signal transfer point (STP) — An intermediate switch on a CCS network that handles signals from one switch to another. In SS7, STPs handle signals between SSPs and SCPs.

signaling — The exchange of information between the components of a telephony system for the purposes of establishing, monitoring, or releasing phone circuits, as well as controlling system operations.

Signaling System No. 7 (SS7) — An ITU standard specifying how switches should exchange alert, addressing, supervisory, and transmission information over a digital network. SS7 is a type of CCS employed on modern telephony networks.

statistical multiplexing — A method of multiplexing that assigns a separate time slot for each node according to priority and need.

subscriber line interface circuit (SLIC) — A component inside a local switch that provides battery power to a subscriber's line and detects when the telephone handset is off-hook.

subscriber loop signaling — The exchange of information about a telephone circuit over the local loop. Many of these signals contain information about the local loop's status.

switching — A method of establishing connections and sending information between nodes on a network. Switching is used in both voice and data communications, and until very recently, telephony switching was quite different from data network switching. The three fundamental types of switching are: circuit switching, message switching, and packet switching.

switching matrix — The internal connections between input and output circuits of a switch (may also be called switching fabric).

switching system — The collection of hardware and software that establishes connections between lines and trunks to complete calls.

tandem switch — A switch that handles calls between central offices. Tandem switches operate at any type of CO other than a Class 5. ILECs, CLECs, and IXCs own and operate tandem switches.

time division multiplexing (TDM) — A method of multiplexing digital signals that assigns a time slot in the flow of communications to every node on the network and in that time slot, carries data from that node.

touch-tone dialing — The process of issuing a combination of two frequencies to convey a number from a telephone's keypad to a local switch.

wavelength division multiplexing (WDM) — A technology that enables one fiber-optic connection to simultaneously carry multiple light signals. Each signal in WDM is assigned a different wavelength, or frequency (similar to FDM).

REVIEW QUESTIONS

1. In an AM wave, which of the following remains constant?

   a. framing

   b. frequency

   c. amplitude

   d. voltage

2. Which of the following per-second sampling rates provides the best sound quality in a digital signal?

   a. 4

   b. 400

   c. 4400

   d. 44000

3. Which of the following waves would be most affected by quantizing noise?

   a. a wave with a maximum amplitude of 2 V

   b. a wave with a maximum amplitude of 20 V

   c. a wave with a maximum amplitude of 220 V

   d. all waves are equally affected by quantizing noise

4. What is used at the transmission end of a communications channel to apply an information signal to a carrier signal?

    a. multiplexer

    b. demultiplexer

    c. modulator

    d. demodulator

5. What technique can convert FM signals into bits?

    a. frequency modulation

    b. frequency phase shifting

    c. frequency shift keying

    d. frequency frame allocation

6. In addition to frequency and amplitude, what third characteristic of a wave can be modulated?

    a. phase

    b. magnetism

    c. time

    d. space

7. What type of modulation are you probably using when you connect to your ISP with a 56 Kbps modem over a phone line?

    a. ASK

    b. FSK

    c. PAM

    d. PCM

8. Explain the difference between duplexing and multiplexing.

9. What does multiplexing achieve?

    a. It scrambles analog signals for improved security.

    b. It allows many signals to be carried over a single channel at once.

    c. It modifies a carrier wave with an information signal.

    d. It translates analog signals into digital signals.

10. Which of the following uses frequency division multiplexing?

    a. cable TV

    b. ISDN

    c. frame relay

    d. ATM

6

11. Which of the following is a disadvantage to using time division multiplexing?

    a. It is slow.

    b. It is error-prone.

    c. It requires expensive multiplexers and demultiplexers.

    d. It is inefficient.

12. How does statistical multiplexing differ from time division multiplexing?

    a. Statistical multiplexing is used only for analog transmission, whereas TDM is used for digital transmission.

    b. Statistical multiplexing relies on fiber optic cable, whereas TDM can be used on wire media.

    c. Statistical multiplexing requires more bandwidth to process signals than TDM does.

    d. Statistical multiplexing makes more efficient use of time slots than TDM does.

13. How is statistical multiplexing similar to time division multiplexing?

    a. Both use fixed cells to carry data from each network node.

    b. Both modify a carrier signal's frequency with an information signal.

    c. Both require fiber optic cable as their transmission medium.

    d. Both assign unique time slots to information from different network nodes.

14. What medium is used with wavelength division

    a. coaxial cable

    b. twisted pair cable

    c. fiber optic cable

    d. satellite

15. What's the difference between WDM and DWDM?

    a. DWDM can accommodate many more channels than WDM.

    b. DWDM can only run on multi-mode fiber.

    c. DWDM can only run on copper wire.

    d. DWDM requires less configuration than WDM.

16. Which type of switching is used for most telephone calls over the PSTN?

    a. circuit switching

    b. message switching

    c. packet switching

    d. time division switching

17. Why is packet switching more efficient than circuit switching?

18. Which of the following uses message switching?

   a. telephony

   b. asynchronous transfer mode (ATM)

   c. e-mail

   d. telnet

19. Which of the following characterizes a private-switching system?

   a. a connection to a Class 5 central office

   b. connections to all telephones in a company

   c. centralized voice mail

   d. the ability to switch calls without using the PSTN

20. Which type of switch provides access to emergency services, such as the Fire Department?

   a. private switch

   b. local switch

   c. tandem switch

   d. layer 3 switch

21. Which of the following functions is performed by a tandem switch?

   a. connecting two trunks

   b. testing a subscriber's line

   c. modifying service attributes for a subscriber

   d. providing dial tone

22. Up to which point in a phone call are the steps for switching both local and long-distance calls identical?

   a. until the intended recipient of the call answers

   b. until the intended recipient's phone begins ringing

   c. until the caller picks up his handset

   d. until the local switch interprets the caller's ten digit number

23. In what year did AT&T's Western Electric division release the first ESS?

   a. 1956

   b. 1965

   c. 1969

   d. 1973

6

24. Which of the following Nortel switches provides local switch services?

    a. DMS500

    b. DMS300

    c. DMS200

    d. DMS100

25. When telephones were new, a caller had to tell the operator what number she wanted to dial. This function, now achieved through signaling, is known as:

    a. numbering

    b. addressing

    c. fingering

    d. pinging

26. Explain how in-band signaling can leave a long-distance carrier vulnerable to telephone fraud.

27. Which of the following signaling functions is not considered part of subscriber loop signaling?

    a. determination of the fastest routes for voice circuits

    b. transmission of dial tone

    c. determination of whether a handset is on- or off-hook

    d. transmission of phone numbers dialed by the calling party

28. What's another word for a service signal that is transmitted to the local switch when a subscriber takes her handset off-hook?

    a. disconnect

    b. off-hook

    c. seizure

    d. alert

29. Which of the following pieces of information would be stored in an SCP?

    a. which subscribers have paid for caller ID service

    b. where network congestion has slowed traffic on an interstate trunk

    c. a central office's inventory of switches according to serial number

    d. date of the last disaster recovery drill for an end office

30. According to ITU SS7 terminology, what is one example of an SSP?

    a. telephone handset

    b. end-office switch

    c. interoffice trunk

    d. local loop

HANDS-ON PROJECTS

Project 6-1

In Chapter 2, you learned that an oscilloscope is an instrument used for measuring a wave's change in voltage over time. In the context of studying electricity and circuits, oscilloscopes can present a graphic view of AC electricity. In the context of telecommunications signaling, oscilloscopes can present a graphic view of electromagnetic waves used in modulation (among other things). Oscilloscopes are commonly used as test equipment by electricians, engineers, and audio/video technicians. However, they are expensive. Modern oscilloscopes typically cost at least several thousand dollars.

In this project, you use a software program that simulates a modern oscilloscope to view wave patterns. Several oscilloscope programs are available on the Web. This project uses Real Time Analyzer RAL, from Yoshimasha Electronics Inc., which can be obtained and used for a nominal shareware fee. Downloading the program requires a computer capable of using the Web. The program works with Windows 98, NT, ME, 2000, or XP desktop operating systems. (You may find or already have access to another oscillator simulation program. If this is the case, you can skip Steps 1–13 and follow along with the remainder of the project.) Your computer should have speakers and also be capable of issuing sound, though a sophisticated sound card is not necessary.

1. Connect to the Internet and go to **www.download.com**. The CNET Downloads Web page appears.

2. In the Search text box, type **RAL**, and then click **Go!**

3. The Search Results page appears, with the RAL/Realtime Analyzer Light 1.011 software listed. Under the Availability column, click **Download now** to copy the program to your hard disk. Note that you may use this software free for a three-day trial before you must pay the nominal licensing fee.

4. The File Download dialog box appears. Choose to save this executable file to your computer's hard disk. (The name of the option you choose to save the file will depend on your computer's operating system and configuration.)

5. The Save As dialog box appears, prompting you to select a location on your hard disk for saving this file. Choose a folder, then click **Save** to save the file to that folder.

6. After the file has been copied to your hard disk, run the file to initiate the RAL installation. (Note: If the entire executable file does not download, you will receive an error with the message: "This file is not a valid Windows 32 application" when you try to run the program. If this happens, delete the file and download it again, according to Steps 3 and 4.)

7. In the Realtime Analyzer RAL – InstallShield Wizard welcome screen, click **Next** to proceed with the installation.

8. The License Agreement dialog box appears. Scroll through the text of the software license. If you agree with the license's terms, select the **I accept the terms in the license agreement** option button and then click **Next** to continue.

9. The Customer Information dialog box appears. If they do not automatically appear, enter your name in the User Name: text box and your school or company affiliation in the Organization: text box. Select the **Anyone who uses this computer (all users)** option under the "Install this application for" prompt. Click **Next** to continue.

10. The Destination Folder dialog box appears. To accept the default program folder of C:\Program Files\RALE, and proceed with the installation wizard, click **Next**.

11. The Ready to Install the Program screen appears. If all the information that appears on this screen is correct, click **Install** to begin the program installation. If some of the information is incorrect, click the Back button to go back and change the information. Wait while files are copied and configured.

12. The InstallShield Wizard Completed dialog box appears. Click **Finish** to close this box.

13. To run the program on a Windows 98, 2000, or XP computer, click **Start**, point to **Programs**, point to **Realtime Analyzer RAL** folder, then click **Realtime Analyzer RAL**. The User License dialog box appears. If you wish to register your program at this time, click **Registration**. If you wish to use the 3-day trial, click **Trial**.

14. At the Realtime Analyzer RAL main screen, click the **Oscilloscope** button to switch to a virtual oscilloscope. The Oscilloscope screen appears. Notice the graph that makes up a majority of the screen. Just as on a real oscilloscope, this graph is where a wave's amplitude over time is depicted.

15. To view a waveform on the oscilloscope, you must first generate a tone. In this program, the Device drop down box allows you to select input from several different types of devices.

16. In the Peak Level Monitor area, make sure the Input check box is *not* selected. (If it is selected, noise from your computer will interfere with the waveform you are about to generate.)

17. Now, you are ready to generate a tone. Click the **Signal Generator** button from the main Realtime Analyzer RAL screen. The Signal Generator dialog box appears. (At the same time, the Oscillator window should remain open, but in the background.)

18. Make sure the **Tone** tab is selected. Under "Frequency," move the sliding pointer to a frequency of **338** Hz (an audible tone at the low end of the human hearing range). If you have trouble positioning the slider precisely at 338 Hz, you may select a frequency close to it. Also, make sure the **Sinusoidal** radio button is selected under "Waveform."

19. Under "Output," click **Start** to begin generating this tone. Adjust the sliding pointers under "Output Level" to adjust the volume up or down. Also, notice the default sampling rate selected for the signal generator. This sampling rate is the one used to generate the digital tone you hear.

20. Now, click anywhere on the Oscilloscope window (which is in the background) to bring it to the foreground. You may need to adjust the Oscilloscope's position so that you can see the entire window on your monitor.

21. To get the best view of the waveform, make sure the sliding pointer under "Sweep Time Range" is on 1 ms/div (millisecond per division on the chart). This "zooms in" on the wave so that you can clearly see its individual cycles.

22. To begin viewing the waveform on the Oscilloscope, click the **Start** button in the lower right corner of the window. The waveform should begin appearing on the oscilloscope's graph. (If the waveform looks like a pattern of vertical lines, you may either wait a few seconds or, if this doesn't correct it, click Stop, and then click Start again.)

23. Notice the spacing of the waveform's cycles. What does the width of this spacing depend on? Also, why do you think the lines of the waveform wiggle slightly? Why is this useful?

24. Now, return to the Signal Generator dialog box by clicking on the Realtime Analyzer RAL (in the background) and clicking the **Signal Generator** button.

25. On the Tone tab, change the frequency of the generated tone.

26. Click on the Oscilloscope window to view this waveform. How does it differ from the 348 Hz wave?

27. Repeat Step 25, choosing a number of different tones, then view each on the Oscilloscope screen. Proceed to Project 6-2 to perform more waveform manipulation on the virtual oscilloscope.

Project 6-2

Recall from earlier in this chapter that, when digitizing a waveform, the higher the sampling rate, the better the sound quality. In the following steps, you investigate the effects of different sampling rates on the waveform. However, the difference between a real oscilloscope and this virtual oscilloscope is that the former can show analog waveforms just as they are input, whereas the latter, because it is computerized, cannot show true, analog waveforms. To simulate analog waves, this program generates a digital facsimile of those waves. Therefore, it is not possible to truly compare an analog wave that has been sampled and converted to a digital wave with the original analog wave. Luckily, however, the program can simulate the effect of using different sampling rates within the Oscilloscope screen.

This project expands on what you learned about signals in Project 6-1. This project requires the same materials and configuration as Project 6-1.

1. If you do not already have it open, open the Realtime Analyzer RAL program and make sure its settings match those listed in Steps 15 and 16 of Project 6-1.

2. Click the **Signal Generator** button. The Signal Generator dialog box opens, with the Tone tab selected.

3. Under "Frequency," move the sliding pointer to select a frequency of **425 Hz**. Make sure the Sinusoidal check box is selected under "Waveform," and leave all other options at their defaults.

4. Click **Start** to begin generating a 425 Hz tone.

5. Click the **Oscilloscope** button on the Realtime Analyzer RAL main screen to open the Oscilloscope screen (if it is not already open). Make sure the sliding pointer under "Sweep Time Range" is on 1 ms/div (millisecond per division on the chart).

6. Click **Start** to begin viewing the 425 tone on the oscilloscope screen. Let the oscilloscope run for at least five seconds while you look closely at the wave's behavior. How much is it affected by the signal noise that your computer generates?

7. Now, under the "Sampling Rate" drop down box, change the sampling rate from the default of 44,100 KHz to the lowest value, **8000 KHz**.

8. Watch the waveform for another five seconds or more. How does it differ from the wave that was sampled at 44,100 KHz? Why is this the case?

9. When you have finished observing the wave, click **Stop** to stop the oscilloscope function and proceed to Project 6-3.

Hands-on
Project

Project 6-3

Recall from this chapter that phase is the relationship between a wave's cycle and time. Just as with frequency and amplitude, phase is a characteristic that can be modulated to carry signals (for example, TV signals). In this project, you use the virtual oscilloscope to demonstrate the concept of phases.

1. Follow Steps 1 – 5 of Project 6-2 to open the Realtime Analyzer RAL program, but this time set the Signal Generator frequency to 338 Hz, and then begin generating a tone.

2. At the Oscilloscope screen, click **Start** to begin viewing this waveform. (If you are proceeding directly from Project 6-2, change the sampling rate back to the default value of 44,100 KHz.)

3. In the "Delay Time" drop down box, make sure the default range within which you can change the delay is set to **1 ms**.

4. Now, move the sliding pointer under "Delay Time" to the right. Watch the wave as you do so. By increasing the delay, you are changing the wave's phase.

5. As you move the delay time sliding pointer, try to align one of the wave's peaks with a vertical bar on the grid and stop moving the wave at that point. Knowing that each vertical line on the graph represents 1 ms, approximately how many milliseconds makes up one full cycle for this wave?

6. Now, move the delay time sliding pointer all the way to the left, so that the delay is 0 ms. Notice where the wave's cycle falls on the oscilloscope's graph.

7. Move the delay time sliding pointer all the way to the right, so that the delay is 1 ms. Notice where the wave's cycle falls on the oscilloscope's graph. Based on what you determined in Step 5 about this wave's cycle, how many degrees have you shifted this wave's phase by increasing the delay from 0 to 1 ms?

8. Continue experimenting with the virtual oscilloscope if you wish. When you are finished, close the program by clicking the Close button in the upper right corner of the main Realtime RAL screen.

Project 6-4

In this project, you bring together all that you have learned about signaling and switching. As you know, each type of telecommunication service may use a different encoding technique (analog or digital), modulation technique (for example, AM, FM, FSK, PSK), multiplexing technique (for example, TDM, FDM, WDM), and switching method (for example, circuit switching, message switching, or packet switching). In the following steps, you characterize each telecommunication service according to the technologies it uses. For this project, you will need a pencil and paper (or if you are familiar with using a spreadsheet program such as Microsoft Excel, you may use that instead).

(Because some of the specific services have yet to be described in detail in this book, feel free to consult the chapter text for references to the services.)

1. On your piece of paper, draw a table that contains five columns and seven rows. In row one, write the following column headings, starting with column one: Service, Encoding, Modulation, Multiplexing, and Switching.

2. In rows two through seven, list the following services in the first column:

   - A telephone conversation between two friends, each of whom is at home using their local phone service.

   - The transmission of a spreadsheet file from one colleague to another over their company's Ethernet LAN, which was installed in 1996 and has not been upgraded since.

   - The transmission of a spreadsheet file from one colleague to another between two company offices that are directly connected with a fiber optic cable. The two offices are part of a WAN that was installed just last year and that relies on ATM transmission.

   - A radio broadcast of jazz music at the 1000 KHz frequency.

   - The transmission of a Web page from a university server on the Internet to a user who has dialed into his ISP. The user's ISP connects to a large, national telecommunications carrier via multiple T-1 lines.

   - A telephone call between two colleagues at the same office. Their company uses a PBX and traditional telephone wire to connect intra-office calls.

3. Complete column two for each service, indicating whether it represents information as analog or digital signals with either an "A" or "D."

4. Complete column three for each service, indicating what type of modulation (if any) this service uses. For example, if the service uses frequency modulation, enter "FM." If you think the service does not use modulation, enter "N/A." In some cases, a service may use more than one type of modulation.

5. Complete column four for each service, indicating what type of multiplexing the service uses. For example, if the service uses time division multiplexing, enter "TDM." If you think the service does not use mutliplexing, enter "N/A."

6

6. Complete column five for each service, indicating what type of switching, if any, the service uses: circuit switching, message switching, or packet switching. If you think the service does not use switching, enter "N/A." In some cases, the transmission for one service may use multiple switching methods.

7. Now, add a seventh column to the table. Name this column "Rank."

8. Review the information you have entered for each service. As best as you can (based on what you have learned about speed and efficiency of different modulation, multiplexing, and switching techniques), rank the services from one to six, with the service potentially capable of transmitting signals the fastest ranked as number one and the service that uses the slowest transmission technology ranked as number 6. What factors might change a service's ranking? (For example, a network experiencing heavy traffic might hamper the potential speed of one type of switching more than another.)

CASE PROJECTS

Case
Project

1. You are a telephone technician who has worked for an RBOC for the last eight years. This RBOC uses the latest 5ESS local and tandem switches and conforms to the SS7 signaling standards. You have been asked to troubleshoot a problem that occurs occasionally with a number of local lines connecting to your CO. Subscribers have been complaining that in the middle of their conversations they sometimes hear a beeping noise, as if they had subscribed to the Call Waiting feature, but they haven't asked for or paid for this service. In what part of the switching system do you start your troubleshooting? Why? If that component shows nothing wrong, what components would you investigate next?

2. Your colleagues are impressed with how quickly you solved the case of the unwanted Call Waiting feature. They have now asked you to help them with a new, more urgent problem. As of 10 a.m., no one in the west half of your CO's territory had a dial tone. What specific components do you investigate first to determine what's causing this problem? What additional questions do you ask your colleagues to gain more clues about the problem? After you find what you think is the cause, how do you go about fixing the problem?

3. You've noticed that more and more subscribers connecting to your CO are using their analog lines to connect to an Internet Service Provider. Your RBOC doesn't offer any high-speed data lines in your area, but you think it would be a profitable thing for the company to do. Searching the Internet, you find that a few CLECs in your area are offering ISDN and DSL services in addition to analog lines. You decide to bring this matter to the attention of your supervisor. Before doing so, you log on to the Internet and research the cost of DSL and ISDN services to subscribers in your area. How does it compare to the cost of an analog line? How much more throughput could a subscriber get with DSL or ISDN? You also research what it would take to upgrade your local CO's 5ESS switch to allow it to handle both ISDN and DSL subscriber lines. Based on your research, compile a fact sheet about the costs and benefits of going into the business of offering DSL and ISDN in your local area.

7

DATA NETWORKING FUNDAMENTALS

After reading this chapter and completing the exercises, you will be able to:

♦ Discuss basic networking concepts, including the elements common to all client-server networks

♦ Provide examples of multiple network services

♦ Describe the differences between LANs, MANs, and WANs

♦ Understand the functions of each layer of the OSI model

♦ Describe the purpose of protocols and list several types of protocols

♦ Recognize the core protocols and addressing scheme for the TCP/IP suite

You already know some things about data networks. For example, you have already learned about communication channels, binary encoding, multiplexing, and packet switching. All of these concepts apply to data networking as well as to telephony. However, data networks involve other technologies that you still need to investigate. You learn about many of these complex technologies in later chapters. First, though, you need to learn about the basic types of data networks and their uses. This chapter introduces you to the basic types of data networks, the elements common to all modern data networks, and the means by which computers on a network exchange data.

BASIC NETWORKING CONCEPTS

Recall that in the context of data communications, a network is a group of computers that are connected in order to share data and devices (such as printers) more easily. Whether small and simple or large and complex, networks share the same terminology and building blocks. The following section provides an introduction to these basic elements. You learn more about these topics throughout this book.

Terminology

Often, in the networking field, a desktop computer is known as a **workstation**. When a workstation is not connected to a network, but relies on its own hard disk for data storage and applications, it is known as a **standalone workstation**. A workstation connected to a network is often called a **client**. A network usually consists of many clients. A person whose workstation is part of a network may also be called a client—or that person may be known more informally as a **user**.

A third definition for the word "client" is the software that allows a networked computer to take advantage of shared resources.

Servers not only store shared data and programs on their hard disks, but can also perform management functions, such as determining which users have access to certain programs. A network that uses a server to enable clients to share data, data storage space, and devices is known as a **client–server network**. You learn more about clients and servers later in this chapter. Because this is the most popular type of network, most of the networking concepts covered in this book pertain to client-server networks. Figure 7-1 shows a diagram of a simple client-server network that includes the components introduced in this section.

Requirements for Connectivity

Recall from Chapter 1 that every system of communication includes a source, a transmitter, a communications channel, a receiver, and a destination. In the context of data networks, the source and destination are computers, and the communications channels are known as transmission media, or simply, media. Examples of transmission media include copper wire, fiber optic cable, and, in the case of wireless communications, the atmosphere. Every network requires some type of media to carry signals between computers.

On a common telephone, the transmitter and receiver are two separate components. However, in most data communications, these two functions are combined in one component known as a **transceiver**. In its capacity as a transmitter, the transceiver encodes a stream of data and sends signals to the transmission medium in a format that the receiver can interpret. As a receiver, the transceiver performs the opposite tasks: It accepts and decodes the stream of data. The device that acts as a transceiver for networked computers is called a **network interface card** (**NIC**, pronounced *nick*). NICs vary depending on the type of computer and network they are used on. For example, a laptop computer requires a much smaller NIC than a desktop computer.

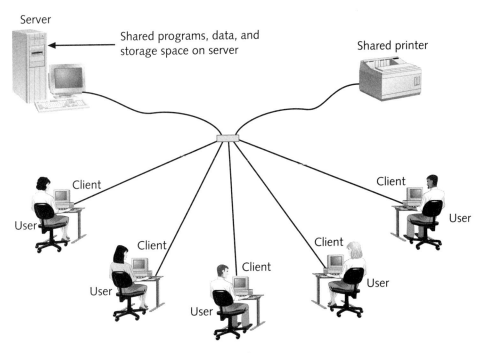

Figure 7-1   A simple client-server network

In the case of tangible transmission media, such as cabling, the transceiver and the medium must be physically connected for a computer's transceiver to issue and accept signals via the transmission medium. To make this connection, each NIC provides at least one receptacle that accepts a **connector** (or **plug**). A connector is the piece of hardware at which a cable terminates. An example of a cable connecting to a NIC is shown in Figure 7-2.

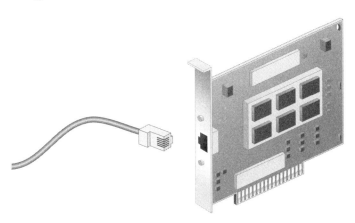

Figure 7-2   A cable connecting to a NIC

Thus, in order to physically connect two computers to form a very simple network, you could affix connectors to each end of a cable, then plug one connector into one computer's NIC and the other connector into the second computer's NIC. However, data could not be exchanged—and this would not constitute a true network—unless you had also implemented the means for the two computers to communicate.

Requirements for Communication

Any device (for example, a server, client, or printer) that can receive a transmission over a network is known as a **node**. To receive data, each node must have a unique **address**, or identifying number, in the same way that your home must have a unique address for the postal service to accurately deliver your mail to you. It is important that each computer on a network have a unique address so that data can be transmitted reliably to and from that computer. Sometimes, a computer with a unique address is known simply as a **host** on the network. A host can be either a client or a server.

Different types of networks use different addressing schemes. The type of address a node uses depends on the network's protocol. A **protocol** is a rule that governs how the parts of a network communicate. For example, protocols define standards for how data will be packaged and when nodes on a network may communicate. Without protocols, devices could not interpret the signals sent by other devices, and data would go nowhere. You learn more about protocols and the addressing schemes they use later in this chapter.

After a computer has a unique address and is equipped to issue data according to certain protocols, it still requires software capable of formatting data according to those protocols. In addition, the computer needs some way to learn the addresses of other computers over the network. These functions are actually divided between different types of software, including the workstation's operating system and the client software, discussed later in this chapter.

After you have fulfilled the requirements for connectivity and communication, you could exchange data over a cable connecting two computers. However, such a small network is unrealistic. Most networks include multiple clients that need to share multiple resources. Such networks benefit from using a server to manage those resources.

Servers

As you learned earlier, a server is a computer on the network that manages shared resources. Servers come in many different varieties. To begin with, two different servers may contain completely different hardware components. Not only does hardware differ according to the make and model, but it may also differ depending on the server's purpose. A server that provides data storage space and programs to hundreds of clients may require significantly more hard disk space than a server designed to simply allow users access to a network. One thing is true of all servers, however: Because they transmit and receive more traffic than most clients, they usually possess more processing power, memory, and hard disk space than clients. Popular server manufacturers include Compaq, Dell, Hewlett-Packard, IBM, and Sun.

As with any other network node, servers require a NIC in order to connect with the transmission media and communicate with other nodes. Some servers contain more than one NIC. Having multiple NICs serves two purposes: It can divide incoming traffic into two paths, allowing the server to handle more requests in a shorter time span and it can help guard against outages by providing a second NIC to take over if the first NIC fails. The practice of using more than one component to guard against outages (or failures) is known as **redundancy**. Redundancy may be used with other components, including memory, processor, and hard disks. It may also be used with devices. For example, a LAN that requires continuous, failsafe access to its resources might incorporate more than one server to manage those resources.

To manage shared resources, servers run a unique type of software known as a network operating system. A **network operating system (NOS)** is software that can manage not only data, but also users, groups, security, and applications on the network. The most popular network operating systems include Microsoft Windows NT, Windows 2000, Windows .NET, Novell NetWare, UNIX, and Linux (a form of UNIX).

Clients

A client computer may take one of several forms. It may be a laptop or desktop computer, a handheld device, a PC or Macintosh, brand name or homemade. However, all client computers share some commonalities: They typically possess less hard disk space, processing power, and memory than a server computer. This makes sense because organizations do not want to spend large sums of money on powerful computers for each desktop when they intend to save money sharing resources via a central server.

Client software is a program or group of programs that tell the client's operating system how to interact with the server's network operating system. Therefore, it follows that versions of client software are specific to both the client's operating system and the server's network operating system. For example, in the case of a network that uses the NetWare network operating system on its server and the Windows 2000 operating system on its clients, Novell recommends installing its "Novell Client for Windows 2000" client software on workstations. Client software interacts with network operating software to allow users to **log on** to a server, or to gain access to shared resources on the network. It is the client software that prompts a user for a logon id and password. After a client supplies the correct logon ID and password, the network operating system attempts to match this information with a valid logon ID and password in its database. If the logon ID and password match, the NOS responds to the client by granting it access to resources on the network, according to limitations specified for this client. This process is known as **authentication**.

After the client has successfully logged on to the network, the client software communicates with the server's network operating system each time the client requests services from the server. For example, if you want to open a file on the server's hard disk, you must choose to open folders on the server via your workstation's operating system interface. When you request to view a file on the server, your client software relays your request to the server's network operating system, which responds by issuing a temporary copy of the file over the network to your workstation.

Now that you are familiar with elements common to all networks, you're ready to learn about the functions they perform.

How Networks are Used

By now, you understand that a network is a collection of computers and other devices (such as printers) that are connected by some type of transmission media. The main purpose for using networks is to share programs, data, and devices, such as printers or fax machines—all of which are known as **resources**. By enabling the sharing of resources, networks help organizations save money. For example, suppose you work at a graphic design firm that employs 15 designers. Each of the 15 designers needs to use five different software programs that cost $1000 per package, plus a high quality printer that costs $12,000. Rather than spend $255,000 ($5000 plus $12,000 times 15) so that all designers can have their own programs and printer, your firm could spend $17,000 to supply one shared copy of each program and one shared printer to service the group of designers.

In addition to saving money, networks help save time. Imagine how long it would take for employees to exchange their large data files if they had to copy them to some type of portable disk (such as a floppy disk) and deliver that disk to a colleague across the building or across the nation. Instead, they can electronically transfer the file over a network. This way, the data arrives in minutes (or less) and employees can quickly move on to the next task.

The many functions that networks perform are known as **services**. Network services can be categorized as follows:

- *File services*—Enable a central computer to share data files, applications (such as word-processing programs or spreadsheets), and disk storage space with other computers over the network. A server that provides file services is called a **file server**. File services accounted for the first use of networks and remain the foundation of networking today, for a number of reasons. As mentioned earlier, it's easier and faster to store shared data at a central location than to copy files to a disk and then pass the disks around. Data stored at a central location is also more secure because **network administrators**, the employees charged with installing, maintaining, and troubleshooting the network, can ensure that everyone's data is secure and continuously available. In addition, using a central computer to store and run applications for multiple users requires that fewer copies of the application be purchased and results in less maintenance work for the network administrator.

- *Print services*—Enable multiple users on a network to share printers. Such services include not only accepting documents from multiple workstations on a network, but also determining the order in which they print, making sure that only users who are authorized to use a printer can print to it, and alerting users when documents have printed. Many networks rely on a dedicated **print server** to manage their printer (or printers).

- *Communication services*—Allow remote users to connect to the network. (The term **remote user** refers to a person working on a client workstation in a different geographical location from the network's centralized storage and application computer.) Less frequently, communications services allow network users to connect to machines outside the network. Businesses and other organizations commonly use communications services to provide network access for workers at home, workers on the road, and workers at satellite offices. In addition, they may use communications services to allow staff from other organizations (such as a software or hardware vendor) to help diagnose a network problem. Communications services are also known as **remote access services**. For remote users to dial into the network, a special server known as a **remote access server** (or **communications server**) is required. A remote access server is dedicated to accepting incoming connections from outside an organization. It requires unique software and, sometimes, unique security measures to accommodate these users.

- *Mail services*—Coordinate the storage and transfer of e-mail between users on a network. Users depend on e-mail for fast, convenient communication both within and outside the organization. Mail services can run on several kinds of systems; they may be connected to the Internet or may be isolated within a company. At most organizations, a computer known as the **mail server** is dedicated to managing mail services. Since businesses first began to use networks, e-mail has been the most popular and frequently used network service.

- *Internet services*—Include World Wide Web servers and browsers (for example, Internet Explorer or Netscape), file transfer capabilities, and a means for directly logging on to other computers on the Internet. You have probably connected to the Internet already without knowing or caring about all of the services running behind the scenes. After you establish a connection, your workstation and the servers it relies upon must run standard protocols to use the Internet's features.

- *Management services*—Coordinate and mange large networks. Networks may be as simple as connecting two workstations in a home office. However, most are much more complex. As networks grow larger, include more devices, and are used for more purposes, they become more difficult to manage. To keep track of a large network, you need to employ special network management services. Network **management services** centrally administer and simplify complicated management tasks on the network, such as making sure that no

7

more than the licensed number of copies of a software package are in use at any one time or that valuable data is regularly archived for safekeeping. Network management services may also include gauging the volume of traffic on a network connection or reporting the utilization of a server's processor or memory resources. Some organizations dedicate a number of servers to network management functions, with each server performing only one or two unique services.

LANs, MANs, and WANs

One way of classifying networks is according to their geographical boundaries. As its name suggests, a **local area network (LAN)** is a network of computers and other devices that is confined to a relatively small space, such as one building or even one office. Small LANs became popular in businesses in the early 1980s. Today's LANs are typically larger and more complex. For example, whereas early LANs might have connected a dozen clients with one server to share two or three applications plus a printer, modern LANs may comprise thousands of clients, dozens of shared applications, multiple shared devices, and many different servers, each with a unique purpose. Contemporary LANs also offer more features than their predecessors—for example, connections to the Internet—which make them more complex.

When multiple networks or multiple parts of one network need to communicate with each other, a **connectivity device** is used to exchange data between them. Examples of connectivity devices include hubs, bridges, switches, and routers. Each of these devices performs different functions. Some, like hubs, are generally much less sophisticated than others, like routers. One important distinction is whether or not a connectivity device separates areas of a network that share the bandwidth of a communications channel, or **segments**. A **hub**, which simply retransmits a digital signal to all its connected devices, does not divide a network into separate segments. Switches, bridges and routers, however, do distinguish between network segments. In Chapter 11 you learn more about the features and applications of these connectivity devices. For the purposes of introduction, Figure 7-3 depicts a simple LAN such as one you might find in a small office. As you progress through this chapter, you see illustrations of more and more complex LANs.

Networks can—and often do—extend beyond the boundaries of a building. A network that connects clients and servers in multiple buildings in a region, for example, a consortium of universities and research facilities in one state, is known as a **metropolitan area network (MAN)**. Although the geographical boundaries for MANs are not officially defined, the range of these networks typically falls between 50 and 150 km. Figure 7-4 depicts a regional MAN.

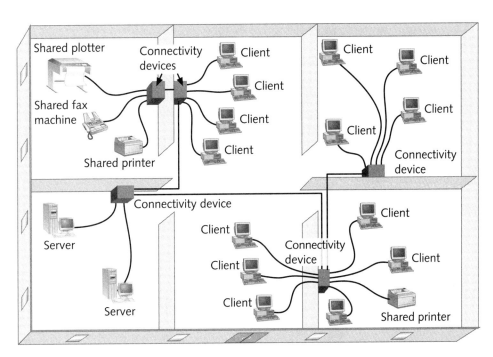

Figure 7-3   A LAN

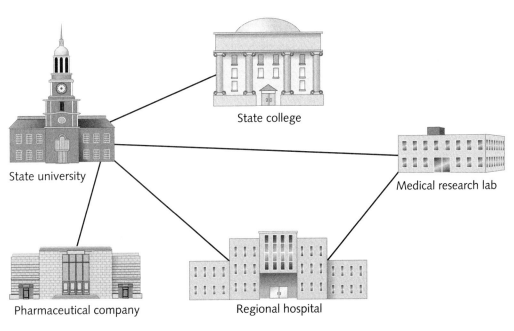

Figure 7-4   A MAN

A network that connects two or more geographically distinct LANs is called a **wide area network (WAN)**. Imagine you work for a nationwide book distributor that keeps its book inventory in warehouses in Los Angeles, California and Knoxville, Tennessee, but your office is located in New York. When a bookstore asks whether you have 20 copies of a recent Pulitzer prize-winning novel available to ship overnight, you must to check the inventory database located on servers at both the Los Angeles and Knoxville warehouses. To access these servers, you could connect from your workstation on the New York LAN to the warehouses through a WAN link, then log on to the warehouse servers. In fact, most organizations use WANs to connect separate offices (and their LANs), whether the offices are across town or across the world from each other. WANs are also distinguished from MANs and LANs in that they almost always rely on a common carrier's network to connect multiple locations. Figure 7-5 illustrates a simple WAN.

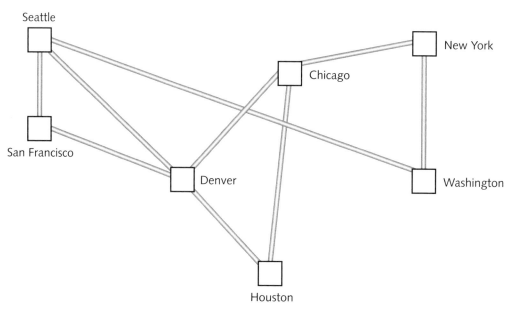

Figure 7-5   A WAN

The main difference between LANs, MANs, and WANs lies in their scope. However, in some cases, the technology best suited to each also differs. Consider, for example, a state hospital, that consists of five buildings, each of which contains its own separate LAN. These buildings might be connected with each other and regional clinics to form a MAN. In addition, the state hospital's MAN may be connected to a WAN that connects all the hospitals and clinics in the state. Because each building's LAN probably carries less traffic than the MAN and the statewide WAN, their transmission media differs. The buildings' LANs probably use copper wire, whereas the MAN and WAN may require both copper wire and fiber optic cable.

Figure 7-6 shows how the LANs, MAN, and WAN might be connected.

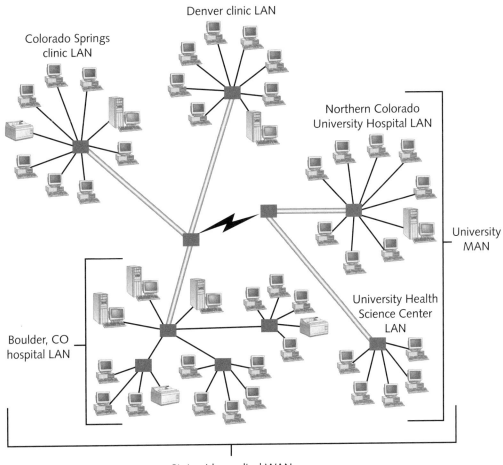

Figure 7-6 Connection of LANs with a MAN and WAN

Another way in which LANs, MANs, and WANs can differ is in the type of connections they rely on and, as a result, the types of switching they use. A LAN nearly always uses private connections and packet switching, in which data is separated into discreet units that may follow any path from the sender to the receiver. MANs and WANs also often use packet switching but they may use circuit switching. In circuit switching, a path is held open and committed to one transmission between the sender and receiver until the transmission is completed. Circuit switching is the type of switching used by the PSTN, and because many WANs rely on the PSTN, they also use circuit switching.

As you progress through this book, you will recognize additional instances in which LANs, MANs, and WANs might differ.

THE INTERNET

The **Internet** is an example of a very large and complex WAN. Although average citizens began using the Internet just over a decade ago, its development began in the 1960s as a project sponsored by the U.S. Department of Defense. At that time, the network was known as the Advanced Research Projects Agency network (ARPANET). It was used mainly by university researchers and other government employees. In the 1990s, the Internet became accessible to anyone with a computer and a phone line, thanks to a mushrooming infrastructure and user-friendly ways to navigate its contents. Today, the Internet is accessed regularly by hundreds of millions of users from around the world. It connects myriad different LANs and WANs and serves as a vital tool for commerce, entertainment, and education.

The Internet is a unique WAN not only because of its size, but also because of its diversity. It encompasses both private and public connections, including some parts of the PSTN. It may carry data, voice, and video over these connections (though the vast majority of Internet traffic consists of data transmissions). It may transmit confidential information between two offices within the same organization, or it may transmit public records to anyone who requests them.

To connect users from around the globe, the Internet relies on a hierarchical structure of connection points, just as the PSTN relies on a hierarchy of central offices. At the bottom of the Internet hierarchy are local **Internet service providers (ISPs)**. An ISP is a company that operates a network and provides consumers with a link to the Internet. For most consumers, this means using a computer's modem to dial into the ISP's access server. In the PSTN analogy, a local ISP is similar to a Class 5 CO. (In fact, many telephone companies have become ISPs by placing Internet access facilities in their COs.)

 Many ISPs are also known as **network service providers (NSPs)**. NSPs are telecommunications companies that provide infrastructure for either public or private traffic. NSPs aren't necessarily ISPs. An NSP may simply provide the infrastructure for connections, without operating access servers for a consumer's initial entry to the Internet. However, most NSPs are ISPs.

ISPs range in size from a few hundred to several million customers. They may or may not own their own facilities, such as fiber optic cable and connectivity devices. Local ISPs typically provide service to customers in one or only a few area codes. Such companies cannot afford to build a network of fiber optic cable to carry their customer's data across the nation. Instead, they connect with regional ISPs. Regional ISPs are larger than local ISPs, serving users in at least a half dozen area codes. Almost all local ISPs forward the traffic from their customers to a larger ISP's network. These larger ISPs may connect to the high-level Internet exchange points or they may rely on yet another ISP to provide that function. There is no formal classification for the different sizes of ISPs as there is with central offices. However, only the very largest ISPs, such as Sprint or WorldCom, do not rely on another ISP or NSP for connections to higher-level access points. Eventually, these top-level ISPs connect with each other, through NAPs and MAEs, as described next.

At the top of the Internet hierarchy sit the **network access points (NAPs)**. NAPs are exchange points for Internet traffic, similar to Class 1 COs in the PSTN. NAPs formed the original backbone of the Internet when it was still maintained by the United States government. In the 1990s, the government handed the operation of NAPs to private companies, with the understanding that those companies would directly link their networks and exchange Internet traffic over those links, a process known as **peering**. NAPs are currently operated and maintained by companies, such as SBC, Sprint, and Worldcom.

Recall that the higher you go in the PSTN hierarchy, the fewer COs you'll find in that level in the hierarchy. The same holds true for the Internet hierarchy. In the United States, there are five large NAPs. They are located in Chicago, New Jersey, San Francisco, San Jose, and in northern Virginia just outside of Washington, DC. Two of these NAPs are also known as **metropolitan area exchanges (MAEs)**. The northern Virginia MAE is known as MAE East whereas the San Jose MAE is known as MAE West.

Because NAPs are a connection point for aggregated Internet traffic, they experience the highest demand for bandwidth. They are also a potential source of network congestion. If you think of data traffic in the same terms as automobile traffic, you can regard NAPs as a point where many different busy highways merge. At rush hour, traffic at this point would become heavy. The required time for traffic to pass through would become exceedingly long. Indeed, the same phenomenon happens at NAPs during periods of heavy traffic (such as 8 a.m. on a weekday). This is why sometimes, even if you have a high-bandwidth connection to your ISP, it takes longer than usual to download a Web page.

Figure 7-7 shows a conceptual drawing of the hierarchy of Internet exchange points. In reality, the network is much more complex. In the United States alone, there are tens of thousands of local ISPs, so the number of interconnections and access points near the bottom of the hierarchy is astounding.

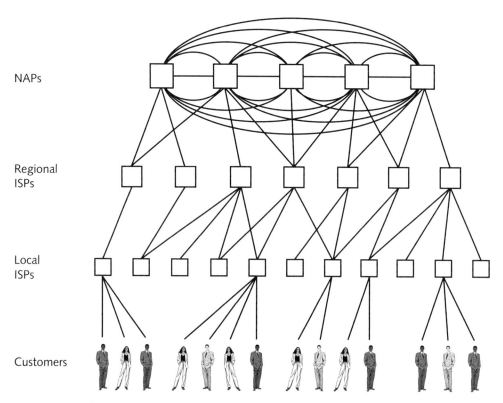

Figure 7-7   The Internet hierarchy

In addition to the five NAPs, large network service providers maintain many other exchange points as part of their own networks. Figure 7-8 depicts a global telecommunication carrier's network of connections and exchange points. As you can imagine, ISPs continually grow their networks as demand for bandwidth rises.

 Countries across the globe maintain their own hierarchies of Internet exchange points. Their top-level exchange points (similar to NAPs in the United States) connect with other countries' top-level exchange points to facilitate international data transmission.

More details about accessing the Internet and transmitting data over the Internet are described in detail in Chapters 10 and 12. Before learning about such specific networking technologies, however, you need to master more networking fundamentals, including the OSI model.

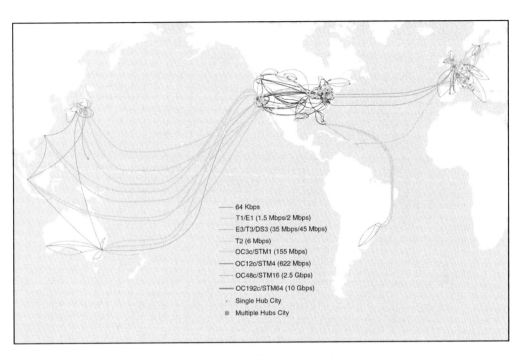

64 Kbps
T1/E1 (1.5 Mbps/2 Mbps)
E3/T3/DS3 (35 Mbps/45 Mbps)
T2 (6 Mbps)
OC3c/STM1 (155 Mbps)
OC12c/STM4 (622 Mbps)
OC48c/STM16 (2.5 Gbps)
OC192c/STM64 (10 Gbps)
Single Hub City
Multiple Hubs City

Figure 7-8   A telecommunication carrier's global network

THE OSI MODEL

Recall that several global and national organizations cooperate to set standards for the telecommunications industry. One such organization is the International Standards Organization, or ISO. In the early 1980s, ISO began work on a universal set of specifications that would enable computer platforms across the world to communicate without obstacles. The organization created a helpful model for understanding and developing computer-to-computer communications. This model, called the **Open Systems Interconnection (OSI) model**, divides communication systems into seven layers: Physical, Data Link, Network, Transport, Session, Presentation, and Application. Each layer has its own set of functions and interacts with the layers directly above and below it. At the top, the Application layer interacts with the software you use (such as a word-processing or spreadsheet program). At the bottom of the OSI model are the transmission media that carry signals. Generally speaking, the layers in between the top and bottom layers ensure that data is delivered in a readable, error-free, and properly sequenced format.

The purpose of a theoretical construct such as the OSI model is to help you understand phenomenon that you can't literally see. For example, in chemistry class, although you can't see a water molecule, you can represent it by drawing two hydrogen atoms connected to an oxygen atom. In the same way, the OSI model is a theoretical representation of what happens between two nodes on a network. It does not prescribe the type of hardware or software that should support each layer. Nor does it describe how software programs interact with other software programs or how software programs interact with humans. It merely separates the process of data communication into separate functions. Figure 7-9 depicts the OSI model and its layers.

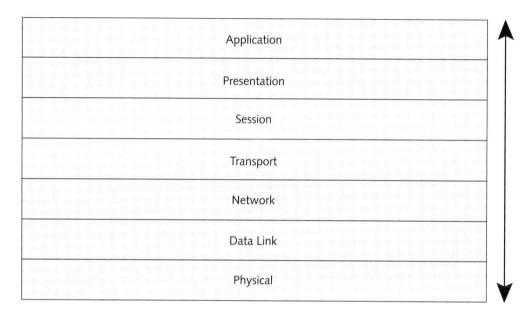

Figure 7-9   The OSI model

Because modern telecommunications rely on computers, everything you learn about modern telecommunications technology can be associated with a layer of the OSI model. Thus, it is critical to memorize not only the names of the layers, but also their functions and the way in which the layers interact. Next, you learn about each layer, its function, and which technologies are associated with it.

People who work in the telecommunications industry often devise their own mnemonics for remembering the seven layers of the OSI model. One strategy is to make a sentence using words that begin with the same first letter of each layer. For example, if your mnemonic started with the Application layer and ended with the Physical layer, you might use the phrase "All programmers strive to not die poor." Or, if your mnemonic started with the Physical layer and ended with the Application layer, you might use the phrase, "Please do not throw sausage pizza away."

Physical Layer

The **Physical layer** is the lowest, or first, layer of the OSI model. Protocols at the Physical layer generate and detect voltage (or in the case of fiber optic transmission, pulses of light) so as to transmit and receive signals carrying data. In other words, they are responsible for applying binary data to the transmission media. Technically, the Physical layer does not include transmission media and connectors, but relies upon them. Transceivers and network interface cards (NICs) perform Physical layer functions. The Physical layer sets the data transmission rate and monitors data error rates, though it does not provide error correction services. Physical network problems, such as a severed wire, affect the Physical layer. Similarly, if you insert a NIC but fail to seat it deeply enough in the computer's circuit board, your computer experiences network problems at the Physical layer.

The IEEE has set standards for protocols used at the Physical layer. The terms "layer 1 protocols" and "Physical layer protocols" refer to the standards that dictate how the electrical signals are amplified and transmitted over the wire.

Data Link Layer

7

The second layer of the OSI model, the **Data Link layer**, controls communications between the Network layer and the Physical layer. Its primary function is to divide data it receives from the Network layer into distinct frames that can then be transmitted by the Physical layer. A **frame** is a structured package for moving data that includes not only the raw data, or "payload," but also the sender's and receiver's network addresses, and error checking and control information. The addresses tell the network where to deliver the frame, whereas the error checking and control information ensures that the frame arrives without any problems.

Figure 7-10 shows a simplified picture of a data frame. Each component of this frame is essential and common to all types of frames.

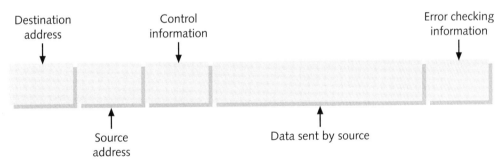

Destination address   Control information   Error checking information

Source address   Data sent by source

Figure 7-10   A data frame

To fully understand the function of the Data Link layer, pretend for a moment that computers communicate as humans do. You might be in a large classroom full of noisy students and need to ask the teacher a question. Your teacher's name is Mr. Stafford. To get your message through, you might say, "Mr. Stafford? Can you explain how Henry Ford's assembly line transformed manufacturing?" In this example, you are the sender (in a busy network) and you have addressed your recipient, Mr. Stafford, just as the Data Link layer addresses another computer on the network. In addition, you have formatted your thought as a question, just as the Data Link layer formats data into frames that can be interpreted by receiving computers.

What happens if the room is so noisy that Mr. Stafford hears only part of your question? For example, he might receive "line transformed manufacturing?" This kind of error can happen in network communications as well (because of electrical interference or wiring problems, for example). The Data Link layer's job is to find out that information has been dropped and ask the first computer to retransmit its message—just as in a classroom setting Mr. Stafford might say, "I didn't hear you. Can you repeat the question?" The Data Link layer accomplishes this task through a process called error checking. Later in this chapter, you learn more about error checking.

In general, the sender's Data Link layer waits for acknowledgment from the receiver that data was received correctly. If the sender does not get this acknowledgment, its Data Link layer gives instruction to retransmit the information. The Data Link layer does not try to figure out what went wrong in the transmission. Similarly, as in a busy classroom, Mr. Stafford will probably say, "Pardon me?" rather than, "It sounds as if you might have a question about assembly lines, and I heard only the last part of it, which dealt with manufacturing, so I assume you are asking about assembly lines and manufacturing; is that correct?" Obviously, the former method is more efficient for both the sender and the receiver.

Another communications mishap that might occur in a noisy classroom or on a busy network is a glut of communication requests. For example, at the end of class, 20 people might ask Mr. Stafford 20 different questions at once. Of course, he can't pay attention to all of them simultaneously. He will probably say, "One person at a time, please," then point to one student who asked a question. This situation is analogous to what the Data Link layer does for the Physical layer. One node on a network (a server, for example) may receive multiple requests that include many frames of data each. The Data Link layer controls the flow of this information, allowing the NIC to process data without error.

To better define shared access for multiple network nodes using the same communications channel (as opposed to simple one-to-one communication between computers), the Data Link layer is divided into two sublayers: the **Logical Link Control (LLC) sublayer** and the **Media Access Control (MAC) sublayer**. The LLC, the upper sublayer in the Data Link layer, provides a common interface and supplies reliability and flow control services. The MAC, the lower sublayer of the Data Link layer, actually appends the address of the destination computer onto the data frame. This address is known as the **MAC address**. It may also be called a **physical address** or a **Data Link layer address**. Figure 7-11 shows how the Data Link layer is subdivided.

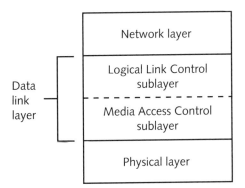

Figure 7-11   The Logical Link Control and Media Access Control sublayers

7

A MAC address is a unique 12-digit hexadecimal number that identifies a network node. A node's MAC address is integrated into its NIC by the NIC's manufacturer. This way, MAC addresses are guaranteed to be unique because industry standards (established and maintained by IEEE) specify which numbers each manufacturer can use. For example, Ethernet NICs manufactured by SMC Systems, Inc. begin with the six-character sequence "0040E2," whereas Ethernet NICs manufactured by D-Link Systems, Inc. begin with "0050BA." The MAC addresses integrated into a NIC cannot be physically changed. The MAC address that a node uses on the network, however, can be changed through software. However, because a manufacturer's pre-assigned MAC addresses are guaranteed to be unique, most network administrators do not attempt to change them.

MAC addresses are divided into two parts. The part of the MAC address that is unique to a particular vendor is called the **Block ID**. Block IDs may also be known as **organizationally unique identifiers (OUIs)** or as the **vendor codes**. Larger manufacturers, such as Intel, have several different Block IDs. The remaining six characters in the MAC address are added at the factory, based on the NIC's model and manufacture date. These six characters form the **Device ID**. An example of a Device ID assigned by a manufacturer might be 004AB6. The combination of the Block ID and Device ID result in a unique, 12-digit MAC address, for example, 0050BA004AB6. MAC addresses may be expressed as one long number, with a hyphen separating the Block ID from the Device ID, or with hyphens between each two numbers. Thus, the above example could be written "0050BA004AB6," "0050BA-004AB6," or divided into its 6 bytes as "00-50-BA-00-4A-B6." Networks rely upon unique MAC addressing to transmit data to their correct destination.

In addition to appending a physical address to the data frame, the MAC address applies error-checking information in the form of a **Frame Check Sequence (FCS)**. FCS is used to calculate whether the bits that arrive at a destination are identical to the bits that were transmitted from the source. When the source node transmits the data, it performs an algorithm called a **Cyclic Redundancy Check (CRC)**. CRC takes the values of all of the preceding fields in the frame and generates a unique four-byte number, the FCS. When the destination node receives the frame, it recalculates the FCS via CRC and makes sure that the frame's fields match their original form. If this comparison fails, the receiving node's Data Link layer assumes that the frame has been damaged in transit and requests that the source node retransmit the data.

The Data Link layer functions independently of the type of Physical layer used by the network and its nodes. It also doesn't care whether you are running Microsoft Word or using the Internet. Most switches—including those used in both data and voice communication—belong to the Data Link layer. Chapters 10 and 11 both discuss elements of the Data Link layer.

Network Layer

The primary function of the **Network layer**, the third layer in the OSI model, is to translate network addresses into their physical counterparts and decide how to **route** data from the sender to the receiver. For example, a computer might have a network address of 10.34.99.12 (if it's using the TCP/IP protocol) and a physical address of 0050BA-004AB6. In the classroom example, this addressing scheme is like saying that "Mr. Stafford" and "U.S. citizen with Social Security number 599-22-7766" are the same person. Even though there may be other people named "Mr. Stafford" in the United States, only one person has the Social Security number 599-22-7766. Within the confines of your classroom, however, there is only one Mr. Stafford, so you can be certain the correct person will respond when you say, "Mr. Stafford?"

Network layer addresses, which reside at the Network layer of the OSI model, follow a hierarchical addressing scheme and can be assigned through operating system software. They are hierarchical because they contain subsets of data that incrementally narrow down the location of a node, just as your home address is hierarchical because it provides a country, state, zip code, city, street, house number, and person's name. Network Layer addresses, therefore, are more useful to internetworking devices, such as routers, because they make sorting data more logical. Network layer address formats differ depending on which protocols the network uses. Network layer addresses are also called **logical addresses** or **virtual addresses**.

Transport Layer

The **Transport layer** is primarily responsible for ensuring that data is transferred from point A to point B (which may or may not be on the same part of a network) reliably, in the correct sequence, and without errors. Without the Transport layer, data could not be verified or interpreted by their recipients. Transport protocols also handle **flow control**, or the method of gauging the appropriate rate of transmission based on how fast the recipient can accept data.

In addition, Transport layer services break arbitrarily long packets into the maximum size that the type of network in use can handle. For example, some types of networks cannot accept packets larger than 1500 bytes.

The Transport layer protocols also accomplish segmentation and reassembly of packets. **Segmentation** refers to the process of decreasing the size of the data units when moving data from a network segment that can handle larger data units to a network segment that can handle only smaller data units. This process is just like the process of breaking down words into recognizable syllables that a small child uses when learning to read. **Reassembly** is the process of reconstructing the segmented data units. To continue the reading analogy, when a child understands the separate syllables, she can combine them into a word—that is, reassemble the parts into a whole.

When the sending node's Transport layer services divide its data into smaller pieces, they assign a sequence number to each piece, so that the data can be reassembled in the correct order by the receiving node's Transport layer services. This process is called **sequencing**. To understand how sequencing works, consider the classroom example again. Suppose you ask the question, "Mr. Stafford? How did railroads lead to the development of the West?" but that the words arrive at Mr. Stafford's ear as "development how West? to the of railroads the did lead." On a network, the Transport layer recognizes this disorder and rearranges the data pieces so that they make sense. In addition, the Transport layer sends an **acknowledgment (ACK)** to notify the sender that data was received correctly. If the data contained errors, the Transport layer requests that the sender retransmit the data. Also, if the data wasn't acknowledged within a given time period, the sender's Transport layer considers the data lost and retransmits it.

Multiplexing, the technology tat combines several data streams onto one communications channel, is a service that belongs to the Transport layer. Another data communications service that works in the Transport layer is TCP (Transmission Control Protocol) of the TCP/IP protocol suite. TCP/IP is the most popular protocol suite in use on modern networks. You learn more about this Transport layer service later in this chapter.

Session Layer

The **Session layer** is responsible for establishing and maintaining communication between two nodes on the network. The term **session** refers to a connection for data exchange between two parties; it is most often used in the context of terminal and mainframe communications, in which the **terminal** is a device with little (if any) of its own processing or disk capacity that depends on a host to supply it with applications and data processing services. Among the Session layer's functions are establishing and keeping alive the communications link for the duration of the session, synchronizing the dialog between the two nodes, determining whether communications have been cut off, and, if so, figuring out where to restart transmission. Often, you will hear the Session layer called the "traffic cop" of network communications. When you dial your Internet service provider to connect to the Internet, the Session layer services at your ISP's access server, and on your PC client, negotiates the connection. If your phone line is accidentally pulled out of the wall jack, the Session layer on your end detects the loss of a connection and initiates attempts to reconnect.

The Session layer also sets the terms of communication by deciding which node will communicate first and how long a node can communicate. In this sense, the Session layer acts as a judge in a debate competition. For example, if you are a member of a debate team and have two minutes to state your opening argument, the judge might signal you after one and a half minutes that you have only 30 seconds remaining. If you try to interrupt a member of the opposing debate team, he tells you to wait your turn. This is similar to the Session layer managing communication on a half-duplex channel. Finally, the Session layer monitors the identification of session participants, ensuring that only the authorized nodes can access the session.

Presentation Layer

The **Presentation layer** serves as a translator between the application and the network. At the Presentation layer, data becomes formatted in a schema that the network can understand; this format varies with the type of network used. For example, if you are working on a PC connected over the network to a mainframe, the data you generate is encoded according to the ASCII coding scheme. However, the mainframe can only interpret EBCDIC-encoded data. Thus, the Presentation layer must translate your data from ASCII to EBCDIC in order for the mainframe to interpret your PC's transmission.

The Presentation layer also manages data encryption. **Encryption** is the use of a mathematical routine to scramble data so that the data can only be read by reversing the formula, or **decryption**. Encryption is used to keep data private. For example, if you retrieve your bank account statement via the Internet, you are use a secure connection, and your account data is encrypted before it is transmitted. On your end of the network, the Presentation layer decrypts the data as it is received. In addition, Presentation layer protocols code and decode graphics and file format information. This function is required, for example, to interpret and display picture files on Web pages as you navigate the Internet with a browser.

Application Layer

The top, or seventh, layer of the OSI model is the Application layer. The **Application layer** provides interfaces to the software that enable programs to use network services. The term "Application layer" does not refer to a particular software application, such as Microsoft Excel, running on the network. Instead, some of the services provided by the Application layer include file transfer, file management, and message handling for electronic mail. For example, if you are running a computer telephony integration (CTI) program on a network and choose to open a customer's personal record, your request for that data is transferred from the CTI software to the network by the Application layer.

The part of the CTI software that handles this request is its **application program interface (API)**. An application program interface is a routine (a set of instructions) that allows a program to interact with the operating system. APIs belong to the Application layer of the OSI model. Programmers use APIs to establish links between their code and the operating system. An example of an API used in a network environment is **Microsoft Message Queueing (MSMQ)**. MSMQ stores messages sent between nodes in queues and then forwards them to their destinations when the link to the recipient becomes available. As a result, programs can run independently of whether the data's destination is connected to the network when the messages are sent.

APPLYING THE OSI MODEL

Now that you have been introduced to the seven layers of the OSI model, you can take a closer look at exactly how the layers interact. For reference, Table 7-1 summarizes the functions of the seven OSI model layers.

Table 7-1 Functions of the OSI model layers

OSI model layer	Function
Application	Transfers information from program to program
Presentation	Handles text formatting and displays code conversion
Session	Establishes, maintains, and coordinates communication
Transport	Ensures accurate delivery of data
Network	Determines delivery routes and handles the transfer of messages
Data Link	Codes, addresses, and transmits information
Physical	Manages hardware connections

SS7, the signaling system that telephone switches use to communicate with each other, performs functions (for instance, flow control and error checking) at every layer of the OSI model.

To learn more about the OSI model, it is useful to follow what happens to data through the layers as two computers communicate. An exemplary process to trace is the retrieval of a message from a server. (Note: this example discusses the less common Token Ring type of network because a Token Ring network best illustrates the functions of each OSI model layer. In Chapter 10 you will learn about the same process as it occurs on an Ethernet network.) After you log on to the network and start your mail program, you can choose to pick up your mail. At that point, the Application layer recognizes your choice and formulates a request for data from a remote node (in this case, the mail server). The Application layer transfers the request to the Presentation layer.

The Presentation layer first determines whether and how it should format or encrypt the data request received from the Application layer. After it has made that determination, it adds any translation or codes required to implement that formatting and then passes your request on to the Session layer.

The Session layer picks up your formatted request and assigns a data token to it. A **token** is a special control frame that indicates to the rest of the network that you have the right to transmit data. (Remember that the Session layer acts as the "traffic cop" for communications between nodes.) The Session layer then passes your data to the Transport layer.

At the Transport layer, your data and the control information it has accumulated thus far are broken down into manageable chunks of data and prepared to be packaged in frames at the Data Link layer. If the data is too large to fit in one frame, the Transport layer subdivides it into several smaller blocks and assigns sequence identifiers to each block. This layer then passes the data blocks, one at a time, to the Network layer.

The Network layer adds logical addressing information to the data it receives from the Transport layer, so that subsequent layers know the source and the destination of the data. (Remember, this addressing information is different from physical addressing information.) It then passes the data blocks, with their Network layer addresses attached, to the Data Link layer.

At the Data Link layer, the data blocks are packaged into individual frames. As you have learned, a frame is a structured format for transmitting small blocks of data. Using frames reduces the possibility of lost data or errors on the network, because each frame has its own built-in error checking field, the FCS. The FCS is inserted at the end of the frame by the Data Link layer. In addition, the Data Link layer adds a header to the frame that incorporates destination and source addresses assigned by the Network layer. The Data Link layer then passes the frames to the Physical layer.

Finally, your request for your mail message hits the NIC at the Physical layer. The Physical layer does not interpret the frame or add information to the frame; it simply delivers the data to the cabling and sends it, as pulses of voltage or light, across the network.

After the data arrives at the Physical layer of the remote system, the mail server's Data Link layer begins to unravel your request, reversing the process just described, until it responds to your request with its own transmission, beginning from its Application layer. Figure 7-12 shows how data is transferred from your system to the server, then back to your system through the OSI model.

In the preceding example, you learned that every successive layer in the OSI model—beginning with the Application layer and ending with the Physical layer—adds some control, formatting, or addressing information to the data it handles. The receiving system then interprets and uses the added information as it reverses the process, passing data from the Physical layer back up to the Application layer. Between your initial software request and the network cable, your blocks of data grow larger as they accumulate more handling information. Figure 7-13 depicts the transformation of data as it travels through the OSI model layers.

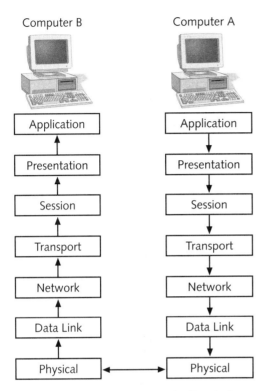

Figure 7-12   Data communication between computers

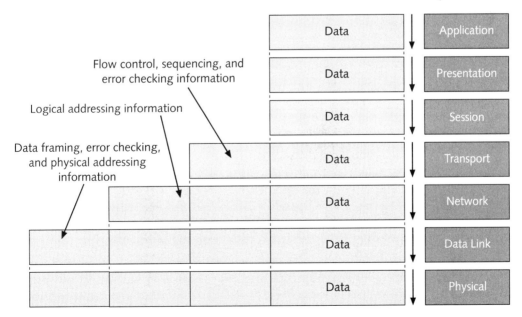

Figure 7-13   Data transformed through the OSI model

INTRODUCTION TO PROTOCOLS

As you learned earlier in this chapter, a protocol is a rule that governs how networks communicate. Protocols define the standards for communication between network devices. Without protocols, devices could not interpret the signals sent by other devices, and data would go nowhere.

You have just learned about the tasks associated with each layer of the OSI model. Each of these tasks is actually carried out by network protocols. In the networking industry, the term "protocol" is often used to refer to a group, or suite, of individual protocols that work together. The protocols within a suite are assigned different tasks, such as data translation, data handling, error checking, and addressing; they correspond to different layers of the OSI model. In the sections that follow, you learn about the most popular networking protocol suite—TCP/IP—and see how its components correspond to the layers of the OSI model.

The protocol (or protocol suite) you use depends on many factors, including the existing network operating environment, your organization's technical expertise, and your network's security and speed requirements. Protocols vary according to their speed, transmission efficiency, utilization of resources, ease of setup, compatibility, and ability to travel between one LAN segment and another. Protocols that can span more than one LAN segment are **routable**, because they carry Network layer and addressing information that can be interpreted by a router. Not all protocols are routable, however.

Following is a list of common protocols and their identifying characteristics:

- *NetBIOS (Network Basic Input Output System)*—A protocol originally designed for IBM to provide Transport and Session layer services for applications running on small, homogenous networks. Microsoft adopted IBM's NetBIOS as its foundation protocol, initially for networks using LAN Manager or Windows for Workgroups.

- *NetBIOS Enhanced User Interface (NetBEUI)*—An Application layer component added on top of NetBIOS On very small networks, NetBEUI is an efficient protocol that consumes few network resources. It also provides excellent error correction, and requires little configuration. It can support only 254 connections, however, and does not allow for good security. Furthermore, because NetBEUI lacks a Network layer and thus, logical addressing information, it is not routable on its own. Therefore, NetBEUI (on its own) cannot be used for data transmissions on WANs, between two LANs or two separate parts of one LAN. Thus, this protocol is not suitable for large networks. In fact, it is rarely used on modern networks.

- *AppleTalk*—The protocol suite used to interconnect Macintosh computers. Although AppleTalk was originally designed to support peer-to-peer networking among Macintoshes, it can now be routed between network segments and integrated with NetWare- or Microsoft-based networks. It may still be used on small

Macintosh-based networks. However, even Macintosh computers have made TCP/IP their default protocol in recent years.

■ *Internetwork Packet Exchange/Sequenced Packet Exchange (IPX/SPX)*—A protocol suite originally developed by Xerox, then modified and adopted by Novell in the 1980s for its NetWare network operating system. IPX/SPX is required to ensure the interoperability of LANs running NetWare versions 3.2 and lower and can be used with LANs running higher versions of the NetWare operating system. In the IPX/SPX protocol suite, **IPX** provides services in the Network layer of the OSI model, while **SPX** provides services at the Transport layer. Addressing in IPX/SPX relies on the MAC address of a node, plus an additional network address assigned by the network administrator.

■ *Transmission Control Protocol/Internet Protocol (TCP/IP)*—A routable, flexible protocol suite that has its origins in ARPAnet, the precursor to the Internet. TCP/IP is still the protocol on which all Internet traffic relies. It is also the protocol of choice for many private LANs and WANs. Because TCP/IP is by far the most popular network protocol in use today, further discussions about protocols in this book focus on TCP/IP.

Additional protocol suites—such as SNA and DLC—do exist, but such suites are used only rarely and in exceptional circumstances.

In addition to the size of the network, you need to consider its interconnection requirements, data security needs, and the technical expertise of personnel who manage the network. Many networks use more than one kind of protocol because they have a mixed hardware or software infrastructure, so it is not only important to know about each protocol, but also to understand how they work together. A network that uses more than one protocol is called a **multiprotocol network**. Multiprotocol networks are common in businesses whose LANs are well established and have evolved from legacy systems to newer, more efficient networks. When designing a new network, however, network administrators are likely to limit their data transmissions to a single protocol suite, TCP/IP.

TCP/IP

TCP/IP is not simply one protocol, but rather a suite of small, specialized protocols—including TCP, IP, UDP, ARP, ICMP, and others—called **subprotocols**. Networking professionals refer to the entire group as "TCP/IP," or sometimes simply "IP." TCP/IP's roots lie with the U.S. Department of Defense, which developed the precursor to TCP/IP for its Advanced Research Projects Agency network (ARPAnet) in the late 1960s (the same network that formed the basis for today's Internet). Thanks to its low cost and its ability to communicate between a multitude of dissimilar platforms, TCP/IP has grown extremely popular. It is a de facto standard on the Internet and in recent years has become the protocol of choice on private networks as well. The latest network operating systems (such as NetWare 6 and Windows 2000) use TCP/IP as their default protocol.

One of the greatest advantages to TCP/IP relates to its status as a routable protocol, which means that it carries network addressing information that can be interpreted by routers. TCP/IP is also a flexible protocol, running on any combination of network operating systems or network media. Because of its flexibility, however, TCP/IP may require significant configuration.

TCP/IP is a broad topic with numerous theoretical, historical, and practical aspects. If you want to become an expert on TCP/IP or its applications (for example, Internet telephony), you should invest in a book or study guide solely devoted to this suite of protocols.

TCP/IP Compared to the OSI Model

The TCP/IP suite of protocols can be divided into four layers that roughly correspond to the seven layers of the OSI model, as depicted in Figure 7-14 and described in the following list. (Unlike the OSI model, which was standardized by ISO, the TCP/IP model is an informal reference. Because there is no universal standard for the TCP/IP model, you may also find it represented as five layers.)

- *Application layer*—TCP/IP's Application layer provides authentication and compression services, and is roughly equivalent to the Application, Presentation, and Session layers of the OSI model. Applications gain access to the network through this layer via protocols, such as the File Transfer Protocol (FTP), Trivial File Transfer Protocol (TFTP), Hypertext Transfer Protocol (HTTP), Simple Mail Transfer Protocol (SMTP), and Dynamic Host Configuration Protocol (DHCP).

- *Transport layer*—TCP/IP's Transport layer roughly corresponds to the Transport layer of the OSI model. This layer holds the Transmission Control Protocol (TCP) and User Datagram Protocol (UDP), which provide flow control, error checking, and sequencing. All service requests use one of these protocols. However, unlike the OSI model's Transport layer services, the TCP/IP model's Transport layer services do not necessarily guarantee reliable delivery of data.

- *Network layer*—TCP/IP's Network layer (sometimes called the Internet layer) is equivalent to the Network layer of the OSI model. This layer holds the Internet Protocol (IP), Internet Control Message Protocol (ICMP), Internet Group Message Protocol (IGMP), and Address Resolution Protocol (ARP). These protocols handle message routing and host address resolution.

- *Link layer*—TCP/IP's Link layer (sometimes called the Network Interface or Network Access layer) is roughly equivalent to the Data Link and Physical layers of the OSI model. This layer handles the formatting of data and transmission to the network wire.

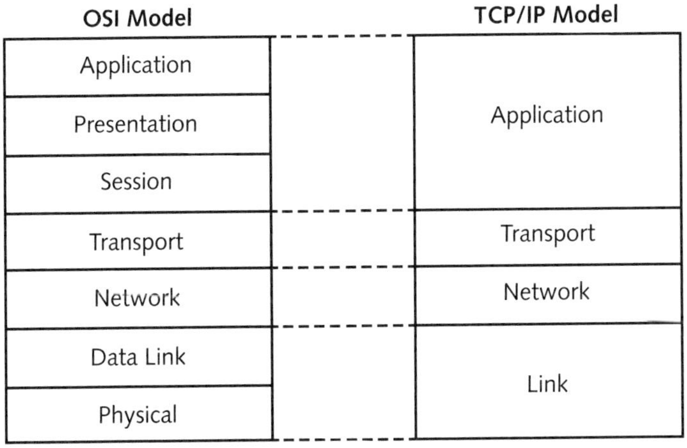

OSI Model		TCP/IP Model
Application		Application
Presentation		
Session		
Transport		Transport
Network		Network
Data Link		Link
Physical		

Figure 7-14   TCP/IP model compared to the OSI model

The TCP/IP Core Protocols

Certain subprotocols of the TCP/IP suite, called **TCP/IP core protocols**, operate in the Transport or Network layers of the OSI model and provide basic services to the protocols in other layers of the four-layer model. These core protocols are required for any data transmission that uses TCP/IP. Of all the core protocols in the suite, TCP and IP are the most significant. These, plus some other important Transport and Network layer protocols, are discussed in the following section.

Internet Protocol (IP)

The **Internet Protocol (IP)** belongs to the Network layer of the OSI model and to the Internet layer of the TCP/IP model. IP provides information about how and where data should be delivered. As such, it is the subprotocol that enables TCP/IP to **internetwork**—that is, to traverse more than one LAN segment and more than one type of network through a router. In an internetwork, the individual networks that are joined together are called subnetworks, or **subnets**. Using subnets is an important part of TCP/IP networking.

The following sections describe the IP subprotocol as it is used in IP version 4 (IPv4), the original version that was used for nearly 20 years and is still used by most networks today. A newer version of the IP subprotocol, called **IP version 6 (IPv6)**, is poised to replace IPv4.

The IP portion of a data frame is called an **IP datagram**. The IP datagram acts as an envelope for data and contains information necessary for routers to transfer data between subnets. The length of the IP datagram including its header and data cannot exceed 65,535 bytes. The components of an IPv4 IP datagram header are described in the following list and depicted in Figure 7-15.

- *Version*—Identifies the version number of the protocol. The receiving work-station looks at this field first to determine whether it can read the incoming data. If it cannot, it rejects the packet. Rejection rarely occurs, however, because most TCP/IP networks use IP version 4 (IPv4). A more sophisticated IP version, called IP version 6 (IPv6), has been developed and will be implemented in coming years.

- *Internet header length (IHL)*—Identifies the number of 4-byte (or 32-bit) blocks in the IP header. The most common header length comprises five groupings, as the minimum length of an IP header is 20 4-byte blocks. This field is important because it indicates to the receiving node where data will begin (immediately after the header ends).

- *Type of service (ToS)*—Tells IP how to process the incoming datagram by indicating the data's speed, priority, or reliability.

- *Total length*—Identifies the total length of the IP datagram, including the header and data, in bytes.

- *Identification*—Identifies the message to which a datagram belongs and enables the receiving node to reassemble fragmented, or segmented, messages. This field and the following two fields, flags and fragment offset, assist in segmentation and reassembly of packets.

- *Flags: don't fragment (DF) or more fragments (MF)*—Indicates whether a message is fragmented and, if it is fragmented, whether the datagram is the last in the fragment.

- *Fragment offset*—Identifies where the datagram fragment belongs in the incoming set of fragments.

- *Time to live (TTL)*—Corresponds to the number of router hops that a datagram can go through; each time a datagram passes through a machine, another second is taken off its TTL, regardless of whether the machine took a whole second to process the data.

- *Protocol*—Identifies the type of Transport layer protocol that will receive the datagram (for example, TCP or UDP).

- *Header checksum*—Determines whether the IP header has been corrupted.

- *Source address*—Identifies the full IP address of the source node.

- *Destination IP address*—Indicates the full IP address of the destination node.

- *Options*—May contain optional routing and timing information.

- *Padding*—Contains filler information to ensure that the header is a multiple of 32 bits. The size of this field may vary.

- *Data*—Includes the data originally sent by the source node, plus TCP information.

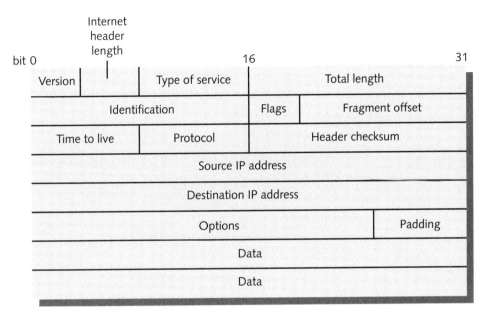

Figure 7-15   Components of an IP datagram

IP is an unreliable, **connectionless** protocol, which means that it does not guarantee delivery of data. Higher-level protocols of the TCP/IP suite, however, can use IP information to ensure that data packets are delivered to the right addresses. Note that the IP datagram does contain one checksum component, the header checksum, which verifies only the integrity of the routing information in the IP header. If the checksum accompanying the message does not have the proper value when the packet is received, then the packet is presumed to be corrupt and is discarded; at that point, a new packet is sent.

Transmission Control Protocol (TCP)

The **Transmission Control Protocol (TCP)** belongs to the Transport layer of both the OSI model and the TCP/IP model. It provides reliable data delivery services. TCP is a **connection-oriented** subprotocol, which means that a connection must be established (at the Session layer of the OSI model) between communicating nodes before this protocol transmits data. TCP sits on top of the IP subprotocol and compensates for IP's reliability deficiencies by providing checksum, flow control, and sequencing information. If an application relied only on IP to transmit data, IP would send packets indiscriminately, without checking whether the destination node is offline, for example, or whether the data becomes corrupt during transmission. TCP, on the other hand, contains several components that ensure data reliability. The fields of the **TCP segment**, the entity that becomes encapsulated by the IP datagram, are described in the following list. Figure 7-16 depicts a TCP segment and its fields.

- *Source port*—Indicates the port number at the source node. A **port** is the address on a host where an application makes itself available to incoming data. One example of a port is port 80, which is typically used to accept Web page requests.

- *Destination port*—Indicates the port number at the destination node.

- *Sequence number*—Identifies the data segment's position in the stream of data segments already sent.

- *Acknowledgment number (ACK)*—Confirms receipt of the data via a return message to the sender.

- *TCP header length*—Indicates the length of the TCP header.

- *Codes*—Includes flags that signal special conditions—for example, if a message is urgent, or if the source node wants to request a connection or terminate a connection.

- *Sliding-window size*—Indicates how many blocks of data the receiving machine can accept.

- *Checksum*—Allows the receiving node to determine whether the TCP segment became corrupted during transmission.

- *Urgent pointer*—Can indicate a location in the data where urgent data resides.

- *Options*—Specifies special options.

- *Padding*—Contains filler information to ensure that the size of the TCP header is a multiple of 32 bits.

- *Data*—Contains data originally sent by the source node.

User Datagram Protocol (UDP)

The **User Datagram Protocol (UDP)**, like TCP, sits in the Transport layer, between the Internet layer and the Application layer of the TCP/IP model. Unlike TCP, however, UDP is a connectionless transport service. UDP offers no assurance that packets will be received in the correct sequence. In fact, this protocol does not guarantee that the packets will be received at all. Furthermore, it provides no error checking or sequence numbering. Nevertheless, UDP's lack of sophistication makes it more efficient than TCP and renders it useful in situations in which data must be transferred quickly, such as live audio or video transmissions over the Internet. In these cases, TCP—with its acknowledgments, checksums, and flow control mechanisms—would add too much overhead to the transmission and bog it down. In contrast to TCP's ten fields, the UDP header contains only four fields: source port, destination port, length, and checksum.

Overhead is a term used by telecommunications professionals to describe the non-data information that must accompany data in order for a signal to be properly routed and interpreted by the network. Overhead is an important networking concept when analyzing a network's performance, because, with all other factors equal, the more overhead a transmission requires, the longer it will take to reach its destination.

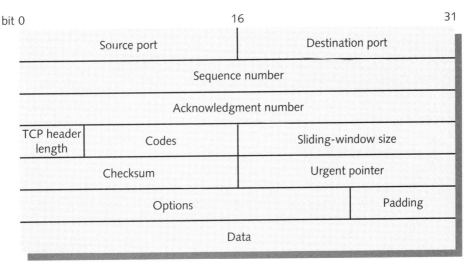

Figure 7-16   A TCP segment

The TCP/IP Application Layer Protocols

In addition to the core Transport and Internet layer protocols, TCP/IP encompasses several Application layer protocols. These protocols work over TCP or UDP and IP, translating user requests into a format the network can read. The following list describes some commonly used Application layer protocols.

- *Dynamic Host Configuration Protocol (DHCP)*—An automated means of assigning a unique Network layer (or IP) address to every device on a network. Using DHCP offers several advantages over manually assigning addresses to each node on the network. DHCP saves a network administrator's time, because it makes it unnecessary to visit every client and device to configure their addresses. It also helps guard against assigning two nodes the same address. Finally, it makes moving clients easier, because if a computer is attached to a different part of the network than it used to be, it can obtain a new address that is valid in its new location on the network using DHCP. You can envision DHCP as a kind of resource manager for IP addresses.

- *File Transfer Protocol (FTP)*—An Application layer protocol used to send and receive files between hosts. FTP is a client-server protocol in which the host running the FTP server portion accepts commands from another host running the FTP client portion. It comes with a set of very simple commands that make up its user interface.

- *Hypertext Transfer Protocol (HTTP)*—The Application layer protocol that enables Web browsers to issue requests to Web servers and then to interpret the Web server's response. You can think of HTTP as the language that Web clients and servers use to communicate.

- *Simple Mail Transfer Protocol (SMTP)*—The protocol responsible for moving messages from one mail server to another over the Internet and other TCP/IP-based networks. SMTP uses a simple request-and-response mechanism to move messages and relies upon more sophisticated protocols, such as the Post Office Protocol (POP), to keep track of storing and forwarding messages.

- *Simple Network Management Protocol (SNMP)*—A communication protocol used to discover information about devices on a TCP/IP network. To use SNMP, each device on the network runs an agent that collects information about that device—for example, the amount of incoming traffic the device is handling. Programs that collect and analyze SNMP data can then issue e-mail or pager alerts to network administrators based on certain criteria, for example, when a critical device is close to being overtaxed. SNMP transports the collected information to a central database. Many network management programs use SNMP.

- *Telnet*—A terminal emulation protocol used to log on to remote hosts using the TCP/IP protocol suite. Often Telnet is used to connect two dissimilar systems (such as PCs and UNIX machines). Through Telnet, you can control a remote host over LANs and WANs, such as the Internet. For example, network managers can use Telnet to log on to their company's routers from home and modify the router's configuration.

In addition to these standard TCP/IP Application layer protocols, new protocols are continuously being developed. For example, the practice of transmitting voice conversations over the Internet has spawned the creation of new voice-specific Application layer protocols. These new protocols address specific challenges, such as making sure data belonging to a phone conversation arrives in a timely manner and is reassembled in the correct order, managing conference calls over the Internet, and connecting an Internet phone call with a PSTN local loop.

Addressing in TCP/IP

As you know, each node on a network must have a unique identifying number called an address. You have also learned that networks recognize two kinds of addresses: logical and physical (or MAC) addresses. MAC addresses are assigned to a device's network interface card at the factory by its manufacturer, but logical addresses depend on rules set by the Network layer protocol standards. In the TCP/IP protocol suite, IP is the core protocol responsible for logical addressing. For this reason, addresses on TCP/IP networks are called **IP addresses**. IP addresses are assigned and used according to very specific parameters.

Each IP address is a unique 32-bit number, divided into four **octets**, or 8-bit bytes, that are separated by periods. An example of a valid IP address is 144.92.43.178. An IP address contains two types of information: network and host. The first octet identifies the network class. Three types of network classes exist: Class A, Class B, and Class C. Table 7-2 summarizes the three commonly used classes of TCP/IP networks.

Table 7-2 Commonly Used TCP/IP Classes

Network Class	Beginning Octet	Number of Networks	Host Addresses per Network
A	1–126	126	16,777,214
B	128–191	>16,000	65,534
C	192–223	>2,000,000	254

Note: Although 8 bits have 256 possible combinations, not every combination is eligible for assignment to a network node. For example, the IP addresses 0.0.0.0 and 255.255.255.255 are reserved for special functions and cannot be used to identify devices on a network. The number 0.0.0.0 is used to identify the default network over which a packet should be routed. The address 255.255.255.255 is reserved for **broadcasts**, or transmissions to all stations on a network.

All nodes on a Class A network share the first octet of their IP addresses, a number between 1 and 126. Nodes on a Class B network share the first two octets, and their IP addresses begin with a number between 128 and 191. Class C network IP addresses share the first three octets, with their first octet being a number between 192 and 223. For example, nodes with the following IP addresses may belong to the same Class A network: 23.78.110.109, 23.164.32.97, 23.48.112.43, and 23.108.37.22. Nodes with the following IP addresses may belong to the same Class B network: 168.34.88.29, 168.34.55.41, 168.34.73.49, and 168.34.205.113. Nodes with the following addresses may belong to the same Class C network: 204.139.118.7, 204.139.118.54, 204.139.118.14, and 204.139.118.31.

Because only 126 Class A networks are available on the Internet, most Class A networks have already been reserved by large corporations, educational institutions, or governments. In addition, some IP addresses are reserved for network functions, like broadcasts, and cannot be assigned to machines or devices. Notice that 127 is not a valid first octet for an IP address assigned to a network node. The range of addresses beginning with 127 is reserved for loopback information, with the IP address 127.0.0.1 being called a **loopback address**. When you try to contact this IP number, you are actually communicating the TCP software running with your own machine. This address can prove useful when you must troubleshoot problems with a workstation's TCP/IP communications. If you receive a positive response from the loopback test, you know that the TCP/IP protocols are installed and in use on your workstation.

The registration and use of Internet addresses are regulated by several different organizations around the globe. You will learn more about such authorities in Chapter 12, which focuses on the Internet. Meanwhile, you should know that to connect with the Internet and obtain the right to use official IP addresses, an organization would typically rely on an ISP. In other words, IP addressing and Internet authorities do not deal directly with Internet users.

For example, suppose that you decide to go into business for yourself, and you hire five staff members who will work on your office network. You want each staff person to have his or her own address to use when communicating with the Internet. You also think that your products will be so successful that you might add five or more new staff members in the coming year. To obtain addresses for all existing staff and allow for growth, you can contract with your ISP to lease a group of 16 official IP addresses that are usable on the Internet.

Alternatively, if the network is behind a firewall, administrators can make up their own IP addressing scheme without adhering to international addressing standards. A **firewall** is a type of software or hardware (typically a router) that secures a network from outside penetration via the Internet; it is commonly used to protect businesses with a presence on the Web. (You learn more about firewalls and other network security measures in Chapter 13.) For example, you could use a firewall to protect your small office network from security breaches related to e-commerce transactions on its Web site. A firewall isolates the network from the Internet (or any public network) at large. As a result, officially registered IP addresses aren't required within the network. If your office machines aren't really using officially registered IP addresses, however, how will your staff get through the firewall and onto the Internet? When staff members request access to machines outside your office LAN, their data transmissions must be assigned valid Internet IP addresses by software running on the connectivity devices that connect the LAN to the public network.

Isolating a network behind a firewall and then using your own address scheme provides useful management benefits. (For example, if you ran a large LAN, you could assign all machines on the third floor of an office building addresses beginning with 10.3.) In addition, this scheme allows an organization to use more IP addresses than it could if it assigned officially registered addresses to each machine.

A secondary number, known as a subnet mask, is also assigned as part of the TCP/IP configuration process. A subnet mask allows large networks to be subdivided into smaller subnetworks known as subnets. The subnet mask identifies to the network software which addresses appear on the same local network and which addresses need to be contacted through a router. Subnetting is a complex, but highly useful aspect of TCP/IP networking.

IP address data is sent across the network in binary form, with each of the four octets consisting of eight bits. For example, the IP address 131.127.3.22 is the same as the binary number 10000011 01111111 00000011 00010110. As you learned in Chapter 2, converting from the dotted decimal notation to binary number is a simple process when you use a scientific calculator.

Every host on a network must have a unique number, as duplicate addresses cause problems on a network. If you add a host to a network and its IP address is already in use by another host on the subnet, an error message is generated on the new client and its TCP/IP services are disabled. The existing host may also receive an error message, but can continue to function normally.

You may assign IP addresses manually, by modifying the client workstation's TCP/IP properties. A manually-assigned IP address is called a **static IP address** because it does not change automatically. It changes only when you reconfigure the client's TCP/IP properties. Alternatively, you can have IP addresses assigned automatically through the Dynamic Host Configuration Protocol (DHCP), an Application layer protocol in the TCP/IP suite. Nearly all modern networks provide the capability of dynamically assigning IP addresses.

You must take care to avoid assigning duplicate addresses. For example, suppose you spend an afternoon manually assigning IP addresses to 50 Windows 2000 Professional machines in a computer lab. After the forty-eighth machine, you feel tired and mistakenly give the same IP address, 193.45.77.112, to machines 49 and 50. The next day, a student uses computer 49 to pick up her e-mail. A few minutes later, a student turns on computer 50. When he tries to connect to the network, he receives an error message effectively saying that "IP address 193.45.77.112 is being used by 00-4B-38-01-AF-4C," where 00-4B-38-01-AF-4C is the MAC address of computer 49. The student at computer 50 cannot proceed until either computer 49 is shut down or changes its IP address or until he changes the IP address of computer 50.

Both Windows 2000 and Windows XP workstations allow users to view their current IP addresses. To view your current IP information on a Windows 2000 or Windows XP workstation connected to a network:

1. Click **Start**, then click **Run**. The Run dialog box opens.

2. In the Open text box, type **cmd**, then click **OK**. The Command Prompt window opens.

3. At the DOS prompt, type **ipconfig /all**. Your workstation's IP address information is displayed, similar to the information shown in Figure 7-17.

4. Type **exit**, then press **Enter** to close the Command Prompt window.

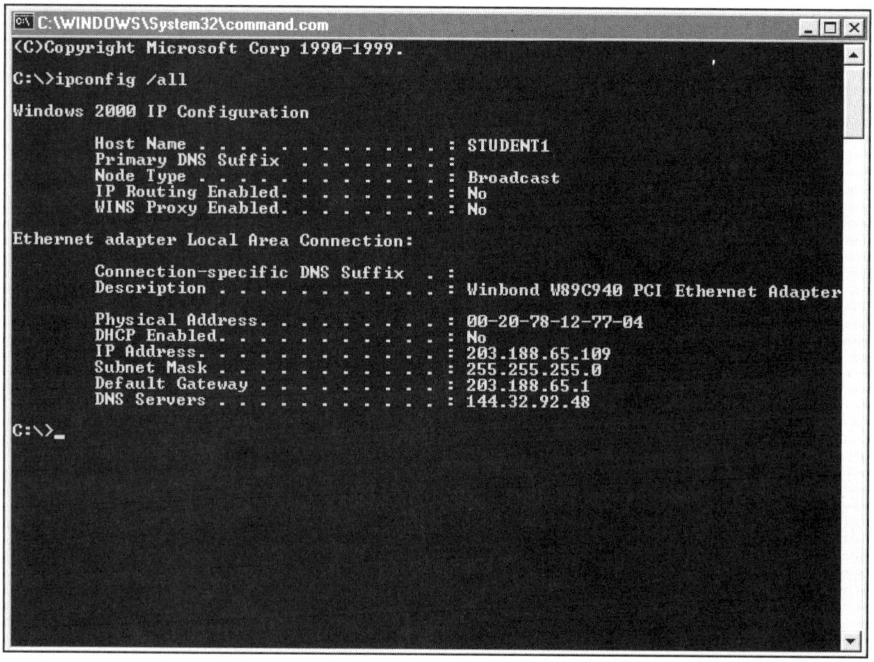

```
C:\WINDOWS\System32\command.com
(C)Copyright Microsoft Corp 1990-1999.

C:\>ipconfig /all

Windows 2000 IP Configuration

        Host Name . . . . . . . . . . . . : STUDENT1
        Primary DNS Suffix  . . . . . . . :
        Node Type . . . . . . . . . . . . : Broadcast
        IP Routing Enabled. . . . . . . . : No
        WINS Proxy Enabled. . . . . . . . : No

Ethernet adapter Local Area Connection:

        Connection-specific DNS Suffix  . :
        Description . . . . . . . . . . . : Winbond W89C940 PCI Ethernet Adapter
        Physical Address. . . . . . . . . : 00-20-78-12-77-04
        DHCP Enabled. . . . . . . . . . . : No
        IP Address. . . . . . . . . . . . : 203.188.65.109
        Subnet Mask . . . . . . . . . . . : 255.255.255.0
        Default Gateway . . . . . . . . . : 203.188.65.1
        DNS Servers . . . . . . . . . . . : 144.32.92.48

C:\>_
```

Figure 7-17   An example of an IP configuration window

In addition to using IP addresses, TCP/IP networks use names for networks and hosts, so as to make them more easily identifiable to humans. Each host (computer on a TCP/IP network) requires a host name. To be recognized on the Internet, each LAN must have a network name, also known as a **domain name**. Together, the host name and domain name constitute the **fully qualified host name**. For example, your host name might be s_atkins while your domain name is course.com. Therefore, your fully qualified domain name would be s_atkins.watc.tec.mn.us. Other users on a TCP/IP network, such as the Internet, would identify you by this name, and other machines would associate your IP address with this name. Your host name, "s_atkins," is a field the network administrator configures on the computer. The rest of the name, "course.com," is the network's domain name. Domain names must follow strict rules and depend on a domain name server to resolve domain names with the network addresses with the domain name assigned to them.

Chapter 12 covers TCP/IP naming services in more detail. For now, it is enough to know that every node on a TCP/IP network requires a unique host name plus a domain name to communicate over the Internet.

CHAPTER SUMMARY

- Workstations on a network typically share data, programs, and devices through a central computer called a server. Servers store shared data and programs on their hard disks and perform management functions. A network that uses a server to enable clients to share data, data storage space, and devices, is known as a client-server network.

- To connect and communicate over a network, nodes must have network interface cards that connect with transmission media and transmit and receive signals. They must also use software that allows them to log on and share resources. Each node must have a unique network address and their transmissions must use appropriate protocols for the network.

- The main purpose for using networks is to share programs, data, and devices, such as printers or fax machines—all of which are known as resources. By enabling the sharing of resources, networks help organizations save money and time.

- The many functions that networks perform are known as services. Network services include: file services, print services, communication services, mail services, Internet services, and management services. In small organizations, one server may perform all these functions. In large organizations, several servers may be dedicated to any one of these functions.

- A local area network (LAN) is a network of computers and other devices that is confined to a relatively small space, such as one building or even one office. A metropolitan area network (MAN) connects several locations in a relatively small area, such as a group of regional healthcare facilities. A wide area network (WAN) connects several distant LANs or MANs.

- To connect users from around the globe, the Internet relies on a hierarchical structure of connection points. At the bottom of the Internet hierarchy are local Internet service providers (ISPs). Local ISPs connect to regional ISPs, which form the next layer in the hierarchy. Regional ISPs connect to the national network service providers via network access points (NAPs). NAPs are where the largest network service providers aggregate and exchange Internet traffic.

- In the early 1980s, ISO created the Open Systems Interconnection (OSI) model for understanding and developing computer-to-computer communications. This model divides communication systems into seven layers: Physical, Data Link, Network, Transport, Session, Presentation, and Application. Each layer has its own set of functions and interacts with the layers directly above and below it.

- The Physical layer is the lowest, or first, layer of the OSI model. Protocols at the Physical layer generate and detect voltage so as to transmit and receive signals carrying data. The Physical layer sets the data transmission rate and monitors data error rates, though it does not provide error correction.

- The second layer of the OSI model, the Data Link layer, divides data it receives from the Network layer into frames that can then be transmitted by the Physical layer. It also provides error-checking information and assigns physical addresses to data frames.

❑ The Network layer, the third OSI model layer, manages addressing and routing data based on addressing, patterns of usage, and availability. Routers belong to the Network layer because they use this information to intelligently direct data from sender to receiver.

❑ The Transport layer is primarily responsible for ensuring that data is transferred from point A to point B reliably and without errors. For example, the Transport layer ensures that data is sent and received in the same order, or sequence. It also establishes the level of error checking.

❑ The Session layer establishes and maintains communication between two nodes on the network. It can be considered the "traffic cop" of network communications. The term "session" refers to a connection for data exchange between two parties; it is most often used in the context of terminal and mainframe communications.

❑ The Presentation layer, the sixth OSI model layer, serves as a translator between the application and the network. At the Presentation layer, data is formatted in a schema that the network can understand; this format varies with the type of network used. The Presentation layer also manages data encryption and decryption, such as the scrambling of passwords.

❑ The top, or seventh, layer of the OSI model is the Application layer. It provides interfaces to the software that enable it to use network services. Some of the services provided by the Application layer include file transfer, file management, and message handling for electronic mail.

❑ Network nodes may be identified by their MAC (or physical) addresses, which are assigned to a NIC by its manufacturer. MAC addresses are 12-digit hexadecimal numbers made of two parts: a Block ID, unique to the manufacturer, and a Device ID.

❑ Network nodes may also be identified by their Network layer (or logical) addresses. Network layer addresses follow a hierarchical addressing scheme and can be assigned through operating system software. An IP address is one type of Network layer address.

❑ The term "protocol" is often used to refer to a group, or suite, of individual protocols that work together. The protocols within a suite are assigned different tasks, such as data translation, data handling, error checking, and addressing; each protocol corresponds to different layer of the OSI model.

❑ Protocols that can span more than one LAN segment are routable, because they carry Network layer and addressing information that can be interpreted by a router. Not all protocols are routable, however.

❑ Some well-known protocol suites include: NetBEUI/NetBIOS, IPX/SPX, AppleTalk, and TCP/IP. The Transmission Control Protocol/Internet Protocol (TCP/IP) suite is a routable, flexible protocol suite that has its origins in ARPAnet, the precursor to the Internet. TCP/IP is still the protocol on which all Internet traffic relies. It is also the protocol of choice for many private LANs and WANs.

❏ One of the greatest advantages to using TCP/IP relates to its status as a routable protocol, which means that it carries network addressing information that can be interpreted by routers. TCP/IP is also a flexible protocol, running on any combination of network operating systems or network media.

❏ Certain subprotocols of the TCP/IP suite, called TCP/IP core protocols, operate in the Transport or Network layers of the OSI model and provide basic services to the protocols in other layers of the four-layer model. These core protocols are required for any data transmission that uses TCP/IP. Of all the core protocols in the suite, TCP and IP are the most significant.

❏ Common TCP/IP Application layer protocols include DHCP, Telnet, FTP, HTTP, SNMP, and SMTP. Many others exist, and new ones are continually being developed.

❏ In the TCP/IP protocol suite, IP is the core protocol responsible for logical addressing. For this reason, addresses on TCP/IP networks are sometimes called IP addresses. Each IP address is a unique 32-bit number, divided into four octets, or 8-bit bytes, that are separated by periods. An example of a valid IP address is 144.92.43.178. An IP address contains two types of information: network and host. The first octet identifies the network class. Three types of network classes exist: Class A, Class B, and Class C.

❏ All nodes on a Class A network share the first octet of their IP numbers, a number between 1 and 126. Nodes on a Class B network share the first two octets, and their IP addresses begin with a number between 128 and 191. Class C network IP numbers share the first three octets, with their first octet being a number between 192 and 223.

❏ IP address data are sent across the network in binary form, with each of the four octets consisting of eight bits. For example, the IP address 131.127.3.22 is the same as the binary number 10000011 01111111 00000011 00010110.

❏ TCP/IP networks use names for networks and hosts, so as to make them more easily identifiable to humans. Each computer on a TCP/IP network requires a host name. Each network must have a network name, also known as a domain name. The combination of a host name and domain name is known as a fully qualified host name.

KEY TERMS

ACK (acknowledgment) — A response generated at the Transport layer of the OSI model that confirms to a sender that its frame was received.

address — A unique number that identifies a node on a network. Addresses may be physical (MAC addresses) or logical (for example, IP addresses).

AppleTalk — The protocol suite used to interconnect Macintosh computers. AppleTalk can be routed between network segments and integrated with NetWare- or Microsoft-based networks.

Application layer — The seventh layer of the OSI model. The Application layer provides interfaces to the software that enable programs to use network services.

application program interface (API) — A routine (or set of instructions) that allows a program to interact with the operating system. APIs belong to the Application layer of the OSI model.

authentication — The process of verifying that a client's logon ID and password are valid and then allowing the client to log on to the network and access defined resources.

Block ID — The first set of six characters (or three bytes) that make up the MAC address and that are unique to a particular vendor. Block IDs are also known as vendor IDs.

broadcast — A transmission to all nodes on a network.

client — A computer on the network that requests resources or services from another computer on a network. In some cases, a client could also act as a server. The term "client" may also refer to the user of a client workstation.

client–server network — A network in which clients (typically workstations) use a central server to share data, data storage space, programs, and other devices.

client software — A program or group of programs that instruct the client's operating system to interact with the server's network operating system. Versions of client software are specific to both the client's operating system and the server's network operating system.

communications server — *See* remote access server.

communication services — The functions of a network that allow remote users to connect to the network (usually through a phone line and modem).

connection–oriented — A feature of some protocols that requires the establishment of a connection between communicating nodes before the protocol transmits data.

connectionless — A feature of some protocols that allows the protocol to service a request without requiring a verified session and without guaranteeing data delivery.

connectivity device — A device that connects and exchanges data between two separate networks or separate parts of a single network. Examples of connectivity devices include switches, bridges, and routers.

connector — The piece of hardware in which a cable terminates. Connectors are plugged into data jacks, or receptacles, to connect transmission media to any part of a network.

Cyclic Redundancy Check (CRC) — An algorithm used to verify the accuracy of data contained in a data frame.

Data Link layer — The second layer in the OSI model. The Data Link layer bridges the networking media with the Network layer. Its primary function is to divide the data it receives from the Network layer into frames that can then be transmitted by the Physical layer.

Data Link layer address — *See* MAC address.

decryption — The process of using an algorithm to decode a transmission and reveal encrypted data.

Device ID — The second set of six characters that make up a network device's MAC address. The Device ID, which is added at the factory, is based on the device's model and manufacture date.

domain name — The symbolic name that resolves to a group of IP addresses. Usually, a domain name is associated with a company or other type of organization, such as a university or military unit.

Dynamic Host Configuration Protocol (DHCP) — An Application layer protocol in the TCP/IP suite that manages the dynamic distribution of IP addresses on a network. Using DHCP to assign IP addresses can nearly eliminate duplicate-addressing problems.

encryption — The use of an algorithm to scramble data so that the data can only be read by reversing the formula (or decryption).

file server — A specialized server that enables clients to share applications and data across the network.

file services — The function of a file server that allows users to share data files, applications, and storage areas.

File Transfer Protocol (FTP) — An Application layer protocol used to send and receive files via TCP/IP.

firewall — A specialized device (typically a router, but possibly only a PC running special software) that selectively filters or blocks traffic between networks. A firewall may be strictly hardware-based, or it may involve a combination of hardware and software.

flow control — A method of gauging the appropriate rate of data transmission based on how fast the recipient can accept data.

frame — A package for data that includes not only the raw data, or "payload," but also the sender's and receiver's network addresses and control information.

Frame Check Sequence (FCS) — The field in a frame responsible for ensuring that data carried by the frame arrives intact. It uses an algorithm, such as CRC, to accomplish this verification. The FCS is inserted at the Data Link layer of the OSI model.

fully qualified host name — In TCP/IP addressing, the combination of a host and domain name that together uniquely identify a device.

host — A computer connected to a network that has a unique address. This term is most often used in the context of networks that rely on the TCP/IP protocol suite.

HTTP (Hypertext Transport Protocol) — The Application layer protocol that enables Web browsers to issue requests to Web servers and then to interpret the Web server's response.

hub — A connectivity device that operates at the Physical layer of the OSI Model and repeats digital signals over a network segment.

Internet — A complex, diverse WAN that connects LANs and individual users around the globe.

Internet Protocol (IP) — A core protocol in the TCP/IP suite that belongs to the Internet layer of the TCP/IP model and provides information about how and where data should be delivered. IP is the subprotocol that enables TCP/IP to internetwork.

Internet service provider (ISP) — A company that operates a network and provides consumers with a link to the Internet.

Internet services — The services that enable a network to communicate with the Internet, including World Wide Web servers and browsers, file transfer capabilities, Internet addressing schemes, security filters, and a means for directly logging on to other computers.

internetwork — To traverse more than one LAN segment and more than one type of network through a router.

Internetwork Packet Exchange (IPX) — A core protocol of the IPX/SPX suite that operates at the Network layer of the OSI model and provides routing and internetwork services, similar to IP in the TCP/IP suite.

Internetwork Packet Exchange/Sequenced Packet Exchange (IPX/SPX) — A protocol originally developed by Xerox, then modified and adopted by Novell in the 1980s for the NetWare network operating system.

IP address — A logical address used in TCP/IP networking. This unique 32-bit number is divided into four groups of octets, or 8-bit bytes, that are separated by periods.

IP datagram — The IP portion of a TCP/IP frame that acts as an envelope for data, holding information necessary for routers to transfer data between subnets.

IP version 6 (IPv6) — A newer version of the IP subprotocol that will replace the existing IP version 4. IPv6 uses more efficient packet headers and allows for 128-bit source and destination IP addresses. The use of longer addresses will allow more IP addresses to be in circulation. IPv6 also includes the IPSec encryption mechanism.

local area network (LAN) — A network of computers and other devices that is confined to a relatively small space, such as one building or even one office.

log on — The act of submitting credentials (such as a username and password) to a server, then being admitted access to shared resources on the network.

logical address — *See* network layer addresses.

Logical Link Control (LLC) sublayer — The upper sublayer in the Data Link layer. The LLC provides a common interface and supplies reliability and flow control services.

loopback address — An IP address reserved for communicating from a node to itself (used mostly for testing purposes). The value of the loopback address is always 127.0.0.1.

MAC address — A number that uniquely identifies a network node. The manufacturer hard-codes the MAC address on the NIC. This address is composed of the Block ID and Device ID.

mail server — A specialized server that manages mail services.

mail services — The network services that manage the storage and transfer of e-mail between users on a network. In addition to sending, receiving, and storing mail, mail services can include intelligent e-mail routing capabilities, notification, scheduling, indexing, document libraries, and gateways to other mail servers.

management services — The network services that centrally administer and simplify complicated management tasks on the network. Examples of management services include license tracking, security auditing, asset management, addressing management, software distribution, traffic monitoring, load balancing, and hardware diagnosis.

Media Access Control (MAC) sublayer — The lower sublayer of the Data Link layer. The MAC appends the physical address of the destination computer onto the frame.

metropolitan area exchange (MAE) — A type of network access point. In the United States, there are two MAEs: MAE East, in northern Virginia just outside of Washington, D.C., and MAE West, in San Jose, California.

metropolitan area network (MAN) — A network that connects clients and servers in multiple buildings within a limited geographic area. For example, a network connecting multiple city government buildings around the city's center.

Microsoft Message Queueing (MSMQ) — An API used in a network environment. MSMQ stores messages sent between nodes in queues then forwards them to their destination when the link to the recipient is available.

multiprotocol network — A network that uses more than one protocol.

NetBEUI (NetBIOS Enhanced User Interface) — The Microsoft adaptation of IBM's NetBIOS protocol. NetBEUI expands on NetBIOS by adding an Application layer component.

NetBIOS — A protocol originally designed for IBM to provide Transport and Session layer services for applications running on small, homogenous networks. Microsoft adopted IBM's NetBIOS as its foundation protocol, initially for networks using LAN Manager or Windows for Workgroups.

network access point (NAP) — A facility operated by one large network service provider where Internet traffic is aggregated and exchanged. In the United States, there are five major NAPs.

network administrator — A professional charged with installing, maintaining, and troubleshooting a network.

network interface card (NIC) — The device that enables a workstation to connect to the network and communicate with other computers. NICs are manufactured by several different companies and come with a variety of specifications that are tailored to the workstation's and the network's requirements.

Network layer — The third layer in the OSI model. The Network layer translates network addresses into their physical counterparts and decides how to route data from the sender to the receiver.

Network layer addresses — The addresses that reside at the Network level of the OSI model, follow a hierarchical addressing scheme, and can be assigned through operating system software.

network operating system (NOS) — The software that runs on a server and enables the server to manage data, users, groups, security, applications, and other networking functions. The most popular network operating systems are Microsoft Windows NT, Windows 2000, UNIX, and Novell's NetWare.

7

network service provider (NSP) — A telecommunications company that provides infrastructure for either public or private traffic. NSPs aren't necessarily ISPs because they may simply provide the infrastructure for connections, but not operate access servers for a consumer's initial entry to the Internet. However, most NSPs are ISPs.

node — A computer or other device connected to a network that has a unique address and is capable of sending or receiving data.

octet — One of the four 8-bit bytes that are separated by periods and together make up an IP address.

OSI (Open Systems Interconnection) model — A model for understanding and developing computer-to-computer communication developed in the 1980s by ISO. It divides networking architecture into seven layers: Physical, Data Link, Network, Transport, Session, Presentation, and Application.

organizationally unique identifier (OUI) — *See* Block ID.

overhead — The non-data information that must accompany data in order for a signal to be properly routed and interpreted by the network. When all other factors are equal, the more overhead a transmission requires, the longer it will take to reach its destination.

peering — An arrangement between network service providers in which they directly link their networks and exchange Internet traffic over those links.

physical address — *See* MAC address.

Physical layer — The lowest, or first, layer of the OSI model. The Physical layer contains the physical networking media, such as cabling and connectors.

plug — *See* connector.

Presentation layer — The sixth layer of the OSI model. The Presentation layer serves as a translator between the application and the network. Here data is formatted in a schema that the network can understand, with the format varying according to the type of network used. The Presentation layer also manages data encryption and decryption, such as the scrambling of system passwords.

port — The address on a host where an application makes itself available to incoming data.

print server — A type of server that manages printers and print services on a network.

print services — The functions of a network that allow printers to be shared by several users on the network.

protocol — The rules a network uses to transfer data. Protocols ensure that data is transferred whole, in sequence, and without error from one node on the network to another.

reassembly — The process of reconstructing data units that have been segmented.

redundancy — The practice of using more than one component to guard against outages (or failures).

remote access server — A specialized server that enables remote clients to log onto a LAN.

remote access services — *See* communications services.

remote user — A person working on a computer in a different geographical location from the LAN's server.

resources — The programs, data, data storage space, and devices (such as printers or fax machines) that are shared on a network and managed by servers.

routable — The protocols that can span more than one LAN segment because they carry Network layer and addressing information that can be interpreted by a router.

route — The action of directing data between networks based on addressing, patterns of usage, and availability of network segments.

router — A type of connectivity device that connects network segments and intelligently directs data based on addressing information contained in the data frame. Routers operate at the Network layer of the OSI model.

segment — Part of a network that shares a fixed amount of capacity and is logically separate from other parts of the network. Layer 2 and Layer 3 devices such as bridges, switches and routers separate network segments, but Layer 1 devices, such as hubs, extend network segments.

segmentation — The process of decreasing the size of data units when moving data from a network segment that can handle larger data units to a network segment that can handle only smaller data units.

Sequenced Packet Exchange (SPX) — A core protocol in the IPX/SPX suite. SPX belongs to the Transport layer of the OSI model and works in tandem with IPX to ensure that data are received whole, in sequence, and error free.

sequencing — The process of assigning a placeholder to each piece of a data block to allow the receiving node's Transport layer to reassemble the data in the correct order.

server — A computer on the network that manages shared resources. Servers usually have more processing power, memory, and hard disk space than clients. They run network operating software that can manage not only data, but also users, groups, security, and applications on the network.

services — The features provided by a network.

session — A connection for data exchange between two parties. The term "session" is most often used in the context of terminal and mainframe communications.

Session layer — The fifth layer in the OSI model. The Session layer establishes and maintains communication between two nodes on the network. It can be considered the "traffic cop" for network communications.

Simple Mail Transfer Protocol (SMTP) — The protocol responsible for moving messages from one e-mail server to another over the Internet and other TCP/IP-based networks.

Simple Network Management Protocol (SNMP) — A communication protocol used to manage devices on a TCP/IP network.

socket — A logical address assigned to a specific process running on a computer. Some sockets are reserved for operating system functions.

standalone workstation — A computer that uses programs and data only from its local disks and that is not connected to a network.

7

static IP address — An IP address that is manually assigned to a device.

subnets — In an internetwork, the individual networks that are joined together by routers.

subprotocols — Small, specialized protocols that work together and belong to a protocol suite.

terminal — A device with little (if any) of its own processing or disk capacity that depends on a host to supply it with applications and data-processing services.

TCP — *See* Transmission Control Protocol.

TCP/IP — *See* Transmission Control Protocol/Internet Protocol.

TCP segment — The portion of a TCP/IP packet that holds TCP data fields and becomes encapsulated by the IP datagram.

TCP/IP core protocols — The TCP/IP subprotocols that belong to the Network layer and upon which higher layer protocols rely.

Telnet — A terminal emulation protocol used to log on to remote hosts using the TCP/IP protocol. Telnet resides in the Application layer of the TCP/IP suite.

token — A special control frame that indicates to the rest of the network that a particular node has the right to transmit data.

transceiver — A component that functions as both a transmitter and receiver. As a transmitter, the transceiver encodes a stream of data and generates signals to the transmission medium in a format that the receiver can interpret. As a receiver, the transceiver performs the opposite tasks: It accepts and decodes the stream of data. Network interface cards, for example, act as transceivers.

Transmission Control Protocol (TCP) — A core protocol of the TCP/IP suite. TCP belongs to the Transport layer and provides reliable data delivery services.

Transmission Control Protocol/Internet Protocol (TCP/IP) — A routable, flexible protocol suite that has its origins in ARPAnet, the precursor to the Internet. TCP/IP is still the protocol that all Internet traffic relies on. It is also the protocol of choice for many private LANs and WANs.

Transport layer — The fourth layer of the OSI model. The Transport layer is primarily responsible for ensuring that data is transferred from point A to point B reliably and without errors.

User Datagram Protocol (UDP) — A core protocol in the TCP/IP suite that sits in the Transport layer, between the Internet layer and the Application layer of the TCP/IP model. UDP is a connectionless transport service.

user — A person who uses a computer.

vendor code — *See* Block ID.

virtual address — *See* Network layer address.

wide area network (WAN) — A network that spans a large distance and connects two or more LANs.

workstation — A computer that typically runs a desktop operating system. A workstation may be standalone or connected to a network.

REVIEW QUESTIONS

1. Which of the following components functions as a transceiver for a workstation?

   a. connector

   b. transmission media

   c. network interface card

   d. client software

2. Why is it important for every network node to have a unique address?

   a. so that data can be reliably delivered to that node

   b. so that network administrators can keep track of their inventory

   c. so that software licenses can be accurately monitored

   d. so that data can be accurately encrypted and decrypted

3. Which of the following is an example of a network operating system?

   a. Excel

   b. SQL Server

   c. Novell NetWare

   d. AppleTalk

4. Of the following specialized servers, which would be responsible for storing spreadsheets used by all of Microsoft Word to several clients on the network?

   a. print server

   b. file server

   c. communications server

   d. management server

5. Of the following specialized servers, which would be responsible for accepting connections from remote users dialing into a LAN?

   a. print server

   b. file server

   c. communications server

   d. management server

6. Which of the following is an example of a connectivity device?

   a. router

   b. printer

   c. server

   d. NIC

7. In the United States, what type of facilities form the backbone of the Internet?

    a. central offices

    b. university data centers

    c. regional ISPs

    d. network access points

8. Which of the following organizations would typically supply a business with a group of IP addresses for its networked devices?

    a. ISP

    b. ITU

    c. ISO

    d. IEEE

9. If you dial into an Internet service provider using your modem, then retrieve a Web page from an Internet server across the globe, what type of switching does your data undergo?

    a. message switching

    b. circuit switching only

    c. packet switching only

    d. both circuit switching and packet switching

10. What standards organization devised the OSI model?

    a. ICANN

    b. ITU

    c. ISO

    d. IEEE

11. Which of the following OSI model layers packages data into frames?

    a. Physical

    b. Data Link

    c. Network

    d. Transport

12. Which of the following OSI model layers assigns logical addressing information to data?

    a. Physical

    b. Data Link

    c. Network

    d. Transport

13. At which layer of the OSI model do routers operate?

    a. Physical

    b. Data Link

    c. Network

    d. Transport

14. Which layer of the OSI model is responsible for encryption and decryption?

    a. Transport

    b. Session

    c. Presentation

    d. Application

15. Which layer of the OSI model is known as the "traffic cop" because it manages which nodes communicate at any point in time?

    a. Transport

    b. Session

    c. Presentation

    d. Application

16. What are the two parts of a MAC address?

    a. Block ID and Device ID

    b. Block ID and vendor code

    c. Device ID and host number

    d. Device ID and node number

17. In a network that relies on fiber optic cable, which layer of the OSI model is responsible for issuing pulses of light to the fiber?

    a. Physical

    b. Data Link

    c. Network

    d. Transport

18. At what layer of the OSI model do switches operate?

    a. Physical

    b. Data Link

    c. Network

    d. Transport

7

19. What makes a protocol routable?

    a. Data Link layer addressing information

    b. Data Link layer error checking information

    c. Network layer addressing information

    d. Transport layer sequencing information

20. Which of the following protocols is not routable?

    a. AppleTalk

    b. NetBIOS

    c. TCP/IP

    d. IPX/SPX

21. Which of the following TCP/IP core protocols makes certain that a connection has been established between the sender and the receiver before issuing a transmission?

    a. IP

    b. TCP

    c. UDP

    d. HTTP

22. Which of the following TCP/IP Application layer protocols enables a remote user to log on to a TCP/IP host?

    a. SNMP

    b. HTTP

    c. SMTP

    d. Telnet

23. Which two of the following are advantages to using DHCP on a TCP/IP network?

    a. It prevents you from having to ensure that each node has a unique IP address.

    b. It minimizes the frame's logical address file size to enable more efficient data transmission between nodes.

    c. It automatically appends the destination node's network location to the data frame, thus expediting routing.

    d. It prevents you from having to manually assign IP addresses, thus minimizing the potential for errors.

24. What is the term for the following special IP address: 127.0.0.1?

    a. loopback address

    b. broadcast address

    c. virtual address

    d. socket address

25. To what class does the IP address "188.72.101.9" belong?

    a. Class A

    b. Class B

    c. Class C

    d. Class D

HANDS-ON PROJECTS

Project 7-1

Large network service providers, such as AT&T, SBC, and Sprint, connect with each other to exchange large amounts of Internet traffic at the highest levels of the Internet's hierarchy. You have learned that congestion in their networks can take a severe toll on network response time. In this project, you get a glimpse into how one of these large carriers, AT&T, assesses and reports the amount of congestion on their backbone network. For this project, you need a computer that can navigate the Internet. You also need Adobe Acrobat reader software, which can be obtained at no cost from *www.adobe.com*.

1. Open your computer's browser and connect to the following Web site: **ipnetwork.bgtmo.ip.att.net/index.html**. The AT&T IP Network Performance Page appears, with a welcome message. On the right side of the screen, in a weather forecast style, the current state of AT&T's backbone network is displayed. One measure of network performance listed on this page is delay, or the time it takes for one packet to travel between nodes. The other measure of network performance listed on this page is loss, or the percentage of data packets that are lost (and must be retransmitted) while en route from one node to another. What is the current condition of AT&T's backbone network?

2. Now click **Current Performance** on the navigation bar on the left side of the page. The current average delay and loss for the network, along with a map of the United States are displayed.

3. In the Select City of Origin drop down box, choose **Washington**. Scroll down the page to see the statistics for connections between Washington and other points on AT&T's backbone. Where is delay the greatest? Why do you suppose this is the case? Are any of the connections on the map not displayed as green (meaning, they are experiencing no problems)? Where is loss occurring?

4. Repeat Step 3 for San Francisco and also for Chicago. How do the delay and loss statistics differ between cities?

5. Notice on the navigation bar an option for the previous month's averages. Click this option. The Monthly Averages Web page appears.

6. Note the value for the network's backbone availability. Click **Modem Connect Success Rate** to read a definition for this measure, then click your browser's **Back** button to return to the Monthly Averages page.

7. Simply reading a list of a carrier's statistics does not give a complete picture of their network's health. You must also understand what the statistics mean and how they are derived. To discover how AT&T generates the statistics you have just viewed, click the **Methodology** option on the navigation bar. The Methodology page appears.

8. Click **Acrobat version** to launch Adobe Acrobat reader software and open the methodology document.

9. After reading about AT&T's methodology, answer the following questions: What factors contribute to delay? Which of those factors cannot be controlled by the network service provider? How does AT&T measure delay without including the effects of factors outside its control? What does it mean when you see a red box for one of the city pair links on the Current Performance page? How long does a link's delay need to be in order to turn red?

Project 7-2

When installing a new client on a network, you may be able to accept the default protocol settings or you may have to install or configure the protocols. In this project, you learn how to install protocols on a Windows 2000 Professional workstation. Because TCP/IP would normally be already installed with the operating system, this project walks you through the process of installing the NetBEUI protocol. The process of installing other protocols on a Windows 2000 Professional workstation is identical.

1. Log on to the Windows 2000 Professional workstation as an Administrator.

2. Click **Start**, point to **Settings**, and then click **Network and Dial-up Connections**.

3. Right-click the **Local Area Connection** icon and then click **Properties** in the shortcut menu. The Local Area Connection Properties dialog box opens.

4. Click **Install**. The Select Network Component Type dialog box opens.

5. Click **Protocol** in the list of Network Component Types.

6. Click **Add**. The Select Network Protocol dialog box opens.

7. In the list of network protocols, click **NetBEUI Protocol**, then click **OK**. Notice that NetBEUI now appears in the list of network components.

8. Click **Close**. The Local Area Connection Properties dialog box closes and your changes are saved.

9. To verify that the NetBEUI protocol was installed, right-click the **Local Area Connection** icon and click **Properties**. The Properties dialog box appears.

10. Verify that the NetBEUI Protocol appears in the list of installed protocols.

11. Click **Cancel** to close the Network dialog box.

Project 7-3

In this project, you discover two ways of finding your computer's MAC address, also known as its physical address. For this exercise, you need a workstation running the Windows 2000 Professional operating system and the TCP/IP protocols connected to a Windows 2000 server. You also need a screwdriver that fits the workstation's cover screws, if the computer's cover is attached with screws.

1. On the Windows 2000 workstation, click **Start**, point to **Programs**, point to **Accessories**, and then click **Command Prompt**. The Command Prompt window opens with a cursor blinking at the C:\> prompt.

2. Type **ipconfig /all** then press **Enter**.

3. A list of your Windows 2000 IP Configuration and Ethernet adapter Local Area Connection parameters appears. Search the list for the Physical Address parameter. This 12-digit hexadecimal number is your NIC's MAC address.

4. Type **exit** and press **Enter** to close the Command Prompt window.

5. Log off the network and shut down your workstation.

6. If necessary, use the screwdriver to remove the screws that secure the workstation's housing. Ask your instructor for help if you can't find the correct screws. Usually there are three to five screws. In some cases, a computer housing may use no screws.

7. Remove the cover from the rest of the CPU.

8. If a cable is connected to your NIC, remove the cable.

9. With the computer open, remove the screw that holds the NIC in place. Gently remove the NIC from its place in the computer's motherboard.

10. In most cases, a NIC's MAC address is printed on a small white sticker attached to the NIC; alternatively, it may be stamped directly on the NIC itself. Find the MAC address and compare it to the one you discovered in Step 3.

11. Reinsert the NIC into its slot so that it is secure and replace the screw that holds it in.

12. Replace the computer's cover and the screws that fasten it to the CPU.

Project 7-4

This project introduces the PING (Packet Internet Groper) utility, which can be used to verify that TCP/IP is running, correctly configured, and communicating with the network. A ping test is typically the first thing network professionals try when troubleshooting a TCP/IP connection problem. The process of sending out a signal is known as pinging. You can ping either an IP address or a host name. (You learn more about PING and other diagnostic TCP/IP utilities in Chapter 12.)

To complete this project, you need a workstation running Windows 2000 Professional that has the TCP/IP protocol installed and that is connected to a Windows 2000 server with Internet access.

1. Click **Start**, then click **Run**. The Run dialog box opens.

2. In the Open text box, type **cmd**, then click **OK**. The Command Prompt window opens.

3. At the DOS prompt, type **ping 127.0.0.1**, and then press **Enter**. (Remember that 127.0.0.1 is the loopback address.) If your workstation is properly connected to the network, you should see a screen that contains five lines. The first line should read "Pinging 127.0.0.1 with 32 bytes of data." Following that, you should see four lines that begin "Reply from 127.0.0.1." If you do not see four positive reply lines, or if you see four lines with the words "Request timed out," check the syntax of your ping command. If you typed the command correctly, check the status of your TCP/IP protocol. Is it properly installed and configured? To reinstall TCP/IP, follow the steps mentioned in Project 7-2 for installing protocols.

4. Because you received these replies to your loopback ping test, you know that your TCP/IP services are installed correctly. The loopback test, however, doesn't indicate whether your workstation can successfully transmit and receive data over the network. In the next step, you try a ping test that can help you determine whether your computer is successfully connected to and can exchange data with the Internet.

5. At the DOS prompt, type **ping www.cisco.com**, and then press **Enter**.

6. What was the response? If you received a "Request timed out" message, why might you have received it? If you received a valid response, with four lines of replies, note the TTL. Why does it differ from the TTL observed when you pinged the loopback address?

7. Type **exit** at the C:\>prompt and press **Enter** to close the window.

CASE PROJECTS

1. You have been asked to consult with a new accounting firm, Wilson and Hayden, about networks. The firm is led by a manager, Laura Hayden, and staffed with 10 accountants. Because they are just planning their office's opening, they haven't purchased any computer equipment yet. In fact, they don't know much about computers at all. Laura has asked you for advice on setting up a network. Before meeting with her, write a list of questions that you plan to ask in order to better determine the services and protocols that should run on the Wilson and Hayden network.

2. As your meeting with Laura gets underway, she questions you about which printers she should purchase for each of the accountants on staff. Explain to her the advantages of client-server networking, and how this pertains to her staff's printing needs. Also describe what type of computer she might consider purchasing as a server, and how this computer will differ from her staff's desktop computers.

3. Laura stresses the importance of connecting her firm's network to the Internet. How does this information affect the protocol that you would recommend using on Wilson and Hayden's network, if at all? Laura is concerned about keeping network maintenance to a minimum. So what type of addressing do you recommend for this protocol. Why?

8

PHYSICAL TRANSMISSION MEDIA

> **After reading this chapter and completing the exercises, you will be able to:**
>
> ♦ Identify the characteristics of wireline transmission
> ♦ Describe the properties and uses of coaxial cable
> ♦ Describe the properties and uses of different types of twisted-pair wire
> ♦ Identify the characteristics of lightwave transmission
> ♦ Describe the properties and uses of fiber optic cable
> ♦ Identify factors to consider when selecting a telecommunications medium
> ♦ Explain and apply cabling standards
> ♦ Describe best practices for installing wire and fiber optic cabling
> ♦ Identify techniques for testing the continuity and performance of physical transmission media

Many seasoned telecommunications technicians agree that the majority of network errors are caused by Physical layer and cabling problems. However, problems with cabling aren't always obvious. For example, network users in one area of a building might experience occasional problems logging on to the network or sending e-mail messages. When you arrive to help troubleshoot the problem, however, it may not recur. Such intermittent data transfer problems could be a sign of poor cabling—perhaps a cable run has exceeded its maximum length limit, been pinched under a cable tie, or loosened from its termination in the telecommunications closet. The best defense against such problems is to install cables properly in the first place. The best answer to problems once they occur is a thorough working knowledge of cable properties, standards, and troubleshooting methods.

CHARACTERISTICS OF WIRELINE TRANSMISSION

In Chapter 2, you learned how electricity travels over circuits and, in the context of telecommunications, creates signals that convey information. Because principles of electricity affect transmission over wire-based media, it is necessary to have a clear understanding of current, voltage, resistance, noise, and attenuation to fully comprehend how signals propagate over physical media. By now, you should also understand throughput and bandwidth and the difference between them. If you have forgotten these concepts from Chapter 2, you should review them before attempting to master the material in this chapter.

In addition to these concepts, several other media and signaling characteristics affect wireline transmission. The following sections describe some of the most significant characteristics you should consider before choosing, installing, or maintaining cables. A discussion of all the potential factors affecting wireline transmission is beyond the scope of this book.

The terms "wire" and "cable" are used synonymously in some situations. Strictly speaking, however, "wire" is a subset of "cabling" because the "cabling" category may also include fiber optic cable, which is almost never called "wire." The exact meaning of the term "wire" depends on context. For example, if you said, in a somewhat casual way, "Since that power spike, nothing's getting through the wire," you would be referring to whatever transmission media helped carry the data—whether fiber, radio waves, coax, or UTP.

Impedance

One important wireline transmission characteristic is impedance. **Impedance**, expressed in ohms, is the combined effect of a circuit's inductance and capacitance. In the case of a DC circuit, the impedance equals the circuit's resistance. Plainly speaking, impedance is a measure of how much opposition current will experience as it traverses the medium. As with resistance, a wire's impedance depends on many factors, including the type of conductor it uses (for example, copper), the quality and size of the wire, and the type of insulation that surrounds the wire.

Impedance is not necessarily problematic, as long as it matches the cable's rated impedance and is consistent throughout a communications channel. However, when a signal encounters changes in impedance, part of the signal reflects back toward its source just as light reflects when it hits a mirror. Small amounts of reflection may not result in noticeable data errors. But, significant reflection of one signal will interfere with subsequent signals attempting to traverse the same wire, resulting in signal loss. **Loss**, in the context of signaling, is a measure of the reduction in strength (or amplitude) of a signal compared to its strength when it was transmitted. The more loss a signal experiences on its way to a destination, the more difficult it is to interpret. The type of loss caused by impedance mismatches is known as **return loss**. Return loss represents the strength of the reflected parts of a signal compared to the strength of the signal as it was originally transmitted. If return loss is high, transmission errors result. In that case, the source may have to retransmit the signal. A high volume of retransmittals causes performance to degrade. Thus, impedance changes in a communications channel contribute to the degradation of a signal. Conversely, if the impedance along a communications channel remains constant, signals travel more efficiently and experience fewer data transmission errors.

A small amount of impedance change is inevitable in a network. It occurs each time a cable terminates or connects with a device or another cable. It also occurs in twisted-pair cables whose twists are not uniform throughout (thus making the case for purchasing higher quality cables whose manufacturing processes guarantee more uniformity). But, larger impedance anomalies arise if cables are improperly terminated (for example, if a wire isn't seated tightly in its connector) or if two cables with different impedance characteristics are spliced together. Impedance anomalies also occur if a network cable is damaged, kinked, or bent sharply. To minimize such changes in impedance, cables should be properly installed according to cabling standards. They must also be securely terminated and connected. Later in this chapter, you learn best practices for cable installation.

Another way to address impedance changes, and the resulting signal degradation, is simply to boost signals along their transmission route. This tactic was used by the Bell System in the mid-twentieth century. To overcome impedance changes in the public telephone system, Bell made liberal use of the transistor, which provides an inexpensive way to amplify signals. Note that simply boosting a signal does not address the causes of impedance mismatches. However, it does help to ensure that a signal reaches its destination in an intelligible form.

As you learn more about different wireline media and connectors, you will learn about their impedance characteristics.

Propagation Delay and Latency

In an ideal world, networks could transmit data instantaneously between sender and receiver, no matter how great the distance between them. Unfortunately, we don't live in an ideal world, and every signal is subjected to a delay between its transmission and its eventual receipt. For example, when you press a key on your computer to save a file to the network, the file's data must travel through your NIC, the network wire, through at least one connectivity device, more cabling, and the server's NIC before it lands on the server's hard disk. Although electrons travel rapidly, they still have to travel, and a brief delay takes place between the moment you press the key and the moment the server accepts the data. The difference in time between a data packet's transmission and its reception over a specific route is known as **propagation delay**. For example, if you send an e-mail message to a colleague, and your NIC issues the first data packet at 9:05:46 a.m. and the hub to which your workstation is connected receives the packet at 9:05:50 p.m., the propagation delay is four seconds. Of course, networks operate much faster than this; therefore, propagation delay is typically expressed in milliseconds (thousandths of a second) or microseconds (millionths of a second).

8

Propagation delay is mainly affected by the distance between a source and a destination. On telephone networks, propagation delay significantly affects calls carried via satellite links or transoceanic cables. If you call someone on another continent, you may experience propagation delay as having to wait a small amount of time before the other party acknowledges your communication. All phone connections experience some degree of delay. However, in local telephone calls, this delay is too brief to notice.

Propagation delay is one factor that contributes to a data or voice network's latency. In telecommunications, **latency** refers to the amount of time it takes a bit of data to traverse a network link. (In other areas of computing, latency may refer to the time required by other functions, for example, a processor loading a file into temporary memory.) Whereas propagation delay refers to the delay in the progress of current or light over a medium, latency also includes the time it takes a server to process or a router to interpret data, for example. Different devices and network types affect latency to different degrees. For example, modems, which must modulate both incoming and outgoing signals, increase a connection's latency far more than hubs, which simply repeat a signal.

Latency is most problematic when a receiving node is expecting some type of communication, such as the rest of a data stream it has begun to accept. If that node does not receive the rest of the data stream, it assumes that no more data is coming. This assumption causes transmission errors on a network. When you connect multiple networks, you increase the latency affecting transmissions between those networks. This makes sense because by connecting networks, you lengthen the communications channel and increase the number of devices through which signals travel.

The most common way to measure latency on data networks is by calculating a packet's **round trip time (RTT)**, or the length of time it takes for a packet to go from sender to receiver, then back from receiver to sender. As with propagation delay, RTT is usually measured in milliseconds. Additional factors besides propagation delay contribute to latency; however, further discussion is beyond the scope of this book.

Distortion

Another category of transmission flaws that affect wireline signals is distortion. **Distortion** is the unintended and undesirable modification of at least one signal component, which makes the signal different from how it was originally transmitted. Many forms of distortion can affect telecommunications transmissions. For example, distortion may occur through changes in a wave's phase, amplitude, or frequency. In this section, you learn about two types of distortion significant to telecommunications: attenuation distortion and delay distortion.

In Chapter 2, you learned that attenuation is the loss of signal strength as it moves away from its source. Further, you learned that attenuation increases with increasing distance (which is why repeaters and amplifiers are necessary to repeat or boost a signal after a certain distance). Attenuation also affects signals with different frequencies differently. Higher frequencies experience more rapid attenuation than lower frequencies. Thus, in waveform signals (in other words, in analog signals or modulated digital signals), the signal components that depend on higher frequencies experience more attenuation over the same communications channel than the components that depend on lower frequencies. The resulting differences in attenuation are known as **attenuation distortion**. Attenuation distortion affects analog signals more than it affects digital signals. It is measured in decibels (dB).

Just as a signal's attenuation varies according to its frequency, its propagation speed also varies according to its frequency. Frequencies in the middle of the transmitted range tend to travel faster than frequencies at the edges of the transmitted range. As a result, signal components follow different frequencies arrive out of phase, a phenomenon known as **delay distortion** (also known as **envelope delay distortion** or **phase distortion**). Because delay distortion is a function of propagation delay, it also varies with the length of a wire. In fact, most data networks have established length limits that help to prevent delay distortion (and attenuation) from impacting transmission. Delay distortion is measured in microseconds.

Delay distortion affects all analog or modulated digital signals that traverse a wire. In analog voice communications, such as an average telephone conversation, delay distortion is not noticeable because the human ear is not sensitive enough to detect phase differences within a range of voice frequencies. However, in digital communications, delay distortion can significantly degrade a signal's quality. For example, consider phase shift keying (PSK), the modulation technique often used by many high-speed data modems. In this modulation scheme, each bit is represented by a change in phase (refer to Figure 6-8 as a reminder of this technique). Because delay distortion causes signals to arrive out of phase, in PSK, signal energy from one bit can spill onto the other bit's position, potentially changing the meaning of the signal. As a result, erroneous data may be transmitted, requiring correction or retransmittal.

Distortion is countered through the use of components called equalizers. In the case of attenuation distortion, equalizers add amplitude (or gain) to the signal frequencies most susceptible to loss. In the case of delay distortion, equalizers artificially delay the frequencies most susceptible to this distortion. In other words, they equalize different parts of the signal so that data is received in sync. Equalizers are usually present at both the sending and receiving ends of a transmission. For example, modems used in high-speed data communications contain equalizers.

Noise

In Chapter 2, you learned that noise is any unwanted interference from external sources, which can degrade or distort a signal. It may manifest as electromagnetic interference (EMI) or radio frequency interference (RFI). Well-known sources of noise include motors, fluorescent lights, and broadcast towers. However, less obvious environmental influences, including heat, can also cause noise. Noise affects and can be harmful to both analog and digital signals. It can be categorized into several different types, including crosstalk, intermodulation noise, impulse noise, and thermal noise. Note that all forms of noise are measured in decibels (dB).

8

Crosstalk

Crosstalk occurs when signals traveling on one wire infringe on a nearby wire's signal. As you learned in Chapter 2, current traveling on one wire can influence current on an adjacent wire by generating an electromagnetic field, a process known as induction. Thus, crosstalk is the result of induction between transmission wires. It is a common form of noise on wires or cables that are strung close to other wires or cables. Figure 8-1 illustrates how crosstalk occurs between wires.

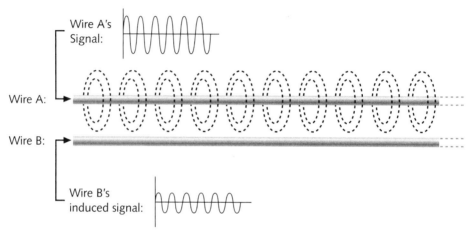

Figure 8-1 Crosstalk between wires

If you have ever been on the phone and heard the conversation on your second line in the background, you have heard the effects of crosstalk. In this example, current carrying a signal on the second line's wire pair imposes itself on the wire pair carrying your line's signal. The resulting noise, or crosstalk, shares the properties of the signal carried by the second line. Crosstalk in the form of overlapping phone conversations is bothersome, but does not usually prevent you from hearing your own line's conversation. In data networks, however, crosstalk can be extreme enough to prevent the accurate delivery of data.

Several different types of crosstalk may affect a signal. One form of crosstalk, called **alien crosstalk**, occurs when signals from adjacent cables (as opposed to adjacent wires) interfere with another cable's transmission. Alien crosstalk becomes a real threat when network administrators bundle several cables into small conduits. We discuss other forms of crosstalk in the discussion of twisted-pair cabling later in this chapter.

Proper cable installation is the best way to limit crosstalk on a network. Such techniques include leaving sufficient space between cables, inserting insulating materials between cables, or surrounding wires within the cables with thicker insulation. Later in this chapter, you learn about proper cable installation.

Intermodulation Noise

Less common than crosstalk is a form of noise called **intermodulation noise**. Recall that some communication channels carry multiple signals through the use of modulation. For example, frequency modulation is used to carry FM radio signals through the air. If the carrier frequencies used for modulation are too close together, their signals may mix. This mixing of one signal with another is a form of intermodulation noise. You may experience intermodulation noise if you listen to the radio and hear another station's signal impose on the signal of the station you set your radio to receive. On data networks, intermodulation noise may be caused by problems with transmission or reception equipment or distortion due to excessive signal strength.

Impulse Noise

Another form of noise is **impulse noise**. Impulse noise is unwanted signal energy that results from sudden spikes in electromagnetic activity. For example, if you are talking on the phone during a lightning storm, and a bolt of lightning strikes a few blocks from your house, you may hear a brief rush of static on the line. This static is impulse noise. Impulse noise affects transmission only briefly, as compared to other types of noise. However, its amplitude is generally higher than other types of noise, and thus, it may significantly distort a signal. Figure 8-2 illustrates how impulse noise affects analog and digital signals.

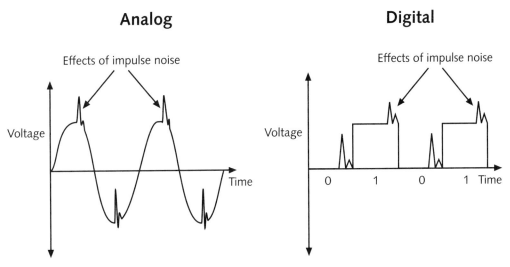

Figure 8-2   Impulse noise affecting analog and digital signals

Thermal Noise

A type of noise that affects signals evenly and consistently is **thermal noise** (also known as **white noise**). Thermal noise occurs when heat or a change in temperature agitates the electrons inside the wire, making them unstable. Figure 8-3 depicts thermal noise affecting both analog and digital signals. Notice how the noise affects all parts of the signals evenly. Thermal noise cannot be eliminated, as it is a natural part of the environment. Engineers compensate for thermal noise by ensuring that the transmitted signal is significantly higher than the noise.

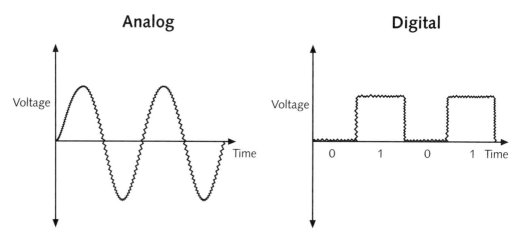

Figure 8-3   Thermal noise affecting analog and digital signals

Bear in mind that one wire (and thus any signal it carries) may be subject to any one or all of the aforementioned types of noise at once. In addition, it may be subject to the transmission flaws you learned about previously, including attenuation, latency, and delay distortion.

Signal-to-Noise Ratio

Sometimes, the level of noise that a communications channel experiences is significant enough to impair the signal. A signal's strength in relationship to the strength of the noise it experiences is known as its **signal-to-noise ratio** (**S/N** or **SNR**). Signal-to-noise ratio is measured in decibels (dB). The higher the signal-to-noise ratio, the clearer the signal.

One way to increase the signal-to-noise ratio is to increase the power of a signal during transmission. Another way to optimize S/N is to make sure a cable is properly grounded. Later in this chapter, you learn techniques for designing and installing cabling systems aimed at limiting the potential for noise. Next, you learn a technique that limits the noise affecting a signal.

Filtering

The most obvious solution to noise is to prevent it from occurring. However, noise cannot be entirely predicted or eliminated. The next best solution is to prevent noise from impairing a signal. One way to accomplish this is through filtering. **Filtering** is the process of modifying a signal so that certain parts of it (in this case, the noise) are removed. One type of filter, a **bandpass filter**, prevents frequencies outside the data-carrying range from being transmitted or received. The result is that only the frequencies carrying data are transmitted or received, and the signal more closely resembles its original form. A bandpass filter may also boost the signal. Thus, due to both its noise reduction and signal amplification, a bandpass filter increases the signal-to-noise ratio. Filters may be present at the transmitting end, the receiving end, or both ends of a communications channel. For example, they are included on high-speed modems used in data communications.

Now that you have added to your knowledge of wireline transmission characteristics, you are ready to learn about three categories of physical media: coaxial cable, copper cable, and fiber optic cable.

COAXIAL CABLE

Coaxial cable, called "coax" for short, was the foundation for cable television systems and data networks in the 1980s and remained a popular transmission medium for many years. Over time, however, twisted-pair cabling (discussed later in this chapter) has replaced coax in most modern LANs. Coaxial cable still forms the foundation for the infrastructure that supplies cable TV and more recently, data signals to many residences.

Coaxial cable consists of a central copper core surrounded by an insulator, a foil or braided metal shielding called **braiding**, and an outer cover called the **sheath** or jacket. Figure 8-4 depicts a typical coaxial cable. The copper core carries the electromagnetic signal, and the braided metal shielding acts as both a shield against noise and a ground for the signal. The insulator layer usually consists of a plastic material, such as polyvinyl chloride (PVC) or Teflon. It protects the copper core from the metal shielding, because if the two made contact, the wire would short-circuit. The jacket, which protects the cable from physical damage, may be PVC or a more expensive, fire-resistant plastic.

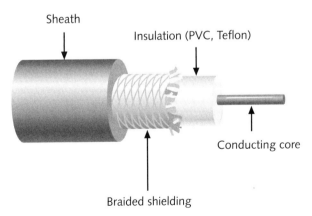

Sheath

Insulation (PVC, Teflon)

Conducting core

Braided shielding

Figure 8-4   Coaxial cable

Because of its insulation and protective braiding, coaxial cable has a high resistance to interference from noise. It can also carry signals farther than twisted-pair cabling before amplification of the signals becomes necessary, although not as far as fiber optic cabling. On the other hand, coaxial cable is more expensive than twisted-pair cable because it requires significantly more raw materials (such as copper for the core, Teflon for the insulation, and so on) to manufacture. Coaxial cable is also less desirable than twisted-pair because in most cases, it supports lower throughput.

Coaxial cabling comes in many specifications, each of which is suited to a unique purpose. All types have been assigned an RG specification number. (RG stands for "radio guide," which is appropriate because coaxial cabling is used to guide radio frequencies.) The significant differences between the cable types lie in the materials used for their center cores, which in turn influence their impedance, throughput, and typical usage. Hundreds of types of coaxial cables exist.

A few types of coaxial cable were used in early data networking: RG-8 and RG-58A/U. Two types are currently used as the last mile for cable TV (and now cable Internet access) installations: RG-59 and RG-6. Because of their different impedance characteristics, you must use the specific type of coaxial cable suited to your purpose. For example, you can not remove the cable that's connected to your home TV, and use it to connect two workstations on a LAN. Doing so causes return loss and, potentially, intermodulation noise. At best, this results in poor data transmission. At worst, it could damage sensitive electronic equipment.

COPPER CABLE

Copper cabling used in voice and data communications consists of color-coded pairs of insulated copper wires, each with a diameter of 0.3 to 0.8 mm. Such copper wire is also known by its American Wire Gauge (AWG) rating. Cable with an AWG rating of 22-28 is commonly used for wires in telecommunications technologies. 22 AWG is approximately .7 mm in diameter, whereas 28 AWG is approximately .3 mm in diameter.

Non-twisted Wire

Until the last few years, traditional telephone wiring used a simple cable containing four insulated copper wires surrounded by a plastic sheath. The four wires may conform to any AWG rating, but are typically 22 to 26 AWG. This type of cable is known to telecommunications technicians as **quad wire**. More formally, it is called **Level 1** cabling (though no organization officially maintains standards for this designation). Because of its low resistance to noise, Level 1 cabling is only appropriate for carrying analog (voice) signals. It is also best used for relatively short connections (for example, from a home's demarcation point to a telephone extension 50 feet away). Although it still works with the PSTN, Level 1 cabling is no longer installed in new homes. This is because more and more, inside wiring is expected to carry data communications or multiple voice lines, and as you will learn later in this section, such applications demand higher-quality copper cable.

Most Level 1 wires are colored red, green, yellow, and black (although this varies from one installation to the next). Recall from Chapter 5 that in telephony, the wire that carries voltage is known as the ring, whereas the ground wire is known as the tip. In a Level 1 cable, the red wire is the ring (used for signaling in the first pair) and the green wire is the tip (used for a ground) in the first pair. If a second line is used, the yellow wire is the ring in the second pair, whereas the black wire is the tip in the second pair. Figure 8-5 depicts a common Level 1 cable, with its tip and ring wires labeled.

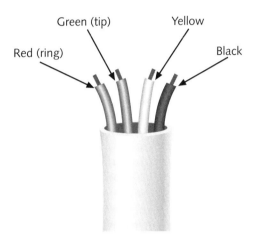

Figure 8-5   Level 1 cable

Level 1 cable terminates in an RJ-11 connector (also known as a jack, or modular plug). You learned about RJ-11 connectors in Chapter 5, which discussed CPE and inside wiring (refer to Figure 5-5 for a simple view of both quad wire and an RJ-11 connector). The individual wire terminations within a connector are called **pinouts**, because pins inside the connector are crimped (or pierced) into the conducting wire. Figure 8-6 illustrates how Level 1 wire is terminated in an RJ-11 connector containing four pins (other RJ-11 connectors may have two or six pins).

Although Level 1 cable is sufficient for analog voice signals, digital communications require a more sophisticated type of copper cable, known as twisted-pair.

Twisted-Pair (TP)

In a **twisted-pair** cable, each two wires are twisted around each other to form pairs. Each different pair is twisted slightly more or less than the next pair. However, the twists within a pair are consistent throughout the cable. All the pairs are collectively encased in a plastic sheath.

Pin number: 1 2 3 4

Pin 1 = Tip (ground), pair 2 (if used)
Pin 2 = Tip (ground), pair 1
Pin 3 = Ring (signal), pair 1
Pin 4 = Ring (signal), pair 2 (if used)

Figure 8-6   Level 1 terminations in an RJ-11 connector

Twisted-pair cable is the most common medium for telephone local loops. It is also the most popular medium for connecting nodes on modern LANs. Twisted-pair cable may contain from 1 to 4200 wire pairs. Cables with over 1000 twisted pairs are used primarily for branch or main feeder routes in a telephone company's outside plant. As you learned in Chapter 4, a cable containing 3600 pairs is a common type of main feeder cable. Traditional consumer telephone wire and network cables installed in the 1980s contain two twisted pairs: one pair for signal transmission and another pair for signal reception. Newer data network cables and telephone wire installed during construction today typically contain at least four twisted pairs, with more than one wire pair both sending and transmitting data simultaneously. Figure 8-7 depicts a modern twisted-pair cable with four wire pairs.

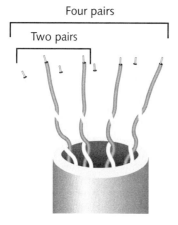

Four pairs

Two pairs

Figure 8-7   Twisted-pair cable

The twists in the wire are designed to reduce the effects of crosstalk. The specific type of crosstalk that occurs within twisted pairs—in other words, in which one wire in the pair affects the other wire—is known as **near-end crosstalk (NeXT)**. If you envision the wire pairs in a single cable as couples in an elevator, you can imagine how one couple speaking very loudly might impair the other couple's ability to converse. Because they are twisted around each other, the release of current from one wire helps to cancel the imposing current from the adjacent wire. Even just one twist between wires every foot reduces near-end crosstalk.

The more twists per inch in a pair of wires, the more resistant the pair is to all forms of noise. Higher-quality, more expensive twisted-pair cable contains more twists per foot. The number of twists per meter or foot is known as the **twist ratio**. Because twisting the wire pairs more tightly requires more cable, however, a high twist ratio can result in greater attenuation (because the signal path is longer in a cable with tightly twisted pairs than it is in a cable with loosely twisted pairs). For optimal performance, cable manufacturers must strike a balance between crosstalk and attenuation reduction.

Because twisted-pair is used in such a wide variety of environments and for a variety of purposes, it comes in hundreds of different designs. Such designs vary in the type of materials used for each part of the cable and in their twist ratio. As a result, the designs also vary in attenuation, crosstalk, impedance, noise immunity, and other wireline transmission characteristics. Twisted-pair cable is relatively inexpensive, flexible, and easy to install, and it can span a significant distance before its signals must be repeated or amplified. Twisted-pair cable easily accommodates several different network designs. Furthermore, twisted-pair can handle the fast networking transmission rates currently being employed. Due to its wide acceptance, it will probably be updated to handle the even faster rates that will emerge in the future. One drawback to twisted-pair is that, because of its flexibility, it is more susceptible to physical damage than coaxial cable. This problem is a minor factor given its many benefits over other transmission media.

All twisted-pair cable falls into one of two categories—shielded twisted-pair (STP) or unshielded twisted-pair (UTP).

Shielded Twisted-Pair (STP)

As the name implies, **shielded twisted-pair (STP)** cable consists of twisted wire pairs that are not only individually insulated, but also surrounded by a shielding made of a metallic substance, such as foil. Some STP uses a braided metal shielding. The **shielding** acts as a barrier to external electromagnetic forces, thus preventing them from affecting the signals traveling over the wire inside the shielding. The shielding may be grounded to enhance its protective effect. The effectiveness of STP's shield depends on the level and type of environmental noise, the thickness and material used for the shield, the grounding mechanism, and the symmetry and consistency of the shielding. Figure 8-8 depicts an STP cable.

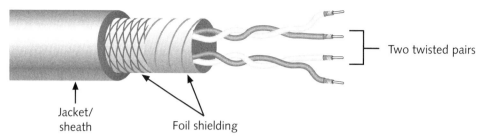

Figure 8-8   STP cable

Unshielded Twisted-Pair (UTP)

Unshielded twisted-pair (UTP) cabling consists of one or more insulated wire pairs encased in a plastic sheath. As its name implies, UTP does not contain additional shielding for the twisted pairs. As a result, UTP is both less expensive and less resistant to noise than STP. Figure 8-9 depicts a typical UTP cable.

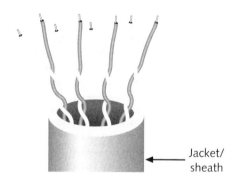

Figure 8-9   UTP cable

The organization responsible for setting twisted-pair standards is the Telecommunications Industry Association/Electronics Industry Alliance (TIA/EIA). The TIA/EIA 568 standard divides twisted-pair wiring into categories, with an individual category referred to as a CAT. The TIA/EIA 568 standard formally defines four types of UTP: CAT3, CAT4, CAT5, and CAT5e. However, manufacturers developing new types of UTP have added their own CAT6 and CAT7 definitions. Modern telephone lines use, at minimum, CAT3. Contemporary LANs and the most advanced telephony installations most frequently use CAT5 or higher wiring. To manage cabling, you need to be familiar with the standards that may be used on such modern networks, particularly CAT3, CAT5, and CAT7. The following list describes the types of UTP wire telecommunication professionals are most likely to encounter on the job.

- *Category 3 (CAT3)*—A form of UTP that typically contains four wire pairs of 22 to 24 AWG. CAT3 can carry up to 10 Mbps of data with a possible bandwidth of 16 MHz. It was used for networks until the mid-1990s, when CAT5 became the medium of choice. Network administrators are gradually replacing their existing CAT3 cabling with CAT5 to accommodate higher throughput. CAT3 is still used for telephone cabling, and is, in fact, the *minimum* standard recommended by the FCC for newly installed telephone lines. Figure 8-10 depicts a typical CAT3 telephone wire with its twisted pairs untwisted, allowing you to see the color coding and the functions of each wire. Notice that wires with solid colors are used for the ring and striped wires are used for the tip. This standard holds true even though the precise wire termination order may vary from one installation to another.

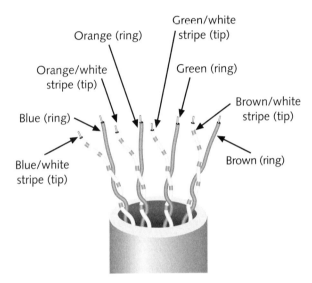

Figure 8-10   CAT3 UTP used in telephony

- *Category 5 (CAT5)*—CAT5 typically contains four wire pairs of 22 to 24 AWG and supports up to 100 Mbps throughput and a 100 MHz signal rate. It contains a higher grade of copper for its conductor and its pairs have a higher twist ratio than CAT3 pairs. It is the most popular medium in use on modern LANs. Figure 8-11 depicts a typical CAT5 UTP cable with its twisted pairs untwisted, allowing you to see their matched color coding. For example, the wire that is colored solid orange is twisted around the wire that is part orange and part white to form the pair responsible for transmitting data.

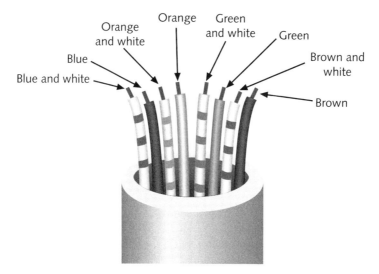

Figure 8-11   A CAT5 UTP used in networking

Most cables have small lettering on their sheaths that indicate the cable's Category, manufacturer, and other specifications. However, some older or less expensive cables do not. Therefore, you may not be able to tell the difference between a CAT3 and CAT5 cable simply by looking at them. Some visual clues can help you decide, however. Because CAT5 almost always has lettering on its jacket, a blank jacket is apt to indicate CAT3. Also, CAT5 wire pairs are twisted more tightly than CAT3 wire pairs. According to TIA/EIA standards, CAT3 may have a twist ratio as low as 3 twists per foot while CAT5 must have at least twelve twists per foot.

- *Enhanced Category 5 (CAT5e)*—A higher-grade version of CAT5 wiring that contains high-quality copper, offers a high twist ratio, and uses advanced methods for reducing crosstalk. Enhanced CAT5 can support a signaling rate as high as 200 MHz, double the capability of regular CAT5.

- *Category 6 (CAT6)*—A twisted-pair cable that typically contains four wire pairs of 22 to 24 AWG, each wrapped in foil insulation. Additional foil insulation covers the bundle of wire pairs, and a fire-resistant plastic sheath covers the second foil layer. The foil insulation provides excellent resistance to crosstalk and enables CAT6 to support at least six times the throughput supported by regular CAT5. Because it is new and because most network technologies cannot exploit its superlative capacity, CAT6 is rarely encountered in today's networks.

- *Category 7 (CAT7)*—A twisted-pair cable that contains multiple wire pairs of 22 to 24 AWG, each surrounded by its own shielding, then packaged in additional shielding beneath the jacket. Although standards have not yet been finalized for CAT7, some cable supply companies are selling it and organizations are installing it. One advantage to CAT7 cabling is that it can support signal rates up to 1 GHz. However, it requires different connectors than other versions of UTP because its twisted pairs must be more isolated from each other to ward off crosstalk. Because of its added shielding, CAT7 cabling is also larger and less flexible than other versions of UTP cable. For the same reasons that CAT6 is not typically found on modern networks, CAT7 is also rare.

 Technically, because CAT6 and CAT7 contain wires that are individually shielded, they are not unshielded twisted-pair. Instead, they are more similar to shielded twisted-pair.

Now that you have learned about characteristics of wireline transmission and the cabling that uses such transmission, you are ready to learn about a different way of transmitting signals—sending pulses of light over fiber optic cable.

8

CHARACTERISTICS OF LIGHTWAVE TRANSMISSION

In contrast to wires, which carry signals as voltage, transmission over fiber optic cable carries discreet pulses of light. And unlike electrical pulses traveling over copper, the light experiences virtually no resistance over the fiber. Therefore, lightwave signals can be reliably transmitted at faster rates than voltage-based signals. In fact, a pure glass strand can accept up to 1 billion laser light pulses per second. And because fiber does not conduct electrical current to transmit signals, it is unaffected by either EMI or RFI. Its impressive noise resistance is one reason why fiber can span such long distances before it requires repeaters to regenerate its signal. Still, lightwave transmission is not perfect. This section introduces some important concepts that you should understand before working with fiber optic cable.

You may already be familiar with the properties of light as it travels. Once it is emitted from a source (for example, the sun, a light bulb, or a candle), light naturally travels in a straight line unless it encounters matter. When light hits something, its rays may be affected one of three ways: they may be reflected, absorbed, or refracted. In reflection, the light bounces off the object. In absorption, the light is absorbed by the object. For example, if you wear a black shirt on a sunny day, your shirt absorbs the sun's light. In refraction, the light passes through the object, but the direction its rays travel are changed as a result. An example of refraction can be seen when you dip a spoon into a tub of water and the spoon appears to be bent below the water line.

Fiber optic cable is designed to take advantage of light's tendency to reflect. However, it must also be designed to account for refraction and absorption, both of which can cause attenuation, delay distortion, and loss. The extent to which a lightwave signal weakens along a length of fiber optic cable is known as **optical loss**. Optical loss is a greater concern to common carriers (such as long-distance telephone companies) and cable TV operators, whose cables traverse long distances, than it is to private data network operators, whose cables traverse shorter distances. Besides the cable's design, good cabling practices, including clean connections, little bending, and the absence of dust, heat, moisture, or pressure on the fiber, help reduce refraction and absorption. By reducing the refraction and absorption of light, these practices also limit the transmission flaws. Next, you learn how fiber optic cable carries data in the form of light.

 Because small particles so severely affect the transmission of light, when a fiber optic connection is suffering performance problems, one of the first things that telecommunications technicians check is the cleanliness of the connection. Cleaning the tip of a fiber optic connector and the receptor into which it is inserted can be a quick way to dramatically improve performance.

FIBER OPTIC CABLE

Fiber optic cable, or simply *fiber*, contains one or several glass fibers in its **core**. Data is transmitted via pulsing light sent from a laser or light-emitting diode (LED) through the central fibers. Surrounding the fibers is a layer of glass called **cladding**. The cladding glass is a different density from the glass in the strands. It acts as a mirror, reflecting light back to the core in patterns that vary depending on the transmission mode. This reflection allows the fiber to bend around corners without diminishing the integrity of the light-based signal. Outside the cladding, a plastic buffer protects the glass cladding and core. Because it is opaque, it also absorbs any light that might escape. To prevent the cable from stretching, and to further protect the inner core, strands of Kevlar (an advanced polymeric fiber) surround the plastic buffer. Finally, a plastic sheath covers the strands of Kevlar. Figure 8-12 shows the different layers of a fiber optic cable.

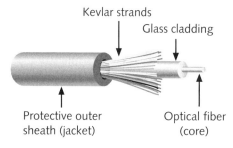

Figure 8-12 A fiber-optic cable

Like twisted-pair cable, fiber comes in a number of different types. Fiber cable variations fall into two categories: single-mode and multimode. **Single-mode fiber** uses a narrow core (between 8 and 10 microns in diameter) through which light generated by a laser travels over one path. Single-mode fiber generally has a graded index of refraction, which means that the glass changes as one moves in all directions outward from the core so that light pulses are refracted back to the core. This refraction, in addition to the single path, means that the light does not disperse as the signal travels along the fiber. This continuity allows single-mode fiber to accommodate high bandwidths and long distances before requiring repeaters. Single-mode fiber may be used to connect a carrier's two facilities. However, it costs too much to be considered for use on typical data networks. **Multimode fiber** contains a core with a larger diameter than single-mode fiber (between 50 and 100 microns in diameter) over which many pulses of light generated by a light emitting diode (LED) travel at different angles. Because light is being reflected many different ways in a multimode fiber cable, the waves become less easily distinguishable the longer they travel. Thus, multimode fiber is best suited for shorter distances than single-mode fiber. It is commonly found on cables that connect devices on the backbone of a network. Figure 8-13 depicts the differences in transmission between single-mode and multimode fiber.

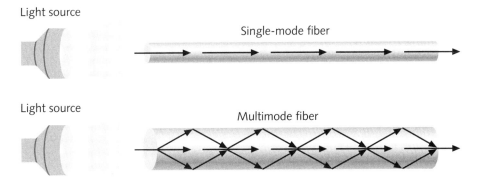

Figure 8-13   Single-mode and multimode fiber-optic cables

Fiber optic cable provides the benefits of nearly unlimited throughput, very high resistance to noise, and excellent inherent security. Because fiber does not conduct electricity like copper wire, it does not emit a current. As a result, the signals it carries stay within the fiber and cannot easily be picked up except at the destination node. Copper, on the other hand, generates a signal that can be monitored by taps into the network.

Fiber can also carry signals for longer distances than can coax or twisted-pair cable. Its overall network length benefits from its need for fewer repeaters than a copper-based network requires. Recommended network length limits vary depending on the type of fiber optic cable used. For multimode fiber, TIA/EIA recommends a length of up to 1 km before a repeater is necessary to repeat the signal. For single-mode fiber, the limit is between 2 km and 25 km, depending on the method of network transmission. Compare these lengths to the recommended 100 meters for a twisted-pair network. In addition, fiber is widely accepted by the high-speed networking industry. Thus, industry groups are establishing standards to ensure that fiber networking equipment from multiple manufacturers can be integrated without difficulty.

The most significant drawback to the use of fiber is its high cost. Fiber is the most expensive type of cable available. The cost of running fiber to every desktop and telephone in an organization is currently prohibitive; consequently, fiber is typically used only for long-distance transmission or network backbones that must bear extraordinary amounts of traffic. Not only is the cable itself more expensive than metal cabling, but connecting individual nodes via fiber optic cable requires installing different types of telephones and workstations. Such fiber optic terminal equipment and connectivity devices can cost as much as five times more than the same type of equipment designed for UTP networks. In addition, hiring skilled fiber cable installers costs more than hiring twisted-pair cable installers. Another disadvantage is that fiber can transmit data in only one direction at a time; to overcome this drawback, each cable must contain at least two strands—one to send data and one to receive it.

Fiber's reliability and high throughput potential makes it well-suited to its original telecommunications purpose, as a cable that connects medium-to large-sized telecommunications carriers. In recent years, however, its cost has decreased to make it attractive for much smaller connections. Some examples of popular uses for fiber optic cable include connecting:

- Regional and local cable TV facilities

- Internet NAPs with other large telecommunications exchange points

- Central offices with other central offices

- Main feeders with central offices

- A telecommunications carrier's network with private LANs

- A telecommunications carrier's network with private switching systems, such as a PBX

- Several private LANs to form a MAN or WAN

- Nodes on a LAN or WAN used for special purposes, such as audio or video conferencing

Like twisted-pair and coaxial cabling, fiber optic cabling comes in a number of different varieties, depending on its intended use and the manufacturer. For example, one type of fiber optic cabling, the D series, is used for underground conduits to high-volume telecommunications carriers (such as AT&T or WorldCom). This cable may contain as many as 1000 fibers, contain pressurized air or gel, and be heavily sheathed, to prevent damage from environmental influences, such as water seepage. At the other end of the spectrum, shorter fiber optic cables for use on LANs may contain only two strands of fiber and be pliable enough to bend easily around corners.

SELECTING APPROPRIATE MEDIA

If you are charged with selecting the type of media for a telecommunications system, a number of practical considerations should come to mind. For example, if you work at a company that wants to provide videoconferencing between offices on its network, one of your primary considerations should be the throughput potential of the media you select. If you work in a brand new office with no existing infrastructure, you do not have to consider whether your selected medium will be compatible with the old media and devices. This section provides a broad view of the factors to consider when choosing telecommunications media.

The following media selection considerations apply to both wireline and wireless transmission media (covered in Chapter 9).

- *Existing Infrastructure*—Rarely does a telecommunications professional have the pleasure of designing a network from scratch. More likely, you will work on a network that has been in operation for many years. Such an environment probably contains many types of media and devices, all of varying ages and conditions. When choosing a transmission medium under these conditions, you must ensure that your selection will integrate well with what is already installed and working.

- *Throughput Potential*—Perhaps the most significant factor in choosing a transmission medium is throughput. As you have learned, the physical nature of every transmission media determines its potential throughput. For example, the maximum throughput allowed over a CAT3 cable is 10 Mbps, a CAT5 cable can handle at least 100 Mbps, whereas a fiber optic cable can handle over ten times the throughput of a CAT5 cable. On the other hand, if you are simply adding a new telephone wall jack to a room in your house, Level 1 cable is sufficient. Throughput requirements naturally depend on the maximum volume of signals your connections must carry at any single point in time. For example, if a network demands only 5 Mbps capacity between midnight and five a.m., but requires 89 Mbps at eight a.m., you must plan to install media that can accommodate at least 89 Mbps. The consequence of not doing so is to accept very slow network performance. Pure data transfer rates are not the only factor when gauging required throughput. As you have learned, noise and devices connected to the transmission media can further limit data flow. A noisy circuit spends more time compensating for the noise and therefore has fewer resources available for transmitting data. Thus, for optimal throughput, choose a high-quality medium with low susceptibility to noise.

- *Cost of Installation*—One cost to consider when selecting a transmission medium is the cost of the materials and labor required to install. Can you install the media yourself, or must you hire contractors to do it? Will you need to move walls or build new conduits or closets? Will you need to lease lines from a service provider? Also consider hidden costs. Although a vendor might quote you the cost per foot of a new type of network cabling, you might also have to upgrade some expensive hardware on your network in order to use that type of cabling. Thus, the cost of installing that cabling includes more than just the cost of the cabling itself. Not only do media costs depend on the hardware that already exists in a network, but they also depend on the length of your network and the cost of labor in your area (unless you plan to install the cable yourself). As you have learned, fiber optic cable is the most expensive medium to purchase, whereas unshielded twisted-pair is the least expensive medium. Fiber is also more expensive to install than twisted-pair cable, because of the special installation techniques and skills required. However, considering the increased number of signals a fiber optic cable can transmit in any given time period, it may in fact result in a lower cost per channel than copper wiring. Ideally, the cost of installation should be secondary to a medium's throughput potential and its ability to be integrated with an existing infrastructure.

■ *Cost of Maintenance*—Installation cost is only one type of cost associated with choosing a transmission medium. You must also consider the cost of the medium's ongoing maintenance—and how quickly it will need to be upgraded. One factor affecting maintenance cost is whether you can service the media yourself or must hire contractors to service it. Fiber optic cable is more likely to require outside help to maintain. On the other hand, an economic cabling installation (for example, the decision to reuse older UTP cabling) does not save any money if it is in constant need of repair or enhancement.

■ *Noise Immunity*—As you have learned, some media are more resistant to the effects of noise than others. For example, if you issue data signals on a bare copper wire, those signals are more susceptible to degradation by external EMI sources than signals traveling over a copper wire surrounded by insulation. The type of media least susceptible to noise is fiber optic cable, because it does not use electric current, but light waves, to conduct signals. Noise considerations are especially important in an environment where noise cannot be reduced—for example, a factory or a power plant.

■ *Security*—If your organization is concerned about intruders attempting to pick up your network's signals (for example, through wire-tapping), you want to choose the transmission media with the highest security. Fiber optic cabling is an excellent choice for this environment. Twisted-pair cabling offers the least protection against eavesdropping, because it has little shielding, and therefore, emits current equal to the signal it carries. Wireless transmission is also susceptible to eavesdropping. Note that the most effective security measures are not dependent on the choice of media, but rather on data encoding and transmission techniques, as you learn in Chapter 13.

- *Size and Scalability*—Each network is limited in size due to transmission flaws, such as attenuation, loss, and latency, which increase with length. Because of this relationship between transmission flaws and distances, different types of networks have different specifications for the number of nodes, the length of a **segment** (how far you can transmit a signal before it must be repeated or amplified), and the overall network length. Such specifications differ according to the medium used. For example, you learned earlier that multimode fiber can extend up to 1 km before the signals it carries must be repeated, whereas UTP can extend up to 100 meters. Current and potential network length, along with **scalability**—or the ease of extending a network—should factor into your media decision.

Table 8-1 compares the media you learned about in this chapter according to their throughput potential, costs, security, scalability, and noise immunity.

Table 8-1   Comparison of physical media

Media	Throughput Potential	Cost of Installation and Maintenance	Security	Scalability	Noise Immunity
Coaxial cable	Up to 10 Mbps	More expensive than twisted-pair cable, but less expensive than fiber	Fair security	In most cases, can extend longer than twisted-pair, but not as long as fiber optic cable before requiring repeaters (depending on transmission method used)	More noise-resistant than twisted-pair, but less noise-resistant than fiber
Shielded twisted-pair (STP)	Up to 1 Gbps, though typically used for up to 100 Mbps	Less expensive than coaxial cable or fiber, but more expensive than UTP	Fair security (not as good as coaxial cable, but better than twisted-pair)	Can extend farther than unshielded twisted-pair networks, but not as far as fiber optic networks	More noise-resistant than UTP, but less noise-resistant than coaxial cable or fiber

8

Table 8-1   Comparison of physical media (Continued)

Media	Throughput Potential	Cost of Installation and Maintenance	Security	Scalability	Noise Immunity
Unshielded twisted-pair (UTP)	Depending on the Category rating, from 128 Kbps to 1 Gbps, though typically used for up to 100 Mbps	The least expensive network medium	The poorest security of all wireline media	Can extend the shortest distance of all media before requiring a repeater; however, due to network design, adding nodes is usually simple	The least noise-resistant medium
Single-mode fiber optic cable	The highest throughput potential of all media; can handle fastest network speed available, 1 Gbps, and more	The highest cost of all network media	Excellent security	Can extend the longest of all media before requiring repeaters; can accommodate more nodes than coaxial or twisted-pair cable	Unaffected by noise
Multimode fiber optic cable	High throughput potential, but not as high as single-mode fiber; can handle fastest network speed available, 1 Gbps, and more	High cost media, second only to single-mode fiber	Excellent security	Can extend longer than twisted-pair or coaxial cable, but not as long as single-mode fiber before requiring repeaters; can accommodate more nodes than coaxial or twisted-pair cable	Unaffected by noise

CABLING STANDARDS

You have learned about several transmission flaws—attenuation, noise, distortion, and latency—that can be minimized by proper cable installation. Now that you know the characteristics and uses for different types of cables, you are ready to learn the best methods for installing these media. The following sections describe two industry standards for cable installations: the TIA/EIA standards and the NEC standards.

TIA/EIA Standards

In 1991, TIA/EIA released its joint 568 Commercial Building Wiring Standard, also known as **structured cabling**, for uniform, enterprise-wide, multivendor cabling systems. (**Enterprise-wide** refers to a network that spans an entire organization and often services the needs of many diverse users. It may include many locations, or it may be confined to one location.) This standard was based on structured cabling guidelines developed by AT&T in 1983. Today, it serves as a guide for installing all types of wiring in all types of buildings.

Structured cabling suggests how voice and data networking media can best be installed to maximize performance and minimize upkeep. It specifies standards without regard for the type of media or transmission technology used. Structured cabling is based on a hierarchical design that divides cabling into six subsystems, described in the following list. You should be familiar with the principles of structured cabling before you attempt to design, install, or troubleshoot an organization's cable plant. Figure 8-14 illustrates how the six subsystems fit together.

- *Entrance facilities*—The point at which a telecommunication carrier's media enters a building. At a LEC's POP, the entrance facility is where aggregated lines, such as the main feeder or interoffice trunks, enter the building's cable vault. At an organization with a private network, for example, the entrance facility separates LANs from WANs and designates where the telecommunications service carrier (whether it's a local phone company, dedicated, or long-distance carrier) accepts responsibility for the (external) wire.

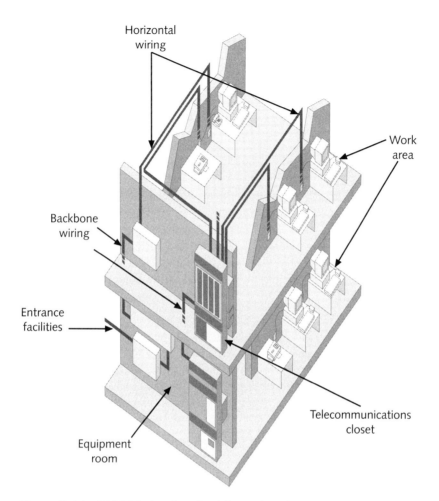

Figure 8-14   TIA/EIA structured cabling subsystems

- *Backbone wiring*—The backbone wiring provides interconnection between telecommunications closets, equipment rooms, and entrance facilities. As you learned earlier, a backbone is essentially a network of networks. On a campus-wide network, the backbone includes not only vertical connectors between floors, or **risers**, and cabling between equipment rooms, but also cabling between buildings. The TIA/EIA standard designates distance limitations for backbones of varying cable types, as specified in Table 8-2. On modern networks, backbones are usually composed of fiber optic or UTP cable. The cross connect is the central connection point for the backbone wiring.

Table 8-2   TIA/EIA specifications for backbone wiring

Cable Type	Cross Connects to Telecommunications Room	Equipment Room to Telecommunications Room	Cross Connects to Equipment Room
UTP	800 m (voice specification)	500 m	300 m
Single-mode fiber	3000 m	500 m	1500 m
Multimode fiber	2000 m	500 m	1500 m

- *Equipment room*—The location where significant hardware, such as the main distributing frame in a common carrier POP, or servers, PBXs, and mainframe hosts on a private network, resides. Equipment rooms usually connect with telecommunications closets over the backbone. On a campus-wide network, each building may have its own equipment room.

- *Telecommunications closet*—A room that contains connectivity for telephones, fax machines, printers, workstations, and other equipment, within a limited geographical area, plus cross connections to equipment rooms. Telecommunications closets may also be called "telco rooms" or "riser closets." Large organizations may have several telecommunications closets per floor. These rooms may contain different types of equipment, depending on whether they are used strictly for voice connections, for data connections, or for both. On voice networks, telecommunications closets house the punch-down blocks that cross-connect horizontal wiring with backbone wiring. On data networks, telecommunications closets are typically larger and may house patch panels, punch-down blocks, hubs or switches, and possibly other connectivity hardware. In Chapter 4's discussion of main distributing frames, you learned that a punch-down block is a panel of data receptors (or contacts) at which individual wires from a cable are terminated. In the context of structured cabling, punch-down blocks are used to accept horizontal cabling from networked devices and cross connect that cabling with backbone cabling. Punch-down blocks used on older telephone networks (for example, those that use Level 1 wiring) are known as **66 blocks**, after the industry standard type 66 punch-down contacts, or clips, they contain. 66 blocks are typically not used on data networks or newer telephone networks. Networks that use CAT5 UTP connect lines via **110 blocks**, named after type 110 punch-down clips they contain. 110 blocks may accommodate different numbers of wire pairs, up to several hundred. Figure 8-15 depicts both a 66 block and a 110 block.

8

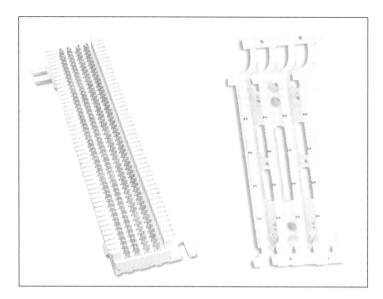

Figure 8-15   66 block (left) and 110 block (right)

On data networks, **patch panels** connect horizontal wiring from networked devices to connectivity devices, such as hubs or switches. A **patch cable** (or **patch cord**) is a relatively short (usually under 50 feet long) copper or fiber optic cable with connectors on each end. Patch panels are distinguished from punch-down blocks in that they contain modular jacks that accept connectors and that they are meant to allow connections to be easily moved (their connections are not as permanent as punch-down block connections). They typically provide 12, 24, 48, or 96 ports. Figure 8-16 shows a patch panel typical of the type used in data telecommunications closets.

- *Horizontal wiring*—The wiring that connects telephones, fax machines, printers, workstations, and other networked equipment to the telecommunications closet. TIA/EIA recognizes three possible cabling types for horizontal wiring: STP, UTP, or fiber optic. The maximum allowable distance for horizontal wiring is 100 m. This span includes 90 m to connect a wall jack to the telecommunications closet plus a maximum of 10 m to connect a workstation to the wall jack. Figure 8-17 depicts horizontal wiring and telecommunications closet connections for both telephones and workstations.

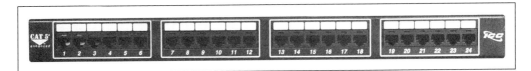

Figure 8-16   Patch panel

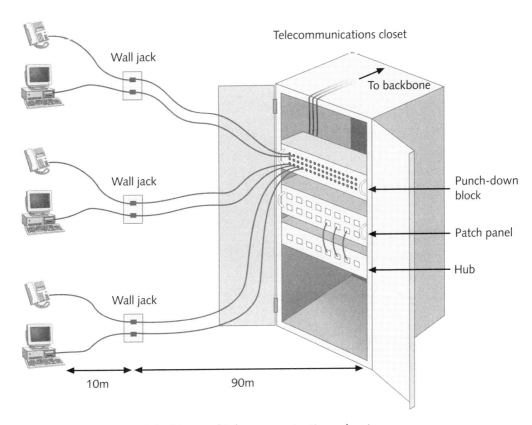

Figure 8-17   Horizontal wiring and telecommunications closet

- *Work area*—An area that encompasses all patch cables and horizontal wiring necessary to connect workstations, printers, and other network devices from their NICs to the telecommunications closet. The TIA/EIA standard calls for each wall jack to contain at least one voice and one data outlet, as pictured in Figure 8-18. Realistically, you will encounter a variety of wall jacks. For example, in a student computer lab lacking phones, a wall jack with a combination of voice and data outlets is unnecessary.

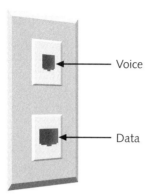

Figure 8-18 A standard TIA/EIA wall jack

Figure 8-19 depicts one possible example of a structured cabling hierarchy. The TIA/EIA standard dictates that a single hierarchy contain no more than two levels of cross-connection wiring.

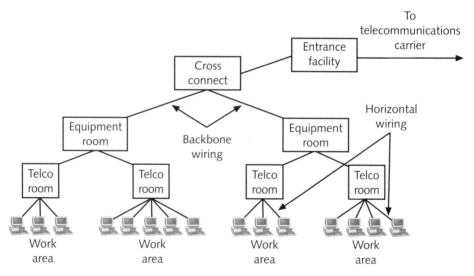

Figure 8-19 A structured cabling hierarchy

Adhering to standard cabling hierarchies is only part of a smart cable management strategy. If you are charged with designing and installing your organization's cable plant, you should also specify standards for the types of cable used by your organization and maintain a list of approved cabling vendors. Keep a supply room stocked with spare parts so that you can easily and quickly replace defective parts.

Create documentation for your cabling plant, including the locations, lengths, and grades of installed cable. Label every wall jack, punch-down block termination, and connector. Use color-coded cables for different purposes (cables can be purchased in a variety of sheath colors). For example, you might want to use pink for patch cables, green for horizontal wiring, and gray for vertical (backbone) wiring. Keep your documentation in a centrally accessible location and be certain to update it as you change the network. The more you document, the easier it will be to move or add cable segments.

Finally, plan your cabling plant to make it easy to expand. For example, if your organization is growing rapidly, consider replacing your backbone with fiber and leaving plenty of space in your telecommunications closets for more racks.

The TIA/EIA 568 standard applies only to telecommunications cabling within commercial buildings. A different TIA/EIA standard, number 570, applies to residential telecommunications cabling systems. This standard does not specify separate equipment rooms and telecommunications closets. Instead, it recommends installing a punch-down block near the entrance facility and connecting telephones and other equipment directly to the punch-down block.

National Electric Code (NEC)

Another telecommunications wiring standard is the **national electric code (NEC)**, a document (or more precisely, a book) which was initially published in 1911 and is updated every three years by the National Fire Protection Association. The purpose of the NEC is to ensure the proper installation of electrical systems to safeguard people and property. This volume addresses all types of wiring systems, including power systems, alarm systems, and communications systems. Section 800 of the NEC is devoted to telecommunications wiring. Other sections, including "IT Equipment," "Optical Fiber," and "Ground Fault Protection" contain information helpful to telecommunications professionals.

Some of the specific installation issues addressed by the NEC standards include proper methods for grounding telecommunications cable, situating cable trays, running cables through walls and ceiling spaces, and the appropriate types of both copper and fiber optic cabling for use in different areas of a building. One of the most important NEC standards is the classification of different types of cables. For example, NEC has established ratings for cables based on how well they resist combustion in the presence of a flame. A NEC type "CMR" cable is suitable for use in the riser area of a building, because it is sufficiently flame retardant to prevent fires from traveling from one floor to another along the cable. A NEC type "CMG" cable is suitable for general purpose use, but not for use in **plenum**, the area above the ceiling tile or below the subflooring, or riser areas, because it does not meet the stringent flame resistance requirements.

Some of the information in the NEC overlaps and complements information contained in the TIA/EIA standards. Although the TIA/EIA standards may be more commonly understood in your organization, you should be aware of NEC standards for safe cabling. Bear in mind that the NEC standard does not equal nor replace your state's wiring codes.

8

INSTALLING CABLE

So far, you have read about the variety of cables used in telecommunications and the limitations inherent in each. You may worry that with hundreds of varieties of cable, choosing the correct one and making it work with your network is next to impossible. The good news is that if you follow both the manufacturers' installation guidelines and the TIA/EIA and NEC standards, you are almost guaranteed success. Many network problems can be traced to poor cable installation techniques. For example, if you don't correctly position and terminate twisted-pair wires in a connector, the cable will fail to transmit or receive data (or both—in which case, the cable will not function at all). Installing the wrong gauge or level of cable can either cause your network to fail or render it more susceptible to damage (for example, using typical, inexpensive twisted-pair cable in areas that might be susceptible to excessive heat). The following sections describe practical guidelines for installing both twisted-pair and fiber optic cable.

Installing UTP

With networks moving to faster transmission speeds, adhering to installation guidelines is a more critical concern than ever. A Category 5 UTP segment that flawlessly transmits data at 10 Mbps may suffer data loss when pushed to 100 Mbps if the cabling is improperly installed. In addition, some cable manufacturers do not honor warranties if their cables were improperly installed. This section outlines the most common method of installing UTP cable and points out cabling mistakes that can lead to network instability.

 When adding new cable to an existing infrastructure, bear in mind that the quality of a connection is limited by its least effective element. For this reason, you should always install cable that at least matches the best quality cable already present on your network. For example, if your network contains CAT5 UTP, you should not add CAT3 cabling. Doing so limits that part of the network to CAT3 standards. For the same reason, you rarely need to install Level 1 telephone wire.

In the previous section, you learned about the six subsystems of the TIA/EIA structured cabling standard. A typical UTP network uses a modular setup to distinguish between cables at each subsystem.

In this example, patch cables connect networked equipment (such as telephones or workstations) to the wall jacks. Longer cables connect wire from the wall jack to a punch-down block in the telecommunications closet. From the punch-down block, patch cables bring the connection into a patch panel. From the patch panel, more patch cables connect to the hub or switch, which in turn connects to the equipment room or to the backbone, depending on the scale of the network. All of these sections of cable make network moves and additions easier. Believe it or not, they also keep the telecommunications closet organized.

Unless they terminate in a punch-down block, modern UTP (and STP) patch cables terminate with **RJ-45** connectors. "RJ" stands for registered jack, a standard originally established by the FCC so that connectors and jacks made by different manufacturers could be used without connectivity problems. RJ-45 connectors look similar to the older, RJ-11 telephone connectors. However, RJ-45 connectors are larger because they are designed to accommodate additional wire pairs.

Although you may never have to make your own patch cables, you might have to repair one in a pinch. Table 8-3 explains how the pins in an RJ-45 connector correspond to the wires in a UTP cable. For example, in wire pair number 3, the green and the white and green striped (often called, simply, "white/green" in cabling specifications) wires are wound around each other. This pair is used for data transmission. The method of UTP coding in Table 8-3 follows the TIA/EIA 568A wiring standard, the most popular wiring standard currently in use for networks. Another standard, the TIA/EIA 568B standard, is similar, but the wire pairs colored orange and orange/white plus green and green/white are reversed. Yet another coding scheme has been established by IEEE. It typically doesn't matter which scheme you choose, but to avoid confusion and transmission errors, you should ensure that you cable all wiring on your LAN according to one standard. In Project 8-2 at the end of this chapter, you have the opportunity to create your own patch cable following these guidelines. Be advised, however, that any imperfection in how you fasten the wires in the connector will prevent the cable from working.

Table 8-3   TIA/EIA 568A pin numbers and color codes for an RJ-45 connector

Pin Number	Pair Number	Use	Color
1	3	Transmit+	White/green
2	3	Transmit-	Green
3	2	Receive+	White/orange
4	1	Unused	Blue
5	1	Unused	White/blue
6	2	Receive-	Orange
7	4	Unused	White/brown
8	4	Unused	Brown

A patch cable in which the terminations at both ends are identical is called a **straight-through cable**, because the wires and the signals they carry pass "straight through." However, in some cases you may want to change the pin locations of some wires. For example, you may want to connect two network devices without using a connectivity device. This can be accomplished through the use of a **crossover cable**, a patch cable in which the terminations locations of the transmit and receive wires on one end of the cable are reversed, as shown in Figure 8-20. Crossover cables can be useful in troubleshooting network problems when you suspect that a single device's networking hardware or software might be at fault.

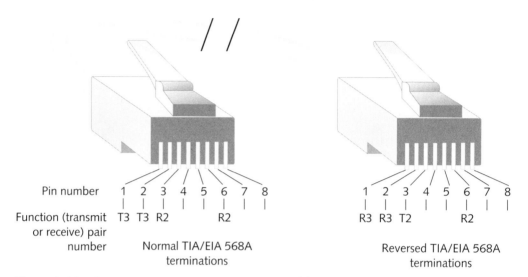

Figure 8-20   RJ-45 terminations on a crossover cable

The art of proper cabling could fill an entire book. If you plan to specialize in cable installation, design, or maintenance, you should invest in a reference dedicated to this topic. As a network professional, you will likely occasionally add new cables to a room or telecommunications closet, repair defective cable ends, or install a data outlet. Following are some cable installation tips for CAT5 UTP that help prevent Physical layer failures:

- Do not untwist twisted-pair cables more than one-half inch before inserting them into the punch-down block or connector.

- Pay attention to the bend radius limitations for the type of cable you are installing. **Bend radius** is the radius of the smallest curve into which you can loop a cable before you impair data transmission. Generally, a twisted-pair cable's bend radius is equal to or greater than four times the diameter of the cable. (Bend radius is typically more of a concern when installing coaxial cable than twisted-pair cable, however.)

- Test each segment of cabling as you install it with a cable tester (these devices are described later in this chapter). This practice prevents you from later having to track down errors in multiple, long stretches of cable.

- Use only cable ties (thin strips of plastic) to cinch groups of cables together. In addition, avoid cinching cables so tightly that you squeeze their outer covering, a practice that leads to difficult-to-diagnose data errors.

- When pulling cable, do not exert more than 25 pounds of pressure on the cable. Such force may stretch the cable and result in data transmission errors.

- Avoid laying cable across the floor where it might sustain damage from rolling chairs or foot traffic. If you must take this tack, cover the cable with a cable protector.

- Install cable at least three feet away from fluorescent lights or other sources of EMI. Also, do not run network cables next to power cables.

- Avoid installing cable in areas of excessive heat or moisture.

- Always leave slack in cable runs. Stringing cable too tightly risks connectivity and data transmission problems.

- If you run cable in the plenum, make sure the cable sheath is plenum-rated and consult with local electric installation codes to be certain you are installing it correctly. A plenum-rated cable is more fire-resistant than other cables, and its sheath will not release noxious fumes if it does start to burn.

- Pay attention to grounding requirements and follow them faithfully.

In addition to heeding these cabling guidelines, pay attention to noise in the environment. On most networks, noise is an ever-present threat, so you should take measures to limit its impact on your network. For example, you should install cabling well away from powerful electromagnetic forces, such as heavy machinery or fluorescent lights. If your environment still leaves your network vulnerable, you should choose a type of transmission media that guards the signal-carrying wire from noise. As a general rule, thicker cables are less susceptible to noise, as are cables coated with a protective shielding. If this doesn't sufficiently ward off interference (for example, if you are installing cable in a factory with machines that run continuously), you may need to use a metal or plastic conduit to contain and further protect the cabling.

Installing Fiber

Almost everything about fiber optic cable and copper-based cable is different, including their connectors and terminations. If you work on a network that uses fiber optic cables, it is critical for you to understand splicing, one of the primary considerations when installing this medium. In the context of fiber optic cable, a physical joining of two facing and aligned pieces of wire or fiber is known as a **splice**. Thus, splicing is the means by which two fiber optic cables are connected to form a continuous communications channel. If you work with fiber optic cable, you may need to splice it in case of a break in the cable. Splicing is also required prior to affixing a connector to a cable end. Three different methods exist for splicing cable: mechanical splicing, fusion splicing, and mass splicing.

In **mechanical splicing**, the two ends of a fiber optic cable are fixed in position within a tube so that they form one continuous communications channel. This is similar to (but much more exact than) setting a broken bone and using a cast to make sure the two parts of the bone remain aligned and immobile. After the fibers are aligned, a small amount of transparent adhesive is applied at the joint to ensure continuity. The tube remains on the splice even after the cable is put into service. Although mechanical splices are considered very stable, over time it is possible for them to be jarred out of alignment. In that case, they can easily be removed and reapplied.

In **fusion splicing**, a connection between fibers is accomplished through the application of heat and the resulting melting and fusion of two fiber strands. To accomplish this, the ends of two cables are first placed in guides that align them so that their cores are perfectly matched. Then, two electrodes are positioned on either side of the exact point where the fibers meet. An electrical arc, or a brief transfer of voltage, is created between the two electrodes. The arc causes sufficient heat to melt and fuse the two strands together. (Other methods may be used to generate such heat; however, the electrical arc method is the most popular.) Because fusion splicing changes the properties of the glass strand, it presents a danger of introducing imperfections. Therefore, it is critical to test fusion splices for attenuation and loss before putting them into service on a network. If a fusion splice is faulty, the fibers must be broken again and the splicing process repeated. However, modern fusion splicing is accomplished by very precise (and expensive) machines. As a result, fusion splices typically result in lower optical loss and less reflection than mechanical splices. Where optimal performance is key, as in long-distance telecommunications, fusion splices are preferred over mechanical splices.

Both mechanical and fusion splicing are used to connect single fiber optic strands within a cable. These two types of splicing are illustrated in Figure 8-21.

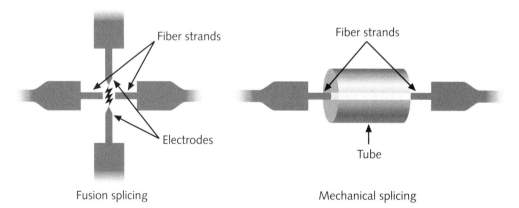

Figure 8-21   Fusion and mechanical splicing

Mass splicing simply refers to the splicing of multiple fiber optic strands at once, whether by fusion or mechanical means. The advantage of mass splicing is the time savings associated with connecting multiple strands over connecting one strand at a time.

All three splicing methods require careful preparation and training. In particular, it is important to clean and polish the ends of the fiber strands before splicing. Further discussion of fiber optic splicing is beyond the scope of this book. However, if you are charged with splicing, you should take a hands-on course to learn how to do it properly.

> Terminating a fiber optic cable is always done in either a connector or splice. In other words, fiber optic cable runs do not have an equivalent of the punchdown block that is used to terminate UTP connections.

With fiber cabling, you can use any of ten different types of connectors. Figure 8-22 shows two popular connector types, an ST connector and an SC connector. ST connectors are the most popular for use with multimode fiber. For short connections, such as a two-foot cable between a connectivity device and a patch panel, you should consider purchasing fiber cables with the connectors pre-installed. For longer connections, either you or the technician who installs your fiber can attach the connectors to the cable.

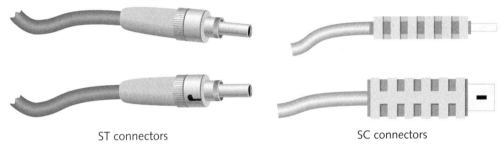

ST connectors   SC connectors

Figure 8-22   ST and SC fiber connectors

As with installing twisted-pair cable, adhering to a few simple rules will help to make the result a path for flawless data transmission. Following are some cable installation tips for fiber optic cable that can prevent Physical layer failures:

- When pulling fiber optic cable, do not exert pressure on the cable. Also, do not leave the cable in a position that forces it to bear tension. Fiber optic cable is typically more fragile and susceptible to damage from tension than UTP.

- Fiber optic cable should be installed within a conduit whenever you are concerned about the potential for environmental damage (for example, heat, moisture, or stress).

- Do not exceed the minimum bend radius. Doing so causes data errors and increases attenuation. For a fiber optic cable containing two or four fibers (such as a patch cable), the minimum bend radius is approximately one inch.

- When installing a fiber optic cabling conduit, consider the likelihood of increasing throughput needs in the future and allow sufficient open space for additional fiber optic cable to be pulled through the same conduit. Some professional installers recommend filling no more than half the capacity of the conduit to begin with.

- When burying conduit, heed these guidelines to prevent subsequent damage from construction machinery or gnawing rodents: bury conduit at least 30 feet deep; in northern climates, bury conduit below the freeze line. Also, avoid utility lines, and use a conduit that is at least 1.5 inches in diameter.

TROUBLESHOOTING CABLE INFRASTRUCTURE

No matter how carefully you follow cable installation techniques and other standard procedures, transmission and connectivity problems will occur. In such circumstances, it is wise to have an established troubleshooting methodology in mind and the proper troubleshooting tools nearby. The following sections describe both the methodology and the tools that will help you solve problems related to telecommunication connections.

Troubleshooting Methodology

Successful troubleshooters proceed logically and methodically. This section introduces a basic troubleshooting methodology, leading you through a series of general problem-solving steps. Bear in mind that experience in your environment may prompt you to follow the steps in a different order or to skip certain steps entirely. For example, suppose you work for a LEC and are asked to troubleshoot a group of lines that cannot obtain a dial tone. If you know that the part of your outside plant's wiring servicing those lines is in an area susceptible to water seepage, you may skip directly to checking that environment before considering recent changes to switching software. In general, however, it is best to follow each step in the order shown. Such a logical approach can save you from undertaking wasteful, time-consuming efforts.

Steps to troubleshooting telecommunication connectivity problems:

1. Identify the symptoms. This step brings you closer to pinpointing the cause of the problem by establishing what is happening and also, by ruling out some potential causes. Carefully document what you learn from people or systems that alerted you to the problem and keep that documentation handy.

2. Identify the scope of the problem. Like identifying symptoms, narrowing down a problem's scope can eliminate some causes and point to others. Are all users experiencing the problem at all times? Or is the problem limited to a specific geographic area (for example, all telephone extensions on the second floor of a building), to a specific demographic group of users (for example, only users who have been granted access to certain network resources), or to a particular period of time (for example, does a telephone subscriber's modem connection drop each time someone tries to call her number)? In other words, is the problem subject to geographic, demographic, or chronological constraints?

3. Establish what has changed on the network. Recent changes are often the cause of connectivity problems. For example, you may have installed a new telephone jack in a residence and the result was that not only does the new

jack not work, but half of the other jacks in the house are also inoperative. This may point to faulty connections in the newly installed jack, if the jacks in this residence are connected in a serial fashion.

4. Determine the most probable cause of the problem. Making this determination may require the following techniques:

   a. Make sure the computer or telephone user is performing operations correctly.

   b. Recreate the problem, and ensure that you can reproduce it reliably.

   c. Verify the physical integrity of the network connection (such as wire terminations, connector seating, and power to devices), starting at the affected workstations, telephones, or other nodes, and moving outward toward the backbone. Use troubleshooting tools as appropriate.

   d. Verify the logical integrity of the network connection (for example, make sure server or PBX software is properly installed and working).

5. Implement a solution. Implementing a solution requires foresight and patience. As with finding the problem, the more methodically and logically you can approach the solution, the more efficient the correction process will be. If a problem is causing catastrophic outages, however, you should solve the problem as quickly as possible, making sure to record your actions and take no action that might inadvertently extend the outage.

6. Test the solution. After implementing your solution, you must test it to verify that it works properly. Obviously, the type of testing you perform depends on the problem and your solution. Some types of solutions can be quickly verified, whereas others may call for a more careful analysis.

7. Recognize the potential effects of the solution. For example, if you place a filter on a telephone line to reduce noise in voice conversations, how might this affect other services used on that line (for example, modulated digital signals)?

8. Document the solution. Make sure that both you and your colleagues understand the cause of the problem and how you solved it. This information should be kept in a centrally available repository, such as an online database.

In addition to the organized method of troubleshooting described in this section, a good, general rule for troubleshooting can be stated as follows: Never overlook the obvious! Although some questions may seem too simple to bother asking, don't discount them.

Next, you learn about troubleshooting tools that help identify problems with cabling infrastructure. Because faults at the Physical layer, including cabling, are responsible for at least half of all network problems (according to some estimates), understanding how and when to use specific cable troubleshooting tools is a valuable skill.

Troubleshooting Tools

You have learned a systematic, trial-and-error method for diagnosing cabling problems. In the real world, however, this technique may lead nowhere or take too much time. In some cases, the most efficient approach is to use a tool specifically designed to analyze and isolate problems with transmission media. Several tools are available, ranging from simple tone generators that help isolate a cable to cable testers that measure crosstalk and attenuation along a cable. The tool you choose depends on the particular problem you need to investigate and the characteristics of your network. This section describes tools that can assist you in identifying a problem with cabling infrastructure.

Crossover Cable

As you learned earlier in this chapter, a crossover cable is one in which the transmit and receive wire pairs in one of the connectors are reversed. This reversal enables you to use a crossover cable to directly interconnect two nodes without using an intervening connectivity device such as a hub. A crossover cable allows you to quickly and easily verify that a node's network adapter is transmitting and receiving signals properly. For example, suppose you are a network technician who has been charged with testing 25 new workstation computers before shipping them to the remote offices where they will be installed. As part of your testing, you must verify that each computer's NIC is functional. Rather than attempting to connect each new workstation to your company's network, you can more easily and quickly verify each NIC's functionality by connecting your workstation's NIC, whose functionality you have verified, directly to the new workstation's NIC using a crossover cable. Once connected, you can perform a simple test to see if the new workstation's NIC can send and transmit signals. If the test results are positive, you can move to the next new workstation.

Tone Generator and Tone Locator

Ideally, you and your networking colleagues would label each port and wire termination in a telecommunications closet so that problems and changes can be easily managed. However, due to personnel changes and time constraints, a telecommunications closet often winds up being disorganized and poorly documented. If this is the case where you work, you may need a tone generator and a tone locator to determine where one pair of wires (out of possibly hundreds) terminates.

A **tone generator** (also called a **toner**) is a small electronic device that issues a signal on a wire pair. A **tone locator** (also called a **probe**) is a type of amplifier that can detect the inductive energy emitted by the tone (current) on a wire. When the tone locator detects this inducted current, it emits an audible tone. By placing the tone generator at one end of a wire and attaching a tone locator to the other end, you can verify the location of the wire's termination. Figure 8-23 depicts the use of a tone generator and a tone locator. When using these devices, you must work by trial and error, guessing which termination corresponds to the wire over which you've generated a signal, until the tone locator indicates the correct choice. This combination of devices is also known as a **fox and hound**, because the locator (the hound) chases the evidence of the generator (the fox).

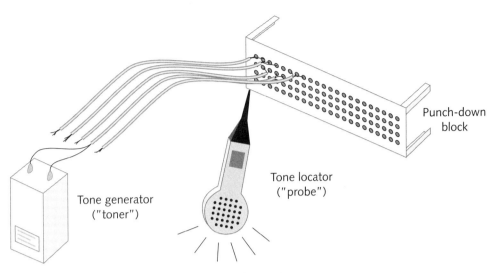

Figure 8-23 Use of a tone generator and tone locator

Tone generators and tone locators cannot be used to determine any characteristics about a cable, such as whether it has defects or whether its length exceeds standards for a certain type of network. They are only used to determine where a wire pair terminates. In fact, because of their limited functionality, tone generators and tone locators are rarely used on modern data networks. However, they are still widely used by telephone technicians.

 A tone generator should never be used on a wire that may connect to a device's port or network adapter. Because a tone generator transmits electricity over the wire, it may damage the device or network adapter.

Continuity tester

Cable testing tools are essential for both cable installers and network troubleshooters, as cables are often at fault when a network problem arises. Symptoms of cabling problems can be as elusive as occasional lost packets or as obvious as a lost connection. You can easily test cables for faults with specialized tools. In this section, you learn about tools that can help isolate problems with network cables. The first cable testing tool you learn about is a **continuity tester**, an instrument that can detect whether electric current is passing unobstructed over a cable. Continuity testers may also be known as **cable checkers**.

Continuity testers simply determine whether your cabling can provide connectivity. To accomplish this task, they apply a small voltage to each conductor at one end of the cable, and then check whether that voltage is detectable at the other end. They may also check whether voltage cannot be detected on other conductors in the cable. Most continuity testers include a set of lights that signal pass/fail. Some also indicate a cable pass/fail with an audible tone. A pass/fail test provides a simple indicator of whether a component can perform its stated function. Figure 8-24 depicts one popular type of continuity tester.

Figure 8-24   A continuity tester

As a telecommunications professional, you might use a continuity tester to:

- Verify that a cable is properly conducting electricity—that is, whether its signal can travel unimpeded from one node on the network to another

- Test for short or open circuits in the wire (by detecting unexpected resistance or loss of voltage)

- Test for connectors or terminations that are miswired—in other words, to test for one or more wires that are not terminated in the correct position

- Test for wires that are paired incorrectly

- Test for wires that are exposed or crossed

- Test for the presence of noise that affects the cable and its signals

When you make your own cables, be sure to verify their integrity with at least a continuity tester (better yet, a performance tester). Even if you purchase cabling from a reputable vendor, you should make sure that it meets your network's required standards. Just because a cable is labeled "CAT5" does not necessarily mean that it will live up to that standard. Testing cabling before installing it may save many hours of troubleshooting after the network is in place.

Continuity testers cannot test the continuity of fiber optic cabling, because fiber cable uses light rather than electric current to transmit data. To test fiber optic cabling, you need a specialized fiber cable tester.

Do not use a cable checker on a live network cable. Disconnect the cable from the network, and then test its continuity.

For convenience, most continuity testers are portable and lightweight and typically use one 9-volt battery. A basic cable checker costs between $100 and $300, but it may save many hours of work. Because continuity testers are much less expensive than performance testers (discussed next), they are also more popular among telecommunications technicians.

Performance Testers

The difference between continuity testers and performance testers lies in their sophistication and price. A **performance tester** performs the same continuity and fault tests as a continuity tester, but also provides the following functions:

- Measures the length of each wire pair
- Ensures that the cable does not exceed recommended maximum lengths
- Measures the distance from the tester to a cable fault
- Measures attenuation along a cable
- Measures crosstalk between wires
- Measures termination resistance and impedance over a distance of cabling
- Measures return loss along a cable
- Issues pass/fail ratings for CAT3, CAT5, CAT6, or even CAT7 standards
- Stores and prints cable testing results

 In data networking, a performance tester is more commonly known as a **cable tester**.

Some performance testers may provide even more features—for example, a graphical output depicting a cable's attenuation and crosstalk characteristics over the length of the cable. Because of their sophistication, performance testers cost significantly more than continuity testers. A high-end unit may cost from $5000 to $8000, and a low-end unit may cost between $1000 and $4000. Figure 8-25 shows an example of a high-end performance tester.

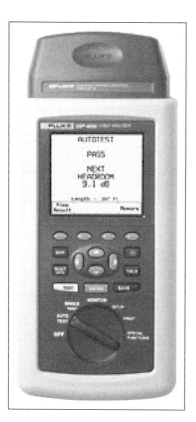

Figure 8-25   A high-end performance tester

Fiber Optic Cable Testers

In addition to continuity and performance testers for coaxial and twisted-pair networks, you can also find cable testers for fiber optic networks. Rather than issue an electrical signal over the cable as twisted-pair cable testers do, a fiber optic cable tester transmits light-based signals of different wavelengths over the fiber. Simple fiber optic cable testers, like continuity testers, measure whether the signal reached its destination unimpeded. More sophisticated fiber optic cable testers can also indicate the following:

- Optical loss along a length of cable
- Attenuation along a length of cable
- Bad splices and connections
- Broken fibers
- Length of a fiber run

Note that because crosstalk does not apply to light-based signals, a fiber tester cannot (and need not) test for crosstalk. Due to the relatively high cost of installing fiber optic cable, you should use a fiber tester on your cable before you install it, as well as after you install it. Figure 8-26 depicts a variety of fiber optic cable testers.

Figure 8-26   Fiber optic cable testers

 Newer performance testers combine the functions of twisted-pair and fiber optic cable testing into a single device. As you can imagine, such devices are much more expensive than purchasing a cable tester meant for only one type of medium.

Time Domain Reflectometers (TDRs)

A **time domain reflectometer (TDR)** is a high-end instrument for testing the qualities of a cable. It works by issuing a signal on a cable and measuring the way the signal bounces back (or reflects) to the TDR. Connectors, crimps, bends, short circuits, cable mismatches, or other defects modify the signal's amplitude before it returns to the TDR, thus changing the way it reflects. The TDR then accepts and analyzes the return signal, and based on its condition and the amount of time the signal took to return, determines cable imperfections. In the case of a coaxial cable network, a TDR can indicate whether terminators are properly installed and functional. A TDR can also indicate the distance between nodes and segments.

As with cable testers, time domain reflectors are also made for fiber optic networks. Such instruments are called **optical time domain reflectometers (OTDRs)**. Rather than issuing an electrical signal, OTDRs issue a light-based signal over the fiber. Based on the type of return light signal, the OTDR can accurately measure the length of the fiber, determine the location of faulty splices, breaks, connectors, or bends, and measure attenuation over the cable. OTDRs differ from fiber optic cable testers in that they are more sophisticated—often providing a graphical view of the transmission characteristics of a cable—and consequently, more expensive. Figure 8-27 depicts an optical time domain reflectometer.

Figure 8-27   Optical time domain reflectometer

Because some loss of a signal is expected with the addition of nodes and connectors, TDRs are a good way of taking a baseline measurement for your network cabling. A **baseline** is a record of how well a system or network operates under normal conditions. Baselines are used for comparison when conditions change. A TDR can provide a baseline for the characteristics and performance of a network's cable infrastructure. Then later, if you suspect cabling problems, you can use the TDR and compare your new results with your baseline measurement to ascertain whether signaling characteristics have changed.

Telephone Test Set

If you have seen telephone technicians on the job, you have probably noticed the oversized telephone-like device that they carry. This device is known as a **telephone test set** (or more commonly, a "butt set" because it used to butt into a conversation). A telephone test set is essentially a rugged and sophisticated telephone. It contains clips that can fasten onto telephone transmission wires, thereby attaching the telephone test set (as a telephone) to the line. It helps a telephone technician working in the field to determine whether a line is functioning, not only by receiving the signal, but also by picking up noise that may be affecting the line. Some sophisticated telephone test sets also perform trivial cable tests. For the most part, however, the telephone test set is a simple means of detecting dial tone on a line. Figure 8-28 depicts a typical telephone test set.

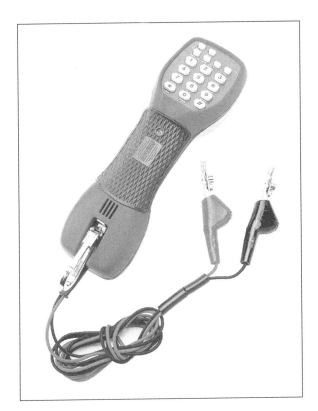

Figure 8-28   A telephone test set

CHAPTER SUMMARY

- In addition to attenuation, resistance, and voltage, characteristics that affect wireline transmission include impedance changes, latency, delay distortion, and noise. Any or all of these may affect a wireline transmission and increase its attenuation or loss, resulting in data errors.

- One of the most common forms of problematic noise in twisted-pair cabling is crosstalk. Crosstalk occurs when the signal traversing one wire induces a current on the adjacent wire.

- Coaxial cable consists of a central copper core surrounded by a plastic insulator, a braided metal shielding called braiding, and an outer plastic cover called the sheath. The copper core carries the electromagnetic signal, and the braiding acts as both a shield against noise and a ground for the signal. The insulator layer protects the copper core from the metal shielding. The sheath protects the cable from physical damage.

- Traditional four-pair, non-twisted copper telephone wiring is known as Level 1 cable or quad wire. It is only appropriate for carrying analog (voice) signals and only for relatively short distances. New telephony installations almost never use Level 1 cable. However, it still exists in most buildings constructed before the mid-1990s.

❏ Twisted-pair cable consists of color-coded pairs of insulated copper wires, each with a diameter of 0.3 to 0.8 mm, twisted around each other and encased in plastic coating. The twists in the wire help to reduce the effects of crosstalk.

❏ Twisted-pair cable may be shielded twisted-pair (STP), which contains foil shielding that surrounds the wire pairs, or unshielded twisted-pair (UTP), which does not contain shielding. UTP is the least expensive and most common.

❏ Category (CAT3) UTP cable is the minimum grade of unshielded twisted-pair cabling for use in telephone systems. However, most newer telephone installations use CAT5 UTP. CAT5 cable is the minimum grade used on modern networks. It typically contains four wire pairs and supports up to 100 Mbps throughput and a 100 MHz signal rate.

❏ Fiber optic cable is designed to take advantage of light's tendency to reflect. However, it must also be designed to account for refraction and absorption, both of which can cause attenuation, delay distortion, and loss.

❏ Fiber optic cable contains one or several glass fibers in its core. Data is transmitted via pulsing light sent from a laser or light-emitting diode through the central fiber(s). Outside the fiber(s), a layer of glass called cladding acts as a mirror, reflecting light back to the core in different patterns that vary depending on the transmission mode. Outside the cladding, a plastic buffer and strands of Kevlar protect the inner core. A plastic sheath covers the braiding.

❏ Fiber cable variations fall into two categories: single-mode and multimode. Single-mode fiber uses a small-diameter core over which light generated by a laser travels mostly down its center, reflecting very few times. Multimode fiber uses a core with a larger diameter over which many pulses of light generated by a light emitting diode (LED) travel at different angles.

❏ Because of its reliability and high throughput potential, fiber is used primarily as a cable that connects many LANs to form a MAN or WAN. Fiber may also be used within a LAN for special purposes. On the Internet, fiber is used to connect NAPs and other large exchange points. In the PSTN, fiber is used to connect large carrier locations, such as Class 1 central offices.

❏ Factors to consider when selecting a transmission medium include: how well it integrates with the existing infrastructure, throughput potential, cost of installation and maintenance, scalability, security, and how well it resists the effects of noise.

❏ The most common standard for installing cable is the TIA/EIA 568 Commercial Building Wiring Standard, also known as structured cabling, for uniform, enterprise-wide, multivendor cabling systems. Structured cabling is based on a hierarchical design that divides cabling into six subsystems: entrance facility, backbone (vertical) wiring, equipment room, telecommunications closet, horizontal wiring, and work area.

❑ The best practice for installing cable is to follow the TIA/EIA 568 specifications and manufacturer's recommendations. Be careful not to exceed a cable's bend radius, subject it to heat or pressure, or untwist wire pairs more than one-half inch. Install plenum-rated cable in ceilings and floors, and run cabling far from power cables or locations where it might suffer physical damage.

❑ Fiber optic cable used to connect geographically distant locations is almost always installed underground, in conduit. Fiber is somewhat more fragile than twisted-pair, so care should be taken when installing it. Splicing, which is required for any fiber termination (in a connector or with another section of fiber cable), can be done through mechanical or fusion splicing. Fusion splicing, in which two fiber strands are instantaneously melted together, is currently the preferred method.

❑ To identify the source of cabling infrastructure problems, follow a logical troubleshooting methodology and have the appropriate testing tools handy. One important tool for testing cables is the continuity tester, which indicates whether a cable is transmitting current efficiently from one end to another. For telephone technicians, an invaluable tool is the telephone test set, which can be connected directly to telephone wires to verify that the line is functioning.

8

KEY TERMS

110 block — A type of punch-down block used for cross-connecting CAT5 or higher UTP, named after the industry standard type 110 punch-down clips they contain. 110 blocks are used on modern voice and data networks.

66 block — A type of punch-down block used for traditional telephone cross-connects, named after the industry standard type 66 punch-down clips they contain. 66 blocks are typically not used on data networks or newer telephone networks.

alien crosstalk — A type of interference that occurs when signals from adjacent cables interfere with another cable's transmission.

attenuation distortion — The distortion of a signal that results from different signal components experiencing different levels of attenuation between the signal's sender and receiver. Attenuation distortion affects analog signals more than it affects digital signals. It is measured in decibels (dB).

bandpass filter — A device that filters a signal so as to remove frequencies higher and lower than the range of frequencies known to carry data.

baseline — A record of how well a system or network operates under normal conditions.

bend radius — The radius of the tightest arc into which you can loop a cable before you cause data transmission errors. Generally, a twisted-pair cable's bend radius is equal to or greater than four times the diameter of the cable. The bend radius of a typical two- or four-fiber cable is approximately one inch.

braiding — A braided metal shielding used to insulate some types of coaxial cable.

cable checker — *See* continuity tester.

cable tester — *See* performance tester.

Category 3 (CAT3) — A form of UTP that typically contains four wire pairs and can carry up to 10 Mbps with a possible bandwidth of 16 MHz. CAT3 is the minimum standard for new telephone wiring. On data networks, CAT3 is being replaced with CAT5 to accommodate higher throughput.

Category 5 (CAT5) — The most popular form of UTP for new network installations and upgrades. CAT5 typically contains four wire pairs and supports up to 100 Mbps throughput and a 100 MHz signal rate.

Category 6 (CAT6) — A twisted-pair cable that contains four wire pairs, each wrapped in foil insulation. Additional foil insulation covers the bundle of wire pairs, and a fire-resistant plastic sheath covers the second foil layer. The foil insulation provides excellent resistance to crosstalk and enables CAT6 to support at least six times the throughput supported by regular CAT5.

Category 7 (CAT7) — A twisted-pair cable that contains multiple wire pairs, each separately shielded then surrounded by another layer of shielding within the jacket. CAT7 can support up to a 1 GHz signal rate. But because of its extra layers, it is less flexible than other forms of twisted-pair wiring. Standards for CAT7 have not been finalized.

cladding — The glass shield around the fiber core of a fiber optic cable. Cladding acts as a mirror, reflecting light back to the core in patterns that vary depending on the transmission mode. This reflection allows fiber to bend around corners without impairing the light-based signal.

coaxial cable — A type of cable that consists of a central copper core surrounded by an insulator, a braided metal shielding, called braiding, and an outer cover, called the sheath or jacket. Coaxial cable, called "coax" for short, was the foundation for Ethernet networks in the 1980s and remained a popular transmission medium for many years.

continuity tester — A simple handheld device that determines whether cabling can provide connectivity. To accomplish this task, a continuity tester applies a small voltage to each conductor at one end of the cable, then checks whether that voltage is detectable at the other end. It may also verify that voltage cannot be detected on other conductors in the cable. A continuity tester may also be called a cable checker.

core — The central component of a fiber optic cable, consisting of one or several pure glass fibers.

crossover cable — A twisted-pair patch cable in which the termination locations of the transmit and receive wires on one end of the cable are reversed.

crosstalk — A type of noise caused by the inducted current of signals traveling on nearby wire pairs. This inducted current infringes on another pair's signal.

delay distortion — The impairment of a signal that results from different frequencies traveling over the same wire at slightly different speeds. When frequencies travel at different speeds, the separate parts of a signal associated with those frequencies arrive at their destination slightly out of sync. Because of their dependence on precise changes in phase, delay distortion affects digital signals more profoundly than analog signals. It is corrected through the use of equalizers.

distortion — The unintended and undesirable modification of at least one signal component (such as amplitude, frequency, or phase), which makes the received signal different than the originally transmitted signal.

enhanced CAT5 (CAT5e) — A higher-grade version of CAT5 wiring that contains high-quality copper, offers a high twist ratio, and uses advanced methods for reducing crosstalk. Enhanced CAT5 can support a signaling rate of up to 200 MHz, double the capability of regular CAT5.

enterprise-wide — The scope of a network that spans an entire organization and often services the needs of many diverse users. It may include many locations (as a WAN), or it may be confined to one location but include many different departments, floors, and network segments.

envelope delay distortion — *See* delay distortion.

fiber optic cable — A form of cable that contains one or several glass fibers in its core. Data is transmitted via pulsing light sent from a laser or light-emitting diode through the central fiber (or fibers). Outside the central fiber, a layer of glass called cladding acts as a mirror, reflecting light back to the core in patterns that vary depending on the transmission mode. Outside the cladding, a plastic buffer protects the core and absorbs any light that might escape. Outside the buffer, strands of Kevlar provide further protection from stretching and damage. A plastic jacket surrounds the Kevlar strands.

filtering — The process of removing unwanted parts of a signal. In the case of analog or digital signals, filters are used to remove frequencies higher and lower than the range of frequencies responsible for carrying data. Filters may be used at either the transmitter, the receiver, or at both locations in a communications system.

fox and hound — *See* tone generator and tone locator.

fusion splicing — A method of splicing fiber optic cables in which the application of heat melts and fuses two aligned fiber strands. The most popular heat source for fusion splicing is an electrical arc. Fusion splicing has the potential to cause material imperfections in the glass. Therefore, it is important to test the splice for attenuation and optical loss.

impedance — The combined effect of a circuit's inductance and capacitance. In a DC circuit, impedance equals resistance. Impedance is expressed in ohms. Every cable possesses a characteristic impedance. Changes in impedance on a network (caused by terminations or connectors) can cause signal loss.

impulse noise — A type of noise caused by sudden spikes in electromagnetic activity. Impulse noise affects a signal only briefly, but often dramatically.

intermodulation noise — A type of noise that is caused by the mixing of one signal and another due to their frequencies infringing on each other.

latency — The delay between the transmission and reception of a data bit. Latency depends on many factors, including the distance between the sender and receiver, as well as the number of connectivity devices in the signal's path. It is often measured in round trip time (RTT).

Level 1 — A cable consisting of four insulated copper wires surrounded by a sheath. In Level 1 cable, wire pairs are not twisted. Also known as quad wire, Level 1 cable formed the basis of most inside telephone wiring until recent years, when data communications have prompted the use of higher quality, twisted-pair cable. In a Level 1 cable, the red wire is the ring (used for signaling in the first pair), the green wire is the tip (used for a ground) in the first pair, and the yellow wire is the ring in the second pair, whereas the black wire is the tip in the second pair.

loss — The extent to which a signal's strength weakens over a distance.

mass splicing — The splicing of multiple fiber optic strands at once, whether by fusion or mechanical means.

mechanical splicing — A method of splicing fiber optic cable in which the two ends of a fiber optic cable are mechanically fixed in position within a tube so that they form one continuous communications channel.

multimode fiber — A type of fiber optic cable that contains a core with a larger diameter over which many pulses of light generated by a light emitting diode (LED) travel at different angles. Because light is being reflected many different ways in a multimode fiber cable, the waves become less easily distinguishable the longer they travel. Thus, multimode fiber is best suited for shorter distances than single-mode fiber.

national electric code (NEC) — A telecommunications wiring standard initially published in 1911 and updated every three years by the National Fire Protection Association. The purpose of the NEC is to ensure the proper installation of electrical systems to safeguard people and property. This volume addresses all types of wiring systems, including power systems, alarm systems, and communications systems.

near-end crosstalk (NeXT) — A type of crosstalk that occurs between two copper wires within a twisted pair (as opposed to the crosstalk that occurs between twisted pairs within a cable). In NeXT, current flowing over one wire in the pair induces a current on the other wire in the pair.

optical loss — The extent to which a light signal weakens over distance on a fiber optic network.

optical time domain reflectometer (OTDR) — A time domain reflectometer specifically made for use with fiber optic networks. It works by issuing a light-based signal on a fiber optic cable and measuring the way in which the signal bounces back (or reflects) to the OTDR.

patch cable — A relatively short section (usually between 3 and 50 feet) of copper or fiber optic cabling, with connectors on both ends. Patch cables may be used to connect patch panels with connectivity devices or to connect a networked node to a data outlet on the wall, for instance.

patch cord — *See* patch cable.

patch panel — A wall-mounted panel of data receptors into which cross-connect patch cables from the punch-down block are inserted.

performance tester — A handheld device that not only checks for cable continuity, but also ensures that the cable length is not excessive, measures the distance to a cable fault, measures attenuation along a cable, measures crosstalk between wires, issues pass/fail ratings for wiring standards, and stores and prints cable testing results. Also known as a cable tester.

phase distortion — *See* delay distortion.

pinouts — The individual wire terminations within a connector.

plenum — The area above the ceiling tile or below the subfloor in a building.

probe — *See* tone locator.

propagation delay — The difference in time between a data packet's transmission and its reception over a specific route. Propagation delay depends mostly on the distance between the sender and receiver.

quad wire — *See* Level 1.

return loss — The loss of signal strength due to the reflection of prior signals along the same communications channel. One cause of return loss is a change in impedance.

risers — The backbone cabling that provides vertical connections between floors of a building.

RJ-45 (registered jack-45) — The standard connector used for modern twisted-pair cables such as CAT5.

round trip time (RTT) — The length of time it takes for a packet to go from sender to receiver, then back from receiver to sender. RTT is typically expressed in milliseconds.

scalability — The ease with which a system or network can be extended, including adding length, nodes, or functions.

segment — The distance a network may carry a signal before the signal must be repeated or amplified.

sheath — The outer cover, or jacket, of a cable.

shielded twisted-pair (STP) — A type of cable containing twisted wire pairs that are not only individually insulated, but also surrounded by a shielding made of a metallic substance such as foil. The shielding acts as an antenna, converting the noise into current (assuming that the wire is properly grounded). This current induces an equal, yet opposite current in the twisted pairs it surrounds. The noise on the shielding mirrors the noise on the twisted pairs, and the two cancel each other out.

shielding — The metallic substance that surrounds an insulated copper wire in shielded twisted-pair cabling.

signal-to-noise ratio (SNR) — The relationship between the strength (or amplitude) of a signal and noise affecting the signal. The higher the signal-to-noise ratio, the clearer the signal.

single-mode fiber — A type of fiber optic cable with a narrow core that carries light pulses along a single data path from one end of the cable to the other end. Data can be transmitted faster and for longer distances on single-mode fiber than on multimode fiber. Single-mode fiber is extremely expensive.

8

splice — The physical joining of two facing and aligned wires or fibers. Most often, a splice refers to the connection of two fibers to form one continuous fiber optic communications channel.

straight-through cable — A twisted-pair patch cable in which the wire terminations in both connectors follow the same scheme.

structured cabling — A method for uniform, enterprise-wide, multivendor cabling systems specified by the TIA/EIA 568 Commercial Building Wiring Standard. Structured cabling is based on a hierarchical design using a high-speed backbone.

telephone test set — A rugged and sophisticated device that resembles a telephone handset and is used by telephone technicians to verify that a line is functioning.

thermal noise — Signal interference caused by heat and changes in temperature agitating the electrons in a wire. Thermal noise is constant and ubiquitous.

time domain reflectometer (TDR) — A high-end instrument for testing the qualities of a cable. It works by issuing a signal on a cable and measuring the way in which the signal bounces back (or reflects) to the TDR.

tone generator — A device that issues a tone over a cable. The combination of a tone generator and tone locator is used to identify one cable among many. It may also be called a toner or a fox and hound.

tone locator — An amplifier that can detect inductive energy issued by a tone on a wire. A tone locator is used in conjunction with a tone generator to identify one cable among many.

toner — *See* tone generator.

twist ratio — The number of twists per meter or foot in a twisted-pair cable.

twisted-pair (TP) — A type of cable similar to telephone wiring that consists of color-coded pairs of insulated copper wires, each with a diameter of 0.4 to 0.8 mm, twisted around each other and encased in plastic coating.

unshielded twisted-pair (UTP) — A type of cabling that consists of one or more insulated wire pairs encased in a plastic sheath. As its name implies, UTP does not contain additional shielding for the twisted pairs. As a result, UTP is both less expensive and less resistant to noise than STP.

white noise — *See* thermal noise.

REVIEW QUESTIONS

1. What happens to an electrical signal as a result of impedance mismatches in a communications channel?

   a. return loss

   b. white noise

   c. delay distortion

   d. intermodulation noise

2. What type of device is used to compensate for delay distortion?

   a. filter

   b. hub

   c. transistor

   d. equalizer

3. A lightning strike near a drop cable causes what type of noise on a telephone signal traversing the cable?

   a. intermodulation noise

   b. crosstalk

   c. impulse noise

   d. white noise

4. Which of the following is caused by the induction of one wire's current on an adjacent wire's signal?

   a. intermodulation noise

   b. crosstalk

   c. impulse noise

   d. white noise

5. What is the outermost covering on a cable called?

   a. cladding

   b. sheath

   c. braiding

   d. insulation

6. Which of the following types of coaxial cable would be used to carry cable TV signals?

   a. RG-5

   b. RG-6

   c. RG-8

   d. RG-58 A/U

7. Which of the following types of wire would most likely be used to form a twisted-pair cable used in a new home's telephony installation?

   a. 24 AWG

   b. 30 AWG

   c. 36 AWG

   d. 48 AWG

8

8. In a CAT3 cable, for example, what type of noise could occur between two wires within the same wire pair?

    a. intermodulation crosstalk

    b. alien crosstalk

    c. near-end crosstalk

    d. thermal crosstalk

9. Which of the following types of twisted-pair cables is most common on modern LANs?

    a. Level 1

    b. CAT3

    c. CAT5

    d. CAT7

10. Which of the following types of twisted-pair cables is rated by the FCC as the minimum standard allowable for new telephony installations?

    a. Level 1

    b. CAT3

    c. CAT5

    d. CAT7

11. What standards organization not only establishes the twisted-pair category levels, but also sets guidelines for uniform cable installation?

    a. TIA/EIA

    b. IEEE

    c. ITU

    d. ISO

12. Shielded twisted-pair is less expensive than unshielded twisted-pair. True or False?

13. How many wire pairs are in a typical CAT5 cable?

    a. 2

    b. 3

    c. 4

    d. 6

14. Why aren't signals traveling over fiber optic cable susceptible to interference from EMI or RFI?

15. What property of light is exploited in transmission over multimode fiber?

    a. absorption

    b. diffusion

    c. refraction

    d. reflection

16. What happens to a lightwave signal as a result of impedance mismatches in the communications channel?

    a. incidence refraction

    b. attenuation

    c. optical loss

    d. impedance mismatches do not apply to lightwave transmission

17. Which of the following is a typical use of fiber optic cable?

    a. connecting a workstation and a connectivity device on a LAN

    b. connecting a server and a connectivity device on a LAN

    c. connecting a switch and an MDF within a central office

    d. connecting a main feeder and a central office

18. Multimode fiber can carry signals longer before they require repeating than can single-mode fiber. True or False?

19. What is the major disadvantage to installing fiber on a network?

    a. It carries signals so fast that connected equipment cannot receive them fast enough, thereby causing data errors.

    b. It is more expensive than any other transmission medium.

    c. It is still an evolving technology, and as such, standards have not been established to allow media from one manufacturer to connect with the media or equipment of another manufacturer.

    d. There is no disadvantage to installing fiber on a network.

20. Which of the following is used to generate and issue signals onto a fiber optic cable?

    a. LED

    b. optical time domain reflectometer

    c. optical filter

    d. fiber optic switch

8

21. If you use CAT5 cabling for backbone wiring and CAT3 cabling for horizontal wiring, what is the maximum throughput that your networked workstations will be able to achieve?

    a. 1 Mbps

    b. 4 Mbps

    c. 10 Mbps

    d. 100 Mbps

22. What is the *maximum* amount you should untwist twisted-pair wires before inserting them into connectors?

    a. ¼ of an inch

    b. ½ of an inch

    c. 1 inch

    d. 2 inches

23. Which of the following might occur if you loop a fiber optic cable tighter than its minimum bend radius?

    a. increased return loss

    b. increased attenuation

    c. increased intermodulation noise

    d. increased impedance

24. Which of the following types of connectors would you use with CAT5 cable?

    a. BNC

    b. ST

    c. RJ-11

    d. RJ-45

25. Which of the following connectors would you use with fiber optic cable?

    a. BNC

    b. ST

    c. RJ-11

    d. RJ-45

26. In which area of a standard structured cabling hierarchy would you find punch-down blocks?

    a. work area

    b. cable entrance facilities

    c. telecommunications closet

    d. plenum

27. According to TIA/EIA 568 standards, what is the recommended maximum length of a cable that connects a workstation's data jack to the punch-down block in the telecommunications closet?

   a. 10 meters

   b. 50 meters

   c. 75 meters

   d. 90 meters

28. What is the first step in a logical troubleshooting methodology?

   a. identify the symptoms

   b. identify the scope of the problem

   c. verify user competency

   d. analyze the potential impact of recent changes

29. What device would you use to isolate one cable's termination among a patch panel full of wire terminations?

   a. continuity tester

   b. cable tester

   c. tone generator and tone locator

   d. telephone test set

30. What device would you use to determine the extent to which optical loss is affecting a signal?

   a. continuity tester

   b. performance tester

   c. TDR

   d. OTDR

HANDS-ON PROJECTS

Project 8-1

As a telecommunications technician, you may work with older, Level 1 wiring when troubleshooting or extending existing residential telephone cabling, for example. However, more often, you will work with newer CAT3 or CAT5 cabling. As you have learned, CAT5 cabling requires RJ-45 connectors. Although in most instances you will purchase cables with the connectors pre-attached, in a pinch you may have to add a connector to a CAT5 cable. In this project, you terminate a length of CAT5 cable in an RJ-45 connector. The process of inserting wires into the connector is called crimping, and it is a skill that requires practice. Even experienced telecommunications technicians occasionally have problems successfully crimping connectors, so don't be discouraged if your first attempt is unsuccessful.

For this project, you need a wire crimper (also known as a crimping tool), a wire stripper, a wire cutter, a 5-foot length of CAT5 or higher UTP that contains four wire pairs, and one RJ-45 modular plug.

1. Using the wire cutter, make a clean cut at both ends of the UTP cable.

2. Using the wire stripper, remove the sheath off of one end of the UTP cable, beginning at approximately one inch from the end. Be careful to not damage the insulation on the twisted pairs inside.

3. Separate the four wire pairs slightly, then unwind each pair no more than ½ inch.

4. Align all eight wires on a flat surface, one next to the other, ordered according to their colors and positions listed earlier in Table 8-3.

5. Keeping the wires in order and in line, gently slide them all the way into the RJ-45 plug.

6. After the wires are fully inserted, place the RJ-45 plug in the crimping tool and press firmly to crimp the wires into place. (Be careful to not rotate your hand or the wire as you do this, otherwise only some of the wires will be properly terminated.) Crimping causes the pins to pierce the insulation of the wire, thus creating contact between the two conductors.

7. Now remove the RJ-45 connector from the crimping tool. Examine the end and see whether each wire appears to be in contact with the pin. It may be difficult to tell simply by looking at the connector. The real test is whether your cable will successfully transmit and receive signals. However, if it is obvious that the pins are not making contact with the wires inside your connector, begin the project again.

8. Repeat Steps 2 – 7 for the other end of the cable. After completing Step 7 for the other end, you will have created a CAT5 patch cable. Proceed to Project 8-2 to test your cable.

Project 8-2

After completing Project 8-1, you probably have a better appreciation for the precision required when adding connectors to cables, as well as the wisdom of carrying ready-made patch cables with you. In this project, you test the success of your patch cable. For this project, you need a Windows 2000 or XP workstation that is already connected to a network via a ready-made (manufactured) CAT5 cable. You also need to know the IP address of another device connected to the network.

1. Begin with the workstation connected to the wall jack via the ready-made CAT5 cable and log on to the workstation as a privileged user (such as Administrator).

2. You will first verify that it can exchange data with the network using a simple PING test. Click **Start**, point to **Programs** (if you are using Windows 2000) or **All Programs** (if you are using Windows XP), point to **Accessories**, and then click **Command Prompt**. The Command Prompt window appears, with a blinking cursor next to the C:\> prompt.

3. At the C:\> prompt, type **ping X**, where X is the IP address of another device connected to the network.

4. The response should result in four lines that begin with the words "Reply from..." and indicate that the device is responding. This is also how you know that your workstation is successfully connected to the network.

5. Now, replace the patch cable connecting the workstation to the wall jack with the patch cable you created in Project 8-1. (Because both ends are identical, it doesn't matter which connector you insert in the workstation's NIC and which you insert in the wall jack.)

6. Repeat Step 3. What response does the PING command produce now? If you receive a message that includes four lines that begin with the words "Reply from...," you have made a successful patch cable. If you receive a message that includes four lines saying "Destination host unreachable," you can conclude that your patch cable is not accurately transmitting or receiving data (or both).

7. Replace your cable with the ready-made patch cable and log off the workstation.

8

Project 8-3

In the previous project (and in Chapter 7), you experimented with the PING command. This utility is a simple way to help troubleshoot connectivity problems on data networks. It also offers some clues to a network's congestion by indicating how long it took a packet to reach a host, then return to your workstation over the network. Recall from earlier in this chapter that this measure of latency is known as round trip time. In this project, you experiment further with the PING command to compare latency in different connections. For this project, you need a Windows 2000 or Windows XP workstation that is connected to a LAN and also the Internet.

1. At the workstation, log on to the network as a user with administrative privileges.

2. Click **Start**, point to **Programs** (if you are using Windows 2000) or **All Programs** (if you are using Windows XP), point to **Accessories**, and then click **Command Prompt**. The Command Prompt window appears, with a blinking cursor next to the C:\> prompt.

3. At the C:\> prompt, type **ping 127.0.0.1**. Recall that this is the loopback address, which means that you are communicating with your own workstation by issuing this command.

4. You should see a reply that contains four lines beginning with the words "Reply from 127.0.0.1:..." Near the bottom of the output, you should see a heading called the "Approximate round trip times in milli-seconds:" These numbers indicate how long it took the PING packets to reach their destination plus how long it took for the reply to reach the PING source. In other words, they indicate the latency. What are the round trip times for the command you just issued? Why?

5. Use the PING command to reach a host elsewhere on your network. How do the round trip times compare to those you observed in Step 4?

6. Use the PING command to reach the Course Technology home page by typing the following command at the C:\> prompt: **ping www.course.com**. Again, observe the round trip times. How do they compare to those of your past tests? Also note the time it took for the first packet to make its journey there and back, compared to the remaining three packets. Why do you think it took the first packet longer?

7. Now, you will ping a host in another country by typing **ping www.itu.ch** (the ITU organization's site). Why is the latency of this connection different than that of all your previous tests?

8. For added interest, repeat Steps 6–7 at different times of the day—for example, at 6 a.m., noon, and then again at 6 p.m. to see how the latency of the Internet varies.

9. Close the Command Prompt window by typing **exit** and pressing **Enter**.

10. Log off the workstation.

CASE PROJECTS

Case
Projects

1. You have installed cable for both telephone and data networking applications for the last ten years. Recently, you have been asked to design cabling for Exeter Enterprises, a plastic parts manufacturer that is opening a new office in your city. Exeter has just leased a building that, up to now, has no telecommunications cabling infrastructure. In the building, Exeter will construct:

   ■ A fabrication lab containing 15 workstations and 2 telephones

   ■ A testing lab containing 22 workstations, 6 telephones, and 2 printers

   ■ 40 research offices, each with its own workstation and telephone, plus two shared printers for all offices

   ■ Two administrative offices with two telephones, one shared workstation, and one shared printer

   All of the workstations need to connect to one of two servers and at least one of six printers. All of the telephones need to connect to Exeter's digital PBX. Also, this Exeter office needs to connect to the company headquarters, which is 500 miles away. To do so, they will lease a high-bandwidth WAN link from the LEC.

   Draw a design of your recommended cabling infrastructure that follows the TIA/EIA 568 commercial building wiring standard. Label the parts of your design according to the six subsystems of structured cabling. Identify the type of cable used in each part. Make sure to draw each cable as it connects each node with its termination point in the hierarchy of structured cabling.

2. Documentation is vital to maintaining a cable plant. As part of your consulting duties, you devise your own logical labeling scheme for Exeter's cable plant. Make sure that each wall jack, punch-down connection, and port on the patch panel has its own identifying code. The codes for each termination point should make sense in relation to other termination point codes. Basing a coding scheme on location is often the most practical approach. For example, the first wall jack (from the door) in the lab might be labeled "LBWK-DJ-1" while the second wall jack might be labeled "LBWK-DJ-2." Next, create a chart that lists each cable, its maximum allowable length (according to TIA/EIA 568 standards), if applicable, and its two termination points (in other words, its starting point and ending point). For example, the cable that connects a work area wall jack to a punch-down block in the telecommunications closet might have starting point code of "LBWK-DJ-1" and an ending point code of "TC1-P3-R5" (which could represent the fifth row on the third column of a punch-down block in telecommunications closet number one). In an additional column, assign each cable its own unique code according to the scheme you devise. Bear in mind that although most cables are left in place after installation, it is possible that they might get moved. For this reason, it is wise to make sure the cable's starting and ending termination codes are incorporated into the cable code.

3. You present your cable infrastructure design and coding scheme to Exeter's top level staff. After reviewing it, they present another piece of information about their office. They plan to run high-temperature molding and parts stamping machines in the fabrication lab. In what ways does this information affect the type of cable you recommend and the way in which it is installed? On your diagram, mark the cables that might be affected by this new information.

8

9

WIRELESS TRANSMISSION AND SERVICES

> **After reading this chapter and completing the exercises, you will be able to:**
>
> ♦ Associate electromagnetic waves at different points on the wireless spectrum with their wireless services
>
> ♦ Identify characteristics that distinguish wireless transmission from wire-bound transmission
>
> ♦ Explain the architecture and access methods used in cellular networks and services
>
> ♦ Understand the differences between wireless and wireline local loops
>
> ♦ Describe the most popular WLAN standards, including their advantages, disadvantages, and uses
>
> ♦ Identify the major satellite positioning schemes and list several telecommunications services that rely on satellite transmission

Wireless transmission offers many advantages over wire-bound transmission. Perhaps most significantly, it is more flexible. Wireless signals can be issued from one transmitter to many receivers without the need for cables and the many potential flaws that cables can introduce. In addition, most wireless systems allow nodes to move freely within a range of a transmitter, whereas physically-cabled nodes are fixed in one location. However, wireless transmission is not perfect. One consideration is that wireless signals must all share the same, limited resource: the airwaves. Radio, television, microwave, cellular, satellite, LAN, and other services travel over the same medium simultaneously. Preventing the myriad electromagnetic waves from interfering with each other is one challenge. Yet another is making sure that the waves reach their destination, despite being limited to no specific path and encountering many obstacles during their journeys. In this chapter, you learn about the characteristics that make wireless telecommunications unique. You are also introduced to the technology behind the most popular forms of wireless communication.

THE WIRELESS SPECTRUM

All wireless signals are carried through the air along electromagnetic waves. In Chapter 2, you learned that electromagnetic waves are waves of energy composed of both electric and magnetic components. Radio broadcasts and light are both examples of electromagnetic waves. The waves that belong to the wireless spectrum (that is, the waves used for broadcasting, cellular telephones, and satellite transmission) are not visible or audible—at least, not until decoded by a receiver.

The **wireless spectrum** is a continuum of electromagnetic waves, with varying frequencies and wavelengths, that are used for telecommunications. (Recall that frequency and wavelength are inversely proportional—that is, the higher the frequency, the smaller the wavelength, and vice-versa.) The wireless spectrum (as defined by the FCC) spans frequencies between 9 KHz and 300,000 GHz. Each type of wireless service is associated with one area of the wireless spectrum. AM broadcasting, for example, involves the low frequency end of the wireless communications spectrum, using frequencies between 535 and 1605 KHz. Its wavelengths are between 560 meters and 190 meters long (from left to right on the wireless spectrum) respectively. Infrared waves make use of a wide band of frequencies at the high frequency end of the spectrum, between 300 GHz and 300,000 GHz. Infrared wavelengths can be between 1 millimeter and 1 micrometer long—potentially as small as a microorganism. Figure 9-1 shows the wireless spectrum and identifies the major wireless services associated with each range of frequencies. Table 9-1 lists the radio band (or "band") name and services associated with each frequency range. Notice that most frequency ranges are used for multiple services (in fact, many more than can be listed in this summary table). Technologies discussed in this chapter fall within the 800 MHz to 50 GHz range.

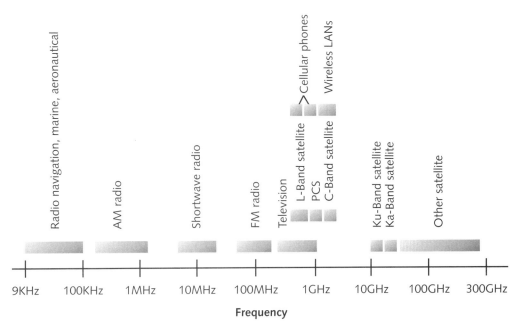

Figure 9-1   The wireless spectrum

Table 9-1   Bands and uses of various frequency ranges

Frequency Range	Band	Notable Uses
3–30 KHz	Very low frequency (VLF)	Marine mobile communications and navigation
30–300 KHz	Low frequency (LF)	Marine and aeronautical mobile communications and navigation
300–3000 KHz	Medium frequency (MF)	AM radio
3–30 MHz	High frequency (HF)	Shortwave, citizen's band (CB) radio
30–300 MHz	Very high frequency (VHF)	FM radio, TV stations 2–13, police and other government transmissions
300–3000 MHz	Ultra high frequency (UHF)	TV channels 14–69, cellular telephone, paging, PCS, wireless LANs
3–30 GHz	Super high frequency (SHF)	Satellite communications, radiolocation
30–300 GHz	Extremely high frequency (EHF)	Point-to-point microwave service, satellite, aeronautical and meteorological communications

The wireless spectrum is a subset of the spectrum of all electromagnetic waves. Electromagnetic waves with higher or lower frequencies exist in nature, but are not used for telecommunications. Frequencies lower than 9 KHz are used for specialized applications, such as wildlife tracking collars and garage door openers. Electromagnetic waves with frequencies higher than 300,000 GHz are visible to humans and, for that reason alone, cannot be used for communication through the air. For example, we recognize an electromagnetic wave with a frequency of 428,570 GHz as the color red. At the very highest end of the electromagnetic spectrum are x-rays and gamma rays. Figure 9-2 depicts the entire electromagnetic spectrum, including the range of frequencies used for telecommunications.

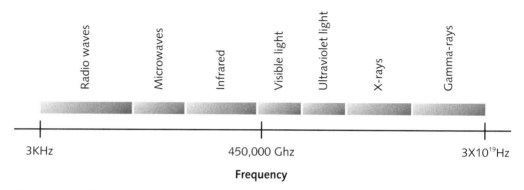

Figure 9-2   The electromagnetic spectrum

In the United States, the collection of frequencies available for communication—also known as "the airwaves"—is a natural resource available for public use. The FCC determines what frequency ranges can be used for what purposes. Some frequencies—those in the 900 MHz and 2.4 GHz portions of the wireless spectrum—are **unlicensed**. The FCC specifies the types of signals that can be issued over unlicensed frequencies, but anyone can use them, without registering with or paying fees to the FCC. Because they are freely available, unlicensed frequency ranges are crowded with signals. Most frequencies, however, are **licensed**, which means an organization must apply to the FCC and pay a fee to issue signals over those frequencies. The FCC grants organizations in different locations exclusive rights to use each frequency. It also determines what frequency ranges can be used for what purposes. For example, the FCC has determined that the range of frequencies between 88 and 108 MHz can be used for FM radio broadcasting. In addition, it has granted exclusive regional use of the 88.7 MHz frequency to a radio station with the call letters "KRVS" in Lafayette, Louisiana and exclusive use of the same frequency to a radio station with the call letters "WXDU" in Durham, North Carolina. Because the 88.7 MHz frequency is a licensed frequency, each radio station must register with the FCC and pay for the right to broadcast over this frequency in its area.

Of course, signals propagating through the air do not necessarily remain within one nation. Therefore, it is important for countries across the world to agree on wireless telecommunications standards. The ITU is the governing body that sets standards for international wireless services, including frequency allocation, signaling and protocols used by wireless devices, wireless transmission and reception equipment, satellite orbits, and so on. If governments and companies did not adhere to ITU standards, chances are that a wireless device could not be used outside of the country in which it was manufactured.

As you proceed through this chapter, you may find it helpful to refer to the wireless spectrum in Figure 9-1. Next, you learn about the unique characteristics of communication signals traveling through the atmosphere.

CHARACTERISTICS OF WIRELESS TRANSMISSION

Although wireline and wireless signals share many similarities—including the use of protocols and encoding, for example—the nature of the atmosphere makes wireless transmission vastly different from wireline transmission. When engineers talk about wireless transmission, they refer to the atmosphere as an **unguided medium**. Because the air provides no fixed path for signals to follow, signals travel without guidance. Contrast this to guided media, such as UTP or fiber optic cable, which do provide a fixed signal path. The lack of a fixed path requires wireless signals to be transmitted, received, controlled, and corrected differently from wire-bound signals.

Just as with wire-bound signals, wireless signals originate from electrical current traveling along a conductor. The electrical signal travels from the transmitter to an antenna, which then emits the signal, as a series of electromagnetic waves, to the atmosphere. The signal propagates through the air until it reaches its destination. At the destination, another antenna accepts the signal, and a receiver converts it back to current. Figure 9-3 illustrates this process.

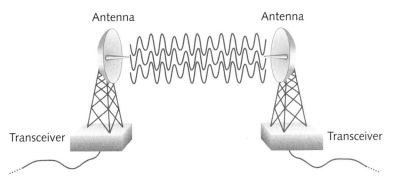

Figure 9-3   Wireless transmission and reception

Notice that antennas are used for both the transmission and reception of wireless signals. As you would expect, to exchange information, the transceivers connected to each antenna must be tuned to the same frequency. Next, you will learn about some fundamental types of antennas and their properties.

Antennas

Each type of wireless service requires an antenna specifically designed for that service. The service's specifications determine the antenna's power output, frequency, and radiation pattern. An antenna's **radiation pattern** describes the relative strength over a three-dimensional area of all the electromagnetic energy the antenna sends or receives. A **directional antenna** issues wireless signals along a single direction. This type of antenna is used when the source needs to communicate with one destination, as in a point-to-point link. A directional antenna may also be used when multiple receiving nodes are arranged in line with each other. Alternatively, it may be used when sustaining the signal's strength over a distance is more important than covering a broad geographical area, because an antenna can either use its power to send signals in more directions or in one direction for a greater distance. Some examples of wireless services that use directional antennas include satellite uplinks and downlinks, wireless LANs, and space, marine, and aviation navigation. Figure 9-4 illustrates a view, from directly above the antenna, of a directional antenna's radiation pattern. Bear in mind that in reality, radiation patterns are three-dimensional.

Figure 9-4   Radiation pattern of a directional antenna (depicted from above)

In contrast, an **omni-directional antenna** issues and receives wireless signals with equal strength and clarity in all directions. This type of antenna is used when many different receivers must be able to pick up the signal, or when the receiver's location is highly mobile. TV and radio stations use omni-directional antennas, as do most towers that transmit cellular telephone signals. Figure 9-5 depicts a birds-eye view of an omni-directional antenna's radiation pattern.

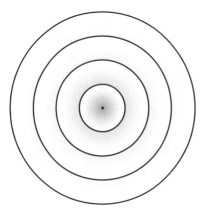

Figure 9-5   Radiation pattern of an omni-directional antenna (depicted from above)

Other types of antennas are not strictly directional or omni-directional, but focus their energy in a few specific directions. For example, a bi-directional antenna issues signals in two directions. Using a bi-directional antenna provides the benefits of a greater coverage area than a directional antenna while sustaining greater signal strength than an omni-directional antenna.

An important consideration in wireless signaling is how far an antenna can transmit a signal that is sufficiently powerful to be clearly interpreted by its receiver. A simple principle of wireless transmission is that a stronger signal will travel farther than a weaker signal. That is, the greater an antenna's power, the farther its range. As you have learned, another way to ensure a signal's strength is to limit the number of directions in which its signals radiate. In addition, engineers may use one of two techniques to maximize an antenna's reach: increasing the antenna's aperture or using a reflector. An **aperture** is the physical area through which an antenna's signal passes as it is transmitted or received. When you increase the aperture, you allow more electromagnetic energy to pass through, resulting in a stronger signal. A reflector strengthens a signal by capturing and concentrating a larger field of energy than could be captured at one point in space. This works on the same principle as the reflector that surrounds a flashlight bulb and serves to concentrate the flashlight's beam of light. Reflectors may be concave disks, parabolas, or grids that surround the antenna. For example, the dish used to receive satellite television signals is actually a reflector that concentrates signals toward a small antenna.

Correct antenna placement is also critical to ensure optimal performance of a wireless system. Antennas used for signaling over long distances are most often mounted on towers or on the tops or sides of tall buildings. Transmitting signals from heights ensures fewer obstructions and better signal reception. Antennas may be built into transmission and reception devices, as is the case with cellular telephones, Walkie-Talkies, and NICs used on wireless LANs. Built-in antennas add to the convenience of such devices, and decrease the device's overall size. In vehicles, the radio receiver antenna is typically built into the glass windshield.

The technical principles that describe antennas can be very complex, and a thorough discussion of antenna theory is beyond the scope of this book. However, a familiarity with the fundamental operation of these critical components will help you understand specific wireless systems.

Signal Propagation

Ideally, a wireless signal travels directly in a straight line from its transmitter to its intended receiver. This type of propagation, known as **line of sight (LOS)**, uses the least amount of energy and results in the reception of a perfectly clear signal. However, because the atmosphere is an unguided medium and the path between a transmitter and a receiver is not always clear, wireless signals do not usually follow a straight line. When an obstacle stands in a signal's way, the signal may pass through the object, be absorbed by the object, or it may be subject to any of the following phenomena: reflection, diffraction, or scattering. The object's geometry governs which of these three phenomena occurs.

Reflection, Diffraction, and Scattering

Reflection in wireless signaling is no different from reflection of other electromagnetic waves, such as light. The wave encounters an obstacle and reflects—or bounces back—toward its source. A wireless signal bounces off objects whose dimensions are large compared to the signal's average wavelength. In addition, signals reflect more readily off conductive materials, like metal, than insulators, like concrete. Consider, for example, a microwave oven. Because microwaves have an average wavelength of less than one millimeter, once the microwaves are issued, they reflect off the inside walls of the oven, which are typically at least 15 centimeters long. Exactly which objects cause a wireless signal to reflect depends on the signal's wavelength. In the context of a wireless LAN, which may use signals with wavelengths between one and 10 meters, such objects include walls, floors, ceilings, and the earth.

In **diffraction**, a wireless signal splits into secondary waves when it encounters an obstruction. The secondary waves continue to propagate in the direction in which they were split. If you could see wireless signals being diffracted, they would appear to be bending around the obstacle. Objects with sharp edges—including the corners of walls and desks—cause diffraction.

Scattering is the diffusion, or the reflection in multiple different directions, of a signal. Scattering occurs when a wireless signal encounters an object that has small dimensions compared to the signal's wavelength. Scattering is also related to the roughness of the surface a wireless signal encounters. The rougher the surface, the more likely a signal is to scatter when it hits that surface. Outdoors, trees and signposts cause scattering of cellular telephone signals. In an office building, objects, such as chairs, books, and computers, cause scattering of wireless LAN signals. The higher the frequency of the wireless signal, the more scattering that occurs, because the signal's wavelength is more likely to be smaller than objects it encounters.

Environmental conditions, such as mist, rain, or snow, may also cause reflection, diffraction, and scattering. This makes sense if you think of drops of precipitation as small objects. In most cases, if precipitation causes a change in a signal's propagation, it results in scattering. If the precipitation is heavy, a signal scatters off several droplets multiple times. Such extreme scattering may result in a badly distorted signal. For example, a television attempts to receive a signal issued from a satellite, heavy precipitation may obscure the picture entirely.

Multipath Signals

Because of reflection, diffraction, and scattering, wireless signals follow a number of different paths to their destination. Such signals are known as **multipath** signals. The generation of multipath signals doesn't depend on how the signals were issued. They may radiate with equal strength in many directions from their source or they may radiate primarily in one direction from their source. Once issued, however, they follow many paths, due to reflection, diffraction, and scattering. Figure 9-6 illustrates multipath signals caused by these three phenomena.

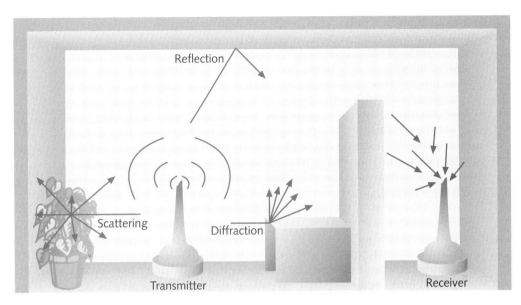

Figure 9-6   Multipath signal propagation

The multipath nature of wireless signals is both a blessing and a curse. On one hand, because signals bounce off obstacles, they have a better chance of reaching their destination. In environments such as an office building, wireless services depend on signals bouncing off walls, ceilings, floors, and furniture so that they may eventually reach their destination. Imagine how inconvenient and inefficient it would be, for example, to make sure you were standing within clear view of a transmitter to receive a paging signal.

The downside to multipath signaling is that because of their various paths, multipath signals travel different distances between their transmitter and a receiver. Thus, multiple instances of the same signal can arrive at a receiver at different times, causing fading and delay—transmission flaws discussed next.

Fading and Delay

Fading is a change in signal strength as a result of some of the electromagnetic energy being scattered, reflected, or diffracted after being issued by the transmitter. In fading, multipath signals encounter obstacles on their way to a receiver and arrive at the receiver at different times. In other words, they arrive out of phase. Due to phase differences, some signal waves may cancel each other out, weakening the overall received signal strength. Most often, the strength of the signal that reaches the receiver is *lower* than its transmitted strength. This makes sense because as more waves are reflected, diffracted, or scattered by obstacles, more are likely to arrive at their destination out of phase. After an antenna issues a signal, the extent of fading the signal experiences continually varies, due to the changing path environment and signal reaction.

As you learned in Chapter 8, delay occurs when different parts of the originally issued signal arrive at the receiver at different times. In a television broadcast, you can recognize delay as "ghosting"—or the faint double of an image that appears next to the primary image.

To compensate for fading and delay caused by multipath signals, wireless systems may use multiple transmitters (placing them some distance apart from each other) or issue multiple instances of the same signal at slightly different times or on different frequencies. The use of multiple antennas or multiple signal transmissions to compensate for fading and delay is known as **diversity**.

Attenuation

In Chapter 2, you learned that as a signal moves farther away from its source, it attenuates, or becomes weaker. This occurs not only in wireline systems, but also in wireless systems. After a signal is transmitted, the farther it moves away from the transmission antenna, the more it weakens. Just as with wire-bound transmission, wireless signals are amplified (if analog) or repeated (if digital) to strengthen the signal so that it can be clearly received. The difference is that the intermediate points through which wireless signals are amplified or repeated are antennas.

However, attenuation—which is only a matter of distance—is not the most severe flaw affecting wireless signals. As you have learned, fading and delay from multipath propagation is a more serious problem. In addition, wireless signals are highly susceptible to interference, as explained in the next section.

Interference

Because wireless signals are a form of electromagnetic activity, they can be hampered by other electromagnetic energy, resulting in interference. Although interference is also a challenge for wire-bound signals, it's usually a greater problem with wireless signals. One reason interference is a significant problem for wireless telecommunication is that the atmosphere is saturated with electromagnetic waves. A cellular telephone signal can be affected by both radio and television broadcast signals. Wireless LANs that use very high frequency transmissions may be affected by microwave ovens or overhead lights. Not only do telecommunications services generate electromagnetic waves, but so do power lines, the sun, and storms. For example, a radio signal can be rendered unintelligible by a lightning strike.

Interference can distort and weaken a wireless signal in the same way that noise distorts and weakens a wire-bound signal. However, because wireless signals cannot depend on a conduit or shielding to protect them from extraneous EMI and RFI, they are more vulnerable to this form of noise. The type of interference a wireless signal experiences depends partly on the type of wireless transmission in use and the density of signals within one area. Cellular networks, for example, may use similar frequencies to serve many customers in the one region or close, neighboring geographical area. Such proximity may result in cellular telephone signals interfering with each other. Naturally, signals that must travel through areas where many wireless communications systems are in use—for example, a downtown financial district—are more apt to suffer interference.

Not only are wireless signals affected by EMI and RFI, but when considered from another viewpoint, they also *are* EMI or RFI. For example, in a hospital, the use of paging and cellular services generates interference that may adversely affect patient monitoring equipment. At the same time, paging services are vital in aiding hospital personnel to respond quickly to medical emergencies. The solution is to adequately shield hospital equipment from EMI and RFI while at the same time limiting wireless signaling to only the most necessary communications.

Narrowband, Broadband, and Spread Spectrum Signals

Transmission technologies differ according to how much of the wireless spectrum their signals use. An important distinction is whether a wireless service uses narrowband or broadband signaling. In **narrowband**, a transmitter concentrates the signal energy at a single frequency or in a very small range of frequencies. In contrast to narrowband, **broadband** (also known as **wideband**) refers to a type of signaling that uses a relatively wide band of the wireless spectrum. The minimum bandwidth necessary for a service to qualify as broadband is ambiguous. Depending on the source, the minimum could be specified at 3 KHz or 6 MHz. The FCC defines broadband services as those capable of at least 200 Kbps throughput in one direction. Most telecommunications professionals agree that to be considered broadband, a service should be at least capable of transmitting a clear voice signal. Examples of broadband wireless services include MMDS and LMDS (discussed later in this chapter). The term broadband is also frequently used to describe wire-bound services such as cable TV. Broadband technologies, as a result of their wider frequency bands, offer higher throughputs than narrowband technologies.

The use of multiple frequencies to transmit a signal is known as spread spectrum technology (because the signal is spread out over the wireless spectrum). In other words, a signal never stays continuously within one frequency range during its transmission. One result of spreading a signal over a wide frequency band is that it requires less power per frequency than narrowband signaling. This distribution of signal strength makes spread spectrum signals less likely to interfere with narrowband signals traveling in the same frequency band.

9

The other result of spreading a signal over more than one frequency is added security. Because signals are distributed according to a sequence known only to the authorized transmitter and receiver, it is much more difficult for unauthorized receivers to capture and decode these signals. To generic receivers, signals issued via spread spectrum technology appear as unintelligible noise. In fact, spread spectrum technology was initially devised for military communications. In 1940, as World War II escalated in Europe, actress-turned-inventor Hedy Lamarr and another inventor, George Anthiel, patented an early form of spread spectrum signaling. The inventors anticipated that this technology would be used to control torpedo launches. But after much experimentation, the military abandoned the idea. When Lamarr and Anthiel's patent expired in 1957, Sylvania assumed the task of developing spread spectrum technology. Sylvania's technology was finally used by the U.S. Navy during the Bay of Pigs Invasion of Cuba in 1962. However, spread spectrum technology remained classified government technology until the 1980s, when it was released for public applications. One of its first public uses was cellular telephone service. As you learn later in this chapter, some modern types of cellular telephone service continue to rely on spread spectrum signaling.

One specific implementation of spread spectrum is **frequency hopping spread spectrum (FHSS)**. In FHSS transmission, a signal jumps between several different frequencies within a band in a synchronization pattern known to the channel's receiver and transmitter. Another type of spread spectrum signaling is called **direct sequence spread spectrum (DSSS)**. In DSSS, a signal's bits are distributed over an entire frequency band at once. Each bit is coded so that the receiver can reassemble the original signal upon receiving the bits.

Fixed vs. Mobile

Each type of wireless communication falls into one of two categories: fixed or mobile. In **fixed** wireless systems, the locations of the transmitter and receiver are static. The transmission antenna focuses its energy directly toward the receiver antenna. One advantage of fixed wireless is that because the receiver's location is predictable, energy need not be wasted issuing signals across a large geographical area. Thus, more energy can be used for the signal. In a wireless network, more available signal energy results in higher potential bandwidth. Fixed wireless links are used both in data and telephone networks. For example, a LEC may set up fixed wireless links between multiple towers to reach remote rural telephone customers, as shown in Figure 9-7. In this example, you can think of the wireless link as a substitute for a wire or fiber optic cable. In cases where a long distance or difficult terrain must be traversed, fixed wireless links are more economical than cabling.

Figure 9-7 Fixed wireless links in the PSTN

Not all communications are suited to fixed wireless, however. For example, cellular telephone users could not use a service that requires them to remain in one spot to receive a signal. Instead, cellular, paging, wireless LANs, and many other services use **mobile** wireless systems. In mobile wireless, the receiver can be located anywhere within a specific range of the transmitter. This allows the receiver to move from one place to another while continuing to pick up its signal. In addition to cellular telephone, paging, and wireless LANs, radio and TV broadcasting are also examples of mobile telecommunications, because receivers can be located anywhere within range of the transmission towers. Receivers that operate in a mobile wireless system (for example, cellular telephones) are known as **mobile stations** or **mobile units**. Figure 9-8 depicts some different types of mobile wireless communication.

In this chapter, you find examples of both fixed and mobile wireless systems. The next section describes the evolution and technology behind one of the most common examples of mobile wireless, cellular telephone service.

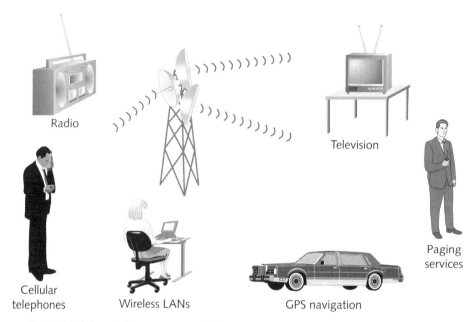

Figure 9-8   Mobile wireless communication

CELLULAR COMMUNICATIONS

All modern wireless technology owes a debt to two vital inventions: the telegraph and the radio (discussed in Chapter 3). Cellular networks are no different. Their roots lie with Marconi's radio, which enabled two-way radio transmission of voice signals as unmodulated radio waves over long distances. Prior to the invention of FM, two-way radio services were dedicated to public safety purposes and employed by ships, the military, and police and fire departments. They weren't highly mobile. The equipment required for these services was too cumbersome to use in an automobile, for example. In addition, the transmission quality was not good enough for signals to overcome obstacles and elevation changes in urban areas.

Thanks to Edwin Armstrong's invention of FM radio in 1935, however, two-way radio equipment became more practical for mobile users. In addition, FM improved the quality of radio wave transmission. The FM frequency range of 88 to 108 MHz was allocated to radio broadcasts, whereas a higher band of frequencies was used for two-way radio communication. Like computer technology, two-way radio communication advanced significantly with the mid-twentieth century inventions of the transistor and integrated circuit. In 1946, AT&T and Southwestern Bell performed the first successful trial of its mobile two-way radio telephone service in St. Louis, Missouri. In 1947, scientists at Bell Labs proposed the idea of cellular telephone networks. **Mobile telephone service** is defined as a system for providing telephone service to multiple, mobile receivers using two-way radio communication over a limited number of frequencies. Although many wireless services use radio frequencies and allow two-way communication, **cellular telephone service** is distinguished by its unique method for reusing a small range of frequencies within a large geographical area.

Despite proving its viability by the middle of the twentieth century, cellular telephone service was not deployed in the United States until after 1984. This delay was partly due to the Bell System's ambivalence about building a wireless network and partly due to the FCC's reluctance to allocate frequencies to cellular services. In addition, cellular technology was slow to evolve, compared to the dizzying pace of today's computer advances. Not until after 1980 did the means exist to allow wide-range roaming, direct dialing, and full-duplex transmission features that finally made cellular service attractive and useful to most people. Furthermore, early cellular telephone sets were too expensive for average telephone subscribers, initially costing thousands of dollars.

Since 1984, cellular technology has rapidly evolved. Telecommunications professionals have roughly subdivided mobile wireless evolution into three stages: first generation (1G), second generation (2G), and third generation (3G). **First generation (1G)** cellular technology is characterized by analog transmission and a simple, relatively inefficient method for using frequencies to transmit and receive signals. To get more voice channels from a limited number of frequencies, **second generation (2G)** cellular technology, introduced in 1990, allows multiple signals access to a limited band of frequencies. It also uses digital encoding, which improves the signal quality and allows for encryption. Second generation cellular networks are what most of today's cellular telephones use. **Third generation (3G)** cellular technology, as yet unavailable to most subscribers, proposes further advances on 2G technology. It features all-digital encoding, provisions for quality of service (guaranteeing that priority signals will arrive intelligibly and on time), more efficient spectrum usage, and faster transmission (at least 128 Kbps). 3G wireless technology, as defined by the ITU in the IMT-2000 standard, is also designed to make wireless devices globally compatible. Next, you learn the basic principles of technology that underlie all three generations of cellular networks.

Principles of Cellular Technology

You have probably used cellular telephone service without thinking about why it's called "cellular." The answer is the technology's use of a network composed of bounded geographical regions called cells.

Cells

Each cell in a cellular telephone network is served by one low-power transmitter that issues signals to the mobile stations located in that cell. This low-power transmitter, along with a receiver and antenna, is located at a **base station**, also known as a **base transceiver station (BTS)** or a **cell site**. Base station antennas may be situated in one of two ways: a single, omni-directional antenna may sit at the center of each cell or three directional antennas may sit at the intersection of three cells, their radiation patterns pointing outward every 120 degrees, as shown in Figure 9-9. The use of low-power transmitters ensures that signals do not have enough strength to travel beyond the cell's boundary (and interfere with another cell's signals).

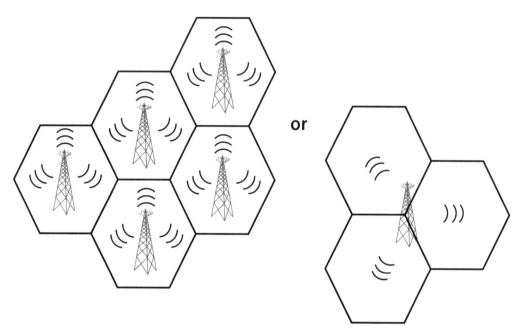

Figure 9-9   Base stations serving cells

Cell sizes vary from 12 to 24 miles in diameter. However, the size of a cell depends on the type of cellular access technology in use, and the region's topology, population, and amount of cellular traffic. An urban area with dense population and high volume of telephone traffic might use cells with a diameter of only two miles. Sparsely populated rural areas might use cells with a diameter greater than 24 miles.

When a mobile cellular user moves from one cell to another, her transmission is changed from a channel in her old cell to an available channel in the new cell. This process is called **handoff**. Ideally, handoff occurs without the user noticing it. (The specific method used for handoff depends on the type of cellular service, as you will learn in following sections.) For example, suppose Jenny is talking with a friend on her cell phone and driving across town, using channel A in cell 1. When Jenny drives across the boundary of cell 1 and into cell 2, her transmission is handed off to a new channel in cell 2. Once the handoff is complete, channel A in cell 1 is available for reuse. Thus, when Eric subsequently drives into cell 1, he may be assigned channel A. Dividing large geographical areas into cells allows the reuse of frequencies for different transmissions. As you learned in the beginning of this chapter, frequencies are a finite resource. Limiting a frequency's usage to small geographical areas allows more callers to simultaneously share this scarce resource.

To ensure that signals do not interfere with each other, the same channels are not reused in adjacent cells. Instead, a cellular network is made of clusters of (typically) seven cells. Each cell within a cluster uses different frequencies. In the previous example, channel A—the channel Jenny was assigned in cell 1—used a particular set of frequencies. When Jenny moves to cell 2, her new channel in cell 2 cannot use precisely the same frequencies as channel A in cell 1 used. However, adjacent *clusters* may use the same frequencies. A network is made of clusters that follow the same pattern of frequency use, so that cells next to each other on the edges of adjacent clusters do not reuse the same signals. For example, cell 1 in cluster 1 may use the same set of frequencies as cell 1 in cluster 2. Figure 9-10 depicts the use of cells and clusters in a cellular telephone network.

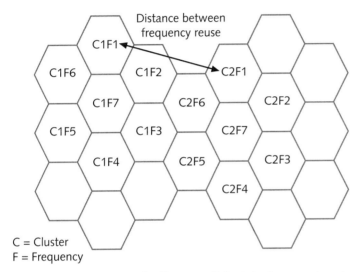

C = Cluster
F = Frequency

Figure 9-10   Layout of cells in a cellular telephone network

 On a typical cellular network diagram, cells are drawn as hexagons. However, in reality, these areas are not perfect geometrical shapes, but rather irregular shapes defined by the reaches of the low power transmitters that serve them.

Cellular Spectrum

Traditional analog cellular networks use the frequency ranges of 824-849 MHz and 869-894 MHz. Together, these ranges are often called "the 800 MHz band." The lower range is used for transmission from a cellular telephone (or mobile station) to a base station. This transmission is also known as the **forward path**. The upper range is used for transmission from a base station to a cellular telephone, also known as the **reverse path**. The 20 MHz separation between the two ranges prevents interference between signals going either direction.

The 800 MHz band is next to the TV broadcasting range on the wireless spectrum, but characterized by slightly a higher frequency. Cellular signals in this range have a wavelength of approximately 12 inches. Such waves are well suited to mobile wireless as they reflect easily off streets, buildings, and cars, allowing them a greater chance of reaching their destination. They are also prone to absorption by obstacles such as trees. This absorption limits the distance cellular signals may travel, which can be an advantage in preventing signals generated in different cells from interfering with one another. However, absorption can be a disadvantage when one cell's signals need to pass through forested areas to reach their destination.

The bandwidth of each analog cellular frequency range (824-849 MHz and 869-894 MHz) is 25 MHz. Adding both ranges results in 50 MHz that was originally allocated to cellular transmission. This is a significant amount of bandwidth, when compared to the 1.17 MHz allocated to AM radio, for example. Also, thousands of communications channels may be carved out of the 50 MHz range. However, cellular signaling requires more bandwidth than AM radio. One reason is that in order to accomplish full-duplex communication, each voice channel actually uses two frequencies: one for a forward path and one for a reverse path. In addition, cellular networks rely on separate **control channels** to convey information other than speech—for example, call setup information, signal timing data, the location of a mobile station, and codes that allow multiple signals to use the same channel. (You learn more about such techniques later in this chapter.) Finally, the bandwidth allocated to each cellular channel is typically 30 KHz—three times wider than AM radio's bandwidth of 10 KHz per channel.

Yet even with thousands of available frequencies in the 800 MHz range, the unpredicted popularity of cellular service led to a shortage of signaling capacity. In 1993, the FCC released the range of 1850 to 1950 MHz frequencies (also known as "the 1900 MHz range") for use with emerging cellular technologies. The addition of this range resulted in a significant increase in the capacity of modern wireless networks. Still, as you will learn, making efficient use of the limited cellular spectrum presents a continual challenge for mobile telephone networks.

Cellular Call Completion

The process of completing a call over a cellular telephone network is similar to, but more complex than completing a call over the PSTN. Because a mobile telephone user is not physically connected to the PSTN, the telephone network first needs a way to determine the user's location. Each time a user turns his cell phone on, the phone sends a signal to a cellular base station. This signal consists of three components: a Mobile Identification Number (MIN), an Electronic Serial Number (ESN), and a System Identification Number (SID). A **Mobile Identification Number (MIN)** is an encoded representation of the mobile telephone's 10-digit telephone number. An **Electronic Serial Number (ESN)** is a fixed number assigned to the telephone by the manufacturer. ESNs cannot be changed by the user or service carrier. Every telephone has a unique MIN and ESN. A **System Identification Number (SID)** is a number assigned to the particular wireless carrier to which the telephone's user has subscribed. Thus, a SID indicates, for example, whether a subscriber's telephone number and equipment used U. S. Cellular's, Verizon's, AT&T's, or Sprint's wireless network.

After a mobile user's identifying numbers are issued to the base station, the base station transmits this information to a **mobile telephone switching office (MTSO)**, which may also be known as a **mobile switching center (MSC)**. You can think of an MTSO as a small central office that only serves mobile users. In some areas, the MTSO is located inside a regular central office. An MTSO not only keeps track of the mobile stations in its area, but it also serves as a switching point for cellular telephone calls. MTSOs are connected to each base station they control via microwave links or wire or fiber optic cable. In addition, MTSOs belonging to the same company may be connected to each other via trunks, allowing simple connection of calls between cellular subscribers who use the same wireless carrier. An MTSO also serves as a gateway between multiple base stations and the PSTN. If an MTSO is not located within a central office, it is connected to a central office (and thus, its switching equipment) via trunks. Because it connects to the PSTN's switches, an MTSO has access to information about telephone users. The MTSO also monitors the locations of cellular telephone users within the cells it serves and controls handoff for callers passing between cells. Furthermore, it collects data about call traffic for billing purposes. You can think of an MTSO as the "brains" of a wireless telephone network, similar to an end office in the PSTN. Figure 9-11 illustrates the relationship between cells, base stations, a mobile telephone switching office, and the PSTN.

9

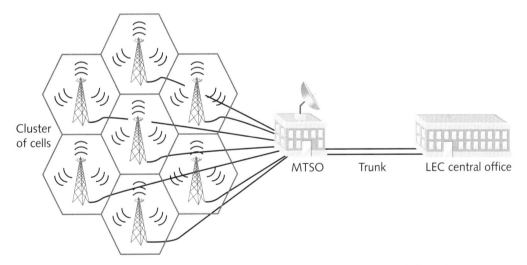

Figure 9-11   Relationship between cells, base stations, an MTSO, and the PSTN

To illustrate how mobile calls are completed, it is helpful to follow the path of a call initiated by a cellular telephone subscriber. For this example, suppose that Lee is calling Alison. After Lee keys in Alison's number, he presses a button on his phone to initiate the call. Lee's telephone (which contains an antenna) then transmits this information to the base station antenna that services the cell he's in. This signal travels over a control channel. His cell's base station receiver accepts the control channel signal and relays it to its MTSO. The MTSO determines whether Alison's number is within its carrier's wireless network or must be passed on to the PSTN. If Alison's number lies within the

MTSO's network, the MTSO forwards the request for a connection to Alison's MTSO. That MTSO issues a broadcast signal to all of its base stations, essentially requesting the attention of Alison's cellular telephone. Cellular telephones contain receivers that continually scan the control channel for incoming signals directed to them. If Alison's telephone is turned on, it detects a signal from her base station. In response to this signal, her phone rings. At this point, the communication between the two MTSOs changes from a control channel to a channel used for voice signals. When Alison pushes a button on her phone to accept the call, the connection is completed.

Figure 9-12 depicts call completion within one carrier's wireless network.

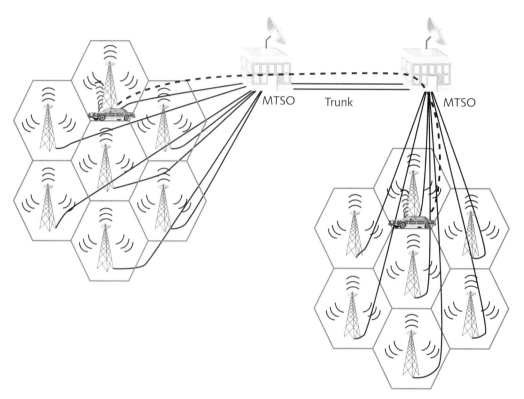

Figure 9-12   Call completion between cellular telephones

If the called number does not lie within the MTSO's network, the MTSO relays the signal to the PSTN's central office over a trunk. The switch at the PSTN's central office accepts the telephone number and determines whether the call can be completed within the central office's switching equipment or needs to be passed to another central office or to another wireless carrier's network. This process is similar to the LEC-to-LEC or LEC-to-IXC interconnection you learned about in Chapter 4.

As the next several sections explain, many different types of cellular telephone systems exist today. These technologies differ according to the ways in which they encode voice signals, modulate radio waves, and conserve and reuse the limited range of frequencies available to cellular service. One of the original forms of cellular telephone service is advanced mobile phone service (AMPS), which is discussed next.

Advanced Mobile Phone Service (AMPS)

Advanced mobile phone service (AMPS) is a first generation cellular technology that encodes and transmits speech as analog signals. The method AMPS uses for creating separate channels out of one frequency band and allowing signals access to these channels is called **frequency division multiple access (FDMA)**. FDMA divides the cellular spectrum into 832 separate communications channels, each with a bandwidth of 30 Hz. When a call is placed under the FDMA scheme, the call's transmission is guaranteed exclusive use of its 30 Hz channel for the duration of the call. As the caller speaks, his voice is modulated (in frequency modulation) along a carrier wave with a frequency in this 30 Hz channel. For each telephone call, one channel is assigned to transmission from a mobile telephone to a base station and another is assigned to transmission from the base station to the mobile telephone. If you imagine cellular signals as conversations, FDMA's technique of assigning each transmission a separate channel is similar to limiting one conversation to a room. Figure 9-13 illustrates the use of FDMA for multiple simultaneous calls within a cell.

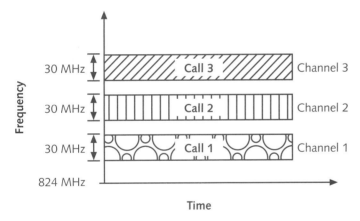

Figure 9-13   FDMA

The primary disadvantage to FDMA is its inefficient use of limited frequencies. Because FDMA requires the exclusive use of two 30 Hz channels for each telephone call, these channels cannot be reused until the caller has left a cell or terminated the call. This severely limits the capacity of an FDMA network. In addition, 30 Hz is a large amount of bandwidth to dedicate to each channel. Newer compression techniques for digital signaling enable cellular signals to fit within a much narrower frequency range. However, because FDMA is used only with analog signals, it cannot make use of this compression, nor can it use smaller channel bands.

Another disadvantage to FDMA is that because signals are analog, noise from interference and delay can lead to poor signal quality. Furthermore, as analog signals attenuate or fade, they can only be amplified. As you have learned, amplification boosts not only the signal, but also the noise that it has accumulated. Thus, on a stormy day or while traveling through areas that present multiple obstacles to a signal's path (such as buildings in a city's downtown), voice signals using FDMA sound garbled or masked by static.

AMPS is still used on some cellular networks today, in conjunction with newer digital encoding techniques, such as TDMA and CDMA, which are discussed next.

Time Division Multiple Access (TDMA)

As with AMPS, **time division multiple access (TDMA)** is a method of wireless network access that divides the cellular spectrum into channels assigned to different frequencies. However, TDMA (a second generation cellular technology) also divides each channel into several time slots. Each TDMA transmission is assigned a different time slot, enabling multiple transmissions to share a single channel. This technique is similar to time division multiplexing used in wireline communications (described in Chapter 6). TDMA also differs from FDMA in that it uses digital signals. Also, TDMA may use frequencies in either the 800- or 1900-MHz frequency ranges. In the United States most popular version of TDMA is called the Interim Standard (IS)-136, also known as **digital advanced mobile phone service (D-AMPS)**. This version of TDMA divides the frequency range into 30 KHz channels.

TDMA assigns three time slots to each 30 KHz channel. Thus, TDMA provides three times more capacity than FDMA. Call signals alternate using the 30 KHz channel in a round-robin fashion. If you think of cellular signals as conversations, TDMA is similar to allowing three conversations in one room, but assigning each speaker a finite time period during which he or she could speak. Figure 9-14 illustrates TDMA for multiple channels within one cell.

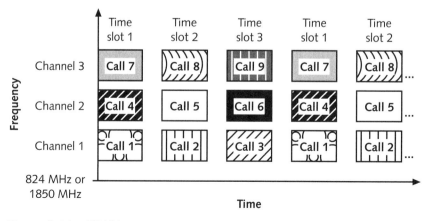

Figure 9-14 TDMA

Because TDMA allows multiple transmissions to share a channel, it makes more efficient use of frequencies than FDMA does. In addition, because TDMA signals are digital, they can be encrypted, checked and corrected for errors, and compressed to better conserve limited bandwidth. Digital encoding requires that synchronization of TDMA systems must be carefully controlled to ensure that bits arrive at the receiver with proper timing. Synchronization bits are issued over a separate control channel. Although TDMA is a digital access technology, it is capable of interpreting and exchanging analog signals. Use of this feature requires a subscriber to have a **dual mode** cell phone, or one that is capable of exchanging both analog and digital signals. This capability is necessary when mobile stations travel through areas (such as remote rural geographies) with base stations that are not equipped for digital signaling. As you might guess, the information indicating whether a call should use digital or analog encoding is exchanged between a telephone and a base station via the control channel.

 Digital encoding does not necessarily equal better sound quality in cellular networks. In fact, due to compression, synchronization, and multiple access techniques, some digital telephone calls sound much worse than their analog counterparts.

Although TDMA wireless is an improvement over FDMA, it still exhibits some inefficiencies, because although channels are subdivided to allow multiple access, only one signal can be transmitted at any given time. Code division multiple access (CDMA), discussed next, addresses this inefficiency.

Code Division Multiple Access (CDMA)

In **code division multiple access (CDMA)** each voice signal is digitized and assigned a unique code, and then small components of the signal are issued over multiple frequencies using the spread spectrum technique. CDMA divides the bandwidth available to a carrier into 1.25 MHz bands. A cell can contain 10 to 15 of these bands. Every transmission in a cell is spread over multiple frequencies within a 1.25 MHz band. As a signal is transmitted, it is modulated with a special code that makes it distinguishable from other signals. The receiver, knowing this code, can interpret its intended signal while ignoring all other signal activity service's frequency range. (The receiver essentially regards extra signals as noise.) In the conversation analogy, CDMA is similar to a number of couples talking at once in the same room. Each couple speaks and understands a different language. In this way, a sender and receiver listen only to the words spoken in their language and tune out words they cannot understand. Figure 9-15 depicts CDMA's use of multiple frequencies to transmit several calls at the same time.

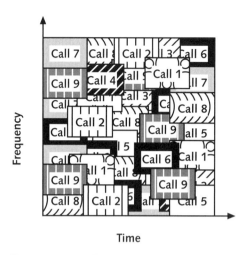

Figure 9-15   CDMA

CDMA's efficient use of a limited spectrum is one of its primary advantages. Because each signal is spread over multiple frequencies according to a special code, frequencies can be reused in nearby cells. This assumes that the codes used in adjacent cells are not the same. In addition, CDMA allows base stations to use very low power transmitters. The use of lower power transmitters means CDMA cells are smaller than TDMA or FDMA cells. This, in turn, allows a greater density of cells. A greater density of cells, combined with the increased potential for frequency reuse, adds up to a larger network capacity in any given region. CDMA can achieve at least three times the capacity of TDMA and at least 10 times the capacity of FDMA.

Like TDMA, CDMA is a digital technology (and like TDMA, CDMA is capable of interpreting and exchanging analog signals). But CDMA's transmission quality is even better than TDMA's because its spread spectrum nature makes it more reliable and less susceptible to noise. In addition, spread spectrum technology makes CDMA signals more difficult to intercept than TDMA signals (though specialized equipment can be purchased to intercept CDMA signals). On many cellular networks, CDMA is replacing TDMA. However, due to the complexity of accurately encoding and decoding CDMA signals, CDMA equipment is typically more expensive than TDMA equipment. Like TDMA, CDMA operates in both the 800- and 1900-MHz frequency bands. The most common implementation of CDMA is Interim Standard (IS)-95. Newer versions of CDMA, including some that use a wider band of frequencies, are proposed for the third generation (3G) mobile wireless standards.

Global System for Mobile Communications (GSM)

Global system for mobile communications (GSM) is a cellular technology popular in Europe since it was made publicly available in 1991, but only recently become common in the United States. Technically, GSM is a version of time division multiple access (TDMA) technology, because it divides frequency bands into channels and assigns signals time slots within each channel. However, GSM makes more efficient use of limited bandwidth than the IS-136 TDMA standard common in the United States. To accomplish this, GSM first divides a channel into smaller timeslots. It separates a 200 KHz channel into eight timeslots (compared to the three timeslots used in the IS-136 TDMA). Although this means that a signal must subdivided into smaller components before transmission, it also means that a signal is less likely to underutilize channel bandwidth. In addition, GSM makes use of silences in a phone call to increase its signal compression, leaving more open time slots in the channel. When time slots are left empty, GSM takes advantage of them by allowing signals to dynamically jump from one frequency to another, using the frequency hopping spread spectrum technique. Base stations and mobile stations keep track of frequency hopping through the use of a special signal on the control channel. Combined, frequency hopping and the use of smaller timeslots give GSM a greater capacity than the D-AMPs version of TDMA. However, GSM does not provide as much capacity as CDMA.

GSM has, since its inception, exclusively used digital signaling. Because it was the first and only mobile wireless network standard across Europe, it didn't need to accommodate older analog signaling, as did versions of TDMA used in the United States. Some organizations are attempting to make GSM the third generation standard for cellular telephone service worldwide. However, many different technologies are competing to be the next cellular technology of choice, as the next section explains.

Emerging Third Generation (3G) Technologies

The cellular technologies discussed thus far were designed to replace wirebound telephony. They conform to the circuit switching method of holding a connection open for as long as a session between a transmitter and receiver lasts. However, new cellular technology, which is based on packet-switching transmission techniques, has been developed. The promise of these technologies is that a user can access all her telecommunication services—including voice calls, e-mail, pages, documents, Internet connections, and even video feeds—from one mobile station. In addition to packet switching, 3G technologies promise higher bandwidth and better reliability than 2G technologies. In Japan, users are already taking advantage of data services on cellular networks, through a subscription-based service known as I-mode. However, in the United States, consumers have shown little interest in 3G services, much to the dismay of cellular equipment manufacturers and wireless carriers. In addition, the FCC has yet to allocate and license frequencies specifically for 3G wireless systems.

Nevertheless, the ITU has established standards for some 3G technologies. One standard, called **CDMA2000**, is based on technology developed by Qualcomm (the company that designed the original CDMA access method). CDMA2000 is a packet-switched version of the CDMA you learned about previously. CDMA2000 will be released in phases. In the first phase CDMA2000 will supply only data transmission (with a maximum throughput of 2.4 Mbps). In the second phase, it will supply both data and voice over the same 1.25 MHz carrier channel. Current CDMA carriers will need to upgrade their base station and MTSO equipment to supply CDMA2000. However, CDMA2000 and CDMA cells can communicate, allowing current CDMA subscribers to take advantage of CDMA2000 services without changing their equipment or service subscription. Carriers and wireless manufacturers in the United States have thus far embraced the CDMA2000 standard.

Wideband CDMA (W-CDMA) is another popular 3G standard. W-CDMA, based on technology developed by Ericsson, and standardized in Europe, shares many similarities with CDMA 2000. W-CDMA is also packet-based and its maximum throughput is also 2.4 Mbps. W-CDMA systems use a channel four times wider than current CDMA systems. Also, W-CDMA systems are capable of synchronizing with each other independent of a satellite-based time source, although CDMA 2000 systems rely on GPS (global positioning system) satellites. And unlike CDMA 2000, W-CDMA will not allow regular CDMA users to connect with their old equipment. On the other hand, W-CDMA is compatible with GSM mobile stations. Other 3G technologies exist; however, W-CDMA and CDMA 2000 appear to be most viable and accepted.

Personal Communications Service (PCS)

Personal communications service (PCS) is a term that may be used to refer to one of a number of technologies, depending on the context and the speaker. Today, PCS is defined by the FCC as a category of digital, mobile wireless services—including telephony and paging—that uses the 1900 MHz frequency band. All PCS services rely on a cellular network structure. However, different PCS services vary in the type of access technologies they use. For example, GSM, TDMA, and CDMA may all be considered a type of PCS.

WIRELESS LOCAL LOOP (WLL)

Wireless local loop (WLL) is a generic term that describes a wireless link used in the PSTN to connect LEC central offices with subscribers. Historically, WLLs have been used in locations where deploying copper local loops is impractical. For example, digging trenches and installing conduit and cables to reach subscribers on a steep, rocky mountain might be physically impossible or prohibitively expensive. Since 1996, when competition for local telephone service was opened, wireless local loops have also provided a way for CLECs to build their own infrastructure. By doing so, a CLEC can avoid having to lease facilities from an ILEC. This allows them rapid access to many new customers. Another common use of WLLs is in countries where wireline local loops have never existed. In this situation it is not only quicker, but also more economical (by some estimates, one-tenth of the cost) to build a WLL infrastructure than to build a wireline infrastructure from scratch.

From a telephone subscriber's point of view, a wireless local loop acts the same as a copper local loop. A home or office contains inside wiring and wall jacks to connect CPE, such as telephones, computers, and fax machines, to the PSTN. The WLL network interface to the PSTN is different, however. WLL subscribers use a small radio transceiver and antenna rather than the drop cable used on the PSTN (as described in Chapter 4). The subscriber's radio transceiver communicates with a PSTN base station using either analog or digital signals (depending on the wireless access technology the WLL uses). The PSTN's base station consists of a power supply, transceiver, and antenna. In most cases, this antenna is directional, because nearly all WLL transmissions are fixed, or point-to-point. The base station transceivers connect with the LEC's facilities through either another wireless link or a wireline trunk.

As with wireline local loops, wireless local loops are used to transmit both voice and data signals. They may be used for phone calls across the city or for downloading data from the Internet. In the United States, where wireline local loops are common, WLLs are being touted as an alternative to forms of high-bandwidth Internet access that depend on physical media. (You learn about this type of Internet access in Chapter 10.) For example, a consumer who already has a wireline connection to his LEC may also choose to lease a WLL connection specifically to obtain a high-speed Internet connection.

9

The technology used to supply wireless local loop connections varies from one carrier to the next and from one country to the next. In some areas, the WLL access technology is identical to that used on cellular networks—for example, TDMA and CDMA. When these technologies are used, the only difference between cellular networks and WLL networks is that the latter serve fixed receivers, rather than mobile ones. Because of congested frequencies within the cellular network bands, additional, higher frequency ranges have been made available to WLLs. These ranges fall between 1.8 GHz to 3.7 GHz on the wireless spectrum. Note that at the lower end of this range, WLL services overlap with newer digital cellular or PCS services, including GSM and emerging 3G offerings.

Rather than using the same access technologies used by cellular networks, some WLL carriers use **broadband wireless**. In this context, broadband refers to a service capable of very high data transfer rates. These access technologies, called local multipoint distribution service (LMDS) and multichannel multipoint distribution service (MMDS), were originally used to transmit television signals. (LMDS and MMDS are discussed in the next two sections.)

With such a variety of WLL access methods and the lack of one clear standard, it is not surprising that WLLs have experienced slow growth in the United States, where the existing wireline infrastructure is adequate for most subscribers' needs. Also, many consumers perceive that a WLL will provide poorer quality than their wirebound connection to the PSTN, though this is not always the case. Nevertheless, many different types of carriers, including LECs, IXCs, and ISPs are touting WLLs as the way of the future and vying for dominance in this market.

Local Multipoint Distribution Service (LMDS)

Local multipoint distribution service (LMDS) is a point-to-multipoint, fixed wireless technology that was conceived to supply wireless local loop service in densely populated urban areas and later used on a trial basis to issue television signals. LMDS operates in the 28, 30, and 31 GHz (microwave) frequency bands. It can deliver both one-way and two-way telecommunications services, including voice, video, and data. One significant benefit to LMDS is its extraordinary throughput. Typical data transmission rates for LMDS are 45 Mbps, and its potential throughput is three times that amount. Because of its capacity, LMDS is often proposed as a wireless alternative to fiber optic transmission technologies.

One disadvantage to LMDS is that its use of very high frequencies, which require considerable power to travel, limits its signals' transmission distance to no more than 4 km between antennas. Also, due to their very small wavelengths, LMDS signals are also highly susceptible to interference caused by factors such as adverse weather conditions. Finally, LMDS requires a line-of-sight path for its signals, which means obstacles, such as buildings and trees, can significantly diminish its performance.

Multipoint Multichannel Distribution System (MMDS)

Similar to LMDS, **multipoint multichannel distribution service (MMDS)** is another high-frequency, point-to-multipoint method of transmitting wireless video, voice, or data signals from one transmitter to multiple receivers. MMDS uses microwaves with frequencies in the 2.1 to 2.7 GHz range of the wireless spectrum. MMDS was originally developed in the mid-1990s to distribute "cable" television signals. More recently, however, it has been considered as a viable access technology for WLLs.

One advantage of using MMDS over LMDS is that because of its lower frequency range (and longer wavelengths), MMDS is less susceptible to interference. In addition, because of its unique method of encoding signals, MMDS does not require a line-of-sight path between the transmitter and receiver. This makes MMDS more appealing in areas with many buildings or dense foliage. Plus, its signals can travel up to 30 miles between antennas. Furthermore, MMDS technology is less expensive than LMDS. However, MMDS cannot achieve the high throughput that LMDS promises. Instead, it offers a maximum of 10 Mbps in one direction.

 Multipoint multichannel distribution service (MMDS) is sometimes also known as **microwave multipoint distribution system (MMDS)**.

In both MMDS and LMDS, the subscriber's receiving antenna is connected to a coaxial cable that then connects with the customer's internal data or telephony network. This arrangement lends itself to use in multi-tenant buildings such as apartment complexes. For example, one LMDS connection to a building could supply hundreds of tenants with Internet access, interactive television, and telephone service combined. The choice between LMDS and MMDS depends on many factors, including budget allowances, the distance between a subscriber and the carrier's transmission facilities, frequency availability within an area, and the relative number of obstacles in the signal's path.

Of all the WLL access technologies available today, perhaps MMDS holds the most promise as the method of choice by both PSTN carriers, Internet service providers, and data networking companies. Although it does not offer the same extraordinary capacity as LMDS, it still offers high throughput rates and can travel farther at a lower cost relative to LMDS.

WIRELESS LANs (WLANs)

A **wireless LAN (WLAN)** is a data network (or part of a data network) that uses wireless signaling for communication between nodes within a limited geographical area. Where a traditional LAN uses coaxial, twisted-pair, or fiber optic cable, a WLAN uses high-frequency radio waves. Today most LANs that use wireless technology do not rely exclusively on wireless communication, but use it only to connect nodes that require mobility. For example, hospital emergency room admissions personnel commonly use wireless connections between laptops and the hospital's network server. This way, they can bring a laptop to a patient, enter the patient's data, and save the data immediately to a centralized database. Healthcare is just one area where WLANs have become popular. Education, retail, manufacturing, and professional services sectors also take advantage of wireless networking.

Thanks to the efforts of many diverse network vendors and professional organizations, a great variety of wireless LAN technologies are now in use. The downside to this growth is a lack of one, dominant standard. In the following sections, you are introduced to basic architecture all WLANs share. You are also introduced to a few of the leading competitive standards used on today's wireless networks.

WLAN Architecture

Wireless LANs follow essentially the same layout as wire-bound LANs, except that the transmission paths between some devices are not physical. Nodes use their own transceiver and antenna, which are incorporated into the device's network interface card (NIC). Wireless NICs come in the same variety of styles as wireline NICS, including PCMCIA, USB, and internal adapter cards. Although wireless NICs cost more than wireline NICs, their prices have dropped significantly in recent years, to approximately $100. Figure 9-16 depicts some wireless NICs.

Figure 9-16   Wireless NICs

The transceiver and antenna used to issue signals from a wire-bound network device to mobile nodes is known as an **access point** or **base station**. Access points may be hardware-based, in which a transceiver and its antenna are one standalone unit, or they may be software-based, in which software installed on a computer with a wireless NIC manages wireless data exchanges. One access point typically serves multiple wireless network nodes, as shown in Figure 9-17. Notice how the access point bridges the wireless and wire-bound portions of the LAN.

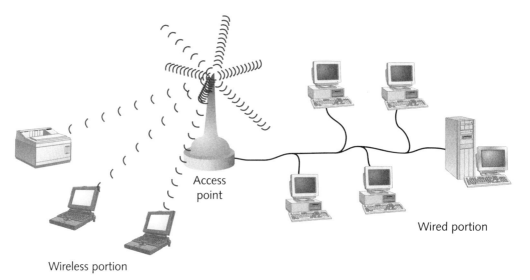

Access
point

Wired portion

Wireless portion

Figure 9-17   Simple wireless LAN architecture

It is common for a WLAN to include several access points. The number of access points depends on the number of wireless nodes a WLAN connects. The maximum number of nodes each access point can serve varies from 10 to 100, depending on the wireless technology used. Exceeding the recommended maximum leads to a greater incidence of errors and slower overall transmission.

As with mobile telephony, mobile networking allows wireless nodes to roam from one location to another within a certain range of their access point. However, unlike mobile telephony, wireless nodes have a much more limited range in which they can roam and maintain reliable connectivity. This range depends on the wireless access method, the equipment manufacturer, and the office environment. As with other wireless technologies, WLAN signals are subject to interference and obstructions that cause multipath signaling. Therefore, a building with many thick, concrete walls, for example, limits the effective range of a WLAN more severely than an office that is divided into a few cubicles. In general, wireless nodes must remain within 300 feet of an access point to maintain optimal transmission speeds.

In addition to connecting multiple nodes within a LAN, wireless technology can also be used to connect two different parts of a LAN or two separate LANs. Such connections typically use a fixed link between two access points, as shown in Figure 9-18. Because fixed links can apply more energy to signal propagation than mobile wireless links, their maximum transmission distance is greater. In the case of connecting two WANs, access points could be as far as 1000 feet apart.

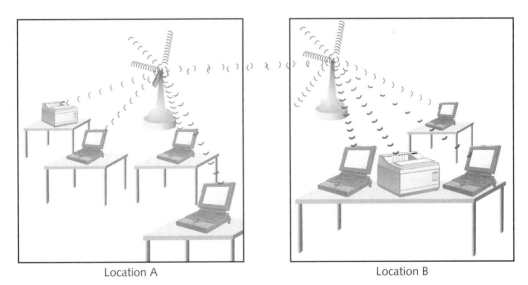

Location A   Location B

Figure 9-18   Wireless LAN interconnection

WLANs run over the same protocols (for example, TCP/IP) and the same operating systems (for example, UNIX, Windows, and Novell NetWare) as wireline LANs. This compatibility ensures that wireless and wireline transmission methods can be integrated on the same network. Only the signaling techniques differ between wireless and wireline portions of a LAN. However, techniques for generating and encoding wireless signals vary from one WLAN standard to another. Next, you learn about the most common wireless network access technologies.

Wireless Networking Standards

Similar to the development of wireline network access technologies, the development of wireless networking standards did not follow one direct and cooperative path, but grew from the efforts of multiple vendors and organizations. Now, a handful of WLAN technologies are competing for dominance. One of the most popular standards is IEEE 802.11.

802.11

As you learned in Chapter 1, IEEE is a professional organization that sets standards for network technology at all layers of the OSI model. IEEE assigns a committee to study and develop standards for every aspect of networking. IEEE's Radio Frequency Wireless networking standards committee is called the **802.11** committee. Each IEEE wireless network access standard is named after the 802.11 task group (or subcommittee) that developed it. Three IEEE 802.11 task groups have generated several wireless standards, of which the most notable are: 802.11b, 802.11g, and 802.11a. All of the 802.11 standards use half-duplex signaling. Thus, a wireless node using one of the 802.11 techniques can either transmit or receive, but cannot do both simultaneously (assuming it has only one transceiver installed, as is usually the case).

In 1999, the IEEE released **802.11b**, also known as "**WiFi**," for **Wireless Fidelity**. 802.11b uses direct sequence spread spectrum (DSSS) signaling. Recall that in DSSS, a signal is distributed over the entire bandwidth of the allocated spectrum. 802.11b uses the 2.4–2.4835 GHz frequency range (also called the 2.4 GHz band) and separates it into 14 overlapping 22-MHz channels. 802.11b provides a maximum of 11 Mbps throughput. To ensure this throughput, wireless nodes must stay roughly within a few hundred feet of an access point (depending on the nature of the signals' paths). Among all the 802.11 standards, 802.11b was the first to take hold and remains the most popular. It is also the least expensive of all the 802.11 WLAN technologies.

IEEE's **802.11g** WLAN standard is designed to be just as affordable as 802.11b while increasing its maximum capacity from 11 Mbps to 54 Mbps through different encoding techniques. 802.11g, like 802.11b, uses the 2.4 GHz frequency band. In addition to its high throughput, 802.11g benefits from being compatible with 802.11b networks. Thus, if a network administrator installed 802.11b access points on her LAN last year, this year she could add 802.11g access points and laptops, and the laptops could roam between the ranges of the 802.11b and 802.11g access points without an interruption in service. Although 802.11g is compatible with 802.11b, a network administrator designing and installing a brand new WLAN would probably consider 802.11a technology, because it offers still more benefits than 802.11g.

IEEE's **802.11a** WLAN standard differs from 802.11b and 802.11g in that it uses multiple frequency bands in the 5 GHz frequency range. Like 802.11g, 802.11a provides a maximum throughput of 54 Mbps. Its high throughput is attributable to its use of higher frequencies, its unique method of encoding data, and more available bandwidth. Perhaps most significant is the fact that the 5 GHz band is not as congested as the 2.4 GHz band. Thus, 802.11a signals are less likely to suffer interference from microwave ovens, cordless phones, motors, and other (incompatible) WLAN signals. However, as you have learned, higher frequency signals require more power to transmit and travel shorter distances than lower frequency signals. As a result, 802.11a WLANs require a greater density of access points between the wireline LAN and wireless nodes to cover the same distance that other versions of 802.11 cover. The additional access points, as well as the nature of 802.11a equipment, make this standard more expensive than either 802.11b or 802.11g. Still, many telecommunications professionals regard 802.11a as the most likely successor to 802.11b.

Just as your car's actual gas mileage varies from the gas mileage specified by its manufacturer, networks typically don't achieve the maximum throughput specified in their standards. In the case of wireless networking, interference and multipath signals can lead to an actual throughput of less than half of the specified maximum. For example, an 802.11g WLAN, although theoretically capable of 54 Mbps throughput, may actually achieve only 22 Mbps. An 802.11b WLAN may achieve only 4.5 Mbps.

Bluetooth

In the early 1990s, Ericsson began developing a wireless networking technology for use between multiple devices, including cordless telephones, computers, and pagers, in a home. It was designed to carry voice, video, and data signals over the same communications channels. Besides being compatible with a variety of devices, this technology was also meant to be low-cost and short-range. In 1994, Intel, Nokia, Toshiba, and IBM joined Ericsson in a consortium whose aim was to refine and standardize this technology. The standard that resulted was named **Bluetooth**. Bluetooth is a mobile wireless networking standard that uses direct sequence spread spectrum (DSSS) signaling in the 2.4 GHz band to achieve a maximum throughput of less than 1 Mbps. The standard recommends that Bluetooth access points and receivers be spaced no farther than 10 meters apart.

Bluetooth was designed to be used on small networks composed of personal communications devices, also known as **personal area networks (PANs)**. An example of a PAN is shown in Figure 9-19. Bluetooth's low throughput and short range makes it impractical for business LANs. Until recently, Bluetooth was slow to catch on with consumers. However, commercial support from several influential vendors in the Bluetooth consortium is making its popularity rise. As a result of Bluetooth's growing popularity, IEEE has recently released a new wireless standard, 802.15.1, that is designed to be fully compatible with the latest version of Bluetooth.

Figure 9-19   Personal area network (PAN)

HomeRF

Another commercially-supported PAN standard is HomeRF. **HomeRF** is a wireless networking specification that also uses DSSS in the 2.4 GHz frequency band to achieve a maximum of 10 Mbps throughput (although the first version of the standard supported no more than 1.6 Mbps). HomeRF proponents predict that with future advances, the technology can achieve up to 100 Mbps.

HomeRF was developed by the HomeRF Working Group, a consortium of mobile wireless companies, including Siemens and Motorola. The aim of the group was to develop a standard for homes and small offices that allowed both voice and data signals to be exchanged on the same wireless network. Therefore, in HomeRF, cordless telephones and laptops, for example, share the same bandwidth, just as in Bluetooth. HomeRF differs from Bluetooth in that its nodes can travel within a 50 meter range of an access point and remain connected to the PAN. However, both technologies target the same end user. In fact, the HomeRF and Bluetooth working groups have combined forces to allow consumers to use both standards on the same home network. Neither HomeRF nor Bluetooth are compatible with 802.11 WLAN technology, however.

> Many organizations and individuals have been reluctant to adopt wireless networking technology because of security concerns. Although it is true that wireless signals can be more easily intercepted than wirebound signals, if proper security measures, such as data encryption, are followed, wireless transmission is not necessarily less secure. You learn the fundamentals of wireless security in Chapter 13.

SATELLITE COMMUNICATIONS

In Chapter 3's discussion of historical telecommunications inventions, you learned about the first satellites that were sent into orbit in the 1960s and 1970s. You also learned that satellites use an uplink to send signals from an earth-based transmitter to an orbiting satellite and a downlink to send signals from a satellite to an earth-based receiver. (Refer to Figure 3-7 for a view of this process.) Since the mid-twentieth century, satellite communication has evolved from a science fiction theory to a vital means of communicating across the globe.

Unlike other technologies discussed in this chapter, such as CDMA, MMDS, or 802.11b, the technologies discussed in this part of the chapter are not access technologies—that is, they do not describe a way of encoding or multiplexing a signal. Instead, they describe unique ways of manipulating a signal's path. In fact, many access technologies, including TDMA, CDMA, FDMA, and GSM are used in satellite transmission. This allows satellite technology to integrate easily with terrestrial mobile wireless networks.

Next, you learn the three ways of positioning satellites.

Satellite Positioning

The original method for positioning satellites above the earth was in a geosynchronous orbit. Recall from Chapter 3 that geosynchronous (GEO) refers to an orbit that progresses at the same rate as the earth's rotation. Therefore, objects in a geosynchronous orbit maintain a constant distance from one point on the earth's surface at all times. Geosynchronous satellites are positioned approximately 35,800 km (22,300 miles) above the earth's equator. Because of their high altitude, they can issue signals over a very wide geographical range. In fact, signals from one GEO satellite can reach all but the most distant polar regions. Their wide range makes them particularly well-suited to long-distance communications.

9

However, high altitude can also be a liability for GEO satellite communications. It takes a tremendous amount of power to transmit signals over such a long distance. Also, high frequency radio waves used in satellite communications require approximately .25 seconds to travel this distance twice—from the satellite to earth and back to the satellite. A sub-second delay may not seem significant, but for services that depend on precisely timed signals, such as voice or video communication, such a delay detrimentally affects the service's quality. You may have experienced this phenomenon if you have made a transatlantic telephone call, for example, and noticed that the person you're talking with does not respond immediately to your voice.

An alternative to GEO satellites are **low earth orbiting (LEO)** satellites. LEO satellites orbit the earth with an altitude roughly between 700 and 1400 kilometers, not above the equator but closer to the earth's poles. Because their altitude is lower, LEO satellites can cover a smaller geographical range than GEO satellites. However, less power is required to issue signals between earth and an LEO satellite than a GEO satellite. Also, signals take less time to travel between an LEO satellite and the earth's surface. The capability of faster transmission has made LEO satellites useful for applications in which signal timing is critical, such as voice and video communications. In fact, LEO satellites are popular for use with mobile telephone service. Several LEO satellites may work in tandem, like base stations in a cellular network, to handoff calls between their coverage areas. LEO satellites are used for data communications as well.

In between the altitudes of LEO and GEO satellites lie **medium earth orbiting (MEO)** satellites. MEO satellites orbit the earth between 10,350 and 10,390 km above its surface. As with LEO satellites, MEO satellites are not positioned over the equator, but over a latitude between the equator and the poles. MEOs have the advantage of covering a larger area of the earth's surface than LEO satellites while at the same time using less power and causing less signal delay than GEO satellites. MEOs are used to convey both voice and data signals. In the next section, you learn about specific telecommunications services that GEO, LEO, and MEO satellites provide.

Figure 9-20 compares the orbits of GEO, LEO, and MEO satellites.

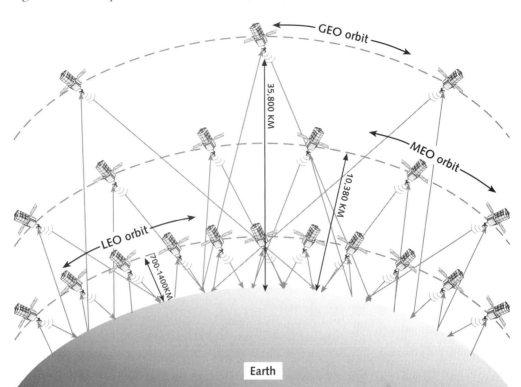

Figure 9-20   GEO, LEO, and MEO satellite orbits

Satellite Services

The first uses of satellites were by the government in military, scientific research, public safety, and global communications applications. However, the proliferation of this technology and reductions in costs have made satellites appropriate and available for more regional (or even local) consumer telecommunications services. Satellites are best suited to services that must travel long distances or cover a wide geographical range. However, they are also used by organizations that simply want to avoid wireline transmission, either because they can't afford to build a cable infrastructure or because cabling cannot reach their users.

Following are only some services that make use of satellite transmission:

- *Analog broadcasting*—Traditional analog television and radio signals can be issued from a terrestrial transmitter to a satellite and then downlinked to another terrestrial location within seconds. Television networks routinely use this capability to present live broadcasts of events happening around the world. Satellites used for broadcasting are apt to be geosynchronous, rather than LEO or MEO.

- *Digital broadcasting*—Digital television and radio services that use satellite transmission are replacing local broadcast and cable services in some areas. To deliver content to subscribers, networks (or other multimedia providers) uplink their audio and video signals to a satellite, which then downlinks the signals, in a broadcast fashion, to earth. Subscribers may have fixed antennas and receivers at their residences, or as in the case of digital radio, they may have mobile antennas and receivers in their cars or on a handheld device. Because it is digital, this type of radio transmission offers the same sound quality as a compact disk recording.

- *Voice communications*—One of the first uses of GEO satellites was to connect transoceanic telephone calls. Voice communications still make up much of the world's satellite traffic.

- *Videoconferencing*—Two-way video transmission between distant locations can easily be accomplished via satellite. Although early videoconferencing services used GEO satellites, satellites with lower orbits, such as LEO and MEO, are better suited to videoconferencing because of their shorter signal delay.

- *Mobile wireless*—Services such as cellular telephone, paging, and other PCS applications are well suited to LEO or MEO satellite transmission. Such services may use CDMA, TDMA, or GSM access methods. Although these services hold promise, early attempts at widespread provision have proved too expensive for most consumers.

- *Tracking and monitoring*—Two-way satellite communications can be used to monitor the whereabouts and condition of wildlife, mobile weather sensors, marine vessels, and so on anywhere in the world.

- *Global positioning service (GPS)*—A service that expands on remote monitoring functions, GPS allows a mobile station on earth to exchange signals with a satellite to determine its precise location. GPS systems are used in automobiles, for example, to help a driver navigate to his destination.

- *Internet access*—Many companies are offering low-cost, high-bandwidth Internet access via LEO or MEO satellite links. In this scenario, each subscriber uses a small satellite dish antenna and receiver to exchange signals with the satellite. Throughput of these services compares favorably to that of wire-bound broadband Internet access services. Alternatively, an ISP may use a satellite link just for its own connection to the Internet.

- *Wide area networks*—Private companies use satellite transmission to connect multiple locations on their WANs. Satellite-enabled WANs are well suited to carrying not only data, but also voice and video traffic. For example, a company may use their satellite WAN links to connect overseas phone calls, transmit faxes between distant offices, and share word processing documents.

Today's satellites typically transmit and receive signals in any of five frequency bands: the L-band, S-band, C-band, Ka-band, or Ku-band, as shown in the following list. Notice that uplink and downlink frequencies differ within each band. This helps ensure that signals traveling in one direction (for example, from a satellite to the earth) do not interfere with signals traveling in the other direction (for example, signals from the earth to a satellite).

- L-band: 1.5–2.7 GHz
- S-band: 2.7–3.5 GHz
- C-band: 3.7–6.5 GHz
- Ku-band: 10.7–18 GHz
- Ka-band: 18–31 GHz

Some of the lower-range satellite frequencies, such as those in the L-band, share bandwidth with wireless technologies discussed earlier in this chapter, such as cellular and WLAN services. Other satellite signals travel at much higher frequencies. As you have learned, the higher the frequency, the more power it requires to issue a transmission and also, the more susceptible the signal is to environmental interference (such as rain or snow).

CHAPTER SUMMARY

- ❏ The wireless spectrum, the range of frequencies within the electromagnetic spectrum that are used for telecommunications services, starts at 9 KHz and ends at 300 GHz.

- ❏ All wireless services use some type of antenna, are susceptible to electromagnetic interference, attenuate as they move farther from their source, experience multipath signaling due to obstacles that cause reflection, diffraction, or scattering, and can be classified as either fixed or mobile.

- ❏ Some wireless services require a line-of-sight (LOS) path between the transmitter and receiver, which means that their effectiveness is reduced by obstructions. Most wireless services (for example, cellular telephone and wireless LAN services) do not require LOS paths.

- ❏ Cellular telephone service is distinguished from other mobile two-way radio services by its use of cells to reuse limited frequencies within a certain geographical area. Each cell is served by a base station that exchanges signals with mobile stations. Each base station communicates with a mobile telephone switching office (MTSO).

- ❏ The MTSO identifies and tracks mobile stations, manages call setup and completion, interfaces with the PSTN, interfaces with other MTSOs in a mobile carrier's network, and controls handoff when mobile stations move between cells.

- ❏ Mobile wireless access technologies can be divided into first generation, second generation, and third generation. Frequency division multiple access (FDMA) is an analog, first generation technology that devotes exclusive use of one 30 KHz channel to each voice signal. FDMA is used in advanced mobile phone service (AMPS).

❐ Time division multiple access (TDMA) divides each channel of the cellular spectrum into multiple time slots, assigning each signal its own time slot. TDMA is more efficient than FDMA. It is also a digital, second generation access technology.

❐ Code division multiple access (CDMA) is another digital, second generation mobile wireless access technology. CDMA divides each channel into small components that are issued over a range of frequencies using the spread spectrum technique.

❐ Global system for mobile communication (GSM) is a form of TDMA standardized in Europe. GSM is more efficient than the IS-136 version of TDMA popular in the United States because it divides channels into smaller time slots and uses frequency hopping to make use of periods of inactivity during a call.

❐ Several technologies are competing for prominence as the favorite 3G cellular technology. All are packet-switched and promise to supply at least voice and data over the same channel. CDMA2000, developed by Qualcomm, is the standard embraced in the U.S. Wideband CDMA (W-CDMA) is the standard embraced in Europe. Both promise a maximum throughput of 2.4 Mbps.

❐ Wireless local loops (WLLs) may use any number of access technologies, including 2G mobile wireless technologies or broadband wireless technologies, such as LMDS and MMDS. Although LMDS offers significantly more capacity than MMDS, MMDS can travel longer distances, is less susceptible to interference, and is less expensive to implement than LMDS.

❐ Wireless LANs (WLANs) use the same protocols and a similar architecture as wirebound LANs. Each wireless node uses a transceiver and antenna (included in its NIC) to communicate with an access point. The access point manages data communication with multiple mobile WLAN nodes or between multiple WLANs. In general, for optimal transmission, the number of nodes served by one access point should remain under 100, while the maximum distance between a mobile node and its access point should not exceed 300 feet.

❐ Several WLAN access technologies are competing for dominance. Three IEEE 802.11 committee standards are appropriate for use on business LANs: 802.11b, 802.11g, and 802.11a. Although 802.11b is the oldest and least expensive technology, it is limited by a maximum throughput of 11 Mbps. The newer 802.11a standard, with a maximum throughput of 54 Mbps, is currently touted as the favorite new WLAN access technology, although it is more expensive than 802.11b or 802.11g.

❐ Bluetooth and HomeRF are mobile wireless access technologies suited to home networks. Both boast the ability to connect multiple devices, including computers, cordless phones, peripherals, and so on. Both use DSSS signaling in the 2.4 GHz range.

❐ Satellites are used primarily for long-distance or wide-range telecommunications. Three major satellite positioning systems are geosynchronous (GEO), low earth orbiting (LEO), and medium earth orbiting (MEO). All may be used for voice, video, or data signals. LEO satellites are the closest to the earth's surface and also cost the least to operate. As such, they have become popular for use with consumer applications, such as Internet access, digital radio, and paging services.

Key Terms

1G — *See* first generation.

2G — *See* second generation.

3G — *See* third generation.

802.11 — The IEEE committee responsible for establishing radio frequency wireless network access standards—or—the group of WLAN standards established by this committee. The most notable 802.11 standards are 802.11b (also known as WiFi), 802.11a, and 802.11g.

802.11a — A WLAN access technology standard that uses multiple frequency bands in the 5 GHz frequency range and offers a maximum throughput of 54 Mbps. Because the 5 GHz band is not as congested as the 2.4 GHz band, 802.11a signals are less likely to suffer interference from microwave ovens, cordless phones, motors, and other (incompatible) WLAN signals than other 802.11 technologies. However, 802.11a WLANs require a greater density of access points between the wireline LAN and wireless nodes to cover the same distance that other versions of 802.11 cover.

802.11b — A WLAN access technology standard that uses direct sequence spread spectrum (DSSS) signaling in the 2.4 GHz band and separates it into 14 overlapping 22-MHz channels. 802.11b provides a maximum of 11 Mbps throughput. It is currently the most popular and cost effective WLAN standard. 802.11b is also known as WiFi (Wireless Fidelity).

802.11g — A WLAN access technology standardized by the IEEE 802.11g working group that uses the 2.4 GHz frequency band and has a maximum throughput of 54 Mbps. 802.11g is compatible with 802.11b.

access point — The transceiver and antenna used to exchange signals between a wire-bound network device and mobile network nodes on a WLAN.

aperture — The physical area through which an antenna's signal passes as it is transmitted or received.

advanced mobile phone service (AMPS) — A first generation cellular technology that encodes and transmits speech as analog signals. The method AMPS uses for creating separate channels out of one frequency band is called frequency division multiple access (FDMA).

base station — (1) A tower, transceiver, and antenna that exchanges signals with all mobile stations within one cell of a cellular network and relays mobile station signals to mobile telephone switching offices. Base stations may also be called base transceiver stations or cell sites. (2) *See* access point.

base transceiver station (BTS) — *See* base station.

Bluetooth — A mobile wireless networking standard that uses direct sequence spread spectrum (DSSS) signaling in the 2.4 GHz band to achieve a maximum throughput of less than 1 Mbps. Bluetooth access points and receivers should be spaced no farther than 10 meters apart. It was designed for use primarily with home networks in which multiple devices (including cordless phones, computers, and pagers) are connected.

9

broadband — A service that spans a relatively wide band of frequencies. Depending on the source, this could mean any width between 3 KHz and 6 MHz. The FCC defines broadband services as those capable of at least 200 Kbps throughput in one direction. Examples of wireless broadband services include MMDS and LMDS.

broadband wireless — A wireless service capable of very high data transfer rates.

CDMA (code division multiple access) — A digital mobile wireless access technology in which each voice signal is digitized and assigned a unique code, then small components of the signal are issued over a 12.5 MHz frequency band using the spread spectrum technique. CDMA can achieve at least three times the capacity of TDMA and at least 10 times the capacity of FDMA.

CDMA2000 — A 3G cellular technology developed by Qualcomm and standardized by the ITU. CDMA2000 is a packet-switched version of CDMA. In its final phase CDMA2000 will supply both data and voice over the same 1.25 MHz carrier channel. Current CDMA subscribers will be able to take advantage of CDMA2000 services without changing their equipment or service subscription. Carriers and wireless manufacturers in the United States have thus far embraced the CDMA2000 standard.

cell site — *See* base station.

cellular telephone service — A system for transmitting wireless voice signals to multiple, mobile receivers using two-way radio communication and reusing a small range of frequencies through the use of cells.

control channel — A communications channel that carries information about how another signal should be managed and interpreted. The control channel is separate from the channel that carries the payload (such as voice, video, or data signals) meant for the receiver.

diffraction — In wireless transmission, the splitting of a signal into secondary waves when it encounters an obstruction. The secondary waves continue to propagate in the direction in which they were split. In diffraction, signals seem to bend around objects. Objects with sharp edges—including the corners of walls and desks—cause diffraction.

digital advanced mobile phone service (D-AMPS) — The most popular form of TDMA technology, a technique of separating each channel into multiple time slots, which follows the Interim Standard (IS)-136.

direct sequence spread spectrum (DSSS) — A transmission technique in which a signal's bits are distributed over an entire frequency band at once. Each bit is coded so that the receiver can reassemble the original signal upon receiving the bits.

directional antenna — An antenna that issues wireless signals along a single direction. Directional antennas are used when the source needs to communicate with one destination, as in a point-to-point link, or when multiple receiving nodes are arranged in line with each other. Alternatively, it may be used when sustaining the strength of a signal over a distance is more important than covering a broad geographical area.

diversity — The use of multiple antennas or multiple signal transmissions to compensate for fading and delay in wireless transmission.

dual mode — A type of cellular telephone that is capable of transmitting and receiving both analog and digital signals.

Electronic Serial Number (ESN) — A fixed number assigned to a mobile telephone by the manufacturer. ESNs cannot be changed by the user or service carrier. The telephone's ESN is transmitted to a base station to identify the mobile station and its location. Every telephone has a unique ESN.

fading — A change in wireless signal strength as a result of some of the originally transmitted electromagnetic energy being scattered, reflected, or diffracted. Fading may be positive, in which the strength of the signal that reaches the receiver is higher than the strength of the signal at the transmitter. This can happen if significant reflection concentrates a signal toward a receiver. Most often, however, fading is negative. That is, the strength of the signal that reaches the receiver is lower than its transmitted strength.

FDMA (frequency division multiple access) — A first generation analog, mobile wireless access technology that divides the cellular spectrum into 832 separate communications channels, each with a bandwidth of 30 Hz. When a call is placed under the FDMA scheme, the call's transmission is guaranteed exclusive use of its 30 Hz channel for the duration of the call. FDMA (used in the AMPS cellular service) is inefficient compared with newer wireless access technologies such as CDMA.

first generation (1G) — The mobile wireless technology developed in the 1980s, which is characterized by analog transmission and a simple, relatively inefficient method for using frequencies to transmit and receive signals. AMPS is an example of 1G technology.

fixed — A wireless system in which the locations of the transmitter and receiver are static and the transmission antenna focuses its energy directly toward the receiver antenna. Because in a fixed wireless transmission the receiver's location is predictable, energy need not be wasted issuing signals across a large geographical area and more energy can be used for the signal.

forward path — In cellular networks, transmission from a mobile station to a base station.

frequency hopping spread spectrum (frequency hopping or FHSS) — A wireless signaling technique in which a signal jumps between several different frequencies within a band in a synchronization pattern known to the channel's receiver and transmitter.

global system for mobile communications (GSM) — A version of time division multiple access (TDMA) that divides a channel into smaller timeslots than the IS-136 TDMA standard. Smaller time slots, in addition to GSM's frequency hopping spread spectrum (FHSS) signaling, mean a signal is less likely to underutilize channel bandwidth. In addition, GSM makes use of silences in a phone call to increase its signal compression, leaving more open time slots in the channel. GSM has been the standard cellular technology in Europe since it was made available there in 1991.

9

handoff — The process of a mobile wireless signal being transferred to a new channel when it passes from one cell to another in a cellular network. Handoff is managed by mobile telephone switching offices (MTSOs). Under ideal conditions, handoff is transparent to the mobile telephone user.

HomeRF — A wireless networking specification that also uses DSSS in the 2.4 GHz frequency band to achieve a maximum of 10 Mbps throughput.

licensed — In the United States, a frequency that requires an operator to apply and pay for exclusive use of a frequency within a specified geographical region. Most frequencies in the wireless spectrum are licensed.

line of sight (LOS) — A wireless link that depends on an unobstructed, direct path between a transmitter and receiver.

local multipoint distribution service (LMDS) — A point-to-multipoint, fixed wireless technology that operates in the 28 GHz and 31 GHz (microwave) frequency ranges. LMDS can deliver both one-way and two-way telecommunications services, including voice, video, and data. Typical data transmission rates for LMDS are 45 Mbps.

low earth orbiting (LEO) — A type of satellite that orbits the earth with an altitude between 700 and 1400 kilometers, closer to the earth's poles than the orbits of either GEO or MEO satellites. Because their altitude is lower, LEO satellites cover a smaller geographical range than GEO satellites and require less power. Also, signals take less time to travel between an LEO satellite and the earth's surface. The capability of faster transmission has made LEO satellites useful for applications in which signal timing is critical, such as voice and video communications.

medium earth orbiting (MEO) — A type of satellite that orbits the earth 10,390 miles above its surface, positioned between the equator and the poles. MEO satellites have the advantage of covering a larger area of the earth's surface than LEO satellites while at the same time using less power and causing less signal delay than GEO satellites.

microwave multipoint distribution system (MMDS) — *See* multipoint multichannel distribution service.

mobile — A type of wireless system in which the receiver may be located anywhere within a specific range of the transmitter. This allows the receiver to roam from one place to another while continuing to pick up its signal.

Mobile Identification Number (MIN) — An encoded representation of the mobile telephone's 10-digit telephone number. The MIN is one number issued from a mobile station (such as a cellular telephone) to a base transmitter that uniquely identifies the mobile station and its location. Every mobile telephone has a unique MIN.

mobile station — A receiver that operates in a mobile wireless system. A cellular telephone is an example of a mobile station.

mobile telephone service — A system for providing telephone service to multiple, mobile receivers using two-way radio communication over a limited number of frequencies.

mobile switching center (MSC) — *See* mobile telephone switching office.

mobile telephone switching office (MTSO) — Similar to an end office in the PSTN, a mobile telephone switching office (MTSO) manages call switching for mobile stations within a cell cluster. It may directly connect mobile stations within a cellular network or, via trunks to the PSTN, connect mobile stations with traditional wireline telephones. MTSOs also control handoff for mobile stations passing between cells. Furthermore, it collects data about cellular call traffic for billing purposes.

mobile unit — *See* mobile station.

multipath — The wireless signals that follow a number of different paths to their destination due to reflection, diffraction, or scattering. The multipath nature of wireless signals cause fading and delay, which can be addressed through antenna and signal diversity.

multipoint multichannel distribution service (MMDS) — A method of transmitting wireless television, voice, or data signals from one transmitter to multiple receivers. MMDS uses microwaves with frequencies in the 2.1 to 2.7 GHz range of the wireless spectrum.

narrowband — A type of radio frequency transmission in which signal energy is concentrated at a single frequency or within a very small range of frequencies.

omni-directional antenna — A type of antenna that transmits and receives wireless signals with equal strength and clarity in all directions. This type of antenna is used when many different receivers must be able to pick up the signal or when the receiver's location is highly mobile. TV and radio stations use omni-directional antennas, as do most towers that transmit cellular telephone signals.

personal area network (PAN) — A mobile wireless network that connects multiple personal communications devices (such as cordless telephones, computers, peripherals, and pagers) within a small geographical area, such as a home. PANs are distinguished from WLANs by a shorter range and a lower maximum throughput.

personal communication service (PCS) — A category of digital mobile wireless services—including telephony and paging—that uses the 1900 MHz (1.9 GHz) frequency band.

radiation pattern — A representation of the relative strength over a three-dimensional area of all the electromagnetic energy the antenna sends or receives.

reflection — In wireless transmission, the bouncing back of an electromagnetic wave (and signal) toward its source. A wireless signal will bounce off objects whose dimensions are large compared to the signal's average wavelength. In addition, signals reflect more readily off conductive materials, like metal, than insulators, like concrete.

reverse path — In cellular networks, transmission from a base station to a mobile station.

scattering — In wireless transmission, the diffusion, or the reflection in multiple different directions, of a signal. Scattering occurs when a wireless signal encounters an object that has small dimensions compared to the signal's wavelength. Scattering is also related to the roughness of the surface a wireless signal encounters. The rougher the surface, the more likely a signal is to scatter when it hits that surface.

9

second generation (2G) — A mobile wireless technology developed in the 1990s that allows multiple signals access to a limited band of frequencies. 2G also uses digital encoding, which improves the signal quality and allows for encryption. TDMA and CDMA are examples of 2G technology.

System Identification Number (SID) — A number assigned to the particular wireless carrier that the telephone's user has subscribed to. Thus, a SID indicates, for example, whether a subscriber's telephone number and equipment used U. S. Cellular's, Verizon's, AT&T's, or Sprint's wireless network.

TDMA (time division multiple access) — A cellular network access technology that divides each channel into multiple time slots and assigns different signals the use of different time slots, thereby conserving the limited number of frequencies in the cellular spectrum.

third generation (3G) — A mobile wireless technology, as yet unavailable to most subscribers, that proposes further advances on 2G technology. It features all-digital encoding, provisions for quality of service, more efficient spectrum usage, and faster transmission (at least 128 Kbps).

unguided medium — A communications channel that provides no fixed path for signals. Wireless transmission relies on the atmosphere, which is an unguided medium.

unlicensed — In the United States, a frequency that may be used by any operator without applying or paying the FCC for its use. Although unlicensed frequencies are freely available, the FCC does restrict what purposes they can be used for. Some unlicensed frequencies are the 900 MHz and 2.4 GHz bands, which are commonly used for cellular telephone service, wireless networks, and cordless telephones.

wideband — *See* broadband.

Wideband CDMA (W-CDMA) — A 3G wireless standard based on technology developed by Ericsson, and standardized in Europe. W-CDMA is packet-based and its maximum throughput is also 2.4 Mbps. W-CDMA systems are capable of synchronizing with each other independent of a satellite-based time source. W-CDMA is compatible with GSM mobile stations.

WiFi (Wireless Fidelity) — *See* 802.11b.

wireless LAN (WLAN) — A data network (or part of a data network) that uses wireless signaling for communication between nodes within a limited geographical area. Where a traditional LAN uses coaxial, twisted-pair, or fiber optic cable, a WLAN uses high-frequency radio waves.

Wireless local loop (WLL) — A generic term that describes a wireless link used in the PSTN to connect LEC central offices with subscribers.

wireless spectrum — A continuum of electromagnetic waves used for telecommunications. On the spectrum, waves are arranged according to their frequency and wavelength. The wireless spectrum (as defined by the FCC) spans frequencies between 9 KHz and 300 GHz. Each type of wireless service can be associated with one area of the wireless spectrum.

REVIEW QUESTIONS

1. Which of the following wireless services uses the lowest range of frequencies?

   a. AM radio

   b. FM radio

   c. cellular telephone service

   d. wireless LANs

2. If a wireless signal collides with an object whose dimensions are much larger than the signal's wavelength, what is the signal most likely to do?

   a. reflect

   b. refract

   c. diffract

   d. scatter

3. Which of the following types of antennas issues signals with equal strength and clarity in all directions?

   a. directional

   b. bi-directional

   c. tri-directional

   d. omni-directional

4. What type of signals are caused as a result of signals responding to obstacles in their paths?

   a. spread spectrum

   b. narrowband

   c. multipath

   d. broadband

5. How can a wireless network compensate for fading and delay?

   a. by using multiple antennas to issue the same signals across a given transmission range

   b. by using exclusively bi-directional antennas pointed toward the receiver

   c. by widening the frequency range in which a signal is transmitted

   d. by using spread-spectrum signaling

6. Which of the following is an example of a fixed wireless service?

   a. AMPS

   b. CDMA

   c. LMDS

   d. wireless LANs

9

7. What type of transmission path does a fixed wireless signal require?

  a. line-of-sight

  b. non-line-of-sight

  c. omni-directional

  d. code divided

8. Which of the following is an advantage of using spread spectrum signaling over narrowband signaling?

  a. Spread spectrum is easier to install.

  b. Spread spectrum is more secure.

  c. Spread spectrum is less expensive to deploy.

  d. Spread spectrum can achieve higher throughput.

9. In a cellular network, adjacent cells must use the same, or nearly the same, frequencies for their voice signal channels in order for handoff to work properly. True or False?

10. What component of a cellular telephone network manages handoffs?

  a. mobile station

  b. mobile telephone switching office

  c. base station

  d. central office

11. What type of mobile wireless access technology uses spread spectrum signaling?

  a. AMPS

  b. FDMA

  c. TDMA

  d. CDMA

12. What type of mobile wireless access technology is the standard in Europe?

  a. FDMA

  b. GSM

  c. D-AMPS

  d. CDMA

13. Which of the following mobile station identifying numbers is the same as a subscriber's 10-digit cellular telephone number?

  a. MID

  b. SID

  c. PIN

  d. ESN

14. Which of the following cellular network access technologies makes the most efficient use of limited frequencies?

    a. AMPS

    b. FDMA

    c. TDMA

    d. CDMA

15. Wireless local loop infrastructure is significantly less expensive to build than wireline local loop infrastructure. True or False?

16. Which of the following broadband wireless technologies offers the greatest potential throughput?

    a. CDMA

    b. GSM

    c. LMDS

    d. MMDS

17. What is one significant difference between LMDS and MMDS?

    a. LMDS requires a line-of-sight path, whereas MMDS does not.

    b. LMDS provides one half the capacity of MMDS.

    c. LMDS can be used with voice, video, or data signals, whereas MMDS is used only with voice signals.

    d. LMDS is less susceptible to interference than MMDS.

18. What was the original purpose for developing MMDS?

    a. radio broadcasting

    b. cable television

    c. Internet access

    d. cellular telephone service

19. The 802.11g WLAN standard is compatible with what other WLAN standard?

    a. Bluetooth

    b. 802.11a

    c. 802.11b

    d. HomeRF

20. What WLAN standard was developed by a consortium of companies that includes Ericsson, IBM, and Intel?

    a. Bluetooth

    b. 802.11a

    c. 802.11b

    d. 802.11g

9

21. What frequency band do 802.11b, 802.11g, Bluetooth, and HomeRF WLANs share?
    a. 1.25 GHz
    b. 2.4 GHz
    c. 5 GHz
    d. 12.5 GHz

22. Which of the following is most likely to interfere with transmissions in the range shared by 802.11b, 802.11g, Bluetooth, and HomeRF?
    a. AM radio waves
    b. FM radio waves
    c. microwaves
    d. Infrared waves

23. Which of the following types of satellites orbits the earth closest to either the South Pole or the North Pole?
    a. GEO
    b. MEO
    c. EEO
    d. LEO

24. At what altitude does a geosynchronous satellite orbit the earth?
    a. 700 km
    b. 1400 km
    c. 10,400 km
    d. 35,800 km

25. What type of satellite is best suited—and most often used—for mobile telephone services (for example, part of a cellular telephone network)?
    a. GEO
    b. MEO
    c. EEO
    d. LEO

HANDS-ON PROJECTS

Project 9-1

You have learned that in the United States, the FCC is the organization responsible for allocating different parts of the wireless spectrum to certain services. It cooperates with ITU, the international frequency allocation authority, in setting national wireless standards. For each frequency range, the FCC designates its use as private (nongovernment) or government, its common service name (for example, "MMDS"), its operational parameters (for example, analog vs. digital), and references to the rulemaking documents (called "rule parts") that govern the service. By maintaining a detailed frequency allocation plan, the FCC ensures that multiple wireless services do not interfere with each other.

In this project, you investigate the FCC's frequency allocation table. For this project, you need a computer that is capable of navigating the Web and reading Adobe Acrobat files with a .pdf extension.

1. With your computer connected to the Internet, open your browser and go to **www.fcc.gov/oet**. The FCC's Office of Engineering and Technology Web page appears.

2. Under "Office Organization" on the left side of the page, click **Radio Spectrum Home Page**. The FCC Radio Spectrum Home Page appears.

3. Read the page's introduction, which describes the wireless spectrum and the FCC's role in regulating its use. Then click on a **description of the FCC's Table of Frequency Allocations**. The Frequency Allocation Table description page appears.

4. Read this page to familiarize yourself with the contents of the FCC's Table of Frequency Allocations, as well as the terminology it uses. For example, note the difference between primary and secondary service specifications. Then, click your browser's **Back** button to return to the FCC Radio Spectrum Home Page.

5. Click the **FCC's Online Table** link near the end of the first paragraph. If your browser is configured to automatically open Adobe Acrobat files, the table begins to load from your browser. Otherwise, your browser prompts you to open or save the file to your hard disk. In this case, choose to open the file.

6. After the entire file has loaded, glance at the first page of the table and notice its date. How recently has the table been updated? Scroll through the first few pages of the table that describe the changes that have been made to it. List the most recent changes to the table. What services and frequencies did these changes apply to?

7. Now scroll through a few pages of the table to familiarize yourself with its design. Each page of the table is divided into three large columns: international frequency assignments, United States frequency assignments, and the FCC Rule Part through which the U.S. frequencies were allocated. At the very top of each page a table heading identifies the frequency range that these frequency assignments fall within. Notice that some frequencies are assigned to different types of services, depending on geographic region or the type of government oversight.

9

8. Earlier in this chapter, you learned that the 2.4 GHz frequency band is crowded with several signals, including those from mobile telephony and wireless LAN services. To see how the FCC has apportioned this band, click the **Search** button (the button with a picture of a pair of binoculars) to open the Find dialog box. In the Find What text box, type **2345–2655 MHz** (which equals 2.345–2.450 GHz), and then click **Find**. The Adobe Acrobat Reader finds and highlights the text you have input. Scroll down the chart to view all the services listed for this frequency range.

9. As you scan the different services listed for this range, notice what name the FCC uses to refer to WLAN technologies, such as 802.11b and Bluetooth. Besides this service, which others are listed in the 2.345 to 2.45 GHz range?

10. Beginning with page 94, the last part of this document includes footnotes about international frequency allocations. Among other things, it highlights some differences between United States policies and those in other countries. To jump to page 94, type **94** in the small text box in the lower left corner of the Adobe Acrobat Reader screen (the text box should indicate which page you are currently viewing, out of a total of 185), and then press **Enter**. Scroll through this section and read some of the footnotes to get an impression of how significantly allocations and rules differ between countries.

11. When you have finished reading the document, you can close it by simply closing your browser.

Project 9-2

In this project, you investigate some of the characteristics and limitations of line-of-sight wireless transmissions. Because the equipment necessary to establish a true point-to-point wireless connection is costly, you simulate such a connection with more common sources of electromagnetic waves. For this project, you need a flashlight with an adjustable beam, a pair of binoculars, and a laser pointer (such as those used for presentations). A laser pointer contains a small diode that emits electromagnetic waves with very high frequencies (higher than microwaves or infrared waves). Laser pointers can be purchased at office supply or consumer electronics stores. It's best to conduct the second part of this project after dark.

1. During the daytime, go outside and find a place to stand where you can clearly see objects at least a mile away, if possible. This will be your transmission location. The farther you can see, the better. Try positioning yourself above trees and small buildings. For example, you might be able to sit on the roof or upper-floor balcony of a building or even a high ladder. When searching for your location, notice how many obstacles are normally in your line of sight—obstacles that may absorb wireless signals or cause them to reflect, diffract, or scatter.

2. After you have decided on a transmission location, identify four objects in your line of sight: one approximately fifty feet away, one approximately two blocks away, one approximately five blocks away, and one approximately a mile away. The objects should be large enough for you to see, and it's best if they have large, flat surfaces. A water tower, a peaked roof, or a large street sign are excellent choices.

The objects do not necessarily have to be in line with one another. On a separate piece of paper, write the names of the objects, along with their relative distance and direction from your transmission location.

3. Later, after dark, return to your transmission location with a flashlight, laser pointer, and binoculars. Turn on the flashlight and adjust its beam to the widest possible setting. Refer to your notes about object distances and directions, then point the flashlight at each of the four objects in turn. Use the binoculars, if necessary, to see how the light acts when it hits an object. What happens to the light beams as they travel farther from their source? What is the technological term for this phenomenon? How far does the flashlight's beam extend before "disappearing?" What happens when the beam hits a flat surface? How do the electromagnetic waves emitted by the flashlight compare to waves used in a point-to-point wireless local loop? What enables WLL signals to travel so much farther? Record your observations on a separate piece of paper.

4. Next, adjust the flashlight's beam to its narrowest setting and try pointing it at the objects again. How does this change affect the beam's range? How is this similar to the use of a directional antenna versus an omni-directional antenna? Record your observations on a separate piece of paper.

9

5. Now turn on the laser pointer and direct its beam at the four objects you identified in Step 2. Use the binoculars, if necessary, to see how the beam acts when it hits an object. How far does the beam extend? What happens when the beam hits a flat surface? How do the electromagnetic waves emitted by the laser pointer compare to waves used in a point-to-point wireless local loop? Record your observations on a separate piece of paper.

When using the laser pointer, be careful not to point it directly at people or animals. Nor should you point it at a highly reflective surface close by. Laser beams can cause temporary blindness or headaches if pointed directly at the eyes.

6. Repeat Step 5, but this time as you point at each different object, make a concentrated effort to keep the beam steadily fixed on one tiny spot. Where is it most difficult to control? What do you predict would happen if the beam had to travel 10 miles instead of only one mile? How does this phenomenon apply to fixed wireless links? What implications does it have for a wireless engineer installing antennas for a point-to-point link? Record your observations on a separate piece of paper.

Project 9-3

One significant drawback to wireless transmission is its high susceptibility to interference caused by EMI or RFI. In addition, due to their unguided nature, wireless signals will encounter obstacles that cause the signals to reflect, diffract, or scatter. As a result, signals suffer fading and delay. In this project, you test the effects of interference and path obstructions on different types of wireless signals. You need a working cellular telephone, television remote channel changer, and cordless telephone. You also need a variety of EMI or RFI sources—for example, a large, fluorescent light, a hand mixer or blender, a garage door opener, or a microwave oven.

1. A television remote control channel changer ("remote") uses infrared waves to communicate with a receiver on the television. Recall that infrared waves have the highest frequency and shortest wavelength of all the telecommunications services. Given the wavelength of infrared waves, and applying what you know about reflection, diffraction, and scattering, what will the remote's signals most likely do when they hit a wall or the ceiling? What will they most likely do over long distances? What types of objects are most likely to block infrared waves? Test your answers by aiming the television remote at different locations and from different distances to determine how they behave. (You will know that they have reflected to a large degree, not been absorbed, and not completely attenuated if pressing the remote's buttons is effective in controlling the television.)

2. Now repeat Step 1 while placing different sources of EMI in front of the remote. (Remember, in order for a device, such as a blender or light, to emit EMI, it has to be turned on and operating.) Which (if any) of your EMI sources affect the remote's operation? Why? How did the distance between the remote and the interference-generating device affect the signal?

3. Next, you will test the effects of path obstructions and electromagnetic interference on cordless telephone signals. First, note the range of frequencies your cordless telephone uses. This specification should be printed in the phone's documentation, if not on the base station itself (newer phones, for example, use the 2.4 GHz range). Attempt to predict how the phone's signals will react. What obstacles will cause the phone's signal to reflect? Which ones will absorb, diffract, or scatter it? Which of your interference-generating devices will cause the signal to suffer?

4. Call a friend from your cordless telephone. Ask the friend to keep talking as you perform the next two steps.

5. Begin by standing close to the cordless phone's base station, then gradually move farther away, behind doors and walls, and even outside the house. Where is the signal best? Where is it worst? Why?

6. Now move close to interference-generating devices. How does each one affect the signal, if at all? How does the proximity between you and the device affect the signal?

7. After completing the call from your cordless phone, call a friend from your cellular telephone. Repeat Steps 5–6. How does the cellular telephone respond to obstacles and interference differently from the cordless phone? Why?

CASE PROJECTS

1. You are a data networking consultant who specializes in emerging wireless technology. A local elementary school has asked you to help them determine whether wireless networking is appropriate for their environment. They currently have 12 classrooms, each of which is equipped with 10 desktop computers. All computers in every classroom are connected to a LAN via CAT5 cabling. This LAN is primarily used to share educational software and peripherals such as printers. The elementary school administrators have been considering investing in a wireless network. Specifically, they want to equip each classroom with a wireless connection so that instructors or guests could move from room to room when making presentations. They are also interested in making printers, copiers, and fax machines compatible with a wireless network. However, they are not sure if a wireless network is indeed the best option for them. Considering their needs and the costs and benefits of a WLAN, do you recommend that the elementary school install a wireless network? Why or why not?

2. Because the school district obtained a large corporate grant to apply to technology, it has decided to go ahead and install a wireless network. However, the grant stipulates that they must use the money within the next six months. School administrators have performed some initial research and are confused by the many WLAN standards that are available. The school board asks you to recommend a standard for their elementary school's WLAN. They have decided to use this WLAN as a prototype for potential WLANs in other schools. What additional questions do you ask the elementary school administrators before deciding which standard to recommend?

3. While the school district is considering your recommendation, you receive a call from a senior manager at Telacc, Inc., a two-year old company that is currently building an MMDS infrastructure to provide local phone service in your area. She received your name from a mutual acquaintance, and she is looking to hire a wireless engineer to help design and install Telacc's MMDS architecture. You tell her you might be interested in such a position. She asks what skills your work with WLANs has provided you that could be transferable to work with MMDS. What do you tell her? What new skills might you need to learn in order to excel as a WLL network engineer? What reservations do you have about accepting a job with a company like Telacc?

9

10

NETWORK ACCESS AND TRANSMISSION METHODS

After reading this chapter and completing the exercises, you will be able to:

♦ Recognize simple and complex physical topologies used in data networks

♦ Describe Ethernet and the CSMA/CD network access method

♦ Understand the different types of Ethernet access methods

♦ Describe the techniques used in the Token Ring, ATM, and FDDI network access methods

♦ Identify the main characteristics of network transmission methods, such as X.25, Frame Relay, T-Carriers, ISDN, DSL, cable, and SONET

Although data and voice networks share many similarities, they also differ significantly in many ways. One noticeable difference is the way their nodes (for example, CPE, NIDS and switches in voice networks and workstations, peripherals, and connectivity devices in data networks) connect to each other. Different types of connections result in differently shaped networks. This chapter introduces you to the fundamental shapes a data network can take.

Another difference between data and voice networks is the way in which the information they carry is switched. You have learned that most data networks use packet switching, whereas most voice networks use circuit switching. In this chapter, you learn more about how data networks are switched, focusing on popular packet-switched data networks, such as Ethernet and ATM. Finally, you also learn about transmission technologies that can transmit both data and voice signals, such as ISDN and T1s.

PHYSICAL TOPOLOGIES

A **physical topology** is the physical layout, or pattern, of the nodes on a network. It depicts a network in broad scope; that is, it does not specify device types, connectivity methods, protocols, or addresses on the network. Physical topologies are divided in three fundamental geometric shapes: bus, ring, and star. These shapes can be mixed to create hybrid topologies. With respect to the OSI model, physical topologies appear underneath the transmission media, which is just below the Physical layer. Physical topologies influence the network access method (for example, Ethernet or Token Ring), cabling design, and the type of network media a network uses. Therefore, when designing a data network, you must carefully consider which physical topology best suits your environment.

Bus

A **bus topology** consists of a single cable connecting all nodes on a network without intervening connectivity devices. This topology gets its name from its single cable, which is called the **bus**. Because a bus topology supports only one channel for communication, every node shares the bus's total capacity. The very first LANs, which used coaxial cabling, incorporated a bus topology. Simple bus topology networks are uncommon today; however, the bus topology may be found on small parts of a modern network.

Each node on a bus network passively listens for data directed to it. When one node wants to transmit data to another node, it broadcasts an alert to the entire network, informing all nodes that a transmission is being sent; the destination node then picks up the transmission. Nodes between the sending and receiving nodes pass along the message without trying to interpret it.

For example, suppose that you work in an organization that uses a bus network and you want to send an instant message to Peter, who works across the hall. You click the Send button after typing your message, and the data stream that contains your message is sent to your NIC. Your NIC then sends a message across the shared wire that essentially says, "I have a message for Peter's computer." The message passes by every NIC between your computer and Peter's computer until Peter's computer recognizes that the message is meant for it and responds by accepting the data.

Because of their linear design, bus networks need a way to stop signals once the signals reach the end of the network. This is accomplished by 50-ohm resistors, known as **terminators**, at the ends of the bus network. Recall from Chapter 2 that resistors are used to create an obstacle to flowing current. In bus networks, terminators stop signals (a form of current) as they reach the end of the wire. Without these devices, signals would travel endlessly between the two ends of the network—a phenomenon known as **signal bounce**—and new signals could not get through. To understand this concept, imagine that you and a partner are standing at opposite sides of a canyon, yelling to each other. When you call out, your words echo; when your partner replies, his words also echo. Now imagine that the echoes never faded. After a short while, you could not continue conversing because all of the previously generated sound waves would still be bouncing around, creating too much noise for you to hear anything else. On a network, terminators prevent this problem by halting the transmission of old signals. Figure 10-1 depicts a bus network with terminators.

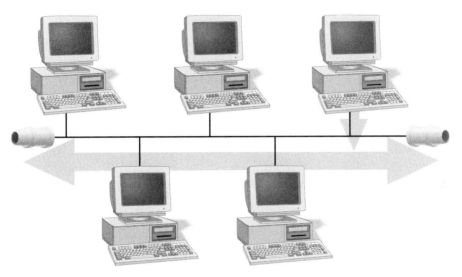

Figure 10-1 A bus network

The primary advantage to a bus topology is that it's very simple to design. However, as you add more nodes to a bus network, the network's performance degrades. Because of the single channel limitation, the more nodes on a bus network, the more nodes that contend for limited bandwidth. And because more modes are contending for limited bandwidth, data delivery to each node will be less frequent. To a user at a workstation on a bus network, the network will seem to get slower. For example, suppose you installed a bus network in your small office, which supports two workstations and a server. Further, suppose that saving a file to the server takes two seconds. During that time, your NIC first checks the communication channel to make sure it is free, then issues data directed to the server. When the data reaches the server, the server accepts it.

Suppose, however, that your business experiences tremendous growth and you add five more workstations during one weekend. The following Monday, when you attempt to save a file to the server, the save process might take five seconds, because the new workstations are also using the communications channel, and your workstation may have to wait for a chance to transmit. As this example illustrates, a bus topology is not practical for a network of more than 200 workstations. In fact, it is rarely practical for networks with more than a dozen workstations.

Another significant disadvantage to bus networks is that they are not very fault tolerant. Because all nodes rely on a single bus, a break or a defect in the bus affects the entire network. Furthermore, bus networks are difficult to troubleshoot. When faults do occur, it is a challenge to identify where. To understand why, think of the game called "telephone," in which one person whispers a phrase into the ear of the next person, who whispers the phrase into the ear of another person, and so on, until the final person in line repeats the phrase aloud. The vast majority of the time, the phrase recited by the last person bears little resemblance to the original phrase. When the game ends, it's hard to determine precisely where in the chain the individual errors cropped up.

Similarly, errors may occur at any intermediate point on a bus network, but at the receiving end, it's possible to tell only that an error occurred. Finding the source of the error can prove very difficult, because you cannot retrace the data's progress from one node to the next; that is, the nodes don't keep a record of the data after they pass it on. (In the telephone game analogy, this situation would be similar to every person in the line forgetting the phrase after he or she passed it on—a situation that makes it impossible to trace the evolution of the phrase as it moved from one person to the next.)

Because of the significant disadvantages associated with this topology, you will rarely see a network run on a pure bus topology. You may, however, encounter hybrid topologies that include a bus component, as discussed later in this chapter.

Ring

In a **ring topology**, each node is connected to the two nearest nodes so that the entire network forms a circle, as shown in Figure 10-2. Data is transmitted clockwise, in one direction (unidirectionally), around the ring. Each workstation accepts and responds to packets addressed to it, then forwards the other packets to the next workstation in the ring. Because a ring network has no "ends," and because data stops at its destination, ring networks do not require terminators. In most ring networks, twisted-pair or fiber optic cabling is used as the physical medium.

One method for passing data on a ring network is token passing. In Chapter 7, you learned that a token is a special control frame that indicates to the rest of the network that a node has the right to transmit data. In **token passing**, a 3-byte token is transmitted from one node to another around the ring. If a computer on the ring has information to transmit, it picks up the token, adds control and data information plus the destination node's address to transform the token into a data frame, and then passes the token on to the next node. The transformed token, now in the form of a frame, circulates around the network until it reaches its intended destination. The destination node picks it up and returns an acknowledgment message to the originating node. After the originating node receives the acknowledgment, it releases a new free token and sends it down the ring. This approach ensures that only one workstation transmits data at any given time. Because each workstation participates in sending the token around the ring, this architecture is known as an **active topology**. Each workstation acts as a repeater for the transmission.

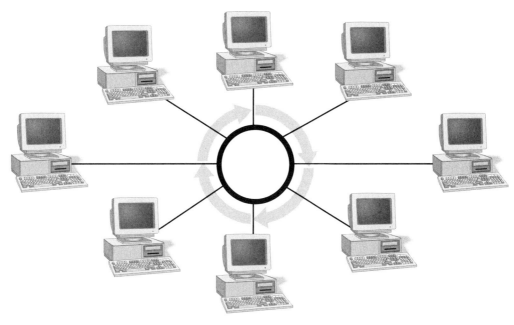

Figure 10-2 A ring network

10

The drawback of a simple ring topology is that a single malfunctioning node can disable the network. For example, suppose that you and three colleagues share a pure ring topology LAN in your small office. You decide to send an instant message to Abe, who works three offices away, telling him that you accidentally received a package addressed to him. Between your office and Abe's office are two other offices and two other workstations on the ring. Your instant message must pass through the two intervening workstations' NICs before it reaches Abe's computer. If one of these workstations has a broken NIC, your message will never reach Abe.

In addition, just as in a bus topology, the more workstations that must participate in token passing, the slower the response time. Consequently, pure ring topologies are not very flexible or scalable.

Contemporary LANs rarely use pure ring topologies. A variation of the ring topology, known as a star-wired ring, is popular for some types of networks, such as Token Ring networks. Star-wired rings and Token Ring technology is discussed later in this chapter.

Star

In a **star topology**, every node on the network is connected through a central device, such as a hub. Figure 10-3 depicts a typical star topology. Star topologies are usually built with twisted-pair or fiber cabling. Any single cable on a star network connects only two devices (for example, a workstation and a hub), so a cabling problem affects two nodes at most. Devices, such as workstations or printers, transmit data to the hub, which then retransmits the signal to the network segment containing the destination node.

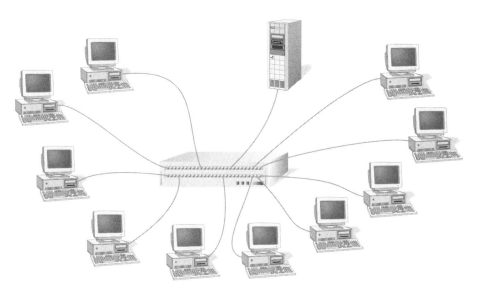

Figure 10-3   A star network

Star topologies require more cabling than ring or bus networks. They also require more configuration. However, because each node is separately connected to a central connectivity device, they are more fault tolerant. (Often, hubs are the central connectivity device that allows multiple nodes to connect in a star topology. You learn more about hubs in Chapter 11.) A single malfunctioning cable or workstation cannot disable star networks. However, failure in the central connectivity device can take down part of a network.

Because they include a centralized connection point, star topologies can easily be moved, isolated, or interconnected with other networks; they are therefore scalable. For this reason, and because of their fault tolerance, the star topology has become the most popular fundamental layout used in contemporary LANs. Many network administrators have replaced their old bus or ring networks with star networks. Single star networks are commonly interconnected with other networks through hubs and switches to form more complex topologies.

Hybrid Physical Topologies

Except in very small networks, you will rarely encounter a network that follows a pure bus, ring, or star topology. Simple topologies are too restrictive, particularly if the LAN must accommodate a large number of devices. More likely, you will work with a complex combination of these topologies, known as a **hybrid topology**. The two most common hybrid topologies—star-wired bus and star-wired ring—are explained in the following sections.

Star-wired Bus

One popular hybrid topology combines the star and bus formations. In a **star-wired bus topology**, groups of nodes (typically workstations and printers) are star-connected to connectivity devices such as hubs. The hubs are then networked via a single bus, as shown in Figure 10-4. With this design, a network can cover longer distances, and administrators can easily interconnect or isolate its different parts. One drawback is that this option is more expensive than using either the star or especially the bus topology alone because it requires more cabling and potentially more connectivity devices. The star-wired bus topology forms the basis for most modern Ethernet networks.

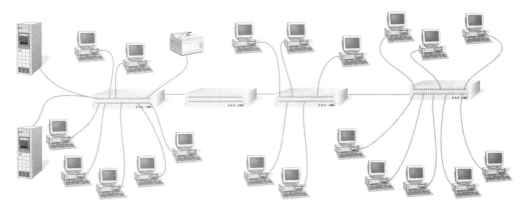

Figure 10-4 A star-wired bus network

Star-wired Ring

The **star-wired ring topology** uses the physical layout of a star in conjunction with the token-passing data transmission method. In Figure 10-5, which depicts this architecture, the solid lines represent a physical connection and the dotted lines represent the flow of data. Data is sent around the star in a circular pattern. This hybrid topology benefits from the fault tolerance of the star topology (data transmission does not depend on each workstation to act as a repeater) and the reliability of token passing. Modern Token Ring networks use this hybrid topology.

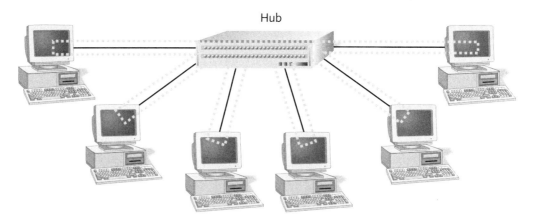

Figure 10-5   A star-wired ring network

Mesh Topologies

In some cases, networks require a more intricate physical topology than even the hybrid topologies. One example is the mesh topology. In a **mesh topology**, connectivity devices are interconnected with other connectivity devices more than once, so that at least two pathways connect each device. The primary advantage of using a mesh network is its fault tolerance. If one connectivity device fails, data can be rerouted to follow another path through a different connectivity device.

Although a simple LAN can be a mesh network, most often this topology is employed for enterprise-wide networks and WANs. On a WAN, a mesh topology directly connects several geographical locations. If one location suffers a problem, routers can redirect data easily and quickly. The most fault tolerant type of mesh topology is a **full-mesh topology**, shown in Figure 10-6. In this configuration, every location is directly interconnected with every other location. Thus, full-mesh networks provide multiple routes for data to follow between any two points. For example, if the link between the Santa Fe and Dallas offices in Figure 10-6 is cut in a construction mishap, the Dallas office could still send and transmit data to and from the Santa Fe office by rerouting it through the Denver office, for example. If, in addition, the Denver office suffered a power outage, traffic between Dallas and Sante Fe could be rerouted through the Phoenix office. The likelihood of several catastrophes at once is small, making the full-mesh WAN extremely reliable.

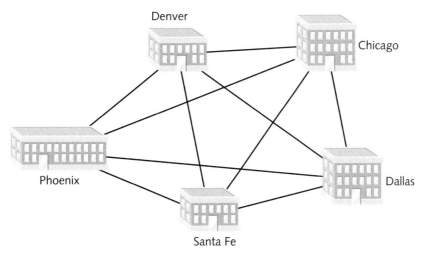

Figure 10-6   A full-mesh WAN

One drawback to a mesh WAN is the cost; connecting every node on a network to every other entails leasing a large number of (potentially pricey) links. With larger WANs, the expense can become enormous. To reduce costs, a professional designing a WAN might choose to implement a **partial mesh**, in which only some WAN nodes are directly connected, as shown in Figure 10-7. An organization may choose to directly connect the nodes that most often share the greatest amount of data. Less critical nodes may be connected to only one other node. Or, to ensure connectivity, less critical nodes may have two connections: one primary connection and one secondary connection. Partial-mesh WANs are more economical and therefore more common in today's business world than full-mesh WANs.

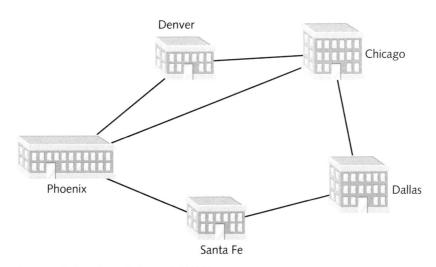

Figure 10-7   A partial-mesh WAN

NETWORK ACCESS METHODS

Earlier in this book, you learned how multiple signals can share the same communications channel. For example, one strand within a fiber optic cable can carry many signals using wave division multiplexing (WDM). In the following sections, you learn how multiple nodes on a network share one communications channel.

Consider that a network has a limited amount of capacity. Maximum capacity may depend on various factors including—most importantly—the network's transmission media, but also its physical topology, length, signaling method, and other factors. Now consider a network with hundreds of nodes, each of which needs to transmit and receive data. Each node must follow the same standard for sharing that capacity. Otherwise, all would be trying to communicate at the same time, and signals from one node would interfere with another node's signals. This standard is known as a **network access method**. If you think of a network's communication channel as a busy highway, a network access method is similar to the highway's on- and off-ramps and the rules for using those ramps (for example, some on-ramps require the driver to wait for a green light before merging with highway traffic). Regulating the flow of traffic helps avoid backups and collisions.

It's important to distinguish between network access methods and other networking technologies you've learned about, such as network protocols, signaling methods, and physical topologies. Using the OSI model as a guide helps. For example, a WAN using the Ethernet network access method could package and transmit data according to the TCP/IP network protocol suite. The same WAN might rely on fiber optic cable in a partial-mesh topology while using WDM to issue multiple signals over one communications channel. Separating this network into layers reveals that at the very bottom, the physical topology (for example, partial mesh) describes how the cabling is arranged. Above that lies the transmission medium—in this case, fiber optic cable. Above the transmission medium lies the Physical layer of the OSI model, where signaling (in this case, WDM) specifies how electric current or light is applied to or guided over the transmission media.

Moving up the OSI model from signaling is the network access method, which belongs to both the Physical and Data Link layers. Recall from Chapter 7 that the Data Link layer is responsible for packaging data into frames. Network access methods set guidelines for data framing, and each network access method uses a different frame type. Also, recall that the Data Link layer is divided into two sublayers: the Logical Link Control (LLC) sublayer and the Medium Access Control (MAC) sublayer. The MAC sublayer is where network access method rules are specified. Here, the network access method (in this example, Ethernet) determines how nodes contend for space on the media. Each node's NIC is responsible for adhering to these rules.

Above the Data Link layer lie the network protocols, such as TCP/IP. Recall that TCP/IP is a protocol suite that contains the main subprotocols TCP, UDP, and IP. At the Network layer, IP is responsible for determining where data should be delivered. TCP performs reliable and error-free transmission of data at the Transport layer. UDP performs connectionless (or, without a guarantee of delivery) transmission of data at the Transport layer. Figure 10-8 illustrates how the different network technologies used in this example fit into the OSI model.

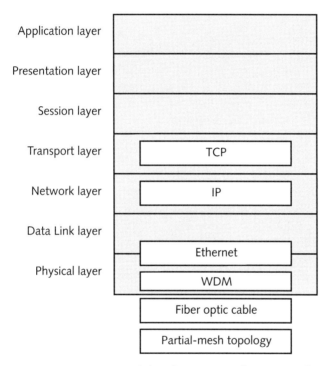

Figure 10-8   OSI model with corresponding network technologies

Note that the Ethernet WAN described in the previous example could have used IPX/SPX instead of TCP/IP or a wireless link instead of fiber optic cable, for example. This is because network access methods are independent of the physical topology, transmission media, signaling, or network protocols used.

IEEE is the standards organization that oversees network access method technology. Several different network access methods have been designed, but in general, two remain in use on modern networks: Ethernet and Token Ring. The following sections describe both of these network access methods, with an emphasis on the more popular of the two, Ethernet.

10

Ethernet

Ethernet is a network access method originally developed by Xerox in the 1970s and later improved by Xerox, Digital Equipment Corporation (DEC), and Intel. This flexible technology can run on a variety of network media, including both wireline and wireless channels. It uses packet switching, which allows data packets to take any number of routes to their destination where they are reassembled into the original message. Ethernet is, by far, the most popular network access method for LANs today. Its popularity is due to its combined attributes of excellent throughput and reasonable cost.

Ethernet has evolved through many variations since the 1970s, and its speed and quality continues to improve. As a result of this history, Ethernet comes in many different versions—so many, in fact, that you will probably find the many variations a little confusing. In this section, you learn about only the versions you are most likely to encounter on modern networks. First, however, you learn about a characteristic that all Ethernet networks share—the use of baseband transmission.

Baseband

Before learning about the different Ethernet versions, it is useful to understand the distinction between broadband and baseband. In Chapter 9's discussion of wireless transmission, you learned that "broadband" refers to a type of transmission that uses a relatively large amount of bandwidth (or, a wide band of RF frequencies). Broadband is a term used in wireline transmission as well. The original sense of this word applied only to analog systems, such as cable TV. It also included data networking technologies that used multiple (analog) frequencies to carry many signals over the same channel at once. For example, a WAN link that employs time division multiplexing is considered broadband. In recent years, the meaning of broadband has evolved to refer to any technology—whether or not it relies on multiple analog frequencies—that supplies a relatively high throughput. You learn about several types of broadband transmission methods, such as DSL and ATM, later in this chapter.

In contrast to broadband, **baseband** is a transmission form in which (typically) digital signals are sent through direct current (DC) pulses applied to the wire. This direct current requires exclusive use of the wire's capacity. As a result, baseband systems can transmit only one signal at a time. In the highway analogy of network access methods, this is akin to a single lane for drivers traveling in both directions. Every device on a baseband system shares the same channel. When one node is transmitting data on a baseband system, all other nodes on the network must wait for that transmission to end before they can send data. Baseband transmission supports bidirectional signal flow, which means that computers can both send and receive information on the same length of wire.

Ethernet is an example of a baseband system found on many LANs. In Ethernet, each device on a network can transmit over the wire—but only one device at a time. For example, if you want to save a file to the server, your NIC submits your request to use the wire; if no other device is using the wire to transmit data at that time, your work-station can go ahead. If the wire is in use, you must wait and try again later. Of course, this retrying process happens so quickly that you, as the user, may not even notice the wait. This process is known as CSMA/CD.

CSMA/CD

According to IEEE 802.3 specifications, Ethernet is defined as an access method that uses the **Carrier Sense Multiple Access with Collision Detection (CSMA/CD)** protocol. All Ethernet networks, independent of their speed or frame type, rely on CSMA/CD. To understand Ethernet, you must first understand CSMA/CD.

Take a minute to think about the full name "Carrier Sense Multiple Access with Collision Detection." The term "Carrier Sense" refers to the fact that Ethernet NICs listen on the network and wait until they detect (or sense) that no other nodes are trans-mitting data on the communications channel before they begin to transmit. (In Ethernet terms, the communications channel is called the carrier.) The term "Multiple Access" refers to the fact that several Ethernet nodes can be connected to a network and can monitor and issue traffic, or access the media, simultaneously.

In CSMA/CD, when a node wants to transmit data, it must first access the transmission media and sense whether the channel is free (in other words, it must wait for a time when no other nodes are transmitting data). If the channel is busy, the node waits and checks again after a random (but very brief) amount of time. If the channel is free, how-ever, the node transmits its data. Any node can transmit data after it determines that the channel is free. This simple method of checking the communications channel is not fool-proof, however. It's possible for two nodes to simultaneously check the channel, deter-mine that it's free, and begin to transmit. As a result, their two transmissions will interfere with each other in what is known as a **collision**.

When a collision occurs, the network performs a series of steps known as the collision detection routine. A collision is indicated when voltage on the wire jumps from a normal 5 volts to 10 volts.

If a station's NIC determines that its data has been involved in a collision, it first propagates the collision throughout the network (in a process known as **jamming**). Jamming ties up the communications channel, ensuring that no other station attempts to transmit. In the highway analogy, this is similar to a single car accident resulting in the closure of all on- and off-ramps. After propagating the collision, the NIC remains silent for a random period of time. Meanwhile, the other NIC whose transmission was involved in the collision also remains silent for a random period of time. After waiting, the node determines if the channel is again available; if it is available, the line retrans-mits its data. Figure 10-9 depicts the way CSMA/CD regulates data flow to avoid and, if necessary, detect collisions.

10

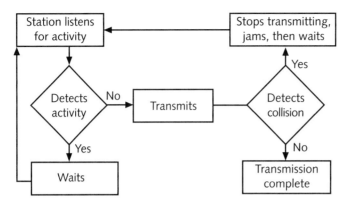

Figure 10-9   CSMA/CD process

Collisions are a normal part of Ethernet data transmission. On networks with sufficient capacity, they are typically resolved in microseconds, and network users are unaware of them. However, the more nodes transmitting data on a network, the more collisions that take place. Whenever a collision takes place, CSMA/CD requires retransmittal of the data. A high volume of retransmittal attempts naturally generates more traffic on the network. Therefore, when an Ethernet network grows to include a particularly large number of nodes, performance may suffer as a result of collisions. This "critical mass" number depends on the type and volume of data that the network regularly transmits. Collisions can corrupt data or truncate data frames, so it is important that the network detect and compensate for them.

The average percentage of all transmissions involved in collisions during a one minute time period is known as the **collision rate**. Although collision rates of up to approximately three percent are tolerable, collision rates greater than this will affect network performance. Assuming they are not caused by a severely overtaxed network, such high collision rates may point to a problematic NIC or poor cabling on the network.

On an Ethernet LAN, an individual segment is known as a **collision domain**, or a portion of a network in which collisions occur if two nodes transmit data at the same time. When designing an Ethernet network, it's important to note that because repeaters simply regenerate any signal they receive, they repeat collisions just as they repeat data. Thus, connecting multiple parts of a network with repeaters results in a larger collision domain. Higher-layer connectivity devices, such as switches and routers, however, can separate collision domains.

Collision domains play a role in the Ethernet cabling distance limitations (which you learn about in the following sections). If the distance between two nodes connected to the same Ethernet network bus exceeds the maximum allowable length, data propagation delays are too long for CSMA/CD to work. A **data propagation delay** is the length of time data takes to travel from one point on the network to another point. When packets take a long time, CSMA/CD's collision detection routine cannot identify collisions accurately. In other words, one node on the segment might begin its CSMA/CD routine and determine that the channel is free even though a second node has begun transmitting, because the second node's data is taking so long to reach the first node. In versions of Ethernet with throughput of 100 Mbps or more, data travels so quickly that NICs can't always keep up with the collision detection and retransmission routines. To minimize undetected collisions, such networks have shorter maximum network lengths than networks that transmit at a maximum of only 10 Mbps. This shorter path reduces the potential propagation delay between nodes.

Ethernet Frames

As you learned earlier, each network access method packages data into its own unique frame type. On Ethernet networks, each frame contains a 14-byte header and a 4-byte Frame Check Sequence (FCS) field. These two fields add 18 bytes to the frame size. The data portion of the frame—that is, the original message that the sender wants to transmit—may contain from 46 to 1500 bytes of information. (If less than 46 bytes of data is carried, the network fills out the data portion with extra bytes until it totals 46 bytes. The extra bytes are known as padding and have no effect on the data being transmitted.) Thus, the minimum Ethernet frame size is 18 + 46, or 64, bytes and the maximum Ethernet frame size is 18 + 1500, or 1518, bytes. Because of the overhead present in each frame and the time required to enact CSMA/CD, the use of larger frame sizes on a network generally results in faster throughput. To some extent, you cannot control frame sizes. You can, however, minimize the number of unnecessary frames on your network (for example, by limiting broadcast transmissions).

Although different Ethernet networks may use slightly different frame types, further discussion about frame types is beyond the scope of this book. For now, it is sufficient to know that all Ethernet networks use frames that vary in size from 64 to 1518 bytes.

10BaseT

The first types of Ethernet networks—known as 10Base2 and 10Base5—used coaxial cabling in a bus topology. (Few of these networks remain in use today; however, if you plan to specialize in LAN maintenance and troubleshooting, you should pursue further information about these Ethernet versions.) As Ethernet technology evolved through the 1980s, a new standard for using this network access method over twisted-pair wire was adopted, **10BaseT**. The "10" represents its maximum throughput of 10 Mbps, the "Base" indicates that it uses baseband transmission, and the "T" stands for twisted pair, the media it uses.

On a 10BaseT network, one pair of wires in the UTP cable is used for transmission, while a second pair of wires is used for reception. Thus, each wire pair, by itself, is capable of half-duplex transmission (recall that in half-duplex transmission signals can only travel in one direction at a time).

However, by using two pairs of wires, 10BaseT networks achieve full-duplex transmission. A 10BaseT network requires CAT3 or higher UTP. But as you have learned, modern networks are more likely to use CAT5 or higher UTP. Because 10BaseT uses twisted-pair cable, it also uses RJ-45 connectors and adheres to structured cabling guidelines, as described in Chapter 8.

Nodes on a 10BaseT Ethernet network connect to a central hub or repeater in a star fashion. As is typical of a star topology, a single network cable connects only two devices. This characteristic makes 10BaseT networks more fault tolerant than earlier Ethernet network types that relied on the bus topology. It also means that 10BaseT networks are easier to troubleshoot because you can isolate problems more readily when every device has a separate connection to the LAN. Figure 10-10 depicts a small 10BaseT Ethernet network.

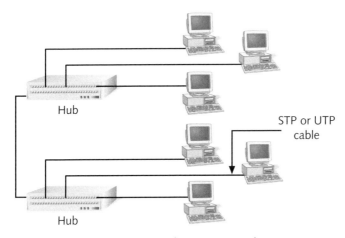

Figure 10-10   A 10BaseT Ethernet network

Earlier, you learned that CSMA/CD only works within a certain distance. Otherwise, data propagation delays make nodes more likely to transmit data simultaneously, and transmission errors result. Therefore, all forms of Ethernet networks are subject to distance limitations. The maximum distance that a 10BaseT segment can traverse is 100 meters. To go beyond that distance, Ethernet star segments must be connected by connectivity devices to form more complex topologies, such as the star-bus hybrid. When used with 10BaseT, this arrangement can connect a maximum of five sequential network segments. Beyond five segments, the overall network length causes transmission errors due to attenuation and delay. Because only five segments can be serially connected, only four repeaters (or hubs) can be used in a serial fashion on a 10BaseT network. Furthermore, only three of the segments may contain user nodes. In other words, two of the segments can be used simply to extend the network's length. Among networking professionals, this guideline for designing an Ethernet network is known as the **5-4-3 rule**. Figure 10-11 illustrates how 10BaseT segments can be interconnected to form an enterprise-wide network.

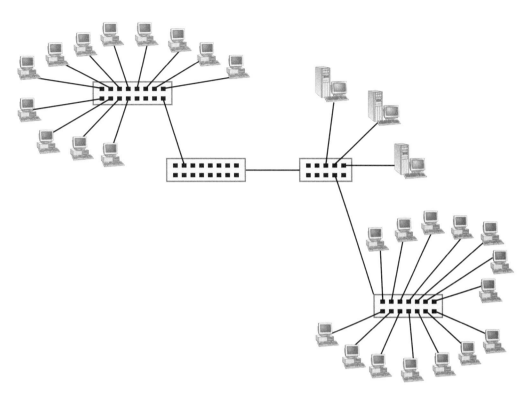

Figure 10-11   Interconnected 10BaseT segments

10BaseF

In the **10BaseF** standard, the "10" represents its maximum throughput of 10 Mbps, "Base" indicates its use of baseband transmission, and "F" indicates that it relies on a medium of fiber optic cable. Just as 10BaseT requires two pairs of twisted copper wire, 10BaseF requires two strands of multimode fiber. One strand is used for data transmission and one strand is used for reception, making 10BaseF a full-duplex technology. 10BaseF also requires ST type of connectors on its patch cables, with ST ports on its NICs and patch panels. In fact, there are at least three versions of 10BaseF. The maximum segment length for a 10BaseF network may be 1000 or 2000 meters, depending on the version used. It may contain no more than two repeaters per network. Like 10BaseT, 10BaseF makes use of the star-wired bus hybrid topology, with nodes connecting to repeaters in a star fashion and its repeaters connected with each other through a bus.

Because 10BaseF uses fiber optic cable, it is less susceptible to noise than 10BaseT Ethernet. However, its higher cost does not usually justify implementing 10BaseF for this reason. Because 10BaseF involves (expensive) fiber and achieves merely 10 Mbps throughput (the same throughput achieved by copper wiring), it is not commonly found on modern networks. Instead, fiber optic cable is used with a faster Ethernet technology, 100BaseF, which you learn about later in this chapter.

100BaseT

As networks become larger and handle heavier traffic, Ethernet's longstanding 10 Mbps limitation becomes a bottleneck that detrimentally affects response time. The need for faster LANs that can use the same infrastructure as the popular 10BaseT technology has been met by **100BaseT**, also known as **Fast Ethernet**. 100BaseT, specified in the IEEE 802.3u standard, enables LANs to run at a 100 Mbps data transfer rate—a tenfold increase from that provided by 10BaseT—without requiring a significant investment in new infrastructure. As its name implies, 100BaseT offers 100 Mbps throughput, uses baseband transmission, and relies on twisted-pair cabling.

Like 10BaseT, 100BaseT uses the star-wired bus hybrid topology. Also, like 10BaseT, the segment length on 100BaseT networks cannot exceed 100 meters. In fact, a diagram of a 100BaseT network looks just like Figure 10-11's drawing of a 10BaseT network—except that 100BaseT networks can practically support a maximum of only three segments connected with two hubs. Because of the fewer segments allowed, a 100BaseT's network maximum length is shorter than a 10BaseT network's overall length. As you learned earlier, higher speed Ethernet networks have a lower tolerance for propagation delay. Thus, 100BaseT networks cannot repeat signals as far as 10BaseT networks. Because 100BaseT relies on twisted-pair cabling, it also uses RJ-45 data connectors. Depending on the type of 100BaseT technology used, it may require a minimum of CAT3 or CAT5 UTP.

 When adding nodes or segments to a 10BaseT network, engineers typically use CAT5 cabling. Because both 10BaseT and 100BaseT can run on CAT5 cabling, this practice allows for a simpler migration from a 10BaseT network to a 100BaseT network in the future. In addition, installing NICs and connectivity devices that are capable of handling either 10BaseT and 100BaseT transmission makes the transition still easier.

Two 100BaseT specifications—100BaseT4 and 100BaseTX—have competed for popularity as organizations move to 100 Mbps technology. The difference between these technologies relates primarily to the way they achieve the 100 Mbps transmission rate, which affects their cabling requirements.

- *100BaseTX*—The most popular version, it achieves its speed by sending the signal 10 times faster and condensing the time between digital pulses as well as the time a station must wait and listen for a signal. 100BaseTX requires CAT5 or higher UTP cabling. Within the cable, it uses the same two pairs of wire for transmitting and receiving data that 10BaseT uses. Therefore, like 10BaseT, 100BaseTX is also capable of full-duplex transmission. Full duplexing can potentially double the bandwidth of a 100BaseT network to 200 Mbps.

- *100BaseT4*—Is differentiated from 100BaseTX in that it uses all four pairs of wires in a UTP cable and, therefore, can use lower-cost CAT3 wiring (rather than only CAT5M as 10BaseTX requires). It achieves its speed by breaking the 100 Mbps data stream into three streams of 33 Mbps each. These three streams are sent over three pairs of wire in the cable. The fourth wire pair is used for control information. Because 100BaseT4 technology uses all four wire pairs for unidirectional signaling, it cannot support full duplexing. This is one reason 100BaseT4 is less popular than 100BaseTX. Another reason is that the cost of CAT5 cabling has decreased since the invention of 100BaseT4 technology. Its cost is nearly as low as CAT3 UTP, so 100BaseT4's reliance on CAT3 cabling is no longer an advantage.

100BaseTX and 100BaseT4 cannot coexist on a single network segment. For example, if you purchase a hub designed for 100BaseTX transmission, you cannot use NICs designed for 100BaseT4 transmission to connect to that hub.

100BaseF

The **100BaseF** standard specifies a network capable of 100 Mbps throughput that uses baseband transmission and fiber optic cabling. Like 10BaseF, 100BaseF requires multimode fiber containing at least two strands of fiber. One strand is used for data transmission while the other strand is used for reception, making 100BaseF a full-duplex technology. 100BaseF networks require one of several types of connectors, including the two most popular connectors, SC and ST. Its maximum segment length is 400 meters, with a maximum of two repeaters allowed to connect segments. The 100BaseF standard uses a star topology, with its repeaters connected through a bus.

100BaseF, like 100BaseT, is also considered "Fast Ethernet." Organizations switching, or migrating, from UTP to fiber media can combine 100BaseTX and 100BaseF within one network. To do this, connectivity devices must have both RJ-45 and SC or ST ports. Alternatively, a 100BaseTX to 100BaseF media converter may be used at any point in the network to interconnect the different media and convert the signals of one standard to signals that work with the other standard.

Switched Ethernet

So far, you have learned that nodes on an Ethernet network share one communications channel in a transmission style known as baseband. (Recall that this is similar to a one-lane highway that must be shared by cars driving in both directions.) In traditional Ethernet technology, known as **shared Ethernet**, the fixed amount of bandwidth supplied by the single channel must be shared by all devices on a segment. Nodes cannot send and receive data simultaneously, nor can they transmit a signal when another station on the same segment is sending or receiving data. On shared Ethernet, all nodes share a segment and connect via a hub or repeater, which, as you know, merely retransmits a signal. In contrast, a **switch** is a device that can separate a network segment into smaller segments (or, in the case of Ethernet, collision domains), with each segment being independent of the others and supporting its own traffic. Comparing data traffic to automobile traffic, switching is similar to subdividing one large lane into several lanes over which drivers may travel in either direction. **Switched Ethernet** is a newer Ethernet

10

model that enables multiple nodes to simultaneously transmit and receive data over different network segments. By doing so, each node can individually take advantage of more bandwidth. Figure 10-12 shows how switches can isolate network segments. You learn more about switches used in data networking in Chapter 11.

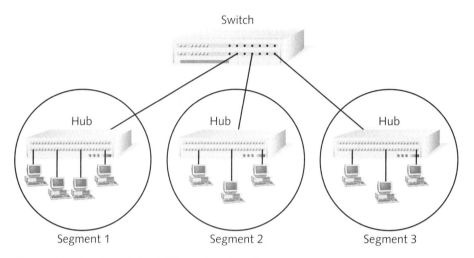

Figure 10-12   A switched Ethernet network

Using switched Ethernet increases the effective bandwidth of a network segment because fewer workstations must vie for the same time on the wire. In fact, applying switches to a 10 Mbps Ethernet LAN can increase its effective data transmission rate to 100 Mbps. For organizations with existing 10BaseT infrastructure, switches offer a relatively simple and inexpensive way to add bandwidth. Switches can be placed strategically on an organization's network to balance traffic loads and reduce congestion.

Note, however, that switches are not always the best answer to heavy traffic and a need for greater speeds. In a case where an enterprise-wide Ethernet LAN is generally overtaxed, upgrading the network's design or infrastructure is a better solution.

Gigabit Ethernet

As you can probably guess, the evolution of Ethernet has not stopped with the development of switched Ethernet and the 100 Mbps standard. The Ethernet version that runs at 1000 Mbps is called **1 Gigabit Ethernet**, or more often, simply, **Gigabit Ethernet**. IEEE has established specifications for Gigabit Ethernet over fiber optic or coaxial cable in its 802.3z project. This form of Gigabit Ethernet, known as 1000BaseF, is the most common form of Gigabit Ethernet. However, Gigabit Ethernet may also run over CAT5 UTP cable, as specified by the IEEE in its 802.3ab project. Using UTP for Gigabit Ethernet is rare partly because of its distance limitations. A segment of Gigabit Ethernet running on UTP can span a maximum of 100 meters, whereas a segment running on fiber can span a maximum of 550 meters. Like other forms of Ethernet, Gigabit Ethernet network uses CSMA/CD transmission and is capable of full duplexing.

You will most likely encounter Gigabit Ethernet as part of a network's backbone. It is well-suited to connecting multiple buildings in a MAN, for example. Currently, this scheme would not typically be used for connecting workstations to hubs, for example, because most workstation users do not require Gigabit throughput on a regular basis. For these users, the increased data rate rarely justifies the cost of upgrading workstations with Gigabit NICs and connections.

But the race for greater throughput has not stopped at 1 Gigabit. In March 1999, representatives from the networking industry began discussing a **10 Gigabit Ethernet** standard. The standards for 10 Gigabit are currently being defined by the IEEE 802.3ae committee and will include full-duplexing and multimode fiber requirements. IEEE is aiming to make the 10 Gigabit Ethernet standard compatible with the Physical layer standards for 1 Gigabit Ethernet to allow organizations to easily upgrade their networks. The 1- and 10-Gigabit technologies compete directly with other fast networking solutions such as Asynchronous Transfer Mode (ATM), which is covered later in this chapter.

Token Ring

Now that you have learned about the many forms of Ethernet, you are ready to learn about Token Ring, a less common, but still important network access method. Token Ring was first developed by IBM in the 1980s. Since that time, the IEEE has developed its own Token Ring standard through its 802.5 task force. Token Ring networks transmit data at either 4, 16, or 100 Mbps over STP or UTP. A Token Ring network using STP may contain as many as 255 addressable stations (or nodes). One using UTP may contain as many as 72 nodes.

In the early 1990s, the Token Ring architecture competed strongly with Ethernet to be the most popular network access method. Since that time, the economics, speed, and reliability of Ethernet have improved, leaving Token Ring behind. Because IBM developed Token Ring, some IBM-centric Information Technology Departments continue to use it. Many other network administrators have changed their former Token Ring networks into Ethernet networks.

Token Ring networks are generally more expensive to implement than Ethernet networks. Proponents of the Token Ring technology argue that, although some of its connectivity hardware is more expensive, its reliability results in less downtime and lower network management costs than Ethernet provides. On a practical level, Token Ring has probably lost the battle for superiority because its developers were slower to agree on a high-speed standard. For a long time, Token Ring was limited to 4 or 16 Mbps. The 100 Mbps Token Ring standard, finalized in 1999, is known as **High-Speed Token Ring (HSTR)**. HSTR can use either twisted-pair or fiber optic cable as its transmission medium. Although it is as reliable and efficient as Fast Ethernet, it is less common because of its more costly implementation.

Token Ring networks use the token-passing routine and a star-ring hybrid physical topology. Recall from the discussion of the ring topology earlier in this chapter that a token designates which station on the ring can transmit information on the wire. On a Token Ring network, one computer, called the **active monitor**, acts as the controller for token passing. Specifically, the active monitor maintains the timing for ring passing, monitors token and frame transmission, detects lost tokens, and corrects errors when a timing error or other disruption occurs. Only one computer on the ring can act as the active monitor at any given time. The token-passing access control scheme ensures high data reliability (no collisions) and an efficient use of bandwidth. It also does not impose distance limitations on the length of a LAN segment, unlike CSMA/CD. On the other hand, token ring passing generates extra network traffic.

The Token Ring architecture is often mistakenly described as a pure ring topology. In fact, it uses a star-ring hybrid topology in which data circulates in a ring fashion, but the physical layout of the network is a star.

Like Ethernet networks, Token Ring networks can take advantage of switching to better utilize limited bandwidth. Token Ring switching products are typically more expensive and more difficult to manage than Ethernet switches, although they perform essentially the same function. A Token Ring switch can subdivide a large network ring into several smaller network rings. For example, if a 16 Mbps Token Ring network supports 40 users, each workstation has access to approximately 0.4 Mbps. Installing a Token Ring switch that is configured to subdivide the network into four logical subnetworks provides each workstation with approximately 1.6 Mbps (under optimal physical conditions). Thus, switching effectively quadruples the bandwidth in this example.

FDDI

FDDI (Fiber Distributed Data Interface) is a network access method whose standard was originally specified by ANSI in the mid-1980s and later refined by ISO. FDDI (pronounced "fiddy") uses a double ring of multimode or single mode fiber to transmit data at speeds of up to 100 Mbps. FDDI was developed in response to the throughput limitations of Ethernet and Token Ring technologies used at the time. In fact, FDDI was the first network transport system to reach the 100 Mbps threshold. For this reason, you will frequently find it supporting network backbones that were installed in the late 1980s and early 1990s. A popular implementation of FDDI involves connecting LANs to form MANs. FDDI links can span distances as large as 62 miles. Because Ethernet and Token Ring technologies have developed faster transmission speeds, FDDI is no longer the much-coveted technology that it was in the 1980s.

Nevertheless, FDDI is a stable technology that offers numerous benefits. Its reliance on fiber optic cable ensures that FDDI is more reliable and more secure than network access methods that depend on copper wiring. Another advantage of FDDI is that it can be integrated with LANs that use Ethernet 100BaseTX technology. For example, if FDDI were used to connect multiple buildings on a college campus, network administrators could easily connect the FDDI parts of the MAN to the 100BaseTX LANs within each building. Finally, some organizations choose FDDI over other high-speed network access methods, such as 100BaseT, because it can span longer distances.

One drawback to FDDI technology is its high cost relative to Fast Ethernet (costing up to 10 times more per connected device than Fast Ethernet). If an organization has FDDI installed, however, it can use the same cabling to upgrade to Gigabit Ethernet, with only minor differences to consider, such as Ethernet's lower maximum segment length.

FDDI is based on a ring physical topology similar to a Token Ring network, as shown in Figure 10-13. It also relies on the same token-passing routine that Token Ring networks use. However, unlike Token Ring technology, FDDI runs on two complete rings. During normal operation, the primary FDDI ring carries data while the secondary ring is idle. The secondary ring assumes data transmission responsibilities should the primary ring experience Physical layer problems. This redundancy makes FDDI networks extremely reliable.

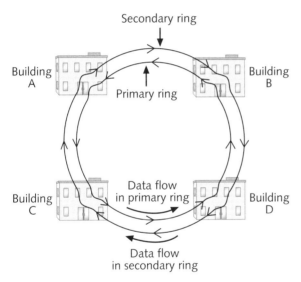

Figure 10-13 A FDDI network

ATM

ATM (Asynchronous Transfer Mode) is a standard that describes both a network access method and a multiplexing technique. Therefore, it performs the same functions as other network access methods (like Ethernet), but it also performs functions that allow multiple signals to share one channel, similar to ISDN and T-carrier transmission methods. ATM is unique not only in its broad scope, but also because it relies on a fixed packet size to achieve data transfer rates up to 9953 Mbps (9.95 Gbps). It was first conceived by researchers at Bell Labs in 1983 as a higher-bandwidth alternative to FDDI, but it took a dozen years before standards organizations could reach an agreement on its specifications. ATM standards are now maintained by the ITU.

ATM may run over specific types of fiber optic or copper networks, such as SONET or T-carriers (which you learn about later in this chapter). It is typically used on WANs, particularly by large data carriers, such as LECs, IXCs and other network service providers. The following sections provide more details about ATM's unique characteristics.

Cells

Like Token Ring and Ethernet, ATM specifies Data Link layer data packaging and Physical layer signaling techniques. But what sets ATM apart from Token Ring and Ethernet is its fixed packet size. The fixed packet in ATM, which is called a **cell**, consists of 48 bytes of data plus a five-byte header, for a 53-byte packet. Compare this to Ethernet's frame size of between 64 to 1518 bytes. ATM's smaller packet size results in more overhead, making ATM transmission less efficient than Ethernet. In fact, ATM's overhead decreases its potential throughput by nearly 10 percent. On the other hand, using a fixed packet size allows ATM to better predict and adjust traffic patterns. As a result, ATM networks can better control bandwidth utilization. The predictability that comes with using cells compensates for some of the inefficiency caused by using small packets.

Virtual Circuits

Another key to ATM's speed is its use of virtual circuits. **Virtual circuits** are logical (as opposed to physical) connections between network nodes. Virtual circuits may follow disparate physical links, but perform like direct links between those nodes. One advantage to virtual circuits is their efficient use of limited bandwidth. Several virtual circuits can be assigned to one length of cable or even to one channel on that cable. A virtual circuit uses the channel only when it needs to transmit data. Meanwhile, the channel is available for use by other virtual circuits. In addition, several virtual circuits can be assigned to a single port on a switch, allowing network managers to make the best use of their overall switching capacity.

Depending on the specific implementation of ATM, one of two types of virtual circuits may be used: switched virtual circuits (SVCs) or permanent virtual circuits (PVCs). **SVCs** are connections that are established when parties need to transmit, then dismantled after the transmission is complete. **PVCs** are connections that are established before data needs to be transmitted and maintained after the transmission is complete. Note that in a PVC, the connection is established only between the two points (the sender and receiver); the connection does not specify the exact route the data will travel. Thus, in a PVC, data may follow any number of different paths to move from point A to point B.

For example, suppose you work at a shipping firm that relies on PVCs to connect its offices and warehouses across the nation. (Note that your firm would lease these PVCs—or pay for their use on a regular basis—from a network service provider, such as AT&T or WorldCom.) Suppose also that you need to e-mail a copy of a shipping confirmation from your Boston location to your colleague, Justin, who works in the Missoula, Montana warehouse. After you click the "Send" button in your e-mail program, your message might go from Boston to New York, to Chicago, to Minneapolis, and then to Missoula. Next, you might decide to send an e-mail to Justin's supervisor, notifying her that you sent Justin the shipping confirmation. This message might go from Boston to Louisville, to Denver, and then to Missoula. However, technically speaking, both messages used the same PVC.

Quality of Service (QoS)

Because ATM packages data into packets before transmission, each of which travels separately to its destination, ATM is typically considered a packet-switching technology. At the same time, the use of virtual circuits means that ATM provides the main advantage of circuit switching—that is, a point-to-point connection that remains reliably available to the transmission until it completes. On an ATM network, switches determine the optimal path between the sender and receiver, then establish this path—or virtual circuit—before the network transmits data. This reliable connection allows ATM to guarantee a specific **Quality of Service (QoS)**. QoS is a standard that specifies that data will be delivered within a certain time period after its transmission.

ATM networks can supply four QoS levels, from a "best effort" attempt for noncritical data to a guaranteed, real-time transmission for time-sensitive data. This is important for organizations using networks for time-sensitive applications, such as voice or video transmissions. For example, suppose a company establishes a network link between two offices located at opposite sides of a state. Over this link, the company carries data traffic between the two offices. At times, this data traffic uses up nearly all the link's capacity. Now suppose the same company wants to take advantage of this link to carry its telephone calls between offices (this assumes the company has the equipment to encode voice signals as data packets). If the company relies on a traditional Ethernet access method, the abundant data traffic hampers voice signals, making conversations nearly impossible to conduct. This is because packets may arrive in the wrong order or too slowly to be properly interpreted by the receiving node. However, if the company uses ATM over this link, it could specify that voice signals should have a higher QoS than data signals. Thus, telephone conversations could be conducted with the same quality offered by PSTN connections.

Compatibility

Because ATM is a comparatively recent technology, its developers have made certain it is compatible with other leading network technologies. Its cells can support multiple types of higher-layer protocols, including TCP/IP and IPX/SPX. In addition, ATM can be integrated with Ethernet or Token Ring networks through the use of **LAN Emulation (LANE)**. LANE operates at the Data Link layer of the OSI model, where it encapsulates incoming Ethernet or Token Ring frames, then converts them into ATM cells for transmission over an ATM network. When the data reaches its destination, LANE converts the ATM cell back to the original Ethernet or Token Ring frame so that the receiver can interpret the data.

10

Currently, ATM is more expensive and more complex than its competitors. Thus, it is rarely used on modest sized LANs. On large WANs, ATM may be preferable because it is not distance-sensitive (as Ethernet is) and requires a telecommunications carrier to spend less on facilities. However, even on heavily trafficked WAN routes, ATM is losing its once dominant position. Gigabit Ethernet—a faster, cheaper, and more standard technology—poses a substantial threat. In addition to having better understood standards, Gigabit Ethernet is less expensive and a more natural upgrade for the multitude of Fast Ethernet users. It overcomes the QoS issue by simply providing a larger pipe for the greater volume of traffic using the network. Although ATM caught on among large carriers in the late 1990s, many networking professionals are now following the Gigabit Ethernet standard rather than spending extra dollars on ATM infrastructure.

NETWORK TRANSMISSION METHODS

Now that you have learned about different ways of accessing a shared communications channel, you are ready to learn about different techniques used to achieve high throughput, given limited bandwidth. Each technique discussed in the following sections varies according to its developer, implementation, media requirement, and maximum throughput. Yet each specifies a way of transmitting data over a particular medium to obtain greater throughput than a simple telephone line can achieve. As you might expect, each of these techniques has its own connectivity requirements. Because, historically, WAN connections were forced to rely on PSTN lines for their transmission media, many of the techniques discussed in the following sections use the PSTN as their foundation.

The transmission methods discussed in this section run over leased lines. The term **leased lines** means that the organization does not own the transmission media, but leases a service on a regular basis from a telecommunications provider. The provider may be a LEC, IXC, ISP, or another nontraditional common carrier. Also, the provider may own the infrastructure through which the service is provided, or the provider may resell another carrier's infrastructure. In exchange for a recurring (usually monthly) fee, an organization has unlimited use of the service. Some services, like T-carriers, may be leased up to a specified maximum throughput.

X.25 and Frame Relay

X.25 is set of protocols designed for long-distance data transmission and standardized by the ITU in the mid-1970s. X.25 transmits analog signals via packet-switched technology. It was developed as a more reliable alternative to the voice telephone system for connecting mainframe computers and remote terminals. The original standard for X.25 specified a maximum of 64 Kbps throughput, but by 1992, the standard was updated to include maximum throughput of 2.048 Mbps. X.25 ensures data reliability over long distances by verifying the transmission at every node. Unfortunately, this verification also renders X.25 comparatively slow and unsuitable for time-sensitive applications, such as audio or video. X.25 was never widely adopted in the United States, but was accepted by other countries and was for a long time the dominant packet-switching technology used on WANs around the world.

Frame relay is an updated, digital version of X.25 that also relies on packet switching. The name is derived from the fact that data is separated into frames which are then relayed from one node to another without any verification or processing. The most significant difference between frame relay and X.25 is that frame relay does not guarantee reliable delivery of data. X.25 checks for errors and, in the case of an error, either corrects the damaged data or retransmits the original data. Frame relay, on the other hand, simply checks for errors. It leaves the error correction up to higher network devices (such as routers). Partially because it doesn't perform the same level of error correction that X.25 performs, frame relay supports higher bandwidth than X.25. It offers throughputs between 64 Kbps and 45 Mbps. Frame relay was standardized in 1984 by the ITU for international communications. It became popular in the United States and Canada (where it is standardized by ANSI) for reliable long-distance WAN connections. The main advantage to using frame relay over other WAN transmission methods is its low cost.

On data networks diagrams, WANs that use packet-switched technologies (such as X.25 and frame relay) are depicted as clouds, as shown in Figure 10-14. The cloud represents the indeterminate nature of their traffic, compared to the circuit-switched PSTN connections that they were designed to replaced. You may see the Internet depicted as a cloud on networking diagrams as well. In its beginning, the Internet relied largely on X.25 or frame relay transmission—hence the similar illustration.

10

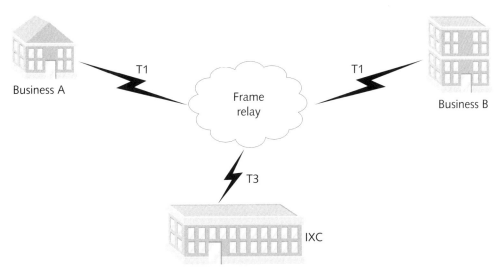

Figure 10-14   A WAN using frame relay

As with ATM, both X.25 and frame relay use virtual circuits during transmission. They may also use either switched virtual circuits (SVCs) or permanent virtual circuits (PVCs), depending on the customer's needs. When a customer leases an X.25 or frame relay circuit from a network service provider, his contract reflects the endpoints he specifies and the amount of bandwidth he requires between those endpoints. (In the ATM example described previously, had the shipping company used frame relay instead, Boston and Missoula would be specified as endpoints.) The network service provider guarantees a minimum amount of bandwidth, called the **Committed Information Rate (CIR)**. Provisions usually account for brief bursts of traffic that occasionally exceed the CIR. When you lease a PVC, you share bandwidth with the other X.25 and frame relay users on the service provider's network.

One advantage to leasing a frame relay circuit (as opposed to leasing a direct connection between two points) is that you only pay for the amount of bandwidth required. Another advantage is that frame relay is much less expensive than the newer, high-bandwidth WAN technologies offered today. Its low cost is partly due to the fact that, unlike other long-distance data services, frame relay's pricing does not depend on the distance you want to transmit data. Another reason for its low cost is its shared (or public) nature. Also, frame relay follows an established, worldwide standard, so it is well-suited to international telecommunications. Because of its low cost and ubiquitous availability, frame relay is often used by businesses that need to transmit small amounts of data from multiple locations. For example, a bank might use frame relay to connect its 50 automatic teller machines located across a city to its central processing facility.

On the other hand, because frame relay and X.25 use shared lines, their throughput remains at the mercy of variable traffic patterns. For example, in the middle of the night, data over your frame relay network may zip along at 4 Mbps; at mid-morning, when everyone is surfing the Web, your throughput may slow down to less than 500 Kbps. In addition, frame relay's shared, virtual circuits are less private than point-to-point connections or circuits used by only one organization.

ISDN

ISDN (Integrated Services Digital Network) is an international standard, established by the ITU for transmitting data over digital lines. ISDN typically relies on the PSTN network, and its connections may be dial-up or dedicated. In a dial-up connection, ISDN users dial their telecommunications provider's network from an ISDN modem, similar to how you might dial into your ISP's network from your computer's modem. A **dedicated** connection is one that is always available to transmit or receive data. ISDN is only one example of a transmission method that uses dedicated connections. Later in this chapter, you learn about others.

Although ISDN relies on the PSTN, it is distinguished from a simple telephone line by the fact that it exclusively uses digital signaling, and also by the fact that it can carry data and voice signals at once. ISDN lines may carry as many as two voice calls and one data connection simultaneously. (To achieve this feat, the ISDN user must have the correct devices to accept all three connections, as described later in this section.) Through their ability to transmit voice and data simultaneously, ISDN lines can eliminate the need to pay for separate phone lines to support faxes, modems, and voice calls at one location. When used for telephone calls, ISDN offers the advantage of much quicker dialing and call completion.

LECs began offering ISDN in the mid-1980s, anticipating that the United States would convert to this all-digital system by the turn of the century. ISDN hasn't caught on as quickly as predicted, and other types of digital transmission methods now compete with it to serve customers who require moderate to fast throughput over phone lines.

All ISDN connections are based on two types of channels: B channels and D channels. The **B channel** is the "bearer" channel, employing circuit-switching techniques to carry voice, video, and other types of data over the ISDN connection. A single B channel has a maximum throughput of 64 Kbps, although it is sometimes limited to 56 Kbps by the ISDN provider's equipment. As you will learn, the number of B channels in a single ISDN connection may vary. The **D channel** is the "data" channel, employing packet-switching techniques to carry information about the call, such as session initiation and termination signals, caller identity, call forwarding, and conference calling signals. A single D channel has a maximum throughput of 16 Kbps or 64 Kbps, depending on the ISDN implementation. Each ISDN connection uses only one D channel. By separating the control signals (the D channel) from the information signals (the B channels), ISDN can transmit voice and data signals more efficiently than a regular phone line, in which control and information signals share the same channel.

In North America, two types of ISDN connections are commonly used: Basic Rate Interface (BRI) and Primary Rate Interface (PRI). A third type of ISDN connection, called Broadband ISDN (B-ISDN), was developed by the ITU in the late 1980s to provide more capacity than BRI or PRI. B-ISDN was the precursor to ATM. Today, organizations in need of the capacity offered by B-ISDN tend to choose newer, high-capacity lines, such as those using xDSL or T1 technology (both described later in this chapter).

BRI (Basic Rate Interface) uses two B channels and one 16-Kbps D channel, as indicated by the following notation: 2B+D. The two B channels are treated as separate connections by the network and can carry voice and data or two data streams simultaneously and separate from each other. In a process called **bonding**, these two 64 Kbps B channels can be combined to achieve an effective throughput of 128 Kbps—the maximum amount of data traffic that a BRI connection can accommodate. Most consumers who subscribe to ISDN from home use BRI, which is the most economical type of ISDN connection.

Figure 10-15 illustrates how a typical BRI link supplies a home consumer with an ISDN link. (Note that the configuration depicted in Figure 10-15 applies to installations in North America only. Because transmission standards differ in Europe and Asia, different

10

numbers of B channels are used in the standard ISDN connections in those regions.) From the telephone company's lines, the ISDN channels connect to a Network Termination 1 device at the customer's site. The **Network Termination 1 (NT1)** device connects the twisted-pair wiring at the customer's building with the ISDN terminal equipment via RJ-11 or RJ-45 data jacks. The ISDN **terminal equipment (TE)** may include cards or standalone devices used to connect computers to the ISDN line (similar to a network adapter used on Ethernet or Token Ring networks).

So that the ISDN line can connect to analog equipment, the signal must first pass through a terminal adapter. A **terminal adapter (TA)** converts digital signals into analog signals for use with ISDN phones and other analog devices. (Terminal adapters are often called ISDN modems, though they are not, technically, modems.) Typically, telecommuters who want more throughput than their analog phone line affords choose BRI as their ISDN connection. For a home user, the terminal adapter would most likely be an ISDN router, such as the 1604 router from Cisco Systems, whereas the terminal equipment would be an Ethernet card in the user's workstation plus, perhaps, a telephone.

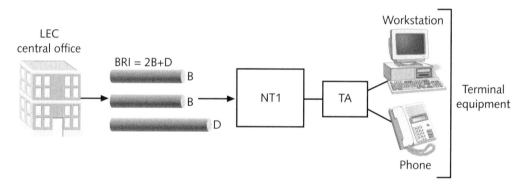

Figure 10-15   A BRI link

PRI (Primary Rate Interface) uses 23 B channels and one 64-Kbps D channel as represented by the following notation: 23B+D. PRI is less commonly used by individual subscribers than BRI is, but it may be selected by businesses and other organizations that need more throughput. As with BRI, the separate B channels in a PRI link can carry voice and data, independent of each other or bonded together. In North America, the maximum potential throughput for a PRI connection is 1.544 Mbps, the same as that for T1; in fact, PRI channels can be carried by T1 trunks.

PRI and BRI connections may be interconnected on a single network. PRI links use the same kind of equipment as BRI links, but require the services of an extra network termination device, called a **Network Termination 2 (NT2)**, to handle the multiple ISDN lines. Figure 10-16 depicts a typical PRI link as it would be installed in North America.

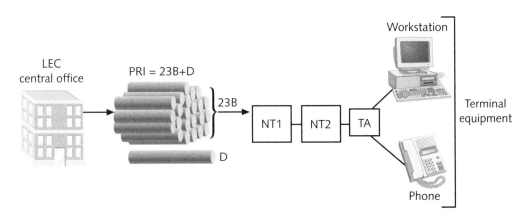

Figure 10-16 A PRI link

Individual customers who need to transmit more data than a typical modem can handle or who want to use a single line for both data and voice commonly use ISDN lines. ISDN, although not available in every location of the United States, can be purchased from most local telephone companies and other network service providers. The cost of using BRI averages $100 to $250 per month, depending on the customer's location. PRI and B-ISDN are significantly more expensive. In addition, no matter what version of ISDN the customer chooses, she must pay setup fees and purchase an ISDN router (unless it is provided by the telecommunications carrier). In some areas, ISDN providers may charge customers additional usage fees based on the total length of time they remain connected.

One disadvantage of ISDN is that it can span a distance of only 18,000 feet before repeater equipment is needed to boost the signal. For this reason, it is only feasible to use for the local loop portion of a connection. In other words, a company with offices across the state might lease separate ISDN lines for each office to connect to the Internet. However, the same company could not lease an ISDN link to connect all the offices with each other to form a WAN. In addition, ISDN requires special, expensive telephone stations to supply voice services. The requirement of purchasing new telephones contributed to ISDN's lack of popularity among consumers. Among businesses, however, the PRI version of ISDN is still in demand. The primary reason for this is because of ISDN's flexibility. The use of one PRI ISDN connection can be dynamically changed from incoming to outgoing lines. For example, suppose a retail catalog company's call center uses a PRI ISDN connection to take calls from customers all day long. During the day, the connection is configured to accept only incoming calls. At 6:00 p.m., however, the retail catalog company uses the call center for a telemarketing. At that time, the lines using the PRI ISDN connection switch to become outgoing lines that only allow representatives to call consumers and market the company's services.

10

T-Carrier Services

Earlier in this chapter, you encountered references to T-carriers. **T-carrier** is the general name for a group of transmission methods that includes T1s, fractional T1s, and T3s. Every type of T-carrier uses time division multiplexing (TDM) over two copper wire pairs (one pair for transmitting and one pair for receiving) to divide a single channel into multiple channels. For example, multiplexing enables a single T1 circuit to carry 24 channels, each capable of 64 Kbps throughput; thus, a T1 has a maximum capacity of 24 x 64 Kbps, or 1.544 Mbps. Each channel may contain data, voice, or video signals.

If you have forgotten the principles behind multiplexing and modulation, it may be helpful to review this material from Chapter 6. In particular, you may want to refresh your understanding of time division multiplexing (TDM) and pulse code modulation (PCM), both of which are used in T-carrier technology.

AT&T developed T-carrier technology in 1957 in an effort to digitize voice signals, thereby enabling such signals to travel long distances. Before that time, voice signals, which were purely analog, were expensive to transmit over long distances because of the number of connectivity devices needed to keep the signal intelligible. AT&T implemented pulse code modulation (PCM) to encode voice signals in a digital format. In the 1970s, many businesses installed T1s to obtain more voice throughput per line. With increased data communication needs, such as Internet access and geographically dispersed offices, T1s have become common WAN links for use in medium to large businesses. Like ISDN, T-carriers are well suited to transmitting voice, video, and data signals together over a single connection.

T-carriers are examples of dedicated leased lines. They are also **private lines**; that is, when you lease a T-carrier from a network service provider, your connection is only available for use between your defined endpoints. The bandwidth over a private line is not shared. This makes private lines, such as T-carriers, well-suited to connections that require reliable and predictable bandwidth. Private lines are also more secure than shared connections, such as frame relay.

The next section describes the various types of T-carriers. After that, you learn about the ways in which T-carriers are connected with customer networks.

Types of T-Carriers

A number of T-carrier varieties are available today, and their differences depend on which signal level they employ. **Signal level** refers to the T-carrier's Physical layer electrical signaling characteristics as defined by ANSI standards in the early 1980s. **DS0 (Digital Signal, Level 0)** is an international standard used to describe one 64-Kbps channel. On this 64 Kbps, signal level standards dictate that voice signals should be digitized using pulse code modulation (PCM) with a sampling rate of 8000 times per second. Compare this low sampling rate to the 44,100 times per second described in

Chapter 6 as the norm for compact disc audio recordings. 8000 times per second is appropriate for encoding conversations when conserving bandwidth is more important that preserving the subtleties of the original analog sound. Many signal levels exist, and each is a multiple of DS0, as shown in Table 10-1. For example, 24 DS0 channels make up a DS1.

In North America, a T-carrier that follows the DS1 standard is known as a T1. A **T1** circuit can carry the equivalent of 24 voice or data channels, giving a maximum data throughput of 1.544 Mbps. A **T3** can carry the equivalent of 672 voice or data channels, giving a maximum data throughput of 44.736 Mbps (its throughput is typically rounded up to 45 Mbps for the purposes of discussion). T1s and T3s are the most common form of T-carriers.

You may hear signal level and carrier terms used interchangeably—for example, DS1 and T1. Technically, T1 is the North American implementation of the international DS1 standard. In Europe, the DS1 standard is implemented as E1. In Japan, it is known as J1.

Table 10-1   T-carrier specifications

Signal level	Carrier	Number of T1s	Number of channels	Throughput
DS0	—	1/24	1	.064 Mbps
DS1	T1	1	24	1.544 Mbps
DS1C	T1C	2	24	3.152 Mbps
DS2	T2	4	96	6.312 Mbps
DS3	T3	28	672	44.736 Mbps
DS4	T4	168	4032	274.176 Mbps

Because a T3 provides 28 times more throughput than a T1, many organizations may find that a few T1s—rather than a single T3—can accommodate their throughput needs. For example, suppose a regional architecture firm needs to transmit blueprints and specifications over the Internet to an engineering firm, and its peak throughput requirement (at any given time) was 10 Mbps. The architecture firm would require 7 T1s (10 Mbps divided by 1.544 Mbps equals 6.48 T1s). Leasing 7 T1s would prove much less expensive for the firm than leasing a single T3. As a telecommunications professional, you are most likely to work with T1 or T3 lines. In addition to knowing their capacity, you should be familiar with their costs and uses. T-carriers typically run over a connection between the consumer and the LEC's end office. Or, if provided by an IXC, they use connections between the consumer and the IXC's POP. Functionally, T1s are used by businesses to connect the business's multiple branch offices or to connect the business with a carrier, such as an IXC or ISP. Telephone companies also use T1s to connect their smaller central offices or to connect end offices with telephone switches located "in the field." Local ISPs may use one or more T1s or T3s, depending on the carrier's size, to connect to regional ISPs. Regional ISPs and larger network service providers, however, are likely to use transmission methods with higher throughput, such as SONET rings.

10

The cost of T1s varies from region to region and depends on the distance between a customer's specified endpoints. On average, a T1 might cost as much as $4000 to install, plus an additional $1000 to $2000 per month in access fees. The longer the distance between the provider (such as an ISP or a telephone company) and the subscriber, the higher a T1's monthly charge. Charges for local T1s may be based on mileage, whereas costs for long distance T1s vary on a city-to-city basis. For example, a T1 between New Orleans and New York costs more than a T1 between Boston and New York. Similarly, a T1 from a Los Angeles suburb to the city center costs more than a T1 from the city center to a business three blocks away. T-carrier pricing does not typically depend on usage. For example, if a company leases a T1 for $1450 per month, they pay that price no matter whether they use an average of 1.33 Mbps or only 400 Kbps over the course of the month.

For organizations that do not need constant bandwidth, a dial-up ISDN solution may prove more cost-effective than a T1. For businesses that *do* need a dedicated circuit, but don't always need as much as 1.544 Mbps throughput, a fractional T1 is a better option. A **fractional T1** lease allows organizations to use only some of the channels on a T1 line and be charged according to the number of channels they use. Thus, fractional T1 bandwidth can be leased in multiples of 64 Kbps. A fractional T1 is best suited to businesses that expect their traffic to grow and that may require a full T1 eventually, but can't currently justify leasing a full T1.

T3s are very expensive and are used by the most data-intensive businesses—for example, computer consulting firms that provide online data backups and warehousing for a number of other businesses or large long-distance carriers. A T3 may cost as much as $8000 to install, plus monthly access fees, which may be as high as tens of thousands of dollars. Of course, T3 costs vary depending on the carrier, the customer's location, and the distance covered by the T3. In any event, however, this type of connection is significantly more expensive than a T1. Therefore, only businesses with significant bandwidth requirements use T3s.

T-Carrier Connectivity

The approximate costs mentioned previously include monthly access and installation, but not connectivity hardware. Every T-carrier line requires connectivity hardware at both the customer site and the local carrier's POP. Connectivity hardware may be purchased or leased. Leasing the connectivity equipment from the telecommunications provider is more common than purchasing. However, if a customer leases the line directly from a local carrier and anticipates little change in his connectivity requirements over time, he may find it more economical to purchase the hardware.

Because of their multiplexing and termination requirements, T-carrier lines use specialized connectivity hardware. In addition, T-carrier lines require different media depending on their maximum potential throughput. In the following sections, you learn about the physical components of a T-carrier connection between a customer and a local telecommunications carrier.

Transmission Media   As mentioned earlier, the T-carrier system is based on AT&T's original attempt to digitize existing long-distance telephone lines. As a result, T1 technology can use unshielded or shielded twisted-pair copper wiring—in other words, plain telephone wire. Because the digital signals require a cleaner connection (that is, one less susceptible to noise and attenuation), however, shielded twisted-pair is preferable. For T1s using shielded twisted-pair, repeaters must regenerate the signal approximately every 6000 feet. Twisted-pair wiring cannot adequately carry the high throughput of multiple T1s or T3 transmissions. Thus, for multiple T1s, coaxial cable, microwave, or fiber optic cabling may be used. For T3s, microwave or fiber optic cabling is necessary.

CSU/DSU (Channel Service Unit/Data Service Unit)   Although CSUs (channel service units) and DSUs (data service units) are actually two separate devices, they are typically combined into a single box called a **CSU/DSU**. The CSU/DSU is the connection point for a T-carrier line at the customer's site. The **CSU** provides termination for the digital signal and ensures connection integrity through error correction and line monitoring. The **DSU** converts the digital signal used by bridges, routers, and multiplexers into the digital signal sent via the cabling. The CSU/DSU box connects the incoming T-carrier with the multiplexer, as shown in Figure 10-17. Plainly speaking, a CSU/DSU performs functions for a T-carrier that are similar to the functions your computer's modem performs for a regular telephone line.

10

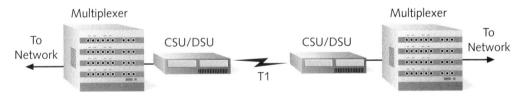

Figure 10-17   A CSU/DSU connecting a T1

Multiplexers   As you learned in Chapter 6, a multiplexer is a device that combines multiple voice or data signals on one line. At a T-carrier customer's location, multiplexers connect a customer's equipment—for example, private telephone switches or routers—with the CSU/DSU. In the context of voice communications, multiplexers separate individual telephone conversations from the T-carrier's multiple channels. For data communications, multiplexers separate individual data streams from the multiple channels. T-carrier multiplexers may be connected to voice or data devices or both. For example, suppose a small community college leases a T1 from a LEC to carry its voice traffic. Also suppose the community college uses a private switching system, such as a PBX, to connect calls between its campus buildings. When a college employee makes a call to an outside number (for example, a student's home), her voice signal is routed through the PBX, then to the T1 multiplexer. The multiplexer combines her signal with other signals and issues all of them to the CSU/DSU. From there, the signal travels over the transmission media (either fiber optic cable or twisted pair) to the LEC's central office, so that it can be issued to the PSTN. Figure 10-18 depicts a typical use of a multiplexer with a T1-connected voice network.

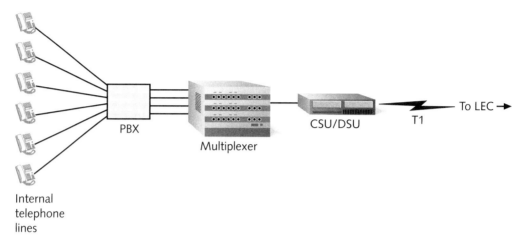

Figure 10-18 Use of a multiplexer on a T1-connected voice network

At the LEC's central office, the T-carrier terminates in CSU/DSU equipment. Next, the T-carrier's channels must be demultiplexed back to their original voice or data streams using another multiplexer. In the community college example, the T1 is divided into its 24 separate 64-Kbps channels, so that the employee's telephone call can be treated as a separate circuit. After the channels are separated, each telephone call can be switched to a telephone subscriber according to the switching process you learned about in Chapter 5.

In T-carrier connections that are wholly digital, the multiplexer is typically incorporated with the CSU/DSU. For example, if the community college in the previous example used a digital PBX, it would not require a separate multiplexing device. However, in T-carrier connections with analog equipment, a different type of multiplexer, called a **channel bank**, is used. If the community college in the previous example used an older, analog PBX, it would require a channel bank. Because many systems are converting their voice communications to digital encoding, channel banks are becoming less common.

Figure 10-19 shows a picture of a channel bank. This channel bank, which is not in service, has some of its adapter cards pulled out for purposes of illustration. Each adapter card is associated with one incoming T-carrier connection.

Figure 10-19 Channel bank

DACS The term **DACS (Digital Access and Cross-connect System)** refers to a method of interconnecting multiple T-carrier lines. DACS makes it possible to split a T-carrier at the DS0 level (in other words, in multiples of 64 Kbps) and recombine several DS0-level channels to form another T-carrier line. For example, suppose the community college described earlier had a remote distance learning center and another remote office used for student counseling. The community college could lease fractional T1s to each of the two remote offices from the same LEC it uses for its T1. At the LEC's facilities, the community college's T1 could be cross-connected through a DACS with its two remote offices' fractional T1s. This would allow the community college's telephone calls to travel between its three locations over the LEC's network without any intervening switching or multiplexing points. The advantages to configuring a WAN in this manner are speed and privacy.

You can think of a DACS as a more sophisticated version of the cross-connects used for telephone lines in an MDF (which you learned about in Chapter 4). But in addition to cross-connecting lines, a DACS allows technicians to remotely monitor the lines it connects and perform maintenance, if necessary. As you can probably guess, a DACS is used in places where many T-carriers converge, such as a network service provider's POP. A DACS would not typically be found at a T-carrier customer's location. Figure 10-20 shows a picture of a modern DACS. Note that the incoming and outgoing connections use fiber optic cable.

Figure 10-20 A modern DACS

DSL

Digital subscriber line (DSL) is a type of high-bandwidth transmission method introduced in the late 1990s that competes directly with ISDN and T1 services. DSL standards are set by the ITU. Like ISDN, DSL can span only limited distances without the help of repeaters and is therefore best suited to the local loop portion of a WAN link But in addition to cross-connecting lines, a DACS allows technicians to remotely monitor the lines it connects and perform maintenance, if necessary. Also, like ISDN, DSL can support multiple data and voice channels over a single line.

DSL uses advanced data modulation techniques to achieve extraordinary throughput over regular phone lines. Recall from Chapter 3 that in data modulation, one signal alters the frequency, phase, or amplitude of another signal to enable multiple signals to traverse the same wire without interfering with each other. Depending on the type, DSL may use any one of these three types of modulation.

Many individuals and businesses are choosing DSL for its low cost, ease of installation, and high throughput. In most areas of the United States, a DSL connection that can supply nearly as much throughput as a T-1 costs less than $100 per month. Consumer-grade DSL, with approximately half as much bandwidth, can cost as low as $20 per month. Because it runs over existing telephone lines, DSL installation is relatively simple, requiring only a special modem and some configuration at the user end. Also, DSL is a dedicated service, which means a connection is always available for use. In the next section, you learn about the many varieties of DSL in use today.

Types of DSL

The term **xDSL** refers to all DSL varieties, of which at least eight currently exist. (The number of DSL standards continues to grow as technology develops and the ITU approves new technologies, making them into standards.) The better-known DSL varieties include Asymmetric DSL (ADSL), G.Lite (a version of ADSL), High Bit-Rate DSL (HDSL), Symmetric or Single-Line DSL (SDSL), and Very High Bit-Rate DSL (VDSL)—the "x" in "xDSL" is replaced by the variety name. DSL types can be divided into two categories: asymmetrical and symmetrical.

To understand the difference between these two categories, you must understand the concept of downstream and upstream data transmission. The term **downstream** refers to data traveling from the telecommunications carrier's end office to the customer. The term **upstream** refers to data traveling from the customer to the carrier's end office. In some types of DSL, the throughput rates for downstream and upstream traffic differ. That is, if you were connected to the Internet via a DSL link, you might be able to pick up your e-mail messages more rapidly than you could send them because the downstream throughput is usually greater. A technology that offers more throughput in one direction than in the other is considered **asymmetrical**. In asymmetrical communications, downstream throughput is usually much higher than upstream throughput. Asymmetrical communication is well-suited to users who download more information off the network than they transmit to it—for example, people watching movies, listening to radio, or downloading files off the Web. ADSL is an example of **asymmetrical DSL**.

Conversely, **symmetrical** technology provides equal capacity for data traveling both upstream and downstream. Symmetrical transmission is suited to users who both upload and download significant amounts of data—for example, a bank's branch office, which sends large volumes of account information to the central server at the bank's headquarters and in turn, receives large amounts of account information from the central server at the bank's headquarters. HDSL and SDSL are examples of **symmetrical DSL**. VDSL comes in both symmetrical and asymmetrical versions.

The types of DSL also vary in terms of their capacity and maximum line length. A VDSL line that carries as much as 52 Mbps in one direction and as much as 6.4 Mbps in the opposite direction can extend a maximum of 1000 feet between the customer's premises and the carrier's POP. This limitation might suit businesses located close to a telephone company's central office (for example, in the middle of a metropolitan area), but it won't work for most individuals. The most popular form of DSL, ADSL, provides a maximum of 8 Mbps in one direction and a maximum of 1.544 Mbps in the other direction; at its highest speeds, it is limited to a distance of 12,000 feet between the customer's premises

10

and the carrier's POP. This distance (more than 2 miles) renders it suitable for most telecommuters. Table 10-2 compares current specifications for five types of DSL.

Table 10-2   Comparison of DSL types

DSL type	Maximum upstream capacity (Mbps)	Maximum downstream capacity (Mbps)	Distance limitation (feet)
ADSL ("full rate")	1	8	18,000
G.Lite (a type of ADSL)	512	1.544	25,000
HDSL	1.544 or 2.048	1.544 or 2.048	12,000
SDSL	1.544	1.544	9,000
VDSL	1.6, 3.2, or 6.4	13, 25.9, or 51.8	1000 - 5000

In addition to their data modulation techniques, capacity, and distance limitations, DSL types vary according to how they use the PSTN. In the following sections, you learn about how DSL connects to a business or residence over the PSTN.

DSL Connectivity

DSL connectivity, like ISDN, depends on the PSTN. To understand how DSL uses the PSTN, it is helpful to recall that telephone lines carry voice signals over a very small range of frequencies, between 300 and 3300 Hz. This leaves higher, inaudible frequencies unused and available for carrying data. Some versions of DSL, such as the popular full-rate ADSL, G.Lite, and VDSL, use the same pair of wires that carry voice signals, but modulate data on the higher frequencies. In the case of full-rate ADSL, a splitter must be installed at the carrier and at the customer's premises to separate the data signal from the voice signal before it reaches the terminal equipment (for example, the phone or the computer). G.Lite, a slower and less expensive version of ADSL, eliminates the splitter but requires the use of a filter to prevent high frequency DSL signals from reaching the telephone. This makes G.Lite easier to install. Other types of DSL, such as HDSL and SDSL, cannot use the same wire pair that is used for voice signals. Instead, these types of DSL use the extra pair of wires contained in a telephone cable (that are otherwise typically unused).

Once inside the customer's office or home, the DSL line must pass through a **DSL modem**, a device that demodulates the signal, extracting the information and passing it on to the computer. The DSL modem may also contain a splitter (for example, in the case of ADSL) to separate the line into multiple channels for voice and data signals. The DSL modem may be external to the computer and connect to a computer's Ethernet NIC via UTP cable or to the computer's USB port. Newer DSL modems come in the form of internal adapters. If the DSL bandwidth is to be shared on a LAN, the DSL modem could connect to a connectivity device, such as a hub or router, rather than just one computer. Figure 10-21 represents a typical DSL connection, including its termination inside an office. Figure 10-22 depicts a DSL modem.

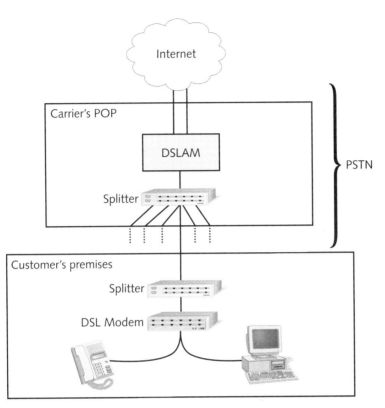

Figure 10-21   A DSL connection

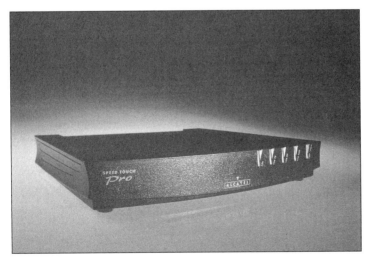

Figure 10-22   A DSL modem

On the other end of the line, the DSL connection terminates at a local telecommunications carrier's facility (for example, an RBOC's end office). If necessary, a splitter is placed between the incoming line and the telephone or data switch. To accept the DSL signals, the carrier must have newer digital switching equipment. In areas of the country where carriers have not updated their switching equipment, DSL service is not available. Inside the carrier's facility, a device called a **DSL access multiplexer (DSLAM)** aggregates multiple DSL subscriber lines and connects them to a larger carrier or to the Internet backbone, as pictured in Figure 10-21.

As mentioned earlier, standards for DSL continue to evolve. Service providers and manufacturers have positioned DSL as competition for T1, ISDN, and cable modem services (discussed next). The installation, hardware, and monthly access costs for DSL are similar to those for ISDN lines but are significantly less than the cost for T1s. Considering that DSL technology can provide faster throughput than T1s, it presents a formidable challenge to the T1 industry, especially given that T1s are typically too expensive for home users.

One drawback to DSL is that it is not available in all areas, and even where it is available, it may be subject to severe distance limitations. Add to that the fluctuating state of DSL standards and providers, and DSL appears to be a technology that requires some time to stabilize. Nevertheless, DSL has won over many consumers and small businesses who want more bandwidth than ISDN or PSTN can afford. As of the year 2000, over 2 million DSL lines were installed in the United States, and by some estimates that number is predicted to grow to over 23 million by 2004.

Cable Modem Technology

While local and long distance phone companies race to make DSL the preferred method of Internet access for consumers, cable companies are pushing their own connectivity option, based on the coaxial cable wiring used for TV signals. Such wiring could theoretically transmit as much as 36 Mbps downstream and as much as 10 Mbps upstream. Thus, cable is an asymmetrical technology. Realistically, however, cable allows approximately 3 to 10 Mbps downstream and 2 Mbps upstream due to its shared nature (described later in this section) as well as bottlenecks that occur either at the Internet carrier's data facilities or on the Internet itself. The asymmetry of cable technology makes it a logical choice for users who want to surf the Web or download data from a network. Some companies are also developing services to deliver music, videoconferencing, and Internet services over cable infrastructure.

Cable connections require that the customer use a special **cable modem**, a device that modulates and demodulates signals for transmission and reception via cable wiring. Figure 10-23 provides an example of a cable modem. The cable modem then connects to a customer's PC via its USB port or through a UTP cable to a (typically Ethernet) NIC. Alternatively, the cable modem could connect to a connectivity device, such as a hub or router, to supply bandwidth to a LAN rather than just one computer. Before customers can subscribe to cable modem service, however, their local cable company must have the necessary infrastructure.

Figure 10-23   A cable modem

Some cable modems are combined with DSL modems into one device. This allows a user to subscribe to both cable modem and DSL connections, terminate the connections at the same device, and connect multiple network nodes to the device.

Traditional cable TV networks supply the infrastructure for downstream communication (the TV programming), but not for upstream communication. To provide Internet access through its network, the cable company must upgrade its existing equipment to support bidirectional, digital communications. For starters, the cable company's network wiring must be replaced with **hybrid fiber-coax (HFC)**, an expensive fiber-optic link that can support high frequencies. The HFC connects the cable company's offices to a node location near the customer. Then, either fiber optic or coaxial cable may connect the node to the customer's business or residence via a connection known as a **cable drop**. All cable drops for the cable subscribers in the same neighborhood connect to the local node. These nodes then connect to the cable company's central office, which is known as its **head-end**. At the head-end, the cable company can connect to the Internet through a variety of means (often via fiber optic cable) or it can pick up digital satellite or microwave transmissions. The head-end can transmit data to as many as 1000 subscribers, in a one-to-many communication system. Figure 10-24 illustrates the infrastructure of a cable system.

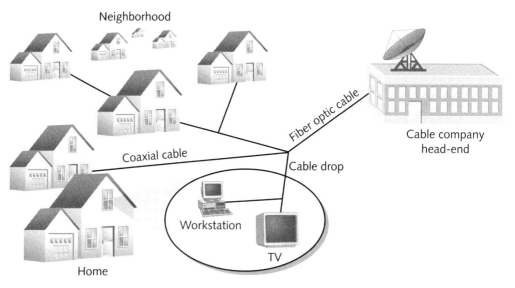

Figure 10-24   Cable infrastructure

One advantage of cable is that, like DSL, it provides a dedicated, or continuous, connection that does not require dialing up a service provider. On the other hand, cable technology requires many subscribers to share the same line, thus raising concerns about security and actual (versus theoretical) throughput. For example, if your cable company supplied you and 10 of your neighbors with cable access to the Internet, your neighbors could capture the data that you transmit to the Internet. Thus, cable users must consider methods of securing their data, such as encryption. Moreover, the throughput of a cable network that serves one neighborhood is fixed. As with any fixed resource, the more one claims, the less that is left for others. In other words, the greater the number of users sharing a single line, the less throughput available to each individual user. Through various means, cable companies are addressing security and bandwidth concerns so that potential subscribers will not hesitate to use their method of Internet access.

Cable technology continues to compete strongly with DSL for servicing consumers who demand higher bandwidth than that offered by a traditional telephone line or ISDN. Cable companies have an advantage of being more stable than many newer DSL providers. On the other hand, the infrastructure (the PSTN) for DSL is (for the most part) already in place and cable is not quite ubiquitous. Cable modems remain a popular choice for residential customers. However, they are less often used in businesses than DSL, partly because of security and bandwidth concerns that arise from cable's shared nature.

SONET and SDH

SONET (Synchronous Optical Network) can provide data transfer rates from 64 Kbps to 39.8 Gbps using the same TDM technique used by T-carriers. Bell Communications Research developed SONET technology in the 1980s to link different phone systems around the world. SONET has since emerged as the best choice for link-ing WANs between North America, Europe, and Asia, because it can work directly with the different standards used in different countries. Internationally, SONET is known as **SDH (Synchronous Digital Hierarchy)**. SONET integrates well with T-carriers, making it a good choice for connecting WANs and LANs over long distances. In fact, SONET is often used to aggregate multiple T1s or T3s. SONET is also used as the underlying technology for ATM transmission.

SONET depends on fiber-optic transmission media to achieve its extraordinary quality of service and throughput. Like T-carriers, it also uses multiplexers and terminal equip-ment to connect at the customer's end. A typical SONET network takes the form of a ring topology, similar to FDDI, in which one ring acts as the primary route for data and the other ring acts as a backup. If, for example, a backhoe operator severs one of the rings, SONET technology would automatically reroute traffic along the backup ring. This char-acteristic, known as **self-healing**, makes SONET very reliable. Companies can lease an entire SONET ring from their local or long distance carrier or they can lease part of a SONET, a circuit that offers T1 throughput, to take advantage of SONET's reliability. Figure 10-25 illustrates a SONET ring and its dual fiber connections.

10

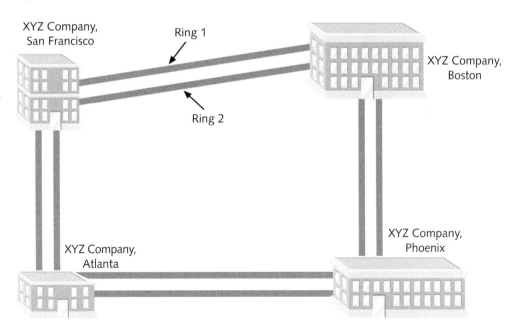

Figure 10-25 A SONET ring

The data rate of a particular SONET ring is indicated by its **Optical Carrier (OC) level**, a rating that is internationally recognized by networking professionals and stan-dards organizations. OC levels in SONET are analogous to the digital signal levels of T1s. Table 10-3 lists the OC levels and their maximum throughput.

Table 10-3   SONET OC levels

OC level	Throughput (Mbps)
OC1	51.84
OC3	155.52
OC12	622
OC24	1244
OC48	2480
OC96	4976
OC192	9953
OC768	39813

SONET technology is typically not implemented by small- or medium-sized businesses, because of its high cost. It is more commonly used by large global companies, IXCs linking metropolitan areas and countries, or other network service providers that want to guarantee fast, reliable access to the Internet. SONET is particularly suited to audio, video, and imaging data transmissions. As you can imagine, given its reliance on fiber optic cable and its redundancy requirements, SONET technology is very expensive to implement.

CHAPTER SUMMARY

❐ Three simple physical topologies (or the layout of nodes on a network) exist: bus, star, and ring. Few organizations use simple physical topologies, but rather use a hybrid of these simple shapes.

❐ The star-wired bus hybrid topology is commonly used on modern Ethernet networks. The star-wired ring hybrid topology is commonly used on modern Token Ring networks. Mesh topologies, in which nodes are directly connected to more than one other node, are commonly used on WANs.

❐ A network access method specifies protocols at the Physical and Data Link layers of the OSI model that determine how multiple nodes share a single network channel. Ethernet is by far the most popular network access method.

❐ Ethernet, as specified in IEEE's 802.3 standard, is a network access method that uses Carrier Sense Multiple Access with Collision Detection (CSMA/CD) to determine how multiple nodes share a single channel. Depending on the type, Ethernet may run over fiber optic cable or twisted-pair wiring. It offers between 10 Mbps and 10 Gbps throughput.

❐ Ethernet types include 10BaseT, 10BaseF, 100BaseT, 100BaseF, and 1- and 10-Gigabit Ethernet. In Ethernet shorthand "T" represents twisted-pair and "F" represents fiber optic cable, the technology's medium. "10" represents a maximum throughput of 10 Mbps and "100" represents a maximum throughput of 100 Mbps.

❑ Most Ethernet networks currently use baseband transmission and the star-wired bus hybrid topology.

❑ Token Ring is a network access method originally designed by IBM and now specified by IEEE in its 802.5 project. Token Ring uses token passing to determine which nodes may transmit over a shared channel. It comes in 4-, 16-, and 100-Mbps versions and typically runs over UTP and relies on the star-wired ring hybrid topology. Token Ring is less popular than Ethernet.

❑ Fiber Distributed Data Interface (FDDI) is a 100-Mbps network access method that runs over double fiber optic rings. Its primary advantage is its reliability, because if one of its rings suffers a fault, data automatically reroutes over the second ring. FDDI was a popular choice for MANs in the late 1980s and early 1990s, when it was essentially the only 100 Mbps solution.

❑ Asynchronous Transfer Mode (ATM) is a unique networking technology that uses fixed packets, called cells, and virtual circuits to transmit information at rates up to 9.95 Gbps. It is primarily used on large network backbones (such as those operated by network service providers). One significant advantage to ATM is that it can guarantee quality of service (QoS), which makes it appropriate for voice and video applications.

❑ X.25 and frame relay are packet-switched technologies that rely on the PSTN to deliver data at higher rates than an ordinary telephone line. X.25 is analog whereas frame relay is digital. Also, X.25 guarantees accurate data delivery and frame relay does not. X.25, therefore, is slower than frame relay. Both are economical solutions for WAN links.

❑ Integrated Services Digital Network (ISDN) is a dedicated, digital network transmission method that runs over PSTN lines. It comes in three varieties: PRI, BRI, and B-ISDN. BRI, which offers a maximum throughput of 128 Kbps, is a popular choice among telecommuters.

❑ T-carrier refers to any transmission method that uses the multiplexing and digitizing techniques first developed by AT&T in 1957 to digitize voice signals. The most popular T-carriers for business use are T1s, with a capacity of 1.544 Mbps, and T3s, with a capacity of 45 Mbps.

❑ T-carriers are dedicated, leased lines that may run over twisted-pair or fiber optic cable or wireless links. They are classified according to their digital signal (DS) level, where DS0 equals one 64-kbps channel. A T1 contains 24 of these channels.

❑ Digital subscriber line (DSL) is a transmission method that uses advanced data modulation techniques to achieve extraordinary throughput over regular phone lines. It comes in several different varieties. Each type has a unique signaling method and as a result, offers a different throughput. Some are asymmetrical, like ADSL, whereas others are symmetrical, like SDSL. DSL is a dedicated service. It competes with ISDN and cable technology.

10

❐ Cable technology uses the existing cable TV infrastructure to offer subscribers access to the Internet. To accomplish this, cable companies must upgrade their networks to allow bidirectional signaling. Cable is an asymmetrical technology that offers at least as much throughput as a T1 for much less money. However, cable is a shared network, meaning that an entire neighborhood may share a fixed amount of bandwidth.

❐ Synchronous optical network (SONET) is a transmission method that can provide data transfer rates from 64 Kbps to 39.8 Gbps using the same TDM technique used by T-carriers. It relies on a dual fiber optic ring, similar to FDDI technology. This makes it highly fault tolerant. SONET rings are costly and are typically used by telecommunications carriers or very large organizations.

KEY TERMS

1 Gigabit Ethernet — A type of Ethernet that achieves 1 Gbps maximum throughput. IEEE has defined two standards for 1 Gigabit Ethernet: one that runs over twisted pair (802.3ab) and one that runs over fiber optic cable (802.3z). It is preferable to run Gigabit on fiber. Gigabit Ethernet is primarily used for network backbones. Also known as Gigabit Ethernet.

10 Gigabit Ethernet — An Ethernet standard currently being defined by the IEEE 802.3ae committee. 10 Gigabit Ethernet will allow 10 Gbps throughput and will include full-duplexing and multimode fiber requirements.

10BaseF — A Physical layer standard for networks that use baseband transmission and multimode fiber cabling and can achieve 10 Mbps throughput. 10BaseF networks have a maximum segment length of 1000 or 2000 meters, depending on the version, and employ a star-wired bus hybrid topology.

10BaseT — A Physical layer standard for networks that use baseband transmission and twisted-pair media and can achieve 10 Mbps throughput. 10BaseT networks have a maximum segment length of 100 meters and use a star-wired bus hybrid topology.

100BaseF — A Physical layer standard for networks that use baseband transmission and multimode fiber cabling and can achieve 100 Mbps throughput. 100BaseF networks have a maximum segment length of 400 meters. 100BaseF may also be called "Fast Ethernet."

100BaseT — A Physical layer standard for networks that use baseband transmission and twisted-pair cabling and can achieve 100 Mbps throughput. 100BaseT networks have a maximum segment length of 100 meters and use the star-wired bus hybrid topology. 100BaseT requires CAT5 or higher UTP.

100BaseT4 — A type of 100BaseT network that uses all four wire pairs in a twisted-pair cable to achieve its 100 Mbps throughput. 100BaseT4 is not capable of full-duplex transmission, but can run on older, lower-cost CAT3 UTP.

100BaseTX — A type of 100BaseT network that uses two wire pairs in a twisted-pair cable, but uses faster signaling to achieve 100 Mbps throughput. It is capable of full-duplex transmission and requires CAT5 or higher media.

5-4-3 rule — A guideline for 10BaseT Ethernet networks that specifies a maximum of five segments connected with four repeating devices, and a maximum of three segments, which may contain connected nodes (such as workstations, printers, servers, and so on).

active monitor — On a Token Ring network, the workstation that maintains timing for token passing, monitors token and frame transmission, detects lost tokens, and corrects problems when a timing error or other disruption occurs. Only one workstation on the ring can act as the active monitor at any given time.

active topology — A topology in which each workstation participates in transmitting data over the network.

asymmetrical (ASDL) — The characteristic of a transmission technology that affords greater bandwidth in one direction (either from the customer to the carrier, or vice versa) than in the other direction.

asymmetrical DSL — A variation of DSL that offers more throughput when data travels downstream—downloading from a local carrier's POP to the customer—than when it travels upstream—uploading from the customer to the local carrier's POP.

Asynchronous Transfer Mode (ATM) — A technology originally conceived in 1983 at Bell Labs, but standardized only in the mid-1990s. It relies on a fixed packet size to achieve data transfer rates up to 9953 Mbps. The fixed packet consists of 48 bytes of data plus a 5-byte header. The fixed packet size allows ATM to provide predictable traffic patterns and better control over bandwidth utilization.

B channel — In ISDN, the "bearer" channel, so named because it bears traffic from point to point. A B channel uses circuit switching to carry digital voice, video, and data signals. Different types of ISDN are characterized by different quantities of B channels.

baseband — A transmission form in which (typically) digital signals are sent through direct current (DC) pulses applied to the wire. This direct current requires exclusive use of the wire's capacity. As a result, baseband systems can transmit only one signal at a time.

bonding — The process of combining more than one bearer channel of an ISDN line to increase throughput. For example, BRI's two 64-Kbps B channels are bonded to create an effective throughput of 128 Kbps.

BRI (Basic Rate Interface) — A variety of ISDN that uses two 64-Kbps bearer channels and one 16-Kbps data channel, as summarized by the following notation: 2B+D. BRI is the most common form of ISDN employed by home users.

bus — The single cable connecting all devices in a bus topology.

bus topology — A topology in which a single cable connects all nodes on a network without intervening connectivity devices.

cable drop — In the context of cable network technology, a fiber optic or coaxial cable that connects a neighborhood cable node to a customer's house.

10

cable modem — A device that modulates and demodulates signals for transmission and reception via cable wiring.

Carrier Sense Multiple Access with Collision Detection (CSMA/CD) — Rules for communication used by shared Ethernet networks. In CSMA/CD, each node waits its turn before transmitting data, to avoid interfering with other nodes' transmissions.

cell — A packet of a fixed size. In ATM technology, a cell consists of 48 bytes of data plus a 5-byte header.

channel bank — A multiplexer used to terminate analog T-carrier connections. Channel banks separate or consolidate multiple channels within a T-carrier.

CIR (Committed Information Rate) — The guaranteed minimum amount of bandwidth selected when leasing a frame relay circuit. Frame relay costs are partially based on CIR.

collision — In Ethernet networks, the interference of one network node's data transmission with another network node's data transmission.

collision domain — The portion of an Ethernet network in which collisions occur if two nodes transmit data at the same time.

collision rate — On Ethernet networks, the average percentage of all transmissions involved in collisions during a one minute time period.

CSU (channel service unit) — A device used with T-carrier technology that provides termination for the digital signal and ensures connection integrity through error correction and line monitoring.

CSU/DSU — A combination of a CSU (channel service unit) and a DSU (data service unit) that serves as the connection point for a T1 line at the customer's site.

D channel — In ISDN, the "data" channel that uses packet-switching techniques to carry information about the ISDN connection, such as session initiation and termination signals, caller identity, call forwarding, and conference calling signals.

DACS (Digital Access and Cross-connect System) — A device that allows for direct connection between T-carriers that terminate at the same carrier's facilities. Through a DACS, for example, an incoming T1 can be divided into multiple channels, with some of the channels forming an outgoing fractional T1.

data propagation delay — The length of time data takes to travel from one point on a network segment to another point. On Ethernet networks, CSMA/CD's collision detection routine cannot operate accurately if the data propagation delay is too long.

dedicated — A continuously available link or service that is leased through a telecommunications provider, such as a LEC. Examples of dedicated lines include ADSL, T1, and T3.

downstream — A term used to describe data traffic that flows from a local carrier's facility to the customer. In asymmetrical communications, downstream throughput is usually much higher than upstream throughput. In symmetrical communications, downstream and upstream throughputs are equal.

DS0 (Digital Signal, Level 0) — An international standard that defines Physical layer signaling standards for transmitting digital voice or data over a 64-Kbps channel. In North America, DS0 is equivalent to one channel in a T-carrier circuit.

DSL (digital subscriber lines) — A dedicated remote connectivity or WAN technology that uses advanced data modulation techniques to achieve extraordinary throughput over regular phone lines. DSL currently comes in seven different varieties, the most common of which is Asymmetric DSL (ADSL).

DSL access multiplexer (DSLAM) — A connectivity device located at a carrier's office that aggregates multiple DSL subscriber lines and connects them to a larger carrier or to the Internet backbone.

DSL modem — A device that demodulates an incoming DSL signal, extracting the information and passing it on to the data equipment (such as telephones and computers) and modulates an outgoing DSL signal.

DSU (data service unit) — A device used in T-carrier technology that converts the digital signal used by bridges, routers, and multiplexers into the digital signal used on cabling. Typically, a DSU is combined with a CSU in a single box, a CSU/DSU.

Ethernet — A network access method that follows the IEEE 802.3 signaling specifications, including CSMA/CD and packet switching. Ethernet comes in several forms. 100BaseT (or Fast Ethernet) is currently the most popular type of Ethernet in use on LANs.

Fast Ethernet — A type of Ethernet network that is capable of 100 Mbps throughput. 100BaseT and 100BaseFX are both examples of Fast Ethernet.

FDDI (Fiber Distributed Data Interface) — A networking standard originally specified by ANSI in the mid-1980s and later refined by ISO. FDDI uses a dual fiber-optic ring to transmit data at speeds of 100 Mbps. It was commonly used as a backbone technology in the 1980s and early 1990s, but lost favor as Fast Ethernet technologies emerged in the mid-1990s. FDDI provides excellent reliability and security.

fractional T1 — An arrangement that allows organizations to lease only some channels on a T1 line and pay for only the channels they lease. Fractional T1s are an economical alternative to full T1s.

frame relay — An updated, digital version of X.25 that relies on packet switching. Because it is digital, frame relay supports higher bandwidth than X.25, offering a maximum of 45 Mbps throughput. It provides the basis for much of the world's Internet connections. On network diagrams, the frame relay system is often depicted as a cloud.

full-mesh topology — A type of mesh topology in which every node is directly connected to every other node on the network. Full-mesh provides the highest fault tolerance, but is also more expensive than other topologies.

Gigabit Ethernet — *See* 1 Gigabit Ethernet.

head-end — A cable company's central office, which connects cable wiring to many nodes before it reaches customers' sites.

10

High Speed Token Ring (HSTR) — A standard for Token Ring networks that operates at 100 Mbps.

hybrid fiber-coax (HFC) — A link that consists of fiber cable connecting the cable company's offices to a node location near the customer and coaxial cable connecting the node to the customer's house. HFC upgrades to existing cable wiring are required before current TV cable systems can serve as WAN links.

hybrid topology — A complex combination of the simple physical topologies.

ISDN (Integrated Services Digital Network) — An international standard, established by the ITU, for transmitting data over digital lines. ISDN uses the PSTN, but it differs from PSTN in that it exclusively uses digital lines and switches. Its connections may be dial-up or dedicated. It comes in three varieties: PRI, BRI, and B-ISDN.

jamming — The process by which a station's NIC first propagates a collision throughout the network so no other station attempts to transmit; after propagating the collision, the NIC remains silent for a period of time.

LAN Emulation (LANE) — A method for transporting Token Ring or Ethernet frames over ATM networks. LANE encapsulates incoming Ethernet or Token Ring frames, then converts them into ATM cells for transmission over an ATM network.

leased lines — Connections or services for which an organization pays a regular (usually monthly) fee to use. Most leased lines are established through a public telecommunications carrier, such as a LEC, IXC, or ISP. T-carriers and frame relay links are examples of leased lines.

mesh topology — A topology that consists of many directly interconnected locations forming a mesh. In a mesh topology, each node is connected to at least two other nodes. Mesh topologies are typically used on WANs. *See also* full-mesh topology and partial-mesh topology.

network access method — A networking technology defined by its Data Link layer data packaging and Physical layer signaling techniques. Also known as network transport system or access method. Ethernet and Token Ring are examples of network access methods.

Network Termination 1 (NT1) — A device used on ISDN networks that connects the incoming twisted-pair wiring with the customer's ISDN terminal equipment.

Network Termination 2 (NT2) — An additional connection device required on PRI to handle the multiple ISDN lines between the customer's network termination connection and the local phone company's wires.

Optical Carrier (OC) level — An international standard used to describe SONET (or SDH) rings according to their maximum throughput.

partial mesh — A physical topology that usually applies to WANs in which only some nodes are directly connected to other nodes. Partial mesh networks are more economical than full-mesh networks, in which every node is directly connected to every other node.

physical topology — The physical layout of a network. A physical topology depicts a network in broad scope; it does not specify devices, connectivity methods, or addresses on the network. Physical topologies are categorized into three fundamental geometric shapes: bus, ring, and star. These shapes can be mixed to create hybrid topologies.

PRI (Primary Rate Interface) — A type of ISDN that uses 23 bearer channels and one 64-Kbps data channel as represented by the following notation: 23B+D. PRI is less commonly used by individual subscribers than BRI, but it may be used by businesses and other organizations needing more throughput.

private line — A connection defined by two endpoints that is available exclusively for use by the customer who leases the line. T-carriers are examples of private lines.

PVC (private virtual circuit) — A point-to-point connection over which data may follow any number of different paths, as opposed to a dedicated line that follows a predefined path. X.25, frame relay, and some forms of ATM use PVCs.

Quality of Service (QoS) — The result of standards for delivering data within a certain period of time after its transmission. For example, ATM networks can supply four QoS levels, from a "best effort" attempt for noncritical data to a guaranteed, real-time transmission for time-sensitive data.

ring topology — A network layout in which each node is connected to the two nearest nodes so that the entire network forms a circle. Data is transmitted unidirectionally around the ring. Each workstation accepts and responds to packets addressed to it, then forwards the other packets to the next workstation in the ring.

SDH (Synchronous Digital Hierarchy) — The international equivalent of SONET.

self-healing — A characteristic of dual-ring topologies that allows them to automatically reroute traffic along the backup ring if the primary ring becomes severed.

shared Ethernet — An implementation of Ethernet in which all nodes on a segment share the same communications channel. Thus, nodes on a shared Ethernet network compete for use of a fixed amount of bandwidth.

signal bounce — A phenomenon in which signals travel endlessly between the two ends of a bus network. Using 50-ohm resistors at either end of the network prevents signal bounce.

signal level — An ANSI standard for T-carrier technology that refers to its Physical layer electrical signaling characteristics. DS0 (Digital Signal, Level 0) is the equivalent of one data or voice channel. All other signal levels are multiples of DS0.

SONET (Synchronous Optical Network) — A WAN technology that provides data transfer rates ranging from 64 Kbps to 39.8 Gbps using the same time division multiplexing technique used by T-carriers. SONET is characterized by its dual fiber optic ring topology, which makes it highly fault tolerant. Internationally, SONET is known as SDH.

star topology — A physical topology in which every node on the network is connected through a central device, such as a hub. Any single physical wire on a star network connects only two devices, so a cabling problem affects only two nodes. Nodes transmit data to the hub, which then retransmits the data to the rest of the network segment where the destination node can pick it up.

star-wired bus topology — A hybrid topology in which groups of workstations are connected in a star fashion to hubs that are connected with each other via a single bus. This topology forms the basis of most modern Ethernet networks.

10

star-wired ring topology — A hybrid topology that uses the physical layout of a star and the token-passing data transmission method. This topology forms the basis of most modern Token Ring networks.

SVC (switched virtual circuit) — Logical, point-to-point connections that rely on switches to determine the optimal path between sender and receiver. ATM and frame relay are examples of technology that use SVCs.

switch — The hardware that manages network switching; used to separate a network segment into smaller segments, with each segment being independent of the others, and supporting its own traffic.

switched Ethernet — An Ethernet model that enables multiple nodes to simultaneously transmit and receive data and individually take advantage of more bandwidth because they are assigned separate logical network segments through switching.

symmetrical — A characteristic of transmission technology that provides equal throughput for data traveling both upstream and downstream and is suited to users who both upload and download significant amounts of data.

symmetrical DSL — A variation of DSL that provides equal throughput both upstream and downstream between the customer and the carrier.

T1 — A T-carrier technology that provides 1.544 Mbps throughput and 24 channels for voice, data, video, or audio signals. T1s may use shielded or unshielded twisted-pair, coaxial cable, fiber-optic, or microwave links. Businesses commonly use T1s to connect to their ISP, and phone companies typically use at least one T1 to connect their central offices.

T3 — A T-carrier technology that can carry the equivalent of 672 channels for voice, data, video, or audio, with a maximum data throughput of 44.736 Mbps (typically rounded up to 45 Mbps for purposes of discussion). T3s require either fiber-optic or microwave transmission media.

T-carrier — Term used to refer to any kind of leased line that follows the standards for T1s, fractional T1s, T1Cs, T2s, T3s, or T4s.

terminal adapter (TA) — Devices used to convert digital signals into analog signals for use with ISDN phones and other analog devices. Terminal adapters are sometimes called ISDN modems.

terminal equipment (TE) — Devices at a communication link's end point that provide a service. For example, on an ISDN connection, the ISDN telephone and network adapter are terminal equipment. On a LAN, the workstations and printers are terminal equipment.

terminator — In the context of bus topology networks, a 50-ohm resistor used to stop a signal at the end of the bus and thereby prevent signal bounce.

token passing — A means of data transmission in which a 3-byte packet, called a token, is passed around the network in a round-robin fashion and used to arbitrate access to the network's shared channel.

upstream — The term used to describe data traffic that flows from a customer's site to the local carrier's facility. In asymmetrical communications, upstream throughput is usually much lower than downstream throughput. In symmetrical communications, upstream and downstream throughputs are equal.

virtual circuits — The connections between network nodes that, while based on potentially disparate physical links, logically appear to be direct, dedicated links between those nodes. Virtual circuits are used in frame relay and ATM technology.

xDSL — The term used to refer to all varieties of DSL.

X.25 — A set of protocols that describes a packet-switched, analog networking technology designed to supply data transmission over the PSTN. The original standard for X.25 specified a maximum of 64 Kbps throughput, but by 1992 the standard was updated to include maximum throughput of 2.048 Mbps. X.25 ensures data reliability over long distances by verifying the transmission at every node.

REVIEW QUESTIONS

1. Which of the following physical topologies requires terminators to prevent signal bounce?

   a. bus

   b. star

   c. ring

   d. mesh

2. Which of the following physical topologies forms the basis of modern Token Ring networks?

   a. bus

   b. ring

   c. star-wired bus

   d. star-wired ring

3. Which of the following physical topologies is most expensive to implement?

   a. star-wired bus

   b. star-wired ring

   c. partial-mesh

   d. full-mesh

4. What occurs when two nodes on a shared Ethernet network transmit data simultaneously?

   a. a glut

   b. a collision

   c. a jabber

   d. a cyclic redundancy check

10

5. In 10BaseT and 100BaseT, what does the "T" stand for?

   a. transmission

   b. technique

   c. twisted pair

   d. token

6. What IEEE standard describes Ethernet networks, such as 10BaseT and 100BaseT?

   a. 802.3

   b. 802.5

   c. 802.8

   d. 802.16

7. What type of UTP is the minimum requirement for 100BaseTX?

   a. CAT3

   b. CAT5

   c. CAT6

   d. CAT7

8. What is the maximum segment length for 100BaseT?

   a. 55 meters

   b. 90 meters

   c. 100 meters

   d. 200 meters

9. What type of transmission media can be used for Gigabit Ethernet?

   a. fiber optic cable

   b. twisted–pair cable

   c. coaxial cable

   d. all of the above

10. What technique do Token Ring networks use to determine what node gets to transmit over a shared channel?

    a. token routing

    b. token skipping

    c. token passing

    d. token competing

11. What makes FDDI more fault tolerant than a typical Ethernet or Token Ring network?

    a. It uses dual fiber optic rings.

    b. It uses the peer-to-peer method of transmitting data.

    c. It uses three methods of error checking and correction.

    d. It uses two forms of modulation for each signal.

12. Which of the following is a characteristic shared by frame relay and ATM?

    a. the use of fixed-sized packets known as cells

    b. the use of virtual circuits

    c. the use of dedicated connections

    d. the use of circuit switching

13. What makes ATM especially well-suited to transmitting voice and video signals?

    a. its use of variable-sized packets

    b. its connectionless nature

    c. its use of time division multiplexing

    d. its quality of service guarantees

10

14. If a network manager wanted to connect his two Ethernet LANs via ATM, what transmission technique must he implement on the ATM link?

    a. TCP/IP encapsulation

    b. LAN emulation

    c. packet-cell translation

    d. CSMA/CD

15. What organization sets standards for frame relay?

    a. ITU

    b. IEEE

    c. IETF

    d. FCC

16. Name two significant differences between X.25 and frame relay.

17. Why is the Internet often depicted as a cloud on network diagrams?

    a. because it uses Ethernet, which derives its name from the early belief that a substance in the air, known as ether, transmitted light and sound

    b. because it is a massive, global WAN that continues to grow without centralized planning

    c. because early Internet connections relied on X.25 and frame relay, packet-switched technologies with an indeterminate route from sender to receiver

    d. because many of its backbone connections rely on wireless, point-to-multi-point links

18. What type of ISDN is most commonly used by home subscribers for Internet access?

    a. BRI

    b. PRI

    c. B-ISDN

    d. A-ISNN

19. What method does a T1 use to achieve high throughput over twisted pair wiring?

    a. frequency division multiplexing

    b. wavelength division multiplexing

    c. statistical multiplexing

    d. time division multiplexing

20. What is the capacity represented by "DS0"?

    a. 56 Kbps

    b. 64 Kbps

    c. 255 Kbps

    d. 768 Kbps

21. How many data or voice channels does a T1 provide?

    a. 2

    b. 6

    c. 18

    d. 24

22. In "ADSL," a version of DSL popular among home subscribers, what does the "A" stand for?

    a. asynchronous

    b. asymmetrical

    c. analog-encrypted

    d. advanced

23. Why is cable Internet access inherently less secure than DSL or ISDN?

24. Which of the following is a likely implementation of SONET?

    a. to connect a hospital's 15 rural clinics to the Internet

    b. to connect five workgroups within an accounting firm's LAN

    c. to connect hundreds of home-based data entry workers with a the LAN at a company's metropolitan headquarters

    d. to connect a regional ISP's five data centers

25. What is the term used to describe SONET's capability to automatically overcome a fault in one of its rings?

    a. self-healing

    b. ring diversity

    c. mode switching

    d. route passing

HANDS-ON PROJECTS

Project 10-1

You have learned that the star-wired bus is the most popular physical topology for modern Ethernet networks. You also know that Ethernet is the most common network access method used on LANs today. The star-wired bus arranges nodes in a star fashion using a hub, then connects these hubs through a bus. In this project, you create a small LAN using a star topology. For this project, you need three workstations running the Windows 2000 or XP or operating system. Each workstation should have an Ethernet NIC that is properly installed, working, and configured for use with a 10 Mbps Ethernet network. The workstations should also have the appropriate client software and TCP/IP installed and configured, so that they can act as a client. Each workstation should be assigned a different IP address. (Normally a star topology would connect clients with a server, but for purposes of demonstration, this project simply connects clients with each other to form a workgroup that allows clients to share data on their hard disks.) You also need three (straight-through) CAT5 or higher patch cables that are at least 3 feet long, plus an Ethernet 10 Mbps hub containing at least four ports.

1. Make sure all of your equipment (the hub, plus the three workstations) is plugged in and turned on. Arrange the machines on a large table so that no workstation is farther than a few feet away from the hub.

2. Label the workstations A, B, and C.

3. Plug one of the patch cable's RJ-45 connectors into Workstation A's NIC. Plug the other end of this patch cable into one of the hub's data ports. (Hubs may have different types of ports. If you are uncertain which ports are data ports on your hub, consult the device's documentation.)

10

4. Repeat Step 2 for the Workstations B and C. You have just created a simple star topology.

5. Next, you need to determine the IP address of each Windows XP computer before you can test your network. Begin at Workstation A. To find the computer's IP address, click **Start**, then click **Run**.

6. In the Open text box, type **cmd**, and then click **OK**. The Command Prompt window opens.

7. At the DOS prompt, type **ipconfig**, and then press **Enter**. The IP configuration information, including the workstation's IP address appears on the screen. Write down Workstation A's IP address so you can remember it later. Leave the Command Prompt window open.

8. Repeat Steps 5–7 for Workstations B and C.

9. Now, you will use the PING command, a simple TCP/IP utility that is frequently used as a way to determine whether a node is connected to a network. (You may recall using this utility in Hands-on Project 7-4). At Workstation A's Command Prompt window type **ping X**, where X is the IP address belonging to Workstation B. What happens? Then type **ping Y**, where Y is the IP address belonging to Workstation C.

10. Repeat Step 9 from Workstation B, pinging Workstation A and C's IP addresses.

11. Repeat Step 9 from Workstation C, pinging Workstation A and B's IP addresses.

12. Was the PING test successful in every case?

13. Now remove Workstation A's CAT5 patch cable from the hub. Attempt to ping Workstation A's IP address from Workstation B. What kind of message do you receive?

Project 10-2

Although many organizations rely on Ethernet and thus, the star-wired bus topology, each organization implements these in slightly different ways. In this project, you have the opportunity to learn about more realistic network layouts and implementations than the ones you created in Project 10-1. For this project, you need a pencil, paper, and access to data networking professionals.

1. Identify four different organizations in your area that rely on networks. For example, you might choose a public school system, a utility company, an accounting firm, and a chain of retail stores. (In this case, it is probably best not to choose telecommunications providers, because their networks are usually atypical.)

2. Contact the Information Technology manager at each of the four organizations and tell him or her that you are working on a student project. Ask whether she or he has time to answer some questions about the organization's network. (If the IT manager doesn't have time to help you, ask whether another employee, such as the network manager, telecommunications manager, or network administrator, can help.) Make sure to obtain the employee's name and address so you can send a thank you card later.

3. Ask the organization's representative the following questions to find out more about the organization's network (and write down the answers):

◻ Does the network use Ethernet or a different network access method? (If different, which one?)

◻ What physical topology does the network rely on?

◻ What is the maximum throughput the network can achieve?

◻ What transmission media does the network use (for example, CAT5 UTP)?

◻ Does the organization connect its private network to the Internet? If so, through what kind of technology (for example, ISDN, DSL, T1)? What was the reason for choosing this technology?

◻ In what ways does the organization plan to upgrade its network in coming years? Why?

◻ Is the voice network integrated with the data network? If not, what kind of physical topology does the voice network rely on?

4. After you have finished gathering information for each organization, compare the answers from each different organization. What, if anything, do all the networks have in common? How do they differ? What surprised you? From their answers to the last question, what assumptions might you make about the direction of networking technology?

5. Follow up with a thank you card to each employee who assisted you in gathering information.

Project 10-3

As you have learned, home users who want to connect to the Internet at faster speeds than a regular telephone line allows have many different access options. They may choose ISDN, DSL, or cable Internet access, for example. For many consumers, comparing the different options, their features, and costs, can be confusing. In this project, you investigate high-speed Internet offerings in your area. You need a copy of your city's or region's (if you live in a sparsely populated area) phone book. (Use one that lists businesses.) You will also need a pencil and some paper, or access to a program that can create tables or spreadsheets (such as Microsoft Word or Microsoft Excel).

1. On your sheet of paper or on a computer, create a table with six columns and four rows. Label the columns (from left to right): Provider, Service, Installation Cost, Monthly Cost, Throughput, Limitations. Make the rows tall enough to accommodate several lines of text.

2. Find the listings for "Internet Access" in your local phone book. Identify at least one ISP, one cable company, and one LEC that provide Internet access.

3. Enter the names of the companies you selected in the second through fourth rows of the first column under "Provider."

4. Call the ISP. Ask to speak with a sales representative, or someone else who can describe the company's services and pricing. Let the person know you are investigating different Internet access options as part of a student project.

5. Ask the sales representative whether the ISP offers DSL, ISDN, T-carrier services, or all of the above. Chances are that the ISP offers more than one type of each service. Pick one type of at least two different services and enter those two in the "Service" column corresponding to the ISP's row.

6. For each service, ask the cost of installation (including both setup and hardware) and enter this figure in the "Installation Cost" column, in line with the name of the service as it appears in column two.

7. For each service, ask the monthly service cost. If the cost is distance-sensitive (that is, if it varies with the customer's location), ask the sales representative to price the service as if it were coming to your home. Next ask the maximum throughput it offers (in the case of DSL, for both upstream and downstream transmission) and what limitations it comes with (for example, certain types of DSL can only be offered within a few miles of a LEC's end office).

8. If the service is available within a limited geographical area, ask the sales representative if the service is available where you live.

9. After you have entered all the information for the ISP's services, thank the sales representative. Repeat Steps 4–8 for the LEC.

10. After you have entered all the information for the LEC's services, thank the LEC's sales representative. Repeat Steps 4–8 for the cable company.

11. Review the data you have gathered. Based on this data, which options are available at your home? Which option offers the fastest throughput? Considering both installation and monthly access costs, which option is most economical?

12. Although much of this information might have been available to you from the service provider's Web site, why might it have been more valuable to talk with a sales representative instead?

CASE PROJECTS

Case Project

1. You have just begun working as a networking consultant with a local consulting firm. One of your first tasks is to help troubleshoot a small Ethernet network at a tax preparation office. The backbone of this network consists of six hubs connected in a bus fashion. Three of the hubs service workgroups of 10 workstations each. One of the hubs services two file servers and two shared printers. In anticipation of tax season and a heavier workload, the organization recently upgraded its network from 10BaseT to 100BaseT. However, they have not witnessed the performance increases they expected. Before even visiting the firm, what can you suggest as reasons for the less than optimal performance?

2. The network managers at the tax preparation office have followed your advice on reconfiguring the network, and as a result, the network is running more smoothly. However, they have now realized that their Internet connection is too slow. They have been using a dial-up BRI ISDN connection. They want to spend no more than $200 per month on an Internet connection. They also need a transmission method with fairly good security and a guarantee of adequate throughput during the daytime hours. What solution can you recommend that will offer them the most throughput at this cost?

3. The Internet connection you have selected for the tax preparation firm is working well. Recently, however, they have learned that their firm will be merging with another firm across town. They need a way to connect the two offices. They have heard about using data lines to carry telephone conversations, and they are interested in adding that to their requirements for the data connection. Also, although they want the connection to be reliable, they are not willing to spend the extra money for an extremely fault tolerant network. On the other hand, now that they have merged with another firm, they have the means to pay up to $2000 per month for a connection. What solution do you suggest?

10

11

DATA NETWORK CONNECTIVITY

> **After reading this chapter and completing the exercises, you will be able to:**
>
> ♦ Explain how NICs operate
>
> ♦ List the most common types of NICs
>
> ♦ Describe the purpose and operation of hubs and repeaters
>
> ♦ Describe the purpose and operation of bridges and switches
>
> ♦ Explain how routers connect dissimilar networks
>
> ♦ Identify other Layer 3 connectivity devices and understand their uses
>
> ♦ Describe how remote users can connect to a LAN or WAN via a modem
>
> ♦ Identify the components necessary for access and carrier network connectivity

In Chapters 4 and 6, you learned about the ways in which subscribers connect to traditional voice networks and how telephone networks connect with each other. In this chapter, you learn about the ways in which computer users connect with data networks and how data networks connect with each other. This chapter is organized according to the layers of the OSI (Open Systems Interconnection) model, beginning with the Physical layer. Material in this chapter builds on the transmission media and methods you learned about in Chapters 8, 9, and 10. By the end of this chapter, you should have a complete view of basic data networking.

LAYER 1 CONNECTIVITY

You are already familiar with functions that occur at the Physical layer, such as network access and signaling. The devices responsible for managing these processes are network interface cards (NICs). Every workstation, printer, or other peripheral that attaches directly to a network requires a NIC to communicate with the network. (Nodes that connect remotely, using a modem, do not necessarily require a NIC, as you learn later in this chapter.) The following sections describe this critical component in detail.

Network Interface Cards (NICs)

In Chapter 7, you learned that network interface cards (NICs), also known as **network adapters**, are the devices that act as transceivers for workstations, servers, connectivity devices, and peripherals on a network. NICs transmit data in a format that other network nodes can interpret. They also receive and interpret encoded data from the network. To transmit signals, NICs issue current, if the transmission media in use is twisted-pair wire, or light pulses, if the transmission media is fiber optic cable. This signaling takes place, as you know, at the Physical layer. NICs also assemble data frames during transmission and disassemble data frames during reception. Both assembling and disassembling data frames are Data Link layer functions. Thus, NICs belong to both the Physical and Data Link layers of the OSI model. NICs are not capable of interpreting the signals they send or receive, however. For example, although a NIC used on an Ethernet network can detect whether its transmission was involved in a collision, it cannot detect whether the collision corrupted the data it was trying to send.

NICs come in a variety of types depending on the network access method (for example, Ethernet versus Token Ring), transmission speed (for example, 10 Mbps versus 100 Mbps), connector interfaces (for example, SC versus RJ-45), type of computer or device, and manufacturer. Popular network adapter manufacturers include 3Com, Adaptec, D-Link, IBM, Intel, Kingston, Linksys, Netgear, SMC, and Western Digital, to name a few. In fact, as a telecommunications professional, you may work with network adapters made by at least a dozen manufacturers.

Before you order or install a network adapter in a network device, you need to know the type of interface required by the device. NICs, as with other computer components (for example, sound cards or modems), may come with one of several different interface types. The most popular NIC interfaces are: adapter card, PC Card, and USB. Each of these three interfaces is discussed in the following sections.

Adapter Card NICs

A desktop or tower workstation typically uses an adapter card for a NIC. An **adapter card** (also known as an **expansion board** or **daughter board**) is a circuit board used to connect a device to the system board (the main circuit board that controls a computer, also known as a motherboard). Adapter cards connect to the system board through

expansion slots, which are openings with multiple electrical contacts into which the adapter card can be inserted. Inserting an adapter card into an expansion slot establishes an electrical connection between the adapter card and the system board. Thus, the device connected to the adapter card becomes connected to computer's main circuit. This connection enables the computer to centrally control its devices.

The circuit that is used by the system board to transmit data to the computer's components is the computer's **bus**. The type of expansion board, and therefore the type of network adapter you choose, must match the computer's bus. Buses differ according to their capacity. The capacity of a bus is defined principally by the width of its data path (expressed in bits) and its speed (expressed in MHz). A data path on a bus equals the number of data bits that it can transmit in parallel at any given time. In the earliest PCs, buses had an 8-bit data path. Later, manufacturers expanded buses to handle 16 bits of data, then 32 bits. Most new computers use buses capable of exchanging 64 or 128 bits of data. As the number of data bits that a bus can handle increases, so too does the speed of the devices attached to the bus.

As computers evolved, bus technology improved. Several different bus types exist, but the most popular of these is the **Peripheral Component Interconnect (PCI)** bus, a 32- or 64-bit bus introduced in the 1990s. PCI buses offer the fastest potential data transfer rate among all bus types. They can also be used in both Macintosh and IBM-compatible workstations. Figure 11-1 shows a typical PCI network adapter. Later in this chapter, you have the opportunity to install a PCI network adapter in a computer.

11

Figure 11-1 A PCI network adapter

You can easily determine which type of bus a network device uses by reading the doc-umentation that came with the device. This information should appear either on the purchase order or in the very beginning of the booklet that lists the computer's speci-fications. Some devices, such as PCs, have more than one bus type on their system boards. In this case, you can usually choose to insert a matching NIC into any of the free buses.

PC Card NICs

Network adapters may connect to interfaces other than a PC's bus. For laptop comput-ers, Personal Computer Memory Card International Association (PCMCIA) slots are frequently used to connect network adapters. **PCMCIA** interfaces were developed in the early 1990s to provide a standard interface for connecting any type of device to a portable computer. PCMCIA devices are now more commonly known as **PC Cards**. Some professionals also call them "credit card adapters" because they are approximately the same size as a credit card. PC Card slots may hold modem cards, network adapters, external hard disk cards, or CD-ROM cards. Most often, they are used for network adapters or modems; in fact, some PC Cards contain both devices. Figure 11-2 depicts a typical PC Card network adapter.

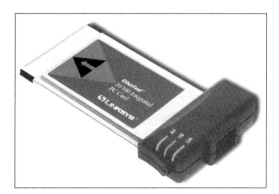

Figure 11-2   A PC Card network adapter

One advantage to using a PC Card network adapter is its simple installation. A PC Card needs only to be inserted into the PCMCIA slot to be physically installed. An expansion board network adapter, on the other hand, requires the user to turn off the computer, remove its cover, insert the board into an expansion slot, fasten the board in place, replace the cover, and turn on the computer. Simple installation makes PC Card network adapters preferable for mobile users and novice users, such as those setting up a home network. This same convenience and simple installation holds true for USB adapters, which are discussed next.

USB NICs

Another type of externally attached network adapter is one that relies on a **USB (universal serial bus) port**. USB is a standard external bus that can be used to connect multiple types of peripherals, including modems, mice, audio players, and network adapters. The original USB standard was developed in 1995 by a group of computer manufacturers working to make a low-cost, simple-to-install method of connecting peripheral devices to any make or model of computer. Since 1998, USB ports have been supplied on most modern laptop and desktop computers. The standard has become so popular that over one hundred different types of devices have been designed to interface with the USB port.

As with a PC Card network adapter, the significant advantage to using a USB NIC is its portability and simple installation. However, the disadvantage of using a USB network adapter is that most USB ports in use today have a maximum data transfer rate of 12 Mbps (a newer, high-speed USB standard that supports up to 480 Mbps throughput has been developed, but is not yet widely used). The traditional 12 Mbps limit means that a USB network adapter cannot be used on a network conforming to the 100BaseT standard, unless the network's connectivity devices are capable of automatically adjusting between 10 Mbps and 100 Mbps. In any case, the USB port's throughput limitation makes this type of network adapter less desirable for networks on which data transfer speed is a critical variable. Figure 11-3 shows an example of a USB network adapter, which has a USB connector on one end and an RJ-45 receptacle on the other end.

11

Figure 11-3   A USB network adapter

More sophisticated devices, such as routers, do not use bus, USB, or PCMCIA network adapters for routine network connections, but rather use ports that make a connection directly with the device's system board. This is one way in which such devices are able to provide fast and efficient network connectivity. The same device may, however provide a peripheral interface, such as a PC Card, which could be used to connect a removable network adapter (though more often, it is used to attach additional system resources, such as memory).

Wireless NICs

As you learned in Chapter 9, networks that use wireless transmission methods require specialized NICs. Such NICs use an antenna (either internal or external) to exchange signals with a base station transceiver or another wireless NIC. Expansion slot network adapters, PC Card network adapters, and USB network adapters can all be wireless. However, the most popular type of wireless network adapter available today comes in the form of a PC Card network adapter.

Wireless network adapters are well-suited to environments in which cabling cannot be installed or in which clients need to move about while staying connected to the network. For example, suppose you work as a quality control specialist in a large chemical production facility. During the day, you might have to visit dozens of different locations to test the quality of chemicals at multiple phases in their production. At each location, you must enter data about the chemicals into a centralized database on the network's server, before moving to the next location. The simplest and most efficient way to accomplish your tasks is by using a laptop that uses a wireless NIC to connect to the network. One disadvantage to using wireless network adapters is that they are generally more expensive than wire-dependent network adapters. (Refer to Figure 9-16 for photos of wireless NICs.)

Now that you have learned about a variety of network adapters used to connect workstations and peripheral nodes to a network, you are ready to learn about the devices that connect all the nodes and segments on a LAN. The simplest of these devices is a repeater.

Repeaters

In Chapter 2, you learned that in order to compensate for the effects of attenuation, analog signals are amplified whereas digital signals are repeated. Repeaters are one type of device used to repeat digital signals. Repeaters operate in the Physical layer of the OSI model, accepting a signal, then retransmitting it to all connected nodes. Repeaters have no means of interpreting the data they retransmit. For example, they cannot improve or correct a bad or erroneous signal. In this sense, repeaters are not "intelligent" devices. Because they cannot read higher-layer information in the data packets, repeaters also cannot interpret MAC addresses (which belong to the Data Link layer) or network addresses (which belong to the Network layer). Therefore, they cannot determine where data is supposed to go. Instead, repeaters simply regenerate a signal over an entire segment. It is up to the receiver to recognize and accept its data.

A repeater is limited not only in function, but also in scope. A repeater contains one input port and one output port, so it is capable of receiving and repeating only one data stream at a time. Furthermore, repeaters are suited only to networks or segments arranged in a bus topology. In addition, because repeaters simply regenerate signals, on an Ethernet network, they create a larger collision domain. That is, any collisions that occur on one side of a segment connected to a repeater are regenerated to the other side. However, the primary advantage to using a repeater is that it can extend the length of a network inexpensively.

For example, suppose that you need to connect a single PC located in a school's performing arts center to the rest of the network, that the nearest data jack is 150 meters away, and that you are using 10BaseT Ethernet, which limits the maximum cable length to 100 meters. In this instance, you could use a repeater to add 100 meters to the existing 100-meter limitation and connect the performing arts center workstation to the network. Bear in mind that the overall network distance limitations still apply. According to 10BaseT's 5-4-3 rule, you cannot use more than four repeaters in sequence to extend the cabling's reach.

Hubs

At its most primitive, a hub is a multiport repeater. A simple hub may contain multiple ports that can connect a group of computers, accepting signals from and repeating signals to all connected nodes. A slightly more sophisticated hub may contain multiple ports for nodes (such as workstations) and one port that connects the hub to a network's backbone. On Ethernet networks, hubs typically serve as the central connection point for branches of a star or star-based hybrid topology. As with repeaters, hubs used on Ethernet networks extend collision domains. On Token Ring networks, hubs are called **Multistation Access Units (MAUs)** and are used to connect nodes in a star-based ring topology. A typical Ethernet hub is shown in Figure 11-4.

11

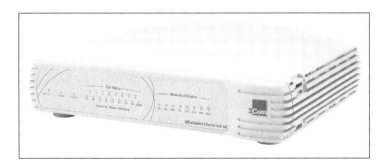

Figure 11-4   An Ethernet hub

In addition to connecting Macintosh and PC workstations, hubs can connect print servers, switches, file servers, or other devices to a network. They can support a variety of different media and data transmission speeds. Some hubs also allow for multiple media connector types or multiple data transmission speeds. As you can imagine, you can choose from a huge number of different hubs. By classifying hubs into categories according to their uses and features, however, you will quickly get the lay of the land and soon learn to understand any hub. Figure 11-5 details the various elements of a hub, some of which are optional. The elements shared by most hubs are described in the following list:

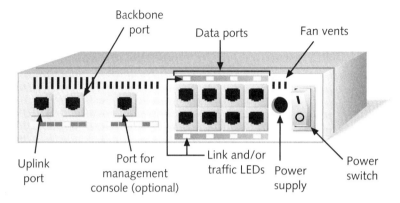

Figure 11-5   Detailed diagram of a hub

- *Ports*—The receptacles where patch cables connect workstations or other devices to the hub. The type of receptacle (RJ-45 versus SC, for example) depends on your network technology. The number of ports on a hub generally ranges from 4 to 24, but can be higher. This number does not include the uplink port, described next.

- *Uplink port*—The receptacle used to connect one hub to another hub. An uplink port may look like any other port, but it should be used only to interconnect hubs. Hubs may be connected with other hubs in serial, along a bus (as in the popular star-wired bus hybrid topology), or in a star formation.

- *Port for management console*—A receptacle used to connect some type of display, or console (such as a laptop PC), that enables you to view the hub's management information, such as the traffic load or number of collisions. Not all hubs provide management information, so not all have a management console port.

- *Backbone port*—The receptacle used to connect a hub to the network's backbone.

- *Link LED*—The light on a port that indicates whether it is in use. If a connection is live, this light should be solid green. If no connection exists, the light is off. If you think that the connection is live but the light is not on, you should check connections, transmission speed settings, and power supplies for both the network adapter and hub.

- *Traffic (transmit or receive) LED*—The light on a port that indicates that traffic is passing through the port. Under normal data traffic situations, this light should blink green. Some hubs include separate LEDs for transmission and receipt of data; others do not even have traffic LEDs for their ports. If they exist, traffic LEDs are normally found adjacent to link LEDs beside each data port.

- *Collision LED (Ethernet hubs only)*—The light that roughly indicates the volume of collisions by blinking. The faster the light blinks, the more collisions are occurring on the network. The hub may include one collision LED for the entire hub or individual lights for each port. If this light is continuously lit, a node is experiencing dire connectivity or traffic problems and may need to be disconnected.

- *Power supply*—The device that provides power to the hub. Every hub has its own power supply. Every hub also has its own power-on light. If the power-on light is not lit, the hub has lost power. The power light is normally found on the front of a hub, and so is not visible in Figure 11-5.

- *Ventilation fan*—A device used to cool a device's internal electronics. Hubs, like other electronic devices, generate heat. To function properly, most hubs must cool their processors, components, and circuitry with a ventilation fan (although very small hubs may not require a ventilation fan). When installing, you should be careful not to block or cover the air-intake vents.

Many hubs—known as **passive hubs**—do nothing but repeat signals. Passive hubs are used to extend the length of a network (just as repeaters are used). Because they have no ability to interpret Layer 2 or Layer 3 information, these hubs cannot determine where data should be directed. However, some hubs are much more sophisticated. For example, they may permit remote management, filter data according to type, or provide diagnostic information about the network. Hubs that can perform any of these functions are known as **intelligent hubs**. As described in detail later in this chapter, the more sophisticated connectivity devices become, the more they resemble other, higher-layer connectivity devices.

Placement of hubs in a network design can vary. One simple implementation is to install a passive hub to connect a workgroup consisting of multiple workstations and peripherals in a star fashion. Multiple workgroup hubs are then connected to another connectivity device, such as a switch or router. Most networks use several hubs to serve different workgroups. One benefit of using several different hubs is that if one hub fails, only some of the network's nodes are affected; nodes that use other hubs are not affected. Because hubs are relatively inexpensive compared to switches or routers, using several hubs can be less expensive than using just one of these devices. As with repeaters, however, the maximum

11

network length limits apply to hubs that are connected along a bus. On a 10BaseT network, no more than four hubs can be used to extend a network. On a 100BaseT network, the limit is two hubs. Figure 11-6 offers one example of how hubs may fit into the overall design of a network.

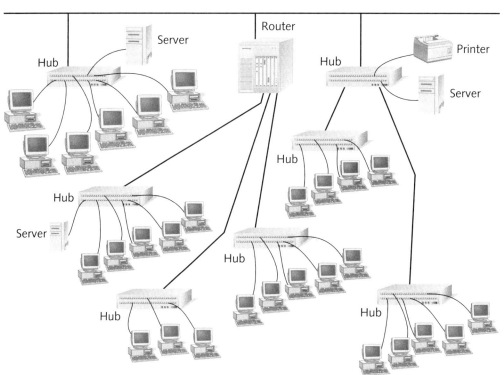

Figure 11-6 Hubs in a network design

LAYER 2 CONNECTIVITY

Recall that Layer 2, the Data Link layer of the OSI model, is responsible for packaging data into frames, inserting physical address information, and adding flow control and error checking fields to the frame. Devices that operate at Layer 2 of the OSI model include bridges and simple switches.

Bridges

Bridges are devices that analyze incoming frames and make decisions about how to direct them to their destination. Bridges look like repeaters in that they have a single input and a single output port. But they differ from repeaters in that they can interpret the data they retransmit. Specifically, bridges read the physical destination (or MAC address) information and decide whether to forward (retransmit) the data packet to another segment on the network or, if the destination address belongs to the same segment as the source address, filter (discard) it. As nodes transmit data through the bridge, the bridge establishes a **filtering database** (also known as a **forwarding table**) of known MAC addresses and their locations on the network. The bridge uses its filtering database to determine whether a packet should be forwarded or filtered, as illustrated in Figure 11-7.

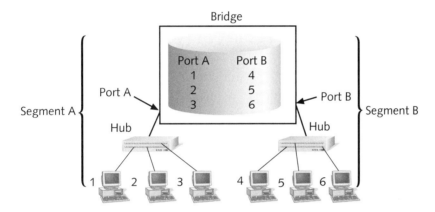

Figure 11-7   A bridge's use of a filtering database

Using Figure 11-7 as a guide, suppose that you sit at Workstation 1 on Segment A of the LAN, and your colleague Frank sits at Workstation 2 on Segment A. When you attempt to send data to Frank's computer, your transmission goes through your segment's hub and then to the bridge. The bridge reads the MAC address of Frank's computer. It then searches its filtering database to determine whether that MAC address belongs to the same segment you're on or whether it belongs on a different segment. The bridge can determine only that the MAC address of Frank's workstation is associated with its port A. If the MAC address belongs to a different segment, the bridge forwards the data to that segment, whose corresponding port identity is also in the filtering database. In this case, however, your workstation and Frank's workstation reside on the same LAN segment, so the data is filtered (that is ignored) and your message is delivered to Frank's workstation through Segment A's hub.

However, if you want to send data to your new employee's computer, which is Workstation 5 in Figure 11-7, your transmission first passes through Segment A's hub and then on to the bridge. The bridge reads the MAC address for your new employee's machine (the destination address in your data stream) and searches for the port associated with that machine. In this case, the bridge recognizes workstation 5 as being connected to port B, and it forwards the data to that port. Subsequently, the Segment B hub ensures delivery of the data to your new employee's computer.

After you install a new bridge, it uses one of several methods to learn about the network and discover where the destination address for each packet it handles resides. After it discovers this information, it records the destination node's MAC address and its associated port in its filtering database. Over time, it discovers all nodes on the network and constructs database entries for each.

Because bridges cannot interpret higher-level data, such as Layer 3 (Network layer) information, they do not distinguish between different protocols. For example, they can forward frames from TCP/IP, IPX/SPX, and other Network-layer protocols with equal speed and accuracy. This flexibility is a great advantage. Because they are protocol-ignorant, bridges can move data more rapidly than traditional routers, for example, which do care about protocol information (as you learn later in this chapter). On the other hand, bridges take longer to transmit data than either repeaters or hubs, because bridges actually analyze each packet, whereas hubs and repeaters do not.

Bridges may follow one of several types of methods for forwarding or filtering packets. A discussion of each of these methods is beyond the scope of this book. However, an overview of the three most common bridging techniques—transparent bridging, source-route bridging, and translational bridging—is useful.

Transparent bridging is the bridging method used on many Ethernet networks. In transparent bridging, a bridge begins polling a network to learn about its physical topology as soon as it is installed on the network. When the bridge receives a packet from an unknown source, it adds the location of that source to its filtering database. Over time, it compiles database entries for each network node and forwards packets accordingly. The primary disadvantage to transparent bridging is that, on large networks that contain multiple bridges, each bridge may recognize a different path to a particular node. When this is the case, data that must traverse more than one bridge to reach its destination may be bounced back and forth among the bridges. This causes packets to travel endlessly over the network and never reach their destination. To avoid this problem, networks may use the spanning tree algorithm. The **spanning tree algorithm** is a routine that can detect circular traffic patterns and modify the way multiple bridges work together, thus eliminating such patterns.

The bridging method used on most Token Ring networks is called **source-route bridging**. In source-route bridging, a bridge polls the network to determine which path is best for a packet to travel from point A to point B. The bridge then adds this information to the data packet. Because forwarding information becomes part of the data, source-route bridging is not susceptible to the circular traffiic problems that transparent bridging introduces. Therefore, source-route bridging is especially well-suited to WANs, in which multiple bridges and long routes are common.

One significant advance in bridges since the 1980s is that, although they initially could only forward packets between homogenous networks, they can now handle data transfer between disparate networks. A method of bridging that can connect networks that use different logical topologies is called **translational bridging**. In translational bridging, the bridge not only forwards packets, but also translates packets between one logical topology and another. Translational bridging may be used, for example, to connect a Token Ring network to an Ethernet network, or a FDDI network to an Ethernet network.

Despite these advances, newer routers and switches are commonly replacing bridges, because the speed of such Layer 3 devices has greatly improved. But bridges are still adequate and appropriate in some situations. The inclusion of a bridge on a network enhances the network performance by filtering traffic directed to the various nodes. In other words, the network's traffic doesn't all share the same channel. Also, a bridge can detect and discard flawed packets that may create congestion on the network.

Perhaps most importantly, bridges offer an inexpensive way to extend a network farther than a Layer 1 device (such as a hub) can. This is because, on an Ethernet network, bridges create separate collision domains. Recall from Chapter 10 that a collision domain is a logically or physically distinct Ethernet network segment on which all participating devices must detect and accommodate data collisions. Because a switch limits the number of devices in a collision domain, it limits the potential for collisions. Therefore, using bridges can circumvent the maximum segment distance limitations that apply to the use of hubs.

For example, suppose you are a network technician for a high school that runs a 100BaseT Ethernet network on CAT5 cabling, and your school has expanded with a new technology wing. The technology wing is 250 meters long, and the distance from the school's main router to the entrance of the technology wing is 160 meters. Thus, the total distance you need to cover between the router and the farthest workstation in the technology wing is 410 meters. However, you can only use up to two serial hubs to extend the length of a 100BaseT network for a maximum of 300 meters. To connect two nodes directly for up to 400 meters, you must rely on a higher-layer connectivity device. By installing a bridge to connect the technology wing to the rest of the school's network, you can easily add the technology wing's nodes to the network.

Data Switches

Throughout this book, you have encountered many references to switching. For example, in Chapter 6, you learned the differences between circuit switching, used in the public telephone network, and packet switching, used on data networks. You have also learned how telephone switches complete calls between two subscribers over the PSTN. Now, you learn one more way of thinking about switches and switching: the use of switches to connect two data network segments. Many types of data switches exist; to begin with, you learn about traditional data switches.

Simply put, a traditional data **switch** subdivides a network into smaller logical segments and facilitates data exchange between those segments. Unlike a telephone switch, a data switch does not try to ensure a completed connection before transmitting, gather information about the nature of the transmission, or determine the best route for a transmission. (On data networks, routers accomplish this last function.) In fact, data switches are much simpler.

Traditional data switches operate at Layer 2 (the Data Link layer) of the OSI model, which means they can interpret MAC address information. In this sense, data switches resemble bridges. In fact, they can be described as multiport bridges. Because they have multiple ports, data switches can make better use of limited bandwidth and prove more cost-efficient than bridges on networks with more nodes. Each port on the switch acts like a bridge, and each device connected to a switch effectively receives its own dedicated communications channel. In other words, a switch can turn a shared channel into several channels. As with bridges, switches separate collision domains. Each dedicated channel created by a switch represents a separate collision domain. A typical data switch is shown in Figure 11-8.

Figure 11-8   Example of a data switch

Switches have historically been used to replace hubs and ease traffic congestion in LAN workgroups. Switches can also be used in place of routers on a network's backbone. The inclusion of switches on a backbone provides at least two advantages. First, switches offer greater security because they isolate one device's traffic from other devices' traffic. Second, switches provide separate channels for (potentially) every device. As a result, applications that transfer a large amount of traffic and are sensitive to time delay, such as videoconferencing applications, can make full use of the network's capacity.

Switches have their disadvantages, too. Although they contain buffers to hold incoming data and accommodate bursts of traffic, they can become overwhelmed by continuous, heavy traffic. In that event, the switch cannot prevent data loss. On a shared environment, in which many nodes share the same data channel, devices can compensate for collisions; on a fully switched network, in which every node uses its own port on the switch and therefore provides a separate data channel, devices cannot detect collisions. Also, although higher-layer protocols, such as TCP, detect the loss and respond with a timeout, others, such as UDP, do not. For those packets, the number of collisions mounts up, and eventually all network traffic grinds to a halt. For this reason, a network professional must plan the placement of switches carefully to match backbone capacity and traffic patterns.

Switches can be classified into a few different categories. One type, a LAN switch, functions on a local area network. LAN switches can be designed for Ethernet or Token Ring networks, although Ethernet LAN switches are more common. LAN switches also differ in the method of switching they use—namely, cut-through mode or store and forward mode. These methods of switching on a LAN are discussed in the next two sections.

Cut-through Mode

A switch running in **cut-through mode** reads a frame's header and decides where to forward the data before it receives the entire packet. Recall from Chapter 10 that every data frame contains a 14-byte header. This header contains the destination MAC address for the data carried by the frame. In cut-through mode, a switch reads the header, then immediately sends the frame to the appropriate port based on its MAC address. It does not bother to hold the frame and match its contents against the Frame Check Sequence (the error-checking field within the frame). Therefore, in cut-through mode, the switch can't verify data integrity in that way. On the other hand, cut-through switches can detect **runts**, or packet fragments. Upon detecting a runt, the switch waits to transmit that packet until it determines its integrity. It's important to remember, however, that runts are only one type of data flaw. Cut-through switches *cannot* detect corrupt packets; indeed, they may increase the number of errors found on the network by propagating flawed packets.

The most significant advantage of the cut-through mode is its speed. Because it does not stop to read the entire data packet, a cut-through switch can forward information much more rapidly than a store and forward switch can (as described in the next section). The time-saving advantages to cut-through switching become insignificant, however, if the switch is flooded with traffic. In this case, the cut-through switch must buffer (or temporarily hold) data, just like a store and forward switch. Cut-through switches are best suited to small workgroups where speed is important and the relatively low number of devices minimizes the potential for errors.

Store and Forward Mode

In **store and forward mode**, a switch reads the entire data frame into its memory and checks it for accuracy before transmitting the information. Although this method is more time-consuming than the cut-through method, it allows store and forward switches to transmit data more accurately. Store and forward mode switches are more appropriate for larger networks because they do not propagate data errors. In contrast, cut-through mode switches do forward errors, so they may contribute to network congestion if one part of a network experiences a number of collisions. In large environments, a failure to check for errors can result in problematic traffic congestion.

Store and forward switches can also transfer data between segments running different transmission speeds. For example, a high-speed network printer that serves 50 employees could be attached to a 100 Mbps port on the switch, thereby allowing all of the employees' workstations to connect to 10 Mbps ports on the same switch. With this scheme, the printer can quickly service multiple jobs. This characteristic makes store and forward mode switches preferable in mixed-speed environments.

VLANs

In addition to improving bandwidth usage, switches can create **virtual local area networks (VLANs)**, logically separate networks within a network, by grouping a number of ports into a broadcast domain. A **broadcast domain** is a combination of ports that make up a Layer 2 segment and must be connected to other segments via a Layer 3 device, such as a router. The ports do not have to reside on the same switch or even on the same physical LAN. A VLAN can include servers, workstations, printers, routers, or any other network device you can connect to a switch. A single switch can create multiple VLANs. Or, multiple switches can be used to create one VLAN.

The great advantage to using VLANs is their flexibility in grouping network nodes. Another advantage of VLANs is their ability to link geographically distant users and create small workgroups from large LANs or WANs. Figure 11-9 depicts three different VLANs formed by two switches.

To create a VLAN, a network administrator must configure the switch properly. In addition to identifying the ports that belong to each logical network, a knowledgeable engineer can specify security parameters, filtering instructions (if the switch should not forward any frames from a certain segment, for example), performance requirements for certain users, and network management options. Clearly, switches are very flexible devices. However, one danger in setting up VLANs is that by creating a logically separate network within the network, you are not merely including a certain group of nodes—you are also excluding another group. As a result, you can potentially cut a group off from the rest of the network. VLAN implementation requires careful planning to ensure that all the groups of users who need to communicate can do so after the VLAN is in operation.

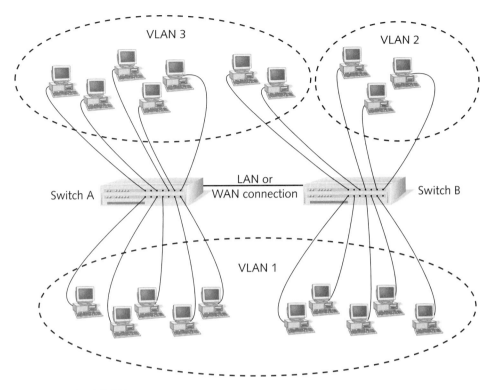

Figure 11-9   VLANs

HIGHER LAYER CONNECTIVITY

Bridges and simple switches are limited in their capabilities because they operate at Layer 2 and can interpret only physical, not logical addresses. However, higher-layer devices, such as routers, can interpret logical addresses, which allows them to make more informed decisions about directing data toward its destination. Other devices, such as gateways, operate at multiple layers of the OSI model. Not only can they integrate networks that use different logical addressing schemes and access methods, but they can also translate between different Layer 5 (Session layer), Layer 6 (Presentation layer), and even Layer 7 (Application layer) protocols. The following sections explain many different higher-layer devices, beginning with routers.

Routers

A **router** is a multiport connectivity device that can integrate LANs and WANs running at different transmission speeds and using a variety of protocols. Routers operate at Layer 3 (the Network layer) of the OSI model. Recall from Chapter 7 that the Network layer applies logical addressing information that helps direct data from one segment or type of network to another. Historically, routers have been slower than switches or bridges because they pay attention to information in Layers 3 and higher. Consequently, unlike bridges and traditional switches, routers are protocol-dependent. That is, they must be designed or configured to recognize a certain protocol before they can handle data transmitted using that protocol.

Features and Functions

A router's strength lies in its intelligence. Not only can routers keep track of the locations of certain nodes on the network, as switches can, but they can also determine the shortest, fastest path between two nodes. For this reason, and because they can connect dissimilar network types, routers are powerful, indispensable devices on large LANs and WANs. The Internet, for example, relies on a multitude of routers across the world.

 As noted in Chapter 7, some protocols are not routable. IPX/SPX and TCP/IP (the protocol used on the Internet) are routable. However, NetBEUI and SNA are not routable. Therefore, routers cannot interpret data transmitted using NetBEUI or SNA.

A typical router has an internal processor, its own memory and power supply, input and output ports for different types of network connectors (depending on the network type), and, usually, a management console interface, as shown in Figure 11-10. High-powered, multiprotocol routers may have several slot bays to accommodate multiple network interfaces (RJ-45, SC, FDDI, and so on). A router with multiple slots that can hold different interface cards or other devices is called a **modular router**.

Figure 11-10   A typical router

A router is a very flexible device. Although any one router can be specialized for a variety of tasks, all routers can do the following: connect dissimilar networks, interpret Layer 3 information, determine the best path for data to follow from point A to point B, and reroute traffic if a primary path is down but another path is available. In addition to performing these basic functions, routers may perform any of the following:

- Filter out broadcast transmissions to alleviate network congestion

- Prevent certain types of traffic from getting to a network, enabling customized segregation and security

- Support simultaneous local and remote connectivity

- Provide high network fault tolerance through redundant components, such as power supplies or network interfaces

- Monitor network traffic and issue statistics to a database

- Diagnose internal or other connectivity problems and trigger alarms

In addition, routers may use one of two methods for directing data on the network: static or dynamic routing. **Static routing** is a technique in which a network administrator programs a router to use specific paths between nodes. Because it does not account for occasional network congestion, failed connections, or device moves, static routing is not optimal. If a router or a segment connected to a router is moved, the network administrator must reprogram the static router's tables. The fact that static routing requires human intervention makes it less efficient and accurate than dynamic routing. **Dynamic routing**, on the other hand, automatically calculates the best path between two nodes and accumulates this information in a routing table. If congestion or failures affect the network, a router using dynamic routing can detect the problems and reroute data through a different path. Most modern networks primarily use dynamic routing, but may include some static routing to indicate a router of last resort (that is, the router that accepts all unroutable packets).

Because of their customizability, routers are not simple devices to install. Typically, an engineer must be very familiar with routing technology to figure out how to place and configure a router to best advantage. Figure 11-11 gives you some idea of how routers fit in a LAN environment, although this example is oversimplified and does not connect with another LAN. If you plan to continue your studies in data networking, you should research router technology further. You might begin with Cisco System's online documentation at *www.cisco.com/univercd/*. Cisco Systems currently provides the majority of networking routers installed in the world.

11

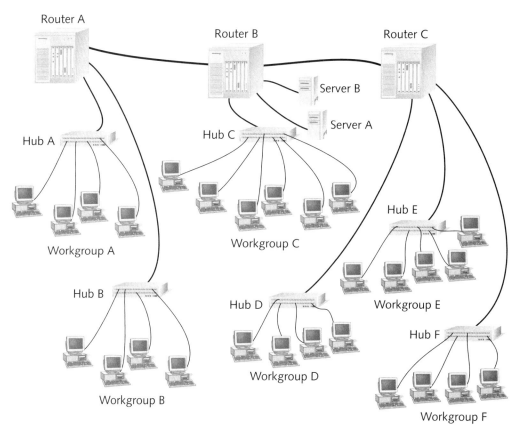

Figure 11-11   Routers in a network design

In the setup depicted in Figure 11-11, if a workstation in Workgroup C wants to print to a networked printer in Workgroup A, it creates a transmission containing the address of the Workgroup A printer. Then, it sends its packets to Hub C. Hub C simply retransmits the signal to router C. When Router C receives the transmission, it temporarily stores the packets as it reads the Layer 3 information. Upon determining that the packets are destined for a printer in Workgroup A, Router C then decides the best way to get the data to the workgroup A printer. In this example, it might send the data directly to Router A.

Before it forwards the packet, however, Router C increments (increases) the number of hops tallied in the packet. A **hop** is the term used in networking to describe each trip data takes from one connectivity device to another. (Usually, the term is used in the context of routing.) For example, a trip from a workstation in Workgroup A to Hub A constitutes one hop, and a trip from Hub A to Router A constitutes another hop. Each time a packet passes through a router, it makes a hop. Packets can only take a certain number of hops before they are discarded. After it increments the number of hops tallied in the packet, Router C forwards the data to Router A. Router A increments the packets' hop counts, reads the packets' destination addresses, and forwards them to Hub A, which then broadcasts the transmission to Workgroup A until the printer picks it up.

Routing Protocols

Finding the best route for data to take across the network is one of the most valued and sophisticated functions performed by a router. The term **best path** refers to the most efficient route from one node on a network to another. The best path in a particular situation depends on the number of hops between nodes, the current network activity, the unavailable links, the network transmission speed, and the topology. To determine the best path, routers communicate with each other through **routing protocols**. Keep in mind that routing protocols are *not* the same as routable protocols, such as TCP/IP or IPX/SPX. Routing protocols are used only by routers and only to collect data about current network status and contribute to selection of best paths. From this data, routers create routing tables for use with future packet forwarding.

In addition to its ability to find the best path, a routing protocol can be characterized according to its **convergence time**, the time it takes for a router to recognize a best path in the event of a change or outage. Its **bandwidth overhead**, the burden placed on the underlying network to support the routing protocol, is also a distinguishing feature.

Although it is not necessary at this point to understand precisely how routing protocols work, you should be familiar with the most common routing protocols: RIP, OSPF, EIGRP, and BGP. (Several more routing protocols exist, but are not widely used.) These four common routing protocols are described in the following list:

- *RIP (Routing Information Protocol) for IP and IPX*—This is the oldest routing protocol, which is still widely used, factors in only the number of hops between nodes when determining a path from one point to another. It does not consider network congestion or link speed, for example. Routers using RIP broadcast their routing tables every 30 seconds to other routers, whether or not the tables have changed. This broadcasting creates excessive network traffic, especially if a large number of routes exist. If the routing tables change, it may take several minutes before the new information propagates to routers at the far reaches of the network; thus the convergence time for RIP is poor. However, one advantage to RIP is its stability. For example, RIP prevents routing loops from continuing indefinitely by limiting the number of hops a packet can take between its source and its destination to 15. If the number of hops in a path exceeds 15, the network destination is considered unreachable. Thus, RIP does not work well in very large network environments in which data may have to travel through more than 15 routers to reach its destination (for example, on the Internet). Also, compared with other routing protocols, RIP is slower and less secure.

- *OSPF (Open Shortest Path First) for IP*—This routing protocol makes up for some of the limitations of RIP and can coexist with RIP on a network. OSPF uses a more complex algorithm for determining best paths. Under optimal network conditions, the best path comprises the most direct path between two points. If excessive traffic levels or an outage preclude data from following the most direct path, a router may determine that the most efficient path actually goes through additional routers. Each router maintains a

11

database of the other routers' links, and if notice is received indicating the failure of a given link, the router can rapidly compute an alternative path. This approach requires more memory and CPU power on the routers, but it keeps network bandwidth to a minimum and provides a very fast convergence time, often invisible to the users. OSPF is the second most frequently supported protocol, after RIP.

- *EIGRP (Enhanced Interior Gateway Routing Protocol) for IP, IPX, and AppleTalk*—This routing protocol was developed in the mid-1980s by Cisco Systems. It has a fast convergence time and a low network overhead, and is easier to configure and less CPU-intensive than OSPF. EIGRP also offers the benefits of supporting multiple protocols and limiting unnecessary network traffic between routers. It accommodates very large and heterogeneous networks, but is only supported by Cisco routers.

- *BGP (Border Gateway Protocol) for IP*—This is the routing protocol of Internet backbones. The demands on routers created by Internet growth have driven the development of BGP, the most complex of the routing protocols. The developers of BGP had to contend with not only the prospect of 100,000 routes, but also the question of how to route traffic efficiently and fairly through the hundreds of Internet backbones.

Layer 3 and 4 Switches

Earlier in this chapter, you learned that switches operate in Layer 2 of the OSI model, routers operate in Layer 3, and hubs operate in Layer 1. You also learned that the distinctions between hubs, bridges, switches, and routers are blurring as the lower layer devices become more sophisticated. One example of this melding of categories is the production of switches that can operate at Layer 3 (Network layer) and Layer 4 (Transport layer), making them act more like routers. A switch capable of interpreting Layer 3 data is called a **Layer 3 switch**. Similarly, a switch capable of interpreting Layer 4 data is called a **Layer 4 switch**. These higher-layer switches may also be called **routing switches** or **application switches**.

Among other things, the ability to interpret higher-layer data enables switches to perform advanced filtering, statistics keeping, and security functions. Layer 3 and Layer 4 switches may also transmit data more rapidly than a router and will probably remain easier to install and configure than routers. However, in general, these switches aren't as fully featured as routers. For example, they typically cannot translate between Token Ring and Ethernet networks or prioritize traffic. These critical differences make switches inappropriate for specific connectivity needs. In other words, if you need to connect a 10BaseT Ethernet LAN with a 100BaseT Ethernet LAN, a switch is adequate. If you want to connect a Token Ring LAN with an Ethernet LAN, you'll want to use a router.

As with other connectivity devices, the features of these Layer 3 and Layer 4 switches vary widely depending on the manufacturer and the price. (This variability is exacerbated by the fact that key players in the networking trade have not agreed on standards for these switches.) Higher-layer switches can cost three times more than Layer 2 switches, and network administrators are only beginning to try them. In general, higher-layer switches are yet another technology to watch closely.

Firewalls

Another higher-layer device you should be familiar with is a firewall. A **firewall** is a specialized computer (typically a router, but possibly only a workstation running special software) that selectively filters or blocks traffic between networks. A firewall relies on a combination of hardware and software (for example, the router's operating system and configuration) to determine which packets it should accept and which it should deny. It can operate at multiple layers of the OSI model, though much of its activity takes place in Layer 3, the Network layer. The term "firewall" is derived from the physical "wall" installed between rooms in a building or in automobiles between the passenger area and the engine to help prevent fires from spreading from one space to another.

Firewalls are an integral part of protecting data networks from unauthorized access. Often, a firewall is placed between a private network, such as a company's LAN, and a public network, such as the Internet, as shown in Figure 11-12. The firewall is then configured to disallow incoming traffic from nodes with network addresses that do not belong to the company's LAN. This is just one example of how firewalls are used. You learn more about firewalls and other network security techniques in Chapter 13.

11

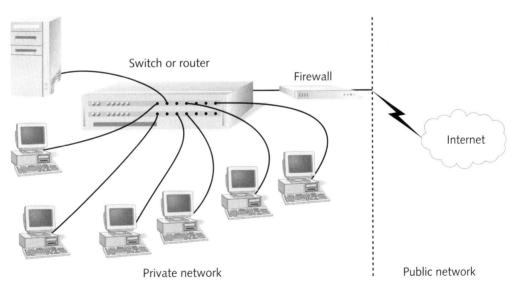

Switch or router

Firewall

Internet

Private network

Public network

Figure 11-12   Placement of a firewall

Gateways

Gateways do not fall neatly into a specific category of connectivity device, nor do they belong to only one layer of the OSI model. They are combinations of networking hardware and software that connect at least two dissimilar kinds of networks. You can think of gateways as entry or exit points into or out of a network, just as physical gates determine access to a bounded geographical area. The networks that gateways connect may use different data formatting, communications protocols, switching techniques, or network access methods. Unlike the connectivity hardware discussed earlier in this chapter, gateways do not simply forward packets. In fact, they repackage information so that it can be read by another system. To accomplish this task, gateways must operate at multiple layers of the OSI model. They must communicate with an application, establish and manage sessions, translate encoded data, and interpret logical (Network layer) and physical (Data Link layer) addressing data.

Gateways can run on servers, workstations, or mainframe computers. They are more expensive than routers because of their vast capabilities, and they are almost always application-specific. In addition, they transmit data much more slowly than bridges, switches, or routers because of the complex translations they conduct. Because they are slow, gateways have the potential to cause extreme network congestion. In certain situations, however, only a gateway will suffice.

You can probably guess that, because of their broad definition, many different types of gateways exist. Following are some common categories of gateways. Each category stands for many different individual gateways, which vary according to a network's specific needs.

- *E-mail gateway*—A gateway that translates messages from one type of e-mail system to another. For example, an e-mail gateway allows a network that uses a Microsoft Exchange mail server to trade mail with a network that uses a Novell GroupWise mail server.

- *Internet gateway*—A gateway that allows and manages access between LANs and the Internet. An Internet gateway can restrict the kind of access LAN users have to the Internet, and vice versa. You learn more about Internet gateways in Chapter 12, which focuses on the Internet.

- *LAN gateway*—A gateway that allows segments of a LAN running different protocols, network access methods, or transmission types to communicate with each other. A router, a single port on a router, or even a server may act as a LAN gateway. The LAN gateway category might also include remote access servers that allow dial-up connectivity to a LAN.

- *Voice/data gateway*—A gateway that allows a data network to issue data signals over a voice network, or vice versa. Among other things, this type of gateway performs translation between packet switching and circuit switching transmissions. It may also translate voice switch signaling (for example, SS7) traffic into a format that can be understood by LANs. Voice/data gateways are necessary to allow consumers to place telephone calls over the Internet, for example. In another instance, a voice/data gateway might be used to allow a company to carry its voice traffic between multiple offices over a T1 or SONET connection. Voice/data gateways are numerous and quickly evolving, due to the increasing integration of voice and data networks. You learn more about them in Chapter 14, which focuses on convergence.

- *Wireless gateway*—A gateway that integrates a wireline network with a wireless network. Wireless gateways translate between wireless and wireline network access methods, formatting, security, and flow control standards. They enable mobile users to connect handheld devices and cellular telephones, in addition to laptops and wireless workstations, with a wire-bound LAN. Wireless gateways are required to fully integrate all kinds of wireless devices with a wire-bound network (as opposed to connecting only laptops and workstations using wireless NICs to a LAN via an access point). For example, to view Web pages on a handheld personal digital assistant (PDA), the Web page's text and graphics must be formatted in a special language designed for PDAs. The wireless gateway translates incoming Web pages into this language, before issuing the page's contents to the PDA.

One network may contain several different types of gateways. In addition, one physical gateway (such as a router or server) may provide the functions of many different types of gateways. For example, suppose you work at an employment agency with several regional offices. The agency might use a voice/data gateway between its PBX and a telecommunications carrier to complete telephone calls over the Internet. In addition, it may use the same computer as an Internet gateway to connect its data LAN with the Internet. For easier management, troubleshooting, and limited risk of downtime, it is advisable to use separate gateways for separate functions, however. This is especially true in a large network environment, in which a single computer failure could affect hundreds of users and dramatically inhibit productivity.

Figure 11-13 depicts the placement of separate voice/data gateways and Internet gateways on a network. Notice that the Internet gateway is located behind (on the private network's side) the firewall. This placement prevents the gateway from having to perform significant security-related functions. Gateways and firewalls are often used in conjunction this way.

11

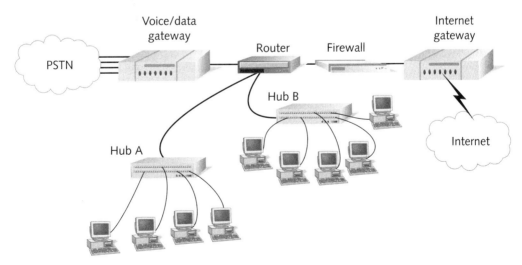

Figure 11-13   Gateways on a network

Up to this point, this chapter has focused on ways of connecting nodes, segments, and different types of networks that are directly and for the most part, permanently, connected. Next, you learn how users can connect to a network on demand from a location outside the network.

REMOTE CONNECTIVITY

The purpose of remote connectivity is to allow geographically distant nodes to log on to a network and perform operations just as if the nodes were directly attached to the network. As a remote user, for example, you may sit at the workstation in your den and retrieve spreadsheet and word processing files from your company's server 50 miles away. As far as the server is concerned, your home computer is no different than a workstation at the office.

Remote Connection Methods

Remote users can connect to networks in one of three ways: by dialing directly to the LAN's access server using a modem, dialing directly to a networked workstation using a modem, or using an Internet connection. Each of these methods offers different advantages and disadvantages, as described in the following list. Bear in mind that the true limiting factor in a remote connection is typically the speed of the modem, PSTN, or other access method that's used. You learn more about modems in the next section of this chapter.

- *Direct dial to a remote access server*—The client uses a dial-in software supplied with its operating system to connect to a remote access server on the LAN, as shown in Figure 11-14. Recall from Chapter 7 that a remote access server (also called a communications server or a dial-in server) is a combination of software and hardware that provides a central access point for multiple users to dial into a network. Many different software and hardware solutions are available for remote access servers. They differ in their complexity, security, ease of use, and method of exchanging data between the PSTN and a network. However, all perform the three main functions of accepting incoming connections, authenticating users who attempt to log on remotely, and translating commands and data between a LAN and the PSTN. In this scenario, the computer dialing into the LAN becomes a **remote node** on the network. Although this remote access method is the most complex to configure, especially on the server side, it can provide the best security. This method does not suffer decreased performance when the Internet becomes congested, as is the case when a remote user relies on a Web interface for connectivity. Also, by using a remote access server, an organization can allow multiple remote users to a network simultaneously.

- *Direct dial to a host workstation*—The remote client uses a dial-in software supplied with its operating system to connect to a workstation that is directly attached to the LAN, as shown in Figure 11-14. Software running on both the remote user's computer and the LAN computer allows the remote user to "take over" the LAN workstation, a solution known as **remote control**. Examples of remote control software include Symantec's pcAnywhere, LapLink.com's LapLink Gold, and the Microsoft Remote Assistance, which comes with Windows XP. After a session has been established, the remote node sends keystrokes to the host workstation (the one directly attached to the network). The host workstation performs the processing and then echoes (or issues a copy of) the screen output to the remote node. This arrangement makes this method well-suited to processing-intensive applications such as databases, because the processing instructions occur on the host workstation and do not have to traverse the slower modem connection to the remote workstation. Remote control is typically not as difficult to configure as dialing directly into a remote access server. One disadvantage to this solution is that it typically allows only one connection to the host workstation (and therefore, to the network) at any given time. This solution is appropriate for providing remote network access to a few employees who occasionally need to work from home. Due to its connection limits, however, this method is not appropriate for an organization that wants to make telecommuting available to all of its employees.

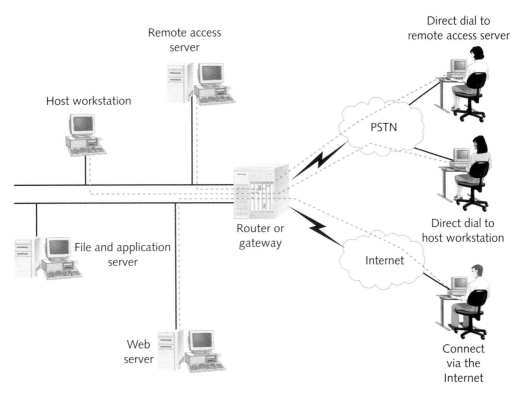

Figure 11-14   Remote connectivity methods

11

- *Connect via the Internet*—The client first connects to the Internet—via any number of methods, including dial-up, DSL, T-carrier, ISDN—then connects to a private network. Depending on the setup, the client may use simple utilities such as FTP to share files with the network, or the client may use special Web-enabled client software. Such client software works through a Web browser, such as Netscape Communicator or Microsoft Internet Explorer. This method requires some setup steps on both the remote workstation and the server, but it is often simpler than a direct-dial configuration. Its security and throughput cannot be controlled as thoroughly as those of the direct-dial solutions, however, because the remote user's connection is not dedicated. Also, it may not offer the full extent of network features that dialing into an access server or a host computer offer. Nevertheless, Internet access is widely available and when used, a Web interface makes resource sharing very simple. Also, many more remote users can simultaneously access the LAN resources using this method, when compared with direct-dial solutions.

Remote connectivity can be established from almost any type of workstation, given the appropriate software and hardware configuration. Some organizations use a combination of techniques, depending on their users' needs. Many different access and host server solutions are also available. Perhaps the simplest dial-in server is the **Remote Access Service** (RAS, pronounced "razz"), which comes with Windows 2000 Server. **Dial-up Networking** is the term that Microsoft uses to describe a remote computer dialing into a LAN's (private) access server or to an ISP's (public) access server to log on to a network. In other words, dial-up networking refers to the type of remote connectivity listed first in the previous list.

In addition to Microsoft's remote access methods, networking hardware manufacturers, such as Bay Networks, Cisco Systems, and 3Com, market their own remote access technologies. Or, instead of using a complete hardware-based solution, a network manager might purchase specialized software that can transform any Windows 2000, NetWare, or UNIX server into a host server. The optimal solution for an organization depends on its requirements for security, throughput, number of connections, and cost. It may also depend on the technical expertise of your users and support staff.

A remote client can use virtually any transmission method to make its connection and log on to a network. More and more telecommuters are using broadband connections, such as DSL or ISDN. However, many users still rely on simple modems to connect over an analog PSTN line. Because modems are so widely used in remote connectivity, the following section describes them in detail.

Modems

Although their technology dates back to the 1950s, modems still form the basis for many modern telecommunications. For instance, the majority of people using the Internet today connect via modem to an Internet service provider. As you just learned, modems are also used to connect directly to private networks via the PSTN. Earlier in this book, you learned some basic information about modems. For instance, you know that modems convert digital signals from your computer to analog signals that can be transmitted over the PSTN. They also convert analog signals from the PSTN into digital signals that can be interpreted by your computer. Because modems are such a critical element of telecommunications connectivity, you should have a thorough knowledge of how they operate.

> Although, technically speaking, any device that performs modulation and demodulation can be considered a modem, this section focuses on the type of modem that dials up another modem to connect two computers via the PSTN.

Modem Standards

The Bell System developed the first modems introduced in the United States. Because they developed the equipment, engineers at AT&T also set the standards for modem communications. The original modem standard issued in the 1950s, known as Bell 103, specified a maximum throughput rate of 300 bits per second. Since that time, modem technology has rapidly evolved, partly due to increased competition among technology manufacturers and partly due to widespread consumer demand for dial-up connectivity. Now, the ITU sets modem standards, and because the ITU is an international organization, these standards are effective worldwide. You can recognize ITU modem standards by their "V" notation. For example, the latest ITU standard for dial-up modem transmission speed is V.92. The latest ITU standard for data compression in modem communications is V.44. However, not all modems use the latest standards. If your telecommunications career includes supporting many dial-up connections across the PSTN, you may encounter over a dozen different modem standards still in use today. The following section discusses the signaling and session technologies that are described by different standards.

11

How Modems Work

You have probably used a modem and heard the familiar series of tones it issues as it connects, without realizing what the tones signify. The tones are performing **session negotiation**, a sequence of routines through which two modems establish rules for communication. These rules govern how the two modems will accomplish data compression, flow control, error correction, and transmission. During session negotiation, the two modems also determine the maximum speed at which they can exchange data. The following sections describe important modem transmission characteristics.

Data Compression

Because of the limited capacity of analog PSTN lines, if a modem were to simply transmit data after receiving it from the computer, the fastest possible connection would be a very slow 600 bits per second. Compare this to the actual maximum throughput of 53,000 bits per second (56 Kbps) we currently enjoy when we dial into an ISP. To obtain higher throughput, modems compress the data they receive from a computer before they transmit it. In compression, familiar, repeated character strings are replaced with symbols or strings that require significantly fewer bits. Modems may use one of several different standards to compress data.

The most popular standard used by new modems is ITU's **V.44**, which in 2000 replaced the previous, and still popular, **V.42bis** compression standard. Proponents of this standard claim that V.44 is capable of compressing a data stream down to one sixth of its original size. Statistics for the V.42bis indicated that it could compress data down to one fourth of its original size. Actual compression varies according to the type of data being compressed, the type of interface the modem uses to connect to a computer, and other factors. Still, V.44 is the most efficient compression scheme employed to date. Yet another standard is the **MNP5 (Microcom Networking Protocol Level 5)**, which can compress data down to one half its original size. Compression is very important in remote connectivity because it is the single most significant factor in expediting data transmission.

 In the ITU standards that describe different aspects of modem data transmission, the word "bis" indicates the second version of a standard. Bis is the Greek word for "double."

Data Transfer Rates

Data transfer rates are the main focus of other ITU standards, such as V.90 and V.92. During the late 1990s, two competing modem manufacturers, US Robotics and Rockwell, manufactured 56 Kbps modems that did not follow an ITU standard, but used different, proprietary standards. Incompatibility between these standards caused numerous problems between dial-up clients and access providers. In February 1998, the ITU issued the V.90 standard for 56 Kbps modems, and nearly all modem manufacturers soon adhered to this new standard. **V.90** defines 56 Kbps, asymmetrical transmission in which one of the modems is assumed to be using a digital line. This assumption fits the model of a modem operating on an ISP's remote access server, for example, which always uses a digital connection to the PSTN. Because the ISP's end of the connection is assumed to be digital, its modem can achieve higher throughput than the user's modem, where the line is assumed to be analog. The result is an asymmetrical connection in which downstream transmission (from the ISP to the user) can reach up to 53 Kbps and upstream transmission (from the user to the ISP) can reach only 33.6 Kbps. Thus, if you connect to your ISP using a V.90-compliant modem, you can retrieve files from the Web faster than you can upload them to the Web.

In November 2000, ITU released **V.92**, the latest dial-up modem speed standard. V.92 improves upon V.90 by increasing the upstream transmission rate to a maximum of 48 Kbps. Therefore, the time it takes to upload files to the Internet is faster with V.92 than with V.90. (The downstream transmission rate remains 53 Kbps.) V.92 also accomplishes faster session negotiation, because modems using this standard keep a record of previous connections and, when connecting to a familiar modem, retrieve the appropriate parameters for that modem. This prevents the modems from having to negotiate error correction and flow control specifics each time they connect. As a result, V.92 modems can connect faster than their V.90

counterparts. Finally, the V.92 standard allows modems to wait "on hold" up to 16 minutes in case a user receives a call while his modem is connected. Users must have call waiting enabled with their local phone service to take advantage of this feature. V.92 modems are also backwards-compatible. In case your ISP has not upgraded its access equipment to accommodate the V.92 standard, V.92 modems can recognize this fact and adjust their transmission to use the V.90 standard.

Flow Control and Buffering

In Chapter 7, you learned that the term "flow control" refers to gauging the rate at which a destination can accept data and adjusting the data transmission rate accordingly. In any type of connection, if one computer is capable of a faster data transfer rate than the other, flow control must be used. The same holds true for connections between modems. In fact, flow control must be employed between the sending computer and its modem, between the two communicating modems, and between the receiving modem and its computer. Every piece of equipment in the communications channel must adhere to the same flow control standard.

Two types of flow control are commonly used with modems: software flow control or hardware flow control. In **software flow control**, also known as **Xon/Xoff**, flow control information is issued over the same channel as the data being sent. For example, to request a pause in the flow of data, a modem issues a specific ASCII character, such as Ctrl-S. The main disadvantage to using software flow control is that noise on the line or corrupt data can inadvertently generate a command character (such as the Ctrl-S) and interfere with flow control. The result is a halt in transmission until the modem issues another control command requesting more data. In the worst cases, such an error could hang up the data transfer entirely.

11

Hardware flow control, on the other hand, separates flow control information from the data being sent. To understand hardware flow control, you must first understand the concept of buffers as they are used with modems. A **buffer** is a logically defined area of a computer's memory where data is temporarily stored until it is requested by software, or until it is cleared. When a computer is turned off, its buffers empty. A modem's buffer collects incoming data (which may come from the computer connected to the modem or from another modem, via a phone line) until the buffer is full. When the buffer is full, the modem signals to the sender to wait before sending more data. When the modem's buffer is nearly empty, the modem signals the sender to begin transmitting again. **Buffering** is the process of issuing data to a buffer.

To illustrate this concept, imagine you dial into your ISP, then open your e-mail program and choose to send a message and a photo to a friend. Suppose the data file that contains the photo is 500 Kb in size. After clicking the Send button in your e-mail program, the software issues a stream of bits representing your message and the photo to your modem. However, your modem's buffer is not large enough to accept the entire photo file at once. When the modem's buffer is full, it tells the computer to stop sending data. The computer complies, and waits to send the rest of the photo file until the modem signals that it is ready to receive more. Meanwhile, the modem empties its buffer as it sends the buffered data over the wire to your ISP's modem. When its buffer is nearly empty, the modem signals the computer to begin sending the rest of the photo. The process repeats until the entire photo file has been transmitted.

Signaling between devices using hardware flow control is accomplished through Request to Send (RTS) and Clear to Send (CTS) signals. Thus, hardware flow control is also known as **RTS/CTS**. These signals are transmitted over the interface between the modem and the computer's system board. Hardware flow control is a more effective method of flow control than Xon/Xoff, because it is less prone to data loss or corruption. Hardware flow control is currently used on nearly all modem connections.

Error Correction

In Chapter 7, you also learned about error correction, which is the process of checking to make sure data arrives just as it was transmitted, and if not, either correcting or requesting another transmission of the data. Because of the amount of noise on analog phone lines, error correction in modem connections is critical to ensure efficient and accurate transmission. The method of error correction used by modems is similar to that used by directly connected LAN devices. Recall that error correction on LANs is achieved through the use of a Frame Check Sequence (FCS) field in each data packet. Modems also use an error correction field in each data packet. But the algorithms used by modems to generate this field and thereby compare received data with transmitted data are different from the algorithms used on directly connected LANs. The latest error correction algorithms are **MNP4 (Microcom Networking Protocol Level 4)** and **V.42** (an ITU standard). Both standards retransmit data that does not match its sent format, plus filter out telephone line noise. Note that if you purchase a new modem for your computer today, it would likely support both error correction methods (and possibly others), thus guaranteeing compatibility with modems that support only one error correction method.

Asynchronous and Synchronous Communication

In addition to accounting for errors and transmission rates, modems must account for the way in which computers time their communications. This timing may be synchronous or asynchronous. Asynchronous and synchronous communications are characteristics that can be applied to any type of data transmission. In modem communications, the distinction is especially relevant, because the software communicating data to the modem must be configured for the appropriate timing scheme.

Asynchronous refers to a communications method in which data being transmitted and received by nodes does not have to conform to any predetermined timing schemes. Asynchronous data is sent in frames. A node can transmit at any time and the destination node must accept the transmission as it comes. To ensure that the receiving node knows when it has received a complete frame, asynchronous communications provide special bits called start and stop bits for each character transmitted. When the receiving node recognizes a start bit, it begins to accept a new character (or byte of information). When it receives the stop bit for that character, it ceases to look for the end of that character's transmission. Asynchronous data transmission therefore occurs in random stops and starts. The first modems used asynchronous communications.

Synchronous refers to a communications method in which data is transmitted in a continuous stream of bits. To interpret this data stream, nodes must conform to a timing scheme. A clock maintains time for all nodes on a network. A receiving node in synchronous communications recognizes that it should be receiving data by looking at the time on the clock. In synchronous communications, start and stop bits are not necessary, because the clocking indicates where transmission should begin and where it should end. As an analogy, imagine a marathon with 1000 participants, in which each runner starts the race precisely five minutes after the previous runner started. The race's official timekeeper keeps track of when each runner begins, so that when a runner arrives at the finish line, his or her total time can be calculated. Runner B, who starts ten minutes after Runner A, will not be expected to arrive at the finish line at the same time as Runner A. In this analogy, the race official is like the clocking mechanism in synchronous communications. Newer, 56 Kbps modems use synchronous data transmission.

Modem Types

As with NICs, modems come in several different varieties. They may be external to a computer or internal. The following list describes a variety of contemporary modem types:

- *Adapter card*—As with NICs, modems can exist as an adapter card that connects to a computer's bus. Such internal modems may follow any of the bus types described earlier in this chapter. The most common bus type used for an internal modem is a PCI interface. Figure 11-15 depicts an adapter card modem.

- *Serial port*—Traditionally, external modems connected to a computer via the serial port, which accepts a 22-pin, RS 232 (Recommended Standard 232) data connector. External modems are simple to install, requiring the user to connect the modem's RS232 cable to the computer's serial port. On IBM-compatible workstations, this serial port may be equivalent to COM1 or COM2 in the computer's operating system configuration. The disadvantage to using this type of modem is that serial interfaces cannot transmit data as fast as other types of interfaces. Figure 11-16 depicts an external, serial-port modem.

- *PC Card*—As with NICs, PC Card (or PCMCIA) modems are an excellent alternative for laptop users. PC Card modems are lightweight, simple to install, and enjoy the fast data transfer rate of a PCMCIA interface. Figure 11-17 depicts a PC Card modem.

- *USB*—Another type of external modem is one that uses the universal serial bus (USB) interface. As with USB NICs, USB modems are an excellent option for both desktop and laptop computer users. Although the USB interface is not as fast as the PCMCIA interface, it is still faster and preferable to an RS232 serial interface. Figure 11-18 depicts a USB modem.

11

Figure 11-15   An adapter card modem

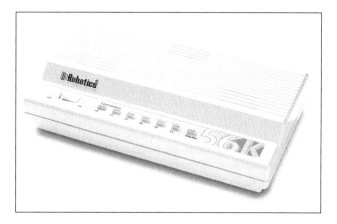

Figure 11-16   A serial port modem

Figure 11-17   A PC Card modem

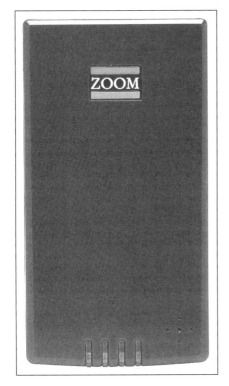

Figure 11-18   A USB modem

Serial Line Internet Protocol (SLIP) and Point-to-Point Protocol (PPP)

Serial Line Internet Protocol (SLIP) and **Point-to-Point Protocol (PPP)** are two communications protocols that enable a workstation to connect to a server using a serial connection (in the case of dial-up networking, *serial connection* refers to a modem). Such protocols are necessary to transport Network layer traffic over serial interfaces, which belong to the Data Link layer of the OSI model. Both SLIP and PPP encapsulate higher-layer networking protocols in their lower-layer data frames. SLIP is a version of the protocol that can carry only IP packets, however, and PPP can carry many different types of Network layer packets, such as IPX or AppleTalk. Another difference between SLIP and PPP is that SLIP supports only asynchronous data transmission and PPP supports both asynchronous and synchronous transmission.

PPP is the more popular communications protocol for dial-up connections to the Internet, because it supports error correction and detection and is faster than SLIP. In addition, PPP requires less client configuration than SLIP does. When using SLIP, you typically have to specify the IP addresses for both your client and for your server in your dial-up networking profile. PPP, on the other hand, can automatically obtain this information as it connects to the server. Because of these disadvantages, SLIP is rarely used.

Virtual Private Networks

Virtual private networks (VPNs) are wide area networks that are logically defined over public transmission systems. VPNs serve an organization's users while at the same time isolating that organization's traffic from other users of the same public lines. In other words, VPNs rely on virtually defined connections between remote nodes. They provide a way of constructing a private and secure network from existing public transmission systems. For example, a brokerage firm with offices across the nation could establish a VPN between its offices, as shown in Figure 11-19. Each office may use a different means of connecting to the Internet, such as ISDN, T-carrier, or even a dial-up connection over analog telephone lines. In this figure, a single cloud represents potentially eight different connections to the public network—as many connections as there are remote nodes. For each connection, a router or firewall encrypts data before it is issued to the public network. This ensures that any nodes other than those that belong to the same VPN cannot interpret the data. After a location receives data from the company's VPN, its router decrypts the transmission so that clients at that location can interpret the data.

Because VPNs do not require leasing a dedicated circuit, for example, or paying for a frame relay system that includes each endpoint on the network, they provide inexpensive solutions for creating long-distance WANs. VPNs employ specific protocols and security techniques to ensure that data can be interpreted only at the WAN's nodes. Depending on the VPN, one of several different methods may be used. The security techniques used may be purely software-based or they may include hardware such as a firewall.

The software required to establish VPNs is usually inexpensive, in some cases being included with other widely-used software. For example, the RAS software that comes with Windows 2000 Server allows you to create a simple VPN. For Novell-based networks, you can use BorderManager, a NetWare add-on product, to construct VPNs. In addition, many other companies offer software that will work with either of these network operating systems to create VPNs. The beauty of VPNs is that they are tailored to a customer's distance and bandwidth needs, so, of course, every one is different.

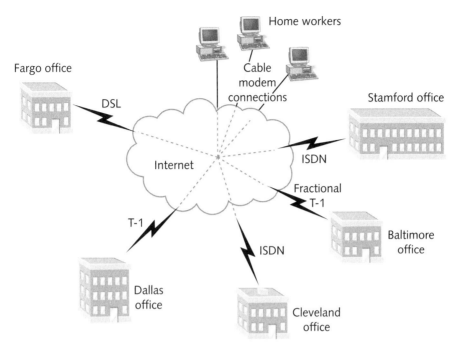

Figure 11-19 A VPN

Note Be careful not to confuse virtual private networks (VPNs) with the virtual LANs (VLANs) discussed earlier in this chapter. VLANs are logically defined LANs created from an organization's existing network infrastructure, usually to serve a particular group of users. VPNs are distinguished from VLANs in that they provide secure, remote connectivity over public transmission systems.

ACCESS AND CARRIER CONNECTIVITY

Until now, you have learned about several connectivity devices used on local and wide area networks, from NICs at the Physical layer to routers at the Network layer of the OSI model. As voice and data networks merge, unique connectivity methods are used to integrate the protocols and transmission methods of each. This section introduces the systems and devices necessary for connectivity between analog and digital networks, building on what you learned about the PSTN in Chapter 4. Whereas that discussion focused on analog technology, the following discussion focuses on digital technology. You also find references to network transmission methods, such as DSL, T-carriers, and SONET, which are discussed in Chapter 10. This section explores modern telecommunications carrier connectivity and prepares you to understand converged networks—or those that carry voice, video, and data signals simultaneously—which are the focus of Chapter 14.

Digital Loop Carrier (DLC)

In Chapter 4, you learned that telephone subscribers access the PSTN via the local loop. More and more, local loops are being used for not only telephone calls, but also for data transmission, as in the VPN connections discussed previously. To accommodate the growing need for more local loops capable of higher bandwidth and longer distances, LECs have implemented **digital loop carrier (DLC)** systems. DLC is a technique for delivering digital signals to a high volume of LEC subscribers over a combination of new and old local loop infrastructure. Most (but not all) new local loop installations rely on DLC.

DLC uses multiplexing to consolidate multiple subscriber lines into fewer, high-capacity digital connections that lead to the LEC's central office. This consolidation is also known as **pair–gain**, because it increases the number of signals that can be issued over a limited number of wire pairs. The point at which the lines are combined is called the **remote subscriber terminal**, or simply, the **remote terminal**. A remote terminal is located either outdoors in an environmentally-protected cabinet or in a pole-mounted enclosure, or sometimes, inside the customer premises. At the remote terminal, circuits from many wires are multiplexed into one or more digital connections. The digital connections are typically a type of T-carrier, but they may also be part of a SONET ring. On most new DLC implementations, these connections rely on fiber optic cable for their transmission. However, other DLC implementations may use twisted-pair wire or coaxial cable. The consolidated connection exits the remote terminal (in underground conduit) and leads to a **local exchange terminal**, also known as a **central office terminal**, which is located at the central office. The central office terminal separates individual subscriber lines into their original circuits. The circuits may then connect to a telephone switch or another type of access node (discussed in the following section). One central office terminal may accept connections from multiple remote terminals, in a star topology. Figure 11-20 illustrates the use of DLC technology on a LEC's network. Compare this figure to depictions of traditional PSTN local loops in Figures 4-4 and 4-6.

Consolidating multiple subscriber lines offers several advantages. First, it addresses the problem of local loop distance limitations. Recall that due to electrical signaling characteristics, a copper local loop cannot exceed 18,000 feet (or approximately three miles). By placing remote terminals between the customer premises and the central office, the length of copper wire in the local loop is minimized. Thus, local loops using DLC technology can span longer distances than traditional local loops. This is particularly advantageous when supplying services such as DSL, which are highly distance-sensitive. Second, consolidation addresses physical installation challenges, such as digging trenches to install new lines, which can be expensive, difficult, and disruptive. In fact, AT&T initiated DLC techniques in the 1970s partly in response to congested cable routes in densely populated areas. Third, because it brings several local lines into one connection, DLC technology can minimize the effort required to troubleshoot faulty connections. And finally, because it minimizes the extent of copper wiring that must be installed, DLC can result in notable cost savings for LECs.

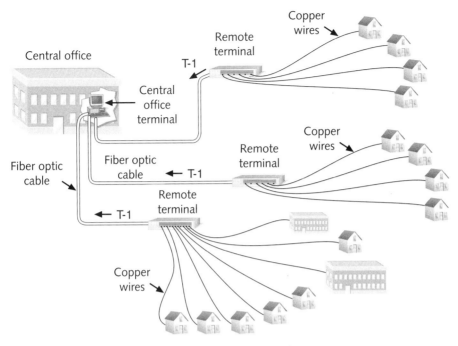

Figure 11-20   DLC technology on a LEC's network

As indicated by the previous example, the entire local loop, from the demarc to the central office, need not be digital for the loop to qualify as a DLC implementation. In fact, signals issued from the subscriber's equipment that traverse traditional copper wire might be analog or digital, until they reach the remote terminal. At that point, any analog signals are converted to digital signals, before being transmitted to the central office. In addition, DLC systems can include more sophisticated transmission media between the remote terminal and the subscriber. In other words, the drop wire may not be copper twisted-pair. In anticipation of delivering high-bandwidth digital services to each home, some LECs have installed HFC, coaxial cable, or even fiber optic cable to subscribers' homes and businesses. However, such advanced connections are expensive to provide and therefore, remain rare.

DLC technology has evolved significantly since its introduction in the 1970s. One major improvement has been the quantity of lines that a remote terminal can accommodate. Although original remote terminals typically accepted 96 subscriber wire pairs, modern remote terminals often accept up to 700. In addition, current DLC technology almost always uses fiber optic cable for connections between the remote terminal and the central office terminal. Early DLC installations may have used coax, twisted-pair, or HFC for this link.

The extent of DLC technology deployed in the PSTN continues to grow, primarily as a result of subscribers demanding multiple services over a single line. For example, DLC enables a subscriber to use a DSL network connection while at the same time using a traditional analog connection for voice telephone calls, both over a single line. A business subscriber can take advantage of DLC to obtain T-carrier, ISDN, DSL, and analog voice connections over the same local loop. To provide this diversity of services, however, the LEC must not only be DLC-capable, but must also have the appropriate connectivity equipment in its central office. Next, you learn about the devices that telecommunications carriers must operate to supply such services.

Access Nodes

In the field of telecommunications, the local loop—or the method by which subscribers access a local exchange carrier's network—is also known as the **access network**. An **access node** is the point at which a user's traffic enters or exits a carrier's network. Because of this broad definition, several different devices qualify as access nodes, and some are more sophisticated than others. For example, in a telecommunications carrier's CO, an access node may be a **digital cross-connect system (DCS)**, which is a device that directly connects multiple digital lines with other digital lines. At its simplest, a DCS can be considered the digital version of the analog cross-connects you learned about in Chapter 4's discussion of a carrier's inside plant. It may simply accept an incoming T-1 (for example, the kind that is used in DLC) before the lines are transferred to a switch. However, most modern DCSs also perform functions at higher layers of the OSI model, such as protocol translation.

Another example of an access node (and in fact, a type of DCS) is the DACS (digital access and control switch), which, as you learned in Chapter 10, is where multiple T-carrier lines are consolidated or separated. Other types of DACS devices integrate lines using multiple types of transmission methods, such as ISDN, T-1, and analog voice connections. Telephone switches, routers, and remote access servers may also be considered access nodes. However, when telecommunications professionals use the term "access node," they are probably referring to a type of DCS. (Not all DCSs are used as access nodes, however; they are frequently used on private networks to integrate many different connections.)

The most sophisticated access nodes are those that perform functions at all layers of the OSI model, supplying digital cross-connections, accepting transmissions from different types of networks, accommodating both voice and data connections, and interpreting data at the highest layers of the OSI model. Such access nodes are sometimes called **integrated access devices (IADs)**, because they integrate a number of functions into one device. Network service providers use IADs to consolidate traffic from many types of incoming connections. IADs form the basis for many converged networks, and thus, are discussed in more detail in Chapter 14.

One specialized use of access nodes is for connecting ILEC local loops with CLEC facilities. Recall that most CLECs still depend on ILEC facilities for the local loop to their customers. Thus, even though a subscriber purchases services from a CLEC, that subscriber's line first connects with an ILEC's POP. Therefore, a means of transferring the subscriber's line from the ILEC's network to the CLEC's network is necessary. An access node provides this function. At the ILEC's central office, the CLEC subscriber's line terminates

❐ A virtual private network (VPN) allows an organization to carve a private WAN over public transmission facilities. VPNs may use one of several different methods of securing data between locations. They are an economical solution to creating long-distance WANs, versus leasing dedicated circuits from a telecommunications carrier, for example.

❐ Digital loop carrier (DLC) is a technology used by LECs to provide more high-bandwidth lines and multiple digital services to a large group of subscribers. DLC installations typically rely on remote terminals to bring fiber optic connections from the central office closer to the customer. This decreases the length of copper in the local loop, saves installation costs, and simplifies maintenance.

❐ Access nodes provide a point of entry for subscriber lines coming into a telecommunications carrier's facility. Many types of devices qualify as access nodes, including DCS, DACS, switches, routers, and gateways. Access nodes are commonly colocated in ILEC POPs to pass local subscriber traffic from an ILEC's facilities to a CLEC's network.

KEY TERMS

access network — The portion of a LEC's network that supplies subscribers with access to multiple services, both analog and digital.

access node — The point at which a user's traffic enters or exits a carrier's network.

adapter card — A circuit board used to connect a device to a computer's system board. Also known as an expansion board or daughter board.

application switch — Another term for a Layer 3 or Layer 4 switch.

asynchronous — A communications method in which data being transmitted and received by nodes does not have to conform to any predetermined timing scheme. Asynchronous data is sent in frames. To ensure that the receiving node knows when it has received a complete frame, asynchronous communications provide start and stop bits for each character transmitted.

bandwidth overhead — The burden placed on the underlying network to support a routing protocol.

best path — The most efficient route for data to follow between two nodes (whether or not they are on the same network). Under optimal network conditions, the best path is the path that requires the fewest hops between two points. Realistically, the best path depends on the volume of network activity, unavailable links, network transmission speed, and topology.

Border Gateway Protocol (BGP) — The routing protocol of Internet backbones. The router stress created by Internet growth has driven the development of BGP, the most complex of the routing protocols. The developers of BGP had to contend with the prospect of 100,000 routes, as well as the goal of routing traffic efficiently and fairly through the hundreds of Internet backbones.

11

bridge — A connectivity device that operates at the Data Link layer of the OSI model and reads header information to forward packets according to their MAC addresses. Bridges use a filtering database to determine which packets to discard and which to forward. Bridges contain one input and one output port, effectively separating a network into two collision domains.

broadcast domain — A group of connected nodes that share broadcast traffic. In a virtual local area network (VLAN), broadcast domains are separated by logically grouping multiple nodes to make up separate Layer 2 segments. Bridges and lower layer connectivity devices simply extend broadcast domains.

buffer — A logically defined area of a computer's memory in which data is temporarily stored. When a computer is turned off, its buffers empty.

buffering — The temporary storage of data in a buffer. Modems, for example, buffer incoming data until their buffer is full, then issue signals to the sending party to pause its transmission until the modem has released nearly all data in its buffer.

bus — The type of circuit used by a computer's system board to transmit data to components. Most new computers use buses capable of exchanging 32 or 64 bits of data. As the number of bits of data a bus handles increases, so too does the speed of the device attached to the bus.

central office terminal — In a DLC system, the point at the central office where multiplexed signals from several subscriber lines are separated.

convergence time — The time it takes for a router to recognize a best path in the event of a change or outage.

cut-through mode — A switching mode in which a switch reads a frame's header and decides where to forward the data before it receives the entire packet. Cut-through mode is faster, but less accurate, than the other switching method, store and forward mode.

daughter board — *See* adapter card.

dial-up networking — The process of dialing in to a network's private or public access server to gain remote access to the network. Dial-up Networking is also the name of the utility that Microsoft provides with its operating systems to achieve this type of connectivity.

digital cross-connect system (DCS) — Any device that directly connects multiple digital lines with other digital lines.

digital loop carrier (DLC) — A technique for delivering digital signals to a high volume of LEC subscribers over a combination of new and old local loop infrastructure. DLC bundles multiple analog lines into fewer, high-capacity digital connections that lead to the LEC's central office.

dynamic routing — A method of routing that automatically calculates the best path between two nodes and accumulates this information in a routing table. If congestion or failures affect the network, a router using dynamic routing can detect the problems and reroute data through a different path. Most modern networks primarily use dynamic routing.

Enhanced Interior Gateway Routing Protocol (EIGRP) — A routing protocol developed in the mid-1980s by Cisco Systems that has a fast convergence time and a low network overhead, but is easier to configure and less CPU-intensive than OSPF. EIGRP also offers the benefits of supporting multiple protocols and limiting unnecessary network traffic between routers.

expansion board — *See* adapter card.

expansion slot — An opening on a computer's system board that contains multiple electrical contacts into which an expansion board (or adapter card) can be inserted.

filtering database — A collection of data created and used by a bridge that correlates the MAC addresses of connected workstations with their locations. A filtering database is also known as a forwarding table.

firewall — A specialized computer (typically a router, but possibly only a workstation running special software) that selectively filters or blocks traffic between networks. A firewall relies on a combination of hardware and software (for example, the router's operating system and configuration) to determine which packets it should accept and which it should deny.

forwarding table — *See* filtering database.

gateway — A combination of networking hardware and software that connects two dissimilar kinds of networks. Gateways perform connectivity, session management, and data translation, so they must operate at multiple layers of the OSI model. Many different types of gateways exist, including e-mail gateways, LAN gateways, Internet gateways, and voice/data gateways.

hardware flow control — A method of gauging the rate at which two modems can exchange data that uses the interface between the modem and the computer to issue flow control information. Hardware flow control information is not combined with the stream of data being exchanged. Because its signals cannot be falsified or corrupted by telephone line noise, it is more effective than software flow control. RTS/CTS is a type of hardware flow control.

hop — A term used in networking to describe each trip data takes from one connectivity device to another.

integrated access device (IAD) — A sophisticated type of access node that performs functions at all layers of the OSI model—for example, supplying digital cross-connections, accepting transmissions from different types of networks, accommodating both voice and data connections, and interpreting data at the highest layers of the OSI model.

intelligent hub — A hub that possesses processing capabilities and can therefore monitor network traffic, detect packet errors and collisions, poll connected devices for information, and issue the information gathered to a database.

Layer 3 switch — A switch capable of interpreting data at Layer 3 (Network layer) of the OSI model.

Layer 4 switch — A switch capable of interpreting data at Layer 4 (Transport layer) of the OSI model.

local exchange terminal — *See* central office terminal.

MNP4 (Microcom Networking Protocol Level 4) — A modem error correction method used on many contemporary modems.

MNP5 (Microcom Networking Protocol Level 5) — A modem compression method that can theoretically compress data streams down to one half of their original size.

modular router — A router that contains multiple slots that can hold different interface cards or other devices.

multistation access unit (MAU) — On a Token Ring network, a device that repeats signals and connects multiple nodes in a star-ring hybrid physical topology.

network adapter — *See* network interface card (NIC).

network interface card (NIC) — The device that enables a workstation to connect to the network and communicate with other computers. NICs are manufactured by several different companies and come with a variety of specifications that are tailored to the workstation's and the network's requirements.

open shortest path first (OSPF) — A routing protocol that makes up for some of the limitations of RIP and can coexist with RIP on a network.

optical switch — A device that connects an optical line with another optical line to switch lightwaves, or that connects an optical line with a line that uses electrical signaling.

pair gain — The consolidation of multiple telephone circuits through multiplexing techniques. In DLC systems, pair gain occurs at the remote terminal.

passive hub — A hub that simply accepts and retransmits signals over the network.

PC Card — *See* PCMCIA.

PCMCIA — An interface developed in the early 1990s by the Personal Computer Memory Card International Association to provide a standard interface for connecting any type of device to a portable computer. PCMCIA slots may hold modem cards, network interface cards, external hard disk cards, or CD-ROM cards. PCMCIA cards are also known as PC Cards or credit card adapters.

Peripheral Component Interconnect (PCI) — A 32-, 64-, or 128-bit bus introduced in its original form in the 1990s. The PCI bus is the network adapter connection type used for nearly all new PCs. It's characterized by a shorter length than ISA, MCA, or EISA cards, but has a much faster data transmission capability.

Point-to-Point Protocol (PPP) — A communications protocol that enables a work-station to connect to a server using a serial connection. PPP can support multiple Network layer protocols, can use both asynchronous and synchronous communications, and does not require much (if any) configuration on the client workstation.

Remote Access Service (RAS) — One of the simplest dial-in servers. This software is included with Windows 2000 Server. Note that "RAS" is pronounced *razz*.

remote control — A remote access method in which the remote user dials into a work-station that is directly attached to the network. Software running on both the remote user's computer and the network computer allows the remote user to "take over" the networked workstation.

remote node — A client that has dialed directly into a LAN's remote access server. The LAN treats a remote node like any other client on the LAN, allowing the remote user to perform the same functions he or she could perform while in the office.

remote subscriber terminal — *See* remote terminal.

remote terminal — In a DLC system, the point at which circuits from many incoming wires are multiplexed into one or more digital connections (for example, a T-1) before connecting to a LEC's central office terminal. Remote terminals are located either outdoors in an environmentally-protected cabinet or in a pole-mounted enclosure, or sometimes, inside the customer premises.

router — A multiport connectivity device that operates at the Network layer of the OSI model and can connect dissimilar LANs and WANs running at different transmission speeds and using a variety of protocols. One of a router's most important functions is to determine the best path for data transmission between nodes. To do this, routers communicate with each other via routing protocols, such as OSPF and BGP. Routers are protocol-dependent devices.

routing information protocol (RIP) — The oldest routing protocol that is still widely used. RIP does not work in very large network environments in which data may have to travel through more than 16 routers to reach its destination (for example, on the Internet). In addition, compared to other routing protocols, RIP is slower and less secure.

routing protocols — The means by which routers communicate with each other about network status. Routing protocols help routers determine the best path for data to take between nodes. Examples of routing protocols include RIP, OSPF, EIGRP, and BGP. Note that routing protocols are different from routable network protocols, such as TCP/IP or IPX/SPX.

routing switch — Another term for a Layer 3 or Layer 4 switch. A routing switch comprises a hybrid between a router and a switch and can therefore interpret data from Layer 2 and either Layer 3 or Layer 4.

RTS/CTS (Request to send/Clear to send) — A method of hardware flow control used in communication between modems and between a modem and a computer, for example. In RTS/CTS, modems use their interface to a computer to send flow control information. In other words, this information is not combined with the data stream exchanged between devices.

runt — A packet fragment. Runts may be caused by collisions or other data transmission errors.

Serial Line Internet Protocol (SLIP) — A communications protocol that enables a workstation to connect to a server using a serial connection. SLIP can support only asynchronous communications and IP traffic and requires some configuration on the client workstation.

session negotiation — A process through which two modems establish rules for communication, including what type of compression, flow control, and error control schemes they will use.

11

spanning tree algorithm — A routine that can detect circular bridging patterns on a network (such as those possible when using transparent bridging) and modify the way multiple bridges work together to avoid such patterns.

software flow control — A method of gauging the rate at which two modems can exchange data that incorporates flow control information within the data stream. The main disadvantage to using software flow control is that noise on the line or corrupt data can inadvertently generate a command character (such as the Ctrl-S) and interfere with flow control. Xon/Xoff is a type of software flow control.

source-route bridging — A bridging technique in which a bridge polls the network to determine a packet's best path between nodes, then adds this path information to the data packet. Source-route bridging is used on most Token Ring networks and on WANs on which multiple bridges and long routes are common.

static routing — A technique in which a network administrator manually programs a router to use specific paths between nodes. Because it does not account for occasional network congestion, failed connections, or device moves, static routing is not optimal.

store and forward mode — A method of switching in which a switch reads the entire data frame into its memory and checks it for accuracy before transmitting it. Although this method is more time consuming than the cut-through method, it allows store and forward switches to transmit data more accurately.

switch — A connectivity device on data networks that logically subdivides a network into smaller, individual collision domains. A switch operates at the Data Link layer of the OSI model and can interpret MAC address information to determine whether to filter (discard) or forward packets it receives.

synchronous — A communications method in which data is transmitted in a continuous stream of bits. To interpret this data stream, nodes must conform to a timing scheme.

translational bridging — A method of bridging that can connect networks that use different logical topologies (such as Ethernet and FDDI or Ethernet and Token Ring).

transparent bridging — A bridging technique in which a bridge begins polling the network to learn about its physical topology as soon as the bridge is installed on the network, then adds information it learns about best paths between nodes to its filtering database. Transparent bridging is susceptible to circular traffic patterns, which can be alleviated through the use of the spanning tree algorithm.

USB (universal serial bus) port — A standard external bus that can be used to connect multiple types of peripherals, including modems, mice, and network adapters to a computer. The original USB standard was capable of transmitting only 12 Mbps of data; a new standard is capable of transmitting 480 Mbps of data.

V.42 — An ITU modem standard that describes a method of error correction. V.42 is compatible with MNP4 error correction.

V.42bis — An ITU modem standard that describes a method of data compression. V.42bis is purported to achieve up to a 4:1 ratio of data compression.

V.44 — An ITU modem standard that describes a method of data compression. V.44 is purported to achieve up to a 6:1 ratio of data compression.

V.90 — An ITU modem standard, issued in February 1998, that defines 56 Kbps, asymmetrical transmission in which one of the modems is assumed to be using a digital line. This standard is appropriate for dial-up connections to access servers (for example, at an ISP). The result is an asymmetrical connection in which downstream transmission can reach up to 53 Kbps and upstream transmission can reach only 33.6 Kbps.

V.92 — The latest dial-up modem speed standard issued by the ITU in November 2000. V.92 boasts an upstream transmission rate to a maximum of 48 Kbps and a downstream transmission rate of 53 Kbps. V.92 also accomplishes fast session connections by keeping a record of previous connections and, when connecting to a familiar modem, retrieving the appropriate parameters for that modem. Also, the V.92 standard allows modems to wait "on hold" up to 16 minutes in case a user receives a call while his modem is connected. Users must have call waiting enabled with their local phone service to take advantage of this feature.

virtual local area network (VLAN) — A network within a network that is logically defined by grouping its devices' switch ports in the same broadcast domain. A VLAN can consist of servers, workstations, printers, routers, or any other network device you can connect to a switch. VLANs serve to not only group nodes together, but also to exclude all other nodes from the group.

virtual private network (VPN) — A logically-constructed WAN that uses existing public transmission facilities. VPNs can be created through the use of software or combined software and hardware solutions. This type of network allows an organization to carve out a private WAN on the Internet (or, less commonly, over leased lines) that serves only its offices, while keeping the data secure and isolated from other (public) traffic.

Xon/Xoff — A type of software flow control used to gauge transmission rates between modems and computers or modems and other modems. Xon/Xoff incorporates flow control information in the data stream.

REVIEW QUESTIONS

1. If you purchase a new desktop workstation from your local computer store today, what type of NIC is it most likely to contain?

    a. PC Card

    b. parallel port

    c. adapter card

    d. USB

2. Which of the following NIC types is best suited to mobile laptop users who require fast throughput?

    a. PC Card

    b. parallel port

    c. adapter card

    d. USB

3. A Token Ring 10 Mbps NIC is interchangeable with an Ethernet 10 Mbps NIC. True or False?

4. To what layer of the OSI model do repeaters belong?

   a. Physical layer

   b. Data Link layer

   c. Network layer

   d. Transport layer

5. Name at least two ways in which hubs and repeaters are similar.

6. On a 100BaseT Ethernet network, what is the maximum number of hubs that can be used to repeat a signal from a router to a workstation?

   a. 1

   b. 2

   c. 3

   d. 4

7. At which layer of the OSI model do bridges operate?

   a. Physical layer

   b. Data Link layer

   c. Network layer

   d. Transport layer

8. Under what circumstances does a bridge discard a packet?

   a. when the packet is determined to be a runt

   b. when the packet belongs to a different network segment than the one from which it originated

   c. when the packet belongs to the same segment as the one from which it originated

   d. when the packet is determined to be carrying corrupt data

9. A bridge that is used to connect an Ethernet network with a FDDI network must be practicing what type of bridging?

   a. cut-through mode bridging

   b. source-route bridging

   c. store and forward bridging

   d. translational bridging

10. Unlike a telephone switch, a traditional data switch does not determine the best path between nodes on the network. True or false?

11. Which of the following switching methods is fastest?

    a. cut-through mode

    b. source route

   c. store and forward

   d. translational

12. What part of a packet does a switch read in order to find the MAC address?

   a. FCS

   b. padding

   c. header

   d. trailer

13. On an Ethernet network, what do all nodes grouped in the same VLAN share?

   a. Internet domain

   b. collision domain

   c. broadcast domain

   d. filtering domain

14. Which of the following types of addresses does a router use to determine the best way to direct a packet to its destination?

   a. MAC address

   b. Data Link layer address

   c. physical address

   d. logical address

15. What kind of router could connect network segments that use CAT5 UTP with other segments that use fiber optic cable?

   a. modular router

   b. translational router

   c. bridge router

   d. terminal router

16. Name three factors that a router must consider when determining the best path for data between two points on a network.

17. What is the routing protocol used by routers connected to the Internet backbone?

   a. EIGRP

   b. RIP

   c. OSPF

   d. BGP

18. Which of the following could *not* be used as a firewall?

   a. hub

   b. router

   c. server

   d. PC

11

19. What type of gateway would be used to connect a company's LAN with the PSTN to carry telephone calls to and from the LAN's clients?

    a. e-mail gateway

    b. LAN gateway

    c. wireless gateway

    d. voice/data gateway

20. Which of the following modem flow control methods is most effective?

    a. Xon/Xoff

    b. TTY/TDS

    c. RTS/CTS

    d. SLIP

21. Which of the following is the most recent ITU standard that describes modem transmission speed and signaling methods?

    a. V.42

    b. V.44

    c. V.90

    d. V.92

22. Which of the following modem types is considered internal?

    a. PCI

    b. USB

    c. PC Card

    d. Serial port

23. What type of remote connectivity requires a user to dial into a workstation on the network and "take over" that workstation?

    a. Internet/Web interface

    b. remote control

    c. access server connectivity

    d. VPN connectivity

24. Which of the following is currently the most popular dial-up protocol for Internet connections?

    a. SLIP

    b. PPP

    c. VPN

    d. Xon/Xoff

25. Which of the following is *not* an advantage to implementing DLC?

   a. In areas of high population density, it offers a more economical method of reaching all subscribers.

   b. For subscribers who want multiple lines to their home or business, it allows more lines to be terminated at any single residence or business.

   c. Because it limits the length of copper in a local loop, it allows a wider distribution of distance-sensitive services, such as DSL.

   d. It affords LEC simpler maintenance and troubleshooting for a greater number of local loops.

HANDS-ON PROJECTS

Project 11-1

Because modems are such an integral part of telecommunications, you should be familiar not only with how they operate, but also with installing them. In this project, you perform a simple modem installation on a desktop workstation. For this project, you need a computer running the Windows XP Professional desktop operating system. The computer must have the minimum hardware requirements to run Windows XP. It should also have a USB port. You also need a USB modem that is both Plug and Play compatible and compatible with the Windows XP Professional operating system (you can search for a list of compatible modems from the following Web site: *www.microsoft.com/hcl*). You should also have a copy of the modem's drivers (the software that enables the operating system to issue commands to the modem). Depending on the way in which Windows XP was installed on your workstation, you may also need the Windows XP installation CD-ROM.

1. With the computer and the modem both plugged in but turned off, first locate the USB port on your computer. For your reference, a USB port is pictured in Figure 11-22.

Figure 11-22   A USB port

2. Connect the modem's USB connector to the workstation's USB port. Turn the modem on.

3. Turn your computer on and log on as an administrator (a user with unlimited privileges on the workstation). This enables you to add or configure devices attached to the workstation.

4. Shortly after you have logged on, the Windows XP operating system displays the desktop and recognizes that a new piece of hardware has been connected to the workstation. At this point, it attempts to install the modem's software automatically. Assuming you have chosen a modem that is on the list of supported hardware for Windows XP, you should not have to provide any further information about your modem.

5. You may be prompted to reboot your computer for the changes to take effect. If so, click **No** to indicate that you do not want to reboot your computer.

6. Next, you need check to make sure the modem has been installed. To do so, click **Start**, then click **Control Panel**. The Control Panel window appears. Make sure the view option in your Control Panel is set to **Classic View**.

7. Double-click the **Phone and Modem Options** icon. The Phone and Modem Options window opens. If you are prompted for dialing information for your location, enter it here, then click **OK**.

8. In the Phone and Modem Options dialog box, select the Modems tab. If your installation was successful, you will see your modem listed here. (If your installation was not successful, the modem will not be listed. If that is the case, click the Add button to start a modem installation wizard. To complete this type of installation, you need your modem's software drivers.)

9. Close the Phone and Modem Options dialog box by clicking **OK**.

Project 11-2

The physical installation of an external device, such as a USB modem or NIC, is much simpler than installing an internal, expansion board device. Although an internal device may already be installed when you purchase a computer, at some point, you may have to install one yourself. In this project, you complete the physical installation of a NIC that uses the PCI bus standard. To complete this project, you need a desktop computer running Windows XP Professional, a PCI NIC that is listed in the Windows XP hardware compatibility list (as referenced in Hands-on Project 11-1), the software (on CD-ROM or floppy disk) that came with the PCI NIC, and some tools. The tools you need depend somewhat on the type of desktop computer you have, because you need to remove the computer's cover, and each computer may use a slightly different way of attaching its cover to the rest of the computer. Most likely, you need no more than a Phillips screwdriver to remove the cover. You also need a ground strap and a ground mat to protect the internal components from electrostatic discharge. Also, make sure that you have ample space in which to work, whether it be on the floor, a desk, or table.

1. Turn off the computer's power switch. In addition to endangering you, opening a computer while it's turned on can damage its internal circuitry.

2. Attach the ground strap to your wrist and make sure that it's connected to the ground mat underneath the computer.

3. Remove the computer's case. To do so, you may have to remove four to six screws. Or, you may be able to slide the cover off after releasing some plastic latches. In other cases, you may have to both remove screws and release latches before you can remove the cover.

4. Locate a PCI slot on the computer's system board where you will insert the network adapter. Remove the metal slot cover for that slot from the back of the PC. Some slot covers are attached with Phillips-head screws; others are merely metal parts with perforated edges that you can punch out with your fingers.

5. Insert the network adapter by lining up its slot connector with the slot and pressing the adapter firmly into the slot. Don't be afraid to press down hard, but make sure the expansion card is properly aligned with the slot when you do so. If you have correctly inserted the network adapter, it should be firmly seated. Although it may flex a little if you try to wiggle it from side to side, it should not be loose. It should also be inserted an equal distance into the slot at all points along its length. If this is not the case, evenly press on the card until it is fully inserted. A loose NIC will cause connectivity problems.

6. The metal bracket at the end of the NIC should now be positioned where the metal slot cover was located before you removed it. Attach the bracket with a Phillips-head screw into the back of the computer cover to secure the network adapter in place.

7. Make sure that you have not loosened any cables or cards inside the PC or left any screws or debris inside the computer.

8. Replace the cover on the computer and reinsert the screws that you removed in Step 3, if applicable.

9. Plug in the computer and turn it on. Proceed to configure the network adapter's software, as described in Project 11-3.

11

Project 11-3

In this project, you perform the software installation for the NIC that you physically installed in Project 11-2. This project's requirements were included in Project 11-2's requirements, so you may proceed without needing to obtain additional hardware or software.

1. After the Windows XP workstation has rebooted, log on as a user with administrator privileges.

2. As happened when you installed the USB modem in Project 11-1, your Windows XP computer will probably automatically recognize the new network adapter, install its drivers, and add the NIC to the list of hardware devices managed by the operating system.

3. Next, you need to make sure the NIC has been properly installed. Click **Start**, and then click **Control Panel**. The Control Panel window opens. Click **Switch to Category View**.

4. Click **Performance and Maintenance**, and then click **System**. The System Properties dialog box opens.

5. Select the **Hardware** tab, then click the **Device Manager** button. The Device Manager window opens. It contains a list of the computer's devices, organized according to type.

6. Find the Network adapters entry in the Device Manager list. Click the **+** sign to the left of the words "Network adapters." Below this entry, you should see the name of the NIC you just installed.

7. Next, you will use the software that came with your NIC to install new drivers for the adapter. In most cases, the drivers that Windows XP chooses for your hardware are satisfactory. However, sometimes you may need to update or supply your own drivers. Right-click on the name of your NIC, then choose **Update Driver...** from the shortcut menu that appears.

8. The Hardware Update Wizard opens, ready to lead you through the steps involved in updating the NIC's device driver software. Insert the floppy disk or CD-ROM that contains your NIC's drivers. Select the **Install from a list or specific location (Advanced)** option.

9. Click **Next** and follow the wizard instructions. Select the **Search removable media (floppy, CD-ROM...)** option, then click **Next**.

10. After the wizard has completed, you will be prompted to reboot your computer for the changes to take effect. Click **Yes** to confirm that you want to reboot your computer.

11. After the computer has rebooted, log on to the computer once again as a user with administrator privileges.

12. Repeat Steps 3–6 to verify that your NIC is still installed properly.

13. Close the Device Manager dialog box by clicking the **Close** button in the upper right corner of the box.

CASE PROJECTS

1. You are a network manager for a metropolitan package delivery service. At your city headquarters, dispatchers maintain a database of customers and items in queue for pickup and delivery. Dispatchers must also have access to information about which couriers are on duty and where they are in order to determine the best delivery routes. In the field, your company's couriers must know where to pick up and deliver items from and to a variety of locations. To be competitive, all employees must work as quickly as possible. To date, the company has relied on cellular telephones to exchange information between the office and employees in the field.

However, the company's IT director is displeased with the number of errors this type of communication results in. He has asked you to design a plan for a wireless MAN that would be accessible to all employees. The MAN must transmit not only messages, but also mapping and routing information for dispatchers and couriers. Given all you know about transmission methods, connectivity devices, and remote connectivity, list the type of hardware that each courier would carry in order to connect to this MAN. What type of interface would this hardware use? Next list the connectivity hardware that would be located at the company headquarters to connect remote couriers to the office LAN. Finally, list the type of hardware that each dispatcher would require to connect to the LAN and MAN.

2. You have successfully established a wireless MAN that connects your company's couriers and dispatchers, and as a result, communication errors have been virtually eliminated. However, you are dubious about the security your solution provides. What measures might you take to improve the security of the data, both on the LAN and on the MAN? What type of hardware would you install and where on the network would you place it?

3. Your IT director is pleased with the way you've designed the company's MAN and LAN. However, he thinks that the company could be even more efficient if its data connections were merged with its voice connections. For example, he thinks the dispatchers could use a CTI system that accepts telephone calls on their computers and automatically routes specific calls to certain dispatchers so that they can concentrate their efforts in specific areas of the city. What type of device (or devices) would be necessary to combine the company's voice and data connections in this manner? What are the potential advantages and disadvantages of achieving this integration?

11

12

INTERNET STANDARDS AND SERVICES

> **After reading this chapter and completing the exercises, you will be able to:**
>
> ♦ Summarize the history of today's Internet
>
> ♦ Identify the organizations that cooperate to set Internet standards
>
> ♦ Explain conventions for Internet domain and host naming
>
> ♦ Describe several popular Internet-based services and identify the protocols on which they rely
>
> ♦ Run and interpret the output of simple TCP/IP-based utilities

The Internet forms the basis for many telecommunications services, from simple e-mail message transfer to highly sophisticated Internet telephony. To fully appreciate these services, you need to understand the technical principles on which the Internet is founded. In Chapter 7, you learned about TCP/IP, the protocol suite responsible for all Internet communication. This chapter builds on that knowledge. Although it does not examine Internet technology in detail, it presents a broad overview of all that the Internet offers, with a focus on technical principles. This chapter prepares you to understand the most complex and current form of telecommunications—convergence—which is the focus of Chapter 14.

THE EVOLUTION OF THE INTERNET

Despite being accessible to average consumers for little more than a decade, the Internet dates back to the mid-twentieth century. Its roots lie with the **Advanced Research Projects Agency (ARPA)**, an organization formed by the United States government in 1958 to investigate and develop new military defense technology. ARPA was a consequence of the escalating Cold War at that time. In 1957, the Soviets launched Sputnik, the first satellite to orbit the earth. This act shook America's sense of security enough to prompt the government's quick allocation of more money and brainpower to defense concerns. ARPA's original mission (as part of the Department of Defense) was to fund research for space, ballistic, and nuclear arms technology. Much of this research took place at universities, such as UCLA, MIT, and Stanford.

Although ARPA's mission did not include computer science research, computers became an integral part of ARPA's work. An obvious reason for this is that computers were essential tools for developing the defense technologies ARPA worked on. Another reason, however, was that the many scientists working for ARPA required a secure means of quickly communicating with each other across the nation. In 1969, they established **ARPANET**, a network that relied on telephone lines to transmit messages that had been fragmented into small packages of data (the precursor to today's packets) between computers. ARPANET initially connected only four universities, but by the early 1970s, it connected 15 universities and 23 hosts.

 Since its inception, ARPA has undergone several name changes. In 1972, it was renamed DARPA (Defense Advanced Research Projects Agency) when its functions were moved under the Office of the Secretary of Defense of the U.S. government. In 1993, as part of President Clinton's technology strategy outline, it was renamed ARPA. Finally, in 1996, through an act of Congress, it was renamed DARPA. Therefore, depending on the source, you may find this research agency—which continues to operate according to its original mission—called ARPA or DARPA.

In 1972, scientists exchanged the first e-mail messages over ARPANET, and in 1974, the set of protocols known as TCP/IP was codified. TCP/IP was designed to facilitate open communication between all computers. This meant that as long as a computer followed TCP/IP rules for operation, it could communicate freely with another computer running the same protocol suite. In addition, TCP/IP's developers decided that information about designing systems and networking with the protocol would be available to everyone at no cost and with no licensing restrictions. This concept of open communication fueled TCP/IP's popularity. Because ARPANET operated via TCP/IP, and because of this protocol's many advantages, the Internet also operates over TCP/IP.

Several independent networks based on TCP/IP emerged during the 1970s and early 1980s. Universities continued to design and operate many of these networks, while corporations such as AT&T and IBM established others. These networks were not limited to a small number of U.S. institutions, but began to include international connections to European and Asian hosts. 1982 marked the introduction of the term "Internet" to refer to the collection of networks that followed TCP/IP. In 1984, the **Domain Name System (DNS)**, a formal, centralized method for automatically associating IP addresses with host names, was established. Prior to DNS, the number of hosts on the Internet was less than 1000—small enough so that a handful of volunteers could maintain the entire database of associations in a single file. Shortly thereafter, organizations were formed to help guide the growth of the Internet. As the next section describes, some of these organizations dealt with technical specifications, whereas others dealt with Internet policies.

National governments recognized the significance of the Internet and began to allocate funds for the network's expansion. In 1986, the U.S. National Science Foundation (NSF) subsidized the creation of supercomputing centers at five universities across the nation, plus a backbone to connect the universities with each other and with other organizations. This network was known as **NSFNET**. NSFNET allowed for access from all public institutions as well as other research-oriented networks (such as ARPANET) that followed TCP/IP. Its mission was to encourage use of the Internet among educational institutions. Indeed, the strategy worked, and use of the Internet grew exponentially over the next several years. By 1989, over 100,000 different hosts were connecting to the Internet, and in 1990, that number swelled to 300,000.

Meanwhile, private organizations continued augmenting their TCP/IP-based network infrastructures, too. Inevitably, private and public networks began to merge. In 1991, the NSF allowed its network to be used for purposes other than education or research. That same year, the U.S. government allocated billions of dollars for further Internet development and expansion. Also in 1991, the **World Wide Web** (**WWW**, or the **Web**) was introduced. The World Wide Web is a collection of multiple Internet servers and a method for organizing and formatting data scattered over these servers. To navigate the Web, a user requires a **browser**, or a program capable of interpreting Web formatting codes and presenting text and graphics to the user's screen. Since the first Web browser, Mosaic, was released in 1994, browsers and formatting codes have undergone significant improvement. For example, they have become more sophisticated. The first browser programs could not display color, much less animated images, as today's browsers can. In addition, the Web became simpler for the average user to follow. (You learn more about Web technology later in this chapter.) Together, the increase in access, funding, and infrastructure, plus the improved navigability, led the way to the Internet's popularity among commercial and personal users.

For a succinct view of the Internet's history over time, visit Hobbes' Internet Timeline at *www.zakon.org/robert/internet/timeline/*. This Web page is maintained by Robert H'obbes' Zakon.

By the mid-1990s, Internet user demographics had shifted from students, professors, and researchers to corporate employees and casual surfers. As a result, the universities and research organizations had to tolerate poor performance on the network that they created. In response, they conceived an exclusive Internet backbone called **Internet2** Internet2 dedicates its capacity to the high-bandwidth applications and fast performance that students, professors, and scientists require. The primary advantage of Internet2 is its speed. Although Internet2's backbone uses virtually the same technology as the public Internet's backbone, because relatively few users access Internet2, its response is much quicker. Also, Internet2 users are typically located at universities or research institutions, and therefore enjoy a direct connection to the backbone. Access to Internet2 costs at least a half-million dollars annually. In addition, participants must promise to use Internet2 for educational or scientific research purposes. Currently its members number close to 200, and Internet2 designers aim to connect all of the public schools in the U. S. to this backbone within the next few years.

INTERNET AUTHORITIES AND STANDARDS

No single country or organization is responsible for setting Internet conventions. Instead, several different organizations—many based in the United States and others that are international—cooperate to establish and enforce them. The number of organizations that participate in setting Internet standards and the relationships between these organizations can be confusing. To help you sort it out, the following sections divide these organizations according to the type of standards they help define: technical specifications (for example, what type of fields are required in an IP datagram) and addressing and domain name policies (for example, who owns rights to post files to a Web page located at "www.course.com").

Technical Specifications

An engineer's idea—for a new method of routing or a new type of TCP/IP subprotocol, for example—follows several steps before it is accepted as an Internet standard. One of the key organizations involved in this process is the Internet Engineering Task Force (IETF), which, as you learned in Chapter 1, is an organization made of technical professionals, companies, and computer researchers from around the world. The IETF is typically the first group involved in the technical standards process. After thoroughly researching an idea (and making sure a standard isn't already available), an engineer determines which IETF working group deals with the technology she proposes to standardize. Then, she writes an **Internet draft**, or a thorough explanation of her proposed standard, and submits it to the appropriate working group. For example, suppose the engineer posits a novel way of extending RIP routing hop count limits for use with IP version 6 (IPv6) networks. First, she submits her idea to IETF's RIP working group. (An Internet draft must follow specific IETF formatting, style, and content guidelines.) Next, members of the IETF working group review the draft. At the same time, IETF volunteers might already be working on a standard for a similar idea. Either way, IETF asks the engineer to cooperate with its working group in developing this standard.

Next, the IETF working group releases the Internet draft to the public for a six-month review period via an IETF Web site. (At any time, hundreds of drafts may be available for review.) During the six-month review period, members of IETF question the engineer about her proposal. Based on the inquiries she receives, the engineer will likely revise the draft several times. At the end of the six months, she requests (or may be requested by the IETF) to present her idea at the next IETF meeting. Finally, she can ask the chair of the working group to release the Internet draft for a "last call"—a final month-long comment period. The working group chair then submits the Internet draft to the **Internet Engineering Steering Group (IESG)**, a committee made of IETF technical area directors that oversees IETF decisions, which determines at its next meeting whether the Internet draft is ready for standardization. If so, the engineer and the working group members collaborate with the RFC editor, a standards publishing group, to write the document as a **Request for Comments (RFC)**. An RFC is a numbered document that articulates some aspect of Internet technology. Many different types of RFCs exist. Some are official standards, whereas others simply describe best practices or proposed standards. Still other RFCs are purely informational. When an Internet draft is transferred to the RFC editor, it is reclassified as a **proposed standard**. The RFC editor may work on the proposed standard for months before the IETF assigns it an RFC number and releases it. If an Internet draft is not revised during its six-month review period or does not become a proposed standard, it is discarded. Roughly one out of every 10 Internet drafts becomes an RFC.

A proposed standard RFC is a more thorough and stable document than an Internet draft. However, the scientist's idea does not have to be empirically proven until the next step in the process—when it becomes a **draft standard**. To qualify for this status, the technology specified by a proposed standard must be successfully demonstrated by at least two independent researchers. In addition, it must conform to and interoperate with other Internet standards. For example, an engineer's idea for revising RIP to offer an unlimited number of route hops on an IPv6 network must conform with every standard previously established for IPv6. If it passes these tests, the proposed standard returns to the RFC editor to be rewritten as a draft standard. Following that, IETF members subject the technology in the draft standard to one more round of scrutiny before it becomes a standard. In this last phase, the technology must prove, through testing by various people in various scenarios, that it is mature (in other words, all the bugs have been worked out as it has been tested), that it is seamlessly interoperable with existing technology, and that it is suitable for large-scale deployment. The path from idea to RFC standard, depicted in Figure 12-1, can last several months or a few years.

The process used to establish Internet technical standards (through IETF and other organizations) is comprehensively detailed in RFC 2026, which you can find at IETF's Web site using the following link: *www.ietf.org/rfc/rfc2026.txt*.

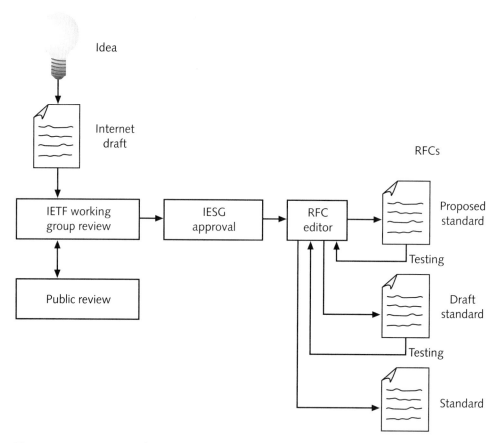

Figure 12-1 Steps in the Internet technical standards process

Although RFCs describe the bulk of Internet standards, they are not official, government-sanctioned policies. Engineers and network administrators normally adhere to RFC standards because it makes sense to do so. If they don't, chances are the parts of their networks that connected with the Internet wouldn't function properly with other Internet-connected networks. The use of standards that everyone can read and follow—not to mention comment on and improve upon, if they wish—is characteristic of the open communication ideology espoused by the Internet's founders.

Another type of unofficial standard is a **de facto standard**. A de facto standard is one that, while not codified, is agreed upon and adhered to nevertheless. (De facto, in Latin, means "from the fact.") Unlike RFC standards, de facto standards are developed independently, by a private corporation or research facility, and then released to the public. For example, the Adobe Acrobat standard for encoding text and graphics in files with a ".pdf" extension is a de facto standard. The software that allows users to read such files, Adobe Acrobat Reader, is publicly available and frequently used to read documents accessed on the Web.

In addition to RFCs and de facto standards, certain government agencies oversee the development of some Internet technical standards. On an international level, the International Telecommunications Union (ITU) investigates technical issues similar to those reviewed by IETF working groups. In fact, many of ITU's "study groups" interact with IETF's working groups on investigating proposed new standards. In particular, the ITU takes a leading role in fostering standards for **IP telephony**, a method of encoding and transmitting voice signals over a data network using TCP/IP. As you know, ITU issues technical standards, in addition to investigating them. Although some overlap exists between IETF and ITU work, the two organizations attempt to coordinate their efforts and avoid releasing redundant standards.

The relationship between the IETF and ITU is described in RFC 2436, which can be found at *www.ietf.org/rfc/rfc2436.txt*.

Another organization that contributes to developing Internet technical standards is the **Internet Architecture Board (IAB)**. IAB is a technical advisory group made of approximately a dozen researchers and technical professionals interested in overseeing the Internet's design and management. The IAB chair appoints members of the IAB. As part of its charter, IAB is responsible for Internet growth and management strategy, for resolution of technical disputes, and for standards oversight. In fact, IETF is the standards-making arm of IAB, and IAB appoints the chair of the IETF. IAB also consults with the IESG in determining whether a proposed standard will become a draft standard. IETF, IAB, and IESG are all related through the umbrella organization, the **Internet Society (ISOC)**. Some current ISOC concerns include how to address rapid growth, security, and the increased need for diverse services over the Internet. ISOC's membership consists of thousands of Internet professionals and companies from around the globe. You can learn more about ISOC at their Web site: *www.isoc.org*.

12

Figure 12-2 depicts the relationships between the technical standards authorities you have learned about so far. However, these are not the only groups that contribute to the standards-making process. In the following section, you learn about organizations that oversee Internet naming and addressing.

Address Assignments and Naming

Now that you have learned how Internet technical standards are generated, you need to understand how the Internet is managed. This section deals with two separate, but related, aspects of Internet management: IP addressing and computer naming. When ARPANET, the Internet's precursor, was very small, an ad hoc group of individuals who worked under the auspices of the United States DoD and NSF assumed these functions. However, as the Internet grew, management tasks were separated and assigned to different organizations. The following discussion describes how IP address assignment and naming have evolved and where they stand today.

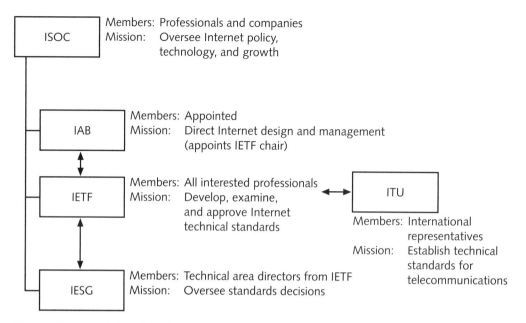

Figure 12-2   Relationships between Internet technical standards authorities

In Chapter 7, you learned that to communicate over the Internet, each computer requires a unique IP address. You also learned that a finite quantity of IP addresses is available. Thus, it makes sense that one central authority is charged with assigning IP addresses and ensuring that no two Internet-connected computers are assigned the same address. In early Internet history, a nonprofit, U.S. government-funded group at the Information Systems Institute (ISI) University of Southern California known as the **Internet Assigned Numbers Authority (IANA)** kept records of available and reserved IP addresses. It also determined how blocks—or groups—of addresses were doled out. Prior to 1997, IANA cooperated with an organization called InterNIC to manage IP address allocation. Starting in 1997, IANA coordinated its efforts with three **Regional Internet Registries (RIRS)**: ARIN (American Registry for Internet Numbers), APNIC (Asia Pacific Network Information Center), and RIPE (Reseaux IP Europeens). An RIR is a not-for-profit agency that manages the distribution of IP addresses to private and public entities. ARIN is the RIR for North, Central, and South America and sub-Saharan Africa. APNIC is the RIR for Asia and the Pacific region. RIPE is the RIR for Europe and North Africa.

For example, a network engineer at an ISP in Dallas might need additional IP addresses because his ISP plans to add new customers who want to host their own Web sites, each of which requires at least one IP address. In that case, the engineer applies to ARIN for a block of IP addresses. ARIN responds and grants the engineer's ISP a group of addresses, in exchange for an annual subscription fee. ARIN, RIPE, and APNIC continue to issue

IP addresses today, and most of their customers are large ISPs or NSPs. These RIRs rarely issue IP addresses to individuals. An individual wanting to reserve an IP address for his home Web server, for example, typically obtains an IP address from his ISP.

In addition to determining how IP addresses were allocated, IANA was also responsible for allocating domain names and maintaining the Domain Name System (DNS). Later in this chapter, you learn more about the structure and operation of DNS. For now, it is enough to understand that as with IP addresses, centralized management is key to smooth operation, because each host connected to the Internet must have a unique host and domain name. IANA worked exclusively with InterNIC and, starting in 1992, Network Solutions (now Verisign, Inc.), a private corporation, to perform the administrative tasks of accepting and fulfilling domain requests from individuals, corporations, and other institutions. For example, if you want to lease the right to post Web pages at *www.course.com*, you supply your technical information plus an annual fee to Network Solutions. In return, Network Solutions coordinates with IANA to make sure that the IP addresses on your network correspond to the "course.com" domain across the Internet.

In the late 1990s, the U.S. Department of Commerce (DOC), which was funding IANA at that time, decided to overhaul the way IP address and domain registration was handled. One reason for this change was that many felt IANA's status as a government-funded organization made it inherently slower and less competitive than a private organization might otherwise be. Another reason was that IANA was run by a small group of individuals, led by the late Dr. Jon Postel, the man responsible for many of the Internet's early technical achievements. Although Postel's work at IANA was highly respected, the government surmised that an organization with broader representation, including international and private interests, would be more just. Finally, the use of Network Solutions as a monopoly domain registrar resulted in perceived abuses in domain registration. For example, a greedy individual might reserve the domain names of several large companies before those companies could apply for the names, then attempt to charge the companies exorbitant fees to use the domain name. IANA didn't have a clear method for dealing with such abuses.

After much public debate, the DOC recommended the formation of the **Internet Corporation for Assigned Names and Numbers (ICANN)**. ICANN is a private, nonprofit corporation that is contracted by the government to oversee IP address and domain name management, plus accomplish specific Internet management improvements. It consists of 19 board members representing every continent in the world, a President and CEO, and At-Large Membership. Technically speaking, IANA continues to perform the system administration. However, these functions are now ultimately managed by ICANN. Domain name registration no longer rests solely with Network Solutions (now Verisign, Inc.), but can be accomplished by any ICANN-accredited registrar, of which there are hundreds.

Since its inception, ICANN has fueled controversy. Some have criticized ICANN's policies and procedures as less democratic than its predecessor, IANA. Domain name registrars protest the large fees ICANN has charged them, complaining that they are not

12

being given sufficient representation in decision-making. Others argue that the formation of ICANN did not take advantage of all opportunities for revamping the Internet management, but was simply re-created according to IANA's model. In addition, because ICANN has been slower than expected to reach its goals, some wonder whether it can respond as quickly as the leaner IANA. Nevertheless, ICANN's current contract with the DOC has been extended to September 2002. At that point, the U.S. Department of Commerce will determine whether ICANN will continue to be the financial and administrative authority for Internet addressing and naming. You can learn more about ICANN by visiting its Web site at *www.icann.org*.

HOST AND DOMAIN NAMING

Material in Chapter 7 introduced you to TCP/IP and the concepts of IP addressing and hosts. Before expanding your knowledge about these technical concepts, you should make certain you understand the following about TCP/IP networking:

- TCP/IP is a protocol suite that contains several subprotocols.

- Some subprotocols, such as TCP, are connection-oriented—that is, they require that a connection be verified before they exchange information, whereas other subprotocols, such as UDP, are connectionless and attempt to exchange data without connection verification.

- Connectionless subprotocols do not guarantee data delivery, but can transmit data faster than connection-oriented subprotocols.

- Every addressable computer connected to a TCP/IP network is known as a host.

- Every host can take a host name, a name that describes the device. For example, if you ran a Web server from your home, you could name the Web server "myWeb."

- Each host belongs to a domain, which also has a name. Together, the host name and domain name constitute the fully qualified host name.

- Every host on a TCP/IP network requires a unique IP address to communicate with other hosts.

- Each IP address is a unique 32-bit number, divided into four octets, or 8-bit bytes (according to the Ipv4 addressing scheme). Often, IP addresses are represented in decimal numbers, rather than binary numbers, with the four octets separated by periods. For example, 63.25.38.239 is a valid IP address.

Computers can manage numbers easily. However, most people can remember words better than numbers. Imagine if you had to identify your friends' and families' Social Security numbers whenever you wanted to write a note or talk to them. Communication would be frustrating at the very least, and perhaps even impossible—especially if you have trouble remembering even your own Social Security number. Similarly, people prefer to associate names with networked devices rather than remember IP addresses. For this reason, engineers who developed the Internet established a naming system for all its nodes. The following sections describe this system, beginning with an explanation of host files.

Host Files

When it was still known as ARPANET, the entire Internet relied on one ASCII text file called HOSTS.TXT to associate names with IP addresses. This file was generically known as a **host file**. Staff at the ISI at the University of Southern California updated this file as necessary. However, the explosive growth of the Internet soon made this simple arrangement impossible—a host file large enough to accommodate the Internet's needs would require constant changes. Furthermore, as more and more computers needed to look up host names, the host file would be queried more often. Such frequent querying from computers all over the nation would strain the Internet's bandwidth capacity. Finally, the entire Internet would fail if the file were accidentally deleted or damaged.

Within a company or university, you may still encounter this older system of straightforward ASCII text files, in which a table is used to associate internal host names with their IP addresses. Such host files must be updated manually, through a simple text-editing program. Figure 12-3 provides an example of a host file. Notice that each host is matched by one line identifying the host's name and IP address. In addition, a third field, called an **alias**, provides a nickname for the host. An alias allows a user within an organization to address a host by a different (and typically, more familiar) name than the full host name. For example, suppose you are the network administrator for a company that relies on three file servers whose host names are: "FileServ1," "FileServ2," and "FileServ3." You might anticipate that not all your employees will remember the file servers' host names. For example, when attempting to reach "FileServ1," an employee might type "server1" or "serv1." In your company's host file, you can assign the aliases "server1" and "serv1" to the "FileServ1" host computer. This allows a user in the company to reach the server using a more familiar name.

In most cases, the first line of a host file begins with a pound sign and contains comments about the file's columns. A pound sign may precede comments anywhere in the host file.

12

```
# IP address          host name               aliases

122.48.77.239         vivaldi.composers.com    vivaldi
122.48.77.240         brahms.composers.com     brahms
122.48.77.241         grainger.composers.com   grainger
122.48.77.242         dvorak.composers.com     dvorak
122.48.77.243         cpebach.composers.com    cpeb
122.48.77.244         jsbach.composers.com     jsb
```

Figure 12-3 A host file

On a UNIX-based computer, a host file is called "hosts" and is located in the /etc directory. On a Windows XP, NT, or 2000 computer, the file is also called "hosts" and is located in the *systemroot*\System32\Drivers\Etc directory, where *systemroot* is the directory in which the operating system is installed. If you are using a host file for name resolution on your network, you should not only master the syntax of this file, but you should also research the implications of using a static method of name resolution on your network. For example, every time you add a new host, you must modify each host file through a text-editing program. If any of the hosts' IP addresses change, you also have to make that change to every host file.

Domain Name System (DNS)

Using host files may be appropriate within a small organization whose IP addresses and host names do not regularly change. However, host files are not appropriate for any sizeable organization, much less for the Internet. Instead, a more automated solution has become mandatory. In the mid-1980s, Internet engineers devised a hierarchical way of identifying domain names and their addresses, called the Domain Name System (DNS). DNS relies on a database, which is distributed over 13 key computers, known as **root servers**, across the Internet. Because it is distributed, DNS will not fail catastrophically if one or a few computers go down.

As you have learned, every host is a member of a domain, or a group of computers that belong to the same organization and have part of their IP addresses in common. A domain is identified by its domain name. Usually, a domain name is associated with a company or other type of organization, such as a university, government organization, or military unit. For example, Cisco's domain name is cisco.com, and the FCC's domain name is fcc.gov. If you worked at the FCC and named your workstation (or host) "debs," your fully qualified host name would be "debs.fcc.gov." As you learned earlier, to be recognized on the Internet, a domain name must be registered with one of ICANN's accredited registrars.

Domain names reflect the hierarchical nature of DNS. In this scheme, each domain name contains a series of labels separated by periods. The last label in a domain name represents a **top-level domain (TLD)**, or the highest level in the DNS hierarchy. For example, in the *www.fcc.gov* domain, the TLD is "gov." A limited number of TLDs have been established, as shown in Table 12-1. The first eight TLDs listed in this table were established in the mid-1980s. In the past few years, organizations have appealed to ICANN to add the remaining seven TLDs. In addition to the TLDs listed in Table 12-1, each country has its own domain suffix, or country code TLD. For example, Canadian domains end with .ca and Japanese domains end in .jp.

Table 12-1 Top level domains

Top-Level Domain	Type of Organization
ARPA	Reverse lookup domain (special Internet function)
COM	Commercial
EDU	Educational
GOV	Government
ORG	Noncommercial organization (such as a nonprofit agency)
NET	Network (such as an ISP)
INT	International Treaty organization
MIL	U.S. Military Organization
BIZ	Businesses
INFO	Unrestricted use
AERO	Air-transport industry
COOP	Cooperatives
MUSEUM	Museums
NAME	Individuals
PRO	Professionals, such as doctors, lawyers, and engineers

After an organization reserves a domain name, the rest of the world's computers know to associate that domain name with that particular organization, and no other organization can legally use it (as long as the reserving organization pays the required annual registration fee to an ICANN-accredited registrar). For example, you might apply for the domain name called "YourName.com;" not only does the rest of the Internet associate that name with your machine, but also no other parties in the world can use "YourName.com" for their machines.

Name Servers and Space

Many name servers across the globe cooperate to keep track of IP addresses and their associated domain names. **Name space** refers to the database of Internet IP addresses and their associated names. Every name server holds a piece of the DNS name space. At the highest level in the hierarchy sit the root servers. A root server is a name server that is maintained by ICANN and that acts as the ultimate authority on how to contact the top-level domains, such as those ending with .com, .edu, .net, .us, and so on.

DNS name space is not a database that you can open and view, like an employer's database of its employees and their salary, performance, and contact information, for example. Rather, this abstract concept describes how the name servers of the world share DNS information. Pieces of it are tangible, however, and are stored on a name server in a **resource record**, which is a single record that describes one piece of information in the DNS database. For example, an **address resource record** is a type of resource record that maps the IP address of an Internet-connected device to its domain name. Resource records come in many different types, depending on their function.

You may wonder how DNS operates on a global scale when its information is distributed over many servers. To route traffic more efficiently, it is divided into three components: resolvers, name servers, and name space. **Resolvers** are any hosts on the Internet that need to look up domain name information and associate that information with an IP address. The resolver client is built into TCP/IP applications such as Telnet, HTTP, and FTP. For example, when you access the Web and point your browser to *www.cisco.com,* your workstation initiates a resolver to associate the host name *www.cisco.com* with the correct IP address. If you have connected to the site before, the information may exist in temporary memory and may be retrieved very quickly. Otherwise, the resolver service queries your machine's name server to find the IP address for *www.cisco.com.*

Name servers (also known as **DNS servers**) are servers that contain databases of names and their associated IP addresses. A name server supplies a resolver with the information it requires. If the name server cannot resolve the IP address, the query passes to a higher-level name server. For example, if you attempted to reach the *www.cisco.com* Web site from your office workstation, the first server that would attempt to provide your client with an IP address associated with that hostname would be your company's DNS server. If it did not have the information, it would pass the request to a higher-level name server on the Internet (for example, one operated by your company's ISP). If that name server could not accommodate your request, it would pass it to another name server. Each name server manages a group of devices, collectively known as a **zone**. In a small company, the DNS server's zone would include all the computers at the company and what version of DNS they are used with. Each resource record contains a name field to identify the domain name of the machine to which the record refers, a type field to identify the type of resource record involved, a class field to identify the class to which the record belongs (usually "IN" or "Internet"), a time to live field to identify how long the record should be saved in temporary memory, a data length field to identify how much data the record contains, and the actual record data. Approximately 20 types of resource records are currently used.

Each resource record type adheres to specific data field requirements, thus ensuring that any name server across the world can interpret it. For example, the data field of a simple network address record includes only the network address, whereas the data field of a mailbox information record includes the name of the mailbox responsible for error messages and the name of the mailbox responsible for mailing lists. In the following fictitious address resource record, "vivaldi.composers.com" is the host domain name, "IN" stands for the Internet record class, "A" identifies the record type as "address," and "122.48.77.239" is the host's IP address:

```
vivaldi.composers.com       IN      A       122.48.77.239
```

Now that you have learned the principles behind locating hosts on the Internet, you are ready to learn more about the technology behind Internet services, such as the World Wide Web, e-mail, and e-commerce, which are probably familiar to you.

INTERNET SERVICES

As the Internet has grown, so has the number of services it supplies, along with personal and professional reliance on those services. The following material describes how these popular services work. In addition, it introduces you to some services, such as Internet telephony, which are still in the development stage, but are expected to become just as popular as the older, more familiar services.

The Use of Ports

In Chapter 7's discussion of TCP segments, you learned that a port is the logical address on a host where an application makes itself available to incoming data. According to Internet standards, every TCP/IP process and service is associated with a port number. For example, 23 is the standard port number for Telnet, the terminal emulation service you learned about in Chapter 7. A Telnet request to a host with the IP address of 128.9.33.67 points to that IP address, but in addition, points to port 23 on that host. This can be represented as 128.9.33.67:23. Note that the port number is expressed as a number following a colon after the IP address.

The use of port numbers simplifies TCP/IP communications and ensures that data are transmitted to the correct application. When a client requests communications with a server and specifies port 23, for example, the server knows immediately that the client wants a Telnet session. No extra data exchange is necessary to define the session type, and the server can initiate the Telnet service without delay. The server will connect to the client's Telnet port and establish a virtual circuit.

As you know, TCP/IP services may use different Transport layer protocols, such as TCP or UDP. Client and server software agree on what Transport layer protocol they will use to exchange data via a service. If a service requires reliable data delivery, it will use TCP. For example, Telnet relies on TCP, a connection-oriented Transport layer protocol. Thus, you can say that Telnet uses TCP port 23. (Although UDP port 23 is also reserved as a Telnet port, because of its reliability requirement, the Telnet service conventionally uses TCP.) DHCP, on the other hand, relies on the connectionless, UDP protocol. UDP is useful when the efficiency and speed of data exchange is more important than its reliability. Although some services may use either TCP or UDP, most consistently rely on one of these protocols.

Port numbers can have any numeric value from 0 to 65536. Most software programs that use TCP/IP (for example, RealAudio, an application that allows a user to listen to music over the Web) choose their own port numbers by default. Port numbers in the range of 0 through 1023 are also known as **well known ports**, because they are the most familiar

12

and frequently used port numbers. These ports are typically reserved for use by servers or processes that require administrator access to a server. Table 12-2 lists the port numbers and Transport layer protocols for services discussed in earlier in the book and in this chapter. You can find a complete and current list of port number assignments on the Web at *www.iana.org/assignments/port-numbers.*

Table 12-2 Some common TCP/IP ports

Service	Port Number Assignment	Transport layer protocol used
DHCP	546 (client) and 547 (server)	UDP
DNS	53	TCP or UDP
FTP	20 (for data) 21 (for control)	TCP
HTTP	80	TCP
IMAP	585	TCP
Kerberos	88	TCP
NNTP	119	TCP
POP3	101	TCP
SMTP	25	TCP
SNMP	161	UDP
Telnet	23	TCP

The port numbers listed for services in Table 12-2 are defaults. That does not mean that a service will only work over one, specific port. In fact, port assignments can be flexible. Most servers maintain a text-based file of port numbers and their associated services. If necessary, a network administrator could change the default port number for the Telnet service on a server from 23 to 2330. Changing a default port number is rarely a good idea, because it violates the standard. For example, if you changed your server's Telnet port to 2330, a client attempting to connect to your server via port 23 would not be able to do so. Instead, the client would have to change its Telnet port to 2330 also. Some network administrators who are preoccupied with security may change their servers' port numbers in an attempt to confuse people who might attempt to access a server without permission.

Now that you understand how TCP/IP services use port numbers, you are ready to learn more about vital Internet services.

World Wide Web (WWW)

Earlier in this chapter, you were introduced to the World Wide Web (WWW, or the Web), a collection of Internet servers that follow specific protocols and methods for sorting and formatting data on the Internet. On the client side, access to the Web requires TCP/IP, a unique IP address, a connection to the Internet, and a browser. On the server side, a

Web site requires TCP/IP, a connection to DNS servers, routers, Web server software, and a connection to the Internet. A Web site must also have an authorized, registered domain name in order to be found by Web browsers.

Hypertext Transfer Protocol (HTTP) and Hypertext Markup Language (HTML)

To interpret data, the Web relies on Hypertext Transfer Protocol (HTTP). As you learned in Chapter 7, HTTP is a protocol that operates in the Application layer of the TCP/IP model. You can think of it as the language that Web clients and servers use to communicate. When you type the address of a Web page in your Web browser's address field, HTTP transports the information about your request to the Web server on the server's port 80, using the TCP protocol. HTTP then interprets your request and returns the Web server's information to you in **Hypertext Markup Language (HTML)**, the Web document formatting language. The **World Wide Web Consortium (W3C)**, a standards organization for Web browsers and languages, developed HTML in 1991 in an effort to make the volumes of information on the Internet more easily accessible. To represent information in a particular manner, HTML uses **tags**, or formatting indicators. For example, to represent text in italics, the "<I>" opener tag precedes the text, and the "</I>" closing tag follows the text. Without formatting tags, a Web browser simply passes along a document as a string of characters—even if the document contains graphics. A special type of HTML tag is the **anchor**, a tag that formats information on a Web page as a hyperlink (or redirection) to another area of the Web page or to another Web page. Although HTML makes the hyperlink available, after clicking on a hyperlink, HTTP accomplishes the connection to those links. Figure 12-4 depicts part of a simple Web page with its HTML codes and then, how it appears in a Web browser.

12

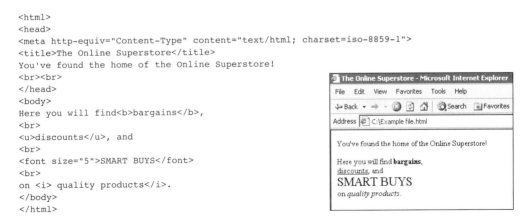

```
<html>
<head>
<meta http-equiv="Content-Type" content="text/html; charset=iso-8859-1">
<title>The Online Superstore</title>
You've found the home of the Online Superstore!
<br><br>
</head>
<body>
Here you will find<b>bargains</b>,
<br>
<u>discounts</u>, and
<br>
<font size="5">SMART BUYS</font>
<br>
on <i> quality products</i>.
</body>
</html>
```

Figure 12-4   Web page in HTML and as it appears in a browser

If you plan to specialize in Web page development or hosting, you should be completely familiar with HTML and HTTP. A thorough exploration of these technical specifications is beyond the scope of this book; however, many excellent references are available in print or on the Web. For example, *Shelly Cashman HTML Comprehensive Concepts & Techniques*, published by Course Technology, is an excellent resource for Web page development using HTML.

As the Internet has matured, both HTTP and HTML have undergone multiple revisions. HTTP/0.9, the original version of HTTP, was released in 1990. This version provided only the simplest means of transferring data over the Internet. Since then, HTTP has been greatly improved to make Web client/server connections more efficient, reliable, and secure. For example, HTTP 1.1, the current version of HTTP, allows servers to transmit multiple objects, such as text and graphics, over a single TCP connection using longer packets. It also allows a client to save Web pages via caching and to compare the saved pages with requested pages. If the two are identical, the Web browser uses the cached copy of the page to save bandwidth and time.

EXtensible Markup Language (XML) and EXtensible Hypertext Markup Language (XHTML)

A successor to HTML is the **eXtensible Markup Language (XML)**. XML is a markup (or formatting) language that does not rely on predefined tags, but rather allows a designer to create her own formatting definitions and embed those definitions in a document. You can think of XML as not truly its own language, but rather a method for defining a language. As a result, an XML document can represent information in a more customized manner than an HTML document. For example, suppose you are the Webmaster for a local school district that posts its lunch menus on the Web. On the lunch menu, your school lists the entrée, side dish, and dessert offered at lunch each day. In HTML, you could create a table that lists the entrée, side dish, and dessert in three separate rows with a column for each day of the week. However, each week you would need to update the text in each cell of that table and repost the menu page to the Web server. In XML, you could define elements—or a named set of data and a method of interpreting this data—for each portion of the Web page: Monday_entrée, Monday_sidedish, Monday_dessert, and so on. In the XML document, these elements would not only be defined, but their placement and formatting could also be specified at the top of the document. Later in the document, you could insert the element where you wanted the lunch menu items to appear. Further, you could define the elements to point to a database of lunch items. Because this database is centralized and directly accessible to only privileged users, you could manage it more easily than the menu Web page. Thus, the Web page does not have to be updated each time the lunch menu changes. This is only a small, simple example of using XML. In fact, XML can be used for programming different applications, not simply Web pages. The requirement of defining codes for each set of documents makes XML more complex than HTML, but also more flexible and sophisticated.

To simplify and standardize the use of XML for Web page creation, the W3C released the **eXtensible Hypertext Markup Language (XHTML)**. XHTML is the latest version of the Hypertext Markup Language, also known as HTML 4.0, written to meet XML specifications. In other words, XHTML is a markup language that has already used XML to define standard elements and their formatting methods. Users familiar with previous versions of HTML will find XHTML much more user friendly than XML.

You can view a Web page's HTML or XHTML coding from Internet Explorer by choosing View from the browser's menu bar, then clicking Source. In Netscape Navigator, choose View from the browser's menu bar, then click Page Source. Much of the time, this reveals information on how the Web page is formatted. However, some organizations mask Web page coding by pointing to another file or script that is not readily accessible.

Uniform Resource Locators (URLs)

You have learned that Web servers and clients transmit content through HTTP and HTML or XHTML. In addition, every Web page is identified by a **Uniform Resource Locator (URL)** that specifies the service it uses, its server's fully qualified host name, and its HTML or XHTML page or script name. For example, a valid URL is *http://www.gao.gov/reports.htm*, where "http" is the service used by the page, "www" is the server's host name (or an alias for the host name), "gao.gov" is the domain name, and "reports.htm" is the content page.

You have already learned how host names and domain names can differ. These differences are reflected in a resource's URL. For example, the URL for a military unit contains the ".mil" TLD, as in the United States Department of Defense Web site: *http://www.defenselink.mil/*. The URL for the Modern Art Museum (MoMA) in New York, on the other hand, is *http://nyc.moma.museum/*, and uses the ".museum" TLD. Besides the identification of a host and domain name, URLs also differ according to the service or protocol used. In other words, not all URLs specify the HTTP protocol. For example, the URL *ftp://ftp.netscape.com/pub* points to a directory on Netscape's FTP server that makes files available for the public to download. Finally, URLs differ according to the type of resource they point to. For example, depending on how a page is encoded, it may end with a .html, .xml, or .xhtml suffix. If a URL does not specify the page name, the Web server displays a default page, called index.html (or index.htm) on most systems.

Notice that the previous examples of URLs do not specify a port number after the server's fully qualified host name. If a port number is not identified, the client and server assume that the default port number is used for exchanging data. However, if a network administrator has used a port other than the default, the URL specified by a client must include the port number. For example, suppose you are developing a new Web server for your company, Low Tennis Nets, which has the domain name of "lowtennisnets.com." You assign the Web server a host name of "web1." You want to be

12

able to access and test this Web server from anywhere, so you make it available to the Internet. Although it doesn't have any confidential information on it, you would prefer that no one else access the Web site for the time being. Therefore, you re-assign the HTTP service for your development Web server to port 9999. When you want to connect to the Web server, you must use the following URL: *http://web1.lowtennisnets.com:9999*. Users who try to connect to *http://web1.lowtennisnets.com* will receive an error message or a blank page, depending on how you configured the Web server software. Figure 12-5 illustrates the makeup of different URLs.

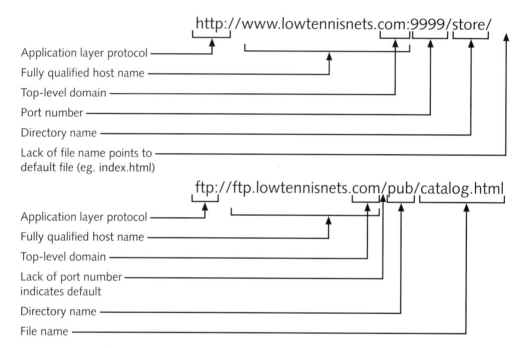

Figure 12-5 Elements of two URLs

E-mail

E-mail was one of the first uses of the Internet and has always been the most popular Internet service. Although several different e-mail client and mail server software packages are available today, all work according to the same technical principles.

Simple Mail Transfer Protocol (SMTP)

In Chapter 3, you learned that the Simple Mail Transfer Protocol (SMTP) is responsible for moving messages from one e-mail server to another over TCP/IP-based networks. SMTP operates in the Application layer of the TCP/IP model and relies on TCP at the Transport layer. It operates from TCP port 25. (That is, requests to receive mail and send mail go through port 25 on the SMTP server.) SMTP, which provides the basis for Internet e-mail service, relies on higher-level programs for its instructions. Although SMTP comes with a set of human-readable commands that you could conceivably use to transport mail from machine to machine, this method would be laborious, slow, and error-prone. Instead, other services, such as the UNIX sendmail software, provide more friendly and sophisticated mail interfaces that rely on SMTP as their means of transport.

SMTP is a simple subprotocol, incapable of doing anything more than transporting mail or holding it in a queue. In the post office analogy of data communications, SMTP is like the mail carrier who picks up his day's mail load at the post office and delivers it to the homes on his route. The mail carrier does not worry about where the mail is stored overnight or how it gets from another city's post office to his post office. If a piece of mail is undeliverable, he simply holds onto it; the mail carrier does not attempt to figure out what went wrong. In Internet e-mail transmission, higher-level mail protocols, such as POP and IMAP, which are discussed in the next two sections, take care of these functions.

When you configure clients to use Internet e-mail, you need to identify the user's SMTP server. (Sometimes, this server is called the mail server.) Each e-mail program specifies this setting in a different place, though most commonly in the Mail Preferences section. Assuming your client uses DNS for name resolution, you do not have to identify the IP address of the SMTP server—only the name. For example, if a user's e-mail address is jdoe@postoffice.com, his SMTP server is probably called "postoffice.com." You do not have to specify the TCP/IP port number used by SMTP, because both the client workstation and the server assume that SMTP requests and responses flow through TCP port 25.

Post Office Protocol (POP)

The **Post Office Protocol (POP)** is a protocol used to retrieve messages from a mail server. It belongs to the Application layer of the TCP/IP model and relies on SMTP. With POP, mail is delivered and stored on a mail server until a user connects—via an e-mail client—to the server to retrieve her messages. As the user retrieves her messages, the messages are downloaded to her workstation. After they are downloaded, the messages are typically deleted from the mail server. Both SMTP and a service such as POP are necessary for a mail server to receive, store, and forward messages and for a mail client to receive them.

Users need an SMTP-compliant mail program to connect to their POP server and download mail from storage. POP does not allow users to store mail on the server after they download it, which can create a problem for users who move from machine to machine. For example, suppose you are the mail system administrator for a call center. Suppose, also that each computer station is used by six different customer service representatives: one user during each of the three shifts on weekdays and one user during each of the three shifts on weekends. You want to allow all customer service representatives to pick up e-mail as they work. If your mail server uses POP, you would need to create six different mailboxes in the e-mail client and six different message storage areas on the hard disk. But what happens if a supervisor, who doesn't normally work at the customer service workstations, needs to fill in for an absent customer service representative one afternoon? With POP, you would have to create yet another area for her mail on the customer service representative's workstation. When the supervisor returns to her computer, however, her mail would not be accessible because it would have been saved on a different PC. Because this was such a significant limitation for POP, programmers and system administrators devised options for circumventing this problem.

One solution is to store users' mail on a LAN server. Another solution is to provide users with Web browser interfaces to the mail server, thus allowing them to read messages without downloading them. However, a more thorough solution has been provided by a new, more sophisticated e-mail protocol called IMAP, described in the next section.

You may have noticed that the acronym "POP" has multiple meanings in the world of telecommunications. In earlier discussions of telecommunications carriers and the PSTN, POP stood for a point of presence. In this chapter's discussion of Internet e-mail, POP stands for Post Office Protocol. Often, the Post Office Protocol is identified with its version number as well—for example, POP2 or POP3.

Internet Mail Access Protocol (IMAP)

The **Internet Mail Access Protocol (IMAP)** is another mail storage and manipulation protocol that also depends on SMTP's transport system. IMAP was developed as a more sophisticated alternative to POP. The most current version of IMAP is version 4 (IMAP4). IMAP4 can replace POP without the user having to change e-mail programs. The single biggest advantage IMAP4 has over POP relates to the fact that IMAP4 allows users to store messages on the mail server, rather than always having to download them to the local machine. This feature benefits users who move from workstation to workstation. In addition, IMAP4 provides the following features:

- Users can retrieve all or only a portion of any mail message. The remainder can be left on the mail server. This feature benefits users who move from machine to machine and users who have slow connections to the network or minimal free hard disk space.

- Users can review their messages and delete them while the messages remain on the server. This feature preserves network bandwidth, especially when the messages are long or contain attached files, because the data need not travel over the wire from the server to the client's workstation. For users with a slow modem connection, deleting messages without having to download them represents a major advantage over POP.

- Users can create sophisticated methods of organizing messages on the server. A user might, for example, build a system of folders to contain messages with similar content. Also, a user might search through all of the messages for only those that contain one particular keyword or subject line.

- Users can share a mailbox in a central location. For example, if several maintenance personnel who use different PCs need to receive the same messages from the Facilities Department head but do not need e-mail for any other purpose, they can all log on with the same ID and share the same mailbox on the server. If POP were used in this situation, only one maintenance staff member could read the message; she would then have to forward or copy it to her colleagues.

- IMAP4 can provide better security than POP because it supports authentication. Security is an increasing concern for network managers as more organizations connect to the public Internet.

Although IMAP provides significant advantages over POP, it also comes with a few disadvantages. For instance, IMAP servers require more storage space and usually more processing resources than POP servers do. By extension, network administrators must keep a closer watch on IMAP servers to ensure that users are not consuming more than their fair share of space on the server. By installing a disk quota manager, a program that automatically ensures clients do not exceed a certain amount of disk space when storing messages, this drawback is simple to overcome. A more significant drawback to using IMAP is that, if the IMAP server fails, users cannot access the mail left there. (IMAP does allow users to download messages to their own PCs, however.)

Until recently, another consideration was that most popular e-mail programs were designed for use with POP servers only. This standard is changing, however, and you should have no difficulty obtaining mail programs that use IMAP4. For example, Eudora Pro, GroupWise, Lotus Notes, Netscape, and Microsoft Outlook all support IMAP4. However, not all ISPs have configured their mail servers to use IMAP.

12

File Transfer Protocol (FTP)

In Chapter 7, you learned that the File Transfer Protocol (FTP) manages file transfers between TCP/IP hosts. The FTP service depends on an FTP server that is always waiting for requests. After a client connects to the FTP server, FTP data is exchanged via TCP using port 20. FTP commands are sent and received through TCP port 21. FTP belongs to the Application layer of the TCP/IP model.

Before the Web provided a friendlier interface for transferring files, FTP commands (typed at the command prompt) were regularly used to exchange data between machines. FTP commands still work from the operating system's command prompt—that is, FTP does not require using browser software or special client software. As a telecommunications professional, you may need to use these commands to download software, such as a new version of a Web browser or a client software update for your networked workstation, from Internet hosts. To do so, you must first start the FTP utility by typing `ftp` at the OS command prompt. The result is an FTP command prompt that appears as follows: `FTP>`. After you have invoked the FTP utility, you can use the open command to connect to an FTP host. For example, to connect to Cisco's FTP server, type `open ftp.cisco.com` at the FTP prompt. However, these two operations—starting FTP and connecting to a host—can be accomplished more simply through a single FTP command. For example, to FTP to Cisco's FTP server from an OS prompt, you could type `ftp ftp.cisco.com`, then press Enter to make the connection.

If the host is running, it responds with a greeting and a request for you to log on, as shown in Figure 12-6. Many FTP hosts, especially those whose purpose is to provide software updates, accept anonymous logons. This means that when prompted for a user name, you need only type the word `anonymous` (in all lowercase letters). When prompted for a password on an anonymous FTP site, you can usually enter your e-mail address, or sometimes, any string of characters. The host's logon screen should indicate whether this is acceptable. On the other hand, if you are logging on to a private FTP site, you must obtain a valid user name and password from the site's network administrator to make a successful connection.

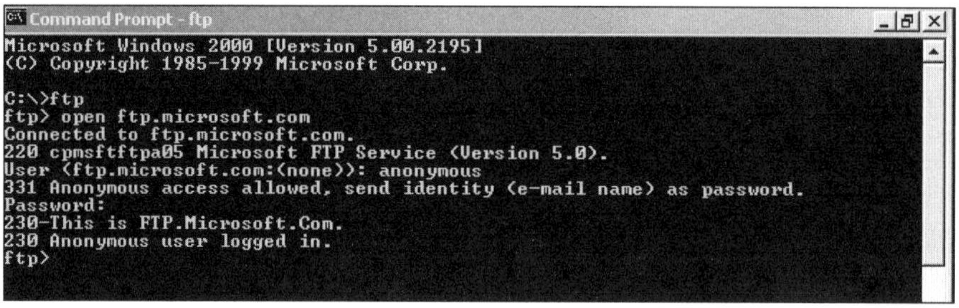

```
Command Prompt - ftp                                          _ |8|X|
Microsoft Windows 2000 [Version 5.00.2195]
(C) Copyright 1985-1999 Microsoft Corp.

C:\>ftp
ftp> open ftp.microsoft.com
Connected to ftp.microsoft.com.
220 cpmsftftpa05 Microsoft FTP Service (Version 5.0).
User (ftp.microsoft.com:(none)): anonymous
331 Anonymous access allowed, send identity (e-mail name) as password.
Password:
230-This is FTP.Microsoft.Com.
230 Anonymous user logged in.
ftp>
```

Figure 12-6   FTP logon screen

After you have successfully connected to a host, additional commands allow you to manage the connection and manipulate files. For example, after you have connected to Cisco's FTP site, you could type: `cd pub` to change your working directory to the "public" directory. Once in that directory, you could download a file by typing: `get XXX`, where "XXX" is the name of the file you want to download. To terminate the connection, simply type `quit`.

Many other FTP commands are available. The following list summarizes a handful of the most common commands and their syntax. To learn more about these and other FTP commands, type `help` after starting the FTP utility.

- `ascii`—Sets the file transfer mode to "ASCII." Most FTP hosts store two types of files: ASCII and binary. Text files are typically ASCII-based and contain formatting characters, such as carriage returns. Binary files (for example, executable programs) typically contain no formatting characters. Before downloading files from an FTP host, you must understand what type of file you are downloading. If you download a file while in the wrong mode (ASCII if the file is binary or vice versa), your file appears as gibberish when you open it. If the file you want to download is an ASCII file, type `ascii` at the FTP prompt and press Enter before starting your file transfer.

- `binary`—Sets the file transfer mode to "binary." If the file you want to download from an FTP is binary (for example, an executable program or a compressed software upgrade), type `binary` at the FTP prompt and press Enter before starting your file transfer.

- `cd`—Changes your working directory on the host machine. For example, if you have logged on to the Cisco FTP site, you can type `cd pub` to switch to the "pub" directory.

- `delete`—Deletes a file on the host machine (provided you have permissions to do so).

- `get`—Transfers a file from the host machine to the client. For example, to transfer the file called program.exe from the host to your workstation, you can type: `get program.exe`. Unless you specify a target directory and file name, the file is saved to your hard disk in the directory from where you started the FTP utility. Therefore, if you want to save the program.exe file to your C:\download\directory, type:

```
get program.exe "c:\download\"
```

(Make sure to include the quotation marks.)

- `help`—Provides a list of commands when issued from the FTP prompt. When used in conjunction with a command, it provides information on the purpose of that command. For example, after typing `help ls`, you learn that the `ls` command lists the contents of a remote directory.

- `ls`—Lists the contents of the directory on the host where you are currently located.

- `mkdir`—Creates a new directory on the FTP host (provided you have permissions to do so).

- `open`—Creates a connection with an FTP host.

- `put`—Transfers a file from your workstation to the FTP host.

- `quit`—Terminates your FTP connection and closes the FTP utility.

The advent of browsers and specialized FTP client software has rendered this command-line method of FTPing files less common. What's more, modern FTP programs provide graphical interfaces for transferring files from a server to a client. Examples of popular, inexpensive (if not free) FTP clients include MacFTP, WS-FTP, CuteFTP, and FTP Voyager. As mentioned earlier, you can also accomplish FTP file transfers directly from a modern Web browser, such as Internet Explorer or Netscape Communicator. To do this, you need only point to a valid a URL that begins with ftp://, which, as you learned earlier, indicates that data should be exchanged using the FTP protocol.

12

From there, you can navigate directories and exchange files just as you do on your desktop OS.

Newsgroups

Newsgroups are similar to e-mail, in that they provide a means of conveying messages; they differ from e-mail in that they are distributed to a wide group of users at once rather than from one user to another. Newsgroups have been formed to discuss every conceivable topic, such as political issues, professional affiliations, entertainment interests, or sports clubs. To belong to a newsgroup, a user subscribes to the server that hosts the newsgroup. From that point forward, the user receives all messages that other newsgroup members post with the newsgroup list as their mail-to address.

Newsgroups require news servers and, on the client side, e-mail programs capable of reading newsgroups or special newsgroup reading software. Rather than using SMTP, as e-mail does, newsgroup messages are transported by the **Network News Transfer Protocol (NNTP)**. NNTP is a protocol that operates via TCP port 119. It supports the process of reading newsgroup messages, posting new messages, and transferring news files between news servers. News servers are organized hierarchically, similar to DNS servers. ISPs, for example, run news servers that use a larger ISP's or an NSP's news server to communicate with other NSP news servers.

E-commerce

One of the fastest growing sectors of the Internet is electronic commerce, or e-commerce. The term **e-commerce** refers to a means of conducting business over the Internet—be it in retail, banking, stock trading, consulting, or training. Any buying and selling of products or services that occurs over the Internet belongs in the e-commerce category. The first industries to take advantage of e-commerce were retail and finance. In the past five years, more and more businesses have realized that e-commerce is critical to their success. Indeed, the number of online purchases has grown exponentially each year since 1996. You have probably used the Web to purchase books, music, clothes, or even furniture.

If you have an interest in Internet technologies, you may want to consider specializing in e-commerce. E-commerce involves customized HTML scripting, software programming, multimedia, graphics, networking, and security skills. Because it often relies on credit card purchases or money transfers over the Internet, security is a significant concern. Web security is becoming more sophisticated to counter hackers who find new ways to break into systems. Personal identification numbers and file encryption, for example, can no longer guarantee that others cannot pick up information in transit. Someday, we may use retinal patterns or fingerprints to provide secure access to Web sites. Chapter 13 discusses network security in more detail.

Next, you are introduced to another advanced service that can run over the Internet, Voice over IP.

Internet Telephony

Throughout this book, you have learned how voice signals are carried over the PSTN. You have also learned that voice signals can be analog (for example, on a traditional telephone line) or digital (for example, when multiplexed over a T-1). But thus far, each voice transmission method you have learned about has relied on circuit switching, in which a communications channel is dedicated to the exchange of signals between two endpoints for as long as a call lasts. Compared with packet switching, circuit switching is an inefficient use of available bandwidth. Telecommunications engineers have devised a way to break voice signals into packets and transmit them over data networks using TCP/IP. This service is called **Voice over IP** (**VoIP**—pronounced "voyp"), or IP telephony.

When VoIP is carried over the Internet, it is known as **Internet telephony**. Internet telephony was introduced in 1995 and has continued evolving, with the result being improved sound quality, efficiency, and availability. But not all VoIP calls are carried over the Internet. In fact, VoIP over private data connections is a very effective and economical method of completing calls between two locations within an organization. In addition, because the line is private, its congestion can be easily controlled, thus resulting in better sound quality than the Internet can provide. But given the Internet's breadth and low cost, it is appealing to consider the Internet for carrying conversations that we currently transmit over the PSTN.

The purpose of this section is simply to introduce you to services, such as IP telephony, that are available over the Internet. Chapter 14 describes IP telephony and other IP-based voice, messaging, and video services in depth. Next, you learn about intranets and extranets, networks that, while not technically Internet services, are built on Internet technology.

12

Intranets and Extranets

All the TCP/IP and Internet services you have learned about can run on private networks as well as the (public) Internet. In other words, a network administrator can establish an HTTP server in an organization to supply "Web" pages only to the employees of that organization. (Technically, because the Web is defined as a collection of Internet-based computers, a private HTTP server is not a Web server. However, employees who use such a server probably refer to it as a Web server.) The HTTP server need not be available to outside, Internet users. In fact, the HTTP server does not even have to be connected to the Internet. A network or part of a network that uses Internet-like services and protocols to exchange information within an enterprise is known as an **intranet**. In addition to supplying HTTP-accessible documents, intranets are used for e-mail, file sharing, document management (for example, indexing several versions of documents), and collaboration (for example, allowing multiple employees to review and modify messages and files pertaining to a particular project). Intranets may also be used for more advanced services such as IP telephony. The flexible, open nature of services and protocols that developed with the Internet and made it popular also makes these services and protocols well-suited to private networks.

An intranet is defined by its boundaries—that is, by the fact that it is contained within a LAN. A network that uses Internet-like services and protocols to exchange information over a broad geographical area (or a WAN) is known as an **extranet**. Extranets provide the same features and advantages as intranets, but on a larger scale. As with any WAN, an extranet may encompass dedicated connections to multiple offices within a company, for example, or dial-up connections for company employees at home or on the road. Or an extranet may make one company's private resources available to another company. For example, a furniture manufacturer in Michigan might open its extranet to a lumber supplier in Washington, so that the lumber company can view the furniture company's requirements for grades and types of wood used in different types of furniture. The furniture company could use the same extranet to accept bids from multiple lumber suppliers.

As with other types of WANs, extranets require added security measures to prevent unauthorized access to restricted information.

Both intranets and extranets are private; that is, they are only accessible to authorized users. Yet, they are often accessible via the Web. For example, a large company might decide to supply its employee handbook via HTML-formatted pages. The network administrator could install an HTTP server at the company's headquarters. The HTTP server would store HTML-encoded files that compose the employee handbook. These files require a user to log on to the HTTP server to gain access. If an employee wants to read about pension benefits while at home, she could connect to the Internet using her home ISP, then type the URL of her company's employee handbook in her browser. The browser directs her to the company's HTTP server, which prompts the employee for a user name and password.

TCP/IP UTILITIES

If your career in telecommunications leads you to network administration or even frequent Internet use, you will sometimes need to assess your Internet connectivity status. Luckily, several utilities are available to help you manage TCP/IP services on a computer. Each utility is built into the TCP/IP suite that comes with the operating system on which it runs. Some utilities can be run from a graphical interface, whereas others are always entered at a command prompt. A utility may be run with its default parameters, or you may choose to tailor the utility's output by using a **switch**, a character or combination of characters that follows a command and instructs the command to format its results in a specific way. For example, if you type the command `netstat` and press Enter, the resulting output lists all the TCP connections to your computer. If you type `netstat -a`, however, the resulting output lists all TCP/IP connections, whether they are UDP- or TCP-reliant.

As described in the following sections, most utilities work identically no matter what operating system you use. However, the syntax for some commands differs slightly depending on whether your client runs Microsoft Windows or a version of UNIX.

Ipconfig

Ipconfig is the TCP/IP administration utility for use with Windows NT, 2000, and XP operating systems. If your computer uses one of these operating systems, you will probably use this tool often to check the computer's TCP/IP configuration. Ipconfig provides information about a NIC's IP address, subnet mask, and default gateway. You may recall using this utility to determine the TCP/IP attributes for the computer in which you installed a NIC in a Hands-on Project in Chapter 7.

In addition to being used alone to list information about the TCP/IP configuration, ipconfig can be used with switches to manage a computer's TCP/IP settings. For example, if you want to view complete information about your TCP/IP settings, including your MAC address, when your DHCP lease expires, the address of your WINS server, and so on, you could type: `ipconfig /all`. Note that the syntax of this command differs slightly from other TCP/IP utilities described later in this section. With ipconfig, a forward slash (/) precedes the command switches, rather than a hyphen.

To use the ipconfig utility from a Windows 2000 computer, click Start, point to Programs, point to Accessories, and then click Command Prompt. (From a Windows XP computer, click Start, point to All Programs, point to Accessories, and then click Command Prompt.) The Command Prompt window opens.

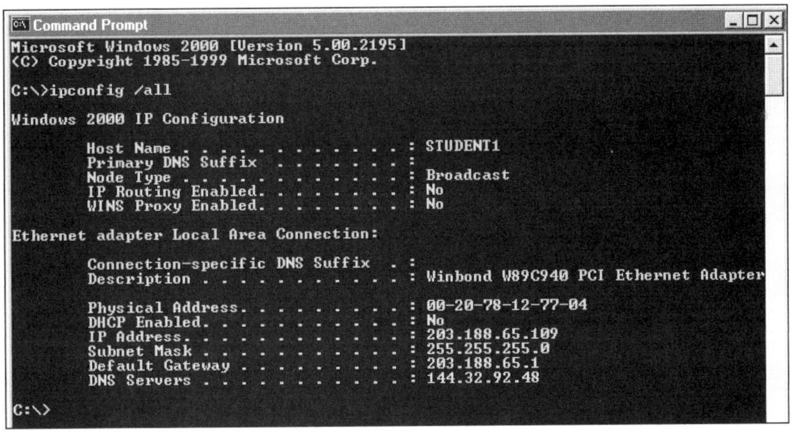

```
Command Prompt
Microsoft Windows 2000 [Version 5.00.2195]
(C) Copyright 1985-1999 Microsoft Corp.

C:\>ipconfig /all

Windows 2000 IP Configuration

        Host Name . . . . . . . . . . . . : STUDENT1
        Primary DNS Suffix  . . . . . . . :
        Node Type . . . . . . . . . . . . : Broadcast
        IP Routing Enabled. . . . . . . . : No
        WINS Proxy Enabled. . . . . . . . : No

Ethernet adapter Local Area Connection:

        Connection-specific DNS Suffix  . :
        Description . . . . . . . . . . . : Winbond W89C940 PCI Ethernet Adapter
        Physical Address. . . . . . . . . : 00-20-78-12-77-04
        DHCP Enabled. . . . . . . . . . . : No
        IP Address. . . . . . . . . . . . : 203.188.65.109
        Subnet Mask . . . . . . . . . . . : 255.255.255.0
        Default Gateway . . . . . . . . . : 203.188.65.1
        DNS Servers . . . . . . . . . . . : 144.32.92.48

C:\>
```

Figure 12-7   Output of an `ipconfig` command on a Windows 2000 workstation

The following list describes some popular switches that can be used with the `ipconfig` command:

- ?—Displays a list of switches available for use with the ipconfig command.

- /all—Displays complete TCP/IP configuration information for each network interface on that device.

12

- /release—Releases DHCP-assigned addresses for all of the device's network interfaces.

- /renew—Renews DHCP-assigned addresses for all of the device's network interfaces.

Next, you learn about ifconfig, the UNIX equivalent of Windows' ipconfig.

> In Windows 95 and 98, the utility that reveals TCP/IP configuration information and allows a user to release and renew DHCP assigned addresses is **winipcfg**.

Ifconfig

Ifconfig is the TCP/IP configuration and management utility used on UNIX systems. As with ipconfig on Windows NT, 2000, and XP systems, ifconfig enables you to modify TCP/IP settings for a network interface, release and renew DHCP-assigned addresses, or simply check the status of your machine's TCP/IP settings. Ifconfig is also a utility that runs when a UNIX system starts to establish the TCP/IP configuration for that system.

As with the other operating systems' TCP/IP configuration utilities, ifconfig can be used alone, or it can be used with switches to reveal more customized information. For example, if you want to view the TCP/IP information associated with every interface on a device, type: **ifconfig -a**. The output resembles the output shown in Figure 12-8. Notice that the syntax of the **ifconfig** command uses a hyphen (-) before some of the switches and no preceding character for other switches. Following are a few of the popular switches you may use with ifconfig:

- **-a**—Applies the command to all interfaces on a device; can be used with other switches.

- **down**—Marks the interface as unavailable to the network.

- **up**—Reinitializes the interface after it has been taken "down," so that it is once again available to the network.

```
% ifconfig -a
eth0      Link encap:Ethernet   HWaddr 00:10:A4:B6:24:82
          inet addr:10.1.1.10  Bcast:10.1.1.255  Mask:255.255.255.0
          UP BROADCAST RUNNING MULTICAST  MTU:1500  Metric:1
          RX packets:38130 errors:1 dropped:0 overruns:0 frame:0
          TX packets:36103 errors:0 dropped:0 overruns:0 carrier:0
          collisions:0 txqueuelen:100
          RX bytes:32055118 (30.5 Mb)  TX bytes:3424759 (3.2 Mb)
          Interrupt:11 Base address:0x200

lo        Link encap:Local Loopback
          inet addr:127.0.0.1  Mask:255.0.0.0
          UP LOOPBACK RUNNING  MTU:16436  Metric:1
          RX packets:374 errors:0 dropped:0 overruns:0 frame:0
          TX packets:374 errors:0 dropped:0 overruns:0 carrier:0
          collisions:0 txqueuelen:0
          RX bytes:29705 (29.0 Kb)  TX bytes:29705 (29.0 Kb)
%
```

Figure 12-8   Detailed information available through ifconfig

Note Other ifconfig switches, such as those that apply to DHCP settings, vary according to the type and version of the UNIX operating system you use. Refer to your operating system's help manual (or man pages) for more information.

Ping

By completing the Hands-on Projects at the end of Chapters 7 and 10, you gained some experience using the Packet Internet Groper (PING) utility. PING can verify that TCP/IP is installed, bound to the NIC, configured correctly, and communicating with the network. It is often employed simply to determine whether a host is responding (or "up"). PING relies on the **Internet Control Message Protocol (ICMP)**, a TCP/IP protocol that notifies the sender that something has gone wrong in the transmission process and that packets were not delivered. Using ICMP, PING sends echo request and echo reply messages that determine the validity of an IP address. These two types of messages work much in the same way that sonar operates. First, a signal, called an **echo request**, is sent out to another computer. The other computer then rebroadcasts the signal, in the form of an **echo reply**, to the sender.

You can ping either an IP address or a host name. For example, to determine whether the *www.course.com* site is responding, you could type: `ping www.course.com` and press Enter. Alternatively, you could type: `ping 198.80.146.30` (the site's IP address) and press Enter. If the site is operating correctly, you receive a response that includes multiple replies from that host. If the site is not operating correctly, you receive a response indicating that the request timed out or that the host was not found. Figure 12-9 gives examples of successful and unsuccessful PING commands on a Windows-based computer.

PING is helpful in diagnosing local connectivity problems, too. By pinging the loop-back address, 127.0.0.1, you can determine whether your workstation's TCP/IP services are running. The loopback address automatically transmits a message back to the sending computer—that is, the message "loops back" to the sender. By pinging a host on another subnet, you can determine whether the problem lies with your Internet gateway or DNS server.

12

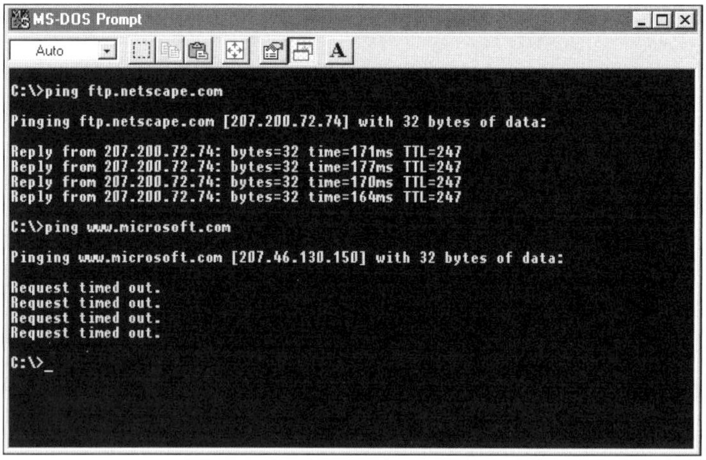

```
MS-DOS Prompt                                    _ □ ×

 Auto       ▼   □ ▦ ▧   ▣   ▧▧   A

C:\>ping ftp.netscape.com

Pinging ftp.netscape.com [207.200.72.74] with 32 bytes of data:

Reply from 207.200.72.74: bytes=32 time=171ms TTL=247
Reply from 207.200.72.74: bytes=32 time=177ms TTL=247
Reply from 207.200.72.74: bytes=32 time=170ms TTL=247
Reply from 207.200.72.74: bytes=32 time=164ms TTL=247

C:\>ping www.microsoft.com

Pinging www.microsoft.com [207.46.130.150] with 32 bytes of data:

Request timed out.
Request timed out.
Request timed out.
Request timed out.

C:\>_
```

Figure 12-9   Example of a successful and an unsuccessful PING commands

For example, suppose that you have just installed a new workstation at your desk and discover that you cannot access the Web. The first test you should perform is pinging the loopback address. If that test is successful, then you know that your workstation's TCP/IP services are installed and operating correctly. Next, you might try pinging the machine belonging to a colleague next to you. If you receive a positive response, you know that your network connection is working. You should then try pinging a machine on another subnet that you know is connected to the network—for example, a computer in the IT Department. If this test is successful, you should try pinging a destination on the Internet. If you can ping an IP address within your organization, but cannot ping an IP address outside your organization, you can safely conclude that you do not have the correct gateway or DNS settings in your TCP/IP configuration or that your organization's gateway is malfunctioning.

As with other TCP/IP commands, PING can be used with a number of different switches. A ping command begins with the word "ping" followed by a hyphen (-) and a switch, followed by a variable pertaining to that switch. For example, if you want to ping Course Technology's Web site with only two echo requests (rather than the standard four that are sent, by default, from a Windows-based computer), you could type the following command: `ping -n 2 www.course.com`. (Unless otherwise instructed, UNIX-based computers continue pinging the host until the user stops the ping process by pressing Ctrl+Z.) The following list describes some of the most common switches used with the PING utility:

- `-?`—Displays the help text for the PING command, including its syntax and a full list of switches.

- `-a`—When used with an IP address, resolves the address to a host name.

- `-n`—Allows you to specify a number of echo requests to send.

- -r—When used with a number from 1 to 9, displays the route taken during ping hops.

- -w—Limits the time to wait for each echo response to a specific number of milliseconds (requires the specification of the number of milliseconds to wait).

Traceroute

Like the PING utility, the **traceroute** command (also known as **tracert** on Windows systems) also uses ICMP. However, traceroute provides more detailed route information than PING. It uses ICMP to trace the path from one host to another, identifying all intermediate hops between the two hosts. This utility is useful for determining router or network connectivity problems.

To find the route, traceroute transmits a series of UDP datagrams to a specified destination, using either the IP address or the host name to identify the destination. The first three datagrams that traceroute transmits have their TTL (time to live) set to 1. Because the TTL determines how many more network hops a datagram can make, datagrams with a TTL of 1 expire as they hit the first router. When they expire, they are returned to the source—in this case, the node that began the traceroute. In this way, traceroute obtains the identity of the first router. After it learns about the first router in the path, traceroute transmits a series of datagrams with a TTL of 2. The process continues for the next router in the path, and then the third, fourth, and so on, until the destination node is reached. Traceroute also returns the amount of time it took for the datagrams to reach each router in the path.

You can infer from traceroute's method and output that this utility can help diagnose network congestion or network failures. Traceroute is not foolproof, however. In fact, its results can be misleading, because traceroute cannot detect router configuration problems or detect whether a router uses different send and receive interfaces. In addition, routers may not decrement the TTL value correctly at each stop in the path. Therefore, traceroute is best used on a network with which you are already familiar. You can then use your judgment and experience to compare the actual test results with what you anticipate the results should be.

The simplest form of the `traceroute` command is `traceroute` *ip_address*. On computers that use the Windows-based operating system, the proper syntax is `tracert` *ip_address*. This command returns a list as shown in Figure 12-10.

12

```
% traceroute www.networksolutions.com
traceroute to www.networksolutions.com (216.168.224.69), 30 hops max, 38 byte packets
 1  * * *

% traceroute -I www.networksolutions.com
traceroute to www.networksolutions.com (216.168.224.69), 30 hops max, 38 byte packets
 1  * * *
 2  10.75.149.1 (10.75.149.1)  21.171 ms  21.026 ms  11.883 ms
 3  bb1-ge2-0.mdsn1.wi.home.net (24.6.204.1)  13.249 ms  14.739 ms  9.679 ms
 4  c2-se3-0-9.chcgil1.home.net (24.7.76.49)  13.511 ms  12.596 ms  18.576 ms
 5  aads.agis.net (206.220.243.19)  18.310 ms  26.789 ms  20.132 ms
 6  at-100100.inindrr01.us.telia.net (206.185.201.6)  68.421 ms  92.255 ms  *
 7  at-0001.dcwdcrr01.us.telia.net (206.84.253.14)  97.508 ms  106.618 ms  100.920 ms
 8  ga011.herndon1.us.telia.net (206.84.235.249)  110.407 ms  108.272 ms  106.386 ms
 9  tii-internic.herndon1.us.telia.net (206.84.235.26)  96.980 ms  95.273 ms  92.744 ms
10  www.networksolutions.com (216.168.224.69)  93.718 ms  89.265 ms  88.828 ms
%
```

Figure 12-10   Output of a traceroute command

As with other TCP/IP utilities, traceroute has a number of switches that may be used with the command. A traceroute command begins with either "traceroute" or "tracert" (depending on the operating system your computer uses), followed by a hyphen, a switch, and then a variable pertaining to a particular switch, if required. The following list describes some of the popular traceroute switches:

- **-d**—Instructs the tracert command not to resolve IP addresses to host names.

- **-h**—Specifies the maximum number of hops the packets should take when attempting to reach a host (the default is 30); this switch must be followed by a variable.

- **-w**—Identifies a timeout period for responses; this switch must be followed by a variable to indicate the number of milliseconds the utility should wait for a response.

Netstat

The **netstat** utility displays TCP/IP statistics and details about TCP/IP components and connections on a host. Information that can be obtained from the **netstat** command include: the port on which a particular TCP/IP service is running, whether or not a remote node is logged on to a host, which network connections are currently established for a client, how many packets have been handled by a network interface since it was activated, and how many data errors have occurred on a particular network interface. As you can imagine, with so much information available, the netstat utility makes a powerful diagnostic tool.

For example, suppose you are a network administrator in charge of maintaining file, print, Web, and Internet servers for an organization. You discover that your Web server, which has multiple processors, sufficient hard disk space, and multiple NICs, is suddenly taking twice as long to respond to HTTP requests. Of course, you should check the server's memory resources as well as its Web server software to determine that nothing is wrong with either of those. In addition, you can use the netstat utility to determine the characteristics of the traffic going in and out of each network interface card. You may discover that one network card is consistently handling 80 percent of the traffic, even though you had configured the server to share traffic equally among the two. This fact may lead you to run hardware diagnostics on the NIC, and perhaps discover that its onboard processor has failed, making it much slower than the other NIC. Netstat provides a quick way to view traffic statistics, without having to run a more sophisticated program such as Windows 2000 Network Monitor.

As mentioned at the beginning of this section, if you use the `netstat` command without any switches, it displays a list of all the TCP connections on your machine. However, as with other TCP/IP commands, netstat can be used with a number of different switches to customize its output. A netstat command begins with the word "netstat," followed by a hyphen and a switch, and a variable pertaining to that switch, if required. For example, the `netstat -a` command displays all current TCP and UDP connections from the issuing device to other devices on the network, as well as the source and destination service ports. The `netstat -r` command allows you to post a listing of the routing table on a given machine. The following list describes some of the most common switches used with the netstat utility:

- `-a`—Provides a listing of all available TCP and UDP connections, even if they are simply listening and not currently exchanging data.

- `-e`—Displays details about all the packets that have been sent over a network interface.

- `-n`—Lists currently connected hosts according to their port and IP address (in numerical form).

- `-p`—Allows you to specify what type of protocol statistics to list; this switch must be followed by a protocol specification (TCP or UDP).

- `-R`—Provides a list of routing table information.

- `-s`—Provides statistics about each packet transmitted by a host, separated according to protocol type (for example, IP, TCP, UDP, or ICMP).

12

CHAPTER SUMMARY

- In 1969, the wide area network that would later become part of the Internet was known as ARPANET. It was funded by the U.S. government and used for communications between scientists and researchers across the nation who were collaborating on defense research projects.

- TCP/IP became the protocol for the Internet after it was codified in 1972. TCP/IP was designed to facilitate open communication between all computers. It remains the basis for Internet data exchange.

- In 1991, the World Wide Web (WWW, or the Web), a collection of many Internet servers and a method for organizing and formatting data scattered over these servers was introduced. To navigate the Web, a user requires a browser, a program capable of interpreting Web formatting codes.

❐ Technical standards for today's Internet are established through a comprehensive application and review process overseen by the IETF. Internet standards are documented in Requests for Comments, or RFCs. Some other Internet-related technical standards are established by government-sponsored organizations such as the ITU.

❐ IP address and domain name management is currently overseen by ICANN, the Internet Corporation for Assigned Names and Numbers. ICANN is a private corporation contracted by the U.S. Department of Commerce. It assumes financial and administrative control of functions previously performed by IANA, the Internet Assigned Numbers Authority, which is based at USC and still performs much of the Internet's top-level system administration.

❐ Individuals wishing to register a domain name apply to an ICANN-accredited registrar. IP addresses are allocated to individuals by ISPs, who obtain blocks of IP addresses from one of ICANN's Regional Internet Registrars (RIRs). ARIN is the RIR for the Americas.

❐ Every host on the Internet needs a way to associate host names with IP addresses across the Internet. This association may be accomplished via a host file—a text file containing a table that associates internal host names with their IP addresses—or more often, by using the Domain Name System (DNS).

❐ DNS is a hierarchical way of identifying domain names and their addresses. It relies on a database, which is distributed over 13 root servers across the Internet. Because it is distributed, DNS will not fail catastrophically if one or a few computers go down.

❐ Domain names reflect the hierarchical nature of DNS. In this scheme, each domain name contains a series of labels separated by periods. The last label in a domain name represents a top-level domain (TLD), or the highest level in the DNS hierarchy.

❐ Many name servers across the globe cooperate to keep track of IP addresses and their associated domain names. Name space refers to the database of Internet IP addresses and their associated names. Every name server holds a piece of the DNS name space. At the highest level in the hierarchy sit the root servers.

❐ Every TCP/IP service is associated with a port through which the client and server exchange data. Ports are numbers from 0 to 65536, and numbers for the most common TCP/IP services are set by default. The Transport layer protocol on which a service relies is a matter of convention, depending on whether the service requires reliable data delivery.

❐ To interpret data, the Web relies on Hypertext Transfer Protocol (HTTP). When you type the address of a Web page in your Web browser's address field, HTTP transports the information about your request to the Web server on the server's port 80 via the TCP protocol.

❑ HTTP interprets Web requests and returns information to the client in Hypertext Markup Language (HTML), the Web document formatting language. The latest version of HTML is XHTML, or HTML 4.0, which combines the flexibility of XML with the simplicity of HTML.

❑ Every Web page is identified by a Uniform Resource Locator (URL) that specifies the service it uses, its server's fully qualified host name, and its HTML or XHTML page or script name. Not all URLs specify the HTTP protocol. They may also specify Telnet or FTP, for example.

❑ Simple Mail Transfer Protocol (SMTP) is responsible for moving messages from one e-mail server to another over TCP/IP-based networks. The Post Office Protocol (POP) runs on top of SMTP and retrieves messages from a mail server. The Internet Mail Access Protocol (IMAP) is a more sophisticated alternative to POP. The single biggest advantage IMAP4 has relative to POP is that it allows users to store messages on the mail server, rather than always having to download them to the local machine.

❑ File Transfer Protocol (FTP) is an Application layer protocol that manages file transfers between TCP/IP hosts. The FTP service depends on an FTP server that is always waiting for requests. After a client connects to the FTP server, FTP data is exchanged via TCP using port 20. FTP commands are sent and received through TCP port 21.

❑ E-commerce is a means of conducting business over the Internet. Any buying and selling of products or services that occurs over the Internet belongs in the e-commerce category.

❑ Telecommunications engineers have devised a way to break voice signals into packets and transmit them over data networks using TCP/IP. This service is called Voice over IP (VoIP—pronounced "voyp"), or IP telephony. When VoIP is carried over the Internet, it is known as Internet telephony.

❑ Intranets (on LANs) and extranets (on WANs) are networks that use Internet-like services and the TCP/IP to provide access to private resources. Intranets and extranets may not connect with the Internet, but often do. They require users to log on and authenticate before gaining access to (private) information.

❑ Several utilities come with the TCP/IP suite to help users and network administrators manage and assess TCP/IP connections. On Windows NT, 2000, and XP computers, the ipconfig utility reveals information about TCP/IP configurations. On a computer running a version of UNIX, ifconfig manages TCP/IP configurations.

❑ PING is a utility that, when run from the command prompt, can verify that a computer's TCP/IP software is installed, bound to the NIC, configured correctly, and communicating with the network. It is often employed to determine whether a host is responding and whether it can reach hosts outside its own network.

12

❑ Traceroute (or tracert on Windows systems) is a utility that traces the path from one host to another, identifying all intermediate hops between the two nodes. This utility is useful for determining router or network connectivity problems.

❑ The netstat utility displays TCP/IP statistics and details about TCP/IP components and connections on a host. It is helpful to determine what services are running and what connections are active.

KEY TERMS

address resource record — A type of DNS data record that maps the IP address of an Internet-connected device to its domain name.

Advanced Research Projects Agency (ARPA) — A government agency formed in 1958 to research and develop space, ballistics, and nuclear arms technology. ARPA established a network for communications between its scientists known as ARPANET.

alias — In a host file, a nickname for a host. An alias allows a user within an organization to address a host by a different (and usually more familiar) name than the full host name.

anchor — An HTML tag that formats information on a Web page as a hyperlink (or redirection) to another area of the Web page or to another Web page.

ARPANET — A rudimentary network established for communication between researchers at universities and other organizations involved contracted by ARPA. ARPANET formed the basis for the Internet.

browser — The software that interprets HTTP-encoded material and provides clients with an easily navigated, graphical interface to the Web. Netscape Communicator and Microsoft's Internet Explorer are examples of common browsers.

de facto standard — A standard that is not an official policy but is adhered to nevertheless. (De facto, in Latin, means "from the fact.") Unlike RFC standards, de facto standards are developed independently, by a corporation or research facility, and then released to the public.

DNS server — *See* name server.

Domain Name System (DNS) — A hierarchical way of tracking domain names and their addresses, devised in the mid-1980s. The DNS database does not rely on one file or even one server, but rather is distributed over several key computers across the Internet to prevent catastrophic failure if one or a few computers go down. DNS is a TCP/IP service that belongs to the Application layer of the OSI model.

draft standard — In the IETF's RFC approval process, a proposed standard that has demonstrated interoperability and functionality and is ready for the last phase of scrutiny before it becomes an RFC standard.

echo reply — The response signal sent by a device after another device pings it.

echo request — The request for a response generated when one device pings another device on the network.

e-commerce — A means of conducting business over the Web—be it in retail, banking, stock trading, consulting, or training. Any buying and selling of products or services that occurs over the Internet belongs in the e-commerce category.

element — In XML, a named set of data and a method of interpreting this data. Using elements rather than tags (as in HTML) makes XML a much more flexible and powerful markup language.

extranet — A network that uses Internet-like services and protocols to make resources available to multiple locations of the same organization or to different organizations.

host file — A text file that associates TCP/IP host names with IP addresses. On UNIX platforms the file is called "hosts" and is located in the /etc directory. On a Windows XP, NT, or 2000 computer, the file is also called "hosts" and is located in the *systemroot*\System32\Drivers\Etc directory, where *systemroot* is the directory in which the operating system is installed.

Hypertext Markup Language (HTML) — The language that defines formatting standards for Web documents.

ifconfig — A TCP/IP configuration and management utility used with UNIX systems (similar to the ipconfig utility used on Windows NT and 2000 systems).

Internet Architecture Board (IAB) — A technical advisory group made up of approximately a dozen researchers and technical professionals interested in overseeing the Internet's design and management. IAB is responsible for Internet growth and management strategy, for resolution of technical disputes, and for standards oversight. IAB appoints the chair of the IETF and consults with the IESG in determining whether a proposed standard will become a draft standard.

Internet Assigned Numbers Authority (IANA) — A nonprofit, U.S. government-funded group that was established at the Information Systems Institute (ISI) University of Southern California and charged with managing IP address allocation and the Domain Name System. The oversight for many IANA's functions was given to ICANN in 1998; however, IANA continues to perform high-level Internet system administration.

Internet Control Message Protocol (ICMP) — A TCP/IP protocol that notifies the sender that something has gone wrong in the transmission process and that packets were not delivered.

Internet Corporation for Assigned Names and Numbers (ICANN) — A private, nonprofit corporation that is contracted by the government to oversee IP address and domain name management, plus accomplish specific Internet management improvements. It consists of 19 board members representing every continent in the world, a President and CEO, and At-Large Membership. ICANN has overtaken many of the responsibilities previously assigned to IANA.

12

Internet draft — A proposed standard that is submitted by a computer networking professional to an IETF working group. After thorough review, an Internet draft may become an Internet technical standard or best practice.

Internet Engineering Steering Group (IESG) — A committee made of IETF technical area directors that oversees IETF decisions. IESG is responsible for finally determining whether an Internet draft is ready to become an RFC.

Internet Mail Access Protocol (IMAP) — A mail storage and manipulation protocol that depends on SMTP's transport system and improves upon the shortcomings of POP. The most current version of IMAP is version 4 (IMAP4). IMAP4 can (and eventually will) replace POP without the user having to change e-mail programs. The single biggest advantage IMAP4 has relative to POP is that it allows users to store messages on the mail server, rather than having to download them to the local machine.

Internet Society (ISOC) — An organization consisting of thousands of Internet professionals and companies from around the globe that helps guide Internet technology and policy. Some current ISOC concerns include how to address rapid growth, security, and the increased need for diverse services over the Internet. ISOC is an umbrella organization for the IETF, IAB, and IESG.

Internet telephony — The provision of telephone service over the Internet.

Internet2 — A network that connects educational and private institutions for the purposes of research and development. Internet2 relies on a backbone separate from the public Internet's backbone, and therefore, Internet2 users enjoy much faster response. To connect to Internet2, an organization must pay a significant annual fee and promise to use access for educational or research purposes.

intranet — A TCP/IP-based network that connects clients with resources within an organization. Intranets use HTTP servers to store and present private information to clients. However, these Web servers require client authentication and are not necessarily connected to the Internet. Intranets are also used for other applications such as e-mail, file sharing, document management, and collaboration.

IP telephony — *See* Voice over IP.

ipconfig — The TCP/IP configuration and management utility for use with Windows NT, 2000, and XP systems.

name server — A server that contains a database of TCP/IP host names and their associated IP addresses. A name server supplies a resolver with the requested information. If it cannot resolve the IP address, the query passes to a higher-level name server. Name servers may also be known as DNS servers.

name space — The database of Internet IP addresses and their associated names distributed over DNS name servers worldwide.

netstat — A TCP/IP utility that displays statistics and details about TCP/IP connections and listening ports on a host.

Network News Transfer Protocol (NNTP) — The protocol that supports the process of reading newsgroup messages, posting new messages, and transferring news files between news servers.

newsgroup — An Internet service similar to e-mail that provides a means of conveying messages, but in which information is distributed to a wide group of users at once rather than from one user to another.

NSFNET — A network established in 1986 by the U.S. National Science Foundation (NSF) that originally consisted of five interconnected supercomputing centers at universities across the nation, plus a backbone network. NSFNET's mission was to increase early use of the Internet by universities and other educational and research institutions.

Packet Internet Groper (PING) — A TCP/IP troubleshooting utility that can verify that TCP/IP is installed, bound to the NIC, configured correctly, and communicating with the network. PING uses ICMP to send echo request and echo reply messages that determine the validity of an IP address.

Post Office Protocol (POP) — An Application layer protocol used to retrieve e-mail messages from a mail server. When a client retrieves mail via POP, messages are downloaded to the client workstation and then deleted from the mail server.

proposed standard — A type of RFC (or Internet document) that describes a technology that has been proposed in an Internet draft but has not yet been proven as an Internet standard.

Regional Internet Registry (RIR) — A not-for-profit agency that manages the distribution of IP addresses to private and public entities. ARIN is the RIR for North, Central, and South America and sub-Saharan Africa. APNIC is the RIR for Asia and the Pacific region. RIPE is the RIR for Europe and North Africa.

resolver — Any host on the Internet that needs to look up domain name information to resolve a name with an IP address.

resource record — The element of a DNS database stored on a name server that contains information about TCP/IP host names and their addresses.

RFC (Request for Comments) — A numbered document that articulates some aspect of Internet or TCP/IP technology. Many different types of RFCs exist. Some are official standards, whereas others simply describe best practices or proposed standards. A searchable index of RFCs can be found at IETF's RFC editor site, *www.rfc-editor.org*.

root server — A DNS server maintained by ICANN that is an authority on how to contact the top-level domains, such as those ending with .com, .edu, .net, .us, and so on. ICANN maintains 13 root servers around the world.

switch — A character or combination of characters that follows a command and instructs the command to format its results in a specific way.

tag — A formatting indicator used in HTML.

top-level domain (TLD) — The highest-level category used to distinguish domain names—for example, .org, .com, .net. A TLD is also known as the domain suffix.

traceroute — A TCP/IP utility that uses ICMP to trace the path from one host to another, identifying all intermediate hops between the two hosts. This utility is useful for determining router or network connectivity problems. On Windows systems, this command is known as tracert.

12

tracert — On Windows systems, a TCP/IP utility that uses ICMP to trace the path from one host to another, identifying all intermediate hops between the two hosts.

Uniform Resource Locator (URL) — A standard means of identifying every Web page, which specifies the service used, its server's host name, and its HTML page or script name.

Voice over IP (VoIP) — A method of encoding and transmitting voice signals over a data network using TCP/IP. An IP telephony system may use the Internet or a private network as a communications channel.

well-known ports — TCP/IP port numbers between 0 and 1023, so called because they were the first to be defined, and are the most familiar and most frequently used. Well-known ports are typically reserved for TCP/IP services that require administrator access to a server.

winipcfg — The TCP/IP configuration and management utility for use with Windows 95 and 98.

World Wide Web (WWW or Web) — A collection of internetworked servers that share resources and exchange information according to specific protocols and formats.

World Wide Web Consortium (W3C) — A standards organization for Web browsers and languages. W3C issues and updates HTML and XHTML standards, for example.

XHTML (eXtensible Hypertext Markup Language) — The latest version of the Hypertext Markup Language, also known as HTML 4.0, written to meet XML specifications. In other words, XHTML is a markup language that has already used XML to define standard elements and their formatting methods. Users familiar with previous versions of HTML will find XHTML much more user friendly than XML.

XML (eXtensible Markup Language) — A markup (or formatting) language that does not rely on pre-defined tags (as HTML does), but rather allows a designer to create her own formatting definitions and embed those definitions in a document. XML is considered to be not simply a language, but a method for defining a language.

zone — In the DNS hierarchical structure, a group of devices collectively managed by one DNS server.

REVIEW QUESTIONS

1. What organization provided funding for ARPANET, the precursor to today's Internet?

   a. the U.S. Department of Defense

   b. the U.S. Department of Education

   c. universities that used ARPANET

   d. the U.S. National Science Foundation

2. In the context of TCP/IP, what does the principle of open communication refer to?

   a. the ability to connect to a host without specifying an address or port

   b. the ability to view, modify, and use TCP/IP code without licensing restrictions

   c. the ability to combine TCP/IP components and elements of other protocol suites within the same datagrams

   d. the ability to freely exchange data without security concerns

3. Which of the following organizations manages IETF decisions and is ultimately responsible for determining when an Internet draft can become a proposed standard?

   a. IRTF

   b. IESG

   c. ICANN

   d. IANA

4. If you want to reserve the domain name that is the same as your first and last names, what organization would you contact?

   a. an IANA agent

   b. an ICANN board member

   c. an ICANN-accredited registrar

   d. an ARIN affiliate

5. If you lived in Dusseldorf, Germany, and worked as a network engineer for a large ISP, to which of the following organizations would you apply for IP addresses?

   a. ARIN

   b. IANA

   c. APNIC

   d. RIPE

12

6. Where would you find a hosts file on a UNIX server?

   a. in the /bin directory

   b. in the /etc directory

   c. in the /root directory

   d. in the /dev directory

7. Why are host files rarely used in any sizeable organization?

   a. because they are difficult to manage—each change in a host file requires a change to every computer on the network

   b. because they have limited capacity—they cannot accurately resolve over a dozen host names and IP addresses

   c. because they are not supported by all of the currently popular operating systems

   d. because they provide poor security compared to DNS—any TCP/IP host user can lookup a host's IP address, while DNS masks this information

8. What is the purpose for distributing the DNS name space over multiple servers?

   a. It allows multiple clients to query DNS simultaneously.

   b. It allows fewer administrators to update the name space more efficiently.

   c. It safeguards against catastrophic Internet failure, should one server go down.

   d. It enables the use of host names for multiple Internet-connected machines.

9. What TLD would be assigned to a federal agency, such as the U.S. Department of Commerce?

   a. .mil

   b. .fed

   c. .gv

   d. .gov

10. What types of computers manage top-level domains in the DNS hierarchy?

    a. root servers

    b. Internet node servers

    c. edge servers

    d. core gateways

11. Which of the following pieces of information is *not* contained in every DNS resource record?

    a. a domain name

    b. a preferred route

    c. time to live data

    d. data length field

12. You are a systems administrator for an auto parts dealer. You create a Web site that allows customers to view your current specials and sales. Instead of accepting the default HTTP port when you configure the Web server software, you assign port 8800 to your Web site. What will your customers have to do to view the Web site?

    a. replace the server's host name with the alias "8800" in the URL

    b. insert a "/8800" after the fully qualified host name

    c. insert a ":8800" after the fully qualified host name

    d. replace the server's TLD with "8800"

13. Describe the differences between XML and HTML.

14. Which of the following is not a valid uniform resource locator (URL)?

    a. ftp://ftp.netscape.com

    b. http://www.course.com

    c. http://shopping.yahoo.com

    d. telnet://telnet.loc.gov

15. What role does SMTP play in exchanging e-mail?

   a. It transports mail from one host to another.

   b. It provides statistics about e-mail usage.

   c. It allows users to view e-mail in HTML format.

   d. It helps prevent junk mail from entering users' e-mail boxes.

16. Which of the following is an advantage of using IMAP over POP?

   a. It requires fewer resources on the server.

   b. It allows users to review and delete mail without downloading from the mail server.

   c. It is more widely used by popular e-mail clients.

   d. It provides guarantees for mail delivery within a specified time period.

17. At what layer of the OSI model do POP and IMAP operate?

   a. Application

   b. Presentation

   c. Session

   d. Transport

18. You are the network administrator for a large company that sells gourmet food baskets. Programmers at your organization have developed an online store. They tell you they have tested its viability and functionality and that it's ready to be connected to the Internet. From a networking perspective, what is one of your top concerns you'll address before the online store goes live?

   a. whether product listings have been accurately associated with your company's inventory items

   b. whether the programmers have designed user interfaces that are easy to understand and navigate

   c. whether the Web site conforms to the most recent release of HTTP

   d. whether the online store provides for secure transactions to protect customer information and to prevent hackers from using the site as a pathway

19. Which of the following ports would FTP use to send files to a host?

   a. 16

   b. 18

   c. 20

   d. 80

12

20. What type of TCP/IP services would use UDP, rather than TCP, for a Transport layer protocol?

    a. those that require all packets to arrive at the destination in order

    b. those that require all packets to arrive at the destination without errors

    c. those that require fast data transmission

    d. those that require a session to be established before transmission can occur

21. Which of the following uses are appropriate for an extranet?

    a. assigning each user within an organization a new system password

    b. offering ftp downloads of publicly available software on the Internet

    c. offering shoppers an online grocery store

    d. supplying company employees with a way of virtually collaborating on projects while they travel

22. If you want to know the IP address assigned to your Windows XP workstation, which of the following commands should you type at the command prompt?

    a. ifconfig

    b. ipconfig

    c. traceroute

    d. ping

23. Which of the following utilities is used to renew a DHCP-leased address on a UNIX computer?

    a. ifconfig

    b. ipconfig

    c. traceroute

    d. ping

24. Which of the following utilities could you use to determine where, in the path between your workstation and a host somewhere on the Internet, your data transmission is slowing down?

    a. ifconfig

    b. ipconfig

    c. traceroute

    d. ping

25. When you type the following command: `ping 127.0.0.1`, what are you communicating with?

    a. your Internet gateway

    b. your DNS server

    c. your own computer

    d. your file server

HANDS-ON PROJECTS

Project 12-1

At the beginning of this chapter, you learned how Internet technical standards are drafted, reviewed, and released by the IETF. Each Internet standard is documented in an RFC (Request for Comments). In this project, you learn how to find and interpret RFCs available on the Internet. You also investigate IETF Internet drafts that currently wait for approval. For this project, you need a computer that is capable of connecting to the Internet and navigating the Web.

1. Verify that your workstation is connected to the Internet.

2. Point your browser to the following URL: **www.rfc-editor.org**. The home page for the RFC-editor appears. Recall that the RFC-editor is the publishing arm of ISOC, the organization that oversees IETF standards activities.

3. From the main menu, click **RFC Search**. The RFC Index Search Engine page appears.

4. First, you will search for the latest RFC that documents specifications for the IMAP mail client protocol. In the Search text box, type **IMAP**, then click the **Search** button.

5. A list of matching RFC documents appears in the bottom half of the screen. Notice that some of the RFCs are designated as informational only, whereas others are proposed standards. Also notice that some older IMAP RFCs have been superseded by newer RFCs. Click on **RFC2060** to open this document in your browser window.

6. RFC 2060 specifies the key features of the IMAP (the Internet Message Access Protocol). Scroll down until you reach the document's table of contents. Read through the table of contents, noting the scope of this standard. If you are interested, scroll through the document and read about this standard.

7. Now that you have seen the list of accepted standards that pertain to IMAP, you will view the Internet drafts pertaining to this protocol. Point your browser to the Internet Engineering Task Force's home page: **www.ietf.org**. The IETF home page appears.

8. From the menu list, click **Internet-Drafts**. IETF's Internet-Drafts page appears.

9. Click **I-D Keyword Search**. The Internet-Drafts Search Engine page appears.

10. Under Query Options: change the Maximum number of hits from 25 to **100**. In the Query: text box, type **IMAP** and then click **Submit**. After a search of the Internet drafts database, the Search Results page appears. Notice how many Internet drafts are pending for the IMAP protocol.

11. Scroll through the list of IMAP Internet drafts. What issues are the authors of these drafts addressing? Are any of them revisions of the IMAP-related RFCs you saw listed in Step 5?

12

12. Click the **Back** button on your browser to return to the Internet-Drafts Search Engine page. Under Query Options: change the Maximum number of hits from 25 to **100**, if necessary. In the Query: text box, type **RTP**, then click **Submit**. RTP is a protocol in the TCP/IP suite used for Voice over IP services.

13. Notice how many Internet drafts are listed for this protocol. Why does the IETF have so many more Internet drafts for RTP than for IMAP? What technical issues are these Internet drafts addressing?

14. Close your browser program.

Project 12-2

After reading this chapter, you now understand how TCP/IP components work together to provide Internet access. In this exercise, you will set up a Windows 2000 or XP workstation with everything it needs to access the Internet. For this project, you need a Windows 2000 or XP workstation that currently has TCP/IP installed and bound to the NIC, but doesn't have any settings specified. You need to obtain the correct settings for your network from your instructor. In this project, it's important to type the numbers exactly as they are given to you; otherwise, the TCP/IP connection will not work. Also, each computer must use a unique IP address and host name.

1. Obtain the following numbers from your instructor: IP address, subnet mask, DNS primary name server, DNS secondary name server, default gateway, and domain name.

2. Click **Start**, point to **Settings**, and then click **Control Panel**.

3. Double-click **Network and Dial-up Connections**. The Network and Dial-up Connections window opens.

4. Right-click the **Local Area Connection** icon and then click **Properties** in the shortcut menu. The Local Area Connection Properties dialog box appears.

5. Highlight **Internet Protocol (TCP/IP)** in the list of installed network components and then click **Properties**. The Internet Protocol (TCP/IP) Properties dialog box opens.

6. Make sure the **Use the following IP address** option is selected.

7. Enter your network's IP address in the space provided.

8. Enter your network's default gateway in the space provided.

9. Enter your network's subnet mask in the space provided.

10. Make sure the **Use the following DNS server addresses** option is selected.

11. Enter the IP address of your primary DNS server in the **Preferred DNS server** text box.

12. Enter the IP address of your secondary DNS server, if you have one, in the **Alternate DNS server** text box.

13. Click **OK** to save your changes to the TCP/IP properties. The dialog box closes.

14. Click **OK** to save the changes to the Network properties. The dialog box closes and your changes are saved.

15. To test whether your change worked, click **Start**, point to **Programs** (or **All Programs** in Windows XP), point to **Accessories**, and then click **Command Prompt**. The Command Prompt window opens.

16. At the command prompt, type: **telnet locis.loc.gov**, and then press **Enter**.

17. If you see a text screen entitled "LOCIS: Library of Congress Information System," you have successfully modified your TCP/IP properties. If you see a window titled "Connect Failed!" you either typed the host name incorrectly or need to retrace your steps from the beginning of this project to ensure that your TCP/IP properties are correct.

Project 12-3

As you have learned, TCP/IP comes with several diagnostic utilities, including ipconfig (on Windows-based computers), ping, netstat, and tracert (or traceroute on UNIX-based computers). In previous projects, you have already experimented with ping and ipconfig. In this project, you will try the tracert and netstat utilities. To complete this project, you need a Windows 2000 or XP workstation that is capable of connecting to the Internet.

1. Connect to the Internet, then click **Start**, point to **Programs** (or **All Programs**, if you are using Windows XP), point to **Accessories**, and then click **Command Prompt**. The Command Prompt window opens.

2. At the command prompt, type **netstat -a** and press **Enter**. Recall that netstat is the command that reveals TCP/IP port connections, and the -a switch instructs the command to list all ports, including those using TCP and UDP, even if they are not actively exchanging data. How many connections are listed on your computer? Of those connections, how many rely on the TCP protocol and how many rely on UDP?

3. Now look at the "State" column of your connection listing. How does the value in this column differ for TCP and UDP connections? Why do you suppose this is the case?

4. Now type **netstat -s** and press **Enter**. Separate lists of statistics for each protocol (for example, IP, ICMP, TCP, and UDP) appear. Which protocol has sent and received the most packets or datagrams?

5. Now, you will experiment with another TCP/IP utility, the traceroute function. At the command prompt, type **tracert www.course.com** and press **Enter**. How many hops does it take to go from your computer to the Course Technology Web server? How many hops are listed as the maximum for the tracert command?

12

6. Now use the traceroute utility but allow it to omit the host names of every hop between your workstation and the destination by typing **tracert -d www.course.com** and pressing **Enter**. Notice how the output differs from the output you received in Step 5.

7. Close the Command Prompt window.

CASE PROJECTS

1. You have been asked to assist with a new Internet project at an established retail business in your area called Sunsource Supplies. Sunsource Supplies sells goods related to recycling, farming, and homesteading. Although the owners are experts at distribution, sales, and marketing, they do not understand technology very well. Their goal is to establish an e-commerce site to sell their supplies on the Web. They also want to instantly share messages and order information between their three regional stores. Currently, each store has a separate dial-up connection to the Internet. The owners of Sunsource Supplies have asked you to list the steps they need to take (with your help) to establish Internet connectivity, set up a simple extranet, and set up a Web server that can one day be used for e-commerce services. Begin by breaking each of these three objectives into at least five smaller tasks. Be sure that the tasks take into account each location and the need to connect those locations. Then arrange the tasks according to the order in which they must be accomplished. Also identify any tasks that depend on other tasks to be completed before they can begin.

2. In response to the list of tasks you presented, the owners of Sunsource Supplies question whether they can manage a Web server themselves. Still, they are willing to build their technical skills if it means having greater autonomy over their system and their business. They ask you to describe the specific technical skills they need to run a simple e-commerce Web server. What skills do you tell them are critical to have before embarking on such a project? What skills, though not critical, would be very useful to have? What alternatives can you suggest to the owners managing a Web server from one of their stores?

3. The owners of Sunsource Supplies decided that the installation and maintenance of a Web server is more effort than they want to expend. Instead, they contracted with an ISP to house their Web server at a data center and have network engineers maintain the server there. However, the owners still have access to their server and still want to learn about it. Specifically, they want to check occasionally to see how many users are connected to the server. They also want to be assured that the server is available at all times of the day or night, as the ISP has guaranteed it will be. In addition, they want to make such checks without purchasing any fancy software. What TCP/IP utilities could help them determine this information?

CHAPTER 13

INFORMATION SECURITY

> **After reading this chapter and completing the exercises, you will be able to:**
>
> ♦ List the key steps in assessing information security risks
>
> ♦ Explain the elements and purpose of a security policy
>
> ♦ Describe strategies for minimizing common security risks associated with people, passwords, physical security, and modem access
>
> ♦ Discuss the most popular, current methods of encrypting data
>
> ♦ Identify security threats to public and private telephone networks and discuss ways to prevent them
>
> ♦ Identify security threats to LAN- and WAN-based telecommunications and discuss ways to prevent them
>
> ♦ Identify security threats to wireless telecommunications and discuss ways to prevent them

Guarding against information security threats has long been a business concern. Back in the 1890s, for example, telegraph messages were subject to eavesdropping. With the advent of electromechanical switches in the early 1900s, AT&T had to guard its national telephone network against individuals who could trick the switches into completing long-distance calls without paying fees. Electronic switching, which depends on computers and out-of-band signaling, solved that problem, but opened new vulnerabilities. The introduction of modems in the 1960s offered yet another way for determined individuals to illicitly access information—in this case, information traversing computer and telephone networks. Internet access, widely available for the last decade, has only exacerbated the problem of information security. These days, large organizations, such as a federal government agencies or Fortune 100 businesses, commonly hire employees who devote all their work hours to network security.

On modern networks, addressing information security is a process; it has no end point. It also offers no guarantees. The best approach, then, is to follow a rigorous methodology and keep a constant vigil over important, sensitive information. In this chapter, you learn the fundamental tools for assessing vulnerabilities and securing information over data and voice networks.

RISK ASSESSMENT

Before you can protect information from unauthorized access or harm, you must first identify what information is at risk, explain why it is at risk, and determine who or what might attack it. In addition, you should attempt to predict the costs to your organization, should its resources be compromised. These findings are the purpose of a **risk assessment**, a thorough analysis of an organization's vulnerability to security breaches and an identification of its potential losses. A risk assessment should lead to recommendations for improving information security and must precede any of the protective measures described in this chapter. Neglecting to perform a risk assessment could result in security policies and procedures that fail to protect a key resource or vulnerability. Alternatively, in the case of a business that has few proprietary resources to protect, neglecting to perform a risk assessment may lead to expensive security measures that exceed the cost of recovering from a security breach.

The desired outcome of a risk assessment is to prevent—or at least to minimize—any damage that might occur from misuse of an organization's resources. In this context, "damage" may be physical, monetary, or related to an organization's reputation. For example, an individual who obtains unauthorized access to a data center and slices a number of network cables causes physical damage. An individual who illegally obtains a list of telephone calling card codes and uses those codes to place long-distance calls at the card owner's expense causes monetary damage. Another form of monetary damage is the cost of paying employees who spend hours, if not weeks, of their time restoring resources compromised in a security breach. In another example, an individual who gains unauthorized access to a company's Web server and replaces the company's regular home page with defamatory text may damage the company's reputation.

Many different terms are used to describe those who break into telephone or data networks. Individuals who manipulate telephone connections or resources to their advantage are known as **phone phreaks**, or **phreakers**. A **hacker**, in the original sense of the word, is someone who masters the inner workings of computer hardware and software in an effort to better understand them. To be called a hacker used to be a compliment, reflecting extraordinary computer skills. To distinguish hackers from people who use their computer skills with malicious intent, those who seek to destroy data or systems are called **crackers**. Today, however, many people use the words hacker and cracker synonymously. Many telecommunications professionals have settled on "hacker" as a general term for phone phreaks—hackers of all kinds. For simplicity's sake, this chapter also uses that term to describe individuals who gain unauthorized access to voice or data networks, with or without malicious intent.

A risk assessment should attempt to answer the following questions:

- *What resources or assets are at risk?* The answer to this question should include any object (for example, a switch, trunk, workstation, server, or router) or electronic resource (for example, e-mail messages, documents stored on a computer or removable storage device, customer information stored in a telephone switching system) that, if it were damaged or accessed by a nefarious individual, could cause harm. The risk to some resources may not be obvious. For example, although a network's system administrator may take pains to prevent hackers from opening confidential documents on a server, if those same documents are stored on floppy disks lying on an employee's desk, they remain vulnerable. To fully answer this question, an organization must generate a complete inventory of its assets, both tangible and intangible. An organization might list its reputation as an asset.

- *What methods could be taken to compromise those resources?* This question addresses the vulnerabilities in your network, systems, and facilities. To adequately answer the question, you must be creative and consider every possible means a hacker (or an unwitting individual) might take to access your resources. For example, a hacker could access your equipment room by posing as a technical support technician and asking an employee to let him in. Once inside the equipment room, he could steal backup tapes, sit at a switch console and reconfigure line ports, download customer data, pull wires, and so on. Other means of access may occur from afar. On a data network, any modem connected to a networked workstation is vulnerable to incoming calls. Once connected to a modem, a hacker might gain access to the network and steal or damage data. Connectivity devices, cabling, service area interfaces, demarcation points, wireless access points, cellular antenna towers, and many other network elements are also prone to unauthorized access, if not properly secured. Throughout this chapter, you learn more about the most common methods used to access restricted resources.

- *Who or what are the most likely threats to resources?* When considering security threats, most people envision a wily and mysterious vandal typing at his or her basement computer, thousands of miles away. Although this person may indeed be a perpetrator, most security threats come from individuals with a personal tie to an organization—be they current employees, contractors, ex-employees, or acquaintances of employees. In other words, most security threats are internal. A recently terminated employee, for example, might still have easy access to a system, either because the organization hasn't disabled her network user ID or because she has obtained a logon ID and password from a former colleague. With such access, she could attempt retribution by deleting files or sabotaging the network. Other internal threats are unintentional, such as employees who simply don't know what they're doing. For example, a novice programmer may inadvertently delete or damage system files while experimenting with a server's configuration. Finally, threats may derive from business competitors or, in the case of national security, from adversarial countries.

13

■ *What is the probability that the organization or its resources will be compromised?* The answer to this question differs greatly depending on the organization. Factors that make an organization more susceptible to attacks include: access to valuable assets (for example, a bank or a repository for government information), provision or transport of a high volume of data or voice traffic (for example, a network service provider), dominance within a business sector (for example, because Microsoft has such a large market share of PC software, it is a popular hacker target), or potentially controversial products or services (for example, a nuclear weapons contractor). The likelihood of being a target for security attacks directly affects how much the organization should invest in security measures. If an organization determines that it is highly likely to be targeted by hackers, it should devote more time and staff to preventing such attacks.

■ *What are the consequences of those resources being compromised?* After you have listed all the resources that are threatened, you can begin to assess the value of each resource. Some resources are more easily quantified than others. For example, you can easily estimate the value of a stolen server. However, it is more difficult to estimate the value of the data on that server. First, if the data cannot be retrieved from backup files, the cost of employees' time required to re-create the data must be considered. (One way to calculate this cost is to estimate the number of hours it takes employees to generate a document, then multiply that times the number of documents on the server, and then multiply that by the employees' hourly rate. Obviously, your sum will only be an estimate.) Second, if the data was obtained by a competitor and used to the competitor's advantage, the cost of the lost server would also include the cost of lost sales opportunities. Finally, if the server's data could be used against an organization to damage its reputation, another cost must be considered. Although it is nearly impossible to place a value on reputation, it may be possible to translate a loss of reputation into a loss in sales, based on historical information about similar breaches that transpired either in your organization's past or to other, similar organizations. For any sizeable organization, estimating the financial consequences of security breaches is a highly complex undertaking. Yet this calculation is vital to determining how much an organization must spend on security.

A risk assessment indicates how much an organization stands to lose if a security breach occurs and how much it can afford to spend protecting its resources. However, a risk assessment is only the first step in securing a voice or data network against threats. After completing this step, engineers and managers at the organization must write a plan for securing resources. The plan should be a roadmap for future security policies and network practices. It may propose a new network design or a new policy for granting rights to certain areas of the network, for example. After the plan is complete, security measures should be deployed. To be certain the security measures are effective, a consultant or another professional who was not involved with deploying the security measures should test them. Providing they are effective, an organization's staff must manage and support the security measures (for example, by making sure the software on a switch is updated to the latest, secure release). Finally, after a period of time, risk assessments should be repeated, along with the rest of the security cycle. Figure 13-1 depicts this cycle. Security policies and common security measures are discussed later in this chapter.

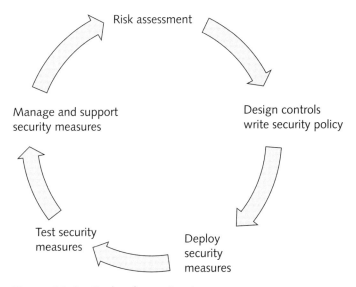

Figure 13-1   Cycle of security steps

It's important to note that risk assessments are not a one-time occurrence, but rather regularly recurring events. The frequency of risk assessments depends on how vulnerable an organization is and how much it stands to lose from a security breach. A law enforcement agency, for example, might perform risk assessments quarterly, whereas an office supply store might perform risk assessments every two years. In addition, an organization should repeat its risk assessment process after any major change, including adding connectivity equipment, reconfiguration, redesign, organizational restructuring, or moving to a new location.

SECURITY POLICIES

After an organization completes its risk assessment, it needs to establish a security policy. This document identifies security goals, risks, levels of authority (for instance, what staff position is allowed to change the administrator's password on the main switch), designated security team members, responsibilities for each team member, and responsibilities for each employee. In addition, it specifies how to address security breaches. However, a security policy does not state exactly which hardware, software, network architecture, or protocols are used to ensure security, or how devices or programs are installed and configured. These details change from time to time and should be shared only with authorized network administrators or managers.

Security Policy Goals

Security policies are often frowned upon by employees who deem the policies as obstacles to productivity, or by managers who think security policies are costly. Therefore, it is often wise to specify why the security policy is necessary and how it serves your organization. Explicitly stating a security policy's goals—and tying those goals to potential cost savings—may convince reluctant staff to embrace the policy. Typical security policy goals include:

- Ensuring that authorized users have appropriate access to the resources they need

- Preventing unauthorized users from gaining access to facilities, cabling, devices, systems, programs, or data

- Protecting sensitive data from unauthorized access, from individuals both internal and external to the organization

- Preventing accidental damage to hardware, facilities, or software

- Preventing intentional damage to hardware, facilities, or software

- Creating an environment in which the network and its connected nodes can withstand and, if necessary, quickly respond to and recover from any type of threat

- Communicating each employee's responsibilities with respect to maintaining information security

After defining the goals of your security policy, you can devise a strategy to attain them. First, you might form a committee composed of managers and interested parties from a variety of departments, in addition to your network administrators. The more decision-making people you can involve, the more effective your policy will be. This committee can assign a security coordinator, who will then drive the creation of a security policy. The security coordinator might assign each authorized technical employee responsibility for managing a handful of different risks. For example, suppose you are the security coordinator for an insurance company's headquarters. You might assign one person responsibility for managing threats to the PBX, telephone lines, and Internet-voice gateway. You might assign another person responsibility for managing threats to the Web and e-mail servers, another person responsibility for managing threats to the internal workstations and file and print servers, and yet another person responsibility for managing threats to the switches, routers, cabling, and WAN gateways.

After you have outlined your security policy's goals and assigned team members responsibility for managing threats, you can write the specific provisions of the policy.

Security Policy Content

If you have completed a thorough risk assessment, a security policy's content will parallel the assessment's findings. A security policy is typically divided into sections, according to the type of assets protected and the measures used for protection. Subheadings for the policy might include the following: Password policy; Software installation policy; Confidential and sensitive data policy; Network access policy; Telephone use policy, E-mail use policy; Internet use policy; Modem use policy; Remote access policy; Policies for connecting to remote locations, the Internet, and customers' and vendors' networks; Policies for use of laptops and loaner machines; and Cable Vault and Equipment room access policy. Although compiling all this information might seem like a daunting task, the process ensures that everyone understands the organization's stance on security and the reasons why it is so important.

The security policy should clearly explain to users what they can and cannot do and how these measures protect the network's security. Clear and regular communication about security policies makes them more acceptable and better understood. One idea for making security policies simpler for employees to understand is to create a separate section of the policy that applies only to users. Within the users' section, divide security rules according to the particular function or part of the network to which they apply. This approach prevents users from having to read through the entire document. For example, a company may impose restrictions on modem use within the company.

Some provisions of a security policy restrict what employees may do with confidential information. Thus, one question to clarify in the security policy is: What type of information is confidential? Each organization's definition of "confidential" differs. In general, information is confidential if it could be used by other parties to impair your organization's functioning, decrease your customers' confidence, cause a financial loss, damage your organization's status, or give a significant advantage to a competitor. If you work in an environment such as an investment firm, where much of the information is proprietary or confidential, however, your security policy should classify information in degrees of sensitivity that correspond to how strictly access is regulated. For example, information marked "for your eyes only" may be accessible only by the organization's top executives, whereas "confidential" information may be accessible only to senior money managers, and information marked "internal only" may be accessible only to research analysts who must modify or create it.

 An organization's security policy may also prescribe safeguards that do not pertain to its voice or data networks. For example, a large bank's security policy may state that employees may not discuss certain, potentially confidential topics in public places, such as on airplanes or in cafés. A chemical research facility's security policy may state that employees must lock confidential lab reports in approved file cabinets before leaving for the day. Aspects of security policies not related to telecommunications are beyond the scope of this chapter, however.

In case a security breach does occur, a company must be prepared to respond to it quickly. This contingency is also addressed by the response policy portion of a security policy.

Response Policy

Part of a security policy, a response policy describes, in detail, a planned response to a security breach. The response policy identifies the members of a response team, all of whom clearly understand the security policy, risks, and measures in place. Each team member is assigned a role and responsibilities. The security response team should regularly rehearse their defense by participating in a security threat drill. Some suggestions for team roles are listed next:

- *Dispatcher*—The person on call who first notices or is alerted to the problem. The dispatcher notifies the lead technical support specialist and then the manager. He or she opens a case for the incident, which includes the time it began, its symptoms, and any other pertinent information about the situation. The dispatcher remains available to answer calls from clients or employees or to assist the manager.

- *Manager*—The team member who coordinates the resources necessary to solve the problem. If internal technicians cannot handle the break-in, the manager should obtain assistance from external sources, such as a company that specializes in security responses. The manager also ensures that the security policy is followed and communicates with others in the organization. As technicians respond to the threat, the manager continues to monitor events and, if necessary, communicates with the organization's public relations specialist. After the incident has been resolved, the manager should convene a meeting to discuss how the breach happened, how the problem was resolved, and what measures are being taken to prevent a recurrence.

- *Technical support specialists*—The team members who strive to solve the problem as quickly as possible. Depending on the threat, this may include isolating a network from further attack, recovering lost data, tracking the intruder's point of entry and source, and applying measures to prevent the same attack from recurring. After the situation has been resolved, the technical support specialist describes in detail what happened and assists the manager in finding ways to avert such an incident in the future. Depending on the size of the organization and the severity of the incident, this role may be filled by more than one person.

- *Public relations specialist*—The team member who acts as official spokesperson for the organization to the public. The public relations specialist depends on the manager for accurate, current information.

After a security breach has been blocked and its consequences fully addressed, the response team should review what happened, determine how it might have been prevented, then implement those measures to prevent future problems. Based on the team's experience and findings, the security policy might require revision.

COMMON SECURITY RISKS

Although this chapter devotes several sections to specific risks associated with telecommunications technology, some risks are common to all systems and networks. These include: risks associated with human error, ignorance, and omission; passwords; physical security; and modem access. Most network administrators agree that their primary security concerns relate to employees who ignore, forget, or do not understand security precautions.

Human Error, Ignorance, and Omission

By some estimates, human errors, ignorance, and omissions cause more than half of all security breaches sustained by voice and data networks. Most of these breaches are inadvertent (for example, a network administrator walks away from her office for lunch and leaves her workstation logged onto the network under her administrator ID). The number one method for gaining unauthorized access to a network is to simply ask a user for his or her logon ID, password, authorization code, or to simply ask for permission to enter a secured equipment room.

For example, imagine an intruder who convincingly poses as a support technician. He calls an unsuspecting employee and says, "This is Jared Milne with Ever-able Technical Solutions, and I've been working on your PBX all morning trying to figure out why it's not letting some long-distance calls through. I need to know your authorization code so I can run a series of tests." The trusting employee gladly offers her authorization code, hoping to be helpful. After the intruder has this information, he can obtain access to an outside line and make long-distance calls at the company's expense. He does not need to be in or even near the building to perpetrate the attack. This strategy is commonly called **social engineering**, because it involves manipulating social relationships to gain access to restricted resources. It happens frequently, through a variety of means. Often, the intruder is successful. The best way to counter social engineering is to educate all employees to ask the supposed technician for his telephone number, agreeing to call him back with the information. Chances are, the intruder will hang up. Next, the employee should alert a supervisor or security personnel.

13

This and other risks associated with human ignorance, errors, and omissions are included in the following list:

- Intruders or attackers using social engineering or snooping to obtain user passwords, authorization codes, or physical access to equipment or facilities. Such intruders might also trick users into logging on to a system for them, at which point the intruder is prepared to take over the system.

- An administrator incorrectly creating or configuring ports, lines, user IDs, groups, or their associated rights on a system, resulting in system or network access vulnerabilities.

- Technicians leaving normally secured facilities, such as service area interfaces, cable vaults, equipment rooms, telecommunications closets, and demarcation boxes, unlocked or open.

- Network administrators overlooking security flaws in network design, hardware configuration, operating systems, or applications.

- An unused computer or terminal left logged on to the network, thereby providing an entry point for an intruder.

- Users or administrators choosing easy-to-guess passwords.

- Users or administrators bypassing security policies to make their jobs easier, for example, by connecting modems to their networked workstations, never changing passwords, transmitting data in an unencrypted format, or using insecure, unauthorized applications to transmit data.

- Staff discarding disks or backup tapes in public waste containers.

- Administrators neglecting to remove access and file rights for employees who have left the organization.

- Users writing their passwords on paper, and then placing the paper in an easily accessible place (for example, taping it to their monitor or keyboard).

As you learned earlier, many people-related risks can be addressed through a clear, simple, and strictly enforced enterprise-wide security policy. Employee orientation should make an organization's security policy clear to every new hire. In some organizations, orientation includes videos, skits, and anecdotes that demonstrate the methods intruders use to manipulate employees. Security personnel may even test employees by posing as intruders attempting social engineering tactics. In any case, regular reminders about security should follow the initial security orientation to make sure employees remain vigilant.

Another significant security threat that can be minimized through proper employee education is the selection of insecure passwords.

Passwords

Choosing a secure password is one of the easiest and least expensive ways to guard against unauthorized access. Unfortunately, too many people prefer to use an easy-to-remember—and easily guessable password. If your password is obvious to you, it may be easy for a hacker to discover. The following guidelines for selecting passwords should be part of your organization's security policy. It is especially important for network administrators not only to choose difficult passwords, but also to keep passwords confidential and to change them frequently. The following list offers guidelines for choosing and keeping passwords secure.

- Always change system default passwords after installing new programs or equipment. For example, every mail box in a voice mail system—including the adminstrator's—might have the same password (such as "1234") after the voice mail system is installed.

- Do not use familiar information, such as your birth date, anniversary, pet's name, child's name, spouse's name, own name or nickname, user ID, phone number, address, or any other words or numbers that others might associate with you.

- Do not use any word that might appear in a dictionary. Hackers can use programs that try a combination of your user ID and every word in a dictionary to gain access to the network. This is known as **dictionary attack**, and it is typically the first technique a hacker uses when trying to guess a password (besides asking the user for her password).

- Make the password longer than six characters—the longer, the better.

- Choose a combination of letters and numbers; add special characters, such as exclamation marks or hyphens, if allowed. Also, if passwords are case sensitive, use a combination of capital and lowercase letters.

- Do not write down your password or share it with others. Do not save a list of your passwords in a document on your computer.

- Change your password at least every 60 days, or more frequently, if desired. If you are a network administrator, establish controls through the network operating system to force users to change their passwords at least every 60 days. If you have access to sensitive data, change your password even more frequently.

Password guidelines should be clearly communicated to everyone in your organization through your security policy. Although users may grumble about having to choose a combination of letters and numbers and change their passwords frequently, you can assure them that the company's sensitive data will be safer as a result. No matter how much your colleagues protest, do not back down from your password requirements. Many companies mistakenly require employees only to use a password, without helping or requiring them choose a good one. This oversight increases the risk of security breaches.

Like choosing secure passwords, ensuring physical security of telecommunications equipment and facilities is a simple way of eliminating common security threats.

Physical Security

Another important element in network security is restricting physical access to network components. A risk assessment should point out every place where valuable assets could be compromised. It should also evaluate the likelihood of an intruder using physical access as a way to gain access to any type of resource—tangible or intangible. For example, one especially vulnerable place for any business's information security is the equipment room, where servers, connectivity devices, private switches, and sometimes even building security and climate controls are housed. At any organization, the equipment room should be tightly secured. Only engineers, managers, and technicians who require access to the equipment should be allowed inside. Conversely, access to work areas, where networked workstations are located, is generally less restricted. Still, unauthorized access to any networked node, including a workstation, can lead to a security breach.

13

The following list suggests some locations on voice and data networks that warrant physical security:

Inside a central office or POP:

- Cable vaults

- Equipment rooms

- Power sources (for example, a room of batteries or a fuel tank)

- Cable runs (ceiling and floor)

- Work areas (anyplace where networked workstations and telephones are located)

Outside telecommunications facilities:

- Serving area interfaces and remote switching facilities

- Exterior cross-connect boxes

- Wires leading to or between telephone poles

- Base stations and mobile telephone switching offices used with cellular telephone networks

- Demarcation boxes

Inside a business:

- Entrance facilities

- Equipment room (where servers, private switching systems, and connectivity devices are kept)

- Telecommunications closet

- Data center and separate data storage areas, if applicable

- Cable runs (for example, risers and horizontal wiring)—especially those used for the network's backbone

- Work areas (anyplace where networked workstations and telephones are located)

- Power sources

Most physical security measures involve a type of lock. Locks may be either physical or electronic. Many large organizations require authorized employees to wear electronic access badges. These badges can be programmed to allow their owner access to some, but not all, rooms in a building. Figure 13-2 depicts a typical badge access security system.

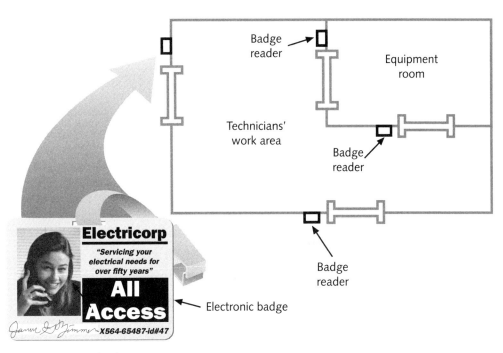

Figure 13-2   A badge access security system

A less expensive alternative to the electronic badge access system consists of locks that require entrants to punch a numeric code to gain access. For added security, these electronic locks can be combined with key locks. A more expensive solution involves **bio-recognition access**, in which a device scans an individual's unique physical characteristics, such as the color patterns in her eye's iris or the geometry of her hand, to verify her identity.

Locked rooms may also require that authorized staff sign in on a log when they enter and sign out when they leave. In addition to using locks, organizations may regulate entrance through physical barriers to their campuses, such as gates, fences, walls, or landscaping. Many IT departments also use closed-circuit TV systems to monitor activity in secured rooms. Surveillance cameras may be placed in computer rooms, telecommunications rooms, supply rooms, and data storage areas, as well as building entrances. A central security office may display several camera views at once, or it may switch from camera to camera. The footage generated from these cameras is usually saved for a specified period of time, in case it's needed in a security breach investigation or prosecution.

As with other security measures, the most important way to ensure physical security is to plan for it. Begin by asking questions related to physical security checks during your risk assessment. Relevant questions include the following:

- Which rooms contain critical systems, transmission media, or data and need to be secured?

- Through what means might intruders gain access to the entrance facility, equipment room, telecommunications rooms, or data storage areas (including not only doors, but also windows, adjacent rooms, ceilings, temporary walls, hallways, and so on)?

- How and to what extent are authorized personnel granted entry? (Do they undergo background or reference checks? Is their need for access clearly justified? Are their hours of access restricted? What is the policy for dealing with lost keys?)

- Are employees instructed to ensure security after entering or leaving secured areas (for example, by not propping open doors)?

- Are authentication methods (such as ID badges) difficult to forge or circumvent?

- Do supervisors or security personnel make periodic physical security checks?

- Are all combinations, codes, or other access means to computer facilities protected at all times, and are these combinations changed frequently?

- What is the plan for documenting and responding to physical security breaches?

Now that you have learned about simple ways to improve your information security by attending to physical security, you are ready to learn about securing modem access, another especially vulnerable aspect of all networks.

Modem Access

In the discussion of risk assessment (earlier in this chapter), you learned the importance of evaluating all the avenues a hacker could use to access your network. This means that, if modems are connected to your voice or data network, you should expect that hackers will try to use them to gain unauthorized access. Modems are notorious for providing hackers with an easy way in. This section explains why that is the case and describes how to combat a hacker's tactics for exploiting modems.

Computer programs that dial multiple telephone numbers in rapid succession, attempting to access and receive a handshake response from a modem, are known as **war dialers**. War dialers are available as freeware from the Internet. Once started, they simply dial different numbers and keep a record of which ones were answered by modems. An intruder can start a war dialer at night, then find a list of modem telephone numbers waiting for him in the morning. Armed with this list, he can dial the modems and attempt to break into systems or networks to which the modems are attached. Note that modems are not only used for remote access to networks; they could also be attached to telephone switches, connectivity devices, building environmental controls, or home security systems, just to name some examples.

Not all modems are at risk for this type of exploitation. On a properly secured network, modems used for general remote access are attached to a remote access server that requires users to log on to the network before gaining rights to resources. Furthermore, the remote access server might be placed in front of a firewall, so that traffic between the server and the rest of the private network is checked for security breaches. However, in cases where individual or special access to a device is needed, modems might be attached directly to network nodes. For example, a PBX contains a modem so that PBX technicians can dial into the system and perform maintenance from remote locations. Similarly, routers contain modems so that they can be remotely managed by network administrators. For security's sake, these modems should be disabled if unused. When such modems are needed, they should be carefully configured to require a secure password before a dial-up connection can be completed, and also to allow incoming calls only at certain times of day, from certain network users, or specific telephone numbers, for example.

Although modem ports on connectivity devices can open access to significant parts of a network, the more common security risks relate to modems that users attach directly to their workstations. For example, suppose Irene in the Shipping Department decides to take a sunny Friday afternoon off, but plans to make up her work over the weekend. Rather than coming into the office on Saturday, she plans to work from home by dialing into her workstation from her home PC. Before leaving work, she attaches a modem to her workstation and initiates the program that allows her remote access. She is not worried about security, because she knows that this program requires a logon ID and password to complete the connection. Her password is "shipping." Within hours of her leaving the office, a war dialer program could discover that her telephone line was answered by a modem. Upon learning her line's number, a hacker could launch an attack to try to access her machine. Because Irene's password is a recognizable word, the hacker would quickly have her password. This allows him access to her machine, which is connected to the network. From her machine, the hacker could try additional methods to gain access to the LAN.

When modems are attached directly to networked modems, they essentially provide a "back door" into the network. That is, they offer the intruder a direct path to the network, without a firewall, router, or PBX in between to slow him down. To prevent employees from using workstation modems, network administrators should rely on security education, security policy enforcement, or best of all, ensure that workstations do not include internal modems and that external modems are not available. On a private LAN that allows employees to dial I, only secure remote access servers should be used as a remote access entry point. Later in this chapter, you learn how telecommunications firewalls can further restrict modem traffic into and out of a network.

13

ENCRYPTION

As you have learned, encryption is the use of an algorithm to scramble data into a format that can be read only by reversing the algorithm—that is, by decrypting the data. The aim of encryption is to keep information private and safe from harm (though remember, virtually no security method is foolproof). Data may be encrypted for transmission over a network, in which case it is encrypted before it is transmitted, and then decrypted when it arrives at its destination. Or, it may be encrypted as it is stored on a computer's hard disk or a removable medium, such as a floppy disk. Many forms of encryption exist, with some being more secure than others. Even as new forms of encryption are developed, hackers develop new ways of hacking their codes.

Encryption acts as the last means of defense against information eavesdropping, theft, or tampering. In other words, if an intruder has exploited all other means of entry, including physical security (for instance, if he has broken into the equipment room) and password security (for instance, if he has logged on to the switch as an administrator), signals can still be secure if they are encrypted. Encryption ensures that:

- Data can only be viewed and voice signals can only be heard by their intended recipient (or at their intended destination).

- Data or voice information was not modified after the sender transmitted it and before the receiver picked it up.

- Data or voice signals received at their intended destination were truly issued by the stated sender and not forged by an intruder.

Key Encryption

The most popular kind of encryption used on data networks today is known as **key encryption**. In this scheme, an algorithm weaves a **key** (a random string of characters) into the original data's bits to generate a unique data block. The best encryption techniques interleave data bits and keys multiple times. The resulting, scrambled data block is known as **cipher text**. In general, the longer the key, the less easily the cipher text can be decrypted by an unauthorized system. For example, a 512-bit key is considered secure, whereas cipher text generated with a 16-bit key could be cracked in no time. The extent to which a key's length improves data security depends on the type of encryption algorithm used, however.

An analogy is useful to better understand key encryption and the effects of key length on security. Key encryption is similar to what happens when you finish a card game and place your five-card hand into the deck, and then shuffle the deck numerous times. After shuffling, it might take you a while to retrieve your hand. As you can imagine, if you shuffled your five cards into four decks of cards at once, it would be even more difficult to find your original hand. In encryption, only the computer, user, or program that is authorized to retrieve the data knows how to unshuffle it. Thus, only the intended recipient can compile the original sequence of data. Figure 13-3 provides a simplified view of key encryption and decryption. (Note that actual key encryption does not simply weave a key into the data once, but rather inserts the key, shuffles the data, shuffles the key, inserts the shuffled key, shuffles the data, and so on for several iterations.)

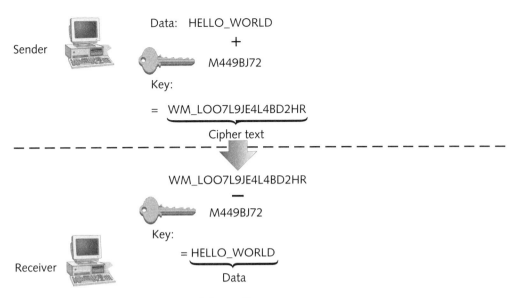

Figure 13-3   Key encryption and decryption

Software that performs key encryption randomly generates keys as needed. Some common programs ship with key encryption capabilities. For example, suppose your computer has a Web browser program that is capable of key encryption and that you use this program to access an online retailer and select some goods for purchase. After entering your personal information and credit card number, you click the "Submit" button to transmit your order to the store's Web server. After clicking "Submit," your Web browser generates a key and weaves this key into your data. That way, your name, address, telephone number, and credit card information is secure while it travels over the Internet. In other cases, special encryption programs are used to generate keys. Such programs work with software packages, such as word processing or spreadsheet programs, to encrypt data files before they are saved or transmitted.

Key encryption can be separated into two categories: private key and public key encryption.

Private Key Encryption

In **private key encryption**, data is encrypted using a single key that only the sender and the receiver know, as depicted in Figure 13-4. This method of key encryption is also known as **symmetric encryption**, because the same key is used during both the transmission and reception of the data. The most popular private key encryption is the **data encryption standard (DES)**, which was developed by IBM in the 1970s.

13

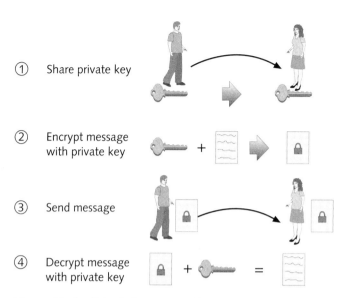

① Share private key

② Encrypt message
with private key

③ Send message

④ Decrypt message
with private key

Figure 13-4   Private key encryption

In private key encryption, for example, before Alicia can decrypt a message that Serge sends, he must share his private key with her. After Alicia receives Serge's encrypted message, she starts a decryption program. The decryption program prompts Alicia for Serge's private key before it will decipher the message and allow her to read it. As you can imagine, one problem with private key encryption is that the sender must somehow share his key with the recipient in advance. For example, Serge could call Alicia and tell her his key over the telephone, or he could send it to her in an e-mail message. However, both telephone conversations and e-mails are subject to eavesdropping. A more secure method for sharing private keys is holding a personal meeting in a private place; but for many reasons, this may not be practical.

Public Key Encryption

To overcome the potential risks of sharing private keys, a method of associating publicly available keys with private keys was developed. This method is called **public key encryption**. In public key encryption, data is encrypted using two keys: One is a key known only to a user (that is, a private key) and the other is a public key associated with the user. A user's public key can be obtained the old-fashioned way—by asking that user—or it can be obtained from a third-party source, such as a public-key server. A **public-key server** is a publicly accessible host (often, a server connected to the Internet) that freely provides a list of users' public keys. A public-key server lists public keys much like a telephone book lists peoples' phone numbers. When a user receives a message encrypted with her public key, her software (for example, her e-mail program) prompts her to enter her private key to decrypt the message. The software already knows what her public key should be, based on her private key. If the public key and private key match, she can open the message. In other words, her public key has an association with her private key, and a message that has been encrypted with her private key can only be decrypted with her private key.

The combination of the public key and private key is known as a **key pair**. In this arrangement, every user has a key pair. One key in a pair is known only to the user, whereas the other key is known to those with whom she exchanges data. Because the two users have a different combination of keys, public key encryption is also known as **asymmetric encryption**. Figure 13-5 illustrates the process of public key encryption.

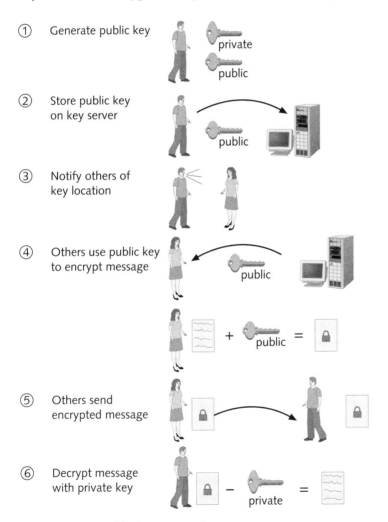

①   Generate public key

②   Store public key
       on key server

③   Notify others of
       key location

④   Others use public key
       to encrypt message

⑤   Others send
       encrypted message

⑥   Decrypt message
       with private key

13

Figure 13-5   Public key encryption

For example, suppose that Alicia and Serge want to use public key encryption to exchange messages over the Internet. Before sending a message to Serge, Alicia looks up Serge's public key on a public-key server. She then uses her encryption software to scramble her message with Serge's public key. When Serge receives the message, his software recognizes that the message has been encoded. Furthermore, the software recognizes that the encryption used Serge's public key. Based on the public key, it then prompts Serge for his private key to decrypt the message. Some examples of public key algorithms include RSA (named after its creators, Rivest, Shamir, and Adleman), Diffie-Hellman, and Elliptic-curve cryptography.

With the abundance of private and public keys, not to mention the number of places where each may be kept, users have found a need for easier key management. **Key management** refers to the way in which two nodes agree on common parameters for the keys they will use. One answer to this problem is using digital certificates. A **digital certificate** is a password-protected and encrypted file that holds an individual's identification information, including a public key. In the context of digital certificates, the individual's public key is used to verify the sender's digital signature. For example, on the Internet, certificate authorities such as VeriSign, will, for a fee, keep your digital certificate on their server and ensure to all who want to send encrypted messages to you (for example, an order via your e-commerce site) that the certificate is indeed yours. Some operating systems contain components that can generate digital certificates for users, such as Windows 2000 Server's Certificate Services. Digital certificates are used in some of the encryption methods discussed in the following sections, such as PGP and SSL.

The following section describes, in general, some public and private key methods of encrypting data as they are transmitted over a network. However, a detailed discussion of encryption techniques is beyond the scope of this book.

Encryption Methods

The history of encryption can be traced back as far as ancient Egypt, where hieroglyphics were used to convey stories. In some senses, today's encryption methods are not much different from those primitive systems. Both involve a substitution of obvious, readable symbols (for example, letters and words) with other symbols that are more difficult to translate. Although this section does not provide a detailed discussion of modern encryption methods, it attempts to summarize those you are most likely to encounter as a telecommunications professional.

Kerberos

Kerberos is a cross-platform authentication protocol that uses key encryption to verify the identity of clients and to securely exchange information after a client logs on to a system. Cross-platform means that Kerberos works equally well on networks that rely on different transmission methods, protocols, or network operating systems. In addition, it supports the exchange of encrypted data between disparate networks. Kerberos is an example of a private-key encryption service.

In Chapter 7, you learned about authentication, the process of a client providing credentials, such as a logon ID and password, to verify the client's rights to access network resources. In traditional client-server authentication, the server only verifies the user's ID against a password in the network operating system's (NOS's) database. In other words, the server assumes that the client is who it says it is. Kerberos, however, does not automatically trust the client. Instead, it requires the client to prove its identity through a third party. This is similar to what happens when you apply for a passport. The government does not simply believe that you are "Paul Morales," but instead requires you to present proof, such as your birth certificate. In addition to checking the validity of a client, Kerberos communications are encrypted and unlikely to be deciphered by any device on the network other than the client. Contrast this type of transmission to the normally unencrypted and vulnerable communication between an NOS and a client.

Kerberos, which is named after the three-headed dog in Greek mythology who guarded the gates of Hades, was designed at Massachusetts Institute of Technology (MIT). MIT still provides free copies of the Kerberos code. In addition, many software vendors have developed their own versions of Kerberos.

PGP (Pretty Good Privacy)

You have probably exchanged e-mail messages over the Internet without much concern for what happens with your message between the time you send it and when your intended recipient picks it up. In addition, you have probably retrieved e-mails sent by friends without thinking that they might actually be sent by individuals who are impersonating your friends over the Internet. In fact, typical e-mail communication is a highly insecure form of data exchange. The contents of a message are usually sent in clear (that is, unencrypted) text, which makes it readable by anyone who can capture the message on its way from you to your recipient. In addition, a person with malicious intentions can easily pretend they are someone else. For example, if your e-mail address is suzy@moldycheez.com, someone else could assume your address and send messages that appear to be sent from suzy@moldycheez.com. To secure e-mail transmissions, a computer scientist named Phil Zimmerman developed PGP in the early 1990s. **PGP (Pretty Good Privacy)** is a public key encryption system that can verify the authenticity of an e-mail sender and encrypt e-mail data in transmission. PGP is freely available both as an open source and proprietary software package. Since its release, it has become the most popular tool for encrypting e-mail.

SSL (Secure Sockets Layer)

Just as clear-text e-mail messages can be intercepted and read while traveling over the Internet, so can Web page text be similarly compromised. For some Web pages, this insecurity might seem insignificant. For example, if your grandmother posts cookie recipes on her home page, she probably doesn't worry about a hacker capturing the information en route when you access the site. However, in the case of exchanging private data—for example, budget figures available via a corporate extranet or personal information sent to a retail Web site during a purchase—security is a significant concern.

13

SSL (Secure Sockets Layer) is a method of encrypting TCP/IP transmissions between a client and server using public key encryption technology. If you trade stocks or purchase goods on the Web, for example, you are most likely using SSL to transmit your order information. SSL is popular in part because it is widely accepted. The most recent versions of Web browsers, such as Netscape Communicator and Internet Explorer, include SSL client support in their software.

Recall from Chapter 12 that Uniform Resource Locators (URLs) for most Web pages begin with the HTTP prefix, which indicates that the Web page is handled by HTTP. When a Web page's URL begins with the prefix **HTTPS**, it is requiring that its data be transferred from server to client and vice versa using SSL encryption. HTTPS uses the TCP port number 443, rather than port 80 (the port used by HTTP). After an SSL connection has been established between a Web server and client, most modern browsers (for example, Internet Explorer and Netscape Communicator versions 4.0 and higher) indicate this connection by showing a padlock in the lower right corner of the screen.

Each time a client and server establish an SSL connection, they also establish a unique **SSL session**, or an association between the client and server that is defined by an agreement on a specific set of encryption techniques. An SSL session allows the client and server to continue to exchange data securely as long as the client is still connected to the server. An SSL session is created by the SSL handshake protocol, one of several protocols within SSL, and perhaps the most significant. As its name implies, the **handshake protocol** authenticates (or introduces) the client and server to each other and establishes terms for how they will securely exchange data. For example, suppose you are connected to the Web and you decide to manage your brokerage account online. After you enter the correct URL, your browser initiates an SSL connection with the handshake protocol. The handshake protocol sends a special message to the server, called a **client_hello** message, which contains information about what level of security your browser is capable of accepting and what type of encryption your browser can decipher (for example, RSA or Diffie-Hellman). The client_hello message also establishes a randomly generated session ID to identify your SSL session. The server responds with a **server_hello** message. The server_hello message confirms the information it received from your client and agrees to certain terms of encryption based on the options your client supplied. Depending on the Web server's preferred encryption method, the server may choose to issue your browser a public key or a digital certificate at this time. After the client and server have agreed on the terms of encryption, they begin exchanging data. In the brokerage account example, this is when your account number and password are finally transmitted to the broker's Web server.

Netscape, the same company that publishes the Communicator Web browser, originally developed SSL. Since that time, the Internet Engineering Task Force (IETF) has attempted to standardize SSL in a protocol called **TLS (transport layer security)**. Besides standardizing SSL for use with software from multiple vendors, IETF also aims to create a version of SSL that will encrypt UDP as well as TCP transmissions. TLS, which will likely be supported by new Web browsers, uses slightly different encryption algorithms than SSL, but otherwise is very similar to the most recent version of SSL.

IPSec (Internet Protocol Security)

In Chapter 12, you also learned that the latest version of the Internet Protocol, IP version 6 (IPv6), inherently provides improved security over the currently used IP version 4. This security is supplied by the **IPSec (Internet Protocol Security)** protocol, which is native to IPv6. Though it is included with the newer IP version, IPSec can also be used with IP version 4. IPSec defines encryption, authentication, and key management for TCP/IP transmissions. It is somewhat different from other methods of securing data in transit. Rather than applying encryption to a stream of data, IPSec actually encrypts data at the packet level by adding security information to the header of all IP packets. Thus, IPSec transforms each data packet. To do so, IPSec operates at the Network layer (Layer 3) of the OSI model.

IPSec accomplishes authentication in two phases. The first phase is key management and the second phase is encryption. As you learned earlier, key management is a way for two systems to agree on the techniques they will use for generating and verifying encryption keys. IPSec relies on **Internet Key Exchange (IKE)** for its key management. After IKE has established the rules for the type of keys two nodes will use, IPSec invokes its second phase, encryption. In this phase, two types of encryption may be used. Both types of encryption provide authentication of the IP packet's data payload through public key techniques. One of the two types also encrypts the entire IP packet for added security.

IPSec can be used with any type of TCP/IP transmission. However, at present it is most commonly used by routers or other connectivity devices in the context of virtual private networks (VPNs). Because VPNs transmit private data over public networks, they require strict encryption and authentication to ensure that data is not compromised. Later in this chapter, you learn more about VPN security measures.

13

TELEPHONE NETWORK SECURITY

Now that you have learned about security risks and precautions common to all telecommunications networks, you are ready to learn about risks inherent in traditional public and private telephone networks. As you read this section, bear in mind that because of the increasing connections between traditionally separate telephone and data networks, some of the following security threats and preventive measures might also apply to data networks.

Eavesdropping

You might have seen advertisements for inexpensive eavesdropping or wiretapping equipment in electronics magazines. The efficacy and legality of these devices is generally questionable; nevertheless, eavesdropping does indeed threaten the security of both individuals and businesses. **Eavesdropping** is the use of a transmission or recording device to capture conversations without the consent of the speakers. This section introduces you to the ways in which telephone connections are vulnerable to eavesdropping.

Although many types of conversations may be subject to electronic eavesdropping—for example, people talking in a closed meeting room—this section only discusses eavesdropping on telephone conversations.

 Eavesdropping, wiretapping, and other security breaches discussed in this book are described solely for the purpose of understanding threats to an organization's resources. Without knowing how such attacks occur, you cannot plan strategies for preventing them. Material in this chapter is not intended to suggest or describe how to conduct security exploits. Be aware that in almost all cases (depending on where you live, whether you have obtained the caller's consent, or whether you have obtained a court's permission), activities such as wiretapping and eavesdropping are illegal, even if you are simply experimenting, and can result in criminal charges.

Three types of individuals or groups characteristically conduct telephone eavesdropping: a family member or close associate (for personal reasons), a government law enforcement official (for legal reasons), or an unknown party with hostile intentions (for competitive reasons, in the case of corporate espionage, or simply for the challenge). Although eavesdropping is generally illegal, it is a useful tool for law enforcement agencies. According to the United States Communications Assistance to Law Enforcement Act (CALEA), if a law enforcement official has obtained a court order to tap a line, telephone companies must provide the official with an undetectable means of eavesdropping on that line. Through the 1990s, the federal government used CALEA to obtain several thousand court orders allowing them to eavesdrop. Most of those orders were justified for use in the war on drugs.

Eavesdropping can be accomplished in one of four ways:

- **Bugging**, or hiding a small microphone or RF transmitter in or on the telephone station to issue conversations via wire or RF waves to a nearby receiver
- Listening on one of the parties' telephone extensions
- Using an RF receiver to pick up inducted current near a telephone wire pair
- **Wiretapping**, or the interception of a telephone conversation by accessing the telephone signal

Of these methods, wiretapping is the most common way to eavesdrop on a telephone conversation. It can occur at any point in the connection between two parties: in the CPE, inside wiring, local loop, a LEC's CO, or another carrier's POP.

One of the most vulnerable parts of the PSTN is the local loop. Recall that the local loop extends from the demarcation point at a residence or business to a central office's entrance facilities. Also recall that demarcation boxes, which contain the connection between outside and inside wires, belong to the LEC and are usually locked. Locking demarcation boxes prevents intruders from connecting to a line from outside. If an intruder gains access, she could, for example, insert wire to create a bridge between the existing transmission and reception wires, and run her wire to an RF transmitter or directly to a tape recorder. Or, she could place an RF receiver in the demarcation box to capture the inducted current from telephone wires, and then transmit the signal to a nearby receiver. Other components of the local loop, such as the wires that lead from a demarcation box to the ground or to a pole, cables strung from pole to pole, and service area interfaces, are vulnerable to similar tactics.

Eavesdropping at the local loop is a serious security threat; however, in almost all cases, only amateurs use this access point. To guard against eavesdropping at the demarcation point, only LEC technicians and in the case of a business, internal telephone technicians should have access to a demarcation box. Individuals and organizations should ensure that the locks on their demarcation boxes couldn't be easily picked or broken (some locks ordinarily supplied by LECs are easy to pick). Other components of the local loop should be restricted to authorized LEC personnel only. To minimize the risk of hackers tapping a signal at a service area interface (a pedestal) or other outdoor cross-connect, such boxes should also be tightly secured. In the case of wires running to or between telephone poles, surrounding the wires in metal conduit lessens the risk of hackers using inducted current to pick up signals. (Using a metal conduit works on the same principle as the shielding that surrounds the core of a coaxial cable and limits the effects of EMI and RFI.)

Despite its name, wiretapping does not always involve splicing wires. In fact, taps used by law enforcement officials are almost always placed directly on the telephone switch. Digital switching makes this method of wiretapping simple and virtually impossible to detect. However, unauthorized parties can also eavesdrop by connecting to the telephone switch. Although telecommunications carriers have strict privacy policies, the fact is that central office personnel can easily connect test equipment to a DACS, for example, and listen to conversations carried by any channel in a T1. Alternatively, a physical security breach at a central office can lead to hackers placing eavesdropping devices or software on a telephone switch for later listening. Figure 13-6 depicts points at which telephone conversations can be easily tapped.

13

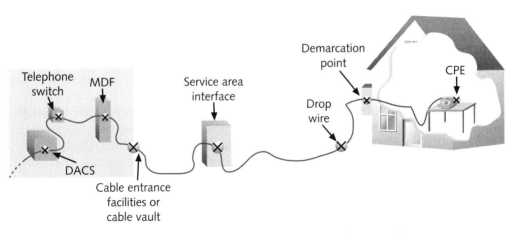

Figure 13-6   Locations where telephone conversations can be tapped

Detecting wiretaps and other eavesdropping methods can be difficult, if not impossible. You cannot tell from the quality of your telephone connection (for example, if you hear static or clicking noises on the line) whether your conversation is being tapped. Some devices claim to detect wiretaps. For example, makers of inexpensive "wiretap detectors" boast that their product can detect any eavesdropper. But these devices are usually nothing more than simple voltmeters or multimeters. The claims are based on the premise that a decrease in your telephone line's normal off-hook voltage indicates a wiretap. However, this principle only holds true if the tap exists between your telephone (or the point at which the wiretap detector is connected) and the LEC's transformer. Attempting to detect wiretaps through a loss in voltage is useless if the tap is closer to the central office, or even within the central office. Furthermore, sophisticated wiretapping equipment can compensate for the weakening effects of a tap, thus keeping the line voltage constant. Finally, normal off-hook voltage can vary throughout the day and from one line to the next. Unless a wiretap detector is expertly calibrated on a line undoubtedly free of taps, it may falsely indicate the presence of a tap during normal voltage fluctuations.

More expensive wiretap detectors measure not only the voltage, but also current and impedance on a telephone circuit. Other wiretap detectors claim to be able to detect and also pinpoint the location of a wiretap. Such devices contain a time domain reflectometer. Still other sophisticated detectors claim to detect bugs by sensing whether an inducted current is being picked up and transmitted. However, such detectors can cost tens of thousands of dollars, and they still cannot detect eavesdropping beyond the local loop.

If your organization has sufficient reason to believe that its telephone lines are being tapped, you may perform a physical inspection to search for taps on the CPE, inside wiring, and around the demarcation box. For example, an extra cable or set of wires exiting the demarcation box might indicate the presence of a wiretap. Take pictures of what looks suspicious, but do not move any wires or attachments. Do not open the demarcation box if it is owned by the LEC (most often, this is the case). Instead, call a local law enforcement official. Together, law enforcement and the telecommunications provider can determine whether a wiretap exists.

Encrypting voice conversations can foil wiretaps. For analog voice signals traversing the PSTN, this encryption requires specialized devices attached to each party's telephone. The devices scramble incoming voice signals at the caller's telephone, and then unscramble the encoded signal at the called party's telephone. Using analog voice encryption is expensive and impractical for most businesses, because every customer, vendor, employee home, business partner, and any other called party requires the same type of encryption attachment as is used on the business's telephones. At the time of this writing, such attachments are cost-prohibitive. On the other hand, voice signals transmitted over data networks are easier and less costly to encrypt. They could use some of the encryption techniques described earlier in this chapter, such as IPSec.

Next, you learn about vulnerabilities inherent in private switches (for example, PBXs) and voice mail systems.

Private Switch Security

Recall from Chapter 5 that private switches route calls between telephones within an organization and from telephones inside an organization to outside lines. They also provide enhanced features, such as automatic call distribution (ACD), computer-telephony integration (CTI), voice mail, and other messaging services. Also recall that the most common type of private switch is the private branch exchange (PBX). Therefore, this section uses PBXs as examples when describing the security risks of private switches. The same vulnerabilities may apply to other types of private switches, such as CENTREX or key systems.

In essence, a PBX is a miniature central office that serves only one organization rather than thousands of consumers. However, whereas a telecommunications carrier's central office is highly secure, often a PBX is left unguarded or insufficiently configured for security. As LECs and IXCs strengthened switch security over the last 30 years, hackers have increasingly targeted the more vulnerable PBXs. A hacker might want to gain access to a PBX to:

- Eavesdrop on telephone conversations, thus obtaining proprietary information

- Capture information about the types of calls an organization makes—for example, to whom, at what times, and with what frequency

- Use the PBX for making long-distance calls at the company's expense, a practice known as **toll fraud** (from the use of the word "toll" to describe long-distance calls)

- Barrage the PBX with such a high volume of signals that it cannot process valid calls, a practice known as a **denial-of-service attack**

- Vandalize PBX equipment, tamper with PBX configurations, logs, or features, or pull pranks, such as leaving objectionable messages in voice mail boxes or interrupting phone calls in progress

- Use the PBX as a connection to other parts of a telephone network, such as voice mail, ACD, or paging systems

- Use the PBX as a connection to another network (for example, a company's LAN), where additional security attacks are launched

13

Hackers often gain access to a PBX through the most common security risks discussed previously in this chapter: social engineering, physical access, and poorly chosen (or default) passwords. For example, a classic PBX toll-fraud technique is known as the **9-0-# scam**. In this scam, an intruder calls an unsuspecting employee at an organization that uses a PBX and says she is a telephone company employee who needs to troubleshoot a telephone problem. She asks the employee to press 9, then 0, then the # key on his telephone, and then hang up (in other words, press the switch hook), to aid in diagnosing the "problem." In fact, on some PBX systems, this is the sequence that transfers a caller to an outside line. (A "9" accesses an outside line, a "0" accesses a local operator, and a "#" cancels the previous request, and pressing the switch hook transfers the caller.) After the intruder has been transferred, she can make long-distance calls at the organization's expense (assuming the organization uses this type of PBX). As with other social engineering techniques, the 9-0-# scam can be countered by educating employees to never respond to the requests from an anonymous technician and, instead, to ask the technician for a number at which he or she can be reached. Because toll fraud is so common and accounts for billions of dollars of lost revenue each year (according to the FCC), this section focuses on ways to detect and prevent this type of PBX security breach.

Another toll-fraud vulnerability on PBXs is the **direct inward system access (DISA)** feature. DISA allows an organization's employees to complete long-distance calls from outside the organization by first accessing the PBX via a toll-free number. For example, a salesperson who regularly travels could call his company's 1-800 number while on the road, and gain access to a long-distance line. Then, he could place calls to another client across the state, and have the charges billed directly to his company. DISA's primary advantage is that it saves businesses money. Per-minute toll costs are lower with DISA than with either direct dialing or a calling card. Also, calls that use a company's DISA feature are included in the company's total call volume, for which they receive a volume discount. The DISA feature is also a convenience to employees. It also makes it unnecessary for employees to pay for calls themselves and then submit the cost of the calls later on an expense report. However, DISA also presents a security risk. Obviously, a company should never divulge its DISA access number. However, hackers may use techniques (such as social engineering) to obtain the number, after which they can make long-distance calls at the company's expense.

One remedy for DISA vulnerabilities is to simply remove the DISA feature and require traveling or remote employees to use calling cards. However, because of DISA's cost and accounting benefits, this might not be the best solution. If DISA is used, it should be configured with security in mind. First, after a PBX receives a DISA line request, it should respond not with a regular dial tone, but with a voice message or with no tone. If a PBX responds with a dial tone, a hacker who is simply trying numbers to see whether he can stumble upon a DISA line knows that he has been successful. Second, a PBX should not respond to an incoming call until after at least four rings. This tactic could foil hackers who are using a program to dial hundreds of numbers in sequence, because such programs do not sustain their attempts for more than a few rings. Finally, employees should be required to enter an authorization code before access to the line is granted.

An **authorization code** is a sequence of numbers that allows an employee to gain access to a certain line through the PBX. Authorization codes are useful for billing purposes. For example, an organization might assign each department a different authorization code. At the end of the month, the PBX can generate a report listing all of an organization's telephone calls according to authorization code, and thus, by department. (Although for security purposes, the authorization code should not appear on the report.) They are also useful for limiting access to long-distance lines. For example, in a manufacturing plant with several shifts of workers, the managers might want to limit access to long-distance lines to supervisors only. Supervisors would then need to press an authorization code before they could be transferred to a line that can complete long-distance calls.

However, authorization codes, like passwords, can be abused. Hackers can commit toll fraud after obtaining DISA or other PBX authorization codes from employees, documents, or lists of codes that have been compromised and publicized by other hackers. As you might guess, when a hacker obtains an authorization code, he, too, can complete long-distance calls at the company's expense.

Authorization codes should be treated like any other passwords. To guard against the abuse of authorization codes, keep the codes private, and take care to educate employees about the importance of authorization code privacy. Also, be sure to eliminate any publicly-available lists of codes. In addition, make sure that authorization codes are difficult to guess and are composed of as many digits as the PBX allows. Codes created for testing purposes (for example, when the PBX was first installed) should be deleted. Configure the PBX to prevent multiple, unsuccessful attempts to enter an authorization code. A hacker who is trying to guess an authorization code will likely make several unsuccessful attempts before stumbling upon the right one. If a PBX is configured to cut the hacker's connection after two or three attempts, his attempts will be disrupted. Issue authorization codes sparingly. Verify that every employee who requests an authorization code can justify the request with a clear, business reason. Cancel unused authorization codes. Finally, as with other passwords, change authorization codes frequently.

To minimize the potential for all types of toll fraud—the 9-0-# scam, abuse of DISA, and abuse of authorization codes—you should configure a PBX to limit access to any long-distance numbers the company does not use. For example, many organizations restrict use of long-distance numbers that begin with a "900" NPAs or a foreign country's code. Access to outside lines can also be blocked entirely during certain times or days. For example, a firm might prevent a PBX from completing any long-distance calls in the evenings or on weekends.

Some PBXs can be configured to help detect and prevent toll fraud. Most PBXs are programmed to deny any future attempts to connect with a port after three unsuccessful connection attempts. If the PBX is not already configured in this manner, a network administrator could program the PBX to recognize instances of multiple, unsuccessful attempts to access a DISA number. Further, she could program the PBX to issue an alarm when this event occurs. Or, organizations may install PBX software or additional devices that help detect toll fraud and attempted toll fraud. Later in this chapter, you learn how one device, a telecommunications firewall, can help detect and prevent toll fraud. Some telecommunications carriers also offer toll fraud prevention services with their telephone service.

Although toll fraud is illegal in the United States, victimized companies are still responsible for paying the charges incurred via unauthorized access to their PBXs.

13

Although the majority of PBX abuses relate to toll fraud, some unauthorized accesses are targeted at stealing information or tampering with a network. Most commonly, these attempts abuse remote access technologies. You are familiar with the concept of remote access from Chapter 7's discussion of remote access servers that operate on LANs. In the context of telephone switches, remote access typically refers to the ability to dial into the device from a telephone not connected to the PBX's network. In other words, the PBX has a port attached to a modem that accepts incoming calls. After the caller has gained access, she can log on to the PBX (given valid credentials) and perform system administration or access other components of the voice network. Some PBXs offer remote access so that the PBX vendor or the company's PBX technician can remotely monitor, troubleshoot, or maintain the switch.

However, remote access also makes the PBX vulnerable to hackers. Therefore, remote access should only be enabled when absolutely necessary (for example, during a period in which PBX vendors must perform maintenance on the system). If used, remote access, as with any other computer system access, should require the user to log on and provide a secure password. Very few people should require remote access. In fact, at some organizations, only the voice network administrator may know how to remotely access the PBX. Or, the PBX's remote access feature can be tailored to allow different levels of access—for example, the administrator has access with full privileges to create, modify, and delete system settings, but the vendor dialing in to troubleshoot a problem might only have rights to view system settings. And with DISA lines, a PBX's remote access lines should answer only after at least four rings and respond with a message or with no dial tone whatsoever.

This section has described many toll-fraud techniques related to the most popular type of private switch, the PBX. However, hackers may also take advantage of other telephone network devices and features to make long-distance calls at someone else's expense.

Voice Mail Security

Private switches are not the only targets for toll fraud. Voice mail, calling cards, and pay phones can be similarly exploited. Voice mail, the service that allows callers to leave messages for later retrieval, is a popular access point for hackers. This presents a risk because once inside the voice mail system, a user can sometimes push a series of buttons to transfer to an outside line. To find a voice mail system number, an intruder starts a computer program, such as a war dialer, that calls potentially thousands of numbers until it finds a line that answers with a voice mail prompt. Once inside the voice mail system, the intruder performs similar techniques to crack the password for a voice mailbox. Or, he might obtain a list of voice mail numbers and mailbox passwords from the Internet. After he has gained access to a voice mailbox, he presses a series of buttons to be transferred to an outside line, and then makes toll calls at the organization's expense.

In another example of voice mail toll fraud, a hacker might not even need to gain mailbox access. Instead, he exploits voice mail systems that use the auto attendant feature.

This is the feature that greets callers with a message and instructs them to, for example, "Press 1 to leave a message for a customer service representative," "Press 2 to leave a message for a sales representative," and so on. Unless a voice mail system is properly secured, hackers may be able to press a digit not advertised by the auto attendant message to access an outside line.

Voice mail presents additional security threats besides toll fraud. Criminals who need an anonymous place to exchange messages make use of mailboxes that they have hijacked. In fact, if a hacker obtains access to a voice mail system's administrator mailbox, she can set up additional mailboxes for her private use. Valid voice mail users will never notice. Often, this is a simple task, because organizations choose easily guessable passwords or neglect to change the default administrator password.

Voice mail abuse can also take the form of privacy breaches. If a hacker guesses the password for a mailbox, naturally, she can listen to the messages in that user's mailbox. But if she gains access to an administrator's mailbox, she can probably listen to any message in the system. Worse, she could have messages left in certain mailboxes automatically forwarded to another mailbox (for example, one that she has set up for herself) or to another system. Imagine how useful this type of attack could be to a company's competitor. For example, an intruder from Company X could break into Company Y's voice mail system, and add a feature that forwards each message left in each executive's voice mailbox to an anonymous mailbox in Company Y's system. Thus, Company X has gained access to potentially confidential information. Meanwhile, managers at Company Y never notice.

To guard against voice mail toll fraud, unauthorized mailbox use, and privacy breaches, voice mail system access numbers should not be publicly available. And as with PBX authorization codes, voice mailbox passwords should be chosen with security in mind. For instance, they should be difficult to guess, as long as possible, changed frequently, and different from the default passwords that are established at installation. In the case of privacy breaches, voice mail system administrators should regularly monitor the mailbox activity for suspicious new mailboxes or feature changes.

Despite your best efforts to enforce policies and secure access points against PBX and voice mail abuses, your telephone network might require more protection. In that case, a telecommunications firewall can provide another layer of security.

Telecommunications Firewalls

As you learned in Chapter 11, a firewall is a specialized computer that selectively filters or blocks traffic between networks. A **telecommunications firewall** is a type of firewall that monitors incoming and outgoing voice traffic and selectively blocks telephone calls between different areas of a voice network. Telecommunications firewalls are typically installed between a private switch, such as a PBX, and the lines or trunks that lead to a telecommunications carrier. This arrangement is pictured in Figure 13-7.

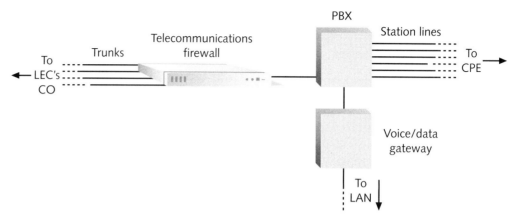

Figure 13-7 Placement of a telecommunications firewall

A telecommunications firewall's primary purpose is to prevent intruders from gaining access to a voice network. To accomplish this, it performs the following functions:

- Prevents incoming calls from certain sources from reaching the PBX—for example, it can prevent fax transmissions from known direct-marketing organizations that issue unsolicited faxes and it can allow only a network administrator's home telephone line to dial into a PBX maintenance port

- Prevents certain types of outgoing calls from leaving the voice network—for example, calls to 900 numbers or foreign countries

- Prevents all outgoing calls during specified time periods

- Collects information about each incoming and outgoing call, including type of originating equipment (for example, telephone, fax, or modem), telephone number, called number, date, start and end time, and duration (note that most, if not all, of this information can also be provided by the LEC)

- Restricts the type of traffic that can be transmitted over a particular line—for instance, on a line designated for voice use, it prevents fax or modem calls from being completed, thus preventing employees from dialing outside ISPs by connecting their desktop telephone to their workstation's modem

- Detects signals or calling patterns characteristic of intrusion attempts, immediately terminates the suspicious connection, and then alerts the system administrator of the potential breach

- Monitors line and trunk status (for example, busy or not answering) and utilization over time

Some of the previously listed tasks are not unique to telecommunications firewalls, but can also be achieved through software on a private switch or by subscribing to a carrier's security services. For example, most PBXs can log detailed information about incoming and outgoing calls. However, most PBXs do not monitor traffic for signs of attempted intrusion and alert staff if a suspected intrusion occurs. In addition, PBX-based call information recording applies to only the PBX(s) on which it is installed. This may not be practical in a large organization that uses several PBXs or PBXs from different manufacturers. Conversely, telecommunications firewalls can be connected to multiple private switches. Thus, a voice network system administrator has a single, centralized interface from which she can configure and apply an entire company's telephone policies.

As with any sophisticated computer, a telecommunications firewall cannot simply be placed on a voice network and be expected to perform exactly as you want it to. Instead, managers and telephone network administrators must first devise security policies specific to the telecommunications firewall. The voice network administrator then applies these policies by creating access controls—or rules—in the firewall configuration. For example, suppose you work for an international firm that manufactures electronic components, headquartered in San Jose, California. The company has locations across the globe, and employs close to 8,000 people. Because the telephone network is so complex, you have recently purchased a telecommunications firewall to improve the voice network's security. Some of the access policies you configure in the telecommunications firewall include: allowing long distance calls between each of the international offices, but only during working hours in the applicable time zone, preventing long distance calls to any "900" number, preventing outgoing modem traffic from any voice extension in any location, preventing incoming modem or fax calls on any voice line, preventing any incoming calls to the PBX maintenance port, alerting network administrators when multiple unsuccessful attempts are made to access a long-distance line using an authorization code, and so on. Because some key employees need special consideration, you also configure exceptions to the rules. For example, you allow managers at the director level and higher to have unlimited outgoing calls from their telephones and faxes. You might also allow the PBX's maintenance port to accept incoming modem traffic from your home computer's modem line only. Finally, you configure the telecommunications firewall to record every detail about call activity for a week, to get a sense of what type of traffic travels over your voice network. Later, you may choose to limit the type of details that are recorded, because amassing such a large amount of information can make distinguishing important events from insignificant events difficult.

The default access levels on each type of telecommunications firewall vary from one manufacturer to another, so be certain you understand how your firewall's policies are structured. For example, some firewalls begin with a default status of allowing all calls into or out of a network. This default policy provides no security whatsoever. Instead, it leaves the network administrator to set all call limits through the configuration. If this is the case with your telecommunications firewall, begin configuration by setting the broadest types of limits (such as disallowing any outgoing long-distance phone calls during the weekend) first, and then applying more specific limits later.

13

LAN AND WAN SECURITY

The following sections describe the ways in which LANs and WANs can be attacked by malicious intruders, and how best to protect your data network. Note that most of the material applies to wireless networks as well as wire-bound networks, although security risks unique to wireless transmission are discussed in the last part of this chapter.

Network Operating System Security

You have already learned about the ways a server can verify a client's identity: through routine NOS authentication and through a more restrictive Kerberos authentication. However, security measures are not complete just because a client has successfully logged on to the network. Given the wealth of resources on a network, an administrator must take care to restrict users' access to them. For example, a network administrator should assume that some of her clients, no matter how much security education they receive, will choose poor passwords or share their logon ID and password with others. This opens the door for hackers to log on to the network. However, logging on to a network as a client should not mean that the hacker can access significant or confidential resources. Access to these resources should be restricted to only those who require it. Regardless of whether your servers run a Novell, Microsoft, or UNIX network operating system, you can implement basic security by restricting what users are authorized to view, modify, erase, or control on a network.

To begin planning client-server security, every network administrator should understand which resources on the server all users need to access. The rights conferred to all users are called public rights, because anyone can have them and exercising them presents no security threat to the network. In most cases, public rights are very limited. They may include privileges to view and execute programs from the server and to read, create, modify, delete, and execute files in a shared data directory.

Next, network administrators typically group users according to their security levels. Just you would guess, a **group** is a collection of users (or other network objects, such as printers or servers) that are associated with each other for the purposes of streamlining network management. Grouping users simplifies the process of granting users rights to resources. For example, all 20 users in an Accounting Department might be collected in the "ACCTG" group. The network administrator grants "ACCTG" rights to a directory on the server that contains budget and forecast spreadsheets. That way, he does not have to assign rights separately to each of the 20 users. Other groups, such as "ENGR" and "ADMIN" on the same network, will not be assigned the same rights, because employees in these groups are not supposed to access those files.

In addition to restricting users' access to files and directories on a server, a network administrator can constrain the ways in which users access the server and its resources.

Following is a list of only some of the additional restrictions that an administrator may use to further protect network resources:

- *Time of day*—Use of logon IDs can be valid only during specific hours, for example, between 8:00 A.M. and 5:00 P.M. Specifying access by time of day increases security by preventing logon IDs from being used by unauthorized personnel after hours.

- *Total time logged in*—Use of logon IDs may be restricted to a specific number of hours per day. Restricting total hours in this way can increase security in the case of temporary IDs. For example, suppose that your organization offers an e-mail training class to a group of visiting teachers one afternoon, and the e-mail program and training files reside on your staff server. You might create IDs that are valid for no more than six hours that day.

- *Source address*—Use of logon IDs can be restricted to certain workstations or certain areas of the network (for example, one LAN within a WAN). This restriction can prevent unauthorized use of logon IDs from workstations outside the network (for example, from hackers attempting to access the network from a modem connection).

- *Unsuccessful logon attempts*—As with PBX security, use of data network security allows administrators to block a connection after a certain number of unsuccessful logon attempts. This guards against hackers who repeatedly attempt to log on under a valid ID for which they do not know the password.

Besides establishing client rights and restrictions to network resources, a network administrator must pay attention to security precautions when installing and using the network operating system. An obvious example is choosing a secure administrator password and changing it frequently. Perhaps less obvious is the strategy of disabling the default administrator account ID that an NOS creates during installation. For example, the default user ID that enables someone to modify anything in Windows 2000 Server is called "Administrator." This default is well known, so if you leave the default ID as "Administrator," you have given a hacker half the information he needs to access your system and obtain full rights.

Also, a vigilant network administrator will take care to keep her servers' NOS software current. With some regularity, hackers find ways to exploit software flaws in network operating system software. In response, the NOS manufacturer issues a software update that, when installed on each network server, fixes the flaw. Network administrators can subscribe to mailing lists or newsgroups to stay abreast of the latest NOS software updates.

Applying protective measures through the network operating system is only a small part of network security. Next, you learn about security considerations that apply to a data network's topology and connectivity.

13

Security Through Network Design

Ask any security expert for the best way to protect your network against intruders, and she will tell you to keep it isolated from the rest of the outside world! Of course, this strategy is impossible in today's business environment. The next best protection, then, is to carefully restrict access at every point at which your network connects to the rest of the world. This principle forms the basis of design-based network security.

This section describes security risks inherent in (roughly) Layers 1 and 2 of the OSI model—the Physical and Data Link layers. Recall that the transmission media, NICs, hubs, and network transmission methods (for example, Ethernet) reside at these layers. At these levels, security breaches require more technical sophistication than those that take advantage of social engineering or poor physical security. You have already learned about one network design risk: the use of modems connected to private networks. Following is a list of additional, significant risks inherent in data network hardware and design:

- *Transmissions can be intercepted*—Wire-bound transmissions emit EMI that can be picked up by a nearby receiver. Fiber-based transmissions are more difficult to intercept, but it is possible for someone with physical access to the cabling to open it and redirect a portion of the signal to another fiber, with a marginal impact on legitimate network transmission. (Wireless transmissions, as you learn later in this chapter, are also in danger of being intercepted.) Physical security of cabling, both inside and outside the organization, should be ensured. And as with telephone eavesdropping, the best solution to thwarting intruders intent on intercepting data signals is to apply strong encryption techniques.

- *Leased lines are vulnerable to eavesdropping*—MANs and WANs that rely on leased public lines, such as T1s or ISDN connections to the Internet, are more vulnerable to eavesdropping than private connections. As you learned earlier, if an intruder gains access to a central office switch, for example, he can intercept any signals traversing a T1. Not only could he easily listen in on voice conversations, but he could also connect a computer to the circuit and capture packets using a computer known as a **sniffer** (or **packet sniffer**). Sniffers are helpful tools when diagnosing network transmission problems, but they are also useful to hackers who want to gather data in transit. If your network uses leased public lines and you are concerned about security, you should encrypt the data at least before it enters the WAN.

- *Shared media and broadcast traffic allow data capture*—You learned in Chapter 10 that Ethernet, the most popular data network access method, broadcasts signals over a shared segment, with only the destination node picking up traffic meant for it. This means that if a network node were designed to do so, it could intercept all packets traveling over its segment. In fact, any workstation can accomplish this if its NIC configuration is changed to **promiscuous mode**, meaning that it indiscriminately accepts all packets on the channel, not only those destined for it. After setting her NIC to run in promiscuous mode, a user could start a network monitoring program to capture the packets and view data traveling over the network. Recall that hubs simply repeat signals, essentially extending a segment. Therefore, they cannot prevent against this type of traffic capturing. Conversely, switches provide logical point-to-point communications, which limit the availability of data transmissions to the sending and receiving nodes.

- *Device ports can be exploited*—As with PBXs, hubs, routers, switches, and servers often have ports (whether physical, like a modem connection, or virtual, like a TCP/IP port) that are used for maintenance. For example, a network administrator might use the Telnet utility to connect to a router's configuration port and perform configuration changes while on the road. If a hacker gains access to this port, she could attempt to log on to the router as the administrator. If she accomplishes that, she could reconfigure the router, access data in transit, or bring down the network, depending on that router's placement in the network's design. In response to this risk, network administrators should disable all unused ports on their connectivity devices. Access to used ports should be highly restricted, and data transmitted to and from these ports should be encrypted.

- *Private IP addresses can be exploited*—On many private networks that connect to the Internet, a gateway or router is used to mask the IP addresses of transmissions sent from individual network nodes. However, if this precaution is not taken, or if the devices are not properly configured to mask internal IP addresses, users on outside networks (such as the Internet) can read the private addresses. If outsiders obtain internal IP addresses, they could use those addresses to pretend that they have authority to access your internal network from the Internet—a process called **IP spoofing**.

- *Private and public hosts on the same network*—Computers hosting very sensitive data may coexist on the same part of a network with computers open to the general public. This presents a significant security risk because if a hacker logs on to the public host (such as a Web server), he is not far from logging on to the private hosts on the same network. To guard against this possibility, place private resources (such as servers) on different subnets from public resources. Also, impose restrictions on connections between the public and private parts of the network (for example, by using a firewall or gateway).

Firewalls, key to any secure data network design, are discussed next.

Firewalls

As you learned in Chapter 11, a firewall is a specialized computer that selectively filters or blocks traffic between networks. A firewall typically involves a combination of hardware and software and may reside between two interconnected private networks or, more typically, between a private network and a public network (such as the Internet). Many types of firewalls exist, and a detailed discussion of each is beyond the scope of this book. However, it is useful to recognize which functions firewalls can provide, where they can appear on a network, and how to decide what you need in a firewall.

13

The simplest and most common form of a firewall is a **packet-filtering firewall**, which is a device that operates at the Data Link and Transport layers of the OSI model. It examines the header of every packet of data that it receives to determine whether that type of packet is authorized to continue to its destination. If a packet does not meet the filtering criteria, the firewall denies it. However, if a packet does meet filtering criteria, the firewall accepts it, or lets the packet pass to the rest of the network connected to the firewall. An example of a popular packet-filtering firewall is pictured in Figure 13-8.

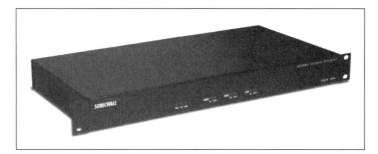

Figure 13-8   Firewall

As with telecommunications firewalls, packet-filtering firewalls do not operate effectively until the administrator has performed a great deal of custom configuration. For packet-filtering firewalls, a network administrator must configure the firewall to accept or deny certain types of data traffic. Some of the criteria that a firewall might use to accept or deny data include the following:

- Source and destination IP addresses

- Source and destination ports (for example, ports that supply TCP/UDP connections, FTP, Telnet, HTTP, and so on)

- Use of the TCP, UDP, or ICMP transport protocols

- A packet's status as the first packet in a new data stream or a subsequent packet

- A packet's status as inbound or outbound to or from a private network

- A packet's status as originating from or being destined for a particular application on a private network

Based on these options, a network administrator could configure her firewall, for example, to prevent any IP address that does not begin with "67.34," the first two octets of the addresses on her private network, from accessing the network's router and servers. Furthermore, she could disable—or block—certain well-known ports, such as TCP ports 20 and 21 which provide the FTP service through the firewall's configuration. Blocking ports prevents *any* user from connecting to and completing a transmission through those ports. This technique is useful to further guard against unauthorized access to the network. In other words, even if a hacker were able to spoof an IP address that began with "67.34," he could not access the FTP ports (which are notoriously insecure) on the firewall. Ports can be blocked not only on firewalls, but also on routers, servers, or any device that uses ports, providing these devices have the correct software installed. For example, if you established a Web server for testing but did not want anyone in your organization to connect to your Web pages through their browsers, you could block TCP port 80 on that server.

You will recognize examples of firewall placement in most VPN architectures. For example, you might design a VPN that uses the Internet to connect your Omaha office with your Hartford office. To ensure that only traffic from Omaha can access your Hartford LAN, you could install a packet-filtering firewall between the Hartford LAN and the Internet that accepts incoming traffic only from IP addresses that match the IP addresses on your Omaha LAN. In a way, the firewall acts like a bouncer at a private club who checks everyone's ID and ensures that only club members enter through the door. In the case of the Omaha-Hartford VPN, the firewall discards any data packets that arrive at the Hartford firewall and do not contain source IP addresses that match those of Omaha's LAN. Unfortunately, this strict configuration also prevents users on the Hartford LAN from viewing any pages on the Internet or receiving mail from anyone outside the company (unless they rely on the Omaha LAN for these services). Therefore, the configuration must be further refined to indicate not only the origin but also the type of traffic that is allowable only on the Omaha-Hartford connection.

In another example, suppose that your Hartford network hosts a server that stores confidential information, such health insurance claims, which only the Hartford-based insurance auditors need to access. You could add a filter in the firewall to block all external traffic (from the Internet as well as the Omaha LAN) from reaching the destination address of that server.

Because you must tailor a firewall to your network's needs, you cannot simply purchase one, install it between your private LAN and the Internet, and expect it to offer much security. Instead, you must first consider what type of traffic you want to filter, then configure the firewall accordingly. It may take weeks to achieve the best configuration—not so strict that it prevents authorized users from transmitting and receiving necessary data, and not so lenient that you risk security breaches. Further complicating the matter is that you may need to create exceptions to the rules. For example, suppose that one of your company's auditors is temporarily working out of the Omaha office and needs to access the Hartford server that stores health insurance claims. In this instance, the WAN's administrator might create an exception to allow transmissions from the auditor's workstation's static IP address to reach that server. That way, even if someone obtained the auditor's logon ID and password, he could not access the health insurance information unless he also obtained her computer or spoofed her IP address.

However, because packet-filtering routers operate at the Network and Transport layers of the OSI model and examine only network addresses, they cannot distinguish between a user who is trying to breach the firewall and a user who is authorized to do so. To ensure that an unauthorized user does not simply sit down at the workstation belonging to an

13

authorized user and try to circumvent the firewall, a more sophisticated technique—such as user authentication—is necessary.

Many more sophisticated firewalls—both hardware- and software-based—exist. Choosing the appropriate firewall for your network can be a difficult task. Among the factors you want to consider when making your decision are the following:

- Does the firewall support encryption?
- Does the firewall support user authentication?
- Does the firewall allow the network administrator to manage it centrally and through a standard interface?
- How easily can you establish rules for access to and from the firewall?
- Does the firewall support filtering at the highest layers of the OSI model, not just at the Data Link and Transport layers?
- Does the firewall provide logging and auditing capabilities, or alert you to possible intrusions?
- Does the firewall protect the identity of your internal LAN's addresses from the outside world?

If you cannot find a firewall capable of blocking traffic at the highest layers of the OSI model, you might choose to add a proxy server to the boundary between your private network and the Internet. Proxy servers are discussed in the following section.

Proxy Servers

One approach to enhancing the security of the Network and Transport layers provided by firewalls is to combine a packet-filtering firewall with a proxy service. A **proxy service** is a software application on a network host that acts as an intermediary between the external and internal networks, screening all incoming and outgoing traffic. The network host that runs the proxy service is known as a **proxy server** or gateway. Proxy servers manage security at all layer's of the OSI model. To understand how they work, think of the secure data on a server as the president of a country, and the proxy server as the secretary of state. Rather than having the president risk his or her safety by leaving the country, the secretary of state travels abroad, acting as the president's substitute. In fact, foreign leaders may never actually meet the president. Instead, the secretary of state always acts as his or her proxy.

On a network, a proxy server (like most firewalls) is placed between the private and public parts of a network. To the outside world, a proxy server appears to be an internal network server. In reality, it is merely another filtering device for traffic leaving and entering the internal LAN. Among other things, a proxy server prevents the outside world from discovering the addresses of the internal network. For example, suppose your LAN uses a proxy server, and you want to send an e-mail message from your workstation to your best friend via the Internet. After clicking the "Send" button, your message travels from your workstation to your internal LAN's mail server. The mail server sends the message to the proxy server. The proxy server repackages the data that makes up the message and replaces the mail server's (the source) IP address with its own IP address. Next, the proxy server passes your repackaged data to the packet-filtering firewall. The firewall verifies that the source IP address in your packets is valid (that it came from the proxy server) and then sends your message to the Internet. Examples of proxy server software include Novell's BorderManager and the Microsoft Internet Security and Acceleration (ISA) Server 2000, an optional service for Windows 2000 servers. Figure 13-9 depicts how a proxy server might fit into a WAN design.

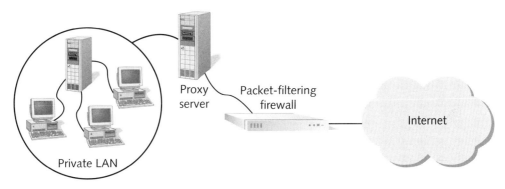

Figure 13-9   A proxy server on a WAN

Virtual Private Networks (VPNs)

As you learned in Chapter 11, virtual private networks (VPNs) are private networks that use public channels to connect clients and servers. Often VPNs integrate a wide variety of clients, from dial-up users at home to networked workstations in offices to Web servers at an ISP. The mix of client types, transmission methods, and services used by VPNs adds to their design complexity, as well as to the complexity of their security needs. Fully describing the nuances of designing VPNs is beyond the scope of this book. In this section, however, you learn about the significant security techniques particular to these unique networks.

VPNs typically use the Internet, PSTN, or both of these public networks to connect multiple sites; obviously, the use of such large public networks presents security hazards. To diminish security threats, VPNs often take advantage of firewalls and special protocols that encrypt the data transmitted over public connections. The following sections describe some of the special protocols used in VPN connectivity.

In the context of Chapter 11's discussion of modem communications, you learned that PPP is a dial-in protocol that belongs in the Data Link layer (Layer 2) of the OSI model and provides transport services over serial and digital communications lines for the TCP/IP and IPX/SPX protocols. PPP originated for use with direct dial-in connections to Windows NT RAS servers. The **Point-to-Point Tunneling Protocol (PPTP)** expands on PPP by encapsulating it so that any type of PPP data can traverse the Internet masked as pure IP transmissions. PPTP supports the encryption, authentication, and LAN access services provided by Windows NT RAS server and by the newer, Windows 2000 RRAS server. Instead of users having to dial directly into a remote access server, however, they can dial into their ISP using PPTP and thereby gain secure access to their corporate LAN via the Internet.

The process of encapsulating one protocol to make it appear as another type of protocol is known as **tunneling**. Essentially, tunneling makes a protocol fit a type of network that it wouldn't normally match. PPTP is easy to install, is available at no extra cost with Microsoft networking services, and supports multiple kinds of protocols. For these reasons, it is the most popular VPN tunneling protocol in use today.

 PPTP is available with both the server and workstation versions of Windows NT, as part of RAS, and Windows 2000, as part of RRAS. PPTP support is included automatically in the Windows 98, Me, and XP operating systems.

Layer 2 Forwarding (L2F) is similar to PPTP in that it is a Data Link layer (Layer 2) protocol that provides tunneling for other protocols and can work with the authentication methods used by PPP. The difference between PPTP and L2F lies in the type of encryption that each supports, and the fact that PPTP was developed by Microsoft, and L2F was developed by Cisco Systems. One disadvantage of L2F compared to PPTP is that the former protocol requires special hardware on the host system end, whereas PPTP works with any Windows NT or 2000 server. On the other hand, L2F can encapsulate protocols to fit more than just the IP format, unlike PPTP.

Both PPTP and L2F, however, will gradually be replaced by a third type of tunneling protocol called **Layer 2 Tunneling Protocol (L2TP)**. This Layer 2 tunneling protocol was developed by a number of industry consortia and codified by the IETF in RFC 2661. L2TP is an enhanced version of L2F that, like L2F, supports multiple protocols. Unlike L2F, however, L2TP does not require costly hardware upgrades to implement. It is also optimized to work with the next generation of IP (IPv6) and IPSec.

WIRELESS SECURITY

The use of wireless, rather than wire-bound, transmission does not dramatically change the type of security risks a network faces. As with traditional telephone and data networks, wireless networks can be compromised through social engineering, password insecurities, and physical security breaches. Breaches are used for toll fraud, to obtain private information, or to disable a network. However, the fact that signals travel through the air—an unguided and openly accessible medium—presents unique challenges to protecting resources on a wireless network. For example, wireless networks are not typically victims of war-dialer attacks, but they are much more susceptible to eavesdropping than wire-bound LANs. As you learn in the following sections, wireless networks require unique encryption methods and, in the case of cellular networks, methods to secure the identity of mobile stations.

Cellular Network Security

When using a cellular phone, you might be in the midst of a conversation with a friend, for example, when suddenly your friend's voice disappears and, instead, you hear a cabbie talking to his dispatcher. This occurs when the frequency used by your friend's cellular connection is assigned to another mobile station. Consider that as a listener, your cellular telephone is simply an RF receiver. It is not difficult to imagine that with the appropriate receiving equipment, you could deliberately pick up voice signals traveling over different channels within a cell. In its simplest form, this is how cellular network eavesdropping occurs.

However, intercepting a cellular network conversation is not necessarily that straightforward. For one thing, even if a hacker obtained a radio scanner, she could only listen to a portion of each conversation. Recall that when a mobile station moves from one cell to another, its signals are almost always handed off to new frequencies in the new cell. Therefore, if a cellular telephone user is mobile, only part of her conversation can be intercepted. Secondly, depending on the transmission technology used, signals might be digitally encoded, multiplexed, and encrypted.

On analog systems, such as AMPS, signals are very simple to intercept. Recall that AMPS uses simple, FM technology to transmit and receive signals. This allows any FM receiver to pick up AMPS signals in a cell. More difficult to intercept are digital technologies, such as TDMA, CDMA, and GSM (a form of TDMA). Because they are digital, signals between mobile stations using these technologies do not exist as waveforms, but as streams of 1s and 0s. Not only that, but the digital data streams are multiplexed to use bandwidth more efficiently. Among other things, this multiplexing separates data streams into time slots. To interpret a multiplexed signal, a hacker needs the same type of demultiplexer on her receiver. Finally, in some cases, the digital data streams exchanged between a mobile station and a base station are encrypted using key encryption algorithms. These factors combined make it a challenge for hackers to intercept and translate digital cellular signals.

Nevertheless, hackers intent on obtaining private information can find ways to listen in on cellular conversations. With some effort, typical radio scanners can be modified to interpret digital cellular signals. And sometimes the efforts pay off. For example, suppose you are driving to work and decide to order tickets for a concert you heard about on the radio. Calling from your cell phone, you offer your name, address, and credit card number to the ticketing agency. It doesn't take you more than five minutes, and during that five minutes, you remained within one cell. If an intruder intercepts your signal and has the means to decrypt it, he has your credit card information. To be safe, never divulge personal or confidential information while speaking on a cell phone.

Potentially more damaging than eavesdropping is cellular telephone fraud. It goes without saying that if a malicious individual steals your cellular phone, he can place calls at your expense. However, the fraud only continues until you discover your phone is missing and call your cellular telephone provider to cancel that phone's service. A more insidious form

13

of fraud is cellular telephone cloning. This occurs when a hacker obtains a cellular telephone's electronic serial number (ESN), and then reprograms another handset to use that ESN. Recall from Chapter 9 that an ESN uniquely identifies a mobile station to a base station. When turned on, a cellular telephone transmits this number to the nearest base station. During this transmission, it is possible for a hacker to capture the ESN. After he has captured the ESN, he uses this number to create a clone. Then he can use the phone for toll calls without raising suspicion with the cellular carrier. The user will not know about the breach until she receives her cellular telephone bill. In the United States, a cellular telephone user is not responsible for the charges incurred through cloning. However, this fraud represents a significant cost to carriers.

To combat cloning fraud, cellular telephones that use CDMA and TDMA technology transmit their ESN numbers in encrypted form. (On AMPS cellular networks, this number is transmitted without any encryption, making AMPS even less secure.) Therefore, to clone a cellular phone that belongs to a CDMA or TDMA, the hacker must decrypt the ESN after capturing it. In addition, cellular telephones that use CDMA and TDMA authenticate with the network before they may place calls. This authentication uses private key encryption, similar to the Kerberos method of authentication you learned about earlier in the chapter. Finally, both CDMA and TDMA employ techniques to make the interception of ESN transmissions more difficult. For example, in CDMA, an ESN is additionally encrypted according to an identifying number assigned to the specific base station to which it initially connects.

Like cellular telephone networks, wireless LANs are also targets for eavesdropping. However, as you learn next, they employ different strategies for protecting signals in transit.

Wireless LAN Security

One technique used to eavesdrop on wireless LAN transmissions is **war driving**. War driving is searching for unprotected wireless networks by driving around with a laptop configured to receive and capture wireless data transmissions. (The term is derived from the term war dialing, which describes similar tactics used with modems.) War driving is surprisingly effective for obtaining private information. Recently, the hacker community publicized the vulnerabilities of a well-known store chain, which were discovered while war driving. The retailer used wireless cash registers to help customers make purchases when the regular, wire-line cash registers were busy. However, the wireless cash registers transmitted purchase information, including credit card numbers and customer names, to network access points in clear text. A war dialer situated in the retailer's parking lot captured the information. By chance, the sniffer program on his laptop obtained several credit card numbers in a very short time. The person who discovered the security breach alerted the retailer to the situation (rather than exploiting the information he gathered). Needless to say, after the retailer discovered its error, it abandoned the use of wireless cash registers until after a thorough evaluation of security techniques.

For an interesting view of how wireless LAN signals extend beyond the perimeter of a building, thus opening signals to potential interception, you can view images generated by the Information & Telecommunications Technology Center of the Kansas Applied Remote Sensing Program by connecting to the following URL: *www.ittc.ku.edu/wlan/*.

By now, you have probably guessed that next to avoiding transmission altogether, the single best way to prevent hackers from obtaining confidential information is to apply strong encryption techniques. This principle certainly holds true for wireless LANs.

As you learned in Chapter 9, most businesses with wireless LANs use one of the 802.11 protocol standards. Encryption for these types of networks follows the **Wired Equivalent Privacy (WEP)** standard. WEP is a key encryption technique that assigns keys to wireless nodes. Those keys are used both to authenticate network clients and to encrypt data in transit. Unfortunately, WEP is not very secure. A hacker with a war dialer can capture data traffic encrypted through WEP and, with the right software analysis tool, discover the key and decrypt the transmission in less than 24 hours. Professional networking organizations have urged computer scientists to develop better alternatives to WEP.

One solution for improved WLAN security is the **Extensible Authentication Protocol (EAP)**, defined by the IETF in RFC 2284. EAP does not perform encryption. Instead, it is used with separate encryption and authentication schemes. In the case of wireless LANs, EAP is used with WEP. (Note that it can also be used with other encryption schemes on wireline networks.) To enhance security, EAP requires the same logon and verification technique that remote WAN clients use to log on to a remote access server. In fact, EAP is an extension to the point-to-point (PPP) remote access protocol you learned about in Chapter 11. It operates in the Data Link layer of the OSI Model.

On wireless networks, EAP prevents any data sent by an unknown source from passing the access point and entering the rest of a network. If a wireless node wants to log onto a network, it first issues a request to the access point. The access point acts as a proxy between the server and client until the client has successfully authenticated with a network access server. Meanwhile, it prevents any direct exchange of data between the two. After obtaining data from an unknown client, the access point repackages the data and then transmits it to the access server. It also repackages data from the access server before issuing it to the client. Thus, in EAP, the client authenticates with the server, and the server also authenticates with the client. One of several authentication schemes can be used with EAP, depending on the type of remote access server an organization uses (for example, a logon ID and password are typically required). After mutual authentication, the access server instructs the access point to allow traffic from the client into the network without first repackaging the data. Next, the client and server agree on the encryption key that they will use with the encryption scheme (for example, WEP). Following that, they exchange data that is encrypted with this key, according to the encryption scheme.

The combination of EAP and WEP provides more security than using WEP alone. However, EAP's greatest advantage is that it can be used with any authentication

13

method. For example, although the typical network authentication involves a user ID and password, EAP would also work with bio-recognition methods, such as retina or hand scanning. EAP is also adaptable to new technology. Therefore, no matter what future wireless encryption schemes are developed, EAP will support them.

CHAPTER SUMMARY

- ◘ In a risk assessment, an organization analyzes its valuable assets, ways in which the assets might be compromised, the sources of threats to those assets, and the consequences that would arise if those assets were stolen or damaged. Data gathered from a risk assessment is used to generate security policies. The more an organization has at stake, the more time and money it should invest in security precautions.

- ◘ Key goals of a security policy include: preventing unauthorized users from gaining access to facilities, cabling, devices, systems, programs, or data; preventing accidental or intentional damage to hardware, facilities, or software; and creating an environment in which the network and its connected nodes can withstand and, if necessary, quickly respond to and recover from any type of threat.

- ◘ To be effective, an organization should appoint a security team and involve technical and managerial personnel in developing the security policy. Among other things, the team communicates each employee's responsibilities with respect to maintaining information security.

- ◘ Part of the security policy, the response policy describes in detail a planned response to possible security breaches. It also identifies the members of a response team, all of whom clearly understand the security policy, risks, and measures in place.

- ◘ The most significant network security threats come from people inside an organization, whether due to human error, ignorance, or omission. The number one method for an intruder to gain access to a network is to simply ask a user for his or her logon ID, password, authorization code, or to request entrance into a secured equipment room. This technique is known as social engineering.

- ◘ Choosing secure passwords is a simple way to augment information security. Secure passwords are as long as possible, contain both numbers and letters (and if allowed, special characters), are never shared with anyone, change frequently, can never be found in a dictionary, do not represent a date or word significant to the user or organization, and never equal the default password established by a software program upon installation.

- ◘ In a highly secure environment, access to equipment rooms, telecommunications closets, cable vaults, demarcation boxes, and even work areas is restricted to only those employees who need it.

- ◘ Modems are often an easy way for hackers to access a network. At greatest risk are modems attached to workstations with no firewall or other device between the network and the outside world.

❐ Encryption acts as the last means of defense against information eavesdropping, theft, or tampering. In other words, if an intruder has exploited all other means of entry, including physical security and password security, signals can still be secure if they are encrypted.

❐ The most commonly used form of encryption on modern data networks is key encryption, in which a string of characters is interleaved with the bits of data that make up a message, according to a predefined algorithm. In general, the longer the key, the more secure the encryption.

❐ Private key encryption requires both the sender and receiver to know the sender's private key. Kerberos, a cross-platform authentication service, uses private key encryption.

❐ Public key encryption uses a combination of a private key, known only to recipient, and a public key, available from a public key server. PGP (most often used with e-mail) and SSL (used in TCP/IP transmissions such as secure Web pages) use public key encryption.

❐ Hackers can easily eavesdrop on telephone conversations in a home or office, at the demarcation point, elsewhere on the local loop, or at equipment (for example, a DACS) in the LEC's central office. Modern wiretaps are difficult, if not impossible, to detect. To be considered truly secure, voice signals should be encrypted before transmission.

❐ Private telephone switches, such as PBXs, are frequent targets of security attacks, such as toll fraud, denial-of-service attacks, and information interception. Or, they may be used as stepping stones to compromising a data network. For optimal PBX security, administrators should disable the DISA feature; limit access to the maintenance port; require long, difficult-to-guess authorization codes; configure the PBX to limit certain incoming and outgoing calls; and separate the PBX from the data network.

❐ Voice mail systems are also subject to toll fraud and information interception. For optimal security, administrators disable unused voice mail boxes, enforce secure mailbox passwords, keep voice mail system access numbers private, and monitor voice mail usage for suspicious activity.

❐ Telecommunications firewalls offer a sophisticated, centralized way of selectively blocking incoming and outgoing calls. They are typically placed between an organization's PBX and the lines or trunks that lead to a LEC's central office.

❐ One way of limiting access to a network's resources is through the network operating system. Administrators can limit user file and directory rights, as well as the time of day, place, and length of time that users can log on to the network.

❐ Network security can be improved through better design. Consider restricting access to transmission media, and separating private and public hosts using a firewall, switch, or gateway. Note areas of the network that share a broadcast domain (in the case of Ethernet), where all traffic can be captured by nodes that share the same channel. Use gateways or proxy servers to mask private IP addresses. For the best security, encrypt data in transit.

13

❐ A common type of firewall is a packet-filtering firewall, which is a router that operates at the Data Link and Transport layers of the OSI model. It examines the header of every packet of data that it receives to determine whether that type of packet is authorized to continue to its destination. Packet-filtering firewalls must be carefully configured to be sufficiently restrictive, yet allow valid traffic to pass through.

❐ Virtual private networks (VPNs) typically use the Internet, PSTN, or both of these public networks to connect multiple sites, which leads to significant security risks. VPNs take advantage of firewalls and special protocols—such as PPTP, L2F, and L2TP—that encrypt the data transmitted over public connections.

❐ Cellular telephone signals are subject to eavesdropping, but in CDMA and TDMA-based transmission, signals are multiplexed and encrypted, making interpretation more difficult.

❐ Cloning cellular telephones, a practice in which a hacker obtains the phone's unique identifying number, and then copies that number to his own cellular phone, presents a significant security risk. After the hacker has created a clone, he can use the phone for toll calls without raising suspicion with the cellular carrier. The user will not know about the breach until she receives her cellular telephone bill.

❐ Wireless LANs rely on secure network design and unique wireless encryption techniques, such as the Wired Equivalent Privacy (WEP), to safeguard information in transit. However, WEP is notoriously easy to crack, and IEEE committees are developing better wireless LAN encryption techniques.

❐ The Extensible Authentication Protocol (EAP) can be used with WEP on wireless networks to improve wireless LAN security. EAP operates at the Data Link layer and specifies a pre-authentication process in which a client and server exchange data via an intermediate node (an access point on a wireless LAN). Only after they have mutually authenticated can the client and server exchange encrypted data.

KEY TERMS

9-0-# scam — A method of PBX toll fraud in which an intruder uses social engineering to trick an unsuspecting employee at an organization that uses a PBX to press 9, then 0, then the # key on his telephone, and then hang up (in other words, press the switch hook). In fact, on some PBX systems, this is the sequence that transfers a caller to an outside line. (A "9" accesses an outside line, a "0" accesses a local operator, and a "#" cancels the previous request, and pressing the switch hook transfers the caller.) After the intruder has been transferred, she can make long-distance calls at the organization's expense (assuming the organization uses this type of PBX).

asymmetric encryption — A type of encryption (such as public-key encryption) that uses a different key for encoding data than is used for decoding the cipher text.

authorization code — In the context of private switching, a sequence of numbers that allows an employee to gain access to a certain line or feature.

bio-recognition access — A method for granting access to restricted rooms in which a device scans an individual's unique physical characteristics, such as the color patterns in her eye's iris or the geometry of her hand, to verify her identity.

bugging — The use of a microphone with a small RF transmitter placed near an audio source (such as a telephone mouthpiece) and a nearby receiver to eavesdrop.

cipher text — The unique data block that results when an original piece of data (such as text) is encrypted (for example, by using a key).

client_hello — In the context of SSL encryption, a message issued from the client to the server that contains information about what level of security the client's browser is capable of accepting and what type of encryption the client's browser can decipher (for example, RSA or Diffie-Hellman). The client_hello message also establishes a randomly generated number that uniquely identifies the client plus another number that identifies the SSL session.

cracker — A person who uses his or her knowledge of operating systems and utilities to intentionally damage or destroy data or systems. Although crackers are technically distinguished from hackers by their malicious intentions, the two terms are often used synonymously.

data encryption standard (DES) — A popular private key encryption technique that was developed by IBM in the 1970s.

denial of service attack — A technique in which hackers barrage a system, network, or device with such a high volume of signals that valid signals cannot be processed or transmitted.

dictionary attack — A technique in which attackers run a program that tries a combination of a known user ID and, for a password, every word in a dictionary to attempt to gain access to the network. This is typically the first technique a hacker uses when trying to guess a password (besides asking the user for her password).

digital certificate — A password-protected and encrypted file that holds an individual's identification information, including a public key and a private key. The individual's public key is used to verify the sender's digital signature, and the private key allows the individual to log on to a third-party authority who administers digital certificates.

direct inward system access (DISA) — A feature of some private switches that allows an organization's employees to complete long-distance calls from outside the organization by first accessing the PBX via a toll-free number. DISA is a security risk often exploited by hackers.

eavesdropping — The use of a transmission or recording device to capture conversations without the consent of the speakers.

Extensible Authentication Protocol (EAP) — A Data Link layer protocol defined by the IETF in RFC 2284. EAP specifies a pre-authentication process in which a client and server exchange data via an intermediate node (an access point on a wireless LAN). Only after they have mutually authenticated can the client and server exchange encrypted data. EAP supports multiple authentication and encryption schemes.

group — On a network, a collection of users (or other network objects, such as printers or servers) that are associated with each other for the purposes of simpler

13

network management. For example, all users in an Accounting Department might be collected in the "ACCTG" group, which is granted rights to the budget and forecast spreadsheets on a server.

hacker — A person who masters the inner workings of operating systems and utilities in an effort to better understand them. Often, hacker is used as a general term for phone phreaks, as well as all types of hackers.

handshake protocol — One of several protocols within SSL, and perhaps the most significant. As its name implies, the handshake protocol allows the client and server to authenticate to (or introduce) each other and establishes terms for how they will securely exchange data during an SSL session.

HTTPS — The URL prefix that indicates that a Web page requires its data to be exchanged between client and server using SSL encryption. HTTPS uses the TCP port number 443, rather than TCP port 80 (the port that normal HTTP uses).

Internet Key Exchange (IKE) — The first phase of IPSec authentication, which accomplishes key management. Once IKE has established the rules for the type of keys two nodes will use, IPSec invokes its second phase, encryption.

IP Protocol Security (IPSec) — A Layer 3 protocol that defines encryption, authentication, and key management for TCP/IP transmissions. IPSec is an enhancement to IPv4 and native to IPv6. IPSec is unique among authentication methods in that it adds security information to the header of all IP packets.

IP spoofing — A security attack in which an outsider obtains internal IP addresses, then uses those addresses to pretend that he or she has authority to access a private network from the Internet.

Kerberos — A cross-platform authentication protocol that uses key encryption to verify the identity of clients and to securely exchange information once a client logs on to a system. It is an example of a private key encryption service. Unlike some other private key encryption services, Kerberos requires the client to prove its identity through a third party.

key — A series of characters that is combined with a block of data during that data's encryption. To decrypt the resulting data, the recipient must also possess the key.

key encryption — An encryption technique that weaves a key into a block of data using a predefined algorithm, so that the same key and algorithm must be used to decrypt the data. Key encryption comes in two forms: public key encryption and private key encryption.

key management — The method whereby two nodes using key encryption agree on common parameters for the keys they will use to encrypt data.

key pair — The combination of a public and private key used to decipher data that has been encrypted using public key encryption.

Layer 2 Forwarding (L2F) — A Layer 2 protocol similar to PPTP that provides tunneling for other protocols and can work with the authentication methods used by PPP. L2F was developed by Cisco Systems and requires special hardware on the host system. It can encapsulate protocols to fit more than just the IP format, unlike PPTP.

Layer 2 Tunneling Protocol (L2TP) — A Layer 2 tunneling protocol developed by a number of industry consortia. L2TP is an enhanced version of L2F. Like L2F, it supports multiple protocols; unlike L2F, it does not require costly hardware upgrades to implement. L2TP is optimized to work with the next generation of IP (IPv6) and IPSec (the Layer 3 IP encryption protocol).

packet-filtering firewall — A router that operates at the Data Link and Transport layers of the OSI model, examining the header of every packet of data that it receives to determine whether that type of packet is authorized to continue to its destination.

packet sniffer — *See* sniffer

phreaker — *See* phone phreak.

phone phreak — A person who manipulates telephone connections or resources to his advantage. For example, a phone phreak could obtain the phone number to a PBX's maintenance port and, by dialing into that port with a modem, launch a denial-of-service attack to prevent the PBX from processing legitimate call traffic.

Point-to-Point Tunneling Protocol (PPTP) — A Layer 2 protocol developed by Microsoft that encapsulates PPP so that any type of data can traverse the Internet masked as pure IP transmissions. PPTP supports the encryption, authentication, and LAN access services provided by RAS. Instead of users having to dial directly into an access server, they can dial into their ISP using PPTP and gain access to their corporate LAN over the Internet.

Pretty Good Privacy (PGP) — A key-based encryption system for e-mail that uses a two-step verification process.

private key encryption — A type of key encryption in which the sender and receiver have private keys, which only they know. Data encryption standard (DES), which was developed by IBM in the 1970s, is a popular example of a private key encryption technique. Private key encryption is also known as symmetric encryption.

promiscuous mode — A setting that allows a NIC to indiscriminately accept all packets traversing the network channel to which it is attached, not only those packets destined for it.

proxy server — A network host that runs a proxy service. Proxy servers may also be called gateways.

proxy service — A software application on a network host that acts as an intermediary between the external and internal networks, screening all incoming and outgoing traffic and providing one address to the outside world, instead of revealing the addresses of internal LAN devices.

public key encryption — A form of key encryption in which data is encrypted using two keys: one is a key known only to a user and the other is a key associated with the user that can be obtained from a public source, such as a public-key server. Some examples of public-key algorithms include RSA (named after its creators, Rivest, Shamir, and Adleman), Diffie-Hellman, and Elliptic-curve cryptography. Public key encryption is also known as asymmetric encryption.

public-key server — A publicly available host (such as an Internet host) that provides free access to a list of users' public keys (for use in public key encryption).

13

risk assessment — A thorough analysis of an organization's vulnerability to security breaches and an identification of its potential losses, should a breach occur.

server_hello — In the context of SSL encryption, a message issued from the server to the client that confirms the information the server received in the client_hello message and agrees to certain terms of encryption based on the options the client supplied. Depending on the Web server's preferred encryption method, the server may choose to issue your browser a public key or a digital certificate at this time.

sniffer — A computer that, once connected to a network, can capture data packets traveling over the channel to which it is attached. Sniffers are useful troubleshooting tools, but hackers can also use them to intercept and interpret data traffic.

social engineering — The manipulation of social relationships to obtain information (for example, a password) that could grant an intruder access to restricted resources.

SSL (Secure Sockets Layer) — A method of encrypting TCP/IP transmissions—including Web pages and data entered into Web forms—en route between the client and server using public key encryption technology.

SSL session — In the context of SSL encryption, an association between the client and server that is defined by an agreement on a specific set of encryption techniques. An SSL session allows the client and server to continue to exchange data securely as long as the client is still connected to the server. SSL sessions are established by the SSL handshake protocol.

symmetric encryption — A method of encryption that requires the same key to encode the data as is used to decode the cipher text.

telecommunications firewall — A type of firewall that monitors incoming and outgoing voice traffic and selectively blocks telephone calls between different areas of a voice network.

TLS (transport layer security) — A version of SSL being standardized by the Internet Engineering Task Force (IETF). With TLS, IETF aims to create a version of SSL that will encrypt UDP as well as TCP transmissions. TLS, which will likely be supported by new Web browsers, uses slightly different encryption algorithms than SSL, but otherwise is very similar to the most recent version of SSL.

toll fraud — The unauthorized use of a telephone line, calling card, switch, or other type of connection to complete long distance calls at another's expense.

tunneling — The process of encapsulating one protocol to make it appear as another type of protocol.

war dialer — A computer program that dials multiple telephone numbers in rapid succession, attempting to access and receive a handshake response from a modem.

war driving — The action of searching for unprotected wireless networks by driving around with a laptop set to receive and capture wireless data transmissions.

wiretapping — The interception of a telephone conversation by accessing the telephone signal. Wiretapping can occur at any point in the telephone connection. Law enforcement personnel perform wiretapping at the telephone switch, where it is undetectable.

Wired Equivalent Privacy (WEP) — A key encryption technique that assigns keys to wireless nodes for authentication and data encryption. Unfortunately, WEP can be easily decrypted with the proper software tools.

REVIEW QUESTIONS

1. List three questions that an organization should consider as part of a risk assessment. For each question, explain what type of data the question is intended to generate.

2. Which of the following events would cause an organization to begin or repeat its cycle of security steps?

   a. A company introduces a new product line.

   b. A company hires five new accountants.

   c. A company upgrades its network from 10BaseT Ethernet to Gigabit Ethernet.

   d. A company rewrites its Web site text.

3. For any organization, who is the most likely source of security breaches?

   a. the organization's current employees

   b. the organization's business competitors

   c. the organization's vendors

   d. people who have no ties to the organization

4. Which of the following is an example of social engineering?

   a. A senior administrator provides a novice employee with the network's administrative password before he leaves for vacation.

   b. An administrative assistant forgets to shred confidential documents before throwing them in the trash.

   c. A system administrator inadvertently leaves the door to the equipment room open for an afternoon.

   d. An intruder posing as a PBX support technician calls an employee and asks him for his PBX authorization code.

5. What is one factor that helps determine whether a particular piece of information should be considered confidential?

   a. how much time staff took to collect or generate the information

   b. how many staff people are allowed to access the information via the network

   c. how old the information is

   d. whether the information could be used by a competitor to limit the organization's sales or profits

6. Which of the following is the most secure password?

   a. ARSENIC

   b. p!Jf8g*df99L

   c. 200000

   d. readytogo

13

7. You are the technical manager for a LEC's end office. Of the following areas of the building, which will you ensure is the most physically secure? (In other words, at what point could a hacker cause the most significant outage, if she breached security?)

   a. cable vault

   b. battery room

   c. foyer

   d. plenum cable runs

8. Which of the following uses of modems would provide the simplest way for a hacker to break into a private network?

   a. A network administrator has enabled the modem on her PBX and configured it so that it will accept connections from her home telephone line.

   b. A network administrator has enabled the modem on a standalone workstation that he uses for a development Web server as he experiments with new Web software from home.

   c. A network user has purchased a PCMCIA modem card for his laptop and uses it to dial into the corporate remote access server to retrieve her e-mail and documents from the LAN.

   d. A network user has attached an external modem to his workstation's serial port so that he can dial his ISP and pick up e-mail from his private, ISP account at any time.

9. What type of attack floods a device with illegitimate traffic so that legitimate signals cannot be processed?

   a. denial-of-service attack

   b. IP spoofing

   c. brute force attack

   d. social engineering

10. In key encryption, a longer key generally means

   a. data takes longer to encrypt

   b. data is more difficult to decrypt, without the key

   c. data is easier to decrypt

   d. data must be broken down into smaller packets before encryption

11. What type of encryption is commonly used between Web browsers and Web servers to secure information over the Internet?

   a. PGP

   b. SSL

   c. IPSec

   d. Kerberos

12. Which of the following types of encryption is included with IP version 6?

   a. PGP

   b. SSL

   c. IPSec

   d. Kerberos

13. At which of the following points in a telephone network would a wiretap be the most difficult for a telephone user to detect?

   a. in the CPE

   b. at the demarcation point

   c. in the drop wire

   d. at the telephone switch

14. Theoretically, how does a voltmeter detect a wiretap on your local loop?

   a. It equates a lower than normal off-hook voltage with the presence of a wiretap.

   b. It equates a higher than normal off-hook voltage with the presence of a wiretap.

   c. It generates a small amount of voltage, and then measures the amount of signal reflection to see if it is equal.

   d. It equates a reverse in current direction with the presence of a wiretap.

15. What makes DISA a security risk?

   a. It offers a toll-free number through which one could access a company's long-distance services

   b. It relies on a PBX's auto-attendant feature, which can be tricked into transferring to an outside line.

   c. It provides network administrators and vendor technicians with a port to control or reconfigure the PBX.

   d. It is not capable of interpreting authorization codes.

16. Which of the following PBX configurations could a network administrator set to guard against toll fraud?

   a. a limit on the number of station lines connecting to the PBX at any given time

   b. a limit on the area and country codes to which long distance calls can be made

   c. a limit on the maximum PBX processor utilization before an alarm is triggered

   d. a limit on the use of certain trunks leading to the LEC

13

17. Where, in a voice network, should a telecommunications firewall be placed to adequately protect an organization's voice network?

    a. between the PBX and the station lines

    b. between the PBX and the LEC's trunks

    c. between the PBX's central processor and its switching module

    d. between the PBX and the gateway to the private data network

18. In addition to toll fraud, name two types of security risks a voice mail system presents.

19. You are the network administrator for a call center that staffs its telephones with three different shifts of customer service representatives. To prevent security breaches on the data network, you allow customer service representatives limited access to the customer and product records on the network. In addition to limiting file rights, how can you use your network operating system to prevent customer service representatives from abusing their network access?

    a. Limit the time of day each customer service representative can be logged on to the network.

    b. Limit the places from which customer service representatives can log on to the network, according to station extension.

    c. Limit the duration of time a customer service representative can be logged on to the network.

    d. All of the above.

20. What is the optimal way of securing a private network from external hackers?

    a. Place firewalls on the perimeter of every subnet.

    b. Do not connect it to any other networks.

    c. Do not integrate telephone and data networks.

    d. Use both firewalls and proxy servers at the connection between the private and public portions of the network.

21. If you want to restrict Internet users from compromising your network using the notoriously insecure FTP service, how would you configure the router at the edge of your private network?

    a. Block all UDP-based transmission.

    b. Block all TCP-based transmission.

    c. Block TCP ports 20 and 21.

    d. Block TCP port 80.

22. What is the primary purpose for using a proxy server?

    a. to encrypt TCP/IP transmissions between private and public networks

    b. to selectively filter incoming traffic according to source address, transport protocol, or port number

    c. to act as a central connection point for multiple VPN clients

    d. to mask the IP addresses of nodes on a private LAN from public discovery

23. Which of the following cellular technologies presents the greatest risk to information privacy?

    a. AMPS

    b. CDMA

    c. TDMA

    d. GSM

24. Which of the following cellular technologies is most susceptible to cellular telephone cloning?

    a. AMPS

    b. CDMA

    c. TDMA

    d. GSM

25. What wireless LAN protocol uses the Wired Equivalent Privacy standard?

    a. Bluetooth

    b. Wi-Fi

    c. HomeRF

    d. 802.11

HANDS-ON PROJECTS

13

Project 13-1

This chapter emphasizes the importance of secure, difficult-to-guess passwords as part of every company's security strategy. You also learned about freely available tools, such as dictionary attack programs, that hackers could use to crack passwords that are not secure. In this project, you experiment with a password-cracking program designed for users of Microsoft Word 2000 to open files that are password-protected, in case the users have forgotten their passwords. Note that this program should be used only for educational purposes, to demonstrate the importance of choosing secure passwords. Keep in mind, though, that similar programs, designed for cracking passwords for many different kinds of software, can be found on the Internet. Individuals with malicious intent frequently use these programs, so you need to be prepared to guard against them.

For this project, you need a Windows 2000 or XP computer that is capable of browsing the Web and extracting files that have been compressed using the WinZip utility. Your computer should have Microsoft Word 2000 installed, and it should have at least 5 MB of free space on the hard disk.

1. First, create three documents in Microsoft Word 2000 and name them **test1.doc**, **test2.doc**, and **test3.doc**. In the following steps, you will assign a different password to each document.

2. Microsoft Word 2000 allows you to use passwords that contain letters or numbers and can be as long as 15 characters. To assign a password to the first file, open **test1.doc**, click **File** on the menu bar, and then click **Save As**.

3. The Save As dialog box appears. Click **Tools** on the menu bar, and then click **General Options**.

4. The Save dialog box appears, as shown in Figure 13-10. Beneath the "File sharing options for test1.doc" prompt, click in the **Password to open** text box, type **bird**, and then click OK.

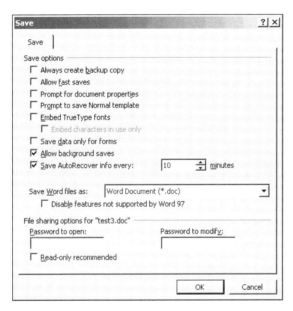

Figure 13-10   The Save dialog box in Microsoft Word 2000

5. The Confirm Password dialog box appears. In the Reenter password to open text box, type the password again, and then click **OK**.

6. Click **Save** to save the document with the password requirement.

7. Close **test1.doc** and then open **test2.doc**. Repeat Steps 2–6 for this document, using the password **pterodactyl**.

8. Close **test2.doc** and open **test3.doc**. Repeat Steps 2–6 for this document, but choose what you consider to be a very secure password, based on the material you read in this chapter.

9. Next, you will download the program that cracks Microsoft Word 2000 document passwords. This program is called Advanced Office 2000 Password Recovery. It is available for a 30-day trial at no charge from the software publisher, ELCOMSOFT, Inc. To connect to ELCOMSOFT's Web site, point your browser to the following URL: **www.elcomsoft.com/ao2000pr.html**.

10. Scroll down the Web page until you find the **Download AO2000PR 1.20 Std** link. Click this link to begin downloading the compressed version of the software.

11. The File Download dialog box appears, prompting you to save or open the file. Click **Save**.

12. The Save As dialog box appears. Choose a directory on your hard disk where you want the compressed files to be installed, and then click **Save**. The file named "ao20pr_s.zip" is copied to your hard disk.

13. Using your WinZip program, extract all the files from the ao20pr_s.zip file into a directory of your choice.

14. From Windows Explorer, open the directory where you extracted the ao20pr_s.zip file, and then double-click the **setup.exe** file to start the program installation. The Advanced Office 2000 Password Recovery Installation Wizard begins with a Welcome message. Click **Next** to continue.

15. The next dialog box presents you with system requirements and overview information. Read this information, and then click **Next** to continue installation.

16. The next dialog box displays the software copyright information. Read the licensing agreement and click **Next** to agree with its terms and continue installation.

17. The Select Destination Directory dialog box appears. The default directory is C:\Program Files\ao2000pr. Click **Next** to accept this directory for the program's installation and continue.

18. The Backup Replaced Files dialog box appears, asking you whether you want to keep copies of all files replaced during the installation process. Click **Next** to accept the default selection (yes), and continue the installation.

19. The Select Backup Directory dialog box appears, prompting you to identify a directory where copies of replaced files will be saved. Click **Next** to accept the default directory, C:\Program Files\ao2000pr\BACKUP, and continue.

20. The Select Components dialog box appears, prompting you to choose which program elements you want to install. To install all the components and continue installation, click **Next**.

21. The Ready to Install! dialog box appears. Click **Next** to begin copying program files to the C:\Program Files\ao2000pr directory.

22. After the files have been copied, the Installation Completed! dialog box appears, confirming that you have installed the Advanced Office 2000 Password Recovery program. Click **Finish** to close the installation wizard.

23. To run the Advanced Office 2000 Password Recovery program, click **Start**, point to **Programs** (or **All Programs**, if you are using Windows XP), point to **Advanced Office 2000 Password Recovery**, and then click **Advanced Office 2000 Password Recovery**.

24. The Advanced Office 2000 Password Recovery opens, displaying the AO2000PR 1.20 dialog box. You will first attempt to crack the password you assigned to the test1.doc document. Click the **open file** icon.

25. The Open dialog box appears. Select the **test1.doc** document and click **Open**.

26. The AO2000PR dialog box appears, asking you to select a type of password attack. Check the box next to "Don't show this message again" and then click **OK**.

27. Under the Type of attack heading, select **Dictionary attack**.

28. Select the Dictionary tab. Notice that the Advanced Office 2000 Password Recovery program has copied an English dictionary to its program directory to use as a reference for a dictionary attack.

29. To begin your password cracking, click **Recovery** on the main menu and then click **Start**. (Remember, this program is designed to help users who have forgotten document passwords recover those documents.)

30. Wait while the program attempts to crack the document's password. Notice what kind of information it responds with. If the test1.doc password was cracked, how long did it take? How many passwords did it attempt *each second* before it found the correct one?

31. Click **OK** to close the Password successfully recovered! dialog box.

32. Repeat Steps 24–30 for test2.doc and test3.doc. How did the results differ?

33. Now try cracking each document's password using a brute force attack, rather than a dictionary attack. How do the results differ?

34. Click the close icon in the upper right corner of the Advanced Office 2000 Password Recovery window. When asked whether you want to save your projects, click **No**.

Project 13-2

Now that you have some experience with simple password cracking, you have a better appreciation for how easily and quickly insecure passwords can be guessed. As a network administrator, you apply policies through the network operating system to ensure that users choose secure passwords. In this project, you work with policies in the Windows 2000 Server network operating system to restrict the type of passwords users can choose.

This project requires a Windows 2000 Server and the capability to log on as Administrator to that server. To test your changes, you need a Windows 2000 or Windows XP client and a valid user ID (other than the Administrator account) that can log on to the Windows 2000 server.

1. Log on to the server as Administrator.

2. Click **Start**, point to **Programs**, point to **Administrative Tools**, and then click **Domain Security Policy**. The Domain Security Policy window appears, as shown in Figure 13-11.

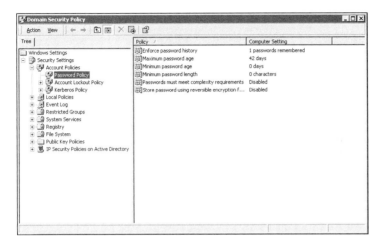

Figure 13-11   The Windows 2000 Domain Security Policy window

3. In the left pane of the Domain Security Policy window, double-click the **Security Settings**, if necessary, to expand the container. In Microsoft networking terminology, a container is an organizational unit that contains other items, such as users or groups of users.

4. Double-click **Account Policies**, if necessary, to expand this option.

5. Click **Password Policy**. A list of password policies and their settings appears in the right pane of the Domain Security Policy window.

6. What is the default maximum password age? Right-click the **Maximum password age** policy and choose **Security** from the shortcut menu. The Security Policy Setting dialog box appears.

7. Change the number of days after which passwords will expire to **30**.

8. Click **OK** to close the Security Policy Setting dialog box.

9. What is the default minimum password length setting? Right-click the **Minimum password length** policy and choose **Security** from the shortcut menu. The Security Policy Setting dialog box appears.

10. Change the minimum number of characters in the password to 12.

11. Click **OK** to close the Security Policy Setting dialog box.

13

12. Right-click on the **Passwords must meet complexity requirements** policy and choose **Security** from the shortcut menu. The Security Policy Setting dialog box appears.

13. Make sure the **Define this policy** option is selected, and then click the **Enabled** radio button to enable the complexity requirements. Click **OK** to close the Security Policy Setting dialog box.

14. In the left pane of the Domain Security Policy window, click the **Account Lockout Policy** option. Account lockout policies appear in the right pane of the Domain Security Policy window.

15. Right-click the **Account lockout duration** policy and choose **Security** from the shortcut menu. The Security Policy Setting dialog box appears.

16. Select the **Define this policy setting** check box, and then change the number of minutes an account will be locked out to 3.

17. Click **OK** to close the Security Policy Setting dialog box. A Suggested Value Changes window may appear, informing you that because the account lockout duration is now 3 minutes, the settings for the "Account lockout threshold" and "Reset account lockout counter after a period of time" will also be changed. Why do you think the number of invalid logon attempts was raised when you lowered the lockout duration?

18. Click **OK** to accept the changes and close the Suggested Value Changes window.

19. Close the Domain Security Policy window.

20. From your Windows 2000 or XP workstation, attempt to log on to the Windows 2000 server with an ordinary user ID. Are you prompted with any messages about your password?

21. Now attempt to change your password, using each of the following character strings: animal, 1000000, and X25kIN63mN73. How does the server respond to each attempt?

22. Log off from the server, and then attempt to log on again, but deliberately enter the wrong password several times in a row. At what point does the server prevent you from attempting to log on again?

23. Wait four minutes and try logging on to the server with the correct password. What happens?

24. Close the Administrative Tools window.

Project 13-3

The Internet holds vast amounts of information about computer security. As you have learned, hackers can exploit this information to break into networks. However, the information is also helpful for telecommunications professionals, who need to stay abreast of new security threats and understand how to prevent security breaches in their environment. In this project, you research one of the best known security alert Web sites, which is run by CERT, a clearinghouse for security risks established by the Carnegie Mellon Software Engineering Institute.

For this project, you need a computer capable of browsing the Web. The computer should also have the Adobe Acrobat Reader software installed, so that you can read files with a .pdf extension.

1. Make certain your computer is connected to the Internet. Start your browser program, then point your browser to the following URL: **www.cert.org/**. The CERT Coordination Center Web page appears.

2. From the Options menu on the left side of the page, click **Vulnerabilities, Incidents, & Fixes**. The Vulnerabilities, Incidents, & Fixes page appears.

3. Notice the latest warnings issued by CERT (listed under the "Current Activity" heading). Then, scroll down the page until you find the Presentations and Reports heading. Click **Overview of Attack Trends** to open that document.

4. Scan through CERT's overview of trends in security attacks. What are some ways hackers are gaining unauthorized access to resources more quickly than they could only 10 years ago? How has Internet access affected a corporation's security risks? In what ways are firewalls being compromised?

5. Click your browser's **Back** button twice to return to the CERT home page. Next, you will search for information about security risks unique to wireless transmission.

6. In the Search the CERT/CC Web site text box (next to the "for" prompt), type **wireless networks**, and then click **GO**. Wait while the CERT server completes your search.

7. How many documents were retrieved by your search? On the results page, click the **sort by date** button to arrange the results with the most recent documents listed first.

8. Click the first document in the list to open it. Read through the security advisory, FAQ, or tip you selected. What software and hardware does the document pertain to? What type of security breaches does it warn against?

9. Click your browser's **Back** button to return to the list of documents pertaining to wireless network security.

10. In the search text box, type **war dialer**, and then click **search**. A list of documents pertaining to war dialer techniques appears, with the result listed by date.

11. Click the **sort by relevance** button to rearrange the documents according to how well they apply to your search request.

12. Now click on the first document in the list to open it. What does this document say about war dialers? According to what you read, do you think that war dialing is being replaced in favor of more sophisticated techniques?

13. When you have finished scanning the document, close your browser.

13

Case Projects

1. You are the telecommunications manager for the local government of Midville, a medium-sized city. You are responsible for designing, implementing, and maintaining Midville's voice, data, and videoconferencing infrastructure. Naturally, you do not accomplish this on your own, but rely on a staff of 10 engineers and technicians. At this time, your voice and data networks are separate. They include:

   ❑ A data MAN that connects two government buildings downtown via fiber-optic cable

   ❑ A wire-bound data LAN in each of the two buildings, with each building containing three Windows 2000 file and print servers and one building containing a UNIX e-mail server and a UNIX Web server

   ❑ A T1 connection between the MAN and your ISP

   ❑ A PBX in one of the buildings that connects to telephone stations in both of the two buildings

   ❑ A T1 connection between the PBX and the local RBOC

   ❑ An emergency dispatching telephone network that connects emergency services, such as police, fire, and 911 callers

   For your own records, you keep detailed diagrams of both your voice and data network infrastructure. However, during a meeting with the city's budget oversight committee, you are asked to sketch your network's design and highlight the security precautions built into that design. Complete your sketch on a piece of paper. Make sure your sketch incorporates the best design practices for protecting network resources.

2. Next month, half of your networking staff will be attending a week-long conference in another state. While out of town, these employees need access to the network. Voice technicians want to be able to check the logs on the PBX and telecommunications firewall. They might also need to perform voice-mail maintenance. Data technicians want to be able to check logs on the firewall. They might also want to perform server and router maintenance. What policies should you establish that will allow employees to remotely access both your voice and data network? What technology must you implement to ensure that these remote connections are secure?

3. Citizens of Midville have recently passed a proposal to install surveillance cameras at local underpasses and busy intersections. The mayor has asked you to investigate ways in which the data captured by these cameras can be economically and securely transmitted to storage devices on the city's LAN. She wonders if wireless transmission is a good idea, or if another type of transmission is better. Also, she asks you to suggest ways to safely keep the media that store the images. What do you suggest?

14

CONVERGENCE OF VOICE, VIDEO, AND DATA

After reading this chapter and completing the exercises, you will be able to:

♦ Identify terminology used to describe applications and other aspects of converged networks

♦ Describe several different applications available on converged networks

♦ Outline possible VoIP implementations and examine the costs and benefits of VoIP

♦ Explain methods for encoding analog voice or video signals as digital signals for transmission over a packet-switched network

♦ Identify the key signaling and transport protocols that may be used with VoIP

♦ Understand Quality of Service (QoS) challenges on converged networks and discuss techniques that can improve QoS

Traditionally, voice and data signals have been carried by separate networks. Through most of the twentieth century, the PSTN, based on Alexander Graham Bell's circuit-switched model, carried telephone calls and fax transmissions. Packet-based networks, such as the Internet, took care of e-mail, Web pages, file transfers, and access to other data resources. In the latter part of the century, the two types of networks began intersecting. For example, when an Internet user dials into his ISP, he is using the PSTN to connect to a data network. However, this intersection is not seamless or efficient. When the user dials his ISP, his system requires modems to convert digital data into analog signals and vice versa. Networks can achieve more unified integration, however, by packetizing voice—that is, digitizing the voice signal and issuing it as a stream of packets over the network. In the last decade, common carriers, network service providers, data equipment manufacturers, and standards organizations have concentrated on ways to deliver voice, video, and data over the same network. These converged networks, as they are called, may bring cost savings, but they also require new technology. This chapter compares the old and new network models and describes the technology behind converged networks. Material in this chapter builds on everything you have learned thus far about telephony, signaling, switching, network architecture, protocols, and access methods.

TERMINOLOGY

Telecommunications professionals use many different terms to refer to services and technologies used on converged networks. In Chapter 1, you learned that convergence is the use of one network to simultaneously carry voice, video, and data communications. In this chapter, you learn about many applications that can operate over converged networks. One example is Internet telephony, the use of the Internet to complete telephone calls, which was introduced in Chapter 12. More generally, the use of any network (either public or private) to carry voice signals using TCP/IP is known as IP telephony or voice over IP (VoIP). VoIP can run over any packet-switched network. When a frame-relay network is used to transport packetized voice signals, the service is called **voice over frame relay (VoFR)**. When ATM is used, the service is called **voice over ATM (VoATM)**. Similarly, when a DSL connection is used to carry packetized voice signals, the service is known as **voice over DSL (VoDSL)**. When speaking in general about issuing voice signals over a network, some telecommunications professionals use the term **voice over network (VON)**. VON encompasses VoIP, VoFR, VoATM, VoDSL, and Internet telephony. (Note that these terms are not mutually exclusive, however. For example, VoIP is considered VoDSL if the packets are transported over a DSL connection.) Packetized voice can be carried over virtually any type of data connection, including T-carriers, ISDN, cable, satellite, and cellular networks. These, too, fall under the umbrella of VON.

Voice is not the only nondata application that can be carried on a converged network. **Fax over IP (FoIP)** uses packet-switched networks to transmit faxes from one node on the network to another. Other applications include radio or TV broadcasts and videoconferencing. To identify networks that use cutting-edge technology to integrate voice, video, and data signals on the same infrastructure, professionals may use one of the following two terms: **next generation networks (NGNs)** and **multiservice networks**. In discussions of convergence, the use of multiple terms to refer to the same technology is common. This is a result of a rapidly developing market in which many different vendors tout their own solutions, using their own, preferred terminology. The terms used throughout the chapter are those most frequently cited by standards organizations, such as the ITU and IETF, that focus on converged network technology.

Because voice services represent the highest volume of nondata traffic on converged networks, this chapter concentrates primarily on VoIP. However, as you progress through the chapter, you should be aware that issues such as bandwidth usage, quality of service (QoS), infrastructure upgrades, and potential cost savings apply to FoIP and video applications as well as to VoIP.

APPLICATIONS

Combining voice and data signals on the same network offers organizations a chance to provide brand new applications and to enhance older, existing applications. On a converged network, a telephone can be a Web browser, a computer can be a TV, and a voicemail box can be a repository for e-mail and faxes. The following sections describe some applications that make use of converged networks. Later in this chapter, you learn about the specific protocols necessary to provide these applications.

Voice over IP (VoIP)

As you know, voice over IP (VoIP) is the use of packet-switched networks and the TCP/IP protocol suite to transmit voice conversations. VoIP has generated great interest among network service providers, equipment manufacturers, and customers. Reasons for implementing VoIP may include one or more of the following:

- To improve business efficiency and competitiveness

- To supply new or enhanced features and applications

- To centralize voice and data network management

- To improve employee productivity

- To save money

Of these reasons for implementing VoIP, one that attracts significant attention is saving money. In the case of private networks, completing calls over a packet-switched network allows an organization to avoid paying long distance telephone charges, a function known as **toll bypass**. However, the costs and benefits of VoIP vary greatly with each customer and implementation. Later in this chapter, you learn about the business considerations of VoIP. First, in this section, you learn about VoIP from an end user's point of view.

14

To conduct a conversation, VoIP callers require either a traditional telephone, a telephone specially designed for TCP/IP signaling, or a computer equipped with a microphone, speaker, and VoIP client software. On any VoIP network, a mix of these three types of clients can coexist.

VoIP and Traditional Telephones

If a VoIP caller uses a traditional telephone, signals issued by the telephone must be converted to digital form before being transmitted on an IP-based network. This conversion can be accomplished in several ways. One way is by using an adapter card within a computer workstation. The traditional telephone line connects to an RJ-11 port on the adapter card. The adapter card, along with its device drivers and software on the computer, converts the voice signals to IP packets, and then issues the packets to the data network.

A second way to achieve this conversion is by connecting the traditional telephone to a switch capable of accepting traditional voice signals, converting them into packets, then issuing the packets to a data network. One example of such a switch is a **digital PBX**, more commonly known as an **IP-PBX** (The term "IP-PBX" implies that TCP/IP is used as the network protocol, as is almost always the case.). In general, an IP-PBX is a private switch that accepts and interprets both analog and digital voice signals (although some IP-PBXs do not accept analog lines). Thus, it can connect with both traditional PSTN lines and data networks. An IP-PBX transmits and receives IP-based voice signals to and from other network connectivity devices, such as a router or gateway. (In addition, some traditional PBXs can be transformed into IP-PBXs with the addition of adapter cards.) Like a traditional PBX, an IP-PBX provides telephones with dial tone and performs telephone setup, supervisory, and call routing functions. It also supplies call management features. **Call management** refers to the group of functions accessed by network managers to monitor telephone traffic, customize calling features and restrictions by line, specify call routes, and analyze calling patterns. Call management also encompasses the user's ability to forward or block calls, to obtain call information, and to change line preferences.

In a third scenario, the traditional telephone connects to an analog PBX, which then connects to a voice-data gateway to convert the signals. Recall that a gateway is a combination of software and hardware that connects two dissimilar networks. In this case, the gateway connects the traditional telephone circuits with a TCP/IP network (such as the Internet or a private WAN). On the PSTN side, a gateway digitizes analog voice signals, compresses the data, assembles the data into packets, and then issues the packets to the packet-switched network. When transferring calls from a packet-switched network to a circuit-switched network, a gateway performs the same functions in the reverse order. To translate between the PSTN and VoIP networks, gateways follow special VoIP signaling protocols, which you learn about later in this chapter. Gateways used on converged networks may also be called **media gateways**. This term implies that the gateway accepts and translates not only voice and data, but also video signals. Some IP-PBXs may contain their own voice-data gateways, eliminating the need for a separate gateway.

Figure 14-1 depicts the different ways traditional telephones can be used to access a converged network. In this figure, the network is not specified. It could be public, such as the Internet, or private, such as a WAN that relies on leased lines. Converged network architectures are discussed later in this chapter.

 In the figures in this chapter, analog connections are represented by wavy lines and digital connections are represented by straight lines.

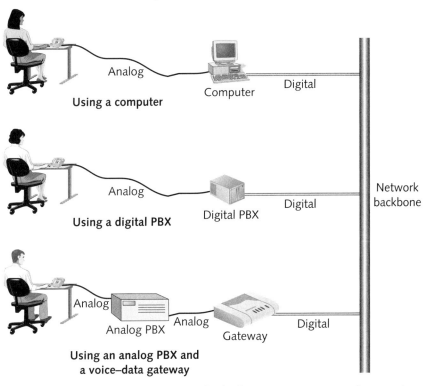

Figure 14-1   Connecting traditional telephones to a converged network

VoIP and IP Telephones

An **IP telephone** (or **IP phone**) is a telephone designed for use on VoIP networks. In new VoIP installations, IP telephones are preferred over traditional telephones. When a caller uses an IP telephone, her voice is immediately digitized and issued from the telephone to the network as a series of packets. To communicate on the network, each IP telephone must have a unique IP address, just as any client connected to the network has a unique IP address. The IP telephone typically connects, via the data network, to an IP-PBX. In other words, the IP telephone is connected to an RJ-45 wall jack, like a computer workstation. And like any other network node, its connection may pass through a connectivity device, such as a hub or switch, before reaching the digital PBX. Rather than connecting directly to an IP-PBX, IP telephones may first connect to an integrated access device (IAD), which, as you learned in Chapter 11, is a device designed to accept and interpret digital signals from many types of network nodes, including IP telephones, fax machines, computers, and various media. The IAD then passes packetized voice signals to an IP-PBX for call management. As previously mentioned, an IP-PBX may contain its own voice-data gateway, or it may connect to a separate voice-data gateway, which is then connected to the network backbone. Figure 14-2 illustrates different ways IP telephones can connect with a data network.

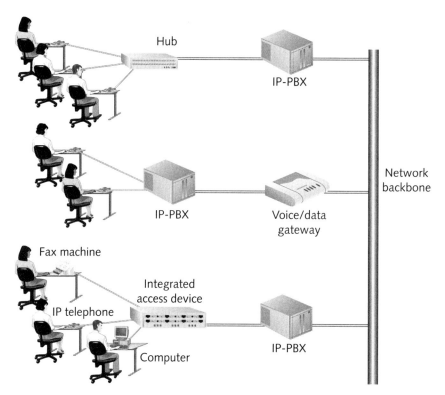

Figure 14-2 Connecting IP telephones to a converged network

The simplest IP telephones appear and act much like traditional telephones. For example, among other things, they feature speed-dialing, call hold, transfer, and forwarding buttons, conference calling, voice mail access, speakers and microphones, and an LCD screen that displays caller ID and call hold information. More sophisticated IP telephones offer features not available with traditional telephones. Because IP telephones are essentially network clients, like workstations, the number and types of customized features that can be programmed for use with these phones is limitless. However, some advanced functions are supplied by the IP telephone vendor. A few popular features unique to IP telephones are provided in the following list:

- Screens on IP telephones can act as Web browsers, allowing a user to open HTTP-encoded pages and, for example, click a telephone number link to complete a call to that number.

- IP telephones may connect to a user's personal digital assistant (PDA) through an infrared port, enabling the user to, for example, view his phone directory and touch a number on the IP telephone's LCD screen to call that number.

- Some IP telephones have speech recognition capabilities, which means that rather than pushing a button, a caller can speak the number he wants to call, and the telephone dials that number. Or, if the caller has activated a browser screen on his IP telephone, he can open a Web page by speaking the name of the URL, or an alias he has programmed the telephone to recognize.

- A user can program her IP telephone to forward calls to another number or to a list of different numbers in the event she is not at her desk. The IP telephone attempts to reach her at each number on the list until the call is answered. Or, the caller can program the IP telephone to forward only calls from certain telephone numbers.

- If a line is busy, an IP telephone can offer the caller the option to leave an instant message on the called party's IP telephone screen.

- An IP telephone can be programmed to accept emergency messages when they are broadcast to all IP telephones in an organization, even as the user is talking over the phone. In this case, the audio signal for the emergency message is combined with the audio signal of the user's call.

One advantage to using VoIP instead of existing PSTN telephony is that VoIP runs over open protocols (the TCP/IP protocol suite), whereas the PSTN runs over proprietary protocols (such as SS7 signaling). Because of this, developers with enough skill and interest can develop their own VoIP applications. VoIP's reliance on open protocols leads to endless possibilities for new VoIP applications. It also means that existing VoIP applications can be modified to suit a particular business's needs.

Another benefit to using IP telephones is their mobility. Because IP telephones are addressable over a network, they can be moved from one office to another office, connected to a wall jack, and be ready to accept or make calls—even if the new office is in another geographic location. Compare this to the traditional method of moving telephone extensions, which may require PBX reprogramming and result in user downtime. In the case of moving to another building or city, the LEC may have to program the change into its switch, a task that can cost a company at least $100. With IP telephones, however, an end user is free to move to any point on the wired network, no matter how distant from his original location, without missing a call and with little or no cost to the organization.

Makers of IP telephones include Alcatel, Avaya, Cisco, Mitel, NEC, Nortel, and Siemens. In the United States, an IP telephone can cost between $150 and $750. However, most IP telephones are sold as part of a package that includes an IP-PBX and call management software. An IP telephone is pictured in Figure 14-3. Note that this IP telephone is a wireline model. Mobile IP telephones, the VoIP equivalent to cell phones, are also available, though less commonly used.

14

Figure 14-3   IP telephone

One issue that faces IP telephones is the need for electric current. Just as with conventional telephones, IP telephones rely on electric current for signaling. Conventional telephones obtain current from the local loop. However, IP telephones are not directly connected to the local loop. Most obtain electric current from a separate power supply. Thus, if an organization suffers a power failure, its IP telephones cease to operate. This means that organizations that rely on IP telephones require assured backup power sources to maintain continual phone service. In some VoIP installations, however, IP telephones can obtain current via an Ethernet connection.

Using IP telephones is not the only way to benefit from a fully digital voice connection. Instead, an off-the-shelf workstation can be programmed to act like an IP telephone, as described in the next section.

VoIP and Softphones

A computer programmed to act like an IP telephone is known as a **softphone**. Softphones and IP telephones provide the same calling functions; they simply connect to the network and deliver services in different manners. To become a softphone, a computer must meet minimum hardware requirements, be installed with an IP telephony client, and communicate with a digital telephone switch.

Typical hardware requirements for a softphone specify a minimum of a Pentium 233 MHz processor, 50 MB of hard disk space, and 128 MB of memory. Virtually all workstations available at home electronics retailers meet or exceed these requirements. In addition, softphone computers must have a sound card capable of full-duplex transmission, so that both the caller and the called party can speak at the same time. For the computer equivalent of a telephone handset, some softphone clients can use the PC's internal microphone and speakers. However, softphone vendors recommend that, instead, the user purchase a special headset that contains higher-quality audio components. Using a headset offers voice sound quality that more closely resembles PSTN sound quality.

After a user starts the softphone client software, she is typically presented with a graphical representation of a telephone dial pad and a list of contacts in her address book. From there, she can click on a contact's name or number to review information about the contact or complete a call. Figure 14-4 shows an example of a softphone interface. Like IP telephones, softphone interfaces also provide buttons for call forwarding, speed dialing, conferencing, and so on—except that on a softphone, these buttons are clickable icons. Unlike other phones, softphones allow the user to customize his graphical interface. For example, a technician who often works at different locations in a company's campus can add to her default interface an option to forward calls to another softphone or IP telephone. An administrative assistant who spends most of his time calling clients and vendors on behalf of his supervisor can position a list of clickable, frequently called numbers in the foreground of his default interface.

Most vendors who supply IP telephones also supply softphone software, but customers do not necessarily have to rely on the same vendor for both. However, the softphone does have to employ signaling, compression, and quality of service protocols compatible with the digital PBX. Some smaller companies specialize in developing softphone clients that are compatible with any vendor's digital PBX.

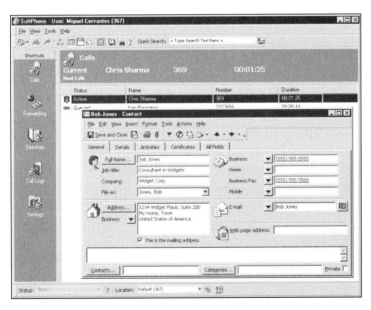

Figure 14-4   Softphone graphical interface

14

Softphones can connect to a converged network through the same means a computer connects to a network—for example, over a LAN, WAN, PPP dial-up, cable, DSL, ISDN, or T-carrier connection. After a softphone issues a voice call to the network, the call is handled by a digital PBX, just as a call from an IP telephone is handled. One difference between IP telephones and softphones, however, is that a softphone's versatile connectivity makes it an optimal VoIP solution for traveling employees and telecommuters. For example, suppose you are a district sales manager with a home office and you supervise dozens of sales representatives throughout the Pacific Northwest. Your company uses VoIP, with an IP-PBX connected to the company headquarters' LAN. At your home office, you have a desktop workstation equipped with a sound card, headset, and softphone software. You also lease a DSL connection to your local carrier, which allows you to log on to your company's LAN from home. After logging onto the LAN, you initiate the softphone client and then log onto the company's IP-PBX. By logging onto the IP-PBX, you access your personal call profile and indicate to the IP-PBX that your calls should be routed to your home computer. However, because you are a district sales manager, you only spend half of the time working from home. The other half of the time, you travel to visit your sales representatives across the region. During that time, you use a laptop that, like your home workstation, is equipped with a sound card, headset, and the softphone client software. While on the road, you dial into your company's LAN and initiate your softphone client, then log onto the company's IP-PBX. Now, your calls are directed to your laptop computer, rather than your home workstation. No matter where you are, you can establish a remote telephone extension, if the computer has the appropriate software and hardware installed. Figure 14-5 depicts the use of softphones on a converged network. As in previous figures, the network architecture is simplified.

Besides their extreme mobility, another advantage of using softphones is the capability for convenient, localized call management. Softphone clients can easily track the date, time, and duration of calls, in addition to their originating number and caller names. A softphone user can export call information to a billing or accounting program on the same workstation. This feature simplifies recordkeeping and billing for professionals—such as lawyers or consulting engineers—who bill their customers by the hour. Of course, the same call data can also be tracked by the IP-PBX to which a VoIP client is attached.

This section described VoIP from an end user's standpoint. Later in this chapter, you learn about VoIP network implementations and protocols. Next, however, you learn about additional applications suited to a converged network. Many of these operate on the same basic principles as VoIP.

Fax over IP (FoIP)

Contrary to some predictions, faxes haven't become obsolete with the proliferation of Web, e-mail, and private WAN services. Although they are less common than they were ten years ago, faxes still meet a unique business need. For example, in areas where digital signatures are not considered legally binding, a lawyer must obtain a signed, paper copy of a document from her client. If time is a concern, the lawyer will probably request a fax rather than wait for the U.S. Postal Service to deliver the document.

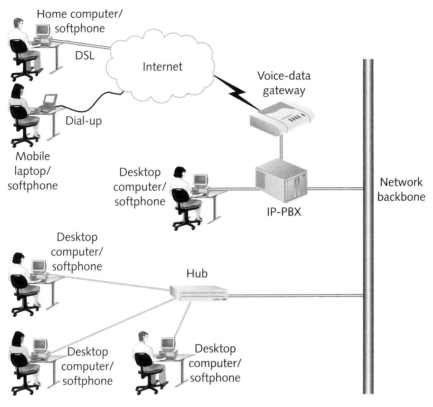

Figure 14-5   Connecting softphones to a converged network

In the same way that organizations can save money by using data networks for telephone calls, they can avoid paying long-distance charges by sending faxes over their existing packet-switched networks. Fax over IP (FoIP) is the use of IP networks to carry fax transmissions. Currently, this can be accomplished through one of two methods: attaching the fax to an e-mail or using IP fax clients that issue the fax data to a packet-based network in real time. Both methods offer advantages over analog fax transmission. However, each FoIP method presents its own advantages and disadvantages, and the choice of method depends on a user's requirements.

The method that attaches faxes to Internet e-mail messages—also referred to as a store-and-forward method—is defined by ITU standard **T.37**. In this scenario, either a computer, an **IP fax machine** (a fax machine designed to exchange fax data over a packet-switched network), or a traditional fax machine can act as a client. If the originating client is a computer, a user first creates a document on the computer. When she's ready to send the document, she starts a software program (this can be either an e-mail program or a fax client that invokes the e-mail program) and addresses the document to her recipient's e-mail address. Or, if the recipient uses a traditional fax machine, she can address the fax to a telephone number. The client software attaches the file, in the TIFF graphical file format, to an e-mail message, and then issues the e-mail message to a **fax gateway**. A fax gateway is a gateway that can translate IP fax data into analog fax data and vice versa. A fax gateway can also emulate and interpret conventional fax signaling protocols when communicating with a conventional fax machine. (Some fax gateways are part of a media gateway that is capable of translating voice, fax, and other communications signals.) When the T.37 standard is used, a fax gateway must also be able to interpret mail server requests through SMTP. It may be combined with a mail server on one machine, or a fax gateway may simply connect to a separate mail server on the same LAN. In addition, a fax gateway used with T.37 must be able to translate telephone numbers into e-mail addresses.

After a sending fax gateway receives a fax attached to an e-mail, it examines the destination e-mail address or telephone number to determine what receiving fax gateway should receive the transmission. Then, the sending gateway addresses the e-mail to the receiving fax gateway and issues it to a packet-switched network, such as the Internet. If the user addressed the fax to an e-mail address, the receiving fax gateway acts as a mail server to accept the fax and deliver it to its recipient. However, if the user addressed the fax to a telephone number, the receiving gateway must translate the telephone number into an e-mail address, and then forward the fax to that e-mail address. Either way, the message waits on the recipient's mail server until he retrieves it. In the case of delivering FoIP-transmitted faxes to conventional fax machines, the receiving fax gateway dials the number of the conventional fax machine. After the fax machine answers, the fax gateway issues conventional fax signals (for example, those that indicate an incoming call and those that indicate at what rate the fax machines will exchange data), convincing the fax machine that it is communicating with another conventional fax machine.

Using an IP fax machine client is similar to using a computer client. The IP fax machine simply encodes the fax as an e-mail attachment and issues it to the network's sending fax gateway. The fax transmission proceeds as described previously. If the client is a conventional, analog fax machine, the user simply feeds the paper into the fax machine and dials the number of the recipient's fax machine, just as she would do with a conventional fax transmission. The fax gateway accepts this analog transmission and converts it into packetized data. (In some configurations, analog lines first terminate at a PBX before connecting to a fax gateway.) It also interprets the destination telephone number and determines which receiving fax gateway should receive it. Then, the sending fax gateway issues the fax to a packet-switched network, such as the Internet. Figure 14-6 illustrates the different ways faxes can be sent to a packet-switched network using the ITU T.37 FoIP standard.

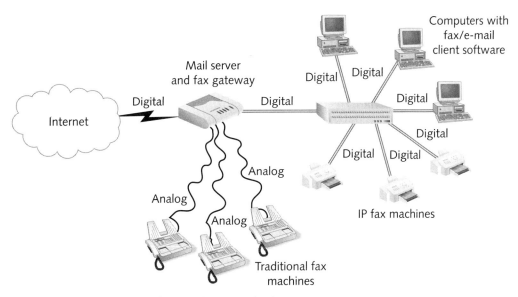

Figure 14-6 FoIP using the ITU T.37 standard

The drawback to the ITU T.37 FoIP method is that the fax sender does not receive any confirmation that the fax arrived without errors, or even that it arrived. For example, a problem with a router or server might damage the fax in transit. Because the transmission does not occur all at once, the sender will not know whether it was halted or damaged on its way to the recipient.

A second FoIP standard, defined by ITU **T.38**, delivers faxes in real time and therefore, provides potentially quicker delivery and verification that a fax was received. The network model for both ITU standards is similar. However, in a T.38 environment, native IP clients, such as computers equipped with FoIP software and IP fax machines, can issue fax transmissions directly to the packet-switched network, rather than connecting through a gateway. Fax gateways are used, however, on a T.38 FoIP implementation when packetized fax data must be sent to or received by conventional fax machines. In that case, the fax gateway emulates fax signaling protocols to establish a connection with the conventional fax machine, and translates FoIP data into analog signals for transmission over a traditional phone line. Figure 14-7 depicts a network using the ITU T.38 standard for FoIP.

14

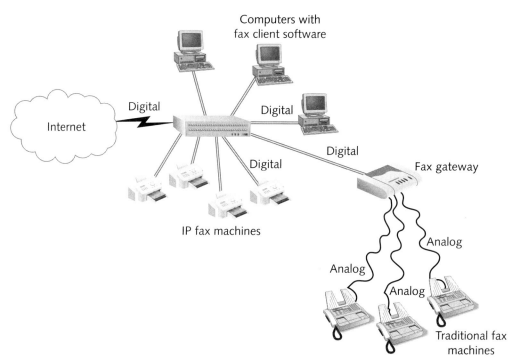

Figure 14-7   FoIP using the ITU T.38 standard

Fax transmissions require the same attention to encoding, signaling, and transport protocols as VoIP requires (as described later in this chapter). However, fax transmissions are more sensitive to the latency, delay, and packet loss inherent in packet-switched networks. A conventional fax machine expects to receive signals nearly constantly. If it detects no signals for more than 75 microseconds, for example, it terminates the call. Such delays are not uncommon on a busy packet-switched network. To overcome this technical consideration, real-time (T.38) FoIP gateways generate "false" signals that imitate real fax signals. By issuing these signals, the gateway prevents the conventional fax machine from dropping the connection. In addition, the fax gateways buffer data they send to conventional fax machines, to maintain a data rate acceptable to the fax machine.

Because of its unique transmission requirements, FoIP is somewhat more complex than VoIP. Next, however, you learn about an even more sophisticated service available on converged networks, videoconferencing.

Videoconferencing

Videoconferencing is the real-time transmission of images and audio between two locations. Videoconferencing is used by educational institutions for distance learning, by healthcare professionals for telemedicine (as described in Chapter 1), and by businesses to share presentations over long distances. One advantage of videoconferencing is obvious: It allows people to avoid travel. The benefits of staying put include saving time, saving money, and avoiding security risks. Videoconferencing also allows organizations to conduct business (which might otherwise be conducted over the phone) in a face-to-face manner; this type of interaction can enhance customer relationships, streamline the hiring process, and fortify business partnerships. The process of issuing real-time video signals from a server to a client is also known as **video streaming**. Most modern videoconferencing implementations use video streaming.

However, transmitting video over a network is complicated. Video is harder to provide on packet-switched networks than on circuit-switched networks. (You'll recall that this same problem applies to VoIP.) This is why, although the technology to transmit video over packet-switched networks has been defined for many years, most organizations continue to use circuit-switched ISDN connections. And like VoIP and FoIP, video over IP cannot provide quality reception when packet delay or loss is present. In addition, videoconferencing requires significant bandwidth—depending on the circumstances, from 10 to 100 times more bandwidth than VoIP. In recent years, thanks to technology innovations, videoconferencing over IP has become viable. But when quality is a concern, it is almost always performed over a private network, in which traffic is more predictable and transmissions can be better controlled. One exception is Internet2, the exclusive backbone designed for educational and research organizations. Because Internet2 does not compete with generic public Internet traffic, it provides sufficient bandwidth and a better path for videoconferencing. In fact, many universities use Internet2 to broadcast lectures to multiple classrooms at different locations.

To participate in a videoconference over the network, each user requires a **video terminal**. Video terminals are the devices that enable users to watch, listen, speak, and capture their image. The video terminal can be a computer equipped with a microphone, speaker, monitor, sound card, camera, and video software. (A camera and microphone are optional if the user is only listening and watching the video.) Or, it may be a separate viewing station connected to a computer via a USB port, for example. Another type of video terminal is a device specially designed to exchange audio and video images. These devices contain a video monitor, camera, speakers, plus a way to connect to the network and interpret videoconferencing signals. The architecture of a videoconferencing network depends on the type of service.

Networks can provide video in three forms: point-to-point (unicast), point-to-multipoint with user registration (multicast), and point-to-multipoint with no user registration requirements (broadcast). In point-to-point videoconferencing, one video terminal connects over the network to another video terminal. If both terminals use the same video-over-IP protocols, each simply connects to the network through an access device, such as an IP-PBX with video signal processing capabilities. If the conference occurs between a terminal on an IP network and another on a circuit-switched network, the signals must be translated. A media gateway performs this translation.

14

The multicast version of point-to-multipoint video requires another connectivity device—a **multipoint control unit (MCU)**, also known as a **video bridge**. The MCU provides a common connection to several clients. To participate in a multicast video-conference, a user connects to the MCU over the network and enters a password to gain access to the conference. Although the sender issues one video signal, the MCU allows several receiving video terminals to tap into that signal. This type of video service is used, for example, to transmit a video presentation from a company's headquarters to its branch offices. In this scenario, not only must clients have MCU credentials, but they must also know when to tap into the videoconference. Figure 14-8 illustrates a multi-cast videoconferencing scenario.

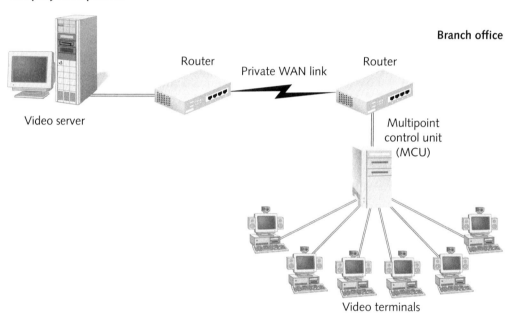

Figure 14-8   Multicast videoconferencing

In the broadcast version of point-to-multipoint video, any number of clients can access a video signal without having to verify their credentials. News agencies use this type of service to broadcast news reports over the Web, for example. In this example, analog video footage (if used) must be encoded in digital format before the streaming server can interpret it. At the same time, the digitally-encoded video is compressed for faster network transmission. The encoded video is stored in a file on a server until a client requests it. MPEG is one of the most popular file formats for video.

Note that unlike multicast video, broadcast video does not use MCUs. Instead, the server issues a separate copy of the video signal to every client, upon the client's request. The advantage of this arrangement is that clients do not have to "log on" to a video session at a particular time. Of course, this type of service is not secure. Another potential disadvantage of this service is that at any point in time, the video server and its network must have sufficient resources to accommodate all the clients that request the video. In other words, if twenty users request a video file, and each user connects to the network at 52 Kbps, the server must be capable of transmitting at least 1.04 Mbps. If you have watched video clips on the Web, you are probably aware that many companies offer free client software for this service—for example RealNetworks' RealOne Player and Microsoft Windows Media Player. Later, in this chapter's Hands-on Projects, you have the opportunity to experiment with broadcast video.

Call Centers

One area in which converged networks promise to streamline communications is in call centers. As you learned in Chapter 1, a call center is a facility designed to accept calls from multiple customers. To efficiently handle their high volume of calls, call centers take advantage of unique telecommunications services, including automatic call distribution (ACD), computer-telephony integration (CTI), and interactive voice response (IVR) software. (These services are discussed in Chapter 5.) In a sizeable call center, combining telephony, Web, e-mail, voice mail, and fax services allows a customer's inquiry to follow the best route to the customer service representative (often known as an agent) who is best able to answer his question. In addition, agents can immediately access, modify, and save details about each customer interaction—for example, what his question was, what the solution was, and how long it took to reach the solution. The program that stores and manages this information is known as a customer relationship management (CRM) database. On a converged network, the CRM program could also be used to initiate follow-up calls or e-mails to the customer.

Call centers have long used Web and e-mail services to interact with customers. However, in organizations in which voice and data travel separate networks, one group of agents is typically assigned to answer telephones while another group of agents responds to Web and e-mail queries. Further, saving the details of a customer interaction in a CRM database requires the agent to work with a separate application on her desktop computer. In this scenario, every method of contact follows a different path, as shown in Figure 14-9. A call center that uses separate voice and data channels requires greater software and hardware investment, more staffing, and arguably provides less customized help than call centers that use converged networks.

14

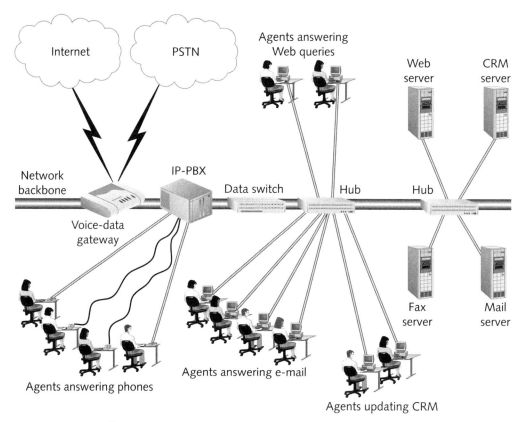

Figure 14-9 Call center activities without a converged network

In contrast, call centers that use converged networks can take advantage of numerous efficiencies and enhanced features. Some examples of call center functions on a converged network include:

- The ability for agents to retrieve a complete customer profile and call history as soon as the customer makes contact with them. For example, if a customer calls via the PSTN, the call center's application server can trigger the CRM to open a customer record based on the customer's incoming telephone number, and then forward that record to the agent who answers the customer's call.

- The ability for a customer inquiry (via PSTN, Web, e-mail, and so on.) to be routed to the most appropriate agent based on the customer's contact information and history. For example, suppose a customer e-mails a PC manufacturer with a question about her computer's sound card. Her e-mail address is associated with her customer history saved in a CRM database. Her customer history indicates that she called the day before with a question about a modem. The database also indicates which agent she spoke with. By integrating the e-mail and CRM applications, her second question about modems could be automatically routed to the same agent who handled her previous question. In other cases, the routing of customer inquiries may be based on an agent's technical specialty, language skills, or availability.

- The ability for a customer to click on a Web page link to connect his telephone line with a customer service representative. After an agent has responded, the agent can also help the customer navigate a Web site by sending that customer certain Web pages. At the same time, the agent might help the customer complete a purchase.

- The ability for customers to click on a Web page link to enable a chat session with a customer service representative. During the chat session, the customer can type questions and immediately receive an agent's typed answer on his Web browser screen.

- The ability for customers and agents to converse via videoconferencing. Although this is less common than voice or e-mail inquiries, it is particularly appropriate for certain applications, such as conducting bank transactions.

- The ability for agents to work anywhere—at the office, at home, or on the road—with the same, comprehensive functionality they enjoy while working at the physical call center. For example, calls that are automatically routed to certain agents based on their technical skills, language skills, or past interactions with a customer can continue to be routed to those same agents, even when they are not at the office.

- The ability for agents and their supervisors to gather real-time statistics on call completion and customer satisfaction rates.

Call centers that use the same network for voice, fax, and data transmission can save money by using the same media, servers, connectivity equipment, station equipment, and network access for all their services. Several combinations of hardware and software can achieve this savings. For example, the fully converged call center network would include all the components of a VoIP and FoIP network, including an IP-PBX (with voice mail capabilities), voice-data gateway, and fax server. In addition, it would include an e-mail server for e-mail and call application servers that run automatic ACD, CTI, and IVR software. Another server might run the customer relationship management database. Note that some vendors offer solutions that combine two or more of these applications on a single server, so that not every function requires its own hardware. The key to efficient call centers is that all of the applications are integrated and available to agents at any place and through a single interface.

Figure 14-10 gives one example of how a call center's converged network might be arranged. Note that there could be many variations on this arrangement, depending on the size and purpose of the organization.

14

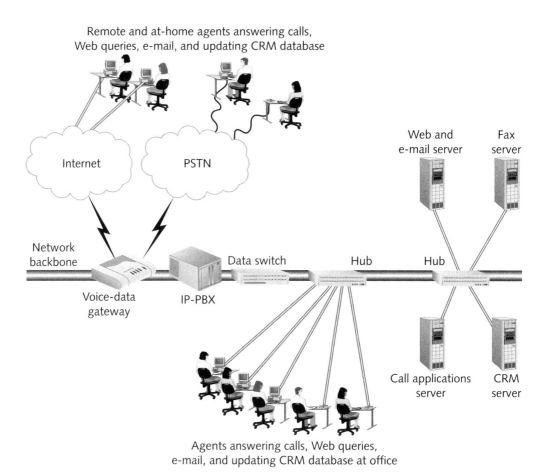

Figure 14-10   Call center activities on a converged network

As you might expect, one challenge to call center converged networks is integrating applications (sometimes from different vendors). Beyond that, however, network administrators must deal with the same technical issues that challenge VoIP, which are discussed later in this chapter. Next, you learn about another converged network application that combines many individual services into a single interface.

Unified Messaging

Unified messaging (sometimes called **unified communication**) is a service that makes several forms of communication available from a single user interface. In unified messaging, a user can, for example, access the Web, send and receive faxes, e-mail messages, voice mail messages, or telephone calls—all from one console. The main console typically exists as a graphical user interface on a computer or an IP telephone. In addition, unified messaging applications allow users to call in and access their messages from an off-site telephone.

The goal of unified messaging is to improve a user's productivity by minimizing the number of devices and different methods she needs to communicate with colleagues and customers. For example, a commuter stuck in traffic could dial one number that accesses her unified messaging inbox. To verify that she is indeed the person authorized to access this inbox, the unified messaging application might prompt her to speak her name, and then use voice recognition software to match her speech patterns with a recording of her voice. After the system grants access, she could choose to listen to voice mail messages or hear her new e-mail messages read to her. By pressing digits on her telephone, she could forward an e-mail or reply to a message by leaving the sender a voice mail message. If she anticipates a long wait in traffic, she could configure her office telephone to forward calls to her cell phone. If she has a wireless fax machine, she could even receive and send faxes from her car. This is only one example of how unified messaging can streamline the several forms of communication common in the modern business world.

Unified messaging can be accomplished through several different means, depending on an organization's needs. For very large organizations, in which it is economically advantageous to purchase equipment and software, a unified messaging solution could include an IP-PBX connected to a messaging server. In this scenario, the IP-PBX provides call management and voice mail services, and a separate messaging server supplies the user interface, Web connectivity, and the storage and management of faxes and e-mail messages. This type of messaging server treats every message and fax as an object in a large database. Alternatively, separate servers could be used for Web, e-mail, and fax services. To integrate with Web, e-mail, and fax servers on other networks, the messaging server (or servers) must run software compatible with common protocols. For example, in the case of e-mail, the mail server software must comply with SMTP mail server standards. Ideally, a mail server used with unified messaging would also support the IMAP mail client protocol (rather than, or in addition to, the POP3 protocol), so that messages can be centrally stored and accessed from anywhere at anytime.

14

Smaller organizations that cannot afford to buy expensive servers and software can instead rely on a service provider to manage their unified messaging. In this scenario, the service provider purchases and maintains the equipment, unified messaging software, and network connectivity. When an organization subscribes to unified messaging, the service provider adds the organization's users to its database. Users can access their messages, calls, faxes, and Web resources by connecting to the service provider's network. Meanwhile, the organization pays a recurring fee, usually per user, for the unified messaging service. In addition, the service provider might charge a variable rate, depending on how much bandwidth an organization requires for its users to access unified messaging. To determine whether this solution is preferable, an organization must assess the number of users who need unified messaging, how frequently they will use it, and how much traffic they will generate as they access and exchange messages.

Now that you have a sense of the variety of applications running on converged networks, you are ready to learn more about what types of organizations implement converged networks and why.

IMPLEMENTING VoIP

Of all the applications discussed previously in this chapter, none has been so widely praised, explored, and debated as VoIP. You have already learned how migrating from traditional telephone service to VoIP allows for new applications, improved efficiency, centralized management, and cost savings. In this section, you learn how organizations can implement VoIP to their advantage, and also how to analyze the costs and benefits of VoIP.

VoIP Over Private Networks

In general, VoIP affords the greatest advantages when implemented on private, rather than public, networks. Earlier, you learned that one benefit of carrying voice signals over an existing data network is toll bypass, or completing long-distance calls without incurring long-distance charges from a telecommunications carrier. Of course, only a WAN (which spans long distances) could complete long-distance calls. To implement VoIP on a WAN, an organization must: install VoIP clients (for example, IP telephones) and connect them to the LAN at each location; install at least one IP-PBX (for example, at the organization's primary location); and provide links between locations with sufficient bandwidth to carry both voice and data traffic. To allow its IP telephone clients to make regular PSTN calls, the organization also requires a voice-data gateway.

Figure 14-11 provides an example of how a private VoIP WAN might be constructed. In this example, IP telephones and softphones at Location B rely on Location A's IP-PBX for call management and also on Location A's voice-data gateway for routing calls to the PSTN. This arrangement works as long as the connection between Location A and Location B is fast and reliable. However, if the connection fails, Location B loses telephone service completely. In an actual implementation, the organization might choose to place a second IP-PBX at Location B (or at least establish redundant connections between the two sites) to minimize the threat of losing telephone service at one location.

VoIP can also be implemented on a virtual private network (VPN), though this is a less common scenario. Recall that a VPN is a logically-distinct private network established via a public network (for example, Internet) connection. Although VPNs use public networks, they are considered private because they incorporate endpoint definitions and stringent security provisions that allow access only to authorized users. In a VPN, locations may connect to the public network via a number of connection types—for example, DSL, ISDN, cable, or T-carrier. A stereotypical VPN is one that connects small branch offices scattered across the country to a company's headquarters. To use VoIP, VPN branch office connects, via a public network, to a media gateway at the headquarters.

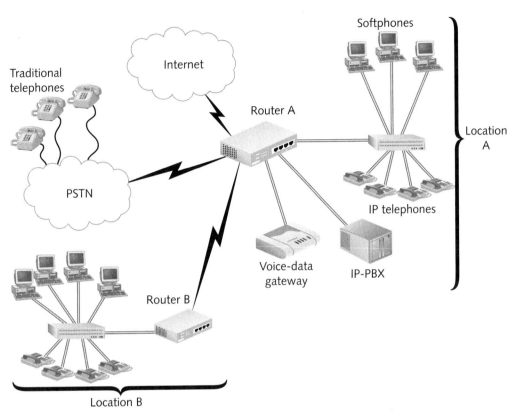

Figure 14-11   VoIP on a private WAN

The challenge in running VoIP over this architecture is that each location's connectivity device (for example, a DSL or ISDN router) must adhere to the same signaling and prioritization protocols as the headquarters' gateway uses. (You learn more about these protocols later in this chapter.) If all the connectivity devices do not conform to a standard, calls cannot be established over the network. Therefore, each branch office requires its own gateway device in addition to the connectivity device supplied by the service provider when the connection was installed. Branch office gateways are smaller and less expensive than the headquarters gateway, but the costs still add up. In addition, because VPNs use a public network, their transmissions compete with other network traffic. As you have learned, during times of heavy usage, a public network experiences more latency than when traffic is light. And although VPN nodes enjoy a private connection over the public network, they cannot do anything to control traffic levels. Thus, VPN transmissions are more susceptible to network delay and packet loss than private WAN transmissions.

14

Not all businesses achieve the benefits of cost savings and greater efficiencies by implementing VoIP. Characteristics that make a business particularly well-suited to running VoIP over a private network include:

- A high number of telephone lines (for example, more than 100)

- Several locations that are geographically dispersed across long distances (for example, over a continent or across the globe)

- A high volume of long-distance call traffic between locations within the organization

- Sufficient capital for upgrading or purchasing new CPE, connectivity equipment, LAN transmission media, and WAN links

- Goals for continued network and business expansion

- Willingness of both technical and nontechnical staff to learn new skills

- Willingness to accept deferred gains (as VoIP investments might not pay off for several years)

The importance of each factor must be weighed against other factors, and of course, each situation varies. However, as you might infer, the profile for an ideal VoIP candidate is a large, growing, international organization that relies heavily on voice communication and has enough capital to invest in VoIP upgrades.

But what if an organization wants to implement VoIP even though it does not meet any of the previously-listed criteria? For example, suppose a small, local engineering firm wants its employees—who are constantly moving from place to place—to be able to use one telephone to receive calls anywhere in the office or at a client's site. In addition, suppose the firm recently moved to a new building, in which voice and data are both cabled with CAT5 UTP, thereby eliminating one of the costs of migrating to VoIP. In that case, the firm could avoid having to buy and build its own VoIP infrastructure and outsource its VoIP services to another provider, such as a public telecommunications carrier. The next section discusses ways in which VoIP is implemented on such public networks.

VoIP Over Public Networks

So far, this chapter has focused on the ways VoIP can be implemented on private networks. However, telecommunications carriers, such as LECs and IXCs, also use VoIP to their advantage. The benefits of VoIP on public networks are similar to those for private networks: potential cost savings, new or enhanced applications, and increased competitiveness. The technology behind a common carrier's VoIP network is also similar to, but operates on a much larger scale than, a private organization's VoIP network.

You have learned how on private networks, IP-PBXs and VoIP (or media) gateways together enable IP telephones to complete calls with analog telephones, and vice versa. On a common carrier's network, VoIP also depends on gateways and packet-based switches. Before learning about this next generation network technology, however, it is useful to review what you know about conventional PSTN switching. Recall from

Chapter 6 that common carrier switches can be divided into two types: end-office switches (also known as Class 5 switches) and tandem switches. An end-office switch supplies dial tone over the local loop and manages call setup, routing, and supervision for subscriber lines. It also provides features, such as caller ID, conference calling, and call waiting. LECs operate end-office switches. In contrast, a tandem switch is used to connect trunks between central offices. It handles inter-carrier and long-distance call routing and supervision. IXCs, LECs, and other common carriers operate tandem switches.

Adding packetized traffic to the public network does not mean that LECs and IXCs can discard their existing switches. Most local loops are still analog and, therefore, require LECs to support this type of connection (and in particular, its SS7 signaling) with traditional Class 5 switches. In addition, existing switches perform specialized functions that are not necessarily available on newer, packet-based switches. However, the growing demand for packet-based transmission compels carriers to introduce new hardware and software to their central offices or POPs.

Because public networks are more complex than their private counterparts, it is difficult to equate a function with a particular device. Instead, it makes more sense to discuss next-generation public networks in terms of the services they perform. Therefore, though the following discussion mentions certain devices, bear in mind that one device might serve several purposes. For example, just as on a private network, a public network's packet-based switch may include a gateway, thus eliminating the need for a separate gateway device. The potential for one device to perform many functions, plus the diversity of connection types and applications a carrier might provide, leads to many permutations of network devices. It also means that two common carrier's networks may look entirely different even though they offer identical services.

 Although this section concentrates on VoIP, Voice over ATM (VoATM) is another common method of transmitting packetized voice signals on public networks.

14

To carry packet-based traffic, common carrier networks incorporate the following:

- *Access service*—Provides endpoints for multiple types of incoming connections (for example IP, ATM, and time division multiplexed (TDM) links, such as T-carriers). Supports as many signaling protocols as are necessary, depending on the types of incoming connections.

- *Media gateway service*—Translates between different Layer 2 protocols and interfaces. Can act as interface between circuit-switched and packet-switched networks. Also handles traffic prioritization and enforces traffic policies (for example, ensuring that high-priority packets are passed on more quickly than low-priority packets). In some architectures, media gateway services incorporate access services.

- *Packet-based signaling*—Provides control and call routing, including functions traditionally performed by end-office and tandem switches. Generates session information for accounting purposes.

- *Signaling gateway service*—Translates packet-based signaling protocols into SS7 signaling protocols (used on circuit-switched PSTN) and vice versa, so that users with packet-based devices can communicate with users with analog devices.

- *Accounting service*—Collects connection information, such as time and duration of calls, for billing purposes. Also tracks use of fee-based applications, such as conferencing.

- *Application (or feature) service*—Provides traditional telephony features to end-users, such as caller ID, 3-way calling, and voice mail, but also provides a host of new features, such as language translation, speech recognition for dialing, and Web-driven applications. Also interacts with packet-based signaling and media gateway services to manage calls based on a feature's requirements (for example, terminating a conference call after the user has chosen this function from the conference call interface).

On many common carrier networks, access and media gateway services are consolidated into one device, the media gateway. In contrast to the media gateways used on private networks, which might contain a few hundred ports, common carrier media gateways have the capacity to accept tens of thousands of connections. Also, common carrier media gateways accept traffic from ATM, IP, and TDM-based links (such as traditional PSTN trunks). The media gateway translates each signal's Layer 2 protocols into the format necessary for call handling, and then passes the signals, in packet form, to a **softswitch**. A softswitch is a computer or group of computers that manages packet-based traffic routing and control. For example, a softswitch processes signals that establish and terminate calls between IP telephones. (You learn more about call signaling later in this chapter.) A softswitch usually also performs call accounting services (unless the carrier uses a separate server to perform accounting). Figure 14-12 shows an example of a media gateway, and Figure 14-13 provides a view of the back of a softswitch computer.

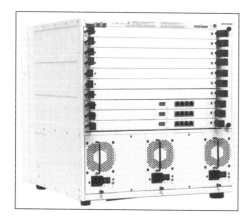

Figure 14-12   Media gateway

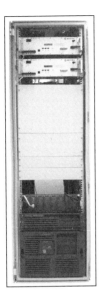

Figure 14-13   Softswitch

Because LECs still rely on their traditional Class 5 switches, softswitches must be capable of exchanging signals with traditional telephony switches. As you probably guessed, a gateway is used to bridge the gap between these two types of switches. In this case, the gateway translates between SS7 signaling protocols used on the PSTN and the signaling protocols used by the softswitch. On some networks, softswitches perform signaling gateway services. Softswitches are also connected with application servers, which supply unique features to VoIP callers. In some cases, softswitches themselves provide the application services. Such enhanced services, along with more straightforward VoIP services, can be profitable offerings for telecommunications carriers. Figure 14-14 illustrates how a LEC might integrate these packet-based networking components.

A long-distance packet-based network shares some of the same elements as the LEC's packet-based network. However, connections between carrier facilities rely on standard interfaces and protocols. In other words, a tandem office only accepts trunks from other central offices. It does not handle local loop connections. Thus, providing access and media gateway services in a tandem office is simpler. Also, softswitches at tandem offices perform different functions than end-office softswitches. For example, tandem switches handle routing for toll-free calls, but do not store customer-billing information.

14

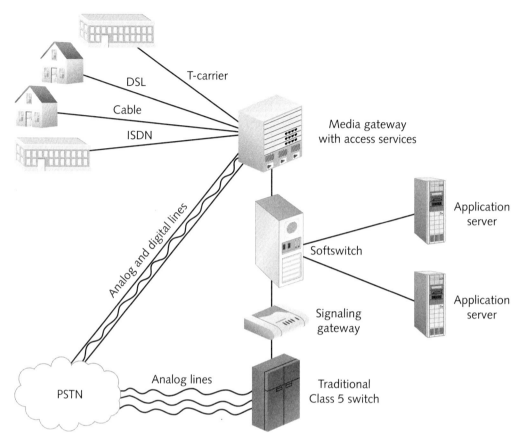

Figure 14-14   Components of a LEC's packet-based network

In most cases, a long-distance packet-based network also requires signaling gateway services to translate between VoIP and PSTN signaling protocols. However, in cases where the POP handles exclusively packet-based traffic and can predict the protocols it receives (for example, a "relay" connection between two large facilities owned by the same carrier), signaling gateways are unnecessary. Figure 14-15 shows an example of the packet-based networking components at a tandem office.

One potential drawback to supplying VoIP on public networks is the lack of clear standards, which can result in interoperability problems between carriers. In the PSTN, all carrier switches use the same signaling protocols for call routing and management. However, packetized voice services can use different signaling protocols (as described later in this chapter). In addition, they can use different prioritization and encoding schemes. However, to complete a call between two carriers' packet-switched networks, both networks must communicate using the same protocols. The lack of clear standards for packetized voice transmission poses a problem. In addition, as engineers continually improve on VoIP technology, protocols continue evolving. Meanwhile, one way to ensure interoperability is for carriers to install media gateways and softswitches capable of interpreting multiple protocols.

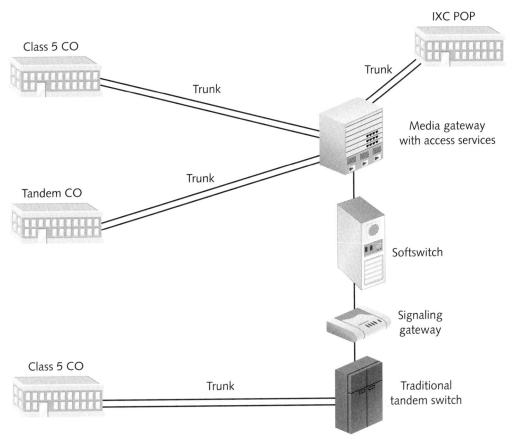

Figure 14-15   Components of a long-distance packet-based network

14

Both LECs and IXCs can lower their operational costs by implementing packet-switched voice networks. In the case of LECs, one significant cost savings comes from off-loading modem calls—that is, redirecting calls from modems away from conventional switches. Conventional switches were designed to provide the optimal number of circuits to support an end office's volume of voice-telephone calls. Engineers based capacity calculations on the fact that the average voice-telephone call lasts approximately five minutes. However, the average dial-up connection to an ISP lasts approximately 30 minutes. As more and more people logged onto the Internet, LECs discovered that their current end-office switch capacity was insufficient. Packet-switched networks and softswitches help LECs address this problem by redirecting Internet dial-up traffic away from the conventional switches currently managing PSTN voice calls. To do this, LECs can assign Internet access numbers (the number a customer's modem dials to connect to an ISP's remote access server) to media gateways or access servers on their packet-based network.

Another advantage to public, packet-switched long-distance networks has to do with the cost of transmitting calls from one carrier's territory to another. As you learned in Chapter 4, LECs and IXCs traditionally hand off calls to another carrier (often, a competitor) when the call terminates in that carrier's territory. This hand-off results in access fees, which can be very expensive. However, by transmitting calls over its own long-distance, packet-switched network, a carrier avoids paying these fees. Instead, calls that originate with that carrier can stay on the carrier's network. This is similar to a private organization bypassing toll charges by using its own packet-based network for voice. Costs saved by using packet-based networks can be substantial, particularly when the traffic travels overseas.

In addition to lowering current operational costs, common carriers expect to gain new revenue from providing data services over packet-based networks. And finally, both LECs and IXCs benefit from a greater port density with packet-based networks. In other words, a traditional switch capable of handling 50,000 lines, for example, could be as large as a delivery truck. A softswitch with the same circuit capacity could be as small as a microwave oven. However, upgrading to VoIP also requires significant investment. Next, you learn some fundamental techniques for determining whether VoIP grants a return on its investment.

Cost-Benefit Analysis

Proponents of VoIP have made bold claims about its potential to save telephony costs. In some cases, VoIP does save money. For example, earlier you learned that an ideal VoIP candidate is an organization with hundreds of telephone lines and a high volume of long-distance traffic. But these measures are still too subjective to predict whether VoIP will truly result in long-term cost savings.

To accurately determine potential savings, an organization must thoroughly analyze its voice and data networks. The analysis begins by identifying an organization's current telephone usage (for example, minutes of long-distance use per month) and the associated costs. These costs should be evident from PBX accounting or from past telephone bills. The next step in analyzing whether VoIP is economically beneficial is to calculate the cost of combining voice and data traffic onto one network. The major costs involved in migrating to and supporting a converged network include:

- Cost of purchasing or upgrading CPE, connectivity devices (for example, media gateways and IP-PBXs), and transmission media for each location

- Cost of installation services and vendor maintenance

- Cost of training technical employees and other staff

- Recurring cost of new or expanded connections (although this may be an area of cost savings, depending on how VoIP is implemented)

- Cost of transmitting voice and data, if part of the connection fees are usage-based

After totaling the costs of establishing a converged network, the analysis should account for the potential economic gains. This sum is more difficult to accurately determine, because certain factors are subjective or intangible. However, you can make an estimate by taking into account the following:

- Bypassing common carriers to make long-distance calls, thus avoiding tolls

- Consolidating traffic over the same connections, which leads to reducing or canceling PSTN or leased-line connections

- Eliminating the need to purchase proprietary and potentially more expensive hardware from a single vendor (for example, a PBX that can only communicate with a similar PBX made by the same company)

- Providing employees with more efficient tools and means of communication

- Increased network management efficiencies through a centralized management interface and the "plug and play" nature of IP telephones

- Potential for more telecommuting (which is simpler on an all-VoIP network) and more long-distance online collaboration

- Increased productivity for mobile employees

- Multiple ways of communicating with and responding to customers, resulting in customer retention and potentially greater sales

- Competitive advantage that potentially leads to increased sales

 Note Additional, less definitive costs and benefits also arise when migrating to VoIP. For example, a LEC saves significant space in its central office by installing softswitches rather than conventional telephone switches. On the other hand, changing to new technology might initially result in greater demands on customer support personnel. Many other variable costs could arise. A more detailed cost-benefit analysis is beyond the scope of this book, however.

14

One organization that has implemented VoIP and video over IP to increase productivity and decrease costs is the United States Census Bureau. In 2001, this federal agency replaced the 30-year old key telephone system at its Maryland headquarters with a complete voice and video over IP solution from Cisco Systems, Inc. The new infrastructure included media gateways, media gateway controllers, 5500 IP telephones, specialized video viewstations, plus management, application, and messaging software. The IP telephones were first installed at Census Bureau call centers. These call centers serve both internal customers (such as employees requesting assistance with their computers) and external customers (such as people requesting the purchase of census data). There, call center employees take advantage of IP telephony to automatically retrieve a caller's history and information, route calls to the most appropriate agent, and connect agents from multiple locations to form one large "virtual" call center. After the improved efficiencies of IP telephony were proven in the call centers, the agency provided IP telephones to end users. In addition to supplying voice over IP, the Census Bureau uses its converged network for distance learning videoconferences and to broadcast live video to employees in Maryland and in other locations, such as its Indiana-based processing center. To provide sufficient bandwidth for the added services, the agency upgraded its LAN's backbone to 1 Gigabit Ethernet and supplied each workstation with a 100-Mbps connection. For videoconferencing, its WAN includes dedicated 768 Kbps links to computers in auditoriums and conference rooms. Although purchasing new cabling, hardware, and software was a significant investment, the Census Bureau predicts that it will pay off. Currently, the organization estimates it saves approximately $200 per telephone for each extension addition or move, plus an additional $150,000 annually by using the same infrastructure for voice, video, and data. Within three years of installation, it expects to save nearly $1 million annually by using a packet-based voice, video, and data network.

Costs and benefits resulting from VoIP implementations naturally depend on the extent to which VoIP is deployed. An organization could utilize VoIP only for toll bypass, only for internal communications (with an IP-PBX), for both of these functions, or for complete, unified messaging. After performing a thorough analysis, some companies find that VoIP will not pay off in their organization—or at least, not for several years. If an organization makes the decision to implement VoIP, it faces decisions about what type of VoIP to implement. In other words, engineers must wrestle with what type of signaling, transport, encoding, and quality of service protocols their network should run.

VoIP Encoding

One important consideration when issuing voice signals over a network is how to represent a human voice, which is analog, in digital format. In Chapter 6, you learned how voice and other audio signals are digitally encoded through pulse code modulation (PCM). Recall that an analog waveform is approximated by sampling its amplitude a certain number of times per second. The sampling rate used on the PSTN is 8000 samples per second. This rate is sufficient to replicate the human voice in conversation (though it would not provide high audio quality on a compact disc, for example). After the wave is sampled, each sample is rounded to a value that can be represented by 8 bits worth of digital information through the process known as quantizing. Multiplying 8000 samples per second by 8 bits per sample results in 64 Kbps, which is the standard capacity of one voice channel, or 1 DS0. (As described in Chapter 10, a T1 contains 24 DS0s, for a total capacity of 1.544 Mbps.) On the PSTN, a telephone switch accomplishes the coding and decoding, or codec, by using a computer chip known as a **digital signal processor (DSP)**. The type of codec used on the PSTN is specified in the ITU **G.711** standard.

The G.711 standard is optimized for use on the circuit-switched PSTN. However, it is not optimal for VoIP networks. One reason is the amount of throughput G.711 requires. Although most packet-based networks can easily handle signals that require 64 Kbps, in an environment where multiple signals vie for the same, limited capacity, using less capacity is preferable if doing so can achieve an acceptable result. A second reason is that G.711 codecs only convert incoming digital signals into good facsimiles of their original, analog waveform as long as the bits arrive intact and in order.

To better understand why G.711 provides better quality on the PSTN, it is helpful to review the key differences between circuit-switched and packet-switched transmission. As you learned in Chapter 6, in circuit switching, a connection is reserved between two endpoints for as long as the parties keep the connection alive. In addition, all circuit-switched signals follow the same path over the network from one point to the other. Because of these characteristics, a PSTN call's signals never lack for bandwidth or arrive out of order. The same is not true, however, for packet switching. Recall that on a packet-switched network, data is divided into small packets that may follow any path to their destination. Packets are delivered according to **best effort**. Best effort means that the network attempts to deliver packets in a timely fashion and in the proper sequence, but does not guarantee either. In fact, best effort offers no guarantees that a packet will arrive at its destination at all. Best effort also means a packet-switched network naturally suffers delays. G.711 cannot withstand such delays and still provide good sound quality. Therefore, a different method of voice encoding is preferable for use on packet-based networks.

The ITU has specified many voice-encoding standards other than G.711. In the following sections, you learn about some techniques that are suited to VoIP networks.

Waveform Codecs

G.711 is known as a **waveform codec** because it obtains information from the analog waveform, and then uses this information to reassemble the waveform as accurately as possible at the receiving end. A waveform codec does not manipulate the signal in any sophisticated way. It simply tries to reconstruct it. All types of PCM are considered waveform codecs. In general, waveform codecs produce excellent sound quality and result in little delay over the network. Furthermore, they demand little effort from a connectivity device's DSP, the computer chip that performs the codec routines. All of these qualities are favorable. However, the drawback to waveform codecs is that they also require a significant amount of throughput, compared to other encoding methods.

A variation on G7.11 that does not require as much capacity is the **G.723** standard. G.723 uses a form of PCM known as **differential pulse code modulation (DPCM)**. In DPCM, the codec samples the actual voice signal at regular intervals. In between, it attempts to predict the value of signal bits that have not yet arrived, based on the value of previously-transmitted bits. When the actual signal differs from the predicted signal, the sending node transmits only the differential, or the difference between the predicted and actual values. Given a predicted signal plus a differential, the receiving end can reconstruct the voice signal with some accuracy.

DPCM codecs work well with human speech because, within very short time spans, our speech patterns are predictable. In addition, because DCPM transmits only the differential between voice samples, it conserves bandwidth. For example, G.723 uses one-tenth of the throughput that G.711 requires, or 6.4 Kbps. On the other hand, G.723 requires more DSP resources and results in moderate network delays, compared to some other codecs. In addition, its voice quality is not as good as G.711. However, G.723 is adequate for packet-based networks and is currently used for VoIP and videoconferencing.

An even more advanced form of PCM is **adaptive differential pulse code modulation (ADPCM)**. In this codec, not only do the nodes base predictions on previously-transmitted bits, but they also factor in human speech characteristics to re-create waveforms. The result is more accurate predictions. More accurate predictions result in less significant differentials between the actual and predicted voice signals. This translates into fewer bits requiring transmission and a lower throughput than with DPCM. ITU's **G.726** codec standard uses ADCPM. G.726 can operate over a 16-, 24-, 32-, or 40-Kbps channel. As you would expect, this codec's voice quality is best on a 40-kbps channel and worst on a 16-Kbps channel. One advantage of using G.726 instead of G.723 is that G.726 requires fewer DSP resources and results in much lower delay. G.726 is also currently used on some manufacturers' VoIP media gateways.

Vocoders

Unlike waveform codecs, **vocoders** do not attempt to replicate a voice signal's original waveform. Rather, they apply sophisticated mathematical models to voice samples, which take into account the ways in which humans generate speech. Based on these models, vocoders predict and then synthesize the voice signal and the receiving node. The particulars of these routines are beyond the scope of this book. However, it is useful to know that this technique requires fewer bits to regenerate the original signal than a waveform codec requires to re-create a signal. In general, vocoders can operate over lower bandwidth than waveform codecs. However, they do not result in the same high voice quality.

One type of vocoder is specified in the ITU **G.729** encoding standard. G.729 further reduces its throughput requirements by suppressing the transmission of signals during silences. In other words, after two samples indicate that no speech is being generated, the codec stops sampling the signal, and does not begin sampling again until it detects speech activity. During this wait, G.729 generates a small amount of background noise so that a caller does not mistakenly think that the connection has been dropped.

Thanks to its conservative use of bandwidth, G.729 can operate over an 8-Kbps channel. Also, G.729 requires only moderate DSP resources and results in only moderate delays. A potential drawback to this standard is that some people complain its voice signals sounds "synthesized," or unnatural. But the sound quality is sufficient for many applications. G.729 is a popular encoding protocol used with VoIP, videoconferencing, wireless, and VoFR network services. In particular, it is recommended for use over WAN links, connections prone to random bit errors, or where bandwidth conservation is a primary concern.

Hybrid Codecs

A third type of codec is known as a **hybrid codec**. As the name implies, a hybrid codec borrows techniques from both waveform codecs and vocoders. Several types of hybrid codecs exist. In general, hybrid codecs incorporate intelligence about the physics of human speech to regenerate a signal. However, rather than apply the same predictive algorithms to all speech signals, a hybrid codec first analyzes a voice's waveform characteristics. Based on this analysis, it then applies specialized algorithms to more accurately predict and synthesize that voice on the receiving end.

Hybrid codecs use lower bandwidth than waveform codecs, but provide better sound quality than vocoders. Because of these qualities, they are emerging as a popular new VoIP encoding method. One example of a hybrid codec is specified in the ITU standard **G.728**. G.728 requires a 16-Kbps channel and introduces very little delay. On the other hand, because of its sophisticated methods of more closely matching a received signal to an actual signal, G.728 requires significant DSP resources.

Table 14-1 summarizes what you have learned about different voice encoding techniques.

Table 14-1   Voice Encoding Techniques

Standard	Codec type	Required Throughput	DSP usage	Voice quality	Delay
G.711	Waveform (PCM)	64 Kbps	Low	Excellent	Negligible
G.723	Waveform (DPCM)	6.4 Kbps	Moderate	Good	High
G.726	Waveform (ADPCM)	16, 24, 32, or 40 Kbps	Low	Varies; good at highest throughput and bad at lowest throughput	Low
G.728	Hybrid	16 Kbps	High	Good	Low
G.729	Vocoder	8 Kbps	Moderate	Fair	Moderate

Voice-encoding techniques are only one factor affecting the quality of VoIP signals. Packet-switched transmission flaws, such as delay and lost packets, must also be considered. Later in this chapter, you learn about techniques used on modern VoIP networks that help ensure that voice or video signals arrive with acceptable quality.

14

When implementing VoIP, network administrators must consider whether all of their network's components can communicate using the same VoIP protocols. In the case of voice encoding, a media gateway (or access server, if it is separate from the media gateway) must be able to interpret the type of codec used by an incoming signal. Thus, if analog lines terminate at the media gateway, the gateway must be capable of interpreting G.711, because PSTN transmission uses G.711. Similarly, if incoming IP telephone lines use G.723, the media gateway must also understand this protocol. Because VoIP encoding standards are still evolving, most media gateways support more than one protocol. When a node connects with a gateway, the two issue signals to negotiate the encoding protocol they will use during data transmission.

In addition to agreeing on voice-encoding protocols, VoIP network devices must agree on standards for call and gateway signaling. As you learn in the next section, these protocols are, like encoding protocols, still evolving.

VoIP Signaling Protocols

In the previous section, you read about protocols that handle the analog-to-digital conversion for VoIP. These protocols operate at the Presentation layer of the OSI model. In this section, you learn about VoIP signaling protocols, which operate at the Session layer of the OSI model. If you remember the call control functions that a traditional end-office switch performs (as described in Chapter 6), you have a good idea of what VoIP call signaling protocols perform—for example, call setup, end-user functions such as call forwarding and call waiting, and call termination. Other signaling protocols described in this section are used between gateways. Although VoIP hardware and software vendors do not agree on a definitive standard for either call or gateway signaling, most support one or more of the following most popular protocols.

H.323

H.323 is an ITU standard that describes not one protocol, but an entire architecture for implementing multiservice packet-based networks. H.323 also specifies several protocols for establishing and managing sessions. In its recommended network architecture, H.323 assigns labels to elements of VoIP networks you have already learned about. For example, in H.323 parlance, an end node such as an IP telephone or softphone is called an H.323 terminal, and an H.323 gateway is a gateway that provides translation between network devices running H.323 signaling protocols and devices running another type of signaling protocol. An H.323 gatekeeper is an optional network device that controls several H.323 terminals.

Among several protocols included in the H.323 specification are the multiservice signaling protocols, H.225 and H.245. Both of these protocols operate at the Session layer of the OSI model. However, each performs a different function. **H.225** is the H.323 protocol that handles call signaling. For instance, when an IP telephone user wants to make a call, the IP telephone requests a call setup (from the gateway) via H.225. The same IP telephone uses the H.225 protocol to announce its presence on the network, to request the allocation of additional bandwidth, and to indicate when it wants to terminate a call.

The other H.323 Session layer protocol, **H.245**, ensures that the type of information—whether voice or video—issued to an H.323 terminal is formatted in a way that the H.323 terminal can interpret. To perform this task, H.245 first sets up logical channels between the sending and receiving nodes. On a VoIP network, these logical channels are identified as port numbers at each IP address. One logical channel is assigned to each transmission direction. Thus, for a call between two IP telephones, H.245 uses two separate control channels. Note that these channels are separate from both the channels used for H.225 call signaling and channels used to exchange the actual data (for example, the words you speak during a conversation).

ITU codified H.323 as an open protocol for multiservice signaling in 1996. At that time, other voice and video signaling protocols existed, but these were proprietary. Early versions of the H.323 protocol suffered from slow call setup, due to the volume of control messages exchanged between nodes. Since that time, ITU has revised and improved H.323 standards twice. The second version of H.323, known as H.323.2, is a popular call signaling protocol on modern VoIP networks. The third version of H.323 has yet to be widely accepted. Since H.323 was first released, another open protocol for VoIP call signaling has emerged.

Session Initiation Protocol (SIP)

The **Session Initiation Protocol (SIP)** is a protocol suite that competes with H.323. SIP was codified by the IETF (in RFC 2543) as a set of Session-layer signaling and control protocols for multiservice, packet-based networks. With few exceptions, SIP performs much the same functions as the H.323 signaling protocols perform. SIP was developed as a more efficient alternative to H.323 before H.323 was revised to expedite its call setup functions. Although SIP is more efficient, because it was released later, it has never enjoyed the same widespread usage as H.323. Still, some VoIP vendors adopt SIP because in general, it is less complex than H.323. Its simplicity makes SIP easier to maintain. In addition, because it requires fewer instructions to control a call, SIP consumes fewer processing and port resources than H.323. Some telecommunications engineers believe SIP also has the potential to adapt better to growing and changing network environments. On the other hand, SIP does not allow for the same quality of service as H.323. Currently, H.323 remains the dominant call signaling and control protocol on VoIP networks.

SIP and H.323 regulate call signaling and control on a VoIP network. However, they do not account for communication between media gateways. This type of communication is governed by one of two protocols: MGCP or MEGACO, which are discussed in the following sections.

Media Gateway Control Protocol (MGCP) and MEGACO (H.248)   14

Earlier in this chapter, you learned that gateways are integral to converged networks. For example, a gateway accepts PSTN lines, converts the analog signals into VoIP format, and translates between SS7, the PSTN signaling protocol suite, and VoIP signaling protocols, such as H.323 or SIP. In another example, to send a real-time fax from one IP network to another, a sending fax gateway must communicate with a receiving fax gateway. You have also learned that information (or "payload," such as the speech carried by a VoIP network) uses different channels from and may take different logical or physical paths than control signals. In fact, to expedite information handling, the use of separate physical paths is often preferable. The reason for this is that if media gateways are freed from having to process control signals, they can dedicate their resources (for example, ports and processors) to encoding, decoding, and translating data. As a result, they process data faster. And as you have learned, faster data processing on a converged network is particularly important, given quality and reliability concerns.

However, gateways still need to exchange and translate call signaling and control information with each other so that voice and video packets are properly routed through the network. To do so, gateways rely on an intermediate device known as a **media gateway controller**. As its name implies, a media gateway controller is a computer that manages multiple media gateways. This means that it facilitates the exchange of call-signaling information between these gateways. It also manages and disseminates information about the paths that voice or video signals take between gateways. (Softswitches, which you learned about earlier, perform the same functions as media gateway controllers, and these two terms are often used synonymously.)

For example, suppose a network has multiple media gateways, all of which accept thousands of connections from both the PSTN and from different types of IP-based connections. When a media gateway receives a call, rather than attempting to determine how to handle the call, the media gateway simply contacts the media gateway controller with a message that essentially says, "I received a signal. You figure out what to do with it next." The media gateway controller then determines which of the network's media gateways should translate the information carried by the signal. It also figures out which physical media the call should be routed over, according to what signaling protocols the call must be managed, and to what devices the call should be directed. After the media gateway controller has processed this information, it instructs the appropriate media gateways how to handle the call. The media gateways simply follow orders from the media gateway controller.

Media gateway controllers are especially advantageous on large VoIP networks—for example, at a LEC's end office. In such an environment, media gateway controllers make a group of media gateways appear to the outside world as one large gateway. This centralizes call control functions, which can simplify network management. Figure 14-16 illustrates this model. (Note that in this figure, as on most large networks, the media gateways supply access services.)

Media gateway controllers communicate with media gateways according to one of several protocols. The most popular protocol is the **Media Gateway Control Protocol (MGCP)**. Technically, MGCP is not a recognized standard, but rather, an IETF Internet Draft, which was originally described in RFC 2705. Nevertheless, it is commonly used on multiservice networks that support a number of media gateways. MGCP can operate in conjunction with either H.323 or SIP call signaling and control protocols.

A newer gateway control protocol is **MEGACO**. MEGACO performs the same functions as MGCP, but uses different commands and processes. MEGACO is considered superior to MGCP because it supports a broader range of network technologies, including ATM. Like MGCP, MEGACO is not a standard, but does have Internet Draft status with the IETF. MEGACO, however, is on its way to becoming a standard, and will probably replace MGCP. The ITU has codified the MEGACO protocol in its **H.248** standard.

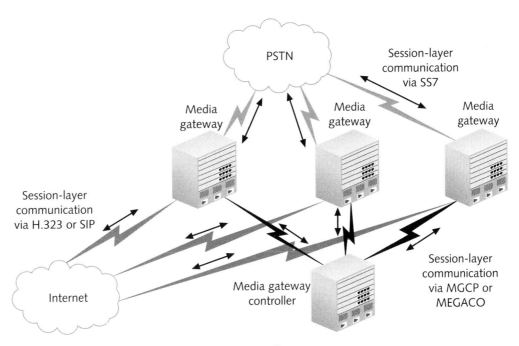

Figure 14-16   Use of a media gateway controller

VoIP Transport Protocols

The protocols you just learned about only govern data exchange at the Session layer of the OSI model. That is, they communicate information about a voice or video *session*. At the Transport layer, a different set of protocols is used to actually deliver the voice or video payload—for example, the bits of encoded voice that together make up words spoken into an IP telephone.

Recall that on a TCP/IP network, the UDP and TCP protocols operate at the Transport layer of the OSI model. Also recall that TCP is connection-oriented, and therefore provides some measure of delivery guarantees. UDP, on the other hand, is connectionless, and does not pay attention to the order in which packets arrive or how quickly they arrive. Despite this lack of accountability, UDP is preferred over TCP for real-time applications, such as voice and video signals, because it requires less overhead and as a result, can transport packets more quickly. In transporting voice and video signals, TCP's slower delivery of packets is intolerable. However UDP's occasional loss of packets is tolerable—that is, as long as additional Transport layer protocols are used in conjunction with UDP.

One protocol that helps voice and video networks overcome UDP's shortcomings is the **Real-Time Transport Protocol (RTP)**. RTP, which is standardized in RFC 1889, operates on top of UDP. It applies sequence numbers to indicate the order in which packets should be assembled at their destination. Sequence numbers also help to indicate whether packets were lost during transmission. RTP also assigns each packet a time-stamp that corresponds to when the data in the packet was sampled from the voice or video stream. This timestamp helps the receiving node to compensate for network delay and to synchronize the signals it receives.

It's important to realize that although RTP can provide information about packet order, loss, and delay, they cannot do anything to correct transmission flaws. Attempts to correct these flaws, and thus improve the quality of a voice or video signal, are handled by Quality of Service (QoS) protocols, which are discussed in the following section.

QUALITY OF SERVICE (QoS)

As you learned in Chapter 10, Quality of Service (QoS) is a measure of how well a network service matches its expected performance. From a VoIP user's standpoint, high QoS translates into an uninterrupted, accurate, and faithful reproduction of both parties' speech. Low, or poor, QoS is often cited as a key disadvantage to using VoIP. Although early attempts at VoIP sounded dreadful, thanks to technology improvements, VoIP now achieves sound quality nearly equal to the PSTN's. Still, VoIP will probably never sound quite as good as PSTN telephony. As you have learned, VoIP's QoS suffers due to voice-compression techniques, the need to conserve bandwidth, the use of shared channels, the reliance on packets to transport data, and the reliance on connectionless transport protocols. However, network engineers have developed several techniques to overcome VoIP's QoS challenges. The following sections describe three of these techniques, all of which are standardized by IETF.

Resource Reservation Protocol (RSVP)

The **Resource Reservation Protocol (RSVP)**, specified in RFC 2205, is a QoS technique that attempts to reserve a specific amount of network resources for a transmission before the transmission occurs. In other words, assuming it is successful, RSVP creates a path between the sender and receiver that provides sufficient bandwidth for the signal to arrive without suffering delay. You can think of RSVP as a technique that addresses the QoS problem by emulating a circuit-switched connection.

To establish the path, the sending node issues a PATH statement via RSVP to the receiving node. This PATH message indicates the amount of bandwidth the sending node requires for its transmission, as well as the level of service it expects. RSVP allows for two service types: Guaranteed service and Controlled-load service. Guaranteed service assures that the transmission will not suffer packet losses and that it will experience minimal delay. Controlled-load service provides the type of QoS a transmission would experience if the network carried little traffic.

Each router that the PATH message traverses marks the transmission's path by noting which router the PATH message came from. This process continues until the PATH message reaches its destination. But the reservation is not yet complete. After the destination node receives the PATH message, it responds with a Reservation Request (RESV) message. The RESV message follows the same path taken by the PATH message, but in reverse. It reiterates information about bandwidth requirements that the sending node transmitted in its PATH message. It also includes information about the type of service the sending node requested. Upon receiving the RESV message, each router between the destination node and the sender allocates the requested bandwidth to the message's path. This assumes that each router is capable of interpreting RSVP messages and also has sufficient bandwidth to allocate to the transmission. If routers do not have sufficient bandwidth to allocate, they reject the reservation request.

After each router in the established path has agreed to allocate the specified amount of bandwidth to the transmission, the sending node transmits its data. It's important to note that RSVP messaging is separate from the data transmission. In other words, it does not modify the packets that carry voice or video signals. Another characteristic about RSVP is that it can only specify and manage unidirectional transmission. Therefore, in order for both telephone users to participate in a conversation over a VoIP network, the resource reservation process must take place in both directions.

As a result of emulating a circuit-switched path, RSVP provides excellent QoS. However, one drawback to RSVP is its high overhead. Because it requires a series of message exchanges before data transmission can occur, RSVP consumes more network resources than some other QoS techniques. Although RSVP might be acceptable on small networks, it is less popular on large, heavily trafficked networks. Instead, these networks use more streamlined QoS techniques, such as DiffServ.

Differentiated Service (DiffServ)

Differentiated Service (DiffServ) is a simple technique that addresses QoS issues by prioritizing traffic. It differs significantly from RSVP in that it modifies the actual IP datagrams that contain payload data. Also, it takes into account all types of network traffic, not just the time-sensitive services such as voice and video. That way, it can assign voice streams a high priority and at the same time assign unessential data streams (for example, an employee surfing the Internet on his lunch hour) a low priority. This technique offers more protection for the time-sensitive voice service.

To prioritize traffic, DiffServ places information in the Type of Service (TOS) field in an IP version 4 datagram. (For a review of the fields in an IP datagram, see the section on IP in Chapter 7.) In IP version 6 datagrams, DiffServ uses a similar field known as the Traffic Class field. This information indicates to the network routers how the data stream should be forwarded. DiffServ defines two types of forwarding: **Expedited Forwarding (EF)** or **Assured Forwarding (AF)**. In EF, a data stream is assigned a

14

minimum departure rate from a given node. This technique circumvents delays that slow normal data from reaching its destination on time and in sequence. In AF, different levels of router resources can be assigned to data streams. AF prioritizes data handling, but provides no guarantee that on a busy network packets will arrive on time and in sequence. This description of DiffServ's prioritization mechanisms is oversimplified, but a deeper discussion is beyond the scope of this book.

Because of its simplicity and relatively low overhead, DiffServ is better suited to large, heavily trafficked networks than RSVP. Another QoS technique that modifies data streams at the Network layer is MPLS.

Multi-protocol Label Switching (MPLS)

As you learned in Chapter 7, every router in a data stream's path makes a determination about where to direct the data stream. It does so by analyzing the destination IP address in the IP datagram header and determining how to best forward the data, according to whatever routing technique it uses (such as RIP, OSPF, and EIGRP, which you learned about in Chapter 11). **Multi-protocol Label Switching (MPLS)** offers a different way for routers to determine the next hop a packet should take in its route. In this sense, MPLS is not strictly a QoS technique, but rather a way of forwarding packets.

To indicate where data should be forwarded, MPLS replaces the IP datagram header with a label at the first router a data stream encounters. The MPLS label contains information about where the router should forward the packet next. Each router in the data stream's path revises the label to indicate the data's next hop. In this manner, routers on a network can take into consideration network congestion, QoS indicators assigned to the packets, plus other criteria. Compared to basing route decisions simply on the destination IP address, MPLS forwarding is also faster. This is because in MPLS, a router knows precisely where to forward a packet. On a typical packet-switched network, routers compare the destination IP address to their routing tables and forward data to the node with the closest matching address. With MPLS, data streams are more likely to arrive without delay. Although this description of MPLS is simplified, it does point out the uniqueness of this technique compared to RSVP and DiffServ.

As with RSVP and DiffServ, a network's connectivity devices and clients must support the same protocols to achieve their QoS benefits. However, networks can—and often do—combine multiple QoS techniques.

To review what you have learned in the second half of this chapter, Table 14-2 summarizes the characteristics of voice communication over the PSTN compared with VoIP networks.

Table 14-2   PSTN Compared with Packet-based Networks

Characteristic	PSTN	VoIP
Switching technique	Circuit-switched (point-to-point connection for duration of conversation)	Packet-switched (signals are divided into packets that can follow different routes)
Quality of Service	Excellent	Varies; several good options for approaching PSTN quality; no single standard yet; standardization between networks requires cooperation between providers
Ubiquity	Existing network covers virtually all of the United States	VoIP networks are scattered, smaller, and less common; some are private, whereas others belong to common carriers
Interoperability	Reliance on a single protocol ensures interoperability between different carriers	Due to different encoding, signaling, and QoS protocols, interoperability between networks cannot be assumed; requires cooperation among competitors
Availability	Almost always available (99.999% of the time)	Availability depends on numerous factors, and is never guaranteed
Bandwidth usage	Fixed at 64 Kbps per channel	Variable, from 6.4 Kbps to 64 Kbps per channel; can be specified according to customer's needs and network availability
Flexibility	Proprietary signaling and switching protocols result in dependence on telecommunications carrier for applications and little opportunity for customization	Open access to protocols for signaling allows customers and developers to devise custom applications; requires significant technical skill to customize
Cost	Potentially more expensive, because of its relatively high bandwidth requirements and dependence on proprietary signaling and switching	Potentially less expensive, due to bandwidth conservation; but also introduces cost of new hardware, software, and work requirements

14

CHAPTER SUMMARY

❐ Several terms describe the transmission of voice signals over packet-switched networks. Voice over network (VON) is one that includes voice over IP (VoIP), voice over frame relay (VoFR), voice over ATM (VoATM), and voice over DSL (VoDSL). On most data networks, voice is transmitted via IP, a service also known as IP telephony.

❐ VoIP can improve efficiency and competitiveness, supply new or enhanced features and applications, centralize voice and data network management, and save organizations money.

❐ End users require an IP telephone or softphone (a computer equipped with VoIP client software) to communicate via VoIP. Analog phones can be used, but must be connected to an IP-PBX capable of translating between analog signals and IP signals.

❐ Fax over IP (FoIP) is commonly implemented according to either the ITU T.37 or T.38 standard. The former, also known as store-and-forward faxing, attaches IP-based faxes as TIFF files to e-mail messages. The latter issues faxes from IP fax machines to fax gateways, which transmit the faxes to other fax gateways across the network. T.38 delivers IP-based faxes in real time.

❐ Video over IP is challenged by the delay and loss characteristics of packet-switched networks. Also, it requires significantly more bandwidth than VoIP or FoIP. It is transmitted in three ways: point-to-point (unicast), point-to-multipoint with user registration (multicast), and point-to-multipoint with no user registration requirement (broadcast).

❐ Call centers are good candidates for converged networks. They can merge telephone calls with e-mail, voice mail, ACD, IVR, CTI, Web communications, and customer relationship management (CRM) software to provide quicker and better customer service.

❐ Unified messaging makes several forms of communication available from a single user interface. In unified messaging, a user can, for example, access the Web and also send or receive faxes, e-mail messages, voice mail messages, or telephone calls—all from one console. The main console typically consists of a graphical user interface on a computer or an IP telephone.

❐ VoIP can be implemented on private or public networks. On private networks, VoIP may include IP telephones connected to an IP-PBX, VoIP connections to common carrier networks, VoIP over private WANs, VoIP over VPNs, or a combination of these.

❐ IXCs use VoIP to avoid paying access fees to other carriers for calls that leave their jurisdiction. It is used by LECs to redirect Internet dial-up calls to a pure data network, thus freeing traditional switches to handle voice calls.

❐ Implementing VoIP does not always save an organization money. Organizations with high volumes of long-distance traffic stand to gain the most from VoIP, due to toll bypass. To determine whether VoIP will pay off, a business should conduct a detailed cost-benefit analysis.

❐ Codecs convert analog voice signals into digital form. They can be divided into three types: waveform codecs, vocoders, and hybrid codecs. The PSTN uses a simple pulse code modulation (PCM) technique—which is a waveform codec—known by its ITU standard as G.711. G.711 provides excellent sound quality, but requires 64 Kbps of throughput.

❐ VoIP networks use codecs that conserve bandwidth but provide lesser sound quality than G.711. They also require more processing resources and introduce some delay as the signal is reconstructed at the receiving end. Examples of VoIP codecs include G.723, G.726, G.728, and G.729. Each standard uses a different technique and results in different sound qualities, delays, and processing burdens.

❐ VoIP networks typically use either the H.323 or Session Initiation Protocol (SIP) call signaling and control protocol. H.323 is actually a set of standards specified for several functions on multiservice networks. Because it is older and more sophisticated, it is more common than SIP. SIP, however, is regarded as potentially more efficient and scalable than H.323.

❐ On networks with multiple media gateways, a media gateway controller is used to offload call control functions from the gateways. This allows the gateways to concentrate their resources on handling payload information translation. Media gateway controllers and media gateways communicate through the Media Gateway Control Protocol (MGCP) or a similar protocol known as MEGACO.

❐ At the Transport layer, voice and video data rely on UDP. Although UDP does not guarantee accurate data delivery, it is faster than TCP. To compensate for UDP's lack of accountability, another Transport layer protocol, the Real-Time Transport Protocol (RTP) is used over UDP.

❐ Quality of Service (QoS) on converged networks can be improved through several different techniques, including RSVP, DiffServ, and MPLS. In RSVP, a path between communicating nodes is established before data is transferred. This method emulates the circuit switching used on the PSTN. In DiffServ, IP datagrams are modified to include indicators about what type of priority the network should assign their data. In MPLS, at each router in the path, IP datagrams are modified to replace the destination IP address with a label that indicates where a packet should be forwarded.

14

KEY TERMS

adaptive differential pulse code modulation (ADPCM) — A waveform analog encoding technique in which nodes first sample a waveform, and then attempt to predict future characteristics of the waveform based on previously-transmitted bits. That way, only differences between the actual and predicted signals must be transmitted between nodes. ADPCM also factors in human speech characteristics as it re-creates waveforms. The result is more accurate predictions than with DPCM, which only predicts signals based on historical signal information.

Assured Forwarding (AF) — In the DiffServ QoS technique, a forwarding specification that allows routers to assign data streams one of several prioritization levels. AF is specified in the Type of Service field in an IP version 4 datagram.

best effort — A characteristic of packet-based transmission in which the network attempts to deliver packets in a timely fashion and in the proper sequence, but does not guarantee either. In fact, best effort offers no guarantees that a packet will arrive at its destination at all.

call management — The group of functions supplied by a PBX that include monitoring telephone traffic, customizing calling features and restrictions by line, specifying call routes, and analyzing calling patterns. Call management also encompasses a user's ability to forward or block calls, obtain call information, and to change line preferences.

differential pulse code modulation (DPCM) — A voice-encoding technique in which the codec samples the actual voice signal at regular intervals, and in between samples, attempts to predict the value of signal bits that have not yet arrived. When the actual signal differs from the predicted signal, the sending node transmits only the differential, or the difference between the predicted and actual values. With the differential, the receiving end can reconstruct the voice signal with some accuracy. DPCM uses far less bandwidth than PCM, but it also requires higher processing resources and results in longer delays. The ITU G.723 standard uses DPCM.

Differentiated Service (DiffServ) — A traffic prioritization technique that helps improve Quality of Service (QoS). DiffServ modifies the Type of Service (TOS) field in IP version 4 datagrams or the Traffic Class field in IP version 6 datagrams to indicate the data's priority. DiffServ defines two types of forwarding: Expedited Forwarding (EF) or Assured Forwarding (AF).

digital PBX — A PBX that is capable of accepting and interpreting digital signals. An IP-PBX is the most common example of a digital PBX.

digital signal processor (DSP) — A computer chip that codes and decodes voice signals.

Expedited Forwarding (EF) — In the DiffServ QoS technique, a forwarding specification that assigns each data stream a minimum departure rate from a given node. This technique circumvents delays that slow normal data from reaching its destination on time and in sequence. EF information is inserted in the Type of Service (TOS) field of an IP version 4 datagram.

fax gateway — A gateway that can translate IP fax data into analog fax data and vice versa. A fax gateway can also emulate and interpret conventional fax signaling protocols when communicating with a conventional fax machine. When the T.37 standard is used, a fax gateway must also be able to interpret mail server requests through SMTP, plus translate telephone numbers into e-mail addresses.

fax over IP (FoIP) — A service that transmits faxes over a TCP/IP network. The ITU recognizes two techniques for FoIP: T.37 and T.38.

G.711 — An ITU standard that specifies the type of pulse code modulation (PCM) voice encoding used on the PSTN. In G.711, a waveform codec samples an analog wave 8000 times per second, then uses 8 bits per sample to represent the information. This results in the requirement of a 64-Kbps channel. The receiving codec attempts to accurately re-create the original waveform using this information.

G.723 — An ITU standard that specifies voice encoding through differential pulse code modulation (DPCM). G.723 requires only 6.4 Kbps of bandwidth, but uses a moderate amount of processing resources and results in moderate network delays, compared to some other codecs. In addition, its voice quality is not as good as other waveform codecs, such as G.711. However, G.723 is adequate for packet-based networks and is currently used for VoIP and videoconferencing.

G.726 — An ITU standard that specifies voice encoding through adaptive differential pulse code modulation (ADPCM). G.726 can operate over a 16-, 24-, 32- or 40-Kbps channel. Its voice quality is best on a 40-Kbps channel and worst on a 16-Kbps channel. G.726 requires fewer DSP resources and results in much lower delay than G.723, another waveform codec used on VoIP networks.

G.728 — An ITU standard that specifies voice encoding using hybrid codec techniques. G.728 requires a 16-Kbps channel and introduces very little delay. On the other hand, because it relies on sophisticated algorithms to closely match and synthesize a signal, G.728 requires significant DSP resources.

G.729 — An ITU standard that specifies voice encoding using a vocoder codec. G.729 further reduces its throughput requirements by suppressing the transmission of voice signals during silences. It can operate over an 8-Kbps channel. Also, G.729 requires only moderate DSP resources and results in only moderate delays compared to other encoding techniques. Although some believe it provides inferior sound quality, G.729 is a popular encoding protocol used with VoIP, videoconferencing, wireless, and VoFR network services. It is recommended for use where bandwidth conservation is a primary concern.

H.225 — A Session-layer call signaling protocol defined as part of ITU's H.323 multiservice network architecture. H.225 is responsible for call setup between nodes on a VoIP network, indicating node status, requesting additional bandwidth, and call termination.

H.245 — A Session-layer control protocol defined as part of ITU's H.323 multiservice network architecture. H.245 is responsible for controlling a session between two nodes. For example, it ensures that the two nodes are communicating in the same format.

H.248 — *See* MEGACO.

H.323 — An ITU standard that describes an entire architecture for implementing multiservice networks, plus several protocols for establishing and managing voice or video transmissions over a packet-based network.

hybrid codec — A voice encoding and decoding method that borrows techniques from both waveform codecs and vocoders. Several types of hybrid codecs exist. In general, hybrid codecs incorporate intelligence about the physics of human speech to regenerate a signal. However, rather than apply the same predictive algorithms to all speech signals, a hybrid codec first analyzes a voice's waveform characteristics. Based on this analysis, it then applies specialized algorithms to more accurately predict and synthesize that voice on the receiving end. ITU's G.728 standard specifies a hybrid codec.

14

IP fax machine — A fax machine designed to exchange fax data over a packet-switched network.

IP-PBX — A private switch that accepts and interprets digital voice signals. Most IP-PBXs can also accept and interpret analog signals, and thus, can connect both traditional PSTN lines and data networks. Like a traditional PBX, an IP-PBX provides telephones with dial tone and performs telephone setup, supervisory, and call routing functions. It also supplies call management.

IP phone — *See* IP telephone.

IP telephone — A telephone designed for use on VoIP networks. To communicate on the network, each IP telephone has a unique IP address and typically connects, via the data network, to an IP-PBX or a media gateway.

media gateway — A gateway capable of accepting connections from multiple devices (for example, IP telephones, traditional telephones, IP fax machines, traditional fax machines, and so on) and translating analog signals into packetized, digital signals, and vice versa.

media gateway controller — A computer that manages multiple media gateways and facilitates the exchange of call control information between these gateways.

Media Gateway Control Protocol (MGCP) — A protocol used for communication between media gateway controllers and media gateways. MGCP is defined in RFC 2507, but it was never officially adopted as a standard. MGCP is currently the most popular media gateway control protocol used on converged networks.

MEGACO — A protocol used between media gateway controllers and media gateways. MEGACO is poised to replace MGCP on modern converged networks, as it supports a broader range of network technologies, including ATM. Also known as H.248.

multipoint control unit (MCU) — In the context of videoconferencing over a network, a device that allows multiple video terminals to receive the same audio-video signals.

Multi-protocol Label Switching (MPLS) — A method of forwarding packets from one router to the next according to priority. To indicate where data should be forwarded, MPLS replaces the IP datagram header with a label at the first router a data stream encounters. The MPLS label contains information about where the router should forward the packet. Each router in the data stream's path revises the label to indicate the data's next hop. In this manner, routers on a network can take into consideration network congestion, QoS indicators assigned to the packets, plus other criteria.

multiservice network — *See* next generation network (NGN).

next generation network (NGN) — A network that provides voice, video, and data services over the same infrastructure.

Real-Time Transport Protocol (RTP) — A Transport-layer protocol used with voice and video transmission. RTP operates on top of UDP and provides information about packet sequence to help receiving nodes detect delay and packet loss. It also assigns packets a timestamp that corresponds to when the data in the packet was sampled from the voice or video stream. This timestamp helps the receiving node synchronize incoming data.

Resource Reservation Protocol (RSVP) — As specified in RFC 2205, a QoS technique that attempts to reserve a specific amount of network resources for a transmission before the transmission occurs. Of the three major QoS techniques, RSVP is the most complex.

Session Initiation Protocol (SIP) — A protocol suite codified by the IETF (in RFC 2543) as a set of Session-layer signaling and control protocols for multiservice, packet-based networks. With few exceptions, SIP performs much the same functions as the H.323 signaling protocols perform. SIP was developed as a more efficient alternative to H.323 before H.323 was revised to expedite its call setup functions. Although SIP is more efficient, because it was released later, it has never enjoyed the same widespread usage as H.323.

softphone — A computer programmed to act like an IP telephone. Softphones present the caller with a graphical representation of a telephone dial pad. Softphones can connect to a network via LAN, WAN, PPP dial-up connection, or a leased line. When installed on laptops or home computers, they offer the unique advantage of mobility for travelers and telecommuters.

softswitch — A computer or group of computers that manages packet-based traffic routing and control. Softswitches also typically handle call accounting services and may provide signaling gateway services to translate between SS7 and packet-based network signaling protocols.

T.37 — An ITU standard that specifies a store-and-forward method of transmitting faxes from one network node to another across a packet-switched network. In T.37, faxes are attached to e-mail messages as TIFF files, then forwarded to a fax/e-mail gateway. The gateway forwards the message to the destination's fax/e-mail gateway, where it is stored until the recipient retrieves it.

T.38 — An ITU standard that specifies a real-time method of transmitting faxes from one node to another across a packet-switched network. In T.38, fax client software or IP fax machines convert faxes to packets, then transmit them to a sending fax gateway. The sending fax gateway transmits them across a network (such as the Internet) to the appropriate receiving fax gateway.

14

toll bypass — A cost-savings benefit that results from organizations completing long-distance telephone calls over their packet-switched networks, thus bypassing tolls charged by common carriers on comparable PSTN calls.

unified communication — *See* unified messaging.

unified messaging — A service that brings several communication services together in a single user interface. In unified messaging, a user can, for example, access the Web, and send or receive a fax, e-mail message, voice mail message, or telephone call all from one console. The console, typically a graphical user interface, may exist on a computer or another sophisticated device such as an IP telephone.

video bridge — *See* multipoint control unit.

video streaming — The act of issuing video signals from a server to a client in real time.

video terminal — A device that enables users to watch, listen, speak, and capture their image.

videoconferencing — The real-time transmission of images and audio between two locations.

vocoder — A voice encoding and decoding that applies sophisticated mathematical models to voice samples, which take into account the ways in which humans generate speech. Based on these models, vocoders predict and then synthesize the voice signal and the receiving node. This encoding technique requires fewer bits to regenerate a voice signal than a waveform codec requires to re-create a signal. One type of vocoder is specified in the ITU G.729 standard.

voice over ATM (VoATM) — A service that uses the ATM network access method (and ATM cells) to transmit voice signals over a network.

voice over DSL (VoDSL) — A service that relies on a DSL connection to transmit packetized voice signals.

voice over frame relay (VoFR) — A service that relies on a frame relay connection to transmit packetized voice signals.

voice over network (VON) — A general term that refers to the transmission of voice signals over a packet-switched network. VoATM, VoDSL, VoFR, and VoIP belong to the VON category, as do voice signals issued over T-carriers, ISDN, cable, satellite, and cellular networks.

waveform codec — A voice encoding and decoding technique that samples an analog waveform at regular intervals and uses sampled data to attempt to reconstruct the waveform at the receiving end. PCM, DPCM, and ADPCM are all waveform techniques. Some examples of waveform codecs are G.711, G.723, and G.726.

REVIEW QUESTIONS

1. What is the difference between VoIP and Internet Telephony?

   a. VoIP uses QoS techniques, but Internet Telephony cannot.

   b. VoIP requires IP telephone clients, but Internet Telephony allows clients to be computers, analog telephones, or IP telephones.

   c. VoIP applies to any type of network, not just the Internet.

   d. They are the same thing.

2. On a VoIP network, what does a user have to do if she wants to move her telephone from her desk to a nearby conference room for the afternoon and continue to receive her calls?

   a. Arrange for the network manager to reconfigure her extension properties in the IP-PBX, then plug her IP telephone into a wall jack in the conference room.

   b. Reconfigure her IP telephone's network properties to specify the wall jack in the conference room, then plug her IP telephone into a wall jack in the conference room.

   c. Submit a reconfiguration request, via a Web interface, to the IP-PBX and after it is granted, plug her IP telephone into a wall jack in the conference room.

   d. Simply plug her IP telephone into a wall jack in the conference room.

3. Which of the following is an example of using VoIP for toll bypass?

   a. A company installs a T1 between two of its buildings on its main corporate campus, and then runs VoIP over the T1 to complete employees' calls from one building to the other.

   b. A LEC reroutes Internet dial-up calls from conventional Class 5 switches to media gateways at the Class 5 offices.

   c. A company allows its salespeople to access the Internet, and then view the company's video presentations, which are saved on a server at the headquarters, over the Web.

   d. A company installs an IP-PBX, and then routes telephone calls over its multiple T1s that connect five different locations across the country.

4. On a private VoIP network, what device determines how a call should be routed?

   a. IP-PBX

   b. router

   c. access server

   d. media gateway

5. Suppose a business is migrating from using analog telephones to using IP telephones. The network manager expects the process to last for a month. During the transition, how does the network manager ensure that employees who use IP telephones can call other employees who use conventional, analog telephones without using an outside line?

   a. She connects both the conventional analog telephone lines and the IP telephone lines to the same hub.

   b. She connects both the conventional PBX and the IP-PBX to a router that performs signal translation.

   c. She connects both the conventional analog telephone lines and the IP telephone lines to the IP-PBX that performs signal translation.

   d. She connects both the conventional PBX and the IP-PBX to a softswitch.

6. A business has fully implemented VoIP on its office's internal telephone network. Next, it wants to allow its telecommuting employees to use their VPN connections to call the office from home. To do this, what new device must each telecommuter have at home?

   a. router

   b. switch

   c. hub

   d. gateway

14

7. What is one drawback to the store-and-forward method of FoIP?

    a. Users cannot verify that the fax was received.

    b. Users cannot issue faxes from their desktop workstations.

    c. Users cannot issue a fax to a conventional, analog fax machine.

    d. Network managers have no means of centrally managing this type of FoIP.

8. What type of device is required for multiple clients to tap into the same video stream issued from one video server?

    a. media gateway

    b. IP-PBX

    c. multipoint control unit

    d. codec

9. When you view a music video on the Web, what type of video service are you using?

    a. unicast

    b. broadcast

    c. multicast

    d. simulcast

10. Which of the following is an example of unified messaging?

    a. An engineer answers calls made to his desktop IP telephone while working at a client's site.

    b. From her home, a supervisor listens in on customer service representatives' conversations with customers, to ensure quality.

    c. A nurse diagnoses a child's flu symptoms through a video session over an IP network that connects a hospital with a remote clinic.

    d. A sales representative dials a number to listen to her voice mail and e-mail messages while she drives to a customer's location.

11. Which of the following organizations stands to gain the most from converting its telephone network to VoIP?

    a. a beverage distributor with five locations in a large metropolitan area, from which sales representatives regularly call customers about their accounts

    b. an electronic components manufacturer with its headquarters in California, production facilities in Singapore and Hong Kong, and district sales offices across the United States

    c. an online auction company that interacts with sellers and buyers over the Internet

    d. a large temporary staffing firm that has an office in New York and another office in Houston

12. On a common carrier's network, which of the following devices performs access services?

    a. DSLAM

    b. router

    c. softswitch

    d. media gateway controller

13. On a Class 5 central office VoIP network, what device stores customer-calling information for billing purposes?

    a. media gateway

    b. softswitch

    c. IP-PBX

    d. router

14. On a Class 5 central office VoIP network, what ensures that devices that rely on SS7 protocols can interpret data following H.323 protocols?

    a. softswitch

    b. application server

    c. access server

    d. signaling gateway

15. A single VoIP channel requires less bandwidth than a single PSTN voice channel. True or False?

16. What ITU-standard waveform codec does the PSTN use?

    a. G.711

    b. G.723

    c. G.726

    d. G.729

14

17. What ITU-standard codec is preferred for use on links that regularly experience high network traffic?

    a. G.711

    b. G.723

    c. G.726

    d. G.729

18. How do DPCM and ADPCM conserve bandwidth?

    a. They crop off signals that occur at the lowest and highest frequencies of the human hearing range, and send only the essential, middle range signals.

    b. They send only some of the bits that make up a full voice stream, and rely on the receiver to fill in the missing data, based on predictions about the actual signal's characteristics.

    c. They issue only the bits that represent a differential between an actual signal and a predicted signal, and rely on the receiving node to reconstruct the signal based on a predicted value plus the differential.

    d. They issue infrequent samples of a voice signal, and then use mathematical models about how humans generate sounds to regenerate the signal at the receiving end.

19. What is one disadvantage to using vocoders to encode speech?

    a. The signals they construct at the receiving end can sound fake.

    b. They consume more bandwidth than waveform codecs.

    c. Their capacity to reconstruct signals at the receiving end is more profoundly affected by delay and loss than other codecs.

    d. They require significant DSP resources.

20. What function does the H.225 protocol provide, as part of the H.323 VoIP specification?

    a. controls communication between media gateways and media gateway controllers

    b. handles call setup, call routing, and call termination

    c. ensures that signals issued to an H.323 terminal are in a format that the terminal can interpret

    d. indicates priority of each IP datagram through the Type of Service field

21. What is one advantage to using SIP over H.323?

    a. SIP uses fewer processing and port resources.

    b. SIP enjoys wider acceptance in the industry.

    c. SIP supports a broader range of Layer 2 protocols.

    d. SIP is compatible with more of the newer QoS protocols.

22. How do media gateway controllers help to improve the performance of media gateways?

a. They offload data translation functions from the media gateways, allowing the gateways to focus on call signaling and routing.

b. They offload QoS functions from the media gateways, allowing the gateways to focus on data translation.

c. They offload access services from the media gateways, allowing the gateways to focus on call signaling and routing.

d. They offload call signaling and routing functions from the media gateways, allowing the gateways to focus on data translation.

23. The RSVP Quality of Service approach emulates a circuit-switched network connection. True or False?

24. What does RTP add to packets that compensates for UDP's lack of reliability?

a. priority indicators

b. loss indicators

c. sequence numbers

d. extended maximum hop counts

25. On a VoIP network that uses the DiffServe QoS technique, which of the following makes certain that a router forwards packet within a given time period?

a. Assured Forwarding

b. Superior Forwarding

c. Expedited Forwarding

d. Best-effort Forwarding

14

HANDS-ON PROJECTS

Project 14-1

As you have probably deduced, the equipment and software that allows packet-switched networks to take advantage of convergence are not inexpensive. However, you can get some sense of the network delay and packet loss that impair voice and video signals over packet networks by experimenting with multimedia services on the Internet. For this project, you need a computer running the Windows 2000 or XP operating system. It should have at minimum the following components: a 233 MHz Pentium processor, 64 MB of memory, a 16-bit sound card, and speakers. The computer should also be capable of accessing the Web. In addition, this project works best if the computer is connected to the Internet via ISDN, cable, DSL, or another broadband connection. (If your computer is on a network that uses a firewall, check to make sure the firewall is configured to accept RealOne Player traffic.)

1. Connect to the Internet and point your browser to the following URL: **www.real.com/realoneplayer.html**. This is the RealNetworks Technology Web page from which you can download a free copy of the RealOne Player client.

2. Click the **Download the Free RealOne Player Only** link in the bottom right of this Web page.

3. The RealOne Player download page appears. Depending on your browser and the way it is configured, a Security Warning dialog box might appear, asking whether you want to trust content from RealNetworks, Inc. Click **Yes** to proceed.

4. The RealDownload Express window opens and the program's installation files begin copying to your hard disk.

5. After the installation files are saved to your hard disk, the RealOne Install Wizard begins, prompting you to choose an install method. Click **Next** to retain the default option of "Express Install" and continue.

6. The License Agreement dialog box appears. After you have read the terms of the agreement, click **Accept** to proceed with the installation.

7. The Internet Connection dialog box appears. Select your type of connection under the Your Connection Speed: heading, and then click **Next**. The RealOne Install Wizard begins copying program files to your hard disk and then configures the program for use on your computer.

8. Click **Finish** to close the RealOne Install Wizard after the files have been copied to your hard disk.

9. After a brief delay, the RealOne Player Welcome screen opens. Click **Cancel**. Click **Cancel** once more to confirm your decision, and then click **Cancel** a third time at the Autoupdate prompt. The RealOne Player starts. Notice that its interface allows access to the Web, plus customized RealNetworks options. However, for the purposes of this project, you need only the audio-video player. To hide everything else, choose **Tools** and then **Preferences** from the RealOne Player menu.

10. The Preferences dialog box appears. Under Category, make sure **General** is selected.

11. On the General part of the Preferences dialog box, select **Player only (no Media Browser)** from the On Startup display: drop-down box.

12. Click **OK** to save your change. Close the RealOne Player program. (The program starts when you choose to view video clips.)

13. Now point your browser to the following URL: **www.nationalgeographic.com/voices/ax/frame.html**. This is the Web page of the National Geographic Society's Voices project, a Web interface that allows users to follow the adventures of National Geographic explorers in the field through text, audio, and video. Only some of the stories provide video clips. Click the **Archives** link on the right side of this page.

14. Under the Field Tales Column heading, click on the story titled **A FIERY DEARTH #95298**, a story about a volcano in Mexico.

15. On the right side of the Web page, click the **Real Video** link to open the video clip.

16. The RealOne Player window opens and begins to accept video signals from the server. (In some cases, it might need to download a codec patch before it can play the clip. Just wait for this process to complete, and the video will begin loading.)

17. The video begins playing in the small RealOne window. Given what you know about packet-switched network transmission, why do you think the window is not full-size?

18. After watching the video for a few seconds, click and drag the lower right corner of the window outward so that you can see the full length of options along the main menu.

19. From the main menu, choose **Tools** and then **Playback Statistics**. The Statistics window opens, with the Bandwidth tab selected by default.

20. Watch the bandwidth graph as the clip plays. What happens to the sound and picture when the line dips and becomes yellow or red? What happens to the statistics about the rate at which the video stream is encoded?

21. As the video is playing, modify the volume controls. How does this affect the picture and sound? Why, if volume has nothing to do with signals traveling over the network, does this affect how you see and hear the video?

22. Now select the **Packets** tab. (If the video has stopped, you can start it again by clicking the Play button—the button on the left side of the control panel that contains one right-facing arrow.)

23. Notice the number of packets that have been transmitted, how many packets were lost, and how many were late. If possible, repeat this test at a different time of day or on a different network connection to see if these statistics vary.

24. Click **Close** to close the Statistics window.

25. Keep your browser and the RealOne Player software open for the next project.

14

Project 14-2

In this project, you will continue to experiment with the video streaming process. However, rather than observing the video and its transmission statistics, you will modify the RealOne Player's network connection properties, and then find out how your changes affect the video. This project has the same requirements as Project 14-1.

1. From the RealOne Player menu, choose **Tools** and then **Preferences**. The Preferences dialog box opens.

2. On the left side of the Preference dialog box, click the plus sign next to Connection. A list of connection preferences appears.

3. Click **Playback Settings**. The Playback settings appear in the right side of the dialog box.

4. Read about the Buffered play and network-timeout parameters. Given the type of connection you're using, would changing either or both of these settings affect your video playback?

5. To test your hypothesis, under Buffered play, change the number of seconds to **5**, and then click **OK** to save your change.

6. Click the **Play** button on the RealOne Player to start the video clip.

7. From the main menu, choose **Tools** and then **Playback Statistics**. The Statistics window opens, with the Bandwidth tab selected by default.

8. Watch the whole clip again. How did your change affect its quality? How did it affect the time it took for the video to begin playing after you pressed Play? Does it affect the image different than it affects the sound?

9. After the clip has stopped, examine the bandwidth graph. How does it vary from the graph you saw in Project 14-1?

10. Now repeat Steps 1–3 to return to the Playback Settings preferences. Change the Buffered play seconds back to its default value of **30**.

11. Under Network Timeout, change the Connection to **50** seconds and the Server to **100** seconds.

12. Click **OK** to save your changes.

13. Repeat Steps 7–9. Did this affect the way the video clip played?

14. Click **Close** to close the Statistics window.

15. Close the RealOne Player program and your browser.

Project 14-3

To assist them in managing a network, network administrators use monitoring tools that can analyze the characteristics of network traffic and alert personnel before serious transmission problems occur. Unique monitoring tools are available to evaluate VoIP services on a network, and in particular, their Quality of Service (QoS). In this chapter you learned about the importance of Quality of Service (QoS) for VoIP applications. In the following project you investigate some VoIP QoS monitoring tools. First, however, you outline specifications for such a tool, anticipating what transmission and voice characteristics such a tool might monitor. For this project, you need a computer that is capable of browsing the Web and that can also open Adobe Acrobat .pdf files.

1. The QoS of a voice call delivered on a packet-based network is directly related to certain packet transmission characteristics. Suppose your task is to design a VoIP QoS monitoring device. Based on what you learned about transmission flaws in Chapter 8, plus what you learned about the causes of poor QoS in this chapter, what network transmission characteristics should your device monitor so that you can predict when VoIP QoS will suffer?

2. A VoIP caller recognizes poor QoS as a "bad connection." However, your monitoring device should be able to quantify what the caller experiences. What call

characteristics will your monitoring device measure to determine the effects of the transmission flaws you listed in Step 1?

3. After you have created a VoIP QoS monitoring device, where would you place it on a small business's network so that it would provide the most accurate and timely information about the entire business's voice traffic? Where would you place it on a WAN used by an international business? Where would you place it on a LEC's central office network?

4. Keeping in mind your device's functionality and its location on the network, would it be possible to add data traffic monitoring functions to VoIP QoS monitoring device? What advantages would this provide, if any?

5. As you design your tool, consider the type of user interface that would be most beneficial to a network manager. What different views would you provide? What filters could you provide that would enable the network manager to isolate and visualize different types of problems?

6. Also consider the effect that your device will have on existing network performance. Will its presence affect QoS?

7. Now that you have outlined the specifications for your own VoIP QoS monitoring tool, you will use the Web to compare what you designed with existing products. First, open your browser and point to the following URL: **www.telchemy.com/ datasheets/vqmon_brochure.pdf**. Read about Telchemy's VQmon Technology. (This information opens in Adobe Acrobat Reader.) Note what this product measures and why. Next, investigate Radcom's Omni Q-Voice Quality system, which is described at **www.radcom-inc.com/radcom/managmnt/q_pro.htm**. Finally, read about Agilent's IP Telephony Reporter product, which is described at the following **URL: literature.agilent.com/litweb/pdf/5988-2098EN.pdf**. (This data sheet also requires Adobe Acrobat Reader.)

8. Compare what you learned about these three products with the monitoring device you designed. What additional factors do the commercial products address that your device does not? How did the recommended placement of these products compare to your recommendation in Step 3? How do these products avoid affecting network performance adversely? For those that offered proactive alarms, what events were given as examples that might trigger alarms?

9. Close the documents you read, and then close your browser program.

14

CASE PROJECTS

1. Tech-on-Call, a large, national computer repair firm, is considering a plan to migrate its current telephony services to its data network. The company's headquarters is in Chicago, with eight branch offices located across the country. The headquarters and branch offices are connected via a VPN. Some of the branch offices connect to the Internet via DSL, and others connect via T1. 50 employees work at the Chicago office, including technical, management, accounting, customer service, sales, and administrative staff. Employees at the Chicago office regularly call the branch offices. Each branch office supports two administrative personnel and ten technicians. Each technician spends approximately 80% of his or her time on the road or at client sites, repairing computers. While out of the office, the technicians rely on pagers and cell phones to communicate with their officemates and clients. Before the company invests in VoIP equipment, Tech-on-Call has asked you to analyze its situation. Based on what you know about the company, what characteristics make Tech-on-Call a good candidate for using VoIP? In what areas could the company save money by making this change? In what areas would it have to spend money to make the change?

2. Acting on your advice, Tech-on-Call has performed some preliminary analysis regarding its current telephone usage. The company's long-distance usage bill, including all its offices, is $34,500 per month. In addition, its monthly connection fees total $12,000 per month. Although upgrading to VoIP doesn't remove the requirement for PSTN lines, Tech-on-Call engineers have estimated that 70% of the PSTN connectivity charges and 50% of the toll charges will disappear after the company migrates to VoIP. In addition, Tech-on-Call plans to eliminate the technicians' cell phone service six months after installing the VoIP system. This will result in a savings of $16,000 per month. The company estimates the cost of adding or upgrading media, telephones, IP-PBX, gateway, and other connectivity devices at $70,000. In addition, some data connections will need to be increased to carry the voice traffic, at an extra cost of $6000 per month. Tech-on-Call wants to make sure its employees understand how to operate the new phone system, so it has allocated $30,000 for training. Based on this information, what one-time costs will Tech-on-Call incur by migrating to VoIP? What is the sum of the monthly costs it will eliminate? What monthly costs will it add? Finally, if all the company's predictions are correct, how many months will it take Tech-on-Call to break even on their VoIP investment? And, assuming things go as planned, how much will Tech-on-Call have saved after one year of using VoIP?

3. After consulting with you about potential cost savings, Tech-on-Call has decided to implement VoIP in the near future. First, the network engineers want to investigate the types of protocols that the network might use. Based on the type of network the company uses, what voice compression scheme, call signaling protocols, and QoS techniques do you recommend and why? Draw a diagram of Tech-on-Call's national network, and indicate where voice and data will share the same connections, where they merge with analog voice services, and where analog voice connections enter the network. Label the connectivity and client devices on the network.

A

DIGITAL ENCODING METHODS

This Appendix serves as a reference for the digital encoding methods introduced in Chapter 2. Recall that the decimal system, which is the common way for humans to represent numbers, is only one encoding method. Computers use binary encoding, which involves combinations of 1s and 0s to exchange information. A simpler and more efficient way for both humans and computers to communicate is by using the hexadecimal numbering system (or hex system), which uses 16 symbols (0 through 9 and A through F) to represent decimal numbers 0 through 15, respectively. Most text messages exchanged between computers are encoded in a simple scheme known as ASCII (pronounced *as-kee*), which stands for American Standard Code for Information Interchange. ASCII is frequently used for basic e-mail messages, but it does not have a mechanism for encoding formatting such as margins, tables, bold, or underline attributes, so it cannot be used for sophisticated documents or spreadsheets. You also learned about Unicode, an internationally standardized code that makes use of 16 binary placeholders, and therefore may represent up to 2^{16}, or up to 65,536 characters. (Whereas ASCII, which is an American standard, can only represent 256 characters.) The first 128 ASCII codes are the same in Unicode. Unicode equivalents for decimal numbers 0 to 32, which are not listed in this table, represent special computer commands.

The following table lists decimal numbers 0 through 255 and their binary, hexidecimal, and ASCII equivalents.

Table A-1   Decimal, binary, hexidecimal, and ASCII codes

Decimal Number	Binary equivalent	Hexidecimal equivalent	ASCII equivalent
0	00000000	0	
1	00000001	1	
2	00000010	2	
3	00000011	3	
4	00000100	4	
5	00000101	5	
6	00000110	6	
7	00000111	7	
8	00001000	8	
9	00001001	9	
10	00001010	A	
11	00001011	B	
12	00001100	C	
13	00001101	D	
14	00001110	E	
15	00001111	F	
16	00010000	10	
17	00010001	11	
18	00010010	12	
19	00010011	13	
20	00010100	14	
21	00010101	15	
22	00010110	16	
23	00010111	17	
24	00011000	18	
25	00011001	19	
26	00011010	1A	
27	00011011	1B	
28	00011100	1C	
29	00011101	1D	
30	00011110	1E	
31	00011111	1F	
32	00100000	20	space
33	00100001	21	!
34	00100010	22	"

Table A-1   Decimal, binary, hexidecimal, and ASCII codes (continued)

Decimal Number	Binary equivalent	Hexidecimal equivalent	ASCII equivalent
35	00100011	23	#
36	00100100	24	$
37	00100101	25	%
38	00100110	26	&
39	00100111	27	'
40	00101000	28	(
41	00101001	29	)
42	00101010	2A	*
43	00101011	2B	+
44	00101100	2C	,
45	00101101	2D	-
46	00101110	2E	.
47	00101111	2F	/
48	00110000	30	0
49	00110001	31	1
50	00110010	32	2
51	00110011	33	3
52	00110100	34	4
53	00110101	35	5
54	00110110	36	6
55	00110111	37	7
56	00111000	38	8
57	00111001	39	9
58	00111010	3A	:
59	00111011	3B	;
60	00111100	3C	<
61	00111101	3D	=
62	00111110	3E	>
63	00111111	3F	?
64	01000000	40	@
65	01000001	41	A
66	01000010	42	B
67	01000011	43	C
68	01000100	44	D
69	01000101	45	E

Table A-1   Decimal, binary, hexidecimal, and ASCII codes (continued)

Decimal Number	Binary equivalent	Hexidecimal equivalent	ASCII equivalent
70	01000110	46	F
71	01000111	47	G
72	01001000	48	H
73	01001001	49	I
74	01001010	4A	J
75	01001011	4B	K
76	01001100	4C	L
77	01001101	4D	M
78	01001110	4E	N
79	01001111	4F	O
80	01010000	50	P
81	01010001	51	Q
82	01010010	52	R
83	01010011	53	S
84	01010100	54	T
85	01010101	55	U
86	01010110	56	V
87	01010111	57	W
88	01011000	58	X
89	01011001	59	Y
90	01011010	5A	Z
91	01011011	5B	[
92	01011100	5C	\
93	01011101	5D	]
94	01011110	5E	^
95	01011111	5F	_
96	01100000	60	`
97	01100001	61	a
98	01100010	62	b
99	01100011	63	c
100	01100100	64	d
101	01100101	65	e
102	01100110	66	f
103	01100111	67	g
104	01101000	68	h

Table A-1   Decimal, binary, hexidecimal, and ASCII codes (continued)

Decimal Number	Binary equivalent	Hexidecimal equivalent	ASCII equivalent
105	01101001	69	i
106	01101010	6A	j
107	01101011	6B	k
108	01101100	6C	l
109	01101101	6D	m
110	01101110	6E	n
111	01101111	6F	o
112	01110000	70	p
113	01110001	71	q
114	01110010	72	r
115	01110011	73	s
116	01110100	74	t
117	01110101	75	u
118	01110110	76	v
119	01110111	77	w
120	01111000	78	x
121	01111001	79	y
122	01111010	7A	z
123	01111011	7B	{
124	01111100	7C	l
125	01111101	7D	}
126	01111110	7E	~
127	01111111	7F	
128	10000000	80	
129	10000001	81	
130	10000010	82	
131	10000011	83	
132	10000100	84	
133	10000101	85	
134	10000110	86	
135	10000111	87	
136	10001000	88	
137	10001001	89	
138	10001010	8A	
139	10001011	8B	

Table A-1   Decimal, binary, hexidecimal, and ASCII codes (continued)

Decimal Number	Binary equivalent	Hexidecimal equivalent	ASCII equivalent
140	10001100	8C	
141	10001101	8D	
142	10001110	8E	
143	10001111	8F	
144	10010000	90	
145	10010001	91	
146	10010010	92	
147	10010011	93	
148	10010100	94	
149	10010101	95	
150	10010110	96	
151	10010111	97	
152	10011000	98	
153	10011001	99	
154	10011010	9A	
155	10011011	9B	
156	10011100	9C	
157	10011101	9D	
158	10011110	9E	
159	10011111	9F	
160	10100000	A0	
161	10100001	A1	
162	10100010	A2	
163	10100011	A3	
164	10100100	A4	
165	10100101	A5	
166	10100110	A6	
167	10100111	A7	
168	10101000	A8	
169	10101001	A9	
170	10101010	AA	
171	10101011	AB	
172	10101100	AC	
173	10101101	AD	
174	10101110	AE	

Table A-1   Decimal, binary, hexidecimal, and ASCII codes (continued)

Decimal Number	Binary equivalent	Hexidecimal equivalent	ASCII equivalent
175	10101111	AF	
176	10110000	B0	
177	10110001	B1	
178	10110010	B2	
179	10110011	B3	
180	10110100	B4	
181	10110101	B5	
182	10110110	B6	
183	10110111	B7	
184	10111000	B8	
185	10111001	B9	
186	10111010	BA	
187	10111011	BB	
188	10111100	BC	
189	10111101	BD	
190	10111110	BE	
191	10111111	BF	
192	11000000	C0	
193	11000001	C1	
194	11000010	C2	
195	11000011	C3	
196	11000100	C4	
197	11000101	C5	
198	11000110	C6	
199	11000111	C7	
200	11001000	C8	
201	11001001	C9	
202	11001010	CA	
203	11001011	CB	
204	11001100	CC	
205	11001101	CD	
206	11001110	CE	
207	11001111	CF	
208	11010000	D0	
209	11010001	D1	

Table A-1   Decimal, binary, hexidecimal, and ASCII codes (continued)

Decimal Number	Binary equivalent	Hexidecimal equivalent	ASCII equivalent
210	11010010	D2	
211	11010011	D3	
212	11010100	D4	
213	11010101	D5	
214	11010110	D6	
215	11010111	D7	
216	11011000	D8	
217	11011001	D9	
218	11011010	DA	
219	11011011	DB	
220	11011100	DC	
221	11011101	DD	
222	11011110	DE	
223	11011111	DF	
224	11100000	E0	
225	11100001	E1	
226	11100010	E2	
227	11100011	E3	
228	11100100	E4	
229	11100101	E5	
230	11100110	E6	
231	11100111	E7	
232	11101000	E8	
233	11101001	E9	
234	11101010	EA	
235	11101011	EB	
236	11101100	EC	
237	11101101	ED	
238	11101110	EE	
239	11101111	EF	
240	11110000	F0	
241	11110001	F1	
242	11110010	F2	
243	11110011	F3	
244	11110100	F4	

Table A-1   Decimal, binary, hexidecimal, and ASCII codes (continued)

Decimal Number	Binary equivalent	Hexidecimal equivalent	ASCII equivalent
245	11110101	F5	
246	11110110	F6	
247	11110111	F7	
248	11111000	F8	
249	11111001	F9	
250	11111010	FA	
251	11111011	FB	
252	11111100	FC	
253	11111101	FD	
254	11111110	FE	
255	11111111	FF	

Glossary

1ESS — The first electronic telephone switch. AT&T's Western Electric division released the 1ESS in 1965.

5ESS — Lucent's most current all-digital switch. A 5ESS may serve as a local or tandem switch, depending on what features are ordered and programmed into its software.

1G — *See* first generation.

2G — *See* second generation.

3G — *See* third generation.

1 Gigabit Ethernet — A type of Ethernet that achieves 1 Gbps maximum throughput. IEEE has defined two standards for 1 Gigabit Ethernet: one that runs over twisted pair (802.3ab) and one that runs over fiber optic cable (802.3z). It is preferable to run Gigabit on fiber. Gigabit Ethernet is primarily used for network backbones. Also known as Gigabit Ethernet.

10 Gigabit Ethernet — An Ethernet standard currently being defined by the IEEE 802.3ae committee. 10 Gigabit Ethernet will allow 10 Gbps throughput and will include full-duplexing and multimode fiber requirements.

10BaseF — A Physical layer standard for networks that use baseband transmission and multimode fiber cabling and can achieve 10 Mbps throughput. 10BaseF networks have a maximum segment length of 1000 or 2000 meters, depending on the version, and employ a star-wired bus hybrid topology.

10BaseT — A Physical layer standard for networks that use baseband transmission and twisted-pair media and can achieve 10 Mbps throughput. 10BaseT networks have a maximum segment length of 100 meters and use a star-wired bus hybrid topology.

100BaseF — A Physical layer standard for networks that use baseband transmission and multimode fiber cabling and can achieve 100 Mbps throughput. 100BaseF networks have a maximum segment length of 400 meters. 100BaseF may also be called "Fast Ethernet."

100BaseT — A Physical layer standard for networks that use baseband transmission and twisted-pair cabling and can achieve 100 Mbps throughput. 100BaseT networks have a maximum segment length of 100 meters and use the star-wired bus hybrid topology. 100BaseT requires CAT5 or higher UTP.

100BaseT4 — A type of 100BaseT network that uses all four wire pairs in a twisted-pair cable to achieve its 100 Mbps throughput. 100BaseT4 is not capable of full-duplex transmission, but can run on older, lower-cost CAT3 UTP.

100BaseTX — A type of 100BaseT network that uses two wire pairs in a twisted-pair cable, but uses faster signaling to achieve 100 Mbps throughput. It is capable of full-duplex transmission and requires CAT5 or higher media.

110 block — A type of punch-down block used for cross-connecting CAT5 or higher UTP, named after the industry standard type 110 punch-down clips they contain. 110 blocks are used on modern voice and data networks.

5-4-3 rule — A guideline for 10BaseT Ethernet networks that specifies a maximum of five segments connected with four repeating devices, and a maximum of three segments, which may contain connected nodes (such as workstations, printers, servers, and so on).

66 block — A type of punch-down block used for traditional telephone cross-connects, named after the industry standard type 66 punch-down clips they contain. 66 blocks are typically not used on data networks or newer telephone networks.

802.11 — The IEEE committee responsible for establishing radio frequency wireless network access standards—or—the group of WLAN standards established by this committee. The most notable 802.11 standards are 802.11b (also known as WiFi), 802.11a, and 802.11g.

802.11a — A WLAN access technology standard that uses multiple frequency bands in the 5 GHz frequency range and offers a maximum throughput of 54 Mbps. Because the 5 GHz band is not as congested as the 2.4 GHz band, 802.11a signals are less likely to suffer interference from microwave ovens, cordless phones, motors, and other (incompatible) WLAN signals than other 802.11 technologies. However, 802.11a WLANs require a greater density of access points between the wireline LAN and wireless nodes to cover the same distance that other versions of 802.11 cover.

802.11b — A WLAN access technology standard that uses direct sequence spread spectrum (DSSS) signaling in the 2.4 GHz band and separates it into 14 overlapping 22-MHz channels. 802.11b provides a maximum of 11 Mbps throughput. It is currently the most popular and cost effective WLAN standard. 802.11b is also known as WiFi (Wireless Fidelity).

802.11g — A WLAN access technology standardized by the IEEE 802.11g working group that uses the 2.4 GHz frequency band and has a maximum throughput of 54 Mbps. 802.11g is compatible with 802.11b.

9-0-# scam — A method of PBX toll fraud in which an intruder uses social engineering to trick an unsuspecting employee at an organization that uses a PBX to press 9, then 0, then the # key on his telephone, and then hang up (in other words, press the switch hook). In fact, on some PBX systems, this is the sequence that transfers a caller to an outside line. (A "9" accesses an outside line, a "0" accesses a local operator, and a "#" cancels the previous request, and pressing the switch hook transfers the caller.) After the intruder has been transferred, she can make long-distance calls at the organization's expense (assuming the organization uses this type of PBX).

ACK (acknowledgment) — A response generated at the Transport layer of the OSI model that confirms to a sender that its frame was received.

access network — The portion of a LEC's network that supplies subscribers with access to multiple services, both analog and digital.

access node — The point at which a user's traffic enters or exits a carrier's network.

access point — The transceiver and antenna used to exchange signals between a wire-bound network device and mobile network nodes on a WLAN.

active device — An electronic component that is capable of controlling voltages or currents it receives.

active monitor — On a Token Ring network, the workstation that maintains timing for token passing, monitors token and frame transmission, detects lost tokens, and corrects problems when a timing error or other disruption occurs. Only one workstation on the ring can act as the active monitor at any given time.

active topology — A topology in which each workstation participates in transmitting data over the network.

adapter card — A circuit board used to connect a device to a computer's system board. Also known as an expansion board or daughter board.

adaptive differential pulse code modulation (ADPCM) — A waveform analog encoding technique in which nodes first sample a waveform, and then attempt to predict future characteristics of the waveform based on previously-transmitted bits. That way, only differences between the actual and predicted signals must be transmitted between nodes. ADPCM also factors in human speech characteristics as it re-creates waveforms. The result is more accurate predictions than with DPCM, which only predicts signals based on historical signal information.

address — A unique number that identifies a node on a network. Addresses may be physical (MAC addresses) or logical (for example, IP addresses).

address resource record — A type of DNS data record that maps the IP address of an Internet-connected device to its domain name.

Advanced Intelligent Network (AIN) — A term coined by telephony manufacturers in the early 1990s to describe the new type of telephony architecture made possible by SS7. The concept behind AIN is that switches rely on vast, centralized databases to make instant decisions on the best available voice circuit path and provide custom services based on individual subscriber preferences.

advanced mobile phone service (AMPS) — A first generation cellular technology that encodes and transmits speech as analog signals. The method AMPS uses for creating separate channels out of one frequency band is called frequency division multiple access (FDMA).

Advanced Research Projects Agency (ARPA) — A government agency formed in 1958 to research and develop space, ballistics, and nuclear arms technology. ARPA established a network for communications between its scientists known as ARPANET.

alias — In a host file, a nickname for a host. An alias allows a user within an organization to address a host by a different (and usually more familiar) name than the full host name.

alien crosstalk — A type of interference that occurs when signals from adjacent cables interfere with another cable's transmission.

alternating current (AC) — An electrical charge flowing in one direction first, then in the opposite direction, then back in the first direction, and so on, in an oscillating fashion over a conductor. To cause this AC, the source sends voltage that varies consistently over regular intervals of time. Home electrical outlets provide AC.

American Standard Code for Information Interchange (ASCII) — An encoding scheme used for simple text messages that represents English letters, numbers, special characters, and punctuation marks as numbers from 0 to 127.

ammeter — An instrument used to measure the current flowing through a circuit.

ampere (amp) — A measure of the amount of current flowing through a conductor. The ampere is named after 19th century French physicist André Marie Ampère.

amplifier — An electronic device that increases the voltage, or power, of a signal.

amplitude — The height, or strength, of a current's or signal's wave. Amplitude is measured in volts.

amplitude modulation (AM) — A method of modulation in which the amplitude of the carrier signal is modified by the imposition of the information signal. In AM, adding the information wave does not change the frequency of the carrier wave.

amplitude shift keying (ASK) — A method for converting analog amplitude modulated signals into digital signals. In ASK, areas with differing amplitude are conveyed as either 0s or 1s.

analog — The signals that use variable voltage to create continuous waves, resulting in an inexact (or approximate) replica of the original sound.

anchor — An HTML tag that formats information on a Web page as a hyperlink (or redirection) to another area of the Web page or to another Web page.

ANSI (American National Standards Institute) — An organization composed of more than a thousand representatives from industry and government who together determine standards for the electronics industry in addition to other fields. ANSI also represents the United States in setting international standards.

AppleTalk — The protocol suite used to interconnect Macintosh computers. AppleTalk can be routed between network segments and integrated with NetWare- or Microsoft-based networks.

Application layer — The seventh layer of the OSI model. The Application layer provides interfaces to the software that enable programs to use network services.

application program interface (API) — A routine (or set of instructions) that allows a program to interact with the operating system. APIs belong to the Application layer of the OSI model.

aperture — The physical area through which an antenna's signal passes as it is transmitted or received.

application switch — Another term for a Layer 3 or Layer 4 switch.

ARPANET — A rudimentary network established for communication between researchers at universities and other organizations involved contracted by ARPA. ARPANET formed the basis for the Internet.

asynchronous — A communications method in which data being transmitted and received by nodes does not have to conform to any predetermined timing scheme. Asynchronous data is sent in frames. To ensure that the receiving node knows when it has received a complete frame, asynchronous communications provide start and stop bits for each character transmitted.

asymmetrical (ASDL) — The characteristic of a transmission technology that affords greater bandwidth in one direction (either from the customer to the carrier, or vice versa) than in the other direction.

asymmetrical DSL — A variation of DSL that offers more throughput when data travels downstream—downloading from a local carrier's POP to the customer—than when it travels upstream—uploading from the customer to the local carrier's POP.

Asynchronous Transfer Mode (ATM) — A technology originally conceived in 1983 at Bell Labs, but standardized only in the mid-1990s. It relies on a fixed packet size to achieve data transfer rates up to 9953 Mbps. The fixed packet consists of 48 bytes of data plus a 5-byte header. The fixed packet size allows ATM to provide predictable traffic patterns and better control over bandwidth utilization.

asymmetric encryption — A type of encryption (such as public-key encryption) that uses a different key for encoding data than is used for decoding the cipher text.

Assured Forwarding (AF) — In the DiffServ QoS technique, a forwarding specification that allows routers to assign data streams one of several prioritization levels. AF is specified in the Type of Service field in an IP version 4 datagram.

ATIS (Association for Telecommunications Industry Solutions) — A North American trade association made of thousands of companies that provide communications equipment and services. Their membership reviews emerging technology and agrees on standards and operating procedures to ensure that services and equipment supplied by multiple companies can be easily integrated.

attenuation — The loss of a signal's strength as it travels farther away from its source.

attenuation distortion — The distortion of a signal that results from different signal components experiencing different levels of attenuation between the signal's sender and receiver. Attenuation distortion affects analog signals more than it affects digital signals. It is measured in decibels (dB).

Audion — A type of vacuum tube invented by Lee DeForest that contained an additional electrode in the middle of the positive and negative electrodes. When subjected to voltage, the third electrode could control current inside the tube. The result was that the Audion could amplify (or boost) a signal.

Automatic Numbering Identification (ANI) — Two digits transmitted with a phone number to identify the number to which the call should be billed.

automated route selection (ARS) — A method of determining over which trunk an outgoing call should be routed to incur the lowest cost.

automatic call distributor (ACD) — A system that uses computerized devices attached to the phone lines to automatically route calls to specific phone extensions.

automatic call distribution (ACD) — A method of distributing incoming calls evenly over multiple stations, according to quantity of calls handled, free time, or availability.

authentication — The process of verifying that a client's logon ID and password are valid and then allowing the client to log on to the network and access defined resources.

authorization code — In the context of private switching, a sequence of numbers that allows an employee to gain access to a certain line or feature.

B channel — In ISDN, the "bearer" channel, so named because it bears traffic from point to point. A B channel uses circuit switching to carry digital voice, video, and data signals. Different types of ISDN are characterized by different quantities of B channels.

backbone — A major, heavily trafficked connection between a carrier's POPs.

band — A subchannel within a communications channel.

bandpass filter — A device that filters a signal so as to remove frequencies higher and lower than the range of frequencies known to carry data.

bandwidth — A measure of the difference between the highest and lowest frequencies that a media can transmit.

bandwidth overhead — The burden placed on the underlying network to support a routing protocol.

base station — (1) A tower, transceiver, and antenna that exchanges signals with all mobile stations within one cell of a cellular network and relays mobile station signals to mobile telephone switching offices. Base stations may also be called base transceiver stations or cell sites. (2) *See* access point. (3) The stationary half of a cordless telephone set. A base station contains wiring to connect to the PSTN, plus a radio antenna, transmitter, and receiver to exchange signals with the cordless telephone handset. Depending on the type of phone, it may use one of several different frequencies and may have a range from 200 to 2000 feet.

base transceiver station (BTS) — *See* base station.

baseband — A transmission form in which (typically) digital signals are sent through direct current (DC) pulses applied to the wire. This direct current requires exclusive use of the wire's capacity. As a result, baseband systems can transmit only one signal at a time.

baseline — A record of how well a system or network operates under normal conditions.

baud — One cycle of an analog wave. Though used to describe modem transmission speeds, a baud is not necessarily equivalent to one bit of data. The term baud is named after French telegrapher Jean-Maurice Baudot who invented an early code for telex transmission.

Bell Communications Research (Bellcore) — The research and development business that was created as a result of the Modified Final Judgment. Bellcore, which was formerly known as Bell Laboratories, was jointly owned by the Regional Bell Operating Companies (RBOCs).

Bell Operating Companies (BOCs) — The 22 telephone companies that belonged to AT&T and provided local service in different regions of the nation (for example, Michigan Bell). As part of the Modified Final Judgment, the Bell Operating Companies were separated from AT&T and transformed into seven Regional Bell Operating Companies (RBOCs).

Bell System — The company initially formed when American Bell took a controlling interest in Western Electric. Later, the Bell System came to refer to AT&T and all its subsidiaries, which controlled U.S. telephone service until the 1984 divestiture.

Bell Telephone Laboratories — The research and development arm of AT&T prior to divestiture. Bell Telephone Laboratories was responsible for innovation and new telephone technology.

bend radius — The radius of the tightest arc into which you can loop a cable before you cause data transmission errors. Generally, a twisted-pair cable's bend radius is equal to or greater than four times the diameter of the cable. The bend radius of a typical two- or four-fiber cable is approximately one inch.

best effort — A characteristic of packet-based transmission in which the network attempts to deliver packets in a timely fashion and in the proper sequence, but does not guarantee either. In fact, best effort offers no guarantees that a packet will arrive at its destination at all.

best path — The most efficient route for data to follow between two nodes (whether or not they are on the same network). Under optimal network conditions, the best path is the path that requires the fewest hops between two points. Realistically, the best path depends on the volume of network activity, unavailable links, network transmission speed, and topology.

binary — A system that uses only 1s and 0s to encode information.

binary coded decimal (BCD) — One of the first code sets that represented a complete English alphabet as binary numbers. IBM devised this code and used this system on its earliest computers. BCD can only use up to 64 symbols to represent letters, numbers, and other characters. It was replaced by EBCDIC.

bio-recognition access — A method for granting access to restricted rooms in which a device scans an individual's unique physical characteristics, such as the color patterns in her eye's iris or the geometry of her hand, to verify her identity.

bit — A pulse in a digital signal which has a value of either 1 or 0. Abbreviation for "Binary Digit."

Block ID — The first set of six characters (or three bytes) that make up the MAC address and that are unique to a particular vendor. Block IDs are also known as vendor IDs.

Bluetooth — A mobile wireless networking standard that uses direct sequence spread spectrum (DSSS) signaling in the 2.4 GHz band to achieve a maximum throughput of less than 1 Mbps. Bluetooth access points and receivers should be spaced no farther than 10 meters apart. It was designed for use primarily with home networks in which multiple devices (including cordless phones, computers, and pagers) are connected.

bonding — The process of combining more than one bearer channel of an ISDN line to increase throughput. For example, BRI's two 64-Kbps B channels are bonded to create an effective throughput of 128 Kbps.

boost — To strengthen a signal.

Border Gateway Protocol (BGP) — The routing protocol of Internet backbones. The router stress created by Internet growth has driven the development of BGP, the most complex of the routing protocols. The developers of BGP had to contend with the prospect of 100,000 routes, as well as the goal of routing traffic efficiently and fairly through the hundreds of Internet backbones.

BRI (Basic Rate Interface) — A variety of ISDN that uses two 64-Kbps bearer channels and one 16-Kbps data channel, as summarized by the following notation: 2B+D. BRI is the most common form of ISDN employed by home users.

braiding — A braided metal shielding used to insulate some types of coaxial cable.

branch feeders — The part of the outside plant that connects service area interfaces to the main feeders in the telephone network's outside plant.

bridge — A connectivity device that operates at the Data Link layer of the OSI model and reads header information to forward packets according to their MAC addresses. Bridges use a filtering database to determine which packets to discard and which to forward. Bridges contain one input and one output port, effectively separating a network into two collision domains.

broadband — A service that spans a relatively wide band of frequencies. Depending on the source, this could mean any width between 3 KHz and 6 MHz. The FCC defines broadband services as those capable of at least 200 Kbps throughput in one direction. Examples of wireless broadband services include MMDS and LMDS.

broadband wireless — A wireless service capable of very high data transfer rates.

broadcast — (1) A type of communication in which one source simultaneously sends a message to multiple destinations. Also called *one-to-many*.

(2) On a data network, a transmission from one node to all other nodes on the same segment.

broadcast domain — A group of connected nodes that share broadcast traffic. In a virtual local area network (VLAN), broadcast domains are separated by logically grouping multiple nodes to make up separate Layer 2 segments. Bridges and lower layer connectivity devices simply extend broadcast domains.

browser — The software that interprets HTTP-encoded material and provides clients with an easily navigated, graphical interface to the Web. Netscape Communicator and Microsoft's Internet Explorer are examples of common browsers.

buffer — A logically defined area of a computer's memory in which data is temporarily stored. When a computer is turned off, its buffers empty.

buffering — The temporary storage of data in a buffer. Modems, for example, buffer incoming data until their buffer is full, then issue signals to the sending party to pause its transmission until the modem has released nearly all data in its buffer.

bugging — The use of a microphone with a small RF transmitter placed near an audio source (such as a telephone mouthpiece) and a nearby receiver to eavesdrop.

bus — (1) The type of circuit used by a computer's system board to transmit data to components. Most new computers use buses capable of exchanging 32 or 64 bits of data. As the number of bits of data a bus handles increases, so too does the speed of the device attached to the bus. (2) The single cable connecting all devices in a bus topology.

bus topology — A topology in which a single cable connects all nodes on a network without intervening connectivity devices.

busy circuit — A signal that indicates that a subscriber's telephone is off-hook (in other words, the line is in use) and the circuit is not available for connection.

busy signal — A tone of two combined frequencies that lasts for .5 seconds and repeats after .5 seconds

of silence. A busy signal is issued to the caller's local switch by the recipient's local switch after it detects that the recipient's line is busy.

byte — The equivalent of eight bits. One byte carries one piece of information, such as a single letter or number.

cable checker — *See* continuity tester.

cable drop — In the context of cable network technology, a fiber optic or coaxial cable that connects a neighborhood cable node to a customer's house.

cable entrance facility (CEF) — The point where a main feeder conduit, which usually contains fiber optic cable, enters a building such as a CO from underground. Also called a *cable vault*.

cable modem — A device that modulates and demodulates signals for transmission and reception via cable wiring.

cable tester — *See* performance tester.

cable vault — *See* cable entrance facility.

call accounting — The process of collecting call information in a database format and making it available through a user interface, such as a software program. Call accounting systems can analyze the collected data and prepare formatted reports.

call center — A facility dedicated to fielding customer calls. A call center usually consists of multiple, trained personnel (also called "agents") and multiple telephone lines.

call forwarding — A feature that allows a user to send a call to another station connected to a private switching system.

call hold — The ability to place an active connection on hold while using the telephone for something else (such as making an outgoing call).

call management — The group of functions supplied by a PBX that include monitoring telephone traffic, customizing calling features and restrictions by line, specifying call routes, and analyzing calling patterns. Call management also encompasses a user's ability to forward or block calls, obtain call information, and to change line preferences.

call pickup — A characteristic of key telephone systems that requires the user to push a button on the telephone station to select a line before placing a call.

call routing — The determination of the path (through switches and COs) that a call's circuit will travel in order to be completed. The route of a call is not necessarily the most geographically direct route. Because of congestion on the public network, or even facilities that happen to be down, a call's route may be indirect. Telephone switches perform call routing.

call setup — The establishment of a circuit between the caller and the party whose number she has dialed.

call supervision — The maintenance of the circuit between a caller and the called party. This function includes tracking when both of the parties have hung up and then terminating the connection. It also includes detecting whether the call needs attention. Telephone switches are responsible for call supervision as long as a call is connected.

caller identification — A feature that displays the name and telephone number of the party who is calling. This feature requires that the switches at the local central office are capable of transmitting this information and that the called party has a telephone set capable of displaying it.

capacitance — The ability for an electric circuit or component to accumulate or store a charge. Capacitance is measured in Farads.

capacitor — A device that stores electrical charges. Capacitors are usually made of two or more thin, conducting plates arranged parallel to each other and separated by an insulator.

capacity — The amount of data that can traverse a communication channel within a given time period.

Carrier Identification Code (CIC) — A unique four-digit number that identifies an IXC as its traffic is handled by LEC facilities. The CIC is used for both call routing and billing between carriers.

Carrier Sense Multiple Access with Collision Detection (CSMA/CD) — Rules for communication used by shared Ethernet networks. In CSMA/CD, each node waits its turn before transmitting data, to avoid interfering with other nodes' transmissions.

carrier wave — In modulation, the wave whose characteristics (for example, amplitude, frequency, or phase) are modified by the addition of an information wave.

Carterfone decision — A 1968 court decision that lifted the restriction against interconnecting to AT&T's telephone network. The Carterfone decision was named after a means of connecting private, radio-controlled telephones to the local telephone lines invented by Tom Carter.

Category 3 (CAT3) — A form of UTP that typically contains four wire pairs and can carry up to 10 Mbps with a possible bandwidth of 16 MHz. CAT3 is the minimum standard for new telephone wiring. On data networks, CAT3 is being replaced with CAT5 to accommodate higher throughput.

Category 5 (CAT5) — The most popular form of UTP for new network installations and upgrades. CAT5 typically contains four wire pairs and supports up to 100 Mbps throughput and a 100 MHz signal rate.

Category 6 (CAT6) — A twisted-pair cable that contains four wire pairs, each wrapped in foil insulation. Additional foil insulation covers the bundle of wire pairs, and a fire-resistant plastic sheath covers the second foil layer. The foil insulation provides excellent resistance to crosstalk and enables CAT6 to support at least six times the throughput supported by regular CAT5.

Category 7 (CAT7) — A twisted-pair cable that contains multiple wire pairs, each separately shielded then surrounded by another layer of shielding within the jacket. CAT7 can support up to a 1 GHz signal rate. But because of its extra layers, it is less flexible than other forms of twisted-pair wiring. Standards for CAT7 have not been finalized.

CDMA (code division multiple access) — A digital mobile wireless access technology in which each voice signal is digitized and assigned a unique code, then small components of the signal are issued over a 12.5 MHz frequency band using the spread spectrum technique. CDMA can achieve at least three times the capacity of TDMA and at least 10 times the capacity of FDMA.

CDMA2000 — A 3G cellular technology developed by Qualcomm and standardized by the ITU. CDMA2000 is a packet-switched version of CDMA. In its final phase CDMA2000 will supply both data and voice over the same 1.25 MHz carrier channel. Current CDMA subscribers will be able to take advantage of CDMA2000 services without changing their equipment or service subscription. Carriers and wireless manufacturers in the United States have thus far embraced the CDMA2000 standard.

cell — (1) A packet of a fixed size. In ATM technology, a cell consists of 48 bytes of data plus a 5-byte header. (2) A geographic area that is serviced by a single low-power transmitter for wireless communications.

cell site — *See* base station.

cellular telephone service — A system for transmitting wireless voice signals to multiple mobile receivers using two-way radio communication and reusing a small range of frequencies through the use of cells.

central control computer — The means by which a telephone switch interprets incoming data, retrieves data, and issues commands to the rest of its components. The central control computer typically includes multiple processors, among other components.

central office — A telephone company facility where lines are terminated and can be connected with other lines to complete calls. Central offices come in different classes depending on the geographic area and type of lines they serve. Central offices are also known as exchanges.

central office terminal — In a DLC system, the point at the central office where multiplexed signals from several subscriber lines are separated.

Centrex — A switching system that provides similar features as a PBX, but the services are supplied from the LEC's central office. The word Centrex is derived from Central Exchange.

channel bank — A multiplexer used to terminate analog T-carrier connections. Channel banks separate or consolidate multiple channels within a T-carrier.

charge — The characteristic of a material that enables it to exert an atomic force on another material.

cipher text — The unique data block that results when an original piece of data (such as text) is encrypted (for example, by using a key).

CIR (Committed Information Rate) — The guaranteed minimum amount of bandwidth selected when leasing a frame relay circuit. Frame relay costs are partially based on CIR.

circuit — A closed connection between an electric source (such as a battery) and a load (such as a lamp) over which electric current may flow.

circuit board — A thin sheet of an insulating material that holds electronic components (for example, resistors and diodes) plus conductive pathways (typically made of copper) to connect those components in a circuit.

circuit switching — A method of switching in which a connection is established between two nodes before they begin transmitting data. In circuit switching, bandwidth is dedicated to the connection and remains available only to the original source and destination nodes until those users terminate communication. While the nodes are connected, all data follows the same path first selected by the switch.

cladding — The glass shield around the fiber core of a fiber optic cable. Cladding acts as a mirror, reflecting light back to the core in patterns that vary depending on the transmission mode. This reflection allows fiber to bend around corners without impairing the light-based signal.

client — A computer on the network that requests resources or services from another computer on a network. In some cases, a client could also act as a server. The term "client" may also refer to the user of a client workstation.

client_hello — In the context of SSL encryption, a message issued from the client to the server that contains information about what level of security the client's browser is capable of accepting and what type of encryption the client's browser can decipher (for example, RSA or Diffie-Hellman). The client_hello message also establishes a randomly generated number that uniquely identifies the client plus another number that identifies the SSL session.

client-server network — A network in which clients (typically workstations) use a central server to share data, data storage space, programs, and devices.

client software — A program or group of programs that instruct the client's operating system to interact with the server's network operating system. Versions of client software are specific to both the client's operating system and the server's network operating system.

coaxial cable — A type of cable that consists of a central copper core surrounded by an insulator, a braided metal shielding, called braiding, and an outer cover, called the sheath or jacket. Coaxial cable, called "coax" for short, was the foundation for Ethernet networks in the 1980s and remained a popular transmission medium for many years.

COCOT (customer-owned coin-operated telephone) — A coin operated telephone (as it is called in the telecommunications industry).

codec (coder/decoder) — A device that can encode and decode a signal. Codecs are found inside switches, for example, to convert an analog signal into a digital signal.

collision — In Ethernet networks, the interference of one network node's data transmission with another network node's data transmission.

collision domain — The portion of an Ethernet network in which collisions occur if two nodes transmit data at the same time.

collision rate — On Ethernet networks, the average percentage of all transmissions involved in collisions during a one minute time period.

collocate (also colocate, co-locate) — To lease space and house equipment at another organization's facilities. Companies usually collocate to take advantage of another organization's superior infrastructure or location.

common carrier — A direct provider of a public telecommunications service that is subject to regulation by the FCC and state public utilities commissions and that is available to any member of the public who wishes to subscribe to the services.

common channel signaling (CCS) — A method of out-of-band signaling developed by AT&T in the 1970s. It is distinguished by the fact that it carries signal information on a dedicated data link between central offices. In CCS, no signal information is carried over the voice connections.

communication — The sharing of information or messages between two or more entities.

communication services — The functions of a network that allow remote users to connect to the network (usually through a phone line and modem).

communications channel — The means of carrying a signal that contains data from the source to the destination (for example, copper wire).

communications server — See remote access server.

companding — The process of compressing and expanding areas of low and high amplitudes, respectively, to better quantize an analog signal that's being converted to a digital signal.

competitive local exchange carriers (CLECs) — The local exchange carriers that have only begun offering local phone service since competition was introduced. CLECs may build their own facilities, but they usually also lease lines from ILECs to cover the local loop portion of their subscribers' connections.

computer-telephony integration (CTI) — A method of combining the features of a PBX with the features of a networked computer.

computing — The automatic manipulation of input based on logical instructions.

conductor — A material over which electric current readily flows.

conduit — A thick tube (usually made of PVC plastic) in which cables are housed to remain protected from environmental damage.

connection-oriented — A feature of some protocols that requires the establishment of a connection between communicating nodes before the protocol transmits data.

connectionless — A feature of some protocols that allows the protocol to service a request without requiring a verified session and without guaranteeing data delivery.

connectivity device — A device that connects and exchanges data between two separate networks or separate parts of a single network. Examples of connectivity devices include switches, bridges, and routers.

connector — The piece of hardware in which a cable terminates. Connectors are plugged into data jacks, or receptacles, to connect transmission media to any part of a network.

continuity tester — A simple handheld device that determines whether cabling can provide connectivity. To accomplish this task, a continuity tester applies a small voltage to each conductor at one end of the cable, then checks whether that voltage is detectable at the other end. It may also verify that voltage cannot be detected on other conductors in the cable. A continuity tester may also be called a cable checker.

control channel — A communications channel that carries information about how another signal should be managed and interpreted. The control channel is separate from the channel that carries the payload (such as voice, video, or data signals) meant for the receiver.

convergence — The combination of voice or video plus data signals traveling on the same network.

convergence time — The time it takes for a router to recognize a best path in the event of a change or outage.

converter — A device (found in most household appliances) that changes AC into DC.

core — The central component of a fiber optic cable, consisting of one or several pure glass fibers.

cracker — A person who uses his or her knowledge of operating systems and utilities to intentionally damage or destroy data or systems. Although crackers are technically distinguished from hackers by their malicious intentions, the two terms are often used synonymously.

crossbar switch — An automatic telephone switch that used a grid of horizontal and vertical bars with electromagnets at their ends. The horizontal bars could rotate up and down to connect to specific vertical bars and thus complete circuits. Each possible permutation of the vertical and horizontal bars' position's represented a different connection.

cross-connect — An arrangement in which wires terminating at two sets of punch-down blocks are interconnected.

crossover cable — A twisted-pair patch cable in which the termination locations of the transmit and receive wires on one end of the cable are reversed.

crosstalk — A type of noise caused by the inducted current of signals traveling on nearby wire pairs. This inducted current infringes on another pair's signal.

CSU (channel service unit) — A device used with T-carrier technology that provides termination for the digital signal and ensures connection integrity through error correction and line monitoring.

CSU/DSU — A combination of a CSU (channel service unit) and a DSU (data service unit) that serves as the connection point for a T1 line at the customer's site.

current electricity — *See* electric current.

customer premise equipment (CPE) — The part of a telecommunications system that resides at the customer's home or business. Usually, but not always, a customer owns and is responsible for CPE. Traditional telephony CPE includes inside wiring, telephones, PBX, and key systems.

cut-through mode — A switching mode in which a switch reads a frame's header and decides where to forward the data before it receives the entire packet. Cut-through mode is faster, but less accurate, than the other switching method, store and forward mode.

cycle — A section of a sine wave, beginning at a starting point, up to the wave's highest amplitude, down to its lowest amplitude, and then back to the starting point. One cycle per second equals one Hertz.

Cyclic Redundancy Check (CRC) — An algorithm used to verify the accuracy of data contained in a data frame.

D channel — In ISDN, the "data" channel that uses packet-switching techniques to carry information about the ISDN connection, such as session initiation and termination signals, caller identity, call forwarding, and conference calling signals.

DACS (Digital Access and Cross-connect System) — A device that allows for direct connection between T-carriers that terminate at the same carrier's facilities. Through a DACS, for example, an incoming T1 can be divided into multiple channels, with some of the channels forming an outgoing fractional T1.

data — Discreet pieces of information. In the context of telecommunications, the term data usually refers to information formatted for and exchanged between computers.

data communication — The sharing of information or messages between electrical or electronic devices.

data encryption standard (DES) — A popular private key encryption technique that was developed by IBM in the 1970s.

Data Link layer — The second layer in the OSI model. The Data Link layer bridges the networking media with the Network layer. Its primary function is to divide the data it receives from the Network layer into frames that can then be transmitted by the Physical layer.

Data Link layer address — *See* MAC address.

data propagation delay — The length of time data takes to travel from one point on a network segment to another point. On Ethernet networks, CSMA/CD's collision detection routine cannot operate accurately if the data propagation delay is too long.

data telecommunication — The use of electrical signals to exchange encoded information between computerized devices across a distance.

daughter board — *See* adapter card.

de facto standard — A standard that is not an official policy but is adhered to nevertheless. (De facto, in Latin, means "from the fact.") Unlike RFC standards, de facto standards are developed independently, by a corporation or research facility, and then released to the public.

decimal system — A numbering system that uses a total of 10 digits, 0 through 9, multiplied by an exponential of 10 to represent any number.

decryption — The process of using an algorithm to decode a transmission and reveal encrypted data.

dedicated — A continuously available link or service that is leased through a telecommunications provider, such as a LEC. Examples of dedicated lines include ADSL, T1, and T3.

delay distortion — The impairment of a signal that results from different frequencies traveling over the same wire at slightly different speeds. When frequencies travel at different speeds, the separate parts of a signal associated with those frequencies arrive at their destination slightly out of sync. Because of their dependence on precise changes in phase, delay distortion affects digital signals more profoundly than analog signals. It is corrected through the use of equalizers.

demarc box — A box (at the demarcation point between a customer's facilities and a service provider's facilities) that contains a network interface device. Demarc boxes prevent both unauthorized tampering and environmental damage to the network interface device. In most cases, the demarc box is the property of the LEC.

demarcation point (demarc) — The place that marks the difference between a LEC's facilities and the subscriber's CPE. On a residence, the demarcation point is usually a small termination box attached to the side of the house.

demodulator — A device that separates the information from the carrier signal at the receiving end of a modulated wave.

demultiplexer (demux) — A device that separates signals combined by multiplexing and regenerates them in their original form at the receiving end.

denial of service attack — A technique in which hackers barrage a system, network, or device with such a high volume of signals that valid signals cannot be processed or transmitted.

dense wavelength division multiplexing (DWDM) — A version of wavelength division multiplexing that can support a larger number of different wavelengths on the same strand of fiber, thus greatly increasing the bandwidth capacity of that fiber.

destination — The person or machine to whom a message is directed.

Device ID — The second set of six characters that make up a network device's MAC address. The Device ID, which is added at the factory, is based on the device's model and manufacture date.

dial tone — A sound made up of two frequencies—350 Hz and 440 Hz—that you hear when you pick up your telephone. Local office switches issue dial tone to a line when they detect that it is off-hook.

dial-up networking — The process of dialing in to a network's private or public access server to gain remote access to the network. Dial-up Networking is also the name of the utility that Microsoft provides with its operating systems to achieve this type of connectivity.

dictionary attack — A technique in which attackers run a program that tries a combination of a known user ID and, for a password, every word in a dictionary to attempt to gain access to the network. This is typically the first technique a hacker uses when trying to guess a password (besides asking the user for her password).

DID (direct inward dialing) trunk — In a PBX, the connection to a central office that allows callers outside an organization to directly dial PBX users inside an organization using a seven-digit number.

difference engine — An automated calculating machine as large as a locomotive and powered by steam that was proposed in 1822 by Charles Babbage, an English mathematics professor. Though a working difference engine was never actually built, Babbage's ideas were adopted by other inventors working on automated calculating machines, which were precursors to modern computers.

differential pulse code modulation (DPCM) — A voice-encoding technique in which the codec samples the actual voice signal at regular intervals, and in between samples, attempts to predict the value of signal bits that have not yet arrived. When the actual signal differs from the predicted signal, the sending node transmits only the differential, or the difference between the predicted and actual values. With the differential, the receiving end can reconstruct the voice signal with some accuracy. DPCM uses far less bandwidth than PCM, but it also requires higher processing resources and results in longer delays. The ITU G.723 standard uses DPCM.

Differentiated Service (DiffServ) — A traffic prioritization technique that helps improve Quality of Service (QoS). DiffServ modifies the Type of Service (TOS) field in IP version 4 datagrams or the Traffic Class field in IP version 6 datagrams to indicate the data's priority. DiffServ defines two types of forwarding: Expedited Forwarding (EF) or Assured Forwarding (AF).

diffraction — In wireless transmission, the splitting of a signal into secondary waves when it encounters an obstruction. The secondary waves continue to propagate in the direction in which they were split. In diffraction, signals seem to bend around objects. Objects with sharp edges—including the corners of walls and desks—cause diffraction.

digital — A method of expressing information in signals composed of pulses of zero voltage and positive voltage that represent values of either 0 or 1, respectively.

digital advanced mobile phone service (D-AMPS) — The most popular form of TDMA technology, a technique of separating each channel into multiple time slots, which follows the Interim Standard (IS)-136.

digital certificate — A password-protected and encrypted file that holds an individual's identification information, including a public key and a private key. The individual's public key is used to verify the sender's digital signature, and the private key allows the individual to log on to a third-party authority who administers digital certificates.

digital cross-connect system (DCS) — Any device that directly connects multiple digital lines with other digital lines.

digital divide — The discrepancy between the greater Internet access enjoyed by more urban and affluent citizens in the United States compared to the lack of access experienced by many rural, disabled, and poor citizens.

digital loop carrier (DLC) — A technique for delivering digital signals to a high volume of LEC subscribers over a combination of new and old local loop infrastructure. DLC bundles multiple analog lines into fewer, high-capacity digital connections that lead to the LEC's central office.

digital PBX — A PBX that is capable of accepting and interpreting digital signals. An IP-PBX is the most common example of a digital PBX.

digital signal processor (DSP) — A computer chip that codes and decodes voice signals.

diode — An active electronic device made from a semiconducting material that allows current to flow in only one direction.

direct current (DC) — An electrical charge flowing steadily in one direction over a conductor. To generate DC, a source must apply a constant amount of voltage to the conductor at all times. Batteries are examples of DC power sources.

direct inward dialing (DID) — A feature that enables parties from outside the organization to dial an extension's seven digit number directly, rather than going through an attendant to complete the call.

direct inward system access (DISA) — A feature of some private switches that allows an organization's employees to complete long-distance calls from outside the organization by first accessing the PBX via a toll-free number. DISA is a security risk often exploited by hackers.

direct sequence spread spectrum (DSSS) — A transmission technique in which a signal's bits are distributed over an entire frequency band at once. Each bit is coded so that the receiver can reassemble the original signal upon receiving the bits.

directional antenna — An antenna that issues wireless signals along a single direction. Directional antennas are used when the source needs to communicate with one destination, as in a point-to-point link, or when multiple receiving nodes are arranged in line with each other. Alternatively, it may be used when sustaining the strength of a signal over a distance is more important than covering a broad geographical area.

disconnect — The indication that a subscriber's telephone is on-hook after being off-hook (in other words, he has hung up the phone).

distance learning — The use of telecommunications technology to inform, educate, or train students across distances.

distinctive ringing — A unique ringing tone or cadence that identifies different types of calls.

distortion — The unintended and undesirable modification of at least one signal component (such as amplitude, frequency, or phase), which makes the received signal different than the originally transmitted signal.

distribution cable — The cabling that connects multiple subscriber drop wires in a neighborhood to a larger conduit.

diversity — The use of multiple antennas or multiple signal transmissions to compensate for fading and delay in wireless transmission.

DMS (Digital Multiplexed System) — A series of local and tandem switches supplied by Nortel. DMS competes with and provides similar features to Lucent's ESS line of switches.

DNS server — *See* name server.

do not disturb — A feature that allows a user to disable her telephone from ringing and accepting incoming calls.

domain name — The symbolic name that resolves to a group of IP addresses. Usually, a domain name is associated with a company or other type of organization, such as a university or military unit.

Domain Name System (DNS) — A hierarchical way of tracking domain names and their addresses, devised in the mid-1980s. The DNS database does not rely on one file or even one server, but rather is distributed over several key computers across the Internet to prevent catastrophic failure if one or a few computers go down. DNS is a TCP/IP service that belongs to the Application layer of the OSI model.

downlink — The transmission of a signal from an orbiting satellite to an earth-based receiver.

downstream — A term used to describe data traffic that flows from a local carrier's facility to the customer. In asymmetrical communications, downstream throughput is usually much higher than upstream throughput. In symmetrical communications, downstream and upstream throughputs are equal.

draft standard — In the IETF's RFC approval process, a proposed standard that has demonstrated interoperability and functionality and is ready for the last phase of scrutiny before it becomes an RFC standard.

drop wire — The cable that runs from a subscriber's demarcation point to a telephone pole or underground conduit.

DS0 (Digital Signal, Level 0) — An international standard that defines Physical layer signaling standards for transmitting digital voice or data over a 64-Kbps channel. In North America, DS0 is equivalent to one channel in a T-carrier circuit.

DSL (digital subscriber lines) — A dedicated remote connectivity or WAN technology that uses advanced data modulation techniques to achieve extraordinary throughput over regular phone lines. DSL currently comes in seven different varieties, the most common of which is Asymmetric DSL (ADSL).

DSL access multiplexer (DSLAM) — A connectivity device located at a carrier's office that aggregates multiple DSL subscriber lines and connects them to a larger carrier or to the Internet backbone.

DSL modem — A device that demodulates an incoming DSL signal, extracting the information and passing it on to the data equipment (such as telephones and computers) and modulates an outgoing DSL signal.

DSU (data service unit) — A device used in T-carrier technology that converts the digital signal used by bridges, routers, and multiplexers into the digital signal used on cabling. Typically, a DSU is combined with a CSU in a single box, a CSU/DSU.

dual mode — A type of cellular telephone that is capable of transmitting and receiving both analog and digital signals.

dual-tone multifrequency (DTMF) — The coding scheme used by touch-tone dialers. DTMF transmits a combination of two frequencies each time a button is pressed.

duplex — *See* full duplex.

duplexing — The simultaneous transmission of a signal in both directions along a single transmission pathway.

Dynamic Host Configuration Protocol (DHCP) — An Application layer protocol in the TCP/IP suite that manages the dynamic distribution of IP addresses on a network. Using DHCP to assign IP addresses can nearly eliminate duplicate-addressing problems.

dynamic routing — A method of routing that automatically calculates the best path between two nodes and accumulates this information in a routing table. If congestion or failures affect the network, a router using dynamic routing can detect the problems and reroute data through a different path. Most modern networks primarily use dynamic routing.

e-business — The use of data telecommunications to conduct business transactions.

e-commerce — A means of conducting business over the Web—be it in retail, banking, stock trading, consulting, or training. Any buying and selling of products or services that occurs over the Internet belongs in the e-commerce category.

e-rate — A program for funding technology in schools and libraries across the nation that was established by the Telecommunications Act of 1996. E-rate money is generated by the universal service fund (USF).

Easily Recognizable Code (ERC) — An NPA in which the second and third digit are identical (for example, the numbers 888 or 411). In the North American Numbering Plan, these NPAs are reserved for special purposes—for example, 888 is reserved for toll-free calls.

eavesdropping — The use of a transmission or recording device to capture conversations without the consent of the speakers.

EBCDIC (Extended BCD Interchange Code) — An 8-bit encoding system developed by IBM and adopted for use with its mainframe computers. EBCDIC can encode up to 2^8, or 256, different characters, including letters, numbers, and punctuation marks.

echo reply — The response signal sent by a device after another device pings it.

echo request — The request for a response generated when one device pings another device on the network.

EIA (Electronic Industries Alliance) — A trade organization composed of representatives from electronics manufacturing firms across the United States that helps establish standards for electronic equipment and services.

electric current — The controlled movement of an electrical charge (or electrons) along the atoms of a conductor (such as wire).

electromagnet — A central conducting core surrounded by a coil that produces an electromagnetic field when current is applied to the coil. An electromagnet is a specific type of inductor.

electromagnetic — A type of force (or wave) that contains a combination of electric and magnetic forces (or waves).

electromagnetic interference (EMI) — A form of noise, or waves that emanate from electrical devices or cables carrying electricity. Motors, power lines, televisions, copiers, fluorescent lights, and other sources of electrical activity (including a severe thunderstorm) can cause EMI.

electromagnetism — The magnetic effect produced by an electric current.

electron — An atomic subparticle that orbits the center of an atom and carries a negative charge.

Electronic Serial Number (ESN) — A fixed number assigned to a mobile telephone by the manufacturer. ESNs cannot be changed by the user or service carrier. The telephone's ESN is transmitted to a base station to identify the mobile station and its location. Every telephone has a unique ESN.

electronic switching system (ESS) — The brand name of Lucent's local and tandem switch that relies entirely on electronics. The first ESS was released in 1965 and since then, the switch has gone through many improvements. Today's ESSs are entirely digital.

electronics — In general, the study of moving electrons. More specifically, electronics is a field that deals with the behavior of electric charge as it flows in a vacuum, in gases, and in semiconductors.

electrostatic charges — The charges inherent in electrons and protons that are bound to balance each other through static electricity.

element — In XML, a named set of data and a method of interpreting this data. Using elements rather than tags (as in HTML) makes XML a much more flexible and powerful markup language.

encode — To modify a set of data into a specific representation that can be interpreted by the receiver (whether it is a software program, piece of hardware, or human).

encryption — The use of an algorithm to scramble data so that the data can only be read by reversing the formula (or decryption).

end office — A Class 5 CO that accepts local loop connections. End offices are the only COs that terminate local subscriber lines.

enhanced CAT5 (CAT5e) — A higher-grade version of CAT5 wiring that contains high-quality copper, offers a high twist ratio, and uses advanced methods for reducing crosstalk. Enhanced CAT5 can support a signaling rate of up to 200 MHz, double the capability of regular CAT5.

ENIAC (Electronic Numerical Integrator and Computer) — An early computer developed in cooperation between the U.S. Army and the University of Pennsylvania. ENIAC was a multipurpose computer so large that it required its own 30 foot by 50 foot room. ENIAC did not contain memory and, therefore, could not retain any information once it was turned off.

Enhanced Interior Gateway Routing Protocol (EIGRP) — A routing protocol developed in the mid-1980s by Cisco Systems that has a fast convergence time and a low network overhead, but is easier to configure and less CPU-intensive than OSPF. EIGRP also offers the benefits of supporting multiple protocols and limiting unnecessary network traffic between routers.

enterprise-wide — The scope of a network that spans an entire organization and often services the needs of many diverse users. It may include many locations (as a WAN), or it may be confined to one location but include many different departments, floors, and network segments.

envelope delay distortion — *See* delay distortion.

equal access — A provision set forth in the MFJ that requires local phone service providers to allow all long distance service providers to access and use their facilities at the same, reasonable cost.

equipment provider — A company that provides telecommunications devices, such as telephones, computers, and network connectors.

Ethernet — A network access method that follows the IEEE 802.3 signaling specifications, including CSMA/CD and packet switching. Ethernet comes in several forms. 100BaseT (or Fast Ethernet) is currently the most popular type of Ethernet in use on LANs.

exchange — (1) *See* central office. (2) The geographical area served by one central office.

expansion board — *See* adapter card.

expansion slot — An opening on a computer's system board that contains multiple electrical contacts into which an expansion board (or adapter card) can be inserted.

Expedited Forwarding (EF) — In the DiffServ QoS technique, a forwarding specification that assigns each data stream a minimum departure rate from a given node. This technique circumvents delays that slow normal data from reaching its destination on time and in sequence. EF information is inserted in the Type of Service (TOS) field of an IP version 4 datagram.

Extensible Authentication Protocol (EAP) — A Data Link layer protocol defined by the IETF in RFC 2284. EAP specifies a pre-authentication process in which a client and server exchange data via an intermediate node (an access point on a wireless LAN). Only after they have mutually authenticated can the client and server exchange encrypted data. EAP supports multiple authentication and encryption schemes.

extranet — A network that uses Internet-like services and protocols to make resources available to multiple locations of the same organization or to different organizations.

facilities-based — A type of carrier that builds its own facilities (such as microwave links and underground cables) in addition to leasing ILEC facilities to provide service under their name.

fading — A change in wireless signal strength as a result of some of the originally transmitted electromagnetic energy being scattered, reflected, or diffracted. Fading may be positive, in which the strength of the signal that reaches the receiver is higher than the strength of the signal at the transmitter. This can happen if significant reflection concentrates a signal toward a receiver. Most often, however, fading is negative. That is, the strength of the signal that reaches the receiver is lower than its transmitted strength.

Farad (F) — A measure of capacitance. The Farad was named after English chemist and physicist Michael Faraday, who experimented with electricity in the early 1800s.

Fast Ethernet — A type of Ethernet network that is capable of 100 Mbps throughput. 100BaseT and 100BaseFX are both examples of Fast Ethernet.

fax gateway — A gateway that can translate IP fax data into analog fax data and vice versa. A fax gateway can also emulate and interpret conventional fax signaling protocols when communicating with a conventional fax machine. When the T.37 standard is used, a fax gateway must also be able to interpret mail server requests through SMTP, plus translate telephone numbers into e-mail addresses.

fax over IP (FoIP) — A service that transmits faxes over a TCP/IP network. The ITU recognizes two techniques for FoIP: T.37 and T.38.

FDDI (Fiber Distributed Data Interface) — A networking standard originally specified by ANSI in the mid-1980s and later refined by ISO. FDDI uses a dual fiber-optic ring to transmit data at speeds of 100 Mbps. It was commonly used as a backbone technology in the 1980s and early 1990s, but lost favor as Fast Ethernet technologies emerged in the mid-1990s. FDDI provides excellent reliability and security.

FDMA (frequency division multiple access) — A first generation analog, mobile wireless access technology that divides the cellular spectrum into 832 separate communications channels, each with a bandwidth of 30 Hz. When a call is placed under the FDMA scheme, the call's transmission is guaranteed exclusive use of its 30 Hz channel for the duration of the call. FDMA (used in the AMPS cellular service) is inefficient compared with newer wireless access technologies such as CDMA.

Federal Communications Commission (FCC) — The primary national regulatory agency involved in telecommunications in the United States.

fiber optic cable — A transmission media that contains thin strands of fiber in its core and uses pulses of light to convey signals. It is capable of carrying higher amounts of data, voice, or video within a given time span than any other type of media.

fiber optic modem (FOM) — A device located at both the transmitting and receiving ends of a wavelength division multiplexed channel. The FOM separates the multiplexed signals into individual signals according to their different wavelengths.

file server — A specialized server that enables clients to share applications and data across the network.

file services — The function of a file server that allows users to share data files, applications, and storage areas.

File Transfer Protocol (FTP) — An Application layer protocol used to send and receive files via TCP/IP.

filtering — The process of removing unwanted parts of a signal. In the case of analog or digital signals, filters are used to remove frequencies higher and lower than the range of frequencies responsible for carrying data. Filters may be used at either the transmitter, the receiver, or at both locations in a communications system.

filtering database — A collection of data created and used by a bridge that correlates the MAC addresses of connected workstations with their locations. A filtering database is also known as a forwarding table.

firewall — A specialized computer (typically a router, but possibly only a workstation running special software) that selectively filters or blocks traffic between networks. A firewall relies on a combination of hardware and software (for example, the router's operating system and configuration) to determine which packets it should accept and which it should deny.

first generation (1G) — The mobile wireless technology developed in the 1980s, which is characterized by analog transmission and a simple, relatively inefficient method for using frequencies to transmit and receive signals. AMPS is an example of 1G technology.

fixed — A wireless system in which the locations of the transmitter and receiver are static and the transmission antenna focuses its energy directly toward the receiver antenna. Because in a fixed wireless transmission the receiver's location is predictable, energy need not be wasted issuing signals across a large geographical area and more energy can be used for the signal.

flow control — A method of gauging the appropriate rate of data transmission based on how fast the recipient can accept data.

forward path — In cellular networks, transmission from a mobile station to a base station.

forwarding table — *See* filtering database.

fox and hound — *See* tone generator and tone locator.

fractional T1 — An arrangement that allows organizations to lease only some channels on a T1 line and pay for only the channels they lease. Fractional T1s are an economical alternative to full T1s.

frame — A package for data that includes not only the raw data, or "payload," but also the sender's and receiver's network addresses and control information.

Frame Check Sequence (FCS) — The field in a frame responsible for ensuring that data carried by the frame arrives intact. It uses an algorithm, such as CRC, to accomplish this verification. The FCS is inserted at the Data Link layer of the OSI model.

frame relay — An updated, digital version of X.25 that relies on packet switching. Because it is digital, frame relay supports higher bandwidth than X.25, offering a maximum of 45 Mbps throughput. It provides the basis for much of the world's Internet connections. On network diagrams, the frame relay system is often depicted as a cloud.

framing — In TDM or statistical multiplexing, a technique of inserting special bits in the data stream to indicate where one series of data-carrying time slots ends and another begins.

frequency — The number of times a wave cycles from its beginning point to its highest amplitude, to its lowest amplitude and back to where it started before it repeats. Frequency is measured in cycles per second, or Hertz.

frequency division multiplexing (FDM) — A method of sending multiple analog signals simultaneously over one channel by separating the channel into subchannels, or bands. Each band in the channel has its own carrier signal with a unique frequency.

frequency hopping spread spectrum (frequency hopping or FHSS) — A wireless signaling technique in which a signal jumps between several different frequencies within a band in a synchronization pattern known to the channel's receiver and transmitter.

frequency modulation (FM) — A method of modulation in which the frequency of the carrier signal is modified by the application of the information signal. In FM, adding the information signal does not change the amplitude of the carrier wave.

frequency shift keying (FSK) — The method by which FM signals are converted into digital signals. In FSK, areas with differing frequency are conveyed as either 0s or 1s.

full duplex — A form of communications in which messages can travel over a communications channel in two directions simultaneously. May also be simply called "duplex."

full-mesh topology — A type of mesh topology in which every node is directly connected to every other node on the network. Full-mesh provides the highest fault tolerance, but is also more expensive than other topologies.

fully qualified host name — In TCP/IP addressing, the combination of a host and domain name that together uniquely identify a device.

fusion splicing — A method of splicing fiber optic cables in which the application of heat melts and fuses two aligned fiber strands. The most popular heat source for fusion splicing is an electrical arc. Fusion splicing has the potential to cause material imperfections in the glass. Therefore, it is important to test the splice for attenuation and optical loss.

G.711 — An ITU standard that specifies the type of pulse code modulation (PCM) voice encoding used on the PSTN. In G.711, a waveform codec samples an analog wave 8000 times per second, then uses 8 bits per sample to represent the information. This results in the requirement of a 64-Kbps channel. The receiving codec attempts to accurately re-create the original waveform using this information.

G.723 — An ITU standard that specifies voice encoding through differential pulse code modulation (DPCM). G.723 requires only 6.4 Kbps of bandwidth, but uses a moderate amount of processing resources and results in moderate network delays, compared to some other codecs. In addition, its voice quality is not as good as other waveform codecs, such as G.711. However, G.723 is adequate for packet-based networks and is currently used for VoIP and videoconferencing.

G.726 — An ITU standard that specifies voice encoding through adaptive differential pulse code modulation (ADPCM). G.726 can operate over a 16-, 24-, 32- or 40-Kbps channel. Its voice quality is best on a 40-Kbps channel and worst on a 16-Kbps channel. G.726 requires fewer DSP resources and results

in much lower delay than G.723, another waveform codec used on VoIP networks.

G.728 — An ITU standard that specifies voice encoding using hybrid codec techniques. G.728 requires a 16-Kbps channel and introduces very little delay. On the other hand, because it relies on sophisticated algorithms to closely match and synthesize a signal, G.728 requires significant DSP resources.

G.729 — An ITU standard that specifies voice encoding using a vocoder codec. G.729 further reduces its throughput requirements by suppressing the transmission of voice signals during silences. It can operate over an 8-Kbps channel. Also, G.729 requires only moderate DSP resources and results in only moderate delays compared to other encoding techniques. Although some believe it provides inferior sound quality, G.729 is a popular encoding protocol used with VoIP, videoconferencing, wireless, and VoFR network services. It is recommended for use where bandwidth conservation is a primary concern.

gateway — A combination of networking hardware and software that connects two dissimilar kinds of networks. Gateways perform connectivity, session management, and data translation, so they must operate at multiple layers of the OSI model. Many different types of gateways exist, including e-mail gateways, LAN gateways, Internet gateways, and voice/data gateways.

generator — A power source that supplies AC.

geosynchronous — A satellite that at every point in its orbit maintains a constant distance from a point on the earth's equator.

giga (G) — A prefix that indicates a quantity multiplied by 2 to the 30th power (1,073,741,824) in the context of data transfer or storage or 10 to the 9th power (1,000,000,000) in the context of mathematics, physics, and electronics.

gigabyte (GB) — A quantity of data equivalent to 2 to the 30th power (1,073,741,824) bytes (1024 megabytes) or 1000 megabytes, depending on the context.

Gigabit Ethernet — *See* 1 Gigabit Ethernet.

global system for mobile communications (GSM) — A version of time division multiple access (TDMA) that divides a channel into smaller timeslots than the IS-136 TDMA standard. Smaller time slots, in addition to GSM's frequency hopping spread spectrum (FHSS) signaling, mean a signal is less likely to underutilize channel bandwidth. In addition, GSM makes use of silences in a phone call to increase its signal compression, leaving more open time slots in the channel. GSM has been the standard cellular technology in Europe since it was made available there in 1991.

grounding — The use of a conductor (such as a wire) to divert unused or potentially harmful charges to an insulator, where they will be stopped or absorbed.

group — On a network, a collection of users (or other network objects, such as printers or servers) that are associated with each other for the purposes of simpler network management. For example, all users in an Accounting Department might be collected in the "ACCTG" group, which is granted rights to the budget and forecast spreadsheets on a server.

guardband — A narrow band of unused frequency that separates two information-carrying bands and ensures that signals do not interfere with each other.

guided wave — An information wave that is added to (and thus, guided by) a carrier wave in the process of modulation.

H.225 — A Session-layer call signaling protocol defined as part of ITU's H.323 multiservice network architecture. H.225 is responsible for call setup between nodes on a VoIP network, indicating node status, requesting additional bandwidth, and call termination.

H.245 — A Session-layer control protocol defined as part of ITU's H.323 multiservice network architecture. H.245 is responsible for controlling a session between two nodes. For example, it ensures that the two nodes are communicating in the same format.

H.248 — *See* MEGACO.

H.323 — An ITU standard that describes an entire architecture for implementing multiservice networks, plus several protocols for establishing and managing voice or video transmissions over a packet-based network.

hacker — A person who masters the inner workings of operating systems and utilities in an effort to better understand them.

half duplex — A form of communications in which messages can travel over a communications channel in two directions, but only one direction at a time.

handoff — The process of a mobile wireless signal being transferred to a new channel when it passes from one cell to another in a cellular network. Handoff is managed by mobile telephone switching offices (MTSOs). Under ideal conditions, handoff is transparent to the mobile telephone user.

handset — The part of the telephone that contains a transmitter and receiver and can be removed from the stationary equipment to allow the user to be mobile while he talks. When a handset is removed from the switch hook, the local loop's circuit is completed.

handshake protocol — One of several protocols within SSL, and perhaps the most significant. As its name implies, the handshake protocol allows the client and server to authenticate to (or introduce) each other and establishes terms for how they will securely exchange data during an SSL session.

hardware flow control — A method of gauging the rate at which two modems can exchange data that uses the interface between the modem and the computer to issue flow control information. Hardware flow control information is not combined with the stream of data being exchanged. Because its signals cannot be falsified or corrupted by telephone line noise, it is more effective than software flow control. RTS/CTS is a type of hardware flow control.

head-end — A cable company's central office, which connects cable wiring to many nodes before it reaches customers' sites.

henry (H) — A unit used to measure inductance. The henry was named after American physicist Joseph Henry who experimented with electricity and magnetism in the early 1800s.

Hertz (Hz) — The unit of measure in which frequency is expressed, equal to cycles per second. The term was named after German physicist Heinrich Hertz who, in the late 19th century, studied electromagnetic theory and radio waves.

hexadecimal numbering system (hex system) — A numbering scheme based on 16 symbols, 0 through 9 and A through F.

High Speed Token Ring (HSTR) — A standard for Token Ring networks that operates at 100 Mbps.

HomeRF — A wireless networking specification that also uses DSSS in the 2.4 GHz frequency band to achieve a maximum of 10 Mbps throughput.

hop — A term used in networking to describe each trip data takes from one connectivity device to another.

host — A computer connected to a network that has a unique address. This term is most often used in the context of networks that rely on the TCP/IP protocol suite.

host file — A text file that associates TCP/IP host names with IP addresses. On UNIX platforms the file is called "hosts" and is located in the /etc directory. On a Windows XP, NT, or 2000 computer, the file is also called "hosts" and is located in the *systemroot*\System32\Drivers\Etc directory, where *systemroot* is the directory in which the operating system is installed.

HTTP (Hypertext Transport Protocol) — The Application layer protocol that enables Web browsers to issue requests to Web servers and then to interpret the Web server's response.

HTTPS — The URL prefix that indicates that a Web page requires its data to be exchanged between client and server using SSL encryption. HTTPS uses the TCP port number 443, rather than TCP port 80 (the port that normal HTTP uses).

hub — A connectivity device that operates at the Physical layer of the OSI Model and repeats digital signals over a network segment.

Hush-a-Phone decision — A 1956 Supreme Court ruling that allowed the attachment of devices not manufactured by AT&T to AT&T telephones as long as the device did not harm the public telephone network.

hybrid codec — A voice encoding and decoding method that borrows techniques from both waveform codecs and vocoders. Several types of hybrid codecs exist. In general, hybrid codecs incorporate intelligence about the physics of human speech to regenerate a signal. However, rather than apply the same predictive algorithms to all speech signals, a hybrid codec first analyzes a voice's waveform characteristics. Based on this analysis, it then applies specialized algorithms to more accurately predict and synthesize that voice on the receiving end. ITU's G.728 standard specifies a hybrid codec.

hybrid coil — A device introduced into telephone sets in the early 1900s to separate the incoming transmit and receive signals into their own two-wire connections.

hybrid fiber-coax (HFC) — A link that consists of fiber cable connecting the cable company's offices to a node location near the customer and coaxial cable connecting the node to the customer's house. HFC upgrades to existing cable wiring are required before current TV cable systems can serve as WAN links.

hybrid telephone system — A private switching system that has some characteristics of a KTS and some characteristics of a PBX. Digital KTSs are considered hybrid telephone systems.

hybrid topology — A complex combination of the simple physical topologies.

Hypertext Markup Language (HTML) — The language that defines formatting standards for Web documents.

idle circuit — An indication that a subscriber's telephone is on-hook (in other words, the line is not in use) and the circuit is available for connection.

IEEE (Institute of Electrical and Electronic Engineer) — An international society composed of engineering professionals. Its goals are to promote development and education in the electrical engineering and computer science fields.

ifconfig — A TCP/IP configuration and management utility used with UNIX systems (similar to the ipconfig utility used on Windows NT, 2000, and XP systems).

impedance — The combined effect of a circuit's inductance and capacitance. In a DC circuit, impedance equals resistance. Impedance is expressed in ohms. Every cable possesses a characteristic impedance. Changes in impedance on a network (caused by terminations or connectors) can cause signal loss.

impulse noise — A type of noise caused by sudden spikes in electromagnetic activity. Impulse noise affects a signal only briefly, but often dramatically.

in-band signaling — A type of switch signaling that uses the same communications channel as the information being exchanged over the channel.

incumbent local exchange carriers (ILECs) — The phone companies, including the RBOCs, that provided local phone service as regulated monopolies before the introduction of competition for intraLATA service.

inductance — The capacity for an inductor (or coiled wire) to create a magnetic field.

inductor — A coil of wire that generates (or induces) a magnetic field as electric current flows over it.

infrastructure — The foundation for a network or system. In the case of the public telephone network, a collection of cables, wires, connectivity devices, and user equipment make up its infrastructure.

information wave — In modulation, the wave that represents the signal to be transmitted. An information wave is added to the carrier wave to result in a unique wave that possesses characteristics of both waves.

inside plant — The cabling and equipment located within a carrier's central offices.

inside wiring — The telecommunications system wiring that is located inside the customer's home or business.

insulator — A material over which electric current doesn't readily flow.

integrated access device (IAD) — A sophisticated type of access node that performs functions at all layers of the OSI model—for example, supplying digital cross-connections, accepting transmissions from different types of networks, accommodating both voice and data connections, and interpreting data at the highest layers of the OSI model.

integrated circuit (IC) — A chip made of a semiconductive material (usually silicon) that contains embedded electronic components, such as resistors, diodes, and transistors.

intelligent hub — A hub that possesses processing capabilities and can therefore monitor network traffic, detect packet errors and collisions, poll connected devices for information, and issue the information gathered to a database.

interactive voice response (IVR) — An automated method of sending and accepting information over a telephone line by pressing buttons in response to recorded voice prompts.

intercom — A feature found in private switching systems that enables users to push a one- or two-digit number to speak directly with a colleague in the same office.

inter-exchange carriers (IXCs) — The service providers that connect calls between LATAs, also known as long distance carriers.

interLATA — The service that is initiated and terminated between LATAs, or long distance service.

intermodulation noise — A type of noise that is caused by the mixing of one signal and another due to their frequencies infringing on each other.

Internet — A complex, diverse WAN that connects LANs and individual users around the globe.

Internet Architecture Board (IAB) — A technical advisory group made up of approximately a dozen researchers and technical professionals interested in overseeing the Internet's design and management. IAB is responsible for Internet growth and management strategy, for resolution of technical disputes, and for standards oversight. IAB appoints the chair of the IETF and consults with the IESG in determining whether a proposed standard will become a draft standard.

Internet Assigned Numbers Authority (IANA) — A nonprofit, U.S. government-funded group that was established at the Information Systems Institute (ISI) University of Southern California and charged with managing IP address allocation and the Domain Name System. The oversight for many IANA's functions was given to ICANN in 1998; however, IANA continues to perform high-level Internet system administration.

Internet Control Message Protocol (ICMP) — A TCP/IP protocol that notifies the sender that something has gone wrong in the transmission process and that packets were not delivered.

Internet Corporation for Assigned Names and Numbers (ICANN) — A private, nonprofit corporation that is contracted by the government to oversee IP address and domain name management, plus accomplish specific Internet management improvements. It consists of 19 board members representing every continent in the world, a President and CEO, and At-Large Membership. ICANN has overtaken many of the responsibilities previously assigned to IANA.

Internet draft — A proposed standard that is submitted by a computer networking professional to an IETF working group. After thorough review, an Internet draft may become an Internet technical standard or best practice.

Internet Engineering Steering Group (IESG) — A committee made of IETF technical area directors that oversees IETF decisions. IESG is responsible for finally determining whether an Internet draft is ready to become an RFC.

Internet Key Exchange (IKE) — The first phase of IPSec authentication, which accomplishes key management. Once IKE has established the rules for the type of keys two nodes will use, IPSec invokes its second phase, encryption.

Internet Mail Access Protocol (IMAP) — A mail storage and manipulation protocol that depends on SMTP's transport system and improves upon the shortcomings of POP. The most current version of IMAP is version 4 (IMAP4). IMAP4 can (and eventually will) replace POP without the user having to change e-mail programs. The single biggest advantage IMAP4 has relative to POP is that it allows users to store messages on the mail server, rather than having to download them to the local machine.

Internet Protocol (IP) — A core protocol in the TCP/IP suite that belongs to the Internet layer of the TCP/IP model and provides information about how and where data should be delivered. IP is the subprotocol that enables TCP/IP to internetwork.

Internet service provider (ISP) — A company that operates a network and provides consumers with a link to the Internet.

Internet services — The services that enable a network to communicate with the Internet, including World Wide Web servers and browsers, file transfer capabilities, Internet addressing schemes, security filters, and a means for directly logging on to other computers.

Internet Society (ISOC) — An organization consisting of thousands of Internet professionals and companies from around the globe that helps guide Internet technology and policy. Some current ISOC concerns include how to address rapid growth, security, and the increased need for diverse services over the Internet. ISOC is an umbrella organization for the IETF, IAB, and IESG.

Internet telephony — The provision of telephone service over the Internet.

Internet2 — A network that connects educational and private institutions for the purposes of research and development. Internet2 relies on a backbone separate from the public Internet's backbone, and therefore, Internet2 users enjoy much faster response. To connect to Internet2, an organization must pay a significant annual fee and promise to use access for educational or research purposes.

internetwork — To traverse more than one LAN segment and more than one type of network through a router.

Internetwork Packet Exchange (IPX) — A core protocol of the IPX/SPX suite that operates at the Network layer of the OSI model and provides routing and internetwork services, similar to IP in the TCP/IP suite.

Internetwork Packet Exchange/Sequenced Packet Exchange (IPX/SPX) — A protocol originally developed by Xerox, then modified and adopted by Novell in the 1980s for the NetWare network operating system.

interoffice signaling — The exchange of alert, supervisory, and other information between switches at different central offices.

intraLATA — The service that initiates and terminates within a LATA, or local service area.

intranet — A TCP/IP-based network that connects clients with resources within an organization. Intranets use HTTP servers to store and present private information to clients. However, these Web servers require client authentication and are not necessarily connected to the Internet. Intranets are also used for other applications such as e-mail, file sharing, document management, and collaboration.

intra-office call — A call in which the local loops from the caller and her intended receiver connect to the same end office. An intra-office call doesn't get passed on to another CO.

ipconfig — The TCP/IP configuration and management utility for use with Windows NT, 2000, and XP systems.

IP address — A logical address used in TCP/IP networking. This unique 32-bit number is divided into four groups of octets, or 8-bit bytes, that are separated by periods.

IP datagram — The IP portion of a TCP/IP frame that acts as an envelope for data, holding information necessary for routers to transfer data between subnets.

IP fax machine — A fax machine designed to exchange fax data over a packet-switched network.

IP Security Protocol (IPSec) — A Layer 3 protocol that defines encryption, authentication, and key management for TCP/IP transmissions. IPSec is an enhancement to IPv4 and native to IPv6. IPSec is unique among authentication methods in that it adds security information to the header of all IP packets.

IP spoofing — A security attack in which an outsider obtains internal IP addresses, then uses those addresses to pretend that he or she has authority to access a private network from the Internet.

IP-PBX — A private telephone switch that accepts and interprets digital voice signals. Most IP-PBXs can also accept and interpret analog signals, and thus, can connect both traditional PSTN lines and data networks. Like a traditional PBX, an IP-PBX provides telephones with dial tone and performs telephone setup, supervisory, and call routing functions. It also supplies call management.

IP phone — *See* IP telephone.

IP telephone — A telephone designed for use on VoIP networks. To communicate on the network, each IP telephone has a unique IP address and typically connects, via the data network, to an IP-PBX or a media gateway.

IP telephony — *See* Voice over IP.

IP version 6 (IPv6) — A newer version of the IP subprotocol that will replace the existing IP version 4. IPv6 uses more efficient packet headers and allows for 128-bit source and destination IP addresses. The use of longer addresses will allow more IP addresses to be in circulation. IPv6 also includes the IPSec encryption mechanism.

ISDN (Integrated Services Digital Network) — An international standard, established by the ITU, for transmitting data over digital lines. ISDN uses the PSTN, but it differs from PSTN in that it exclusively uses digital lines and switches. Its connections may be dial-up or dedicated. It comes in three varieties: PRI, BRI, and B-ISDN.

ISO (International Organization for Standardization) — A collection of standards organizations representing 130 countries with its headquarters located in Geneva, Switzerland. Its goal is to establish international technological standards to facilitate global exchange of information and barrier-free trade.

ITU (International Telecommunications Union) — A specialized United Nations agency that regulates international telecommunication usage, including radio and TV frequencies, satellite and telephony specifications, networking infrastructure, and tariffs applied to global communication. It also provides developing countries with technical expertise and equipment to advance their technological base.

jamming — The process by which a station's NIC first propagates a collision throughout the network so no other station attempts to transmit; after propagating the collision, the NIC remains silent for a period of time.

jumper wires — The short cables often used to complete circuits between punch-down blocks.

Kerberos — A cross-platform authentication protocol that uses key encryption to verify the identity of clients and to securely exchange information once a client logs on to a system. It is an example of a private key encryption service. Unlike some other private key encryption services, Kerberos requires the client to prove its identity through a third party.

key — A series of characters that is combined with a block of data during that data's encryption. To decrypt the resulting data, the recipient must also possess the key.

key encryption — An encryption technique that weaves a key into a block of data using a predefined algorithm, so that the same key and algorithm must be used to decrypt the data. Key encryption comes in two forms: public key encryption and private key encryption.

key management — The method whereby two nodes using key encryption agree on common parameters for the keys they will use to encrypt data.

key pair — The combination of a public and private key used to decipher data that has been encrypted using public key encryption.

key service unit (KSU) — A centralized, wall-mounted control console that provides the intelligence behind a KTS. A KSU connects to the organization's internal phones and to the telephone company's end office. It signals the telephone attendant about incoming calls, controls busy indicator lights on line buttons, and tracks call information, among other tasks.

key telephone system (KTS) — A device that provides centralized line and intercom access, plus other enhanced services, for multiple telephone users within an organization. Unlike a PBX, a KTS relies on the telephone company's CO to supply its users with dial tone.

kilo (k) — A prefix that indicates a quantity multiplied by 2 to the 10th power (1024) in the context of data transfer or storage or 10 to the 3rd power (1000) in the context of mathematics, physics, and electronics.

kilobyte (KB) — A quantity of data equivalent to 2 to the 10th power (1024) bytes or 1000 bytes, depending on the context.

Kingsbury Commitment — The 1913 agreement between AT&T and the U.S. Department of Justice (and named after the AT&T vice president who drafted the proposal) that forced AT&T to divest itself of Western Union, stop buying independent telephone companies, and allow independent telephone companies to connect to its infrastructure. AT&T initiated the settlement, fearing that if it didn't take proactive measures, the government would use anti-trust laws against it.

LAN Emulation (LANE) — A method for transporting Token Ring or Ethernet frames over ATM networks. LANE encapsulates incoming Ethernet or Token Ring frames, then converts them into ATM cells for transmission over an ATM network.

last mile — *See* local loop.

latency — The delay between the transmission and reception of a data bit. Latency depends on many factors, including the distance between the sender and receiver, as well as the number of connectivity devices in the signal's path. It is often measured in round trip time (RTT).

Layer 2 Forwarding (L2F) — A Layer 2 protocol similar to PPTP that provides tunneling for other protocols and can work with the authentication methods used by PPP. L2F was developed by Cisco Systems and requires special hardware on the host system. It can encapsulate protocols to fit more than just the IP format, unlike PPTP.

Layer 2 Tunneling Protocol (L2TP) — A Layer 2 tunneling protocol developed by a number of industry consortia. L2TP is an enhanced version of L2F. Like L2F, it supports multiple protocols; unlike L2F, it does not require costly hardware upgrades to implement. L2TP is optimized to work with the next generation of IP (IPv6) and IPSec (the Layer 3 IP encryption protocol).

Layer 3 switch — A switch capable of interpreting data at Layer 3 (Network layer) of the OSI model.

Layer 4 switch — A switch capable of interpreting data at Layer 4 (Transport layer) of the OSI model.

leased lines — Connections or services for which an organization pays a regular (usually monthly) fee to use. Most leased lines are established through a public telecommunications carrier, such as a LEC, IXC, or ISP. T-carriers and frame relay links are examples of leased lines.

Level 1 — A cable consisting of four insulated copper wires surrounded by a sheath. In Level 1 cable, wire pairs are not twisted. Also known as quad wire, Level 1 cable formed the basis of most inside telephone wiring until recent years, when data communications have prompted the use of higher quality, twisted-pair cable. In a Level 1 cable, the red wire is the ring (used for signaling in the first pair), the green wire is the tip (used for a ground) in the first pair, and the yellow wire is the ring in the second pair, whereas the black wire is the tip in the second pair.

licensed — In the United States, a frequency that requires an operator to apply and pay for exclusive use of a frequency within a specified geographical region. Most frequencies in the wireless spectrum are licensed.

line — A circuit used for voice or data transmission. Line may also refer to the physical wire used to complete a circuit.

line group controller (LGC) — A part of a local switch's central control computer that monitors the status of hundreds of SLICs (which are attached to subscribers' lines).

line of sight (LOS) — A wireless link that depends on an unobstructed, direct path between a transmitter and receiver.

local access and transport area (LATA) — A geographical area that defines local phone calls. LATAs were established by Judge Harold Greene as part of the MFJ. They were roughly equivalent to area codes at that time, and a total of 160 LATAs were established across the United States.

local area network (LAN) — A network of computers and other devices that is confined to a relatively small space, such as one building or even one office.

local exchange carrier (LEC) — A carrier that supplies subscribers with intraLATA telephone connections. CLECs and ILECs are two types of LECs.

local exchange terminal — *See* central office terminal.

local loop — The portion of a subscriber's connection to a carrier's network that links a residence or business to its local phone company's central office.

local multipoint distribution service (LMDS) — A point-to-multipoint, fixed wireless technology that operates in the 28 GHz and 31 GHz (microwave) frequency ranges. LMDS can deliver both one-way and two-way telecommunications services, including voice, video, and data. Typical data transmission rates for LMDS are 45 Mbps.

local office — *See* local switching center.

local switch — A switch that receives and interprets the signal from a subscriber's telephone at the central office where a subscriber's local loop terminates (a Class 5 CO, or end office). ILECs, CLECs, and local wireless carriers own and operate local switches.

local switching center — An exchange where multiple phone lines from homes and businesses in one geographic area converge and terminate. It may also be called a local office.

log on — The act of submitting credentials (such as a username and password) to a server, then being admitted access to shared resources on the network.

logical address — *See* network layer addresses.

Logical Link Control (LLC) sublayer — The upper sublayer in the Data Link layer. The LLC provides a common interface and supplies reliability and flow control services.

loopback address — An IP address reserved for communicating from a node to itself (used mostly for testing purposes). The value of the loopback address is always 127.0.0.1.

loss — The extent to which a signal's strength weakens over a distance.

low earth orbiting (LEO) — A type of satellite that orbits the earth with an altitude between 700 and 1400 kilometers, closer to the earth's poles than the orbits of either GEO or MEO satellites. Because their altitude is lower, LEO satellites cover a smaller geographical range than GEO satellites and require less power. Also, signals take less time to travel between an LEO satellite and the earth's surface. The capability of faster transmission has made LEO satellites useful for applications in which signal timing is critical, such as voice and video communications.

MAC address — A number that uniquely identifies a network node. The manufacturer hard-codes the MAC address on the NIC. This address is composed of the Block ID and Device ID.

magnetic field — A region of magnetic force. Electrons moving through a wire cause a magnetic field that radiates outward from the wire.

mail server — A specialized server that manages mail services.

mail services — The network services that manage the storage and transfer of e-mail between users on a network. In addition to sending, receiving, and storing mail, mail services can include intelligent e-mail routing capabilities, notification, scheduling, indexing, document libraries, and gateways to other mail servers.

main distributing frame (MDF) — The place where numerous individual incoming lines first terminate at a central office. The MDF contains several punch-down blocks that allow incoming lines to be cross-connected with another set of lines that leads to the carrier's switching equipment.

main feeder — The part of the outside plant that connects all the aggregated branch feeders to a central office.

management services — The network services that centrally administer and simplify complicated management tasks on the network. Examples of management services include license tracking, security auditing, asset management, addressing management, software distribution, traffic monitoring, load balancing, and hardware diagnosis.

manhole — *See* utility access hole.

many-to-many — A type of communication in which multiple sources simultaneously send messages to multiple destinations.

mass splicing — The splicing of multiple fiber optic strands at once, whether by fusion or mechanical means.

mechanical splicing — A method of splicing fiber optic cable in which the two ends of a fiber optic cable are mechanically fixed in position within a tube so that they form one continuous communications channel.

media — *See* transmission media.

Media Access Control (MAC) sublayer — The lower sublayer of the Data Link layer. The MAC appends the physical address of the destination computer onto the frame.

media gateway — A gateway capable of accepting connections from multiple devices (for example, IP telephones, traditional telephones, IP fax machines, traditional fax machines, and so on) and translating analog signals into packetized, digital signals, and vice versa.

media gateway controller — A computer that manages multiple media gateways and facilitates the exchange of call control information between these gateways.

Media Gateway Control Protocol (MGCP) — A protocol used for communication between media gateway controllers and media gateways. MGCP is defined in RFC 2507, but it was never officially adopted as a standard. MGCP is currently the most popular media gateway control protocol used on converged networks.

medium earth orbiting (MEO) — A type of satellite that orbits the earth 10,390 miles above its surface, positioned between the equator and the poles. MEO satellites have the advantage of covering a larger area of the earth's surface than LEO satellites while at the same time using less power and causing less signal delay than GEO satellites.

mega (M) — A prefix that indicates a quantity multiplied by 2 to the 20th power (1,048,576) in the context of data transfer or storage or 10 to the 6th power (1,000,000) in the context of mathematics, physics, and electronics.

megabyte (MB) — A quantity of data equivalent to 2 to the 20th power (1,048,576) bytes (1024 kilobytes) in the context of data transfer or storage or 10 to the 6th power (1,000,000) bytes (or 1000 kilobytes) in the context of mathematics, physics, and electronics.

MEGACO — A protocol used between media gateway controllers and media gateways. MEGACO is poised to replace MGCP on modern converged networks, as it supports a broader range of network technologies, including ATM. Also known as H.248.

memory — In the context of computing, a feature or component of a computer that enables it to store information for later retrieval.

mesh topology — A topology that consists of many directly interconnected locations forming a mesh. In a mesh topology, each node is connected to at least two other nodes. Mesh topologies are typically used on WANs. *See also* full-mesh topology and partial-mesh topology.

message switching — A method of switching in which each intermediate node between the source and its target accepts and stores the data before passing it on. This "store and forward" routine continues until the message reaches its destination.

message waiting — A light on the telephone that indicates if a party has a message waiting in his voice mail.

metropolitan area exchange (MAE) — A type of network access point. In the United States, there are two MAEs: MAE East, in northern Virginia just outside of Washington, D.C., and MAE West, in San Jose, California.

metropolitan area network (MAN) — A network that connects clients and servers in multiple buildings within a limited geographic area. For example, a network connecting multiple city government buildings around the city's center.

micro (μ) — A prefix that indicates a quantity multiplied by 10 to the -6th power (.000001).

microprocessor — A special kind of integrated circuit that contains all the components and intelligence necessary to accept and carry out all of the incoming instructions on a computer.

Microsoft Message Queueing (MSMQ) — An API used in a network environment. MSMQ stores messages sent between nodes in queues then forwards them to their destination when the link to the recipient is available.

microwave link — A path used for transmitting signals via microwaves.

microwave multipoint distribution system (MMDS) — *See* multipoint multichannel distribution service.

milli (m) — A prefix that indicates a quantity multiplied by 10 to the -3rd power (.001).

MNP4 (Microcom Networking Protocol Level 4) — A modem error correction method used on many contemporary modems.

MNP5 (Microcom Networking Protocol Level 5) — A modem compression method that can theoretically compress data streams down to one half of their original size.

mobile — A type of wireless system in which the receiver may be located anywhere within a specific range of the transmitter. This allows the receiver to roam from one place to another while continuing to pick up its signal.

Mobile Identification Number (MIN) — An encoded representation of the mobile telephone's 10-digit telephone number. The MIN is one number issued from a mobile station (such as a cellular telephone) to a base transmitter that uniquely identifies the mobile station and its location. Every mobile telephone has a unique MIN.

mobile station — A receiver that operates in a mobile wireless system. A cellular telephone is an example of a mobile station.

mobile telephone service — A system for providing telephone service to multiple, mobile receivers using two-way radio communication over a limited number of frequencies.

mobile switching center (MSC) — *See* mobile telephone switching office.

mobile telephone switching office (MTSO) — Similar to an end office in the PSTN, a mobile telephone switching office (MTSO) manages call switching for mobile stations within a cell cluster. It may directly connect mobile stations within a cellular network or, via trunks to the PSTN, connect mobile stations with traditional wireline telephones. MTSOs also control handoff for mobile stations passing between cells. Furthermore, it collects data about cellular call traffic for billing purposes.

mobile unit — *See* mobile station.

modem — A device that derives its name from its function as a *mod*ulator/*dem*odulator, modulating analog signals into digital signals at the transmitting end, then demodulating digital signals into analog signals at the receiving end.

Modified Final Judgment (MFJ) — A 1982 government ruling that split AT&T into multiple, smaller companies, some of which, like Regional Bell Operating Companies (RBOCs), that provided local phone service, would continue to be regulated monopolies and others of which (such as AT&T's long-distance arm) would be open to competition.

modular router — A router that contains multiple slots that can hold different interface cards or other devices.

modulation — A signal-processing technique in which an information wave is imposed on a carrier wave to create a unique wave pattern.

modulator — The device that imposes an information wave on a carrier wave at the transmission end.

Morse code — A method of representing characters with a series of dots and dashes. Morse code is named after Samuel Morse, the inventor of the telegraph.

multimeter — An instrument that can measure multiple characteristics of an electrical circuit, including its current, resistance, and voltage.

multimode fiber — A type of fiber optic cable that contains a core with a larger diameter over which many pulses of light generated by a light emitting diode (LED) travel at different angles. Because light is being reflected many different ways in a multimode fiber cable, the waves become less easily distinguishable the longer they travel. Thus, multimode fiber is best suited for shorter distances than single-mode fiber.

multipath — The wireless signals that follow a number of different paths to their destination due to reflection, diffraction, or scattering. The multipath nature of wireless signals cause fading and delay, which can be addressed through antenna and signal diversity.

multiplexer (mux) — A device that can combine and transmit many signals on a single channel.

multiplexing — The process of simultaneously transmitting multiple signals over one circuit.

multipoint control unit (MCU) — In the context of videoconferencing over a network, a device that allows multiple video terminals to receive the same audio-video signals.

multipoint multichannel distribution service (MMDS) — A method of transmitting wireless television, voice, or data signals from one transmitter to multiple receivers. MMDS uses microwaves with frequencies in the 2.1 to 2.7 GHz range of the wireless spectrum.

Multi-protocol Label Switching (MPLS) — A method of forwarding packets from one router to the next according to priority. To indicate where data should be forwarded, MPLS replaces the IP datagram header with a label at the first router a data stream encounters. The MPLS label contains information about where the router should forward the packet. Each router in the data stream's path revises the label to indicate the data's next hop. In this manner, routers on a network can take into consideration network congestion, QoS indicators assigned to the packets, plus other criteria.

multiprotocol network — A network that uses more than one protocol.

multistation access unit (MAU) — On a Token Ring network, a device that repeats signals and connects multiple nodes in a star-ring hybrid physical topology.

multiservice network — *See* next generation network (NGN).

music on hold — A feature found in some private switching systems that plays music or promotional recordings while a caller is placed on hold.

mutual inductance — A phenomenon in which one inductor (that has current flowing through it) produces a magnetic field and thereby induces a voltage on a nearby coil. Also known as the *transformer effect*.

name server — A server that contains a database of TCP/IP host names and their associated IP addresses. A name server supplies a resolver with the requested information. If it cannot resolve the IP address, the query passes to a higher-level name server. Name servers may also be known as DNS servers.

name space — The database of Internet IP addresses and their associated names distributed over DNS name servers worldwide.

nano (n) — A prefix that indicates a quantity multiplied by 10 to the -9th power (.000000001).

narrowband — A type of radio frequency transmission in which signal energy is concentrated at a single frequency or within a very small range of frequencies.

national electric code (NEC) — A telecommunications wiring standard initially published in 1911 and updated every three years by the National Fire Protection Association. The purpose of the NEC is to ensure the proper installation of electrical systems to safeguard people and property. This volume addresses all types of wiring systems, including power systems, alarm systems, and communications systems.

near-end crosstalk (NeXT) — A type of crosstalk that occurs between two copper wires within a twisted pair (as opposed to the crosstalk that occurs between twisted pairs within a cable). In NeXT, current flowing over one wire in the pair induces a current on the other wire in the pair.

NetBEUI (NetBIOS Enhanced User Interface) — The Microsoft adaptation of IBM's NetBIOS protocol. NetBEUI expands on NetBIOS by adding an Application layer component.

NetBIOS — A protocol originally designed for IBM to provide Transport and Session layer services for applications running on small, homogenous networks. Microsoft adopted IBM's NetBIOS as its foundation protocol, initially for networks using LAN Manager or Windows for Workgroups.

netstat — A TCP/IP utility that displays statistics and details about TCP/IP connections and listening ports on a host.

network — A group of computers and other devices (such as printers) that are connected by communications channel. Networks enable multiple users to easily share resources and exchange data.

network access method — A networking technology defined by its Data Link layer data packaging and Physical layer signaling techniques. Also known as network transport system or access method. Ethernet and Token Ring are examples of network access methods.

network access point (NAP) — A facility operated by one large network service provider where Internet traffic is aggregated and exchanged. In the United States, there are five major NAPs.

network adapter — *See* network interface card (NIC).

network administrator — A professional charged with installing, maintaining, and troubleshooting a network.

network interface card (NIC) — The device that enables a workstation to connect to the network and communicate with other computers. NICs are manufactured by several different companies and come with a variety of specifications that are tailored to the workstation's and the network's requirements.

network interface device (NID) — The physical point at which a subscriber's facilities connect with a service provider's facilities.

Network layer — The third layer in the OSI model. The Network layer translates network addresses into their physical counterparts and decides how to route data from the sender to the receiver.

Network layer addresses — The addresses that reside at the Network level of the OSI model, follow a hierarchical addressing scheme, and can be assigned through operating system software.

Network News Transfer Protocol (NNTP) — The protocol that supports the process of reading newsgroup messages, posting new messages, and transferring news files between news servers.

network operating system (NOS) — The software that runs on a server and enables the server to manage data, users, groups, security, applications, and other networking functions. The most popular network operating systems are Microsoft Windows NT, Windows 2000, UNIX, and Novell's NetWare.

network service provider (NSP) — A telecommunications company that provides infrastructure for either public or private traffic. NSPs aren't necessarily ISPs because they may simply provide the infrastructure for connections, but not operate access servers for a consumer's initial entry to the Internet. However, most NSPs are ISPs.

Network Termination 1 (NT1) — A device used on ISDN networks that connects the incoming twisted-pair wiring with the customer's ISDN terminal equipment.

Network Termination 2 (NT2) — An additional connection device required on PRI to handle the multiple ISDN lines between the customer's network termination connection and the local phone company's wires.

neutrons — An atomic subparticle found at the center of an atom, which possesses no charge (and is said to be neutral).

next generation network (NGN) — A network that provides voice, video, and data services over the same infrastructure.

newsgroup — An Internet service similar to e-mail that provides a means of conveying messages, but in which information is distributed to a wide group of users at once rather than from one user to another.

node — A computer or other device connected to a network that has a unique address and is capable of sending or receiving data.

noise — Unwanted interference from external sources, such as fluorescent lights, cathode ray tubes, or broadcast towers, that may degrade a signal. Noise may include electromagnetic interference or radio frequency interference.

North American Numbering Plan (NANP) — The scheme for assigning unique numbers to every telephone line in North America. NANP was originally developed by AT&T in 1947. Due to the increasing need for new numbers, NANP standards are continually being assessed and revised.

NSFNET — A network established in 1986 by the U.S. National Science Foundation (NSF) that originally consisted of five interconnected super-computing centers at universities across the nation, plus a backbone network. NSFNET's mission was to increase early use of the Internet by universities and other educational and research institutions.

number portability — The ability of telecommunications service users to retain their same telephone number, no matter what service provider they choose, without impairment of quality, reliability, or convenience. The Telecommunications Act of 1996 required that every local service provider allow for number portability.

Numbering Plan Areas (NPAs) — The geographically divided regions that indicate the first three digits of a North American phone number. NPAs are more commonly known as area codes.

NXX number — A prefix that represents a line's central office prefix, the NXX comes after the NPA in the North American Numbering Plan.

octet — One of the four 8-bit bytes that are separated by periods and together make up an IP version 4 address.

ohm — A measure of resistance.

ohmmeter — An instrument used to measure the resistance of a circuit.

Ohm's Law — A principle of electricity that states that the amount of current flowing in an electric circuit is directly proportional to the voltage and inversely proportional to the resistance. Ohm's Law is named after German scientist Georg Simon Ohm.

off-hook — A telecommunications term that means the condition of the line when a telephone handset is lifted, or taken off its hook. An off-hook condition closes the local line circuit, causing a small amount of current to flow over the line.

omni-directional antenna — A type of antenna that transmits and receives wireless signals with equal strength and clarity in all directions. This type of antenna is used when many different receivers must be able to pick up the signal or when the receiver's location is highly mobile. TV and radio stations use omni-directional antennas, as do most towers that transmit cellular telephone signals.

on-hook — A telecommunications term that means the condition of the line when a telephone handset is resting on its hook. While a telephone is on-hook, its local line circuit cannot be closed.

one-to-many — A type of communication in which one source simultaneously sends a message to multiple destinations.

one-to-one — A type of communication in which one source sends a message to only one destination.

open shortest path first (OSPF) — A routing protocol that makes up for some of the limitations of RIP and can coexist with RIP on a network.

Optical Carrier (OC) level — An international standard used to describe SONET (or SDH) rings according to their maximum throughput.

optical loss — The extent to which a light signal weakens over distance on a fiber optic network.

optical switch — A device that connects an optical line with another optical line to switch lightwaves, or that connects an optical line with a line that uses electrical signaling.

optical time domain reflectometer (OTDR) — A time domain reflectometer specifically made for use with fiber optic networks. It works by issuing a light-based signal on a fiber optic cable and measuring the way in which the signal bounces back (or reflects) to the OTDR.

oscillation — A type of wave motion in which the amplitude of the wave varies regularly as time passes. Oscillation is present in AC current, analog signals, and other natural phenomena.

oscilloscope — An instrument that measures the change in voltage over time (or oscillation) on an AC circuit or an analog signal.

OSI (Open Systems Interconnection) model — A model for understanding and developing computer-to-computer communication developed in the 1980s by ISO. It divides networking architecture into seven layers: Physical, Data Link, Network, Transport, Session, Presentation, and Application.

organizationally unique identifier (OUI) — *See* Block ID.

overhead — The non-data information that must accompany data in order for a signal to be properly routed and interpreted by the network. When all other factors are equal, the more overhead a transmission requires, the longer it will take to reach its destination.

out-of-band signaling — A technique in which signals between switches, including all status and routing information, are communicated over a separate path on the network than voice signals use. Out-of-band signaling offers greater security and reduced call setup time than if signaling were carried over voice network paths.

outside plant — The system of cabling, poles, towers, and other connectivity equipment between the demarcation point and central offices (in other words, the physical components that make up the local loop).

packet — A small group of data organized according to standards. Packets are used in packet switching.

Packet Internet Groper (PING) — A TCP/IP troubleshooting utility that can verify that TCP/IP is installed, bound to the NIC, configured correctly, and communicating with the network. PING uses ICMP to send echo request and echo reply messages that determine the validity of an IP address.

packet-filtering firewall — A router that operates at the Data Link and Transport layers of the OSI model, examining the header of every packet of data that it receives to determine whether that type of packet is authorized to continue to its destination.

packet sniffer — *See* sniffer.

packet switching — A method of switching in which data are separated into packets before they are transported. Packets are free to travel any path on the network to their destination, because each packet contains a destination address and information about where its data belongs in the data stream. Packets are reassembled in their proper order at the receiving end.

pair gain — The consolidation of multiple telephone circuits through multiplexing techniques. In DLC systems, pair gain occurs at the remote terminal.

partial mesh — A physical topology that usually applies to WANs in which only some nodes are directly connected to other nodes. Partial mesh networks are more economical than full-mesh networks, in which every node is directly connected to every other node.

passive device — An electronic component that contributes no power gain to a circuit; in other words, it does not modify the current or voltage it receives from the power source.

passive hub — A hub that simply accepts and retransmits signals over the network.

patch cable — A relatively short section (usually between 3 and 50 feet) of copper or fiber optic cabling, with connectors on both ends. Patch cables may be used to connect patch panels with connectivity devices or to connect a networked node to a data outlet on the wall, for instance.

patch cord — *See* patch cable.

patch panel — A wall-mounted panel of data receptors into which cross-connect patch cables from the punch-down block are inserted.

pay telephone (pay phone) — A telephone provided for public use that requires coin, collect, or credit card payment to complete telephone calls.

PC Card — *See* PCMCIA.

PCMCIA — An interface developed in the early 1990s by the Personal Computer Memory Card

International Association to provide a standard interface for connecting any type of device to a portable computer. PCMCIA slots may hold modem cards, network interface cards, external hard disk cards, or CD-ROM cards. PCMCIA cards are also known as PC Cards or credit card adapters.

peering — An arrangement between network service providers in which they directly link their networks and exchange Internet traffic over those links.

performance tester — A handheld device that not only checks for cable continuity, but also ensures that the cable length is not excessive, measures the distance to a cable fault, measures attenuation along a cable, measures crosstalk between wires, issues pass/fail ratings for wiring standards, and stores and prints cable testing results. Also known as a cable tester.

Peripheral Component Interconnect (PCI) — A 32-, 64-, or 128-bit bus introduced in its original form in the 1990s. The PCI bus is the network adapter connection type used for nearly all new PCs. It's characterized by a shorter length than ISA, MCA, or EISA cards, but has a much faster data transmission capability.

personal area network (PAN) — A mobile wireless network that connects multiple personal communications devices (such as cordless telephones, computers, peripherals, and pagers) within a small geographical area, such as a home. PANs are distinguished from WLANs by a shorter range and a lower maximum throughput.

personal communication — The sharing of information between humans.

personal communication service (PCS) — A category of digital mobile wireless services—including telephony and paging—that uses the 1900 MHz (1.9 GHz) frequency band.

phase — The relationship between a wave's cycle (specifically, the point in the cycle when the wave crosses the zero voltage line) and time.

phase distortion — *See* delay distortion.

phase modulation — A method of modulation in which an information wave is applied to a carrier wave to modify the carrier wave's phase. Phase modulation is used to transmit color information in TV signals and for other specialized functions.

phase shift keying (PSK) — A method by which analog, phase modulated waves are transformed into digital signals. In PSK, changes in phase indicate a change in the value of bits to either 1 or 0.

phone phreak — A person who manipulates telephone connections or resources to his advantage. For example, a phone phreak could obtain the phone number to a PBX's maintenance port and, by dialing into that port with a modem, launch a denial-of-service attack to prevent the PBX from processing legitimate call traffic.

phreaker — *See* phone phreak.

physical address — *See* MAC address.

Physical layer — The lowest, or first, layer of the OSI model. The Physical layer contains the physical networking media, such as cabling and connectors.

physical topology — The physical layout of a network. A physical topology depicts a network in broad scope; it does not specify devices, connectivity methods, or addresses on the network. Physical topologies are categorized into three fundamental geometric shapes: bus, ring, and star. These shapes can be mixed to create hybrid topologies.

pinouts — The individual wire terminations within a connector.

Plain Old Telephone System (POTS) — *See* Public Switched Telephone Network.

plenum — The area above the ceiling tile or below the subfloor in a building.

plug — *See* connector.

point of presence — A carrier's facility, where they typically have either a switch or router to connect to a network.

point-to-point — Communication on a network that involves one source and one destination.

Point-to-Point Protocol (PPP) — A communications protocol that enables a workstation to connect to a server using a serial connection. PPP can support multiple Network layer protocols, can use both asynchronous and synchronous communications, and does not require much (if any) configuration on the client workstation.

Point-to-Point Tunneling Protocol (PPTP) — A Layer 2 protocol developed by Microsoft that encapsulates PPP so that any type of data can traverse the Internet masked as pure IP transmissions. PPTP supports the encryption, authentication, and LAN access services provided by RAS. Instead of users having to dial directly into an access server, they can dial into their ISP using PPTP and gain access to their corporate LAN over the Internet.

port — The address on a host where an application makes itself available to incoming data.

Post Office Protocol (POP) — An Application layer protocol used to retrieve e-mail messages from a mail server. When a client retrieves mail via POP, messages are downloaded to the client workstation and then deleted from the mail server.

power — In an electrical circuit, a multiple of the circuit's current and voltage (in other words, voltage x current = power). Power is measured in watts.

Presentation layer — The sixth layer of the OSI model. The Presentation layer serves as a translator between the application and the network. Here data is formatted in a schema that the network can understand, with the format varying according to the type of network used. The Presentation layer also manages data encryption and decryption, such as the scrambling of system passwords.

Pretty Good Privacy (PGP) — A key-based encryption system for e-mail that uses a two-step verification process.

PRI (Primary Rate Interface) — A type of ISDN that uses 23 bearer channels and one 64-Kbps data channel as represented by the following notation: 23B+D. PRI is less commonly used by individual subscribers than BRI, but it may be used by businesses and other organizations needing more throughput.

print server — A type of server that manages printers and print services on a network.

print services — The functions of a network that allow printers to be shared by several users on the network.

privacy — A feature standard in most private switching systems that prevents other parties from picking up a line that is in use.

private branch exchange (PBX) — A private switching system owned and operated by a business or other organization that connects multiple phone lines within an organization to one or more central offices. You can think of a PBX as a miniature CO. It provides call setup and routing within an organization, plus a host of enhanced features.

private key encryption — A type of key encryption in which the sender and receiver have private keys, which only they know. Data encryption standard (DES), which was developed by IBM in the 1970s, is a popular example of a private key encryption technique. Private key encryption is also known as symmetric encryption.

private line — A connection defined by two endpoints that is available exclusively for use by the customer who leases the line. T-carriers are examples of private lines.

private switching — A method of switching in which calls within an organization are completed independent of the local telephone company's CO. Private switching enables organizations to set up and route internal calls at a much lower cost.

private switching system — A means of routing calls from source to destination independent from the telephone company's facilities. A private-switching system may interact with a public-switching system. Or, in the case of one employee calling another employee within the same building, they may never connect with the telephone company's facilities.

probe — *See* tone locator.

promiscuous mode — A setting that allows a NIC to indiscriminately accept all packets traversing the network channel to which it is attached, not only those packets destined for it.

propagation delay — The difference in time between a data packet's transmission and its reception over a specific route. Propagation delay depends mostly on the distance between the sender and receiver.

proposed standard — A type of RFC (or Internet document) that describes a technology that has been proposed in an Internet draft but has not yet been proven as an Internet standard.

protocol — The rules a network uses to transfer data. Protocols ensure that data is transferred whole, in sequence, and without error from one node on the network to another.

proton — An atomic subparticle found at the center of an atom, which carries a positive charge.

proxy server — A network host that runs a proxy service. Proxy servers may also be called gateways.

proxy service — A software application on a network host that acts as an intermediary between the external and internal networks, screening all incoming and outgoing traffic and providing one address to the outside world, instead of revealing the addresses of internal LAN devices.

public key encryption — A form of key encryption in which data is encrypted using two keys: one is a key known only to a user and the other is a key associated with the user that can be obtained from a public source, such as a public-key server. Some examples of public-key algorithms include RSA (named after its creators, Rivest, Shamir, and Adleman), Diffie-Hellman, and Elliptic-curve cryptography. Public key encryption is also known as asymmetric encryption.

public-key server — A publicly available host (such as an Internet host) that provides free access to a list of users' public keys (for use in public key encryption).

Public Service Commission (PSC) — A state regulatory agency responsible for setting intrastate telecommunications policy. PSCs are known as Public Utilities Commission (PUC) or the state Commerce Commission in some states.

Public Switched Telephone Network (PSTN) — The collection of local and long distance providers' switching facilities and networks that are available for public voice communications, also known as the Plain Old Telephone System (POTS).

public switching system — A means of routing calls and interconnecting telephone subscribers across the PSTN.

Public Utilities Commission (PUC) — *See* Public Service Commission.

pulse amplitude modulation (PAM) — The assembly of multiple analog wave samples to create a wave that approximates the original wave.

pulse code modulation (PCM) — The process of converting analog signals into digital signals.

punch-down blocks — An array of small metallic clips (or receptors) that accept wire terminations.

PVC (private virtual circuit) — A point-to-point connection over which data may follow any number of different paths, as opposed to a dedicated line that follows a predefined path. X.25, frame relay, and some forms of ATM use PVCs.

quad wire — *See* Level 1.

Quality of Service (QoS) — The result of standards for delivering data within a certain period of time after its transmission. For example, ATM networks can supply four QoS levels, from a "best effort" attempt for noncritical data to a guaranteed, real-time transmission for time-sensitive data.

quantizing — The process of converting the sampled amplitude of an analog wave into its binary equivalent.

rack — A heavy metal frame designed to hold equipment (such as switches) and keep equipment stable.

radiation pattern — A representation of the relative strength over a three-dimensional area of all the electromagnetic energy the antenna sends or receives.

radio frequency interference (RFI) — A form of noise, or waves that emanate from electrical devices or cables carrying electricity. RFI may also be caused by strong broadcast signals from radio or TV towers.

Real-Time Transport Protocol (RTP) — A Transport-layer protocol used with voice and video transmission. RTP operates on top of UDP and provides information about packet sequence to help receiving nodes detect delay and packet loss. It also assigns packets a timestamp that corresponds to when the data in the packet was sampled from the voice or video stream. This timestamp helps the receiving node synchronize incoming data.

reassembly — The process of reconstructing data units that have been segmented.

receiver — A device that captures a message from the communications channel and converts it into a form that the destination can understand. May also be called a decoder.

redundancy — The practice of using more than one component to guard against outages (or failures).

reflection — In wireless transmission, the bouncing back of an electromagnetic wave (and signal) toward its source. A wireless signal will bounce off objects whose dimensions are large compared to the signal's average wavelength. In addition, signals reflect more readily off conductive materials, like metal, than insulators, like concrete.

regeneration — The process of retransmitting digital signals in their original, pure form. Regeneration is used by repeaters to compensate for attenuation.

Regional Bell Operating Companies (RBOCs) — The seven local phone service carriers created from the 22 former Bell Operating Companies as part of the MFJ that broke up AT&T in 1984. These seven new companies were called: NYNEX, Bell Atlantic, Bell South, Ameritech, Southwestern Bell Corporation, US West, and Pacific Telesis.

Regional Internet Registry (RIR) — A not-for-profit agency that manages the distribution of IP addresses to private and public entities. ARIN is the RIR for North, Central, and South America and sub-Saharan Africa. APNIC is the RIR for Asia and the Pacific region. RIPE is the RIR for Europe and North Africa.

regional office — A Class 3 central office. Regional offices service large regions of the country and handle toll calls from tandem COs.

regulated monopoly — A company that is allowed to exist without competition, but is subject to a great deal of constraints dictated by the government.

relay center — A centralized call center with live operators who translate input typed into a TDD for the non hearing-impaired party, listen to the response, then type the response for reception by the hearing-impaired party's TDD.

relay rack — *See* rack. (The term "relay rack" is more commonly used in the telephony field, because of the rack's role in relaying cables from the cable vault to the switching equipment.)

remote access server — A specialized server that enables remote clients to log onto a LAN.

Remote Access Service (RAS) — One of the simplest dial-in servers. This software is included with Windows 2000 Server. Note that "RAS" is pronounced *razz*.

remote access services — *See* communications services.

remote control — A remote access method in which the remote user dials into a workstation that is directly attached to the network. Software running on both the remote user's computer and the network computer allows the remote user to "take over" the networked workstation.

remote node — A client that has dialed directly into a LAN's remote access server. The LAN treats a remote node like any other client on the LAN, allowing the remote user to perform the same functions he or she could perform while in the office.

remote subscriber terminal — *See* remote terminal.

remote terminal — In a DLC system, the point at which circuits from many incoming wires are multiplexed into one or more digital connections (for example, a T-1) before connecting to a LEC's central office terminal. Remote terminals are located either outdoors in an environmentally-protected cabinet or in a pole-mounted enclosure, or sometimes, inside the customer premises.

remote user — A person working on a computer in a different geographical location from the LAN's server.

repeater — A device inserted at intervals in the communications channel that regenerates a digital signal or amplifies an analog signal that has been degraded by attenuation.

reseller — A type of telecommunications carrier that leases links or other facilities in wholesale amounts from another carrier and resells the service to consumers under its name.

resistance — The opposition to electric current. Resistance is a fundamental property of conductors that depends on the conductor's structure and size. It is also caused by loads or resistors in a circuit. Resistance is measured in ohms.

resistor — A passive electronic device that is inserted into a circuit to provide a specific amount of resistance and thus help control current.

resolver — Any host on the Internet that needs to look up domain name information to resolve a name with an IP address.

resource record — The element of a DNS database stored on a name server that contains information about TCP/IP host names and their addresses.

Resource Reservation Protocol (RSVP) — As specified in RFC 2205, a QoS technique that attempts to reserve a specific amount of network resources for a transmission before the transmission occurs. Of the three major QoS techniques, RSVP is the most complex.

resources — The programs, data, data storage space, and devices (such as printers or fax machines) that are shared on a network and managed by servers.

return loss — The loss of signal strength due to the reflection of prior signals along the same communications channel. One cause of return loss is a change in impedance.

reverse path — In cellular networks, transmission from a base station to a mobile station.

RFC (Request for Comments) — A numbered document that articulates some aspect of Internet or TCP/IP technology. Many different types of RFCs exist. Some are official standards, whereas others simply describe best practices or proposed standards. A searchable index of RFCs can be found at IETF's RFC editor site, *www.rfc-editor.org*.

ring — The wire in a telephone wire pair that carries a negative charge (48 V) from the central office's battery to a telephone.

ring topology — A network layout in which each node is connected to the two nearest nodes so that the entire network forms a circle. Data is transmitted unidirectionally around the ring. Each workstation accepts and responds to packets addressed to it, then forwards the other packets to the next workstation in the ring.

ringback — A repeating pattern of combined 440 Hz plus 480 Hz tones that ring for two seconds, then are followed by a four-second silence. Ringback is issued by an end office telephone switch. Ringback is also known as ringing tone.

ringer — The device that sounds a bell or tone on a subscriber's telephone to indicate an incoming call.

ringing tone — *See* ringback.

risers — The backbone cabling that provides vertical connections between floors of a building.

risk assessment — A thorough analysis of an organization's vulnerability to security breaches and an identification of its potential losses, should a breach occur.

RJ-11 (registered jack number 11) — The jack used to terminate two- or three-pair telephone connections.

RJ-45 (registered jack-45) — The standard connector used for modern twisted-pair cables such as CAT5.

root server — A DNS server maintained by ICANN that is an authority on how to contact the top-level domains, such as those ending with .com, .edu, .net, .us, and so on. ICANN maintains 13 root servers around the world.

rotary — A dialing scheme in which the turning and releasing of a numbered wheel alternately opens and closes the local loop circuit, issuing a series of pulses as the dial returns to its position. The local central office's switch can translate those pulses into numbers. Rotary dialing was replaced by touch-tone dialing in the late twentieth century.

round trip time (RTT) — The length of time it takes for a packet to go from sender to receiver, then back from receiver to sender. RTT is typically expressed in milliseconds.

routable — Term used to refer to protocols that can span more than one LAN segment because they carry Network layer and addressing information that can be interpreted by a router.

route — To direct data between networks based on addressing, patterns of usage, and availability of network segments.

router — A multiport connectivity device that operates at the Network layer of the OSI model and can connect dissimilar LANs and WANs running at different transmission speeds and using a variety of protocols. One of a router's most important functions is to determine the best path for data transmission between nodes. To do this, routers communicate with each other via routing protocols, such as OSPF and BGP. Routers are protocol-dependent devices.

routing information protocol (RIP) — The oldest routing protocol that is still widely used. RIP does not work in very large network environments in which data may have to travel through more than 16 routers to reach its destination (for example, on the Internet). In addition, compared to other routing protocols, RIP is slower and less secure.

routing protocols — The means by which routers communicate with each other about network status. Routing protocols help routers determine the best path for data to take between nodes. Examples of routing protocols include RIP, OSPF, EIGRP, and BGP. Note that routing protocols are different from routable network protocols, such as TCP/IP or IPX/SPX.

routing switch — Another term for a Layer 3 or Layer 4 switch. A routing switch comprises a hybrid between a router and a switch and can therefore interpret data from Layer 2 and either Layer 3 or Layer 4.

RTS/CTS (Request to send/Clear to send) — A method of hardware flow control used in communication between modems and between a modem and a computer, for example. In RTS/CTS, modems use their interface to a computer to send flow control information. In other words, this information is not combined with the data stream exchanged between devices.

runt — A packet fragment. Runts may be caused by collisions or other data transmission errors.

runway — An overhead tray designed to hold cables.

Rural Area Network Design (RAND) — The method of organizing outside plant in rural areas according to a distribution scheme, in which individual lines aggregate into pools of local lines, which aggregate into larger conduits, which together feed into a central office.

sampling — The process of measuring the amplitude of an analog wave at regular, multiple instants to generate an approximation of that wave in digital form.

sampling rate — The number of samples of an analog wave's amplitude taken each second in order to create a digital representation of the wave. For example, the sampling rate of an audio CD is 44,100 samples per second.

scalability — The ease with which a system or network can be extended, including adding length, nodes, or functions.

scattering — In wireless transmission, the diffusion, or the reflection in multiple different directions, of a signal. Scattering occurs when a wireless signal encounters an object that has small dimensions compared to the signal's wavelength. Scattering is also related to the roughness of the surface a wireless signal encounters. The rougher the surface, the more likely a signal is to scatter when it hits that surface.

SDH (Synchronous Digital Hierarchy) — The international equivalent of SONET.

second generation (2G) — A mobile wireless technology developed in the 1990s that allows multiple signals access to a limited band of frequencies. 2G also uses digital encoding, which improves the signal quality and allows for encryption. TDMA and CDMA are examples of 2G technology.

segment — Part of a network that shares a fixed amount of capacity and is logically separate from other parts of the network. Layer 2 and Layer 3 devices such as bridges, switches and routers separate network segments, but Layer 1 devices, such as hubs, extend network segments.

segmentation — The process of decreasing the size of data units when moving data from a network segment that can handle larger data units to a network segment that can handle only smaller data units.

seizure — The request for service signal that is transmitted to the local switch when a subscriber takes her handset off-hook and closes the local line circuit.

self-healing — A characteristic of dual-ring topologies that allows them to automatically reroute traffic along the backup ring if the primary ring becomes severed.

semaphore — A type of signaling in which visual cues (for example, flags) represent symbols, such as letters. The word semaphore comes from the Greek *sema*, which means "signal" and *phoros*, which means "carrying".

semiconductor — A material (such as silicon) that has some ability to conduct electricity. A semiconductor conducts electricity better than an insulator, but not as well as a conductor.

Sequenced Packet Exchange (SPX) — A core protocol in the IPX/SPX suite. SPX belongs to the Transport layer of the OSI model and works in tandem with IPX to ensure that data are received whole, in sequence, and error free.

sequencing — The process of assigning a placeholder to each piece of a data block to allow the receiving node's Transport layer to reassemble the data in the correct order.

Serial Line Internet Protocol (SLIP) — A communications protocol that enables a workstation to connect to a server using a serial connection. SLIP can support only asynchronous communications and IP traffic and requires some configuration on the client workstation.

server — A computer on the network that manages shared resources. Servers usually have more processing power, memory, and hard disk space than clients. They run network operating software that can manage not only data, but also users, groups, security, and applications on the network.

server_hello — In the context of SSL encryption, a message issued from the server to the client that confirms the information the server received in the client_hello message and agrees to certain terms of encryption based on the options the client supplied. Depending on the Web server's preferred encryption method, the server may choose to issue your browser a public key or a digital certificate at this time.

service area interface (SAI) — A cabinet in which multiple wires from a limited geographical area terminate. SAIs are also known as *terminal boxes*, or colloquially as "terminals," "boxes," or "cabinets."

service control points (SCP) — Databases that store information about customer preferences, which are used in SS7 signaling.

service provider — A company that provides the communication channel for voice, video, or data transmission.

service switching points (SSP) — Central switches, as defined in the SS7 signaling protocol, or any telecommunications switching facility, according to ITU standards.

services — The features provided by a network.

serving area — The geographical boundary that includes all of a central office's or a carrier's subscribers.

Serving Area Concepts (SAC) — The method of organizing outside plant in suburban and urban areas according to a distribution scheme, in which individual lines aggregate into pools of local lines, which aggregate into larger conduits, which together feed into a central office.

session — A connection for data exchange between two parties. The term "session" is most often used in the context of terminal and mainframe communications.

Session Initiation Protocol (SIP) — A protocol suite codified by the IETF (in RFC 2543) as a set of Session-layer signaling and control protocols for multiservice, packet-based networks. With few exceptions, SIP performs much the same functions as the H.323 signaling protocols perform. SIP was developed as a more efficient alternative to H.323 before H.323 was revised to expedite its call setup functions. Although SIP is more efficient, because it was released later, it has never enjoyed the same widespread usage as H.323.

Session layer — The fifth layer in the OSI model. The Session layer establishes and maintains communication between two nodes on the network. It can be considered the "traffic cop" for network communications.

session negotiation — A process through which two modems establish rules for communication, including what type of compression, flow control, and error control schemes they will use.

shared Ethernet — An implementation of Ethernet in which all nodes on a segment share the same communications channel. Thus, nodes on a shared Ethernet network compete for use of a fixed amount of bandwidth.

sheath — The outer cover, or jacket, of a cable.

shielded twisted-pair (STP) — A type of cable containing twisted wire pairs that are not only individually insulated, but also surrounded by a shielding made of a metallic substance such as foil. The shielding acts as an antenna, converting the noise into current (assuming that the wire is properly grounded). This current induces an equal, yet opposite current in the twisted pairs it surrounds. The noise on the shielding mirrors the noise on the twisted pairs, and the two cancel each other out.

shielding — The metallic substance that surrounds an insulated copper wire in shielded twisted-pair cabling.

signal — A method for representing information in order to convey the information from one entity (such as a person or computer) to another. A signal may be formed by manipulating an electric current.

signal bounce — A phenomenon in which signals travel endlessly between the two ends of a bus network. Using 50-ohm resistors at either end of the network prevents signal bounce.

signal level — An ANSI standard for T-carrier technology that refers to its Physical layer electrica signaling characteristics. DS0 (Digital Signal, Level 0) is the equivalent of one data or voice channel. All other signal levels are multiples of DS0.

signal-to-noise ratio (SNR) — The relationship between the strength (or amplitude) of a signal and noise affecting the signal. The higher the signal-to-noise ratio, the clearer the signal.

signal transfer point (STP) — An intermediate switch on a CCS network that handles signals from one switch to another. In SS7, STPs handle signals between SSPs and SCPs.

signaling — (1) The exchange of information between the components of a telephony system for the purposes of establishing, monitoring, or releasing phone circuits, as well as controlling system operations. (2) The movement of signals, or electrical charges that represent encoded information, along a communications channel.

Signaling System No. 7 (SS7) — An ITU standard specifying how switches should exchange alert, addressing, supervisory, and transmission information over a digital network. SS7 is a type of CCS employed on modern telephony networks.

Simple Mail Transfer Protocol (SMTP) — The protocol responsible for moving messages from one e-mail server to another over the Internet and other TCP/IP-based networks.

Simple Network Management Protocol (SNMP) — A communication protocol used to manage devices on a TCP/IP network.

simplex — A form of communication in which messages can only travel in one direction.

single-mode fiber — A type of fiber optic cable with a narrow core that carries light pulses along a single data path from one end of the cable to the other end. Data can be transmitted faster and for longer distances on single-mode fiber than on multimode fiber. Single-mode fiber is extremely expensive.

sniffer — A computer that, once connected to a network, can capture data packets traveling over the channel to which it is attached. Sniffers are useful troubleshooting tools, but hackers can also use them to intercept and interpret data traffic.

social engineering — The manipulation of social relationships to obtain information (for example, a password) that could grant an intruder access to restricted resources.

socket — A logical address assigned to a specific process running on a computer. Some sockets are reserved for operating system functions.

softphone — A computer programmed to act like an IP telephone. Softphones present the caller with a graphical representation of a telephone dial pad. Softphones can connect to a network via LAN, WAN, PPP dial-up connection, or a leased line. When installed on laptops or home computers, they offer the unique advantage of mobility for travelers and telecommuters.

softswitch — A computer or group of computers that manages packet-based traffic routing and control. Softswitches also typically handle call accounting services and may provide signaling gateway services to translate between SS7 and packet-based network signaling protocols.

software flow control — A method of gauging the rate at which two modems can exchange data that incorporates flow control information within the data stream. The main disadvantage to using software flow control is that noise on the line or corrupt data can inadvertently generate a command character (such as the Ctrl-S) and interfere with flow control. Xon/Xoff is a type of software flow control.

SONET (Synchronous Optical Network) — A WAN technology that provides data transfer rates ranging from 64 Kbps to 39.8 Gbps using the same time division multiplexing technique used by T-carriers. SONET is characterized by its dual fiber optic ring topology, which makes it highly fault tolerant. Internationally, SONET is known as SDH.

source — In the communication process, the originator of a message or data.

source-route bridging — A bridging technique in which a bridge polls the network to determine a packet's best path between nodes, then adds this path information to the data packet. Source-route bridging is used on most Token Ring networks and on WANs on which multiple bridges and long routes are common.

space division switching — A technique for switching calls that manipulates the physical space between two lines, thereby closing a circuit. Space division switching was electromechanical and required that the switch be dedicated to a connection until the subscriber terminated the call.

spanning tree algorithm — A routine that can detect circular bridging patterns on a network (such as those possible when using transparent bridging) and modify the way multiple bridges work together to avoid such patterns.

splice — The physical joining of two facing and aligned wires or fibers. Most often, a splice refers to the connection of two fibers to form one continuous fiber optic communications channel.

spread spectrum — A method of transmission in which a signal is separated and its separate pieces distributed over a wide range of frequencies. Using spread spectrum in wireless transmission is more secure than using a single frequency.

SSL (Secure Sockets Layer) — A method of encrypting TCP/IP transmissions—including Web pages and data entered into Web forms—en route between the client and server using public key encryption technology.

SSL session — In the context of SSL encryption, an association between the client and server that is defined by an agreement on a specific set of encryption techniques. An SSL session allows the client and server to continue to exchange data securely as long as the client is still connected to the server. SSL sessions are established by the SSL handshake protocol.

standalone workstation — A computer that uses programs and data only from its local disks and that is not connected to a network.

standards — Documented agreements containing technical specifications or other precise criteria that stipulate how a particular product or service should be designed or performed.

star topology — A physical topology in which every node on the network is connected through a central device, such as a hub. Any single physical wire on a star network connects only two devices, so a cabling problem affects only two nodes. Nodes transmit data to the hub, which then retransmits the data to the rest of the network segment where the destination node can pick it up.

star-wired bus topology — A hybrid topology in which groups of workstations are connected in a star fashion to hubs that are connected with each other via a single bus. This topology forms the basis of most modern Ethernet networks.

star-wired ring topology — A hybrid topology that uses the physical layout of a star and the token-passing data transmission method. This topology forms the basis of most modern Token Ring networks.

static electricity — The sudden transfer of an accumulated charge from one material to another.

station equipment — Any type of telephone and its ancillary parts.

station message detail recording (SMDR) — A method used by PBXs for recording and printing call details for each connected station, such as the caller's and the call recipient's identification, when the call was made, how long the call lasted, and so on.

station restriction — A feature available in most private switching systems that can prevent specific telephones from making certain types of calls or using certain features.

station protector — A device attached to incoming LEC lines at the network interface that prevents a customer's telephone equipment from being damaged in case excessive current affects the line.

static IP address — An IP address that is manually assigned to a device.

static routing — A technique in which a network administrator manually programs a router to use specific paths between nodes. Because it does not account for occasional network congestion, failed connections, or device moves, static routing is not optimal.

statistical multiplexing — A method of multiplexing that assigns a separate time slot for each node according to priority and need.

straight-through cable — A twisted-pair patch cable in which the wire terminations in both connectors follow the same scheme.

step-by-step switch — An automatic telephone switch developed by Almon Strowger in 1889. The step-by-step switch used a cylinder with an arm that brushed against rows of electrical contacts in a ratcheting motion. The movement of the arm was controlled directly by pulses that were issued by a subscriber's telephone.

store and forward mode — A method of switching in which a switch reads the entire data frame into its memory and checks it for accuracy before transmitting it. Although this method is more time consuming than the cut-through method, it allows store and forward switches to transmit data more accurately.

structured cabling — A method for uniform, enterprise-wide, multivendor cabling systems specified by the TIA/EIA 568 Commercial Building Wiring Standard. Structured cabling is based on a hierarchical design using a high-speed backbone.

subnets — In an internetwork, the individual networks that are joined together by routers.

subprotocols — Small, specialized protocols that work together and belong to a protocol suite.

subscriber — A telephone company customer (so called because they subscribe to telephone service).

subscriber line interface circuit (SLIC) — A component inside an end office telephone switch that provides battery power to a subscriber's line and detects when the telephone handset is off-hook.

subscriber loop signaling — The exchange of information about a telephone circuit over the local loop. Many of these signals contain information about the local loop's status.

SVC (switched virtual circuit) — Logical, point-to-point connections that rely on switches to determine the optimal path between sender and receiver. ATM and frame relay are examples of technology that use SVCs.

switch — (1) An electronic or electromechanical device that can open and close a circuit. (2) A character or combination of characters that follows a command and instructs the command to format its results in a specific way. (3) A connectivity device on data networks that logically subdivides a network into smaller, individual collision domains. A switch operates at the Data Link layer of the OSI model and can interpret MAC address information to determine whether to filter (discard) or forward packets it receives.

switch hook — The device that holds a handset and closes a switch when the handset is lifted to complete the local loop circuit. In modern telephony, depressing and releasing switch hooks may

provide additional functions, such as accepting an incoming call while using the call waiting feature.

switched Ethernet — An Ethernet model that enables multiple nodes to simultaneously transmit and receive data and individually take advantage of more bandwidth because they are assigned separate logical network segments through switching.

switching — A method of establishing connections and sending information between nodes on a network. Switching is used in both voice and data communications, and until very recently, telephony switching was quite different from data network switching. The three fundamental types of switching are: circuit switching, message switching, and packet switching.

switching matrix — The internal connections between input and output circuits of a switch (may also be called switching fabric).

switching system — The collection of hardware and software that establishes connections between lines and trunks to complete calls.

symmetric encryption — A method of encryption that requires the same key to encode the data as is used to decode the cipher text.

symmetrical — A characteristic of transmission technology that provides equal throughput for data traveling both upstream and downstream and is suited to users who both upload and download significant amounts of data.

symmetrical DSL — A variation of DSL that provides equal throughput both upstream and downstream between the customer and the carrier.

synchronous — A communications method in which data is transmitted in a continuous stream of bits. To interpret this data stream, nodes must conform to a timing scheme.

System Identification Number (SID) — A number assigned to the particular wireless carrier that the telephone's user has subscribed to. Thus, a SID indicates, for example, whether a subscriber's telephone number and equipment used U. S. Cellular's, Verizon's, AT&T's, or Sprint's wireless network.

T1 — A T-carrier technology that provides 1.544 Mbps throughput and 24 channels for voice, data, video, or audio signals. T1s may use shielded or unshielded twisted-pair, coaxial cable, fiber-optic, or microwave links. Businesses commonly use T1s to connect to their ISP, and phone companies typically use at least one T1 to connect their central offices.

T3 — A T-carrier technology that can carry the equivalent of 672 channels for voice, data, video, or audio, with a maximum data throughput of 44.736 Mbps (typically rounded up to 45 Mbps for purposes of discussion). T3s require either fiber-optic or microwave transmission media.

T.37 — An ITU standard that specifies a store-and-forward method of transmitting faxes from one network node to another across a packet-switched network. In T.37, faxes are attached to e-mail messages as TIFF files, then forwarded to a fax/e-mail gateway. The gateway forwards the message to the destination's fax/e-mail gateway, where it is stored until the recipient retrieves it.

T.38 — An ITU standard that specifies a real-time method of transmitting faxes from one node to another across a packet-switched network. In T.38, fax client software or IP fax machines convert faxes to packets, then transmit them to a sending fax gateway. The sending fax gateway transmits them across a network (such as the Internet) to the appropriate receiving fax gateway.

T-carrier — Term used to refer to any kind of leased line that follows the standards for T1s, fractional T1s, T1Cs, T2s, T3s, or T4s.

tag — A formatting indicator used in HTML.

tandem office — *See* tandem switching center.

tandem switch — A switch that handles calls between central offices. Tandem switches operate at any type of CO other than a Class 5. ILECs, CLECs, and IXCs own and operate tandem switches.

tandem switching center — An exchange where lines from multiple local switching centers converge and terminate.

TCP — *See* Transmission Control Protocol.

TCP/IP — *See* Transmission Control Protocol/Internet Protocol.

TCP segment — The portion of a TCP/IP packet that holds TCP data fields and becomes encapsulated by the IP datagram.

TCP/IP core protocols — The TCP/IP subprotocols that belong to the Network layer and upon which higher layer protocols rely.

TDD (Telecommunications Device for the Deaf) — A specially designed device that uses a TTY and a visual interface to help speech- and hearing-impaired people communicate over the PSTN.

TDMA (time division multiple access) — A cellular network access technology that divides each channel into multiple time slots and assigns different signals the use of different time slots, thereby conserving the limited number of frequencies in the cellular spectrum.

telecommunication — Communication that spans a distance.

telecommunications firewall — A type of firewall that monitors incoming and outgoing voice traffic and selectively blocks telephone calls between different areas of a voice network.

telegraph — An electromechanical device that uses a wire to convey electrical pulses that represent letters or numbers over a distance.

telemedicine — The use of voice, video, and data telecommunications to enable patients and healthcare professionals to exchange information over distances.

telephone test set — A device that resembles a telephone handset and is used by telephone technicians to verify that a line is functioning.

telephony — The study of telephone, or voice telecommunication, technology.

Telnet — A terminal emulation protocol used to log on to remote hosts using the TCP/IP protocol. Telnet resides in the Application layer of the TCP/IP suite.

tera (T) — A prefix that indicates a quantity multiplied by 2 to the 40th power (1,099,511,627,776) in the context of data transfer or storage or 10 to the 12th power (1,000,000,000,000) in the context of mathematics, physics, and electronics.

terabyte (TB) — A quantity of data equivalent to 2 to the 40th power (1,099,511,627,776) bytes (1024 gigabytes) or 1000 gigabytes, depending on the context.

terminal — A device with little (if any) of its own processing or disk capacity that depends on a host to supply it with applications and data-processing services.

terminal adapter (TA) — Devices used to convert digital signals into analog signals for use with ISDN phones and other analog devices. Terminal adapters are sometimes called ISDN modems.

terminal block — *See* punch-down block.

terminal box — *See* service area interface.

terminal equipment (TE) — Devices at a communication link's end point that provide a service. For example, on an ISDN connection, the ISDN telephone and network adapter are terminal equipment. On a LAN, the workstations and printers are terminal equipment.

termination — The place where a wire ends (for example, in a connector) or is connected with another part of the network (for example, at a punch-down block).

terminator — In the context of bus topology networks, a 50-ohm resistor used to stop a signal at the end of the bus and thereby prevent signal bounce.

thermal noise — Signal interference caused by heat and changes in temperature agitating the electrons in a wire. Thermal noise is constant and ubiquitous.

third generation (3G) — A mobile wireless technology, as yet unavailable to most subscribers, that proposes further advances on 2G technology. It features all-digital encoding, provisions for quality of service, more efficient spectrum usage, and faster transmission (at least 128 Kbps).

throughput — The amount of data that a communications channel can carry during a given time period. Throughput may also be called "capacity."

TIA (Telecommunications Industry Association) — A standards organization established in 1988 from a subgroup of the EIA and the former United States Telecommunications Suppliers Association (USTSA). TIA helps establish standards for information technology, wireless, satellite, fiber optics, and telephone equipment. It also has a special subcommittee devoted to multimedia standards development.

tie trunk — A dedicated circuit that connects two PBX systems.

time domain reflectometer (TDR) — A high-end instrument for testing the qualities of a cable. It works by issuing a signal on a cable and measuring the way in which the signal bounces back (or reflects) to the TDR.

time division multiplexing (TDM) — A method of multiplexing digital signals that assigns a time slot in the flow of communications to every node on the network and in that time slot, carries data from that node.

time division switching — A switching technique in which samples from multiple incoming lines are digitized, then each is issued to the same circuit, in sequence, at a different time interval, and finally transmitted to the correct outbound line. This method of switching did not require a continuous electromechanical connection and meant that one switch could handle hundreds of thousands of calls.

tip — The wire in a telephone wire pair that supplies the ground (or nearly zero charge) from the central office's battery to the telephone.

TLS (Transport layer security) — A version of SSL being standardized by the Internet Engineering Task Force (IETF). With TLS, IETF aims to create a version of SSL that will encrypt UDP as well as TCP transmissions. TLS, which will likely be supported by new Web browsers, uses slightly different encryption algorithms than SSL, but otherwise is very similar to the most recent version of SSL.

token — A special control frame that indicates to the rest of the network that a particular node has the right to transmit data.

token passing — A means of data transmission in which a 3-byte packet, called a token, is passed around the network in a round-robin fashion and used to arbitrate access to the network's shared channel.

toll bypass — A cost-savings benefit that results from organizations completing long-distance telephone calls over their packet-switched networks, thus bypassing tolls charged by common carriers on comparable PSTN calls.

toll fraud — The unauthorized use of a telephone line, calling card, switch, or other type of connection to complete long distance calls at another's expense.

toll office — *See* toll switching center.

toll switching center — An exchange where lines from multiple tandem switching centers converge and terminate. This facility is called a toll office because it handles long-distance, or toll, calls.

tone — *See* touch tone.

tone generator — A device that issues a tone over a cable. The combination of a tone generator and tone locator is used to identify one cable among many. It may also be called a toner. Together, a tone generator and a tone locator may also be known as a fox and hound.

tone locator — An amplifier that can detect inductive energy issued by a tone on a wire. A tone locator is used in conjunction with a tone generator to identify one cable among many.

toner — *See* tone generator.

top-level domain (TLD) — The highest-level category used to distinguish domain names—for example, .org, .com, .net. A TLD is also known as the domain suffix.

totalizer — A device inside a coin operated telephone that determines what type of coin was deposited and relays that information to the switch through pulses of brief dual-frequency tones.

touch tone — A method of dialing that uses dual-tone multifrequency encoding, in which pressing any number on the telephone keypad transmits a combination of two frequencies. These frequencies can be translated into numbers by the end office switch.

touch-tone dialing — The process of issuing a combination of two frequencies to convey a number from a telephone's keypad to a local switch.

traceroute — A TCP/IP utility that uses ICMP to trace the path from one host to another, identifying all intermediate hops between the two hosts. This utility is useful for determining router or network connectivity problems. On Windows systems, this command is known as tracert.

tracert — On Windows systems, a TCP/IP utility that uses ICMP to trace the path from one host to another, identifying all intermediate hops between the two hosts.

transceiver — A component that functions as both a transmitter and receiver. As a transmitter, the transceiver encodes a stream of data and generates signals to the transmission medium in a format that the receiver can interpret. As a receiver, the transceiver performs the opposite tasks: It accepts and decodes the stream of data. Network interface cards, for example, act as transceivers.

transformer — An electrical device that contains two electromagnetic coils and transfers electric energy from one coil to another coil through electromagnetic induction.

transformer effect — *See* mutual inductance.

transistor — An active electronic device made from a semiconducting material that allows current to overcome the resistance of a component. A transistor can be used as an amplifier or a switch.

translational bridging — A method of bridging that can connect networks that use different logical topologies (such as Ethernet and FDDI or Ethernet and Token Ring).

Transmission Control Protocol (TCP) — A core protocol of the TCP/IP suite. TCP belongs to the Transport layer and provides reliable data delivery services.

Transmission Control Protocol/Internet Protocol (TCP/IP) — A routable, flexible protocol suite that has its origins in ARPAnet, the precursor to the Internet. TCP/IP is still the protocol that all Internet traffic relies on. It is also the protocol of choice for many private LANs and WANs.

transmission media — The communication channel used to exchange information between electrical or electronic devices.

transmitter — The equipment that modifies a message (either data or voice) into the form required for transmission. May also be called an encoder.

transparent bridging — A bridging technique in which a bridge begins polling the network to learn about its physical topology as soon as the bridge is installed on the network, then adds information it learns about best paths between nodes to its filtering database. Transparent bridging is susceptible to circular traffic patterns, which can be alleviated through the use of the spanning tree algorithm.

transponder — A piece of equipment on a satellite that receives an uplinked signal from earth, amplifies the signal, modifies its frequency, then retransmits it (in a downlink) to an antenna on earth.

Transport layer — The fourth layer of the OSI model. The Transport layer is primarily responsible for ensuring that data is transferred from point A to point B reliably and without errors.

trunk — A transmission route between switches, either within one central office or between different central offices. Trunks typically have a great deal more capacity than feeders.

TTY (TeleTYpewriter) — A device invented by the Teletype Corporation that uses alphanumeric characters entered through a keyboard to communicate over a voice or data network.

tunneling — The process of encapsulating one protocol to make it appear as another type of protocol.

twist ratio — The number of twists per meter or foot in a twisted-pair cable.

twisted-pair (TP) — A type of cable similar to telephone wiring that consists of color-coded pairs of insulated copper wires, each with a diameter of 0.4 to 0.8 mm, twisted around each other and encased in plastic coating.

unguided medium — A communications channel that provides no fixed path for signals. Wireless transmission relies on the atmosphere, which is an unguided medium.

Unicode — An internationally recognized 16-bit encoding scheme developed in the early 1990s. Because Unicode can make use of 16 binary placeholders, it may represent up to 2^{16}, or up to 65,536 characters and encode the letters of many different languages.

Unicode transformation format (UTF) — The way in which a software program uses Unicode encoding.

unified communication — *See* unified messaging.

unified messaging — The combination of telephone, voice mail, e-mail, fax, and paging services so that users only need consult one source to pick up their messages.

Uniform Resource Locator (URL) — A standard means of identifying every Web page, which specifies the service used, its server's host name, and its HTML page or script name.

UNIVAC (Universal Automatic Computer) — The first computer designed for business (and not merely scientific purposes). UNIVAC became available in 1951. It weighed 16,000 pounds and performed approximately 1000 calculations per second. It was used to predict the outcome of the 1952 election based on only 1% of the total poll data. However, UNIVAC was still too large and expensive to be practical for widespread use.

universal service fund (USF) — A fund established by the Telecommunications Act of 1996 to subsidize telecommunications services in less populated areas and to which each telecommunications carrier and business user contributes a small fee on a monthly basis.

unlicensed — In the United States, a frequency that may be used by any operator without applying or paying the FCC for its use. Although unlicensed frequencies are freely available, the FCC does restrict what purposes they can be used for. Some unlicensed frequencies are the 900 MHz and 2.4 GHz bands, which are commonly used for cellular telephone service, wireless networks, and cordless telephones.

unshielded twisted-pair (UTP) — A type of cabling that consists of one or more insulated wire pairs encased in a plastic sheath. As its name implies, UTP does not contain additional shielding for the twisted pairs. As a result, UTP is both less expensive and less resistant to noise than STP.

uplink — A connection from an earth-based transmitter to an orbiting satellite. (Also, a broadcast over such a connection.) Often uplink information is scrambled (in other words, its signal is coded) before transmission to prevent unauthorized interception.

upstream — The term used to describe data traffic that flows from a customer's site to the local carrier's facility. In asymmetrical communications, upstream throughput is usually much lower than downstream throughput. In symmetrical communications, upstream and downstream throughputs are equal.

USB (universal serial bus) port — A standard external bus that can be used to connect multiple types of peripherals, including modems, mice, and network adapters to a computer. The original USB standard was capable of transmitting only 12 Mbps of data; a new standard is capable of transmitting 480 Mbps of data.

user — A person who uses a computer.

User Datagram Protocol (UDP) — A core protocol in the TCP/IP suite that sits in the Transport layer, between the Internet layer and the Application layer of the TCP/IP model. UDP is a connectionless transport service.

utility access hole — An access point to underground tunnels that house branch feeder or main feeder conduits plus other utility lines and equipment. Utility access holes are also known as manholes.

V.42 — An ITU modem standard that describes a method of error correction. V.42 is compatible with MNP4 error correction.

V.42bis — An ITU modem standard that describes a method of data compression. V.42bis is purported to achieve up to a 4:1 ratio of data compression.

V.44 — An ITU modem standard that describes a method of data compression. V.44 is purported to achieve up to a 6:1 ratio of data compression.

V.90 — An ITU modem standard, issued in February 1998, that defines 56 Kbps, asymmetrical transmission in which one of the modems is assumed to be using a digital line. This standard is appropriate for dial-up connections to access servers (for example, at an ISP). The result is an asymmetrical connection in which downstream transmission can reach up to 53 Kbps and upstream transmission can reach only 33.6 Kbps.

V.92 — The latest dial-up modem speed standard issued by the ITU in November 2000. V.92 boasts an upstream transmission rate to a maximum of 48 Kbps and a downstream transmission rate of 53 Kbps. V.92 also accomplishes fast session connections by keeping a record of previous connections and, when connecting to a familiar modem, retrieving the appropriate parameters for that modem. Also, the V.92 standard allows modems to wait "on hold" up to 16 minutes in case a user receives a call while his modem is connected. Users must have call waiting enabled with their local phone service to take advantage of this feature.

vacuum tube — A sealed container made of glass, metal, or ceramic, that contains, in a vacuum, a charged plate that transmits current to a filament.

vendor code — See Block ID.

video bridge — See multipoint control unit.

video streaming — The act of issuing video signals from a server to a client in real time.

video telecommunication — Any means of electrically transmitting moving pictures and sound across a distance, such as TV broadcasting or distributing live feeds of an event to the screens of networked computers.

video terminal — A device that enables users to watch, listen, speak, and capture their image.

videoconferencing — The real-time transmission of images and audio between two locations.

virtual address — *See* Network layer address.

virtual circuits — The connections between network nodes that, while based on potentially disparate physical links, logically appear to be direct, dedicated links between those nodes. Virtual circuits are used in frame relay and ATM technology.

virtual local area network (VLAN) — A network within a network that is logically defined by grouping its devices' switch ports in the same broadcast domain. A VLAN can consist of servers, workstations, printers, routers, or any other network device you can connect to a switch. VLANs serve to not only group nodes together, but also to exclude all other nodes from the group.

virtual private network (VPN) — A logically-constructed WAN that uses existing public transmission facilities. VPNs can be created through the use of software or combined software and hardware solutions. This type of network allows an organization to carve out a private WAN on the Internet (or, less commonly, over dedicated lines) that serves only its offices, while keeping the data secure and isolated from other (public) traffic.

vocoder — A voice encoding and decoding that applies sophisticated mathematical models to voice samples, which take into account the ways in which humans generate speech. Based on these models, vocoders predict and then synthesize the voice signal and the receiving node. This encoding technique requires fewer bits to regenerate a voice signal than a waveform codec requires to re-create

a signal. One type of vocoder is specified in the ITU G.729 standard.

voice mail — A computerized system of recording messages for later retrieval, used when a party does not answer an incoming call.

Voice over IP (VoIP) — A method of encoding and transmitting voice signals over a data network using TCP/IP. An IP telephony system may use the Internet or a private network as a communications channel.

voice over ATM (VoATM) — A service that uses the ATM network access method (and ATM cells) to transmit voice signals over a network.

voice over DSL (VoDSL) — A service that relies on a DSL connection to transmit packetized voice signals.

voice over frame relay (VoFR) — A service that relies on a frame relay connection to transmit packetized voice signals.

voice over network (VON) — A general term that refers to the transmission of voice signals over a packet-switched network. VoATM, VoDSL, VoFR, and VoIP belong to the VON category, as do voice signals issued over T-carriers, ISDN, cable, satellite, and cellular networks.

voice recognition — A feature of some computers that enables them to recognize a user's voice and respond to spoken commands. To recognize these commands, a voice recognition system needs to be "trained" to understand the user's voice patterns.

voice telecommunication — Any means of using electrical signals to transmit human voice across a distance, such as telephones and radio broadcasts.

volt (v) — A measure of voltage, or current strength.

voltage — The pressure that the electric current exerts on its conductor. Voltage is measured in volts.

voltmeter — An instrument that is connected to a circuit to measure its voltage.

Walkie-Talkie — A two-way communication device developed by Motorola that uses frequency modulation techniques.

war dialer — A computer program that dials multiple telephone numbers in rapid succession, attempting to access and receive a handshake response from a modem.

war driving — The action of searching for unprotected wireless networks by driving around with a laptop set to receive and capture wireless data transmissions.

watt — A unit for measuring electrical power. The watt was named after James Watt, a Scottish engineer who experimented with engines in the mid-1700s.

waveform codec — A voice encoding and decoding technique that samples an analog waveform at regular intervals and uses sampled data to attempt to reconstruct the waveform at the receiving end. PCM, DPCM, and ADPCM are all waveform techniques. Some examples of waveform codecs are G.711, G.723, and G.726.

wavelength — The distance between corresponding points on a wave's cycle. Wavelength is expressed in meters and is inversely proportional to frequency.

wavelength division multiplexing (WDM) — A technology that enables one fiber-optic connection to simultaneously carry multiple light signals. Each signal in WDM is assigned a different wavelength, or frequency (similar to FDM).

well-known ports — TCP/IP port numbers between 0 and 1023, so called because they were the first to be defined, and are the most familiar and most frequently used. Well-known ports are typically reserved for TCP/IP services that require administrator access to a server.

Western Electric Company — The firm that was founded in 1856 as Western Union Telegraph. Within two decades, Western Electric had established a national network of telegraph wires. In 1882, Western Electric's competitor, American Bell gained a controlling interest in the company. Combined, Western Electric and American Bell became known as The Bell System.

white noise — See *thermal noise*.

wide area network (WAN) — A network that spans a large distance and connects two or more LANs.

wideband — *See* broadband.

Wideband CDMA (W-CDMA) — A 3G wireless standard based on technology developed by Ericsson, and standardized in Europe. W-CDMA is packet-based and its maximum throughput is also 2.4 Mbps. W-CDMA systems are capable of synchronizing with each other independent of a satellite-based time source. W-CDMA is compatible with GSM mobile stations.

WiFi (Wireless Fidelity) — *See* 802.11b.

winipcfg — The TCP/IP configuration and management utility for use with Windows 95 and 98.

wire-bound — *See* wireline.

Wired Equivalent Privacy (WEP) — A key encryption technique that assigns keys to wireless nodes for authentication and data encryption. Unfortunately, WEP can be easily decrypted with the proper software tools.

wireless — A communications technology that transmits and receives signals via the atmosphere.

wireless LAN (WLAN) — A data network (or part of a data network) that uses wireless signaling for communication between nodes within a limited geographical area. Where a traditional LAN uses coaxial, twisted-pair, or fiber optic cable, a WLAN uses high-frequency radio waves.

Wireless local loop (WLL) — A generic term that describes a wireless link used in the PSTN to connect LEC central offices with subscribers.

wireless spectrum — A continuum of electromagnetic waves used for telecommunications. On the spectrum, waves are arranged according to their frequency and wavelength. The wireless spectrum (as defined by the FCC) spans frequencies between 9 KHz and 300 GHz. Each type of wireless service can be associated with one area of the wireless spectrum.

wireline — A communications technology that depends on physically connected wires to transmit and receive signals.

wiretapping — The interception of a telephone conversation by accessing the telephone signal. Wiretapping can occur at any point in the telephone connection. Law enforcement personnel perform wiretapping at the telephone switch, where it is undetectable

workstation — A computer that typically runs a desktop operating system. A workstation may be standalone or connected to a network.

World Wide Web (WWW or **Web)** — A collection of internetworked servers that share resources and exchange information according to specific protocols and formats.

World Wide Web Consortium (W3C) — A standards organization for Web browsers and languages. W3C issues and updates HTML and XHTML standards, for example.

xDSL — The term used to refer to all varieties of DSL.

X.25 — A set of protocols that describes a packet-switched, analog networking technology designed to supply data transmission over the PSTN. The original standard for X.25 specified a maximum of 64 Kbps throughput, but by 1992 the standard was updated to include maximum throughput of 2.048 Mbps. X.25 ensures data reliability over long distances by verifying the transmission at every node.

XHTML (eXtensible Hypertext Markup Language) — The latest version of the Hypertext Markup Language, also known as HTML 4.0, written to meet XML specifications. In other words, XHTML is a markup language that has already used XML to define standard elements and their formatting methods. Users familiar with previous versions of HTML will find XHTML much more user friendly than XML.

XML (eXtensible Markup Language) — A markup (or formatting) language that does not rely on pre-defined tags (as HTML does), but rather allows a designer to create her own formatting definitions and embed those definitions in a document. XML is considered to be not simply a language, but a method for defining a language.

Xon/Xoff — A type of software flow control used to gauge transmission rates between modems and computers or modems and other modems. Xon/Xoff incorporates flow control information in the data stream.

zone — In the DNS hierarchical structure, a group of devices collectively managed by one DNS server.

Index